W9-ACN-788

Early Childhood Education in the Schools

Jerold P. Bauch, Editor

nea PROFESSIONAL LIBRARY

National Education Association
Washington, D.C.

To my mother—
for a safe and
happy childhood.
—J.P.B.

The editor and publisher wish to extend their thanks to the authors and publishers who granted permission to use the material in this publication. Please see pp. 318–51 for a detailed listing of publishers and other copyright holders.

Copyright © 1988
National Education Association of the United States

Printing History
 First Printing: September 1988

Note

The opinions expressed in this publication should not be construed as representing the policy or position of the National Education Association. Materials published by the NEA Professional Library are intended to be discussion documents for educators who are concerned with specialized interests of the profession.

LIBRARY OF CONGRESS
Library of Congress Cataloging-in-Publication Data

Early childhood education in the schools / Jerold P. Bauch, editor.
     p.   cm.—(NEA aspects of learning)
  Includes bibliographies
  ISBN 0–8106–1464–2
  1. Early childhood education—United States.   2. Public schools—
United States.   I. Bauch, Jerold P.   II. Series
LB1140.23.E18 1988
  372'.21—dc19   88-19569
                                                     CIP

372.21
E12

90-1652
18134976

CONTENTS

Section Six: Evidence and Evaluation

Section Seven: Electronic Technology for Early Childhood Programs

Section Eight: Parents and Community Involvement

CONTENTS

Section Nine: Child Behavior and Discipline

Section Ten: The Future

INTRODUCTION

A new baby in a family is always cause for great excitement, reorganization, and emotional reaction. The field of early childhood education is like that too: each new event makes waves, causes extensive communication, and serves to renew the field and the people who work with young children. There is a surprising continuity in the main ideas and basic qualities of early education, however. This book marks the end of a quarter century of wild innovation, astounding growth, and rapid change. Yet what remains from all that "newness" is a better-informed commitment to the very qualities that have marked early childhood education for centuries. This is not to say that all the issues have been resolved; far from it. It may fairly be said that the more things change, the more they stay the same in early education.

The education of our youngest continues to progress in a state of dynamic equilibrium, where the dialectic between seemingly contradictory ideas produces new insight. From the very beginning, the balance between the needs of the child and the expectations of the society have been a primary source of argument. There is agreement that every young child has a right to optimal development in a safe and nurturant environment. There is disagreement about what is optimal, how we can assure security and support for every child, and what is the right blend of family roles and organized education in the process.

There is agreement that young children progress through developmental stages with unique characteristics, but disagreement even about the names of the stages and the meaning of their effects on child growth. There is agreement that young children master their environment through a complex of thought, language, social relationships, and physical exploration. There is disagreement about how parents and teachers should guide this process, when intervention is necessary or desirable, and how to facilitate development. There is agreement that every planned educational experience should help prepare the child for success in the future, but disagreement about how to make an enduring contribution to the child that is vital for the present and the future.

It is the intent of this collection to represent both the agreements and disagreements that cause excitement and perennial interest in the education of young children in the schools. In the true sense of the dialectic, the answers are the source of the new questions. A thorough reading of this book should produce numerous answers and many intriguing questions. The diversity that makes the field dynamic is well represented, and the consensus on major themes is also present. As in the child, each reader must construct a reality from interactions with the information and ideas that are presented here. There is no point in flipping to the last pages to find the ultimate answer, because the search for excellence in the education of our youngest is a journey, not a destination. Thus, the collection offers readers a chance to construct or reconstruct views on how young children should be educated, and to find places where what they bring to the reading connects with what the authors have to say.

As if developing an individual perception of the field and finding one's place in it were not difficult enough, the internal and external forces that shape early childhood education are also represented. Ideas have a history and that history is represented in Section One. Policy decisions, especially those of economic, social, and philosophical importance are sampled in Section Two. Unanswered questions and sources of conflict and choice are the topics organized in Section Three. Section Four goes to the heart of the issues represented in the title—younger children in school programs. It is highly representative of the seeming diversity of viewpoint that adds up to sensible agreement about the nature and quality of any early educational experience.

Section Five is intended to challenge and lead the reader to further study. What to teach, why, how, and how not to are the themes of these presentations; each one should be provocative. Section Six summarizes some of what we know so far, and what we should be evaluating in the future. Since early childhood education in the schools is a prime candidate for electronic technology in the learning setting, Section Seven explores both research and common-sense frameworks for thinking about computers. Because parents are certainly the child's first teachers, Section Eight is about parent involvement and partnerships between parents and teachers. Section Nine is obviously a biased group of chapters that stand together in favor of a nonviolent childhood for our children. And the final section, Ten, uses some of today's realities as stepping stones toward the near-term future. It will come as no surprise to the reader that writers about the future connect their speculations to the past, to trends and issues, to policy questions, to curriculum and instruction themes, and to other topics found in earlier chapters. Remember, this is a field that makes progress by seeking new insight from old arguments.

We hope that this collection provides some fuel to the fires of discussion and some illumination to help light the way for early childhood education in the schools.

—JEROLD P. BAUCH
Professor of Early Childhood Education
Peabody College of Vanderbilt University
Nashville, Tennessee

Section One: Historical Perspectives of Early Childhood Education

EDITOR'S OVERVIEW

Early childhood education in the schools is an idea with a diverse and interesting history; this section explores that history. The authors discuss social reform, religious beliefs, national policy, and common sense as some of the sources of our historical heritage.

The past is an important touchstone for all professionals; therefore, the historical selections included here span a period of several hundred years. Since the emphasis is on recent developments in the field of early childhood education, however, the writers concentrate on those events that give shape and substance to the present. Spodek sets the stage by giving the broad perspective and Woodill fills in the details. Hinitz's quick summary is a transition to the most dramatic period of our past: 1960 to the present—a short period of time, historians remind us, that saw more change than any other period in human history. Finally, Lawler and Bauch trace the specific history of the kindergarten, documenting the changes that have taken place.

As our society and our culture are re-created through the education of young children in the schools, the need for thoughtful and informed decisions is essential. The history of the field provides a critical context for evaluating the present and planning the future; we are not likely to do either very well without an accurate understanding of what has gone before.

1. EARLY CHILDHOOD EDUCATION'S PAST AS PROLOGUE: ROOTS OF CONTEMPORARY CONCERNS

by Bernard Spodek

I have come to better understand myself *and* the nature of the early childhood field in the historical context of my own developmental experiences. My growing identification with my culture and country from celebrating holidays is an example of this process.

Passover has always been a very special holiday. It celebrates the flight of the Jewish people from slavery in Egypt, an event with symbolic meaning for many people. Each year, Jewish families gather at home, retell the story of the Exodus, and eat special foods. Even as a child, I could feel that each generation of my family had struggled for such freedom. The ritual provides me with a direct sense of my history, back to the survivors of the flight from Egypt.

Thanksgiving is another holiday that I remember vividly, although it was mostly a school event during my childhood. Each November, we heard the story of the joint celebration of Pilgrims and Indians, drew pictures, made paper hats and collars, and cooked a feast. Nevertheless, Thanksgiving seemed an alien, somewhat empty holiday to me because I grew up with different rituals: my parents came from Eastern Europe, not England. When I became a teacher of young children, I often wondered if those students with different ethnic backgrounds had as much difficulty relating to the Pilgrims as I did.

Interestingly, Thanksgiving has now become an important ritual for my family. Celebrating this tradition has made the history of these cultures a part of me, just as in retelling the story of Passover each new generation of Jews feels a sense of participation in the Exodus. The repeated rituals and retelling of legends helps to acculturate us.

People come to identify with a profession in much the same manner as they come to identify with a culture or country— by becoming immersed in its history and traditions. This [chapter] will explore the roots of and recurring themes in early childhood education that strengthen our sense of professional identity and commitment.

See page 318 for acknowledgment and references.

FINDING OUR ROOTS

As early childhood educators we are committed to the education, development, and well-being of young children because they cannot protect themselves. We can better understand our field by seeing how it, like other organizations or individuals, has become a distinctive institution within society.

According to Clark (1970), an institution initially achieves its character either by drifting into or actively seeking its role. The organization's *mission* grows out of its statement of purpose and lends a sense of direction. This common sense of mission—commitment to the education, development, and well-being of young children—holds the field of early childhood education together.

A successful mission in time builds an *organizational saga* which undoubtedly is an embellished understanding of the organization's development! This saga further defines the organization and suggests that its members, past and present, share common characteristics.

An organizational saga captures the allegiance and commitment of its members as they proudly bind together for a common cause. As we immerse ourselves in early childhood education's saga—and see how many historical issues remain relevant today—we can strengthen our identity as early childhood educators.

SCHOOL ENTRANCE AGE

The idea of children starting school before age 5 is not new. The Puritans were concerned that children should learn to read the Bible as soon as possible, so they were often taught to read at age 3 or 4. In 1647, Massachusetts enacted a law requiring that towns establish schools for young children.

By the beginning of the 19th century, most Massachusetts towns offered schooling to the young. In 1826, 5 percent of all children enrolled in these schools were below the age of 5 (Kaestle and Vinovskis, 1978). At about this time the Infant School, developed in Britain by Robert Owen, was introduced into the United States. These schools enrolled children as young as eighteen months and were more activity oriented than the primary schools. Many parents felt that their children could be taught more effectively in infant schools than at home or in primary schools.

During the 1830s the infant school movement faded. There was a sharp reduction in the enrollment of very young children in public schools because of an increased emphasis on the role of the mother at home as educator of her young children. Many voiced concern for balanced development, fearing that excessive intellectual activity in young children would cause insanity. In addition, schools sought to exclude children less than 6 years old for bureaucratic reasons and to save money (May and Vinovskis, 1977).

Kindergarten was introduced in the latter half of the 19th century as a more humane approach to educating young children. Also, kindergartens were more closely related to the family than either the early primary schools or infant schools.

KINDERGARTEN AND EARLY READING

A great deal of attention has been given in recent years to changes in kindergarten programs (Spodek, 1982). The demand to emphasize cognitive development in kindergarten seems to have heightened.

> ...the 1980's may see more and more kindergartners poring over readers, workbooks and ditto sheets. Pressure to cover academic subjects so early, most kindergarten teachers agree, is coming from anxious parents. Parental insistence on pre-first-grade reading programs may stem in part from general mistrust of educational institutions. . . .
> While some teachers support this shift in kindergarten curriculum, many fear that the urgency with which it is carried out may not be in the best interest of their charges. (Mittenthal, 1982, p. C1)

The pressure to include reading in kindergarten is more than 100 years old. Anna Coe conducted a demonstration kindergarten at the 1876 Philadelphia Exposition encouraging such activities as reading and writing. Elizabeth Peabody, then the leading advocate of the Froebelian kindergarten, felt that this class was falsely advertised as an exhibit of kindergarten methods. Coe's program was defended as providing a way to Americanize the kindergarten idea (Ross, 1976).

To this day, we face the same dilemmas of determining what an American kindergarten should be like and when reading instruction should begin. While the decision cannot be made on research alone, it is imperative that we study not only the consequences of introducing such instruction on children, but on the school system as well.

SOCIAL CHANGE AGENT

Head Start is often seen as the first early childhood program to serve the needs of low income families (Zigler and Anderson, 1979). While Head Start was and is a unique resource, child development programs designed to help children and their parents cope with poverty and social evils began with the infant school more than 150 years ago, and continued in the nursery school in this country with its comprehensive program of medical care, nutrition, hygiene, social service, and education.

Owen's Infant School, part of his Institution for the Formation of Character, was rooted in social reform. He believed that character was developed through teaching as well as through the environment. In addition, he believed that early learning had serious consequences for the developing individual.

The infant schools were felt to embody the humane innovations and principals of education that could prove valuable to the public primary schools. They were underwritten by social reformers who saw them as ways to combat the ills of urban life. Infant schools, they believed, would permanently eliminate poverty by educating and socializing young children from low income families, while freeing mothers for work (May and Vinovskis, 1977).

Owen's infant school idea spread, and by 1827 infant schools were established in several cities in the United States. Owen lectured extensively here and purchased a settlement in Indiana where he and his son tried to establish a communitarian society which included an infant school. The community, New Harmony, had serious problems and failed. The infant school movement in America faded by the mid-1830s.

Less than a quarter century after the demise of the infant school movement, the Froebelian kindergarten was introduced to the United States. Churches, The Women's Christian Temperance Union, businesses, charities, settlement houses, and labor unions sponsored kindergartens for a wide variety of purposes.

The first nursery school was established in London at the turn of the century to serve children in poverty. Its founder, Margaret McMillan, felt that children could not develop properly unless they were healthy in their formative years. She also placed a premium on teaching for creativity, believing that imagination was as important for children of workers as for children of managers, especially if working class children were to become leaders.

Thus, early childhood educators have supported a variety of programs intended to change society. Throughout this history, the role of women has been a critical factor.

WOMEN'S ROLES

Child care services in the United States have grown tremendously in the past decade. This growth can, in part, be attributed to the increase in the number of mothers in the work force and to the changing role of women in our society. But this is not the first time. As noted earlier, a large proportion of young children were enrolled in educational programs until about the mid-1800s. The drop in enrollment then can be partly attributed to what was called *Fireside Education*.

The women and clergymen who promoted Fireside Education viewed the nuclear family as a sacred institution, and saw the home more important than the church in preserving religious values (Strickland, 1982). The home was seen as the repository for love, warmth, and intimacy in contrast to the cold competitiveness of the marketplace. Women were endowed by nature, the parent educators insisted, with superior moral character, intuitive insight, tenderness, and sensitivity to others.

This picture of the Victorian woman and family was erroneous. In reality, many women had to work outside of the home and could not dedicate themselves wholeheartedly to their children. Strickland suggests that the idealized picture of the education of the young at the knees of their mothers has led to a neglect of the needs of many children in our society.

This period's definition of the role of women still haunts us. Calls for the development of child care centers are countered by the argument that prematurely wresting young children from the bosom of their families plays havoc with our social, cultural, and economic system. Child care has been accused of destroying family life, and of taking children away from the close warm relationships found only in the home. Women are often burdened with guilt for seeking services for their children outside the home just as they were in the pre-Civil War days of "Fireside Education."

CONCEPTS OF KNOWLEDGE

From the time of the middle ages, the Bible was seen as a source of knowledge in Western society. When theories or observations were not consistent with the Bible's teachings, they were considered erroneous. With the Bible as the source of all knowledge, literacy was the key to being an educated person.

As the period of the Enlightenment developed, it became more generally accepted that there were other views of the world and other ways of validating knowledge. During this Age of Reason, rationalism and empiricism evolved as significant ways of conceiving knowledge. This is reflected in changes in early childhood education.

Rationalism provided the epistemological basis for the Froebelian kindergarten. Rationalism holds that truths are composed of self-evident premises that are logically and undeniably true rather than derived from experience.

Froebel's view of the world suggested that the key idea was the unity of man, God, and nature. This and related ideas were presented to children through a set of materials and activities that symbolized them, called the Gifts, Occupations, and the Mother's Songs and Plays. There was little concern with helping children understand objective reality. Gaining access to ideas and thinking logically from given premises were seen as critical to developing knowledge.

Empiricism, on the other hand, is the belief that sense perceptions play a central role in knowledge. The information generated by one's experiences is believed to be internalized through the senses. The development of the Montessori Method reflected the belief that one's knowledge results from one's experiences. Montessori education is sensory education. Children are trained through apparatus which isolate particular attributes of experiences, helping children learn to order the resultant sensations. For example, children differentiate and order objects by their color, size, weight, or shape.

Sensations, however, do not generate meanings. The structure that we apply to our experiences to give them *meaning* is equally important when understanding how one comes to know things.

A more integrated approach to the construction of knowledge can be found in the research and theory of Jean Piaget. He viewed knowledge as resulting from the application of mental processes *and* personal experiences. Knowledge is neither simply the accumulation of sensory experiences nor the accumulation of innate ideas but a *human* creation using sensory data—information resulting from experiences—to create ideas that can be tested against additional experience, discarded, elaborated, modified, or affirmed.

In recent years early childhood programs have been basing their programs upon this theory of constructivism. Constructivism requires that children actively accumulate experiences and act upon or think about those experiences to create their own mental structures. These programs represent not only a progression in our conceptions of child development, but a progression in our conceptions of knowledge.

These issues represent a part of the saga of early childhood education. Knowing the roots of these issues helps us put our relationship with other early childhood educators into perspective. We are not and have not been the only ones who have been confronted with these issues.

When we became early childhood educators, each of us accepted as our own, either deliberately or implicitly, the mission that is central to our field: We are committed to enhancing the education, development, and well-being of young children. Our saga helps renew our sense of identity and commitment to our profession.

DISCUSSION QUESTIONS

1. How does the history of early childhood education provide perspective and guidance?

2. When should young children start ''school''?

3. Are there similarities between social needs of the past and the present?

4. Has early childhood education responded to social concerns?

5. Should decisions about the future be based on experiences from the past?

2. THE EUROPEAN ROOTS OF EARLY CHILDHOOD EDUCATION IN NORTH AMERICA

by Gary Woodill

SUMMARY

Early childhood education in North America is currently in a state of flux. While Piagetian approaches to early childhood education curricula seem to predominate in North America today, some of the influences of the other paradigms discussed below are still in evidence. The idea of nurturing children as well as educating them has endured, even with the new cognitive focus. The concept of curricula appropriate to a child's developmental level, first introduced by Froebel, has remained an important idea. The Montessori method has enjoyed a renaissance in North America, and specially designed curricula for the disabled have been re-established as the norm, after Itard's and Seguin's pioneering examples.

Yet, new issues in early childhood education have arisen in North America. There is a great debate on the effects of day care, the changing family, the possibility of "hurried children," and the role of state support in a "universal" child care system. The recent Report of the task force on child care in Canada reviewed many of these issues, and used data on child care arrangements in a number of European countries compared to Canada and the United States in much of its discussion. It is not surprising, given the history of models of child care which have come from Europe to North America, that North Americans are once again looking across the Atlantic for fresh ideas.

History is not a smooth continuous flow of events. Rather it is characterized by periods of sameness, broken by ruptures, revolutions and regressions. From science to social practices a society lives by a given "paradigm" (Kuhn, 1967) which directs the thinking of the age and colours the perceptions of most members of the society. Change usually occurs when rising tensions and contradictions reach a point where the dominant paradigm no longer seems to work and a new way of conceptualizing the world is sought, usually from the outside.

Early childhood education in North America is a case in point. Its beginnings reflected the dominant ideas of Christian education found in the colonizing countries of Europe during the sixteenth and seventeenth centuries. Later, as the industrial revolution created victims of child labour, the "child saving" movement, which originated in Europe, resulted in many legislative and institutional changes for children in North America. In the nineteenth and early twentieth centuries, innovative models of early childhood education were exported from Europe to North America, and paved the way for the present system of early childhood education with its heavily psychological orientation.

Of course, the European models have always been adapted to the new environment and have been extended by contributions made by North American educators and psychologists. The documentation of the assimilation and adaptation in North America of European paradigms of early childhood care and education is the subject of this [chapter].

CHANGING CONCEPTIONS OF CHILDHOOD

While the ancient Greeks and Romans had a conception of early childhood education and its importance in the formation of the adult, these ideas were lost in the period known as the Dark Ages (Cubberley, 1920; Postman, 1982). The rediscovery of early childhood education had to wait until the seventeenth century when conditions in Europe made possible the rediscovery of childhood itself, and with it the need for the care and education of the young.

Until the end of the sixteenth century, schools in Europe were elite institutions run by the Church to educate the clergy and the leaders of society (Cremin, 1970). During the Dark Ages and the medieval period, monasteries and churches were the main repositories of ancient learning, Latin and Greek, and the doctrines of Christianity that formed the curriculum of schools of that period.

See pages 318–19 for acknowledgment and references.

Towards the end of the medieval period, the purposes of schooling expanded to include preparation for university, and training for commercial needs of the late medieval economy. Yet schools continued to be clerkish, pedantic and narrow in scope, and "they had managed to trivialize or lose much that was essential in the very classical wisdom they attempt to convey" (Cremin, 1970).

The 1400s and 1500s represented a period of changing sensibilities toward religion, education, childhood, human nature, and science. According to Postman (1982), the most precipitous event in this shift was the invention of the printing press. Knowledge which was hidden in a few places, and interpreted by a small number of scholars, could now be disseminated to the public at large, provided, of course, that the public could read.

The printing press invoked the possibility of a reading culture as opposed to an oral culture, and documents such as deeds, maps, promissory notes, and contracts quickly became the norm in the worlds of exploration and commerce. Since young children could not read, adulthood and childhood could now be seen as separate categories of existence, with the critical difference being the presence of adult "secrets" only accessible after a number of years of education.

The printing press not only enabled the creation of adult literature, but also gave us school textbooks and children's literature. It was John Comenius, the Moravian Bishop who wandered throughout Europe, who designed the first textbook for children. In 1628 he also wrote *School of Infancy*, which included the "school of the mother's lap" from birth to six. Comenius's work underscored the seventeenth century idea that young children should be taught by their mothers at home, rather than by outside institutions. This was to change in the eighteenth century with the coming of the industrial revolution. If the printing press can be seen as starting the process of defining childhood, the exploitation of children in factories, and the disruption of family life caused by industrialization and urbanization, made the separation and protection of children a grim necessity.

The rediscovery of childhood in the sixteenth and seventeenth centuries has been well documented (Aries, 1962; deMause, 1974; Postman, 1982). Whereas children had previously been exposed to adult behaviours and language, and were treated as "miniature adults," European children in this period of history came to experience "dependence, separation, protection, and delayed responsibilities" (Rooke and Schnell, 1983, p. 10). The implication of the new category of childhood was

both "rescue" and "restraint" of a group which had previously not known either condition. Although rescue and restraint were first conceptualized in terms of custodial care and habit training, the element of intellectual learning soon became established especially in Protestant societies. Schools were institutions which both controlled children and enabled them, through learning, to escape the circumstances of their birth. It was natural that social and religious reformers would turn to them for carrying out the changes they envisaged in society.

CHILD CARE AS CHRISTIAN TRAINING

The reformation in religion which occurred in the 1500s precipitated a corresponding reformation in education. The dissolution of monasteries and chantries in England, for example, and their replacement by grammar schools reduced ecclesiastical control of education in that country. However, the Protestant reformation did not dilute the religious content of education. Rather, the relationship with God was no longer mediated through the clergy, as each individual had a personal relationship with God, and everyone was responsible for his or her own salvation. The early Lutherans and Calvinists saw reading the Bible as the road to salvation. They believed that each person was born in utter depravity, and needed to know the signs of God's offering of grace and salvation. Not everyone was chosen, but if you were, and missed the opportunity out of ignorance of God's Word, then you were lost forever.

In Catholic countries, however, there was a counter-reformation in education spearheaded by the Jesuits in France and elsewhere which sought to keep control of education in the hands of the clergy. Instead of trying to make possible the individual reading of the Bible, the Jesuits sought to use education to increase the power of the clergy and to widen the range of influence of the Catholic Church through missionary work.

As the various European nations colonized the New World in the 1600s, they brought with them the idea that religion and education were closely connected. The children of the first European settlers were generally educated at home in religion, morals, culture and behavior. Only a few children attended the first schools in the colonies, and in many areas there were no formal educational institutions.

In addition to the indoctrination of the young into the Christian faith, both the Jesuits in New

France and the founders of New England colonies discovered a new purpose of education—enculturation of a native population. The Jesuits established the first *petit ecole*, or elementary school, in Quebec City in 1635, with the aim of changing the native population into a loyal Frenchified, Catholic peasantry (Anderson, 1985). The removal of native children from their tribes to attend school in Quebec City was part of that plan. To complement the work of the Jesuits among native boys, the Ursuline nun, Marie de l'Incarnation, founded a school for young native girls in Quebec City in 1639. This school is still operated by the Ursulines today.

In the New England colonies, the first educational institutions were for older students, beginning with the founding of Harvard College in 1636. There is evidence that Comenius's textbooks were used at Harvard College by native students (Young, 1932), and the printing of the New England Primer, a mainstay of elementary education in the seventeenth century, followed Comenius's pioneering example.

However, until the nineteenth century, education for young children in New England remained either the sole responsibility of the parents, or lessons were given in a home of a local prominent woman or clergyman. These "dame schools" and "petty schools" were the forerunners of elementary education in North America. The main purpose of these schools was to teach reading and morals, in keeping with Calvinistic views of education. Shapiro (1983) lists the five basic tenets of Calvinism as divine sovereignty, total depravity, limited atonement, predestination, and irresistible grace and contends that until the mid-nineteenth century these principles "continued to determine the basic attitudes of American parents and teachers toward the nurture and early education of their children" (p. 2). For Calvinists, the nature of the child was ignorant and corrupt. Harsh discipline was an accepted part of their pedagogy.

By the eighteenth century the North American Evangelical movement had softened the Calvinist doctrine somewhat by incorporating John Locke's philosophy into their view of the child. In 1690 John Locke wrote *Some Thoughts Concerning Education* emphasizing the importance of a "natural education," a theme later taken up and extended by Rousseau. Locke's concept of *tabula rasa* meant that the child was not born in total depravity, but neutral. However, the Evangelicals believed that the child was predisposed toward evil and needed to be trained in Biblical teachings at an early age in order that his or her soul could be "saved"

from eternal hell-fire. It was only a short step from concern about the salvation of one's own children to the saving of children in general.

CHILD CARE AS RESCUE

Locke's writings had a profound effect on Western sensibilities. The Calvinistic ideas of predestination and utter depravity came to be replaced in the mainstream of the Protestant community by a belief in progress and human improvability.

It was his belief in the improvability of the poor that led the Protestant pastor Jean-Frederic Oberlin, 1770, to hire Sarah Banzet as the first day care teacher. The day care centres started by Oberlin and the several women who worked with him in the Alsace region of France were known as "knitting schools" because the teachers taught the children to knit as part of the program. The skills learned by the children resulted in the development of a local textile industry (Deasy, 1978; Kurtz, 1976).

Rescue from poverty was also the aim of Heinrich Pestalozzi in opening an industrial school for destitute children from six to sixteen on his farm near Zurich, Switzerland in 1774. While his experiment led to financial ruin, and the school closed in 1780, Pestalozzi was to become famous as an innovator in elementary education in the early 1800s. From the examples of both Oberlin and Pestalozzi, the idea of "caring" for the child, as well as "educating" the child, has remained a part of early childhood education to the present day.

Based on the knowledge of Oberlin's pioneering work in the Alsace, Madame de Pastoret opened an "asile" or "refuge" for infants (under three) of working mothers in Paris about 1800. (Later, infant centres were known as *creches*.) News of Pastoret's centre spread to England, and the first infant "asylum" was opened in London. Deasey (1978) suggests that the London centre was the inspiration for Robert Owen's pioneering work with young children at his factories, and in his utopian communities.

The day care centres in France and England, initially modeled on Oberlin's example, soon became large warehouses for children, and used the monitor system developed by Bell and Lancaster in England. Long tiers of children sat with their hands behind their backs, moved to bells or whistles, and even blew their noses in unison (Deasey, 1978). This, then, was the initial institutional model for day care in North America—the removal of children from the streets and the factories to large institutions providing custodial care.

The child rescue movement increased in strength until the middle of the nineteenth century. By then the self-righteous middle class saw the presence of the devil everywhere, especially in the lives of the poor. It became a moral imperative to save souls, especially those of children, even if this meant kidnapping, confinement to orphanages and poorhouses, or forced immigration to the New World as apprentices to Canadian farmers (Bagnell, 1980). Rooke and Schnell (1983) describe the spirit of the nineteenth century "child saving" movement in England:

> The removal of children from environments which were described more often in terms of being vice-ridden, profane, irreligious, and turgid, rather than brutalized and impoverished, frequently consisted of snatching them away from relatives, friends and even parents. The people involved believed that the more extreme the removal the more effective the rescue. Moreover, effective rescue implied restraining those common and base elements that were all too obvious in the coarsened lives of the *restless* poor or the totally destitute. Thus order could be imposed on the disorder apparent in the vermin infested hovels, the meanest streets, the drunken licentious[ness] of the wharves and the surly looks of the masses (p. 67).

The child rescue movement spread from Europe to North America because the same conditions as in Europe—rapid industrialization, child labour, and middle-class moralism—were present in both Canada and the United States. The first *salles d'asile* and the first *creches* were established in Montreal; the New York Hospital established its "Nursery for the Children of Poor Women," which provided care for children of working parents and for the children of wet nurses. Because of the economics of the situation, children of wet nurses often died for lack of sufficient milk (Fein and Clarke-Stewart, 1973). Women who worked in the nineteenth century did so out of necessity, and often faced great poverty and stigma.

Sometimes the children of working women were taken away from them and became "orphans." Many orphanages were built for these children, where they lived until they could be apprenticed or sent to work. According to Quiney (1982), the orphanages also admitted "semi-orphans," neglected children who could be sent home for the night. In a real sense, orphanages operated as day care centres for the children of the poor. In 1856 in Toronto, for example, a "public nursery" was attached to the Protestant Girls' Home and was run by the Female Aid Society (Rooke and Schnell, 1983).

The North American day care programs run by the hospitals and orphanages in the 1800s were, for the most part, custodial in nature. The staff and inspectors were concerned with physical surroundings, hygiene and good behaviour, not with what the children were learning. Fein and Clarke-Stewart (1973) describe the New York City Hospital program established in 1854:

> The children, whose ages ranged from 15 weeks to 3 years, received regular medical examinations and were under the supervision of experienced nursemaids. This concern for the child's physical well-being was soon expanded to concern for proper habits, orderliness, and manners. In some nurseries older children were trained to use a napkin, were expected to eat their meals in silence, and were marched about in line whenever it was necessary to leave the nursery room.

Although an educative element became part of the program of some day care centres, day care continued to be associated with the "care" of children of working women, while kindergarten and nursery schools were seen mainly as educational programs. This was not to change until World War II, when day care became a service for women working in the war industries, rather than a "necessary evil" for women who were forced by circumstances to go to work.

In 1943, for example, New York City established "comprehensive" day care centres (Osborn, 1980). Unlike many day care centres of that period, these centres moved far beyond physical care for children and were designed to care for the child's health and social-emotional needs. They actively promoted the value of educational experiences for the child and this model became the norm in North America. No longer was day care seen as primarily for the purpose of rescuing either the child or the mother.

CHILD CARE AS NATURAL EDUCATION

While the initial motivation of both Oberlin and Pestalozzi was to rescue children from poverty, each contributed new ideas in educating young children. Both men were greatly influenced by Rousseau's *Emile* and believed that natural experiences were vastly superior to book learning for young children. The methods they used contrasted sharply with the pedagogy of the day, where instruction was often given in the schoolmaster's living room, or in overcrowded and badly ventilated schoolrooms. Pupils memorized the words of the books and recited them to the teacher. Flogging was common. With both Oberlin and Pestalozzi, exercise, play and object learning were the main methods used.

The idea of educating young children through interaction with real objects rather than memorization and recitation, or custodial care and control, came slowly to both Europe and North America. It started with changes to primary education in the early 1800s, was furthered with the mid-century development of kindergartens and became firmly established with the nursery school movement of the early 1900s. Pestalozzi in Switzerland, Froebel in Germany, Montessori in Italy and MacMillan in England were the most influential pioneers of these new methods of early childhood education.

Pestalozzi's work had a profound impact on the course of primary education throughout Europe and North America and an indirect impact on early childhood education on both continents. His methods entered North America in three "waves," of which the third was the most successful in reaching primary school teachers.

The earliest presentation of Pestalozzi's work in the United States was an article by William MacClure in the *National Intelligencer* in 1806. A few years later MacClure hired Joseph Neef, a colleague of Pestalozzi's in Switzerland, to come to Philadelphia and open a Pestalozzian school. Both MacClure and Neef joined Robert Owen's utopian community in New Harmony, Indiana, in 1824. After only two years, the community failed and this introduction to Pestalozzi had little impact on the course of American education.

The second route for Pestalozzian ideas to reach North America was through a few prominent New England educators who either travelled to Switzerland to visit Pestalozzi's school or who studied his work (Munroe, 1907). William Russell, founder of the *American Journal of Education* in 1826, included translations of the writings of Pestalozzi and some of his followers in his journal. Reverend Charles Brooks visited Pestalozzian schools in Germany and used Pestalozzian methods at the Massachusetts Normal School. William Woodbridge, who visited Pestalozzi twice in the 1820s, worked for the improvement of common schools, teacher training and the education of women in Connecticut. Henry Barnard, who visited Pestalozzi while studying in Europe in 1835, published a monograph in 1839 entitled "Pestalozzi, Franklin and Oberlin." Barnard also organized a six week teacher training institute, the first in North America, where he lectured on Pestalozzi.

A. Bronson Alcott, the father of Louisa May Alcott, and a Connecticut school teacher from 1823 to 1828, was part of a small circle who subscribed to Pestalozzi's ideas known as the Transcendentalists. Alcott's hope was to make education a more pleasurable experience, so he *improved classroom furniture, eliminated corporal punishment, and introduced songs and games into the classroom* (Shapiro, 1983, p. 11). He opened the Boston Infant School in 1828, for children between the ages of 18 months and 4 years. Its stated purpose was to relieve mothers of a part of their domestic work, to enable them to seek employment. In addition, the children "would be removed from the unhappy association of want and vice, and be placed under better influences" (Steinfels, 1973, p. 36). A few years later Alcott opened the Temple School in Boston, with Elizabeth Peabody as a teacher. However, the people of Boston were not ready for him and his school closed in 1839 in a cloud of controversy. In general, while a number of prominent New England educators became familiar with Pestalozzi in the early 1800s, his ideas did not spread across the North American continent because of this fact.

The third route for Pestalozzian ideas to come to North America was from Switzerland to England via the British Home and Colonial Infant School Society, and then to Canada through Reverend Egerton Ryerson, the first superintendent of schools in the Canadian province of Ontario. Charles Mayo, an Englishman who had studied with Pestalozzi in Switzerland, and his sister Elizabeth, became prominent in the Home and Colonial Infant School Society in the early 1800s. Their goal was to prepare and disseminate a graded course of instruction based on a simplification of Pestalozzi's method. Munroe (1907) gave an opinioned assessment of the difference between the Society's approach and the original Pestalozzian ideas:

> It was thus that Pestalozzianism was "misunderstood and dragged downward," to borrow Emerson's words. Pestalozzi taught without books, and chiefly in the open air; and the moment the English attempted "to reduce his principles and methods to a practicable shape," in the preparation of manuals *about* objects, which manuals were to be studied and the lessons on the objects learned and said to the teachers, that moment a wide gulf separated the Pestalozzianism of Switzerland . . . from the Pestalozzianism of England. (pp. 36–37)

The influence of the Society was felt in Canada as early as the 1830s when its followers established infant schools in the cities of Quebec, Montreal and Charlottetown (Corbett, 1968). During this period Ryerson made several trips to Europe to collect materials for an educational museum in Toronto. He brought back "many of the pictures, models, objects and appliances used by the Home and Colonial School Society in their Pestalozzian schools in England'' (Munroe, 1907, p. 171).

On a visit to Toronto in 1860, Edward Sheldon, superintendent of schools in Oswego, New York, viewed the materials that Ryerson had brought from England. Sheldon was so inspired that he ordered the materials from London, and hired a teacher from England to introduce the British version of Pestalozzian methodology to the teachers of Oswego. In 1863, his teacher training department became the Oswego Normal School. Through the graduates of the Oswego Normal School and the involvement of Sheldon with the National Teachers' Association, Pestalozzian methodology became well known through the United States.

According to Vandewalker (1908) the growth of the ''psychological conception of education,'' especially as taught at the Oswego Normal School, paved the way for the successful introduction of kindergartens in the United States. ''The success and enthusiasm of the graduates of the Oswego Normal School was such that they were sought for in nearly every state of the Union. With the gradual acceptance of the new views the kindergarten began to assume significance, and its message no longer fell on unheeding ears'' (p. 5).

The kindergarten originated with Friedrich Froebel, who spent two years (1808-1810) working with Pestalozzi at his school in Yverdon, Switzerland. It was there that Froebel first recognized the educational value of play. Froebel's kindergartens had spread throughout Germany and Western Europe by the middle of the nineteenth century, and were introduced into the United States by German expatriots in the 1850s. The first American kindergarten was opened by Mrs. Schurz in Watertown, Wisconsin, in 1855.

Because the sentiment of child rescue was strong in the nineteenth century, a number of ''charity kindergartens'' were founded in Boston, New York, and San Francisco to ''give the slum child a chance he would not otherwise have to enable him to rise above the disadvantages of poverty and neglect'' (Ross, 1976, p. 19). However, the primary motivation for kindergartens was an educative one, based on ''the flowering of the child's mind.'' Froebel's educational philosophy represented a pantheistic idealism, whereby carefully contrived ''gifts'' and ''occupations'' were seen to elicit the true, but hidden, nature of the young child.

Given an initial impetus by the writings and work of Elizabeth Peabody, the number of kindergartens in Canada and the United States grew quickly in the last half of the century. The first kindergarten opened as part of a public school system in St. Louis, Missouri, 1873. A kindergarten opened in Toronto in 1878, and according to Corbett (1968), in 1887 the province of Ontario became one of the first governments in the world to recognize officially and support financially kindergartens for four and five year old children as part of the public school system.

The reputation of the new movement was greatly enhanced when Patty Smith Hill conducted a kindergarten class at the 1893 Chicago World's Fair. Yet Patty Hill represented the American adaptation of Froebel's ideas, rather than a strict adherence to the master. Hill changed some of Froebel's materials, added the concept of free play to the kindergarten, and maintained a flexible schedule of activities. The American kindergarten movement became split into two camps—the conservatives, such as Elizabeth Peabody and Susan Blow who didn't want deviations from Froebel's prescriptions, and the progressives, such as Patty Hill and John Dewey, who favoured a freer interpretation. Eventually the progressives won the day and free play, child centered discovery learning, and flexibility came to characterize both the kindergartens and the nursery schools of North America.

EARLY CHILDHOOD EDUCATION AND SOCIAL-EMOTIONAL GROWTH

A 1908 health study in England showed that 80 percent of British infants were well at birth while only 20 percent were healthy upon entering public schools (Osborn, 1980). Margaret MacMillan and her sister Rachel responded to this report by establishing an open air nursery school in the London slums in 1911. MacMillan originated the term ''nursery school,'' and these new organizations emphasized play, nurturing of children, and support of parents. The differences among the approaches of nursery schools, kindergartens, day care centres at the beginning of the twentieth century are described by Osborn (1980):

> In contrast to most public schools of the day, the nursery school opened its doors to parents and invited them to participate in the total program. Unlike day care programs, the nursery school was viewed as an educational experience for the child and his family. Emphasis was also placed on the child enjoying the ''here and now'' and the uniqueness of being his age. Unlike kindergarten (and, other grades), little thought was given to ''readiness'' but rather to the satisfaction of exploration at two or three or four years of age (p. 118).

In the United States, Patty Hill became aware of the British nursery schools and in 1921 she sent social worker Abigail Eliot to England to study the new methods. At the same time, Hill started a laboratory nursery school at Columbia University in New York City. The attachment of nursery schools to research centres continued with the 1921 opening of a laboratory preschool at the Iowa Child Research Station and the founding of the Merrill-Palmer Institute in Detroit in 1922. In Canada, the University of Toronto's Institute of Child Study was started in 1925.

The philosophy of the progressives in early childhood education was that the social-emotional life of the child, as well as learning, was enhanced under the conditions of freedom to explore a stimulating environment. The psychoanalytic influence, after the popularization of Freud in the United States in the 1920s, added to the emphasis on the social-emotional growth of the young child.

In 1915, Margaret Naumberg, a psychoanalytically inclined teacher, opened a program for young children at the Walden school in New York City, that was described as "audaciously radical" (Weber, 1969). According to Osborn (1980), the effects of the psychoanalytic movement on the nursery school were manifested in the establishment of habit clinics, the first being set up in Boston in 1922. "The purpose of these clinics was to prevent maladjustments in young children" (p. 102.)

Freud's work on repression in early childhood, inner conflict and reenactment of disturbing fantasies in play, resulted in the development of play therapy and art therapy. In England, Susan Isaacs, Melanie Klein, and Anna Freud developed treatment methods for emotionally disturbed young children that eventually became known and adopted in North America. Even when early childhood education in North American programs was no longer being called psychoanalytic, many of the attitudes and beliefs of the neo-Freudians became embedded in the methods used in the early childhood education of the 1930s and 1940s (Omwake, 1971). The result of this emphasis on the emotional side of childhood is described by Weber (1970):

> What seemed to emerge from early studies was the need for the young child to experience sympathetic understanding, patient support, and tenderness so that he could accept the process of socialization without becoming resentful, hostile, or overly aggressive. Guided with gentleness and wisdom, it was expected that the child would be free of the mechanisms of adjustment which foster aberrant behaviour. One response to this was a move from repressive discipline to an extreme permissiveness. Another response was freeing the avenues of artistic expression from any adult dictation so that painting, dramatic play, creative rhythms, etc., could serve as a release for feelings. This, too, seemed to imply a "hands off" attitude. (p. 16).

In the 1960s, however, there was another "paradigm shift" in early childhood education in North America. The progressive model became known as the "traditional nursery school," in contrast to the "academic preschool" (Elkind, 1970), a model which has its roots in the cognitive psychology movement.

EARLY CHILDHOOD AND COGNITIVE GROWTH

The idea of early child[hood] education as having a profound impact on cognitive growth, began with the work of Jean Itard in France with "Victor," the wild boy of Aveyron. Itard, who worked in the Deaf and Dumb Institute in Paris, first saw Victor in 1799. He and Madame Guerin spent many long hours trying to teach Victor to speak and to read. They were only partly successful, but their methods, along with those evolved in Itard's successor, Edouard Seguin, started a tradition which drew attention to the importance of sense-training and stimulation in the development of the child's cognitive abilities. Seguin used Itard's methods to teach mentally retarded children to read, write and draw, and devised ingenious teaching apparatus to aid his students. In 1848 he immigrated to the United States where he helped set up educational programs for mentally retarded children in the newly formed training schools.

Itard and Seguin were the main inspirations for Maria Montessori's ten years of work with mentally retarded children in Rome and her opening of the *Casa dei Bambini* in 1906. Montessori wrote many books on her method and visited the United States and Britain, lecturing on her approach to the education of young children.

However, both Seguin and Montessori were eclipsed by hereditarian Darwinism and the belief in the immutability of intelligence which characterized American psychology of the early twentieth century. Consequently, Seguin's enlightened educational approach was eclipsed by the eugenics movement of the 1920s and the resulting institutionalization and forced sterilization of many of the mentally retarded population in North America. During the same period, the Montessori method was severely criticized especially by W. H. Kilpatrick of Columbia University in New York. The Montessori nursery school in the city closed and the Montessori method lay dormant until its rediscovery in the 1950s and 1960s.

The hereditarian view of intelligence was the majority position among psychologists at the beginning of the twentieth century, although Alfred Binet in France, who developed the first intelligence test, was an exception in this regard. Binet believed that intellectual levels could be improved over time through "mental orthopedics," a series of exercises designed to improve the intelligence level of mentally retarded children. Binet's many investigations into children's thought influenced his young assistant, Jean Piaget, to become a psychologist. While Piaget wrote most of his books on cognitive development in young children in the 1920s and 1930s, he too would have to wait until the 1960s to be "discovered" in North America.

Binet's work reached the United States in 1908 through Henry Goddard, an outspoken hereditarian who had been appointed director of research at the Training School for the Feebleminded in Vineland, New Jersey. Goddard, who advocated a unitary view of intelligence determined by heredity, was also an enthusiastic supporter of eugenics. Lewis Terman, the American who developed the Stanford-Binet Intelligence Test, shared similar views to Goddard. In the 1930s, Gesell's extensive work on the "ages and stages" of maturation in children was also based on the hereditarian position.

The most famous proponents of the hereditarian position in recent years have been Sir Cyril Burt and his student H. J. Eysenck in England and Arthur Jensen in the United States. While conceding that environment plays a minor role in the development of intelligence, all have argued that heredity contributes most of the input to intellectual development. Much of the data for this position was provided in the post World War period by Burt's identical twin studies.

The challenge to the hereditarian position has come from two sources, the compensatory education movement in the United States in the 1960s and the statistical analysis of Leon Kamin. Kamin's (1974) book documents the evidence that showed that much of Burt's data and collaborators were faked. Since many of Eysenck's and Jensen's arguments were based on Burt's data, their positions have been considerably weakened.

The compensatory education movement, exemplified by the Head Start Program, has been based on a contrasting belief system, that of optimistic environmentalism. Its basic premise is that intelligence is not a fixed entity, but can be improved by stimulating and systematic programming. David Elkind (1976) cites several reasons for the paradigm shift to environmentalism that occurred in North American education and psychology in the 1960s.

One prominent force for change in the 1960s was the civil rights movement. The substandard quality of education in inner city schools in the United States was brought to the attention of the public. The search for a solution led educators and psychologists in the United States to the discovery of the informal education approach in British primary schools of that time. These schools were based on Piaget's theory of child development, and Piaget's writings rapidly became well known in the United States and Canada. Montessori was rediscovered, and hundreds of Montessori schools opened across North America in a short period of time.

A second impetus for change in the United States was the shock of the *Sputnik* launching in 1957. Critics of education pointed to the progressive philosophy of the American school system as the reason the Russians were ahead of the Americans in space. The emphasis in progressivism was the social integration of the child into the community. "In its stead, a new philosophy of education, which held that the aim of education was to help children develop their mental abilities, to teach them how to think, came into prominence" (Elkind, 1976, p. 19). Educational criticism and educational reform were the order of the day.

At the same time North American psychology was examined by the educational reformers and was found to be inadequate for curriculum development. Learning theory and maze psychology, heavily based on animal research, provided little inspiration for the new cognitivism. Consequently, American psychology was forced to broaden in the 1960s to include more emphasis on developmental psychology, ego psychology, social psychology, and information processing psychology.

DISCUSSION QUESTIONS

1. How have our conceptions of children and childhood changed over the history of civilization?

2. What has been the influence of religion on the education of young children?

3. How was early childhood education used to "rescue" children from poverty and other social problems?

4. What are the sources of our current ideas about early education?

5. How did early ideas about socio-emotional and cognitive growth shape the way we teach young children today?

3. A MINI-HISTORY OF EARLY CHILDHOOD EDUCATION

by Blythe F. Hinitz

Three historical figures prominent in the early centuries of childhood education were Comenius, Rousseau and Pestalozzi. Johann Comenius (1592–1671), creator of the first known picture book, *Orbus Pictus* (1658), and writer of *School of Infancy* and *The Great Didactici*, advocated a "mother school" to train parents and felt the child should learn at home from birth to age six. He believe firsthand experiences are important for children. Jean Jacques Rousseau (1712–1788) was the author of *Emile*, the "children's charter" (1760), which advocates learning through experience rather than instruction and also advocates negative reinforcement. Johann Pestalozzi (1746–1826) is considered the father of modern education. He was a developer of teaching aids and object lessons, and author of *How Gertrude Teaches Her Children*.

The first recorded factory day nursery was instituted in Scotland by Robert Owen (1771–1858). His nursery emphasized dance, song and outdoor play. Owen believed that children could be trained without corporal punishment or fear. In 1906 Maria Montessori (1870–1952) opened the "Children's House" in an Italian slum area housing project. She used her own materials and methods. She believed the "directress" should be a facilitator of children's learning in the areas of Practical Life, Sensorial and Academic Exercises. Her "Method" was not widely accepted in the United States until the 1950s.

Friedrich Froebel (1787–1852) was the father of the kindergarten. He founded his school in Germany in 1837. He wrote *Mother Plays and Nursery Songs*, which includes many fingerplays and songs in use in early childhood classrooms today. He devised "gifts (of small table blocks) and occupations," which were used by many kindergarten teachers after they were brought to the United States by Margaretha Schurz for use in her school in Wisconsin in 1855. The first English speaking kindergarten was a private school kindergarten begun by Susan Blow in St. Louis in 1873. Faculty wives at the University of Chicago founded the first parent cooperative nursery school in the United States in 1915.

During the 1920s several great strides were taken in early childhood education. Carolyn Pratt, founder of the City and Country School (now Bank Street School) originated the unit blocks now in use in most early childhood classrooms. Her school was based on firsthand experiences and creative teaching and learning. The curriculum utilized neighborhood excursions and child-run enterprises, such as the school store and post office. Abigail Adams Eliot founded the Ruggles Street Nursery School in Boston in 1922. She brought the philosophy and practices of England's McMillan sisters to the United States.

Patty Smith Hill (1868–1946), a professor at Teachers College, Columbia University, was the originator of large building blocks "big enough so that children could build houses to play in or set up a store or fire engine house" (*Dauntless Women*, p. 261). She was the author of *Happy Birthday*, and the representative of the Progressive Wing of the International Kindergarten Union (now the Association for Childhood Education International). In 1925 she called a meeting in New York City which led to the founding in 1929 of the National Association for Nursery Education (since 1964 the National Association for the Education of Young Children).

Every decade since 1909 there has been a White House Conference on Children. The first one led to the formation of the Children's Bureau, now a part of the Administration for Children, Youth and Families. During the 1930s and 1940s day care was a federal priority. This led to the W.P.A. nurseries (1933–42) and the Lanham Act War Nurseries (1940–46).

The 1960s saw the renaissance of early childhood education in the United States. Jean Piaget's theories were accepted by many. The federal government funded Head Start (1965), followed by Follow Through, Parent Child Centers and Home Start. There has been "wide movement in history's view of its children. From a nonentity (which permitted infanticide) to a miniature adult (which permitted slavery and sweatshops) to current proposals for a Children's Lobby in Washington" (Osborn, p. 71).

See page 319 for acknowledgment and suggestions for further reading.

Over the years various "parts" of the child have been emphasized—his religious development, his character development, his physical, social, emotional, and intellectual development. Zigler has pointed out the dangers of emphasizing one facet of growth to the exclusion of total development.

Of course, the concept of the "Whole Child" has been around for many years. Perhaps as we view the panorama of historical events we can place all areas of development in their proper perspective and learn the true meaning of this concept (Osborn, p. 71).

DISCUSSION QUESTIONS

1. Who were the important people who first presented the key ideas in early childhood education?

2. What contribution did prominent individuals and organizations make to the development of early education in the United States?

4. THE KINDERGARTEN IN HISTORICAL PERSPECTIVE

by S. Dianne Lawler and Jerold P. Bauch

The title "Father of the Kindergarten" has been assigned to Friedrich Wilhelm Froebel (Hewes 1985). Froebel had experimented with occupations from farmer to forester, and had studied subjects from history to mineralogy. When he announced his concept of the kindergarten in 1836, he viewed it as the second phase of a coordinated lifetime education from birth through adulthood. His approach to teaching young children was aimed at helping the child understand the complex world by playing with concrete objects in an environment of exploration (Ransbury 1982). He also tried to organize parent support groups and instituted training programs for young women to prepare them to become "kindergartners" using the philosophy and practice of the Froebelian method. Froebelian kindergartens became the norm for early education in the major cities of Europe. They were patronized by both the common people and royalty.

KINDERGARTEN IN THE UNITED STATES

Between 1880 and 1900 over ten million Europeans arrived in America. One of these new immigrants, Margaretha Schurz, a student of Froebel, brought his kindergarten ideas with her to the United States. Her husband, Carl, was a revolutionary political leader in Germany. With her sister, Mrs. Schurz had taught children in England, using Froebelian methods. After moving to Watertown, Wisconsin, Mrs. Schurz opened the first kindergarten in the United States in 1856. It served her own children and the children of her neighbors. Classes were conducted in German, the native language of the teacher and most of the children. According to Snyder (1972), Schurz introduced Bostonian Elizabeth Peabody to Froebel's writings in 1859. Peabody and her sister (the widow of famous educator Horace Mann) opened the first English-language kindergarten in Boston in 1860. Henry Barnard, the first U.S. Commissioner of Education, had endorsed the Froebelian concept in 1854, and later urged that kindergarten be the entry grade for the public schools (Hewes

See page 319 for references.

1987). As kindergartens began to spread across the nation, Connecticut and Vermont were the first states to authorize early childhood education as an official part of their public schools.

During the introductory period (1856–1890), the social purpose of kindergarten changed. At first people sent their children to these classes because of the similarity to their early educational experience in their countries of origin. The Froebelian kindergarten, developed by a dreamer to help the young child understand the natural order of the world, quickly became "Americanized," however. Social reformers saw it as a way to help the less fortunate, probably because they intuitively recognized the value of its humane treatment of young children. Professional educators saw it as an effective preparation for children to begin the formal learning process. It was viewed as an appropriate transition from the home atmosphere to the structured classroom, although the early kindergartens seldom resembled the more formalized primary grade programs.

By 1870, kindergartens were becoming instruments of social reform. The first "charity" or "rescue" kindergartens were provided to children of low-income parents, and they expanded rapidly. In fact, wealthy women of the period applied their volunteer spirit to the spread of the kindergarten as a philanthropic service to the poor. The number of classes grew from about 400 in 1880 to 4,000 in 1894 (Vandewalker 1908).

In the early charity kindergartens, it was not possible to use the traditional play program and individualized approach that Froebel had developed. Because these classrooms served what is now called a day-care function, both infants and children who would be eligible for today's elementary schools were enrolled. The teachers, originally taught to consider the unique needs of children, were faced with large groups of youngsters of unknown age from low-income families and speaking a variety of languages. In fact, these classrooms probably had much in common with some Head Start programs of the 1960s, where children from varied backgrounds were taught under conditions that were less than ideal.

AMERICAN KINDERGARTENS MOVING AHEAD

Froebel's ideas, then, did not transfer into the public school system in their original form. "Despite retention of the kindergarten name, many of the public school classes bore little resemblance to the original play garden concept." (Hewes 1985, p. 13). Most public school kindergartens operated as cheaply as possible, including large enrollments, improvised facilities, and underqualified teachers. As Lazerson (1971) noted, kindergarten teachers continued to use Froebel's books for texts and inspiration, but they were no longer able to provide the informality and fun that had characterized the original model. Time and economy led to double shifts, where two groups of children were taught in half-day sessions by one teacher. This plan was the norm in many states, and it was not uncommon to expect the kindergarten teacher to serve 60 or more children per day.

When installed as a regular part of the public school program, kindergarten served five-year-olds for the most part. As nursery schools developed, and rapidly spread in the 1920s, they served children younger than five. However, these schools were able to adopt and retain some of the Froebelian approach because they were usually small, private or parochial, and less subject to the pressure of mass education.

THE 1950s TO THE 1980s

In the mid-1950s, Emma Sheehy's book, *The 5s and 6s Go to School* (1954), was used as a model in child development and teacher training classes. It was a practical guide for kindergarten and nursery school teachers and brought some of Froebel's original ideas into the modern context. It asked teachers to provide children with a rich atmosphere in a room that could attract their interest. Sheehy recommended such ideas as conferences with parents, careful planning, teaching children how to learn, and providing a situation in which children may "grow naturally" (Sheehy 1954, p. 82). She suggested that the teacher's efforts should focus on observing, listening, helping, and most of all, guiding. Overall, the book emphasized concern for each child's whole being and uniqueness. Thus, the kindergarten philosophy had weathered the revolution of progressive education and the brief interest in Montessori's methods, retaining many of Froebel's ideas. In practice, however, certain elements of the approach had to give way to the practical realities of the day, the demographic changes in society, and the resulting changes in children's background knowledge and experiences prior to kindergarten entrance.

When in the summer of 1965 Project Head Start enrolled about 560,000 children, another revolution in early childhood education began. Early intervention was again viewed as a tool of social reform as the five-year-olds of the poor were enrolled. The original Head Start curriculum was vague; teachers were guided by eclectic suggestions; most classrooms were staffed by people without extensive teacher training. The 1960s were also the period of wide-ranging experimentation; "old" ideas were rejected in favor of variety. This was especially true of models that were developed on university campuses for research purposes. This era also saw an expansion of the smorgasbord approach in which children were allowed and encouraged to select activities of interest from a broad array displayed as learning centers in the kindergarten classroom. The philosophy appeared to emphasize "child choice" and the assumption that each child could select appropriately while teachers served as "observant guides."

While the Head Start movement and other early education experimental programs were in the news, the well-established kindergartens in the public and private schools went relatively unnoticed. In some very stable communities, for example, it is likely that as many as three generations of children from the same families attended kindergarten in the same room, were taught in much the same way, and, sometimes, even by the same teacher.

The seemingly endless alternatives of Head Start, Home Start, Infant Intervention Programs, and British Infant Schools appeared to carry over into the literature of the 1970s. Instructional objectives and skill lists were "in," and the term "accountability" was heard for the first time (Webster 1984). During this period, Bloom (1981) advocated mastery learning as the key concept in education. Teachers were no longer considered "observant guides," but were asked to articulate specific skills that children would be learning during a kindergarten day, and, generally, throughout the kindergarten year.

CURRENT ISSUES

After weathering more than one hundred years of educational change and reform, the stability of the Froebelian philosophy may be facing its last challenge during the current educational revolution. As the "basic skills" curriculum in the elementary schools is being systematically moved down into the kindergarten classroom, and public school programs for four-year-olds are being added, the traditional kindergarten is being squeezed out of existence. Thus, the pendulum of change has again performed its rhythmic swing and kindergarten appears to represent only a downward extension of the primary grades—not the unique educational experience its inventor had intended.

The earlier function of the kindergarten was to provide children with their first formalized school experience, using methods that matched their curiosity and interests. "The new function of kindergarten," according to Naron (1981), "requires more instructional time and better instructional tools than existed in traditional half-day kindergarten settings" (p. 307). Naron also emphasized that children who enter kindergarten today are different from those of a decade ago—a change caused by an increase in the number of children attending preschool programs. And Davis (1980) recognized the alarming fact that kindergarten appears to be taking on more and more of the characteristics of the first-grade classroom.

Bartolini and Wasem (1985) found a consensus among current scholars in early childhood education that a major shift in kindergarten has occurred over the past 15 to 20 years. The academic-based curriculum is more prevalent than the original Froebelian developmental curriculum in which children were taught cognitive skills as a part of the "whole" curriculum and were supported socially, physically, emotionally, and intellectually. As Spodek (1981) noted, the curriculum appears to have shifted from concern for continuity of children's development to concern for continuity of achievement.

Current concerns regarding shifts in kindergarten curriculum from developmentally appropriate practices to more academic content are present in the literature. According to Bartolini and Wasem (1985), there is no substantive body of research that directly compares the academically oriented kindergarten curriculum with one that is developmentally appropriate on student outcome measures. There is general agreement, however, that the pressures of the academically oriented curriculum are a major contributor to failure and frustration among kindergarten children (Belgrad 1984; Federlein 1984; Seefeldt 1985; Spodek 1981; Webber 1986; Werner 1984). In addition, Spodek (1981) argued that available research does not demonstrate the superiority of an academically oriented curriculum in terms of long-term achieve-

ment. After examining differences between half-day, full-day, and alternate-day kindergarten programs, Gullo, Bersani, Bayless, and Clements (1985) concluded that "it is crucial to reevaluate what an appropriate kindergarten experience is—the standards of the past no longer apply" (p. 21).

While in agreement that accumulated evidence suggests that there is much that young children learn prior to first grade, Spodek (1981) argued that there has been no unanimity on the issue of what, specifically, young children should learn during that time period. Etheridge (1986) postulated that young children are quantitatively and qualitatively different from adults. He further stated: "When considering what is absolutely necessary for young children to learn, we do not conclude that any fact, concept, or skill is crucial. The facts, skills, and academic content are only tools which teachers may utilize to actively engage the development of the 'whole' child." (p. 25). Webber (1986) added that today's children consume many experiences vicariously and lack the actual concrete realization of the experience itself. Webber noted, too, that the children have changed, but the environment in which they live has also changed. In this fragile environment, pressures for early academic achievement can destroy the purpose, value, and benefits of kindergarten for children (Seefeldt 1985).

IMPLICATIONS FOR THE FUTURE OF THE KINDERGARTEN

Washington (1988) cited five major trends that can be expected by the 1990s: (1) larger populations of Black or Hispanic children, (2) the need for children to be prepared for future complexities and uncertainties, (3) increased potential for polarization and conflict between age and ethnic groups (i.e., the need for multicultural education), (4) instructional issues coming to the forefront (i.e., developmentally appropriate education), and (5) increased concern regarding the "quality" of teaching.

For over one hundred years kindergarten has been an integral part of early childhood education in the United States. While specialists in early childhood education (Cruikshank 1986; Etheridge 1986; Seefeldt 1985; Spodek 1981) have emphasized its importance and goals, there is insufficient research to describe its specific content, procedures, and strategies. Early childhood research is in its infancy; it should continue to grow and thrive with changing times and expressed concerns. One indicator of the growing research interest in this area is *The Early Childhood Research Quarterly*. First published in 1986, this journal prints empirical research conducted in kindergarten classrooms as well as research concerning children younger than five in preschool and day care settings.

Although the research concerning kindergarten teaching practices and curriculum trends is fragmented and sparse, Lawler (1987) recently discovered that kindergarten teachers, using direct instruction for reading readiness activities, utilized "whole group or whole class" instruction as their primary teaching and management strategy. Lawler (1987) also determined that although instructional patterns of kindergarten teachers in the study were identical to those of first-grade teachers during reading and/or language arts lessons, the construct of the kindergarten day still included an average of 45 to 75 minutes of free play and/or learning center time, when children may make choices, socially interact with one another, and engage in manipulation and discovery with a variety of materials and activities.

Specific teacher training and further research in early childhood education can be major contributors to change or reform in kindergarten for the 90s. David Elkind is a current advocate of examining children's reactions to educational practices. His newest publication, *Miseducation* (1987), highlights demographic changes, parental reactions, and children's stress during preschool and kindergarten education. Elkind (1981) previously argued that children are feeling "hurried" to learn abstract concepts and skills during a period of their lifespan in which they are developing concrete realizations and accommodating new information. Perhaps Elkind (1981), as well as others in the field of early childhood (Cruikshank 1986; Etheridge 1986; Seefeldt 1985; Spodek 1981; Washington 1988; Webber 1986), is again advocating the insightfulness of the "Father of the Kindergarten," Froebel. It is neither possible nor desirable to return to the past. But it is both desirable and necessary to study changes taking place in the kindergarten in order to decide how the best ideas of the past can be integrated with the best practices of today and transformed into the best programs for the future.

DISCUSSION QUESTIONS

1. Have the original ideas about the kindergarten been retained since Froebel?

2. What were the social purposes of the kindergarten during the last century?

3. Does the current kindergarten program fulfill some of the original goals and purposes?

4. How will changes in school curriculum and organization affect the kindergarten?

5. Is the modern kindergarten still a unique element of the child's learning experience?

6. What are the research findings about kindergarten?

7. Should early educators try to preserve the original flavor and purpose of the kindergarten?

Section Two: Policy Decisions About Present and Future Issues

EDITOR'S OVERVIEW

The decisions that teachers, administrators, parents, and the general public must make about early childhood education in the schools are seldom made without the influence from many sources. From the classroom to the Congress, the decisions that guide, direct, and control the practice of good education should consider the welfare and needs of the child as a first priority. But these decisions cannot be made in isolation, and the sources of educational policy are very complex. For example, there is clear evidence that international finance and local economics influence program development and expansion. Political considerations, population dynamics, the status of families, and social issues all drive policy. And policy sets the direction and tone for programs, eventually influencing how and to what extent we will prepare our young for their future.

Those professionals who help make the policies, translate them into guidelines, or are guided by them are not without their own personal beliefs, value systems, and viewpoints. The contributors to this section are no exceptions; they represent a range of arguments from statistical evidence to impassioned zeal. But all are bound by one common thread; they speak for improvement and high quality in the way we educate our children.

When Schweinhart, Koshel, and Bridgman list the choices that "policy makers" must consider, they do not mean that only legislators and educational leaders should consider these options; their list is an action agenda for everyone with an interest in and a concern for young children. Schweinhart and Weikart are the leading proponents of improved policy decisions based on evidence. In particular, their contribution explores results and cost/benefit ratios in favor of financial investment in high-quality programs. Cheever and Ryder continue the theme of quality in planning early education in the schools. These authors raise many policy questions that should be considered as schools expand their attention to young children.

Policy decisions that are made some distance from the school classroom are no less influential on the way we organize and provide education to young children. Since decisions at the building, system, state or national level all have direct bearing on the teaching and the taught, teacher and parent input is necessary. Policy is the way "they" either restrain or enable high-quality education for children, and the elusive "they" ought to be subject to the direct participation of the front line: the teachers and parents who live with the children on a daily basis.

5. POLICY OPTIONS FOR PRESCHOOL PROGRAMS

by Lawrence J. Schweinhart, Jeffrey J. Koshel, and Anne Bridgman

A host of new governors, state legislators, state education leaders, and members of Congress assumed office in January [1987]. As was true of their recent predecessors, these newcomers will probably find that they must take a position on programs aimed at early childhood development — especially those that are designed for children from low-income families. Since strong evidence exists that such programs provide both short-term and long-term gains for young participants, legislators and school administrators in almost every state will continue to deliberate during the coming year about how to establish or expand programs that serve children under the age of 5.

Several facts illustrate the increasing activity and financial commitment in this area. In 1984, for example, eight states appropriated approximately $160 million to fund early childhood programs, aimed especially at children living in poverty. In 1986, by contrast, 22 states spent $330 million for similar programs. These programs currently provide some 150,000 families with early childhood education and day care or with parent education.[1]

The momentum for early childhood programs remains strong. State legislatures and other policy-making bodies in the United States seem more willing than ever to consider investing in high-quality early childhood programs. A growing constituency, which includes chief executive officers as well as welfare mothers, considers public spending for such programs worthwhile.

• In its 1983 report, *Investing in Our Children*, the Committee for Economic Development noted, "It would be hard to imagine that society could find a higher yield for a dollar of investment than that found in preschool programs for at-risk children."[2]

• Mayor Edward Koch, in announcing an initiative to provide early childhood education for all 4-year-olds in New York City, said he was "struck by the near unanimity among experts that, of all the educational and social programs initiated in the last 20 years, there is one that holds more promise than any other, an intervention on which there is solid and compelling research indicating its measurable and long-term positive effects on children's success in school and in life."

• Governor Michael Castle of Delaware, who chair[ed] the Committee on Human Resources of the National Governors' Association, pledged that his committee [would] focus in 1987 on early childhood development programs. "Across the board, we're shifting our focus to attack problems early," he said. "We believe that, if we eliminate problems early, young people will have a much better chance to become productive citizens. The education component is the most important, of course; it begins to teach children how to learn and, equally important, it provides an early opportunity to identify problems."

• An editorial in the *Chicago Tribune* on 8 October 1985 stated, "A wealth of experimental projects proves that children from the most disadvantaged homes will thrive academically and socially if they are stimulated early enough in special preschool programs." The writer concluded that "in a few years, early learning programs will pay for themselves many times over in the reduced costs of school failures, delinquency, dependency, and violent behavior."[3]

As more and more federal, state, and local policy makers begin to realize that a constituency — motivated by solid research data — supports early childhood programs, public funding for such programs should grow. But those who are responsible for directing the debate and shaping the programs must have continuing access to pertinent information from research and experience. As they plan and implement new programs, governors, state and national legislators, local policy makers, and educators must consider all the available options. The important questions that they must answer include the following:

• Which children should be served?
• For what part of the day should early childhood programs operate?
• How much money should be invested in programs?
• Through what structures should the money be channeled?

See page 320 for acknowledgment and references.

WHICH CHILDREN SHOULD BE SERVED?

Policy makers must determine the age range and characteristics of the children to be served by early childhood programs. They must also define the program requirements, both for school districts and community agencies and for program participants and their families.

Age range. Policy makers might begin their consideration of this issue by dividing early childhood into two age groups: infants and toddlers (birth through age 2) and preschoolers (ages 3 and 4). Approximately half of the mothers of children in each of these two age groups are employed outside the home, and about two-thirds of the employed mothers work full-time. Consequently the need for child care in each of the age groups is roughly equivalent.[4]

There are fewer good child-care programs for infants and toddlers than for preschoolers. But there is also more evidence of lasting benefits for preschoolers enrolled in such programs than for infants and toddlers.[5] Lawmakers and administrators would be wise, then, to commit funds first to programs for 4-year-olds from low-income families. The second priority should be expanding such programs to serve 3-year-olds from low-income families.

Characteristics of the children to be served. Legislators and educators may decide to make an early childhood program available to all children within the age group to be served. The principal disadvantage of this decision is expense. New funding of this magnitude is difficult to come by. Moreover, the investment potential of early childhood programs has been documented only for children from low-income families. Since the benefits of early childhood programs for children from middle- and upper-income families have not been documented, it is more difficult to make a persuasive case for public funding of programs for these youngsters.

Policy makers might decide instead to provide early childhood programs for all children in the age group but to pay program fees only for low-income children at risk of school failure. This option conserves public funds while providing an opportunity for universal enrollment.

If policy makers choose not to adopt either of these options, they must establish specific criteria for participation in early childhood programs. Children might be selected for enrollment because they are living in poverty, because a screening procedure has shown them to be at risk of school failure, or because they meet both criteria. Policy makers should be aware of the fact that poverty has proved a much better predictor of school failure than any existing screening procedure. At the same time, they should carefully consider the political implications of the selection criteria they establish. Programs to serve children who are "at risk of school failure" may win more public acceptance than programs to serve children who are "living in poverty." Perhaps the best option is to target children who are at risk of school failure but to give considerable weight to environmental factors in identifying the children who fall into this category.

Program requirements. Legislators and school administrators must decide just what the early childhood program requires of school districts or community agencies and of young children and their families. One of the questions to be addressed is, Should the program be voluntary or compulsory? Government involvement in areas related to children and families can be a sensitive issue. Thus policy makers must carefully consider who is required to do what with respect to early childhood programs.

Kindergarten programs in the public schools are the primary state-level efforts in early childhood education, and the legislation attending such programs illustrates the range of options available to policy makers. Some state laws have made kindergarten attendance compulsory; others have made attendance voluntary. Many states have made kindergarten universally available to 5-year-olds. Others have said that demonstrated scholastic readiness is a condition for entry to first grade.

FOR WHAT PART OF THE DAY?

Length of the school day is the primary policy variable that determines whether or not early childhood programs meet families' child-care needs. Policy makers have three options to consider: a part-day program (two to three hours in length), a program that matches the school day (five to six hours in length), or a program that matches the workday (eight to 10 hours in length).

Part-day programs. When they are offered at least four days a week, for approximately eight months a year, high-quality preschool programs have positive, long-term effects on participants.[6] Chief among their immediate benefits are the facts that such programs may spare children the fatigue of full-day programs and that they may be less costly (because of fewer hours of teacher/child contact).

However, part-day programs do not fully meet parents' child-care needs. Moreover, in the public schools, such programs may create special transportation demands. Particularly in rural areas, part-day programs can also cause children to spend more time on a school bus than in class. These disadvantages can be addressed, of course. One solution is to organize satellite day-care homes around a center that offers a part-day early childhood program. This begins to solve children's transportation problems, as well as making the training and networking needs of those who provide the day care easier to satisfy.

Programs geared to the school day. This is a convenient option for early childhood programs based in the public schools. Programs geared to the school day make preschoolers' transportation needs the same as those of other schoolchildren. Such programs also reduce families' child-care needs; however, parents who are employed full-time will still need after-school care for their youngsters.

One of the primary disadvantages of programs geared to the school day is that — unless they are high-quality programs, responsive to children's needs and based on principles of child development — they can produce fatigue and behavioral problems in young children.

As early childhood programs geared to the school day grow in popularity, it is important to caution those individuals who interpret recent research findings as evidence that school-day-length programs are superior to part-day programs in their effects on children's later success in school. A recent study of Chicago kindergarten programs showed that class size is a better predictor of school achievement than length of the school day. When kindergarten classes contain more than 16 students, according to that study, reducing class size should be the primary concern of school officials. Only when kindergarten classes are smaller than 16 will lengthening the school day pay off in later school achievement.[7]

Programs geared to the workday. Such programs are clearly the best way of reducing transportation problems and meeting families' child-care needs. (Remember that some 54 percent of mothers with children under the age of 6 are in the workforce.)

But early childhood programs geared to the workday are costly. When these programs are of sufficient quality to meet children's developmental needs, they can easily cost $3,500 to $4,500 annually per child.[8] By contrast, under its payment schedule for Aid to Families with Dependent Children, the typical state spends only $1,300 per year to support a child at home.[9]

Since funds are limited, policy makers are faced with a difficult choice. If they spend the available funds on part-day programs aimed at developing the intellectual and social skills of economically disadvantaged children, they will be doing little to meet the child-care needs of parents who work full-time. But if they allocate the funds to programs that serve low-income children and that are geared to the workday, they run the risk that these programs will omit essential developmental components and that they will fail to address the needs of those children whose mothers do not work full-time outside the home.

Legislators and school administrators might consider a compromise: the establishment of high-quality early childhood programs geared to the workday just for those children whose mothers work full-time outside the home but live in poverty nonetheless. (In 1985, 732,000 mothers in the United States with children under the age of 6 were employed but earned too little to raise them above the poverty level.[10]) This option meets the child-care needs of some parents and the developmental needs of some disadvantaged children, while signaling a commitment by the state or local government to addressing the increased incidence of poverty among children.

HOW MUCH MONEY SHOULD BE INVESTED?

With regard to early childhood programs, perhaps the thorniest issue that policy makers must address is the matter of funding. Most states prefer to start with pilot projects at a few demonstration sites and to expand these efforts gradually. The level of funding for early childhood programs depends on a state's resources and its level of commitment to early childhood education. Policy makers implementing early childhood programs should carefully consider personnel costs and the inevitable link between level of funding and quality of program.

Personnel costs. The cost of a fully implemented, statewide early childhood program can be determined by multiplying the average cost of the program per child — which is most of the per-child cost of the teaching staff — by the total number of children served by the program. The staff/child ratio depends largely on the size of the classes. Thus the size of the classes is a major determinant of both the cost and the quality of early childhood programs. The National Day Care Study has shown that classes containing no more than 20 4-year-olds and staff/child ratios no higher than 1:10 are associated with desirable classroom behavior and improved cognitive performance.[11]

The National Day Care Study also found that only one teacher characteristic predicts program quality and effectiveness: the amount of job-related training in early childhood education that a teacher has received. Yet teachers with such training continue to be paid less than their colleagues who have specialized in other areas of education. The average annual salary of Head Start staff members in 1985 was $7,700, substantially lower than the average *starting* salary of teachers in the public schools ($14,500) and a mere one-third of the average annual salary of all public school teachers, which stood at $23,500.[12]

Policy makers can help to solve this problem in two ways. First, they can work on making early childhood education a hierarchical profession that gives practitioners opportunities for career development. Second, they can increase funding levels of programs, emphasizing their vast potential to prevent later educational and social problems.

Funding and program quality. Most policy makers who are familiar with the research on early childhood education know that it makes little sense to fund early childhood programs at levels insufficient to provide the high quality that insures program effectiveness. Indeed, unless program quality is carefully defined and maintained, an early childhood classroom is just another place for a child to be. When funds are limited, it is better to provide high-quality programs to some children than to provide inferior programs to all preschoolers.

If an early childhood program is to promote children's intellectual, social, and physical development, it must not only meet high standards of quality but also be administered by competent specialists in child development who can establish an environment that supports active learning. This premise is supported by a 15-year study, conducted by the High/Scope Educational Research Foundation, which found evidence that those preschool programs in which children initiate their own activities are most effective in preventing later juvenile delinquency. Youngsters who participated in child-directed preschool programs appeared to be better adjusted as teenagers; those who took part in highly academic, largely teacher-controlled preschool programs reported more social and educational problems during early adolescence.[13]

Developers of early childhood programs should consider adopting staff/child ratios of 1:10 and enrollment limits of 20 children per classroom; hiring teachers who hold academic degrees in early childhood development, competency-based Child Development Associate (CDA) credentials, or their equivalents; and using curriculum models, derived from principles of child development, that have been evaluated and found to have positive intellectual and social outcomes. They should also try to insure that their programs feature: (1) support systems aimed at maintaining the curriculum model, including inservice training and evaluation of teachers; (2) collaboration between the teaching staff and parents; and (3) sensitivity and responsiveness to children's health and nutrition needs and to families' needs for child care or other services.

THROUGH WHAT STRUCTURES SHOULD FUNDS BE CHANNELED?

As they develop early childhood programs, state officials and local school administrators will have to decide which agencies will receive the funds to carry out these programs. In making these decisions, they should bear in mind the diverse needs of young children and their families for child care and early childhood education. Any public investment in early childhood programs should take this diversity into account. Public officials should also remember that it is not necessary for any single program to meet all the needs of all children.

Regardless of whether providers receive funds directly or parents receive funds and select programs through a voucher system, the question remains: Who should be authorized to receive funds to provide programs? The three types of agencies that policy makers should consider are public schools, such federally funded programs as Head Start, and such other community agencies as day-care centers or associations of day-care homes. Policy makers should also consider the funding of programs through open sponsorship, which allows funds to go to any of these agencies.

Public schools. Developers of early childhood programs might look at state-funded kindergartens as examples of programs sponsored by the public schools. However, they should remember that public school programs for 4-year-olds should be quite different from some of today's kindergarten programs. They should also remember that early childhood programs in public schools will have the very same advantages and disadvantages as other public school programs.

Early childhood programs funded through the public schools would be universally available, governed by elected community representatives (the school board members), and highly professional (since the public schools have certification standards for teachers and salary schedules that guarantee pay increments for extra training and experience). Moreover, the public schools have a vested interest in early childhood programs, because these programs give children better preparation for K-12 schooling.

The disadvantages of offering early childhood programs through the public schools include a tradition of high student/staff ratios (at least 20:1 in the public schools, though a ratio of 10:1 has been shown to be the most effective for preschoolers) and the historic tendencies of the public schools to exclude parents from the educational process, to fail to meet the needs of nonwhite ethnic groups, and to fail to meet the child-care needs of working parents. Those who oppose funding early childhood programs through the public schools also point out that the schools might adopt a narrow focus on direct instruction in academic skills, instead of a broad focus on child development, and that the schools might overlook (or even threaten) existing child-care services in the community.

These concerns must be innovatively addressed, if the public schools are to serve a legitimate function in early child development. Smaller classes, greater parental involvement, and stronger emphasis on broad intellectual and social development must characterize kindergarten and prekindergarten programs in the public schools, if these programs are to yield results like those of exemplary child development programs.

Federally funded programs. Another option is to use state money to supplement existing federally funded early childhood programs, such as Head Start and Chapter 1. States may already be doing this to some extent, since most federal programs require some matching funds from states or from local school districts or community agencies.

Sources of federal grants for early childhood programs include special education funds, the Social Services Block Grant, the Child Care Food Program, and several employment-related grants programs. Another source, the federal tax credit for dependents (retained in the new federal tax policy) has analogues in the income tax policies of some states.

Providing additional funding to the Head Start programs within a state has several advantages.

Head Start is the nation's foremost publicly funded program for meeting the child development needs of low-income families, and it has a relatively stable institutional structure. Designed to repond to a wide range of needs, Head Start focuses on education, nutrition, health care, social services, and parent involvement.

One of the disadvantages of providing state funding for early childhood programs through Head Start stems from the fact that state government has not previously played an important role in that program. Head Start dollars travel from the nation's capital, through regional offices, to local grantees and delegate agencies, which operate the programs. Therefore, policy makers are often unfamiliar with the operations of Head Start in their states. Moreover, Head Start teachers tend to be undertrained; fewer than 10 percent of them hold four-year degrees in early childhood education, and only 18 percent have CDA credentials.[14]

Policy makers could probably ovecome some of these disadvantages by earmarking the state funds they give to Head Start for special purposes such as training, evaluation, or program expansion. Head Start currently serves only 24 percent of the 3- and 4-year-olds who are living in poverty in the U.S.[15]

Community agencies. A third option would be to provide state funds for early childhood programs to community agencies not associated with Head Start. Any child-care program licensed by the state's department of social services—whether based in a center or in a home—could be eligible for funding. The funds could be allocated through competitive programs or through site visits aimed at identifying those agencies that run the best programs.

This option has the advantage of enabling agencies in the private sector that run good early childhood programs to serve larger numbers of children. One disadvantage, however, is that private agencies are less subject to public scrutiny and control. Moreover, a lack of sufficient public funding in the past has deterred private agencies from serving low-income neighborhoods. Therefore, the early childhood programs funded through private agencies are not as accessible to low-income families as the early childhood programs in the public schools.

Open sponsorship. A fourth option is to provide funding for early childhood programs to public schools, Head Start, and other community agencies through open sponsorship. This approach helps to minimize the battles over turf that inevitably occur when funds are exclusively assigned to one type of agency. It also recognizes the fact that there are a variety of existing program providers. Of course, a designated agency or department must still be selected to distribute the funds impartially, at both the state and the local levels.

The number of young children living in poverty in the United States is rapidly increasing. Simultaneously, federal spending on this population has been cut back. Meanwhile, research has convincingly demonstrated a connection between childhood poverty and school failure. Research has also demonstrated the existence of a link between school failure and a variety of social problems, including teenage pregnancy, drug and alcohol abuse, crime, and poverty among adults. Because such problems pose threats to the society, policy makers are very much aware of the need to reduce children's risk of school failure.

Research has shown that good early childhood programs help to prevent school failure among children of the poor. Therefore, an increasing number of states and local governments are planning and implementing early childhood programs for children from low-income families. Such pro-grams are a sound investment because they *prevent* problems in high-risk children — and thus save society the cost of trying to correct these problems later. For state and local legislators and policy makers who are concerned about budgetary constraints, this is perhaps the most compelling argument in favor of funding high-quality early childhood programs.

An assessment of the Perry Preschool Program, conducted by the High/Scope Educational Research Foundation, showed that a good one-year preschool program for disadvantaged children returns to taxpayers six dollars for every dollar invested.

As they begin their new jobs or return to office, governors, state legislators, state education leaders, and members of Congress would be wise to consider carefully the research findings related to early childhood education, as well as the viewpoints and the experiences of specialists in that field. If a dialogue begins at once, the programs that are developed can reflect everything that is known about high-quality early childhood education. Such programs will benefit both our children and U.S. society as a whole.

DISCUSSION QUESTIONS

1. What are the most recent trends and changes in early childhood education?

2. How are major policy decisions made? What sources of information do policymakers use?

3. Is early childhood education for all children or is it to be used to intervene only with children who have special needs or problems?

4. How should states plan and organize programs for younger children in the schools?

5. Is quality early education an *expense* or *investment*?

6. What are some of the options for providing universal early education in the United States?

7. What is the difference between early childhood education as *intervention* and as *prevention*?

6. EARLY CHILDHOOD DEVELOPMENT PROGRAMS: A PUBLIC INVESTMENT OPPORTUNITY

by Lawrence J. Schweinhart and David P. Weikart

The raising of young children is changing dramatically in our time. Parental roles are shifting as unprecedented numbers of mothers are joining the work force. Single-parent families and poverty among children are both on the increase. Amid these changes, early childhood development programs have emerged as a response to immediate family needs, as well as a potential public investment that can improve the quality of life for the next generation of children.

Early childhood development programs, providing education or supplemental care, have increased dramatically in recent years. Between 1970 and 1984, the percentage of three- and four-year-olds enrolled in programs identified as "nursery schools" or "kindergartens" increased from 21 to 36 percent, serving 2.6 million of the nation's 7.2 million three- and four-year-olds in 1984 (U.S. Bureau of the Census 1985). The percentage of families using supplemental child care arrangements, while difficult to estimate directly, is closely tied to the labor force participation rate of mothers. Between 1950 and 1985, the percentage of mothers in the labor force with children under 18 increased from 14 to 62 percent, with similar rates for mothers of three- and four-year-olds (U.S. Bureau of the Census 1983 and unpublished updates). Thus, 4.3 million three- and four-year-olds today require supplemental child care arrangements while their mothers and fathers are working. Nursery schools and kindergartens serve about one-third of these children, providing some or all of the supplemental care that they need.

Public schools serve 85 percent of kindergarten children and 91 percent of students in grades 1-12 (U.S. Bureau of the Census 1985). In contrast, only one out of three nursery school enrollments is in a publicly funded program. The primary source of public funding for programs for three- and four-year-olds is the federal government, which provides at least 85 percent of the total public funds for these programs while spending only about 7 percent of the total public funds for elementary and secondary schools (National Center for Education Statistics 1985, p. 36). Federal spending includes about $1 billion a year for Project Head Start and about $1 billion a year for various other education and supplemental care programs for young children (Schweinhart 1985). Also, the federal dependent care tax credit leaves parents with about $2 billion a year to cover expenses of supplemental care for young children.

State, county, and municipal governments and school boards have recently renewed their interest in public investment in early childhood programs prior to kindergarten. State funding for these programs has grown to over a quarter-billion dollars annually. In the past two years, 19 states have initiated, maintained, or expanded their own investments in early childhood programs—Alaska, California, Florida, Illinois, Louisiana, Maryland, Maine, Massachusetts, Michigan, Minnesota, Missouri, New Jersey, New York, Oklahoma, Pennsylvania, Rhode Island, South Carolina, Texas, and Washington. Large cities—such as Chicago, New York, Philadelphia, and Washington, D.C.—are making significant investments of their own in early childhood programs. County and municipal funding is widespread, since school districts and local agencies, in the process of administering federal and state funds, often contribute their own funds.

Early childhood programs are particularly valuable for young children living in poverty. One of every four children under six is poor (U.S. Bureau of the Census 1984). Early childhood poverty is rampant among minorities, extending to half of all black children and two of every five Hispanic children. Figure 1 illustrates the growth in the poverty rate from 1969-1983. This growth, over and above the general poverty rate, may be attributed largely to the growth in single-parent families, resulting from the high divorce rate and the growing rate of never-married mothers.

Early childhood poverty often leads to children's failure in school (e.g., see Education Commission of the States 1984), which in turn often results in their dropping out of high school (National Center for Education Statistics 1983) and eventual socioeconomic failure and poverty in adulthood. In this

See pages 320–21 for acknowledgment and references.

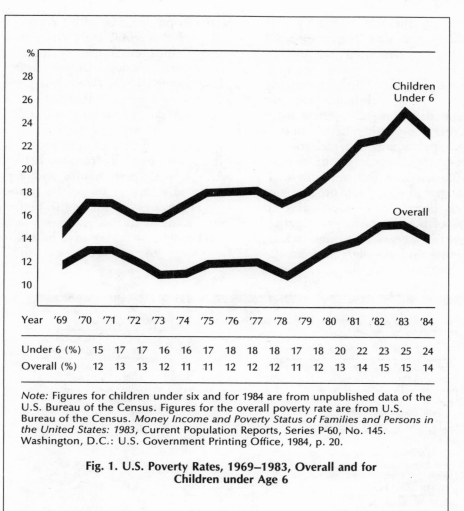

Year	'69	'70	'71	'72	'73	'74	'75	'76	'77	'78	'79	'80	'81	'82	'83	'84
Under 6 (%)	15	17	17	16	16	17	18	18	18	17	18	20	22	23	25	24
Overall (%)	12	13	13	12	11	11	12	12	12	11	12	13	14	15	15	14

Note: Figures for children under six and for 1984 are from unpublished data of the U.S. Bureau of the Census. Figures for the overall poverty rate are from U.S. Bureau of the Census. *Money Income and Poverty Status of Families and Persons in the United States: 1983*, Current Population Reports, Series P-60, No. 145. Washington, D.C.: U.S. Government Printing Office, 1984, p. 20.

Fig. 1. U.S. Poverty Rates, 1969–1983, Overall and for Children under Age 6

country, continuing poverty from generation to generation is not inevitable, but the connection remains strong. Two out of five children from the poorest fifth of families remain in the poorest fifth as young adults; seven out of ten remain in the poorest two-fifths (Hill and Ponza 1983). Poverty and school failure are also correlated to some extent with high rates of both juvenile delinquency (Loeber and Dishion 1983) and teenage pregnancy (Guttmacher Institute 1981).

POTENTIAL BENEFITS OF EARLY CHILDHOOD DEVELOPMENT PROGRAMS

The 1960s saw a renaissance of interest in early childhood education as a means of addressing the consequences of poverty for children. Martin Deutsch in New York, Susan Gray in Tennessee, and David Weikart in Michigan initiated the first of this new wave of experimental early childhood programs for children from low-income families. The designers of these experimental programs all employed curriculum approaches specifically geared to the perceived needs of young children living in poverty. They also used research methods to evaluate their programs and continued these evaluations for some years after children had completed the programs. Thus, the fortunes of early childhood education for children from low-income families became linked to longitudinal research findings.

As might be expected, many studies have addressed the short-term effects of early childhood programs, while only a handful have been able to examine effectiveness ten years or more after program completion. Yet, the weight of the evidence from carefully designed studies suggests that effective programs help children from low-income families do better in school and avoid the later problems that have their roots in school failure.

Table 1 summarizes the findings of some of the better-designed studies, most with random assignment of subjects to program and comparison groups. Each study compared two groups of children from low-income families. One group was placed in some type of early childhood program; the other group attended no program. These studies found that the early programs help improve children's intellectual performance as school begins, though this advantage appears to be temporary. The programs also reduce the need for children to be placed in special education programs or to repeat grade levels because they are unable to do the work expected of them. Third, participation in these programs leads to a lower high school dropout rate. Additional evidence, largely from the High/Scope Foundation's Perry Preschool study, indicates that good early childhood programs can lead to consistent improvement in poor children's achievement throughout schooling, reduced rates of delinquency and arrest and teenage pregnancy; an increased employment rate at age 19; and a decreased rate of welfare dependency at age 19.

To understand how early childhood experiences can affect children throughout their lives, look at life as a series of interactions between persons and settings, with performance and experience in one setting affecting access to the next setting, and so on. For example, successful performance in first grade leads to second grade, while failure may lead to repetition of first grade. Success occurs not only from year to year, but day to day, and even

Table 1
Documented Effects of Good Preschool Programs for Poor Children

Finding Study	Program Group	Control Group	Probability of Error[a]
Intellectual ability (IQ) at school entry			
Early Training	96	86	<.01
Perry Preschool	94	83	<.01
Harlem	96	91	<.01
Mother-Child Home	107	103	—
Special education placements			
Rome Head Start	11%	25%	<.05
Early Training	3%	29%	<.01
Perry Preschool	16%	28%	<.05
New York Prekindergarten (age 9)	2%	5%	<.01
Mother-Child Home (age 9)	14%	39%	<.01
Retentions in grade			
Rome Head Start	51%	63%	—
Early Training	53%	69%	—
Perry Preschool	35%	40%	—
Harlem	24%	45%	<.01
New York Pre-Kindergarten	16%	21%	<.05
Mother-Child Home	13%	19%	—
High school dropouts			
Rome Head Start	50%	67%	<.05
Early Training	22%	43%	<.10
Perry Preschool	33%	51%	<.05
Additional Perry Preschool findings			
Functional competence			
(average or better score)	61%	38%	<.05
Postsecondary enrollments	38%	21%	<.05
Detentions and arrests	31%	51%	<.05
Teenage pregnancies per 100 girls	64	117	<.10
19-year-olds employed	50%	32%	<.05
19-year-olds on welfare	18%	32%	<.05

Note: Adapted from John R. Berrueta-Clement, Lawrence J. Schweinhart, W. Steven Barnett, Ann S. Epstein, and David P. Weikart. *Changed Lives: The Effects of the Perry Preschool Program on Youths through Age 19,* (Monographs of the High/Scope Educational Research Foundation, 8.) Ypsilanti, Mich.: High/Scope Press, 1984, pp. 2 and 102.

[a]Statistical likelihood that the difference between the groups could occur by chance; "<.01" means that a particular group difference could occur by chance less than 1 time out of 100.

minute to minute. Early childhood experiences stand at the gateway of schooling—a formal cultural system with clear norms of right and wrong activities. Good early childhood experiences help a child to acquire an interest in learning, a willingness to try new things and to trust adults, a strong sense of independence. They also help children avoid negative behaviors such as misconduct, rejection of school and adults, and an inability to respond properly to adult requests.

In seeking to understand the long-term effects of early childhood development programs for at-risk children, we proposed and tested a causal model of early childhood program effects over time (Schweinhart and Weikart 1980, Berrueta-Clement et al. 1984). The model builds on a simple framework that links short-, mid-, and long-term preschool effects:

1. Poor children who attend a good early childhood development program are better prepared for school, intellectually and socially.

2. A better start in school helps children achieve greater school success, as demonstrated by a decreased need for attending special education classes or repeating a grade.

3. Greater school success leads to greater success in adolescence and adulthood, as demonstrated by lower rates of delinquency, teenage pregnancy, welfare, and unemployment.

The evidence for short-term effects of good early childhood programs is abundant (e.g., see McKey et al. 1985, the final report of the Head Start Synthesis Project). The evidence for mid-term effects comes largely from the Consortium for Longitudinal Studies (Lazar et al. 1982, Consortium 1983), a collection of follow-up studies of early childhood programs that operated in the 1960s. The evidence for long-term effects comes from High/Scope's Perry Preschool study and a few other studies. We anticipate more of this same pattern—many studies identifying short-term effects, a modest number of studies establishing mid-term effects, and a few studies indicating long-term effects.

An economic cost-benefit analysis was conducted with data from the High/Scope Perry Preschool study (Berrueta-Clement et al. 1984, Barnett 1985). Since the data from this study are consistent with other studies, the economic findings may well apply to some extent to other good early childhood programs for low-income children.

The analysis indicates that, strictly in financial terms, such programs can be an excellent investment for taxpayers. One way to represent the program's investment potential is its internal rate of return, equivalent to the real interest rate that the investment earns. This rate was 8 percent for the two-year program and over 11 percent for the one-year program. (The two-year program had the same effects as the one-year program, but its operational costs were about twice as much.)

Another way to represent the returns to taxpayers of the Perry Preschool program is to depict its per-child profits in constant dollars over and above some reasonable standard of investment profitability. Figure 2 presents the value of the program investment in constant 1981 dollars discounted at 3 percent annually. The 3 percent discount rate is equivalent to the long-term growth rate of the U.S. economy. The major cost of the program was the initial investment of about $5,000 per participant per program year. Major benefits to taxpayers were reduced costs of about $5,000 per preschool participant for special education programs, $3,000 for crime, and $16,000 for welfare assistance. Additional postsecondary education of preschool participants added about $1,000 to costs. Participants were expected to pay $5,000 more in taxes because of increased lifetime earnings resulting from their improved educational attainment.

Thus, total benefits to taxpayers amounted to about $28,000 per participant, nearly six times the initial cost of the one-year program or three times the cost of the two-year program. The return is large enough that even a two-year program that was only half as cost-effective as the program studied would still yield a positive return on investment at the 3 percent discount rate.

WHO SHOULD BE IN PUBLIC PRESCHOOL PROGRAMS?

In responding to the demonstrated potential of good early childhood programs, policymakers and administrators must decide whether to provide these programs for all children or only for some—and, if only for some, which children shall be eligible.

Some educational leaders have advocated that publicly funded preschool programs should be made available to all four-year-olds. Serving everyone of a certain age has obvious appeal. The age criterion is widely accepted, and no one protests that they have been unjustly or improperly excluded. The public schools select this option for older students almost exclusively. When they do serve special populations, such as the handicapped, schools provide the service in lieu of another service received by the rest of children.

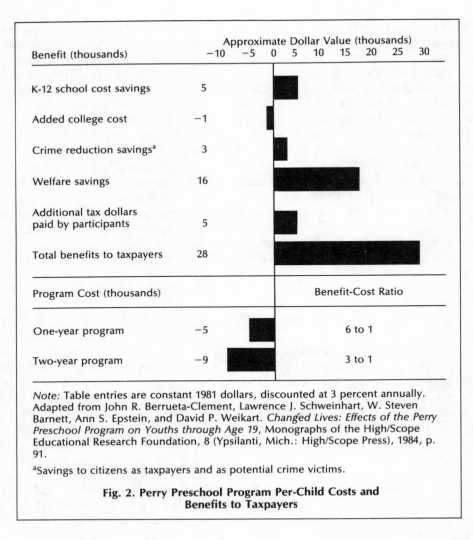

Benefit (thousands)	Approximate Dollar Value (thousands)
K-12 school cost savings	5
Added college cost	−1
Crime reduction savings[a]	3
Welfare savings	16
Additional tax dollars paid by participants	5
Total benefits to taxpayers	28

Program Cost (thousands)		Benefit-Cost Ratio
One-year program	−5	6 to 1
Two-year program	−9	3 to 1

Note: Table entries are constant 1981 dollars, discounted at 3 percent annually. Adapted from John R. Berrueta-Clement, Lawrence J. Schweinhart, W. Steven Barnett, Ann S. Epstein, and David P. Weikart. *Changed Lives: Effects of the Perry Preschool Program on Youths through Age 19*, Monographs of the High/Scope Educational Research Foundation, 8 (Ypsilanti, Mich.: High/Scope Press), 1984, p. 91.

[a]Savings to citizens as taxpayers and as potential crime victims.

Fig. 2. Perry Preschool Program Per-Child Costs and Benefits to Taxpayers

Evidence from the Brookline Early Education Project (BEEP) in Massachusetts indicates that the school problems of middle-class children are lessened somewhat by experience in good early childhood programs. At the end of grade two, 14 percent of BEEP participants exhibited inappropriate classroom learning behaviors, as compared to 28 percent of a control group: 19 percent of BEEP participants had difficulty in reading, as compared to 32 percent of the control group (Pierson et al. 1984). These are certainly significant, but not as profound in magnitude or in economic effect as the positive impact of early childhood programs for children living in poverty.

Ironically, nursery school enrollment rates are lower for children living in poverty than for more affluent children. One national survey found that the preprimary enrollment rate for three- and four-year-olds was only 29 percent for families with annual incomes below $10,000 but that it was 52 percent for families with annual incomes above $20,000. Parents' educational level also plays a role: the enrollment rate for three- and four-year-old children of elementary school dropouts was 23 percent, but for children of college graduates it was 58 percent (National Center for Education Statistics 1982).

A possible policy alternative is to offer early childhood programs that are open to all children, but to provide funding only for low-income children at special risk of school failure. This option conserves public funds while maintaining universal enrollment opportunity. The prekindergarten programs in Texas exercise a variation on this approach, making state funds for four-year-olds universally available, with districts required to provide programs if they contain 15 or more four-year-olds who are either "unable to speak and comprehend the English language" or "from a family whose income . . . is at or below subsistence level" (Texas

House Bill 72, Section 1).

If all children are not served or do not receive funding, they must be selected for the program or for funding by some criteria. These criteria generally focus in some way on risk of school failure, for example, children living in poverty or those identified by a screening test as being at risk. Perhaps the best option is to use the poverty criterion supplemented by screening test information.

However, screening tests should only be used if they meet the psychometric criteria of reliability and validity, particularly the ability to predict accurately which children will later fail in school and which will succeed. One recent review of screening instruments recommends only four of the many that are on the market—Denver Developmental Screening Test, Early Screening Inventory, McCarthy Screening Test, and Minneapolis Preschool Screening Instrument (Meisels 1986).

ONLY HIGH-QUALITY PROGRAMS ARE A GOOD INVESTMENT

Unless program quality is carefully defined and maintained, an early childhood program is just another place for a child to be. There is no intrinsic value in a young child's leaving home for a few hours a day to join another adult and a group of children. If an early childhood program is to promote healthy child development, research and experience show that it must be conducted to high standards of quality by competent child development professionals who establish an environment that supports active learning by the child (see Epstein et al. 1985). To achieve this goal, a program should have a child development curriculum, proper staffing, and adequate attention to child and family needs.

A CHILD DEVELOPMENT CURRICULUM

Unlike a solely academic approach that does not take full advantage of the potential for positive influence on long-term habits of social behavior, a child development curriculum enhances social, intellectual, and physical development. There are many kinds of early childhood curriculum models based on principles of child development, particularly the notion that children learn actively from their surroundings. Roopnarine and Johnson (1986) have recently compiled a book of curriculum models for young children, containing at least eight variations of the child development curriculum approach.

The High/Scope Educational Research Foundation has developed its own version of a child development curriculum. The fundamental premise of the High/Scope curriculum (Hohmann et al. 1979), which is based on Piaget's ideas, is that children are active learners who learn best from activities that they plan and carry out themselves. The teachers arrange interest areas in the classroom and maintain a daily routine that permits children to plan and carry out their own activities. During these activities the teachers ask children questions that encourage them to think. The teachers encourage various key experiences that help children learn to place things in categories, rank things in order, predict consequences, and generally engage in thinking at their own levels of development.

Teachers who use the High/Scope curriculum must be committed to providing settings in which children learn actively and construct their own knowledge. Their knowledge comes from personal interaction with the world, from direct experience with real objects, and from the application of logical thinking to this experience. The teacher's role is to supply experiences with real objects and to help children think about them logically. In a sense, children are expected to learn by the scientific method of observation and inference, at their own level of understanding, something that even very young children can do.

Child progress in the curriculum is reviewed around a set of key experiences that include active learning, using language, representing experiences and ideas, classification, seriation, number concepts, spatial relations, and time. These categories help teachers organize their interaction with children, just as children organize their activities through the daily routine of the plan-do-review sequence. Those key experiences help the teacher to support and extend the child's self-designed activities. They provide a way of thinking about curriculum that frees the teacher from schedules of teacher-imposed activities, as well as promoting the growth of rational thought in children.

Unlike many curriculum models, the High/Scope curriculum does not require any special materials; the only cost is that of equipping the classroom, as would be typical of any good nursery school program. The High/Scope curriculum lends itself to training and supervision and shares its emphasis on the child as active learner with historic early childhood methods like those of Froebel and Montessori. It differs from them in its use of cognitive-developmental theory to place primary emphasis on problem solving and independent thinking, instead of focusing primarily on social development and relationships. In social development approaches, the child's active learning occurs because the teacher stands out of the way and permits it to take place, not because the teacher encourages it to happen. In some Montessori programs, for example, teachers view themselves almost as guests in the child's classroom environment. Using the High/Scope model, teachers continuously gauge the child's developmental status and present intellectual challenges to stretch awareness and understanding.

Teachers or caregivers cannot maintain a child development curriculum without a support system. The administrators to whom they report are the key individuals in providing that support, both personally and institutionally. Above all, those administrators must be curriculum leaders who understand and agree with program goals and who communicate these beliefs to staff and parents.

Further, the evaluation techniques and inservice training provided must support and enhance the child development curriculum. It is essential to evaluate the progress of children and the success of the program with observational and testing techniques that are sensitive to children's developmental status and needs. Teaching staff should be able to use the feedback from evaluations in developing their teaching strategies. The program of inservice training provided to all the teaching staff should be directly applicable to the early childhood curriculum in use. As more and more staff are required for growing early childhood programs, a sound inservice training program in child development and early childhood education is absolutely essential to program quality.

STAFFING

A second characteristic of quality programs pertains to the number and qualifications of their staff members. Smaller classroom group sizes were found to be associated with desirable classroom behavior and improved cognitive performance in the National Day Care Study conducted by Abt Associates in the 1970s (Ruopp et al. 1979). This large-scale study found the most favorable outcomes for groups with fewer than 16 preschool-age-children enrolled, with positive outcomes extending to groups of up to 20 children enrolled; larger groups had negative outcomes. Study findings also led to a recommendation of two adults per group. The only teacher characteristic found to predict

program processes and effectiveness in the National Day Care Study was amount of early childhood training. No other teacher characteristic was found to be related to effectiveness—*not* college degrees and *not* amount of experience, whether in teaching or in child care.

If teaching young children is to be a valued and stable function in our society, we must create a hierarchical profession that permits viable careers. Teaching assistants making lower wages should see the promise of salaries for master teachers that permit them to support their families at a reasonable standard of living. If this is an issue for the teaching profession in general, it is much more of an issue for early childhood teachers. The average annual salary of Head Start staff members in 1985 was $7,700, substantially below the average *starting* public school salary of $14,500 and a mere one-third of the average public school salary of $23,546 (quoted by Hymes, 1986). While some of this disparity is attributable to a greater use of teaching assistants in Head Start, much of it is due to an undervaluing of the early childhood teaching specialization. This specialization has been accorded very low stature because of society's failure to recognize the vast potential of early childhood development programs, when properly implemented, to contribute to preventing educational and social problems.

CHILD AND FAMILY SERVICES

Third, a good relationship between teaching staff and parents in early childhood development programs is crucial to program success. Parents placing their children in these programs retain primary responsibility for their children and have unique and profound psychological influence over them. In terms of sheer contact time, most children spend the majority of their waking hours with their parents, even if their parents work full-time.

Parents are best viewed as partners or colleagues of early childhood teachers, with both parent and teacher having their own areas of responsibility and expertise. The parent-teacher relationship should be built on mutual respect and a pooling of knowledge about individual children and child development principles. For example, if a parent tells the teacher to teach a three-year-old reading skills for which the child is not ready, the teacher should explain to the parent why the child is not ready to learn those skills and identify for the parent the skills that the child can and will be developing.

42

Maintaining a broad focus on the whole child rather than a narrow focus on academics has long been a rallying cry for early childhood educators. The phrase has implications not only for classroom curriculum but for support services needed by children and families. As the number of U.S. children living in poverty increases, so does the need for early childhood educators who are sensitive to children's health and nutrition needs and to their families' needs for various social services. Head Start has proven that such needs can be met in the context of early childhood programs. But even if the services are not integrated into the early childhood program delivery system, educators should know how to gain access to them.

Today the majority of families with young children need supplemental child care services. Some early childhood programs are designed to partially meet the need by providing programs either part-day (2–3 hours) or full-school day (5–6 hours). Families needing full-time supplemental child care (typically 8–9 hours a day) must make additional child care arrangements, which frequently call for transportation by someone other than the parent.

The supplemental child care needs of families must somehow be met, and the quality of these services will have a significant effect on the children we are raising.

NEW HOPE FOR YOUNG CHILDREN AT RISK

High-quality early childhood programs offer new hope to children at risk. With the help of these programs, they can avoid to some extent the school failure that may otherwise plague their lives. Since school failure is at the root of many of our social problems, preventing it can benefit our society as well as the children involved. The research and experience of the past two decades has given us the knowledge we need to make these programs work. All that we need is the political will to invest the necessary resources to serve all children at risk of school failure and the abiding commitment to do the programs well—with proper staffing, sufficient attention to child and family needs, and a well-implemented child development curriculum.

DISCUSSION QUESTIONS

1. How has early childhood education expanded in recent years?

2. What are the reasons for expansion? What are the research results?

3. What economic benefits can come from high-quality early education?

4. What constitutes a quality program that might produce the economic and developmental benefits?

5. What is the relationship between child care and quality early childhood education?

7. QUALITY: THE KEY TO SUCCESSFUL PROGRAMS

by Daniel S. Cheever, Jr., and Anne E. Ryder

. . . Yes, after all the years of experiment and disappointment American society does know one sure way to lead poor children out of a life of poverty.

It has different names—Project Head Start, developmental day care, nursery school—but the idea is the same: high quality preschool education. And it works.

(*New York Times*,
September 13, 1984)

Suppose your school district was offered an educational program proven to produce successful long-term results. Targeted at preschool children, it would promote the development of intelligence, academic skills, competence, and positive self-concept during the critical years of their development. It would help them achieve greater school success, reduce the need for special education or remedial services, and lessen retention in grade.

For disadvantaged children, it would promote school success which, in turn, would lead to greater success in adolescence and adulthood—including significantly lower rates of delinquency, teenage pregnancy, and welfare usage, and higher rates of high school graduation and long-term employment.

Sound too good to be true? A lot of people seem to think so, which may be one reason why successful models of quality early childhood programs have not been adopted in many places.

But the facts speak for themselves. A variety of studies—including careful analyses of Head Start programs and longitudinal studies of the effects of other early childhood education programs—confirm the educational advantages and cost-effectiveness of high-quality early childhood programs. And the message is beginning to attract national attention.

More than 20 states have passed legislation either mandating or encouraging early childhood programs in the public schools as a matter of public policy, and more are expected to follow suit soon. In the next few years, the schools' role will become even more critical as dramatic changes in family life force them to take action. Consider these demographics:

- By 1990, almost half the American labor force will be women.
- 60 percent of the mothers of children aged three to five are currently employed.
- In 1983, almost one in four American children was poor, and that percentage is increasing.
- 45 percent of the children born in the 1980s will live in a single-parent household by age 18.
- 33 percent of all marriages are now remarriages, and one child in four is growing up in a blended family.

These facts point to the need for an entirely new type of family support system in the near future. Combined with the growing evidence of educational and financial benefits from high-quality early childhood programs, the argument for schools to develop such programs—or to utilize programs developed by others—becomes even more persuasive.

Although there are many types of early childhood programs, most high-quality programs share common characteristics. The National Association for the Education of Young Children (NAEYC) defines a high-quality program as "one which meets the needs of and promotes the physical, social, emotional, and cognitive development of the children and adults—the parents, staff, administrators—who are involved in the program. Each day of a child's life is viewed as leading toward the growth and development of a healthy, intelligent, and contributing member of society."

A similar broad definition of quality is included in the National Day Care Study by ABT Associates in 1979. This definition notes that the welfare of children is central to quality. Custodial care is not sufficient; a good early childhood program must actively promote social, emotional, and cognitive development. The ABT Study reported that the most important determinants of such a program were:

Group Size. The size of the group directly affects the quality of care-giving, and small groups are best.

See page 321 for acknowledgment.

Qualifications and Training of Staff. Although formal education or years of experience are not essential, special training in child development and care-giving is vital if a professional staff is to provide high-quality services.

Stability of Care. The establishment of a nurturing, ongoing relationship between the child and the care-giver is essential.

Adult-Child Ratio. The ratio of adults to children and, correspondingly, the opportunity for care-givers to interact with children, is important. Higher ratios are necessary for children under three.

Quality early childhood education takes many forms, and quality programs may have different philosophies, goals, structures, and settings. There is no set formula. There are quality early childhood programs for all ages of children, and some school districts have special programs for the children of teenage parents or for the children of teachers and staff members. The issue is not so much the age or parentage of the child as it is the needs of the family and the quality of the care.

Children of different ages have unique needs that a quality program, through its environment and teaching staff, must address and serve. Infants, for instance, need a quietly stimulating environment, full of pleasant sounds, colors, and with a caring person who will hold, talk to, and nurture them. Toddlers require opportunities for safe exploration to discover all that is suddenly exciting and inviting. Their teachers must appreciate their curiosity and must lovingly, but firmly, establish appropriate behavioral limits. Preschoolers need opportunities for socialization, creative expression, cognitive development, and physical activity. Teachers of preschoolers know that play is the most effective medium for active learning, and they help the growing child become more self-assured and independent.

Quality programs must also address the needs of adults. Teachers need ongoing training with decent wages and benefits. The parents of young children need frequent communication and collaboration with the staff concerning the events of their children's lives.

An examination of quality in early childhood education would not be complete without addressing the costs of such programming. Quality child care is labor-intensive, requiring the energies of knowledgeable, committed, and positive people who deserve appropriate salaries. As school districts compete for money with other important institutions in our society, it is tempting to skimp on the quality of early childhood programs. After all, these children are still very young and we can always help them catch up later. Their needs and potential difficulties are less obvious or demanding of immediate attention than those of older students. And young children do not speak out for themselves.

But cutting quality in early childhood programs is a grave and expensive mistake. The importance of primary learning is well established and good early childhood programs can promote it. Indeed, many would argue that the care, nurture, and education of the young should be our highest priority because they represent the future of our society.

There are practical reasons to provide programs of high quality as well. As American families and the nature of the work force change dramatically, even cost-conscious corporations are starting to make available quality day care programs for the high percentage of parents—particularly mothers—who work. Corporate programs vary from the provision of on-site day care centers to IBM's extensive national child care referral service, operated by Wheelock College's Work/Family Directions for IBM employees across the country.

Finally, there are clear economic benefits to investing in quality early childhood programs, particularly for disadvantaged students. The Perry Preschool Project in Ypsilanti, Michigan, monitored and compared the life experience of two similar groups of poor black children over a 16-year period from the age of three. One group had participated in an exemplary preschool program, the other had not. At age 19, 59 percent of the group that had been enrolled in the preschool program were employed, compared to only 32 percent of children who were not enrolled. More than two-thirds of the preschool group had graduated from high school, compared to only 32 percent of the others, and 38 percent of the preschool group had continued on to college or post-secondary schools. More than 60 percent of the preschool group demonstrated above-average functional competence, compared to only 38 percent of the control group. While 31 percent of the preschoolers had police records at age 19, the comparable figure was 51 percent for the non-preschool group. The teenage pregnancy rate among the preschool group was less than half of the non-preschool group.

The Perry Preschool Project estimated that taxpayers eventually saved $3,100 on *each* student who had been enrolled in the preschool program, the result of lower unemployment rates, fewer brushes with the law, and fewer demands for welfare and other social services.

As schools face the challenge of designing quality early childhood programs for young children, principals frequently ask, ''What should be taught?'' Herein lies a trap, because that is the wrong question. While it is tempting to think of preschool children only as smaller versions of their older brothers and sisters, we know that these children are developmentally different in significant ways.

Particularly significant is the fact that young children's learning occurs primarily as a result of direct experience rather than from mastery of abstract concepts. The understanding of numbers and enumeration, for example, comes most readily from sorting and counting actual objects. Most young children have not yet developed the ability to think abstractly, or to generalize from one set of experiences to others based upon the same underlying principle. Learning occurs as the result of activity which, while it often resembles play, provides the experience from which learning occurs.

Most important, the early years are when fundamental habits, skills, and attitudes toward learning can be promoted. For example, a program that includes opportunities for listening to stories, dictating stories to a teacher, and scribbling on paper will develop an enthusiasm for language and the foundation for learning specific reading and writing skills. By contrast, a program which emphasizes grammatical rules, drill and practice activities, and which is not connected to actual experiences may well doom the child to failure.

There are three key questions that must be answered when staffing early education programs in the public schools: How many adults are needed? What qualifications should they have? How much should they be paid? Let's consider them in that order.

In private preschool programs, there are generally at last two adults for every 20 children. Public schools, which are used to providing only one adult in a classroom, will need to be more flexible about meeting staffing needs for younger children.

If there are two adults in a preschool classroom, at least one should be a certified teacher. However, teachers certified at the elementary level often lack a critical requirement for teaching young children: a comprehensive knowledge of early childhood development. If certified early education teachers are not utilized, it may be possible to provide appropriate training to elementary teachers through intensive development courses conducted by specialists in early childhood.

A CRITICAL DECISION

In determining how its early childhood staff shall be paid, a school system must decide whether to provide compensation according to the district's existing salary schedule for professionals or paraprofessionals, or to pay according to prevailing day care rates—which generally tend to be lower than those in most school systems. This is a critical decision, one that will affect both the quality of staff and the program's ultimate cost. In most cases, particularly if parents can pay part or all of the program costs to supplement public funds, there are many advantages to paying early childhood program staff according to existing salary schedules: it attracts better trained staff, upgrades the status and respect of the staff, avoids difficult bargaining issues with unions or employee associations, and contributes to the overall professionalization of this field.

Before designing a program for young children, a community needs assessment is important. It is crucial to know how many children in your community are and are not getting the preschool services they need. A community service instrument is needed, to survey your population by phone, mail, or home delivery. Some of the important issues to be addressed are: parents' preferences for type of program, ability and willingness to pay, location preference, and other programs in which preschool children are currently enrolled. Often, parents of young children are enthusiastic volunteers in helping to survey existing resources and develop a needs assessment.

By preparing a good needs assessment, public schools will have a more realistic sense of available programs, the number and location of children in need or preschool services, and the potential demand for different types of programs. At this point, the schools are ready to develop a feasibility study, presenting program alternatives that can then be tested with both school officials and the community. There are many planning models, and each district must decide for itself the planning approach most suited to its traditions, existing procedures, and resources.

In our experience a shared planning approach, which involves all members of key constituencies in an advisory committee, is likely to be most successful. Presumably the advisory committee would include interested parents as well as professional staff, school or central office personnel, representatives of community agencies, and even elected officials if their ultimate support might be important. Such an advisory committee needs a strong chairperson as well as a clearly defined timetable with expected outcomes identified for each step in the planning process. The advisory committee must take care to report regularly to whatever decision-making bodies—such as the local school board, city council, or other funding source—may be called on to provide financial or political support.

THE REWARDS

For years, early childhood pioneers have struggled through a wilderness of indifference outside their immediate profession. By and large, neither schools nor other community agencies have shown much interest in early childhood programs of high quality for young children.

Now the picture is beginning to change dramatically. It is time for schools to respond. We think a convincing case can be made for the development of quality early childhood programs in local schools. Most schools already have adequately equipped facilities which meet state and local codes, often a serious problem for small, private programs. Many schools have well-trained professional staff who can provide the human resources necessary for an exemplary early childhood program. Schools also have in place procedures for hiring and supervising employees, providing benefits, and other support necessary for a successful program.

In many communities, local schools have relationships with colleges and universities that can make available the latest research to early childhood education staff. Schools also have credibility in their local community, as well as access to public resources and the media—both essential for the long-term health of an early childhood program. Finally, and most important for the child, early childhood programs in local schools provide a logical progression for the young child from preschool or nursery school to kindergarten and the early elementary grades. This opportunity allows the schools, in turn, to consider the young child's long-term development.

To those who question why public schools should promote early childhood programs now—either in alliance with existing programs in the community or on their own—we can give these answers:

Early childhood programs are good education, and have proven they can promote the cognitive and social development of the young child.

Early childhood programs are cost-effective, particularly for disadvantaged children, and lead to substantial long-term savings for society.

Early childhood programs meet the new needs created by dramatic changes in family life, changes that will not disappear and that require new services if we are to maintain or strengthen the stability of families.

Finally, our youngest citizens have an equal claim to the attention and resources of our society. It is both fair and just to make them available.

DISCUSSION QUESTIONS

1. What are the essential issues in determining a quality early childhood program?

2. How does good early education contribute to the child and to society?

3. What are some of the decisions that must be made to plan and implement a quality program?

4. Can improved early education programs be justified from recent experience, research evidence, and social needs?

Section Three: Issues, Trends, and Directions

EDITOR'S OVERVIEW

The present state of early childhood education and its new relationships with the schools are challenging. This section contains recommendations about what we should do, should not do, and might consider doing to reconcile the needs of children with the intentions of the society through its schools. These recommendations represent a high level of optimism on the one hand, and are intended to raise alarms on the other. If the schools are to be the central coordinating and delivery system for early childhood education, the issues raised here demand serious attention. If the informed professional is to be supportive of excellent new program ideas, some of the trends described here will have to be reversed. And if the new directions are to make the first school years of the next generation optimal experiences, we had better respond to the concerns that are represented in the following pages.

We start with a two-part status report about our child population by Washington. The first part sets the demographic trends as one way to view the big picture; the second part deals with instruction. Next, Jorde gives a broad overview of the field that will leave the reader with questions about the purpose and the practice of early education. Then, Elkind's first piece challenges the reader to ponder a variety of considerations.

The next two chapters raise questions and issues about the public schools, early education, and the child care function. Strother reviews practice, research, and expert opinion about preschool children in the schools. Caldwell describes a promi-

nent and successful model for integrating educational day care into the public school framework.

Since the earlier entrance of children into the schools is one of the primary considerations of this collection, the next group of chapters sample viewpoints on this issue. Parsons urges the administration to unhook from chronological age as the critical factor for beginning school. She finds considerable support from the most outspoken critic of early education in the following chapter, in which Moore proposes age eight as a good point for the child to enroll. He argues against organized early childhood education in favor of the idealized home as the best setting for educational opportunity. Then, Elkind returns to make the case for the defense of a reasoned and enlightened approach to educating young children in school.

The successful progress of children once they are enrolled in school programs is the issue for the next two chapters. If a wide variety of younger children enter the school, will all be successful? Shepard and Smith draw insight from the research on readiness and retention in kindergarten. And the interplay between Meisels and the Gesell Institute about school readiness is presented in the form of "point/counterpoint" arguments.

The last chapter in this section raises questions about the way early childhood education programs in the schools might effectively serve handicapped and exceptional children. Widerstrom describes a possible dichotomy between the way early childhood teachers and special education teachers might view and provide the curriculum.

8. TRENDS IN EARLY CHILDHOOD EDUCATION—PART I. DEMOGRAPHICS

by Valora Washington

Demographic and technological changes in our society are occurring with unprecedented speed. The ability of early childhood educators to anticipate shifts in population, changes in the ecological context of human development and ethnic or instructional tensions influences the continuing relevance and effectiveness of our work. Indeed the rapid pace of change highlights the imperative to understand the demographic and social forces which have, and will continue to, influence research, theory and practice.

As early childhood educators approach the 1990s, five trends can be expected:

• Demographic shifts in population due to increases in the number of children, a large share of whom will be Black or Hispanic;

• Changes in the ecological context of childhood, suggesting the need to prepare children to adapt to future complexities and uncertainties;

• Increased potential for polarization and conflict between age or ethnic groups as the proportion of the young grows relative to the elderly, and the proportion of children of color rises with respect to that of white children;

• Tension related to instructional issues, such as the appropriate school age, length of the school day, curriculum content and computer use; and

• Increased concern about the quality of teaching and the effectiveness of educational programs.

Each of these trends will have an impact on the decisions and innovations which characterize early childhood education in the next decade. In this [chapter] each of these trends and the challenges they present to early childhood educators will be explored. Public policy implications of each trend are highlighted given the growing influence of legislation in affecting the direction of early instruction and the allocations of funds to support professional practice.

See pages 321–22 for acknowledgment and references.

DEMOGRAPHIC SHIFTS IN AMERICAN SOCIETY

Substantial demographic change is now occurring which will have a direct bearing on the field of early childhood education in the American population. A dramatic increase in the number of children to be served will occur in the next decade. A larger proportion of these children will be from lower- or working-class families, or members of nonwhite racial groups.

The Baby Boomlet

In the recent past, there was a significant decline in the American birthrate. Between 1970 and 1978, the number of children under age 14 dropped over 13 percent from 54 million to 47 million; the number of children under age five decreased 10½ percent, from about 17 million to 15 million (U.S. Dept. of Health and Human Services, 1980).

By 1976, the Census Bureau had already anticipated a reversal in birth statistics between 1980 and 2000. According to that projection, there would be 70,577,000 children under age 14 (a 40 percent increase) and 24,654,000 children under age five (a 51 percent increase) (U.S. Dept. of Commerce, 1976).

In fact, the population under five years old grew three times faster than the general population from 1980 to 1983 (Feistritzer, 1985). Demographers now anticipate a 20 percent increase in the number of children under age 10 by the end of the 1980s (AAAS, 1982). By 1990, there will be an estimated 23.3 million preschool children in this country, 23 percent more than in 1980 (CDF, 1982). The number of children in each family, however, remains small with an average of 1.8 compared to 3.9 in the 1950s (Washington and Oyemade, 1984).

School Enrollments

The increase in the number of births will lead to an unprecedented demand for nonparental, out-of-home care for young children. Nursery school enrollments jumped 83 percent from 1972 to 1983 (Feistritzer, 1985). One-third of three- or four-year-olds were enrolled in school in 1983 compared to one in five in 1970 and one in 10 in 1965 (Feistritzer, 1985). Further, preschool enrollment is expected to approach seven million by 1989 (Macado and Myer, 1984).

Over 9,000 elementary schools closed in the past decade (McNett, 1983), but the Department of Education accurately projected that elementary enrollments would climb in 1985 for the first time in 15 years (Ornstein, 1982). Indeed, an NEA report (1985) found that 1984 fall enrollment in U.S. elementary schools underwent a substantial increase for the first time since the 1970-71 school year. While secondary schools continued their enrollment declines, elementary enrollments grew to 23,716,623 pupils in 1984 from 23,200,897 pupils in 1983. Elementary enrollments should continue to increase through the early 1990s.

Changes in the Racial Mix of Young Children

There will be increases in the number of young children and a corollary demand for early education services, but the children who will be served in the next 20 years will be markedly different from those produced during the post-World War II baby boom. The present baby boomlet has a greater proportion of nonwhite and lower or working class children than the nation as a whole (Ornstein, 1982). There were 400,000 fewer white children under five in 1984 than in 1970, which had the highest number in a decade, but there were 280,000 more Black children under five. The Census Bureau's 12 percent growth projection from 1985-2000 reflects increases of 23 percent among Blacks and 9 percent for whites (Feistritzer, 1985).

To illustrate the growing cohort of nonwhite children, one can examine trends in school enrollment in the nation's 25 largest school districts. In 1950, one in 10 students in these school systems was a minority child; in 1960, it was one in three; in 1970, it was one in two (Ornstein, 1982). Today, minorities constitute the majority of school enrollments in 23 out of 25 of the nation's largest cities (McNett, 1983).

Implications for Early Childhood Educators

These demographic shifts in the American population, headed by the increase in births, have the potential to generate renewed interest and excitement in the field of early childhood education. Public attention to our field also brings the possibility of expanding financial support. Parents with moderate and high incomes have demonstrated their willingness to invest in the early education of their children; an appropriate increase in the share of public resources must be allocated for programs which serve the poor, such as Head Start. Thus, early educators can look realistically to the mid-1980s and beyond for a reversal of previous population trends which led to school closings and mergers, staff dismissals, a shrinking job market, and budget cuts (Ornstein, 1982).

Moreover, the expanding proportion of Black and Hispanic children challenges early educators to devote explicit attention to maximizing the cognitive and social skills of children in ways compatible with cultural diversity. Decades of research have demonstrated clearly that early education can yield impressive long-term benefits for poor Black children (Berrueta-Clement et al., 1984; Cole and Washington, in press). Priority attention to the needs of poor or minority children is further justified since Black preschoolers are enrolled in full day programs at two to three times the rates for white preschoolers (CDF, 1985). It is imperative that all children are prepared to live, work and play in a multicultural environment.

Also, it is clear that the expansion of early childhood in the 1980s and 1990s will be followed by another period of decline as the proportion of women of childbearing age again decreases. Although school enrollment declines and increases are fairly predictable, a major problem is now to plan appropriately for growth and decline (McNett, 1983).

Changes in Human Ecology

The increasing number of children is occurring at the same time as major changes in the ecology of childhood. Foremost among these ecological changes is diversity in family lifestyles. For example, births to unmarried women have increased to 11 percent of all births to white women and 55 percent of all births to Black women. Twenty percent of all children live in female-headed households. Today, only 11 percent of American families fit the traditional form of male worker with a homemaker wife and two children.

For the first time in history, more than half of all children under age 18 have a working mother. Moreover, mothers with young children are almost as likely to be employed full time as are mothers with older children. In 1950, only 12 percent of mothers with children under age six worked; by 1982, 50 percent were in the labor force. In 1974, 34 percent of mothers with children under age three worked, compared to 46 percent in 1982. Among children under age one, one-third of the married mothers and 40 percent of single mothers are working (Washington and Oyemade, 1984).

Rapid changes in family life, parenting styles, the role of women, and population shifts lead to a clearer focus on the continuing nature of development and the subsequent need to prepare children to adapt to social change. This focus can be tied to the current emphasis on a "life span" approach to human development; however, it contrasts sharply with the previous impetus for early learning based on a stringent focus of early childhood as a "critical period" which irreversibly establishes a trajectory leading to future success or failure for the child.

A life span perspective of early childhood assumes that equally important antecedents and processes of development may occur at later periods of the life course. As a consequence, it is clear that predictions about development from childhood to later periods of life are always inconclusive or partial. Failing to fully predict adulthood from childhood is not necessarily a scientific debacle, but an important life span assumption. Child development represents but one subset of "developmental" antecedents for later ontogeny (Baltes and Brim, 1982).

From this perspective, early childhood educators have the challenge of preparing today's children for tomorrow's world. Inherent in this challenge is the broader question: What kind of people do we want in the 21st century? In addressing this question, one must relinquish the notion that there are "normal" modes of behavior that should be expected from children.

Child development researchers have too often proceeded as if the development of children occurs in a stable or invariant culture. This assumption is refuted by longitudinal studies and an increased appreciation of the significance of the cultural or historical context surrounding child development (see Elder, 1979). Children develop in a changing society and they themselves later become active contributors to social change. Thus, changes in the macro-ecological context of child development

need to be considered in charting and accounting for the when, how, and why of child development and in preparing children for later life (Baltes and Brim, 1982).

Implications for Early Childhood Educators

Karen Hartman (1977) used four approaches to prepare her preschool pupils for increased complexities and future uncertainties: (1) to help children develop the focusing skills necessary to deal with a highly stimulating world, children were trained to focus on a task with few materials at a time; (2) to facilitate the development of decision-making skills before facing the many choices of the future, children were offered a carefully selected limited supply of materials; (3) to foster independence, children were helped to cope effectively with the environment provided for them; and (4) to keep their curiosity and inner resources alive, children were offered first-hand, rather than vicarious, experiences.

Young children also need to receive the continuity of care and stability which facilitates their confidence in the future. Unfortunately, staffing patterns in all types of child care settings often mitigate against creating a totally continuous and stable environment for children. Stability may be particularly hard to achieve in day care because of the very high rate of staff turnover. A further compilation is the length of the day in full day group day care, which makes it inevitable that the children will be in the center longer than the teachers (Jones and Prescott, 1982).

Nevertheless, as the ecological context of childhood changes, early education must be clearly relevant to the times. For example, given the expanding number of children from diverse family situations, early childhood educators must more explicitly plan programs to work with single or adolescent parents, fathers and children who may be undergoing stress as a result of family dynamics (Washington and Oyemade, 1985). Indeed, if child care and instruction cannot adapt to changing conditions and social forces, how can those settings expect to produce people who can? (Ornstein, 1982).

An important aspect of ecological change relates to children's formation of their initial social patterns, and their attitudes toward their own and other racial groups. Since these attitudes develop in preschool years (Washington, 1976), children must be exposed early to the rich multiplicity of heritages that is America. Sadly, the actual implementation of multicultural education is still only beginning, in both elementary schools (Washington, 1982) and in preschool programs (Washington and Oyemade, 1985). There is a serious and immediate need for teaching and learning using multicultural materials and methods augmented by a clear theoretical understanding of ethnic differences in learning styles and discontinuities between the home and school (Hale, 1982).

Moreover, to further the instructional and professional goals of early childhood educators, practitioners and researchers must receive more training in the ecology of developmental psychology. That is, practitioners and researchers need to learn to view and interact with the child considering the relationship between home, school, community and the broader society. In the past, this need has perhaps been most vivid to those early educators who have worked with diverse cultural groups; Blacks, for example, were among the pioneer advocates and implementers of both kindergarten and nursery education in the United States (Cunningham and Osborn, 1979).

POTENTIAL POLARIZATION AND CONFLICT

Ironically, while increases in the child population should heighten public attention to the needs of the young, the changing complexion of children may limit public action for children as a result of racial bias. Indeed, demographic and ecological changes hold the potential for polarization and conflict based on age, ethnicity, family status and social class.

Age and Ethnicity

For example, the average age of the white population is growing older while that of the minority population is much younger. Since the older generation will be mostly majority, and the younger generation mostly minority, the potential for increased conflict in priorities (such as day care vs. retirement) seems obvious (McNett, 1983).

Family Status

Moreover, demographic projections create a probability that the ''childless haves'' will be called upon to pay for the education of the ''fertile have nots.'' The fastest growing household populations in this nation are people who are single and childless ''nonfamily householders.'' Nearly half of all households added since 1980 have been nonfamily. About 64 percent of all households today do not have children, compared with 54 percent 15 years ago (Feistritzer, 1985).

Social Class

Further, there are growing class disparities among people who do have children. The number of highly educated, high income parents is growing and many of these parents are sending their children to private schools. Unless this trend stops, children in public schools, by and large, will be the offspring of single, uneducated, low income minority parents who are producing the most children today, proportionately (Feistritzer, 1985).

Implications for Early Childhood Educators

America, and early childhood education in America, are becoming more diverse, not more homogeneous (McNett, 1983). Questions arise as to whether nonfamily householders, parents sending their children to private schools, the elderly, childless couples, or the affluent will be willing to support early education for urban, minority children.

Indeed, one may wonder whether it is a mere coincidence that the growing majorities of Black and Hispanic children in urban schools coincides with mounting public dissatisfaction with schools and the corollary demands for tuition tax credits and educational vouchers. Whereas educational policy has heretofore attempted to resolve equity issues, it may become increasingly difficult to tax the affluent to support the education of nonaffluent children. Analysis of social policies for children clearly reveals the fact that the needs of minority children are often obscured or ignored (Washington, 1985; Laosa, 1984).

If unmatched by adequate policy initiatives at the federal, state and local levels, public response to the expected demographic trends may perpetuate and harden division of American society among social class and racial or ethnic lines. There is an urgent need for flexible and creative education policies matched by cooperation among all segments of the population (McNett, 1983).

Personal and national self-interest may encourage the elderly and/or whites to make investments in early education for minority children. Clearly, the retirement income of today's workers will depend on the productive employment of the minority youngsters. The growing ethnic populations represent an underdeveloped national resource that will become increasingly important to the nation's economic, political, and military strength as the majority population ages (McNett, 1983). Therefore, ensuring a foundation for success among poor minority children becomes an essential imperative for early educators.

DISCUSSION QUESTIONS

1. What are the major demographic trends that may influence early childhood education programs?

2. How will trends in population affect early education?

3. Will increased cultural diversity change the way early education programs will be planned and run?

4. How can we assure that tomorrow's programs will be responsive and appropriate for tomorrow's children?

9. TRENDS IN EARLY CHILDHOOD EDUCATION— PART II: INSTRUCTION

by Valora Washington

INSTRUCTION IN EARLY CHILDHOOD

Demographic realities will no doubt heighten public and professional debate about the appropriate types and levels of instruction for young children. While early instruction is sought for both poor and affluent children, each is based on distinct philosophies and rationales. Early experiences for the poor have been sought to mitigate the presumed deleterious effects of the home and social environment (Almy 1985; Zigler and Valentine, 1979), schooling for today's affluent child apparently seeks to extend and augment existing advantages.

Part of the motivation for early enrollment is no doubt that "schooling" is an integral part of the child care arrangement for working parents. Yet, many parents are also motivated by concern for their children's futures. . . .

When Should Schooling Begin?

Of current interest is the issue of lowering the public school entrance age to four, particularly for disadvantaged youth. Educators are divided on the question of whether three- and four-year-olds are ready to benefit from any type of formal instruction. There is concern about the "hurried child" (Elkind, 1982) and fear that early education places excessive demands on young children, inevitably causing frustration and failure. Rather, three- and four-year-olds are thought to thrive in the home where they receive the warmth and continuity which is the foundation for later learning.

Nevertheless, a growing number of state legislatures are ready to invest in public education for four-year-olds (Bland, 1985). The South Carolina Education Improvement Act of 1984 supports programs for four-year-olds who have "predicted significant readiness deficiencies." Both New York and Connecticut's Commissioners of Education support starting school at the age of four. Texas and Missouri have enacted legislation to provide programs for four-year-olds who are low income, developmental delayed or have English deficiencies.

Full-Day Kindergarten

Similarly, there is rising debate over whether full-day kindergarten should be routinely available. About 46 percent of Black five-year-olds, and 21 percent of white five-year-olds, now attend full-day programs. Conversely, about 34 percent of Black, and 65 percent of white five-year-olds attend part-day programs (CDF, 1985). In the fall 1985 school year, an estimated 3.5 million American five-year-olds entered kindergarten, with more attending full day than ever before (Morse, 1985).

The rapid shift to full-day kindergarten is widely viewed as one of the most important recent developments in early education, although its impact and purpose are the subjects of fierce debate (Mittenthal, 1982). Critics see the program more as an attempt to meet parental needs for day care. Ames and Chase (1980) argue vigorously that children are not physically ready for the routine and academic pressure concomitant [with] full-day kindergarten. Advocates of full-day kindergarten stress the mental and physical maturity and exposure of today's young children. And one of the few longitudinal studies of students attending full-day kindergarten suggests that the children do well (Morse, 1985).

Basic Education

Pressure for a back-to-basics curriculum is apparently growing (Nimnicht, 1981). Partly fueled by a series of reports on the crisis in our educational system, there is a new emphasis on drill, recitation, homework, discipline, testing, traditional grading systems, and the elimination of social promotion (Morrison, 1984). Advocates of an academic approach to early learning feel that it will reduce educational costs, take advantage of the child's learning facility and eagerness to learn, and maximize the rapid intellectual growth that is occurring in the preschool years. In this view, the failure to provide cognitive stimulation may curtail the child's ultimate level of achievement (Elkind, 1970).

Elkind (1970) also notes that there is no prepon-

See pages 322–23 for acknowledgment and references.

derance of evidence that formal instruction is more efficient, more economical, more necessary or more cognitively stimulating than the traditional program. Further, advocates of a "whole child" approach are concerned that the back-to-basics movement will make learning an unpleasant, dull, monotonous, and rote task. There is also concern that basic skills (reading, writing, and arithmetic) will become the curriculum with no time left for social sciences, art, and music (Morrison, 1984). Haiman (1984) argues that "reason" constitutes only a small part of the human being; from the point of view of the child's development needs, the most important dynamics of life are emotional and social.

Computers in Early Education

Part of the excitement for the back-to-basics movement in early education is the potential created by the use of computers (Moorsund, 1981). Yet, despite the trend toward state-mandated computer literacy (Barbour et al., 1984), there is not widespread use of computers in the primary grades (Morrison, 1984), although this situation may change rapidly. Two commonly recognized barriers to computer use in early education are the cost of hardware and the fact that many educators fear that the technology lends itself best to instructional programming based on behavioristic theory (see Leeper, Witherspoon and Day, 1984; Berkman, 1972). Nevertheless, computers have been found to be an effective teaching tool in kindergarten and first grades (School Tech News, 1984).

Major studies have found that predominantly white schools have twice as many computers as minority schools. Also, computers in low income predominantly minority schools tend to be used for drill and practice in basic skills; computers in upper income/predominantly white schools tend to be used for programming, problem solving and as learning tools (Reingold, 1985; McPhail, 1985; Bracey, 1985). Computer inequity is a serious problem that threatens to separate groups and communities by providing some children with more effective tools in the age of computer information systems.

Implications for Early Childhood Educators

There is growing concern that childhood is disappearing and that children are increasingly viewed as "pseudo adults" in terms of clothing, behavior, and academic expectations (Postman, 1982). The instructional issues in early childhood challenge teachers to use their knowledge of child develop-

ment to create an appropriate balance between intellectual, social-emotional, and physical growth. A further dilemma is how teachers can use children's own interests and abilities to promote a love of learning and to preserve their emerging confidence in themselves as learners while addressing the back-to-basics concerns of the taxpayer. The introduction of technologies such as computers in the early education curriculum serves to intensify these debates.

Clearly, public policy will affect early education in the coming years as legislators seek educational reform and attempt to balance inequities. Yet, the perceived benefits of public attention to early childhood education must not obscure a host of instructional concerns. For example, Blank (1984) notes that while policymakers seem to quickly grasp the potential economic impact of early intervention, they are less likely to allocate the cost per child that has been necessary to achieve the desired results. Newly proposed initiatives in early education appear unlikely to replicate the comprehensive models of nationally lauded programs for poor children, including health care, nutrition, parent involvement and social services as well as education components. And, the staff-child ratios of some proposed programs for four-year-olds (1:22 in Texas) are unacceptable. The provisions for children of working parents for part-day programs and the criteria used to grant entry into four-year-old programs need to be examined (Blank, 1984).

Early childhood educators have the training or experience necessary to offer a professional and long-term perspective in public policy related to children. Further, early childhood educators are uniquely prepared to respond to current crises or fads in the ecological context of childhood.

Therefore, early educators must encourage moderation and caution in private sector efforts to develop "superbabies." It is important to bear in mind that conflicting theories and concepts about children have arisen through time that are accepted and then rejected, reconsidered and reformulated as educators and parents search for the optimum techniques for working with young children (Stevens and King, 1976).

THE PROFESSIONAL STATUS OF EARLY CHILDHOOD EDUCATION

There has been growing concern about the professional status of early childhood educators. Many consumers view teaching young children as an extension of mothering (Silen, 1985). According to Silen (1985), this concern has led to a new awareness of the need to communicate to the public at large (Caldwell, 1984) and a search for common nomenclature within the field (Hostetler and Klugman, 1982; NAEYC, 1984). One objective of teacher professionalism is to upgrade existing conditions for teachers thus benefiting the children, their families and society as a whole (Machado and Myers, 1984).

Teacher Quality

Between 1983 and 1985, at least 30 national reports and 250 state reports on the status of schooling have been issued (Pipho, 1985), many of which blame the decline in the quality of American education on teachers or colleges of education (Tucker and Mautz, 1984). Moreover, Joyce and Clift (1984) observe that the field of teacher education "is not just surrounded by critics, it is inhabited by them" (p. 5). The criticisms of teacher education typically concern the quality of prospective teachers and teacher training programs (Schlecty, 1982; Atkin, 1980; Joyce, Bush and McKibbin, 1981).

These concerns may be even more prominent about day care or early childhood education teachers, most of whom do not have college degrees. The low status of teachers of young children is widely recognized (Lightfoot, 1978). Joffe (1977) calls early education a weak and marginal profession lacking the necessary mandate for the services that it promises. Indeed, the demand for professional recognition for early childhood educators involves the development of increased conceptual clarity among child care workers themselves as to who they are and what they do (Caldwell, 1984; Joffe, 1977).

Nevertheless, many observers (e.g., Ade, 1982; Silen, 1985; Katz, 1977) continue to question whether professionalism is the only legitimate, a realistic, or a desirable agenda for early childhood educators. The concept of certifying a semi-skilled profession of child development associates (CDA) developed partly due to the recognition that it would be expensive and impractical to employ college-trained teachers in most preschool programs. However, the hope that the federal government would ultimately make the CDA a minimum requirement in staffing federally financed programs for young children has never been realized. Nevertheless, over 17,000 child care workers have been certified through the CDA program. Sixty percent of the states now mention the CDA in their licensing requirements. Indeed, CDA now provides credentials for family day care providers, home

visitors, and infant/toddler programs. In its 10th anniversary year, the CDA now holds substantial promise for revitalization; effective September 1, 1985, the National Association for the Education of Young Children will assume the management, and future refinement of the CDA program (Phillips, 1985).

Program Effectiveness

Although the recent spate of educational reform reports have focused on high schools, genuine and permanent educational reform efforts must begin at the preschool and elementary levels with a concentration of resources in those year[s] (Sava, 1985). The long-term benefits of preschool (e.g. Berrueta-Clement et al., 1984) and Kindergarten (Woodruff, reported in Sava, 1985) provide impressive evidence on the wisdom of investing "reform" efforts in the early years.

Nevertheless, there is a tremendous gap between what is known and what is practiced in early childhood education. This is largely due to the fact that child development concepts, theories, research, and methods have been developed independently of educational practice (Elkind, 1981; Williams, 1984; Almy, 1982; Katz, 1977). This lack of clear congruence between research and practice is often cited as having kept early childhood education from achieving the status of a profession.

Reform in early childhood also must be related clearly to measures of effectiveness. Brookover (1985) defines an effective school program as one in which essentially all students, regardless of family income or race, achieve at acceptable levels of mastery. Despite numerous problems involved in doing definitive research on school effects and effective schools (Sizemore, 1985), researchers have now identified some of the correlates of school effectiveness related to school ideology, organizational structure and instructional practices (Brookover, 1985; Lezotte and Bancroft, 1985).

Implications for Early Childhood Educators

Without question, issues related to teacher or program quality are capturing the public attention. However, because much of early education occurs outside of the public school, issues related to the training and qualification of teachers, program certification, working conditions, child-staff ratios and prestige have been ignored. Indeed, while teaching at every level has stressful dimensions, the impact of stress on the teacher of young children has just begun to be examined (Hyson, 1982).

Movement toward professional status may be enhanced by more effective collaboration between research and practice in the field. It is also important to relate the growing body of early childhood education information to an ever-widening ecological context. Moreover, early childhood teacher training and certification programs must ensure that teachers are prepared to instruct poor or minority youth.

The low "minimum" standards among preschool or day care providers raise additional concerns in view of the acute shortage of infant, toddler and after-school care, and the increase in the number of teachers needed to meet demographic projections. The urgent need for affordable care may encourage unqualified entrepreneurs to render child care services. Unfortunately, the demand is so high that good programs cannot drive inferior ones from the marketplace. As a profession, early childhood educators must establish and enforce criteria through which every child will be reasonably assured of high quality, developmental care, rather than custodial care.

Conclusion

The coming decade challenges early childhood educators to prepare to serve larger numbers of children from diverse family backgrounds and ethnic groups. While the growing numbers of children should result in increased attention to their welfare, it is uncertain whether the emerging racial mix of young children will influence negatively public commitment to devote a proportional share of our nation's resources to the young.

To date, there is scant recognition of the public responsibility for the education and care of young children except to ameliorate the conditions of poverty.

Neither parents nor early childhood professionals have reached consensus positions on important issues in the field such as child care, licensing requirements, and staff qualifications. However, we can more clearly specify policy alternatives, devise criteria for analyzing these alternatives, and provide concise analysis of the political, educational and economic factors involved. The applicability of child development concepts and principles to social policy evaluation has been adequately demonstrated (Phillips, 1984). We must be willing to advance a clear statement about the practical and policy implications of the current state of the art in early childhood education.

Trends related to demographic shifts, changing human ecology, ethnic polarization, early instruction, and teacher or program quality highlight the need to anticipate and adapt to—indeed, influence—social forces. Three themes emerge from this analysis of trends in early childhood education for the 1990s:

• the importance of increased involvement by early childhood educators in advocacy and policy activities, consistent with tradition in this field (May and Vinoskis, 1977; Ziegler and Valentine, 1979; Almy, 1975;

• the need for fundamental change in the beliefs and theories with respect to the distribution of human ability and the role of racial minorities in American society; and

• the need for early educators to anticipate, plan for and work toward the implementation of instructional change.

As long as society is dynamic and composed of a conglomeration of cultural and social groups, Americans will be forced to live with some disagreement about the philosophy and goals of education (Ornstein, 1982). The 1990s present a window of opportunity which can advance public opinion, research, theory, and practice in early education if we are prepared to address realistically the foreseeable trends.

DISCUSSION QUESTIONS

1. Is there a disparity between the expectations of high-income and low-income parents about the purpose of early childhood education?
2. How does differential educational experience (e.g., full-day vs. half-day program) relate to the concept of equal educational opportunity?
3. Will new educational programs for young children be narrow in focus, or will they be comprehensive like some of the models of the present?
4. Should the teachers of young children be fully qualified professionals, or is there justification for reduced or narrow training?
5. How will the diversity and mix of young children in tomorrow's programs affect public perception and public support for early childhood education?

10. EARLY CHILDHOOD EDUCATION: ISSUES AND TRENDS

by Paula Jorde

Historically, the field of early childhood education has always been closely tied to changes in society. Like a barometer, early childhood programs respond to changes in the social, political, and economic climates. Child care practices have had to adapt to changing social values, beliefs, needs, and concerns as each generation gives way to the next. Over the past decade, for example, we have seen how the delivery of child care services has been dramatically altered to meet the needs of single parents, as well as dual career families, and provide many more options for working parents with infants, toddlers, and preschoolers. But early childhood education does more than merely respond to societal changes, and may in fact serve as an important agent of change. In the mid-1960s, to cite an example, compensatory education programs such as Head Start were viewed by many as a panacea for social inequality, a way to intervene and break the cycle of poverty for disadvantaged children. Today, with the latest wave of school reform measures sweeping the country, we again hear the familiar rhetoric about early childhood education as a change agent. Many view early education as the most promising vehicle for preventing poor academic performance by students during their later school years.

In both responding to, and initiating changes, early childhood education seems once again at the forefront of America's consciousness. This [chapter] will attempt to synthesize the most recent developments in this field and provide a framework for understanding the key issues and trends that will be likely to dominate the attention of educators during the coming decade. The overview touches upon five themes of early childhood education: the changing scope and nature of programs, the governmental role in support and regulation, new models for the delivery of services, quality as a central concern, and the professionalization of personnel.

THE CHANGING SCOPE AND NATURE OF EARLY CHILDHOOD PROGRAMS

In years past, the definition of the field was a rather narrow one, referring to the planned educational experiences of young children ages three through five in group settings. Today, the term early childhood education is used to reflect a far more inclusive view of children and their educational experience. Some go so far as to say that early education includes virtually "everything" that happens to the young child from birth through the initial years of formal schooling. This expanded view has evolved in large part because of two coinciding events. First, a wealth of research has emerged over the past two decades, documenting the foundational role of the earliest years in achieving full intellectual, social, emotional, and physical functioning, and the importance of early childhood programs in the child's development.[1] Second, the changing structure of the American family has forced educators to accept a broader domain of responsibility.[2] Early childhood teachers have always talked about educating the "whole" child, but today that concept takes on an even more important meaning as we address the needs of children from single parent families, dual career families, and families in crisis. Since the mental health of children is closely related to that of their parents, it has been imperative that programs move from mere custodial care to a far more comprehensive one that provides support to parents in their parenting role.

We thus see that the scope and the nature of early childhood education is being redefined to encompass infant, toddler, and preschool-age children attending programs that may be either half-day or full-day, public or private, and of differing philosophical orientations. Early childhood education is no longer conceived of as a set of curricular experiences happening in the exclusive context of a group setting at a preschool, but as including all those influences that affect a child's development at home as well and in other care arrangements in the community. The child as an organism has not changed, but our perception of his or her environment certainly has. As its sphere of action and professional responsibility has expanded, the field has taken on a distinctly multi-disciplinary approach. It now encompasses the interests of, among others, education, psychology, sociology,

See pages 323–24 for acknowledgment and references.

anthropology, nutrition, pediatrics, social work, and family welfare. The changing scope and nature of early childhood education has important implications for individuals thinking of entering the field. No longer can early childhood educators view their role with the same specificity as in years past. They must now consider the child in the intersecting contexts of family, school, and community.[3]

THE CHANGING ROLE OF GOVERNMENT IN FUNDING AND REGULATION

What we are witnessing here is clearly a return to local control. The early childhood movement is reluctantly being forced to become more self-sufficient in meeting local needs by returning to its traditional grass roots model for program development and funding. In the 1960s, there was a massive infusion of Federal dollars as part of the goals of the Great Society, but that underwriting of early education was shortlived. During the 1970s, three bills for expanded national child care and family services were defeated, and the funding and commitment to early education slowly began to evaporate. Perhaps more fundamentally, the notion of social entitlement, i.e., the right by virtue of societal membership to a minimum family support for child care, was seriously challenged.[4] In the early childhood community, nevertheless, the expectations for Federal involvement and support were still strong, since it had learned to depend on governmental assistance. Now, in the 1980s, a new awareness has finally taken hold, and program administrators have resigned themselves to the probability that the kind of support for social programs seen in the 1960s will never happen again. A universally available day care service for all low income parents is now clearly unlikely given the prevailing social, political, and economic climates.[5]

Meanwhile, the needs of young children and their families for support and services persist. Existing programs such as Head Start, Title XX, the Work Incentive Program (WIN), and Aid to Families with Dependent Children (AFDC) day care payments provide scattered government subsidy to low income families, but it has been estimated that subsidized child care is available for less than 20 percent of those eligible.[6] Child care funding has never been adequate, and it is still suffering from Congressional approval of President Reagan's request for a 21 percent reduction in the Federal block grant to states for social services in 1981.[7] Funding for fiscal 1984 was $600 million less than

in fiscal 1980. Most of the present Administration's child care initiatives focus on encouraging the private sector and state and local governments to replace the Federal role in funding. This shift toward a decentralized funding policy has taken its toll on individual programs, and the effects will continue to be highly disruptive through the next decade. Many centers relying on public subsidies will have to close their doors for lack of funding, and the technical assistance once available for beginning new programs and training staff has all but disappeared. This also has had important ramifications for the quality of those programs surviving budget cuts. In addition, the Federal government is less likely than ever to promulgate national day care standards. Since it dropped action in revising and expanding the Federal Interagency Day Care Regulations (FIDCR), there has been action taken in many states to deregulate day care and disarm state licensing agencies altogether.[8]

THE DEVELOPMENT OF NEW MODELS FOR THE DELIVERY OF SERVICES

During the past few years we have seen an unprecedented demand for child care created by the increasing number of females who have joined the labor force. Simultaneously, the population of children of appropriate age to attend infant, toddler, and preschool programs has increased by nearly 20 percent. Both these trends are expected to continue during the next decade.[9] This demand, coupled with a shrinking Federal commitment to subsidize child care, has spawned the development of many new models for the delivery of child care services. The next decade will continue to be characterized by an increased need for child care options. The following is a brief overview of some of the caregiving models that exist today.

Employer-sponsored programs. Employer sponsorship of child care is not a new phenomenon. Indeed, during World War II when more than three million married women entered the work force, child care became imperative and many defense plants provided such services. After the war, however, most of these programs closed, and industry sponsorship of child care was limited to a few scattered industries. During the 1970s, in response to the influx of women into the work force, business and labor began again to explore the feasibility of providing day care as a fringe benefit to employees.[10] In the last few years, such employer-supported child care programs have grown significantly from only 100 programs in

1978 to an estimated 1500 programs in operation today.[11] However, not all of these provide direct services to children in on-site or near-site programs, since they encompass a broad range of options reflecting the differing characteristics of businesses, labor force compositions, company goals, and family needs, to include flexible personnel policies, information and referral programs, and voucher payments to parents. Proponents of employer-sponsored child care report that such policies directly benefit the employer, as such programs pay good dividends on the investment in terms of increased productivity, staff morale and loyalty, enhanced public image, improved recruitment, and reduction in turnover, absenteeism, and tardiness. Of course not all employers are impressed with the results, and point out that many parents do not want to commute on public transportation during rush hour with their young children. They are also concerned about the high start-up costs of providing services, as well as the equity considerations for employees who do not have children.

Family day care. Over the past few years family day care in private homes, referring to any arrangement where up to eight children are cared for under one roof, has gained a new respectability. Many parents prefer this smaller, home-like environment for infants, and it has indeed been estimated that well over half of all child care for children under the age of five is provided by family day care providers.[12] Unfortunately, only a fraction of these facilities are licensed, perhaps less than 20 percent.

Public-sponsored programs. There are several different types here. Many school districts, for example, provide comprehensive child care services to parents of children at risk (those with physical handicaps, of extremely young parents, and from low-income families). Funding for these programs comes from a variety of sources including Title XX block grant monies, local taxes, AFDC reimbursements, and sliding-scale fees paid by parents. Several states are considering legislation to increase the public school's role in serving young children.[13] Another type is offered at many of the high schools or vocational training sites throughout the country. These programs, most often half-day, provide a dual role of training high school age students in the principles of child development and early childhood education, and of providing a preschool experience for the young children enrolled in the program. Still another type is offered under the auspices of local park districts. These programs, usually low cost and part time, provide enrichment activities for young children (e.g., kin-dergym), or custodial care for young-children for a few hours each week (e.g., Mother's Day Out).

Church-sponsored programs. It is estimated that as much as 50 percent of the center-based care provided in this country is housed on religious property.[14] In 1983, the National Council of Churches of Christ conducted a national study to determine the extent and nature of church-based child care. One striking finding was that local churches are taking the initiative in providing child care without the support or urging of the national hierarchy.[15] Church involvement thus seems to be entirely a grass-roots phenomenon, a response to an overwhelming community need.

Programs sponsored by social service agencies. Numerous programs are sponsored by nonprofit social service agencies such as the YMCA, YWCA, Salvation Army, and Community Centers. Many of these are half-day enrichment programs for young children, while others provide full-day care for children of working parents. Funding generally comes from a variety of sources including Head Start, United Way, parent fees, and local foundations. In years past, many of these relied heavily on Comprehensive Employment Training Act (CETA) funding from the Federal government and have now had to cut back services.

Programs sponsored by institutions of higher education. Colleges and universities have for many years run laboratory (demonstration) preschools for teacher training and research, but the structure, funding, and clientele of these programs has gradually changed over the past few years. Few colleges now have the financial resources to subsidize lab schools, and many demonstration schools have closed. Others have had to find alternative sources of funding by expanding hours and services and opening enrollment beyond the children of faculty and students to include those from the immediate community.

Private proprietary and corporate programs. The increase in demand for child care has dramatically affected the private sector during the past decade, including small, individual enterprises like Mary Jane's Nursery School, as well as large, corporate chains such as Daybridge Learning Centers or Kinder Care. Most demographic analysts project a continuation of the growth in the private sector well into the 1990s.[16] These programs run the gamut in philosophical orientations as well as the kinds of services they provide. Some remain half-day nursery schools for preschool children, and others provide comprehensive full-day care for infants, toddlers, and preschoolers, as well as after-school care for school-age children. These programs also vary widely in the quality of services they offer. There appears to be a general bias in the public's belief that nonprofit programs have better qualified staff, pay their teachers more, and generally provide a higher quality of care. There are indeed many programs that have well-prepared and -paid staff to give excellent care for young children, even though some private proprietary programs are singularly motivated to maximize profits.

Information and referral programs. These are also referred to as resource and referral programs and increasingly are seen as a viable way to make the delivery of child care services more efficient and effective. Such programs are generally run by nonprofit community organizations or state and local social service agencies, and they gather and disseminate information on enrollment trends, needed services in the community, different programs, and staff employment possibilities. Several states have taken the initiative to appropriate seed money for information and referral centers.[17]

ENSURING QUALITY— A CENTRAL CONCERN

Beyond the mere provision of child care for parents, the concern of early childhood educators extends to the *quality* of the services.[18] With cutbacks in financial support for enforcing and upgrading child care licensing standards, monitoring the quality of programs is becoming increasingly difficult. Although recent reports of child abuse in center-based programs have focused national attention on the issue, very little action has been taken to date to remedy the situation. The issue of regulating and licensing early childhood centers is a complex one, however. The quality of child care has typically been conceptualized as a continuum with harm at one end and optimum child development at the other end. It is obvious that cramped space, inadequate heating, or negative teacher actions would be towards the harm end, but specifying the quality end is not that easy.[19] While evaluation researchers often use different yardsticks to measure expected outcomes of early childhood programs, most child care licensing practices are only concerned with enforcing minimal standards that usually have to do with the health and safety of children. As center-based child care has grown, so too have several interest groups that question the right of the state to set any standards at all. Many center owners from the private sector consider regulation and licensing a threat to the free

enterprise system, and many church-sponsored programs view licensing as a violation of the separation of church and state.

One promising development with respect to the quality issue occurred in 1984, when the National Association for the Education of Young Children (NAEYC) launched a nationwide voluntary accreditation system for early childhood programs.[20] A set of guidelines developed for this new accreditation system involves all aspects of a program, including staff-child interaction, curriculum, staff-parent interaction, staff qualifications, health and safety, nutrition, and program evaluation. The procedure involves three steps: (1) The center director, staff, and parents examine the program's operations to identify strengths and weaknesses. This self-study culminates in a descriptive report noting areas of compliance and improvements that have been made. (2) Validators make an on-site visit to the program to verify the accuracy of the center's report. (3) A commission reviews the program report and makes a decision. At this point, the NAEYC accreditation system is still a voluntary procedure, but it holds considerable promise for upgrading program services and ensuring quality throughout the country.

A final point needs to be made—quality is intricately linked to the content of the early childhood education curriculum, but it does *not* equal academics. Educators who see the detrimental effects of excessive stress in young children placed in an academic pressure cooker are becoming increasingly concerned about those who view early learning in its narrow cognitive context.[21] Most child development experts agree that the emphasis must be on developing a broad-based competence in the young child, involving those capacities or processes, cognitive, social, emotional, and physical, which determine effective functioning in a wide range of situations. Here, educating the public becomes imperative.

THE PROFESSIONALIZATION OF EARLY CHILDHOOD EDUCATORS

High quality programs are run by well-prepared, competent, and dedicated staff with a firm understanding of human development and learning. Studies conducted in a variety of settings have repeatedly shown that the staff quality is a critical determinant of overall program quality.[22] Thus any attempt to improve early childhood programs must look at the professional qualification of both the classroom teacher and the program director. Unfortunately, political and economic realities work against the creation of a well-prepared child care work force. Requirements for certification are minimal, and current licensing standards do not require advanced academic work. Less than optimal working conditions and low occupational status work against the recruitment of competent and dedicated personnel. There is little incentive for potential workers to enter the field where, upon completion of a four-year college degree, teachers can expect to earn only slightly more than minimum wage. Any further schooling rarely makes a difference in compensation. Moreover, the low pay is seldom balanced by a short work week or other benefits such as health coverage, paid vacations, or retirement.

Given this situation, it is not surprising that disillusionment is widespread among early childhood workers. Low morale, job stress, and burnout are not uncommon as many dedicated teachers and directors find themselves frustrated, and many simply leave their positions to look for more lucrative and less stressful jobs.[23] Staff turnover in child care centers averages 30 to 40 percent a year, far greater than in other human service professions. Indeed, the Bureau of Labor Statistics reports that child care work is among the country's top 10 job categories with the highest turnover.[24] This puts a tremendous strain on programs that must search out and retrain new staff, thus disrupting continuity and risking compromises in quality. Opportunities for further professional development are one effective way to retain the best and most capable in the profession. In-service training for teachers and directors not only helps them expand their knowledge base and improve skills, but also has the ancillary benefit of increasing commitment to the profession. Despite the clear link between quality child care and staff qualification, there appears to be virtually no government support for funding the professional development of child care workers. What little money allocated to centers subsidized by Title XX was totally eliminated by the Omnibus Budget Reconciliation Act of 1981. Most programs are not in a position to fill this void and to provide comprehensive in-service training for their staff, or financial assistance to those

wishing to enroll in local colleges and universities. Recent tightening of Federal student loan monies has further aggravated the difficulty.

The professionalization of early childhood workers will remain a central issue for the next decade. Some efforts are underway to help improve the situation. On a national level, the Child Care Employee Project and the Day Care Workers Connection publish newsletters and offer information about employee rights. These organizations also conduct workshops and provide materials for program directors on how to improve personnel policies and upgrade working conditions. Many colleges of education are also focusing attention on the issue. At the author's institution, for example, an Early Childhood Professional Development Project has recently been launched to give financial assistance for program directors to pursue studies in early childhood leadership and advocacy and to conduct in-service training for teachers and directors on a variety of early childhood topics. Some important strides are also being made at the state level. The Illinois Association for the Education of Young Children, for example, has just initiated the Society of Early Childhood Professionals. The Society's goals are to expand the public's awareness of the importance of early childhood education and give recognition to those who promote high quality work.

Professionals in early childhood education talk about a kind of quiet revolution taking place in their field. Welcome or not, recent social, political, and economic developments have forced them to reexamine their functions and devise different ways through which to serve young children and their caregivers better. Changes are apparent in the scope and nature of programs, the funding and regulatory roles of the government, forms and varieties of service delivery, means and manners of quality monitoring, and professionalization efforts of personnel. Early childhood education is clearly in a state of flux, searching for greater legitimacy and a sense of identity, and the next decade will prove vital in determining just what that identity will be.

DISCUSSION QUESTIONS

1. Do social and family changes influence the scope and nature of early childhood programs in the schools?
2. Will the federal and state governments have a larger role in planning and funding programs?
3. How will an increased variety in program sponsorship influence program coordination, quality control, and delivery?
4. How will the preparation of teachers and other personnel respond to some of the current trends?

11. EDUCATING THE VERY YOUNG: A CALL FOR CLEAR THINKING

by David Elkind

Education theorists from Plato to Maria Montessori have recognized that the education of preschool children is on a continuum with the formal education provided by the schools—and that, indeed, there can be meaningful schools for preschool children.

In our own day, there is a growing demand for out-of-home programs for preschool children. But this demand does not grow out of a Platonic concern for the proper upbringing of the young or even out of a Montessorian concern that young children be given the kind of intellectual stimulation needed to nurture their budding mental abilities. Rather, the contemporary demand for out-of-home programs for young children derives first and foremost from parents' need for quality child care while they work and pursue careers. Theorists like Plato and Montessori wanted professionals to rear young children because they felt it was too important a task to be left to parents. Today's parents want professionals to care for their young children because they do not have the time to do so themselves.

The difference is very important. For the theorists, providing young children with a sound education was justification for separating a young child from its parents. For today's parents, however, work and career are the reasons they put young children into out-of-home programs. Providing children with early childhood education is often merely a rationalization for putting young children in out-of-home programs.

It is because today's parents—and to some extent teachers and educational administrators—do not fully appreciate the nature and value of early childhood education that there is so much confusion in the field today. In some respects, schools are involved in early childhood education for the wrong reasons. They're responding to the demand of parents for quality child care facilities, rather than to convictions about the benefits of early childhood education. To help clarify the nature and value of early childhood education and its place within the educational enterprise, I will address some of the most frequently asked questions about the education of young children.

Can early childhood education be more than custodial care?

It seems to me that this question raises an artificial dichotomy between education and child care. At all levels of education, there is some degree of child care. This is true even at the university level, where the concept of *in loco parentis* was generally accepted until the revolutions of the 1960s and seems to be reemerging now. And the child-care functions of the public schools are increasing as more and more of them provide before- and after-school programs for children of parents who work. And, of course, in boarding schools the child care responsibility of the schools is very large indeed.

PRESCHOOL PREP SCHOOL?

So the issue is not education versus child care but rather what proportion of each of these two components should be provided at any particular level of schooling. It is certainly true, that programs for young children must, of necessity, involve more child care than must programs for elementary school children, but the difference is relative, not absolute. Teachers at the preschool level must do more comforting, more limit setting, more crisis intervention than teachers at the higher grade levels. But they are also helping young children acquire the fundamental concepts of space, time, number, causality, relations, and nature—concepts that form the essential data base for all later learning. In addition, preschool teachers help children acquire the preacademic language and social skills, such as paying attention and taking turns, that formal education presupposes.

Does an early start mean an early finish?

Is education a race? In a race, it is certainly true that an early start may give the competitor a better chance of winning. But education is not a race. There is certainly not a starting point—nor is there a finish line. A diploma does not signify that one

See page 324 for acknowledgment, footnotes, and suggestions for further reading.

has won a race but only that one has learned enough to go on learning at a particular level. Education, in the broadest sense, is an ongoing adaptation to our social and physical environment; it ends only when we do.

The idea of early childhood education as an early start that insures an early finish in an educational race is, in part at least, an unfortunate byproduct of the Head Start programs. Numerous studies, including one done in 1983 by the Consortium of Longitudinal Studies, show that Head Start programs have provided much-needed health and education benefits for millions of disadvantaged preschool children. There is no question as to their value for the families they serve. Nonetheless, the choice of the phrase "Head Start" was unfortunate. "Head Start" does imply a race. And not surprisingly, when middle-income parents heard that low-income children were being given a "Head Start," they wanted a similar "Head Start" for their children.

But education is not a race. There is absolutely no evidence that a child who is taught to read at the age of three has any lasting advantage over a child who learns to read at age six or seven.* Indeed, the evidence all points in the other direction. In the 1930s Carlton Washburn compared classes of children who had been taught to read in first grade with children who had been taught to read at ages seven and eight. He found that when these young people reached adolescence, both groups read at comparable levels. But the late reading group were more interested, spontaneous readers than were the early reading group.

Starting children in formal academics too early may, in fact, do more harm than good. Cross-cultural data (described in *Comparative Reading: Cross-National Studies of Behavior and Processes in Reading and Writing*, Macmillan, 1973) are quite convincing in this regard. In Denmark, where reading instruction follows a language experience approach and formal instruction is delayed until age seven, there is almost no illiteracy. In contrast, in France, where state-mandated formal instruction in reading begins at age five, some 30 percent of the children experience reading problems. Likewise the data from two studies (one by Benjamin Bloom and one by June Cox and others) and a recent Gallup survey of people who have attained eminence make it very clear that the parents of gifted children did not impose their learning priorities upon their young offspring. Rather they followed the child's lead, emphasizing play and a rich, stimulating environment rather than formal instruction. Education, then, is not a race, and

teaching the wrong things at too early an age constitutes miseducation, putting children at risk for short-term stress and long-term learning problems—for no purpose.

THE DISADVANTAGED

Is preschool education crucial for disadvantaged children?

This question has to be answered in both the broad and narrow sense of *crucial*. In the broadest sense, healthy early childhood education is crucial for all children. All young children will benefit from the opportunity and support for fully developing their intellectual, emotional, and social abilities. To the extent that disadvantaged children are perhaps less likely to receive such education at home or at school than are advantaged children, special efforts need to be made in order to insure that disadvantaged children get off to a good start.

There is, however, a narrower sense in which the word *crucial* is used. Is early childhood education crucial for disadvantaged children to succeed academically as students and occupationally as adults? This is a more complex question, with social and political overtones. It harks back to some of the motivations for introducing early childhood education into this country during the last half of the 19th century. The first early childhood programs were for the children of immigrants, whose parents had to work. It was hoped that these early childhood programs would socialize children and keep them from becoming delinquent teenagers.

I feel strongly that the schools, at whatever level, should not be used to solve social problems that do not originate in the schools. My objection to busing was not that I was in any way opposed to integration, but that I could not see how busing was going to change adult attitudes. It seemed unlikely to me that a child who went to an integrated school but who never saw Blacks (or whites) in his or her home or community was going to be any less prejudiced than a child attending a nonintegrated school. Without parents making an attempt at integration, integration in the schools alone was bound to fail, at least as a way of solving the problems of racial prejudice and discrimination.

In the narrow sense of whether early childhood education is crucial for resolving the problems of poverty, unequal opportunity, cultural bias, and racial prejudice in our country, the answer is quite clearly no! Early childhood education should not be expected any more than education in general to solve social problems whose roots and dynamisms lie elsewhere. I dearly wish we could stop using education to ease our guilty consciences about the social ills in our society.

On the other hand, healthy early childhood education *in combination with* comprehensive health care, education, and job training for parents would go far towards alleviating some of the social problems of our society.

PRESCHOOL CURRICULUM

What skills, if any, should a preschool teach?

A basic misunderstanding about the education of preschool children is that it should be involved with teaching—albeit at a more elementary level—the skills that are taught in first grade. The error here is the assumption that young children are lacking in learning skills! This is not at all the case. In many ways, the four- and five-year old child is like the nine- or 10-year-old child who has mastered reading and math and can now put these skills to use acquiring more information.

Young children have a variety of learning skills at their command. What they need is the opportunity to exercise these skills, not to learn new ones. Consider the learning skills preschool children have at their disposal. First of all, they can *discriminate* large from small, black from white, soft from hard, and so on. In addition, they can *match to sample*, that is, given a picture of a boat they can select a similar boat from a group of pictures of different objects. They can also *classify* like objects—put all the brown beads in one pile and all the white ones in another. And they can begin to *seriate* according to size, indicating the smallest, next smallest, and so on. What young children need are the materials and the opportunities to use these skills to acquire a variety of concepts.

This is not to say that young children do not have to learn anything in the way of math or language, but only that they have to learn math and language *concepts* that will then make it possible to learn higher order math and language skills. For example, through classifying and seriating many different materials, children eventually get to the point where they can construct a notion of a "unit," something that is both like and different from something else.** A true unit concept is basic to performing all arithmetic operations and hence to the attainment of all math skills.

Young children are already equipped with the skills they need to construct the concepts on which to base the further skills they will acquire through formal instruction. Teaching young children academic skills is miseducation, because it fails to take account of the child's existing skills and the concepts the child must construct with them.

Young children do need to learn some skills, but not the formal reading and math skills that are more appropriately and effectively taught at later age levels.

Should the preschool program reproduce the structure of kindergarten?

The answer to this question depends upon what is meant by the "structure" of the kindergarten. In education, structure tends to be a very ambiguous word, used in many different ways by many different people. If a kindergarten is a true kindergarten, that is, if it provides a developmentally appropriate curriculum, then such a program would, with some slight modifications, be appropriate for four-year-olds. An age-appropriate program for young children takes account of their specific modes of learning and provides an environment—a structure—that enables children to fully exploit these learning modes.

The learning of young children is *manipulative* and *fundamental*, as opposed to the learning of older children and adults, which is primarily *symbolic* and *derived*. Young children learn through direct interaction with persons, places, and things. They must learn firsthand about hot and cold, sweet and sour, green and red, square and round, up and down, and much more. This is manipulative fundamental learning for which there really is no substitute. A congenitally blind person can be told about red or green but can never really get a true idea of color. The blind person's learning of color is symbolic, by way of words, and derived from the experience of others, rather than fundamental, constructed from the blind person's own experience.

The young child's learning is also *permeable* rather than *compartmentalized*, as it is in older children and adults. The categories of reading, math, science, social studies, and art are really not appropriate for young children, whose minds are not organized according to adult categories. Partly because their learning is permeable, and partly because what they are learning is at such an entry level, they are always learning in many different domains at once. Accordingly, young children learn in "spreads" rather than in "steps." Children making soup, for example, are learning the names of the vegetables (language), the shapes of the vegetables (geometry), the weights of the ingredients (math), and the effect of heating up the contents (science)—not to mention social cooperation in making and enjoying a consumable product.

Young children are also guided by what I have called the *structural imperative*, a need to find stimuli to exercise their emerging mental abilities. To illustrate, young children who are just acquiring quantitative skills spontaneously count any set of things they can find. And some children—about one or three per 100—have a structural imperative for reading. They teach themselves to read and ask adults for help when they need it.

Finally, *play* is an important learning mode that serves a somewhat different function among young children than it will at a later age. Young children have few ego defenses; they frequently lose self-esteem. Play is a means of asserting their competence and restoring their self-esteem. While young children may learn something academic from, say, playing with dinosaurs, that learning is secondary to what they gain in self-confidence and self-esteem by being able to assert their competence over those large creatures. In short, we must not attempt to transform a young child's play into a lesson.

The structure of an effective kindergarten classroom provides an environment conducive to the full utilization of these modes of learning. Such a classroom is organized into "interest" (not subject matter) areas, where children can acquire fundamental concepts through active manipulation. The teacher works with small groups of children and helps to guide their inquiry. Providing a balance scale and then asking children to predict what happens when a nail is put in one cup and a feather in another is an example of teacher-guided inquiry.

Group activities and a readily accessible play area are other components of healthy early childhood programs. A teacher-child ratio of not more than 1 to 15 is still another ingredient. All these components help the child maximize fundamental and manipulative learning, encourage permeability, provide nourishment for the structural imperative, and support the child's dramatic play.

If a kindergarten is designed and taught so as to encourage the basic learning modes of the five-year-olds, it is easily adapted to accommodate four-year-olds, who share the same learning modes but who may need a little more direction and a few more limits than their older siblings.

PRESCHOOLERS AND CHOICE

To what extent should preschool children choose the activities they will engage in?

The question of how much choice and responsibility children should have for the curriculum is one that has to be asked at all levels of education. One of the criticisms that the 1983 report *A Nation at Risk* leveled at high schools is that they offer a "smorgasbord" curriculum that caters to the demands of students rather than the "core" curriculum demanded by educational theory and practice.

The issue of choice always has at least two dimensions. One of these is the freedom of the student to choose among educational offerings; the other, the depth, variety, and appropriateness of the offerings. In a small college, the student has less freedom of choice than in a large university only because he or she has fewer options to choose from. In the same way, good preschool programs provide children with more freedom than poor ones, in part because they provide more educational choices.

The issue of choice is thus really no different at the preschool level than at other levels of education. There is a very definite core curriculum, a set of skills, concepts, and values that it is desirable for all children to acquire. There are also various "elective" activities, which permit children to follow their own inclinations. The core curriculum of the preschool includes such skills as paying attention, following instructions, taking turns, and completing a task. With respect to knowledge, children should know numbers and letters, the basic colors and forms, and have a substantial passive vocabulary and a good working active vocabulary by the time they leave preschool. They should also have a beginning sense of weights and measures, know basic plants and animals, and have had exposure to music, songs, and rhythmic activities.

The preschool teacher insures that all young children acquire this basic curriculum by encouraging all the children to participate at one time or another in activities where these basic skills and concepts are emphasized. For example, a child who spends too much time in the block corner is encouraged to move to the reading and science area to give other children a chance with the blocks. In this way, the child learns to take turns at the same time that he or she is directed to move on to another curricular area.

So, as at all levels of education, the preschool child's opportunities for choice are limited by the curricular offerings and by the demands of the core curriculum. In a good preschool program, the child has considerable freedom in deciding *when* he or she will pursue a particular activity (curricular area), but much less freedom in deciding *what* curricular areas are available for exploration. The *what* is determined by how the classroom is arranged and by how the teacher encourages children to move from one activity area to another. In short, the way in which the preschool environment is prepared limits the child's choices, as does the teacher, who insures that each child sample all the activities available.

Does it really matter if a child attends preschool before entering kindergarten?

One way to answer this question is to ask whether it really matters if a child attends elementary school before junior high or junior high before high school.

The analogy is not as absurd as it first appears. Parents who are extraordinarily competent and dedicated and who have both the time and the energy can provide the essentials of formal education to their children at home. It is true, of course, that the more advanced the schooling, the less able the home is to provide equivalent expertise, equipment, and facilities. A parent might come close to duplicating what a nursery school offers much more easily than he or she could duplicate the offerings of, say, a high school.

If parents possess the competence to provide young children with a variety of learning experiences, with exposure to other children and adults (perhaps by means of neighborhood play groups), along with opportunities for small and large motor play, then home schooling may suffice to prepare children for kindergarten. But if parents do not have the commitment, the time, the energy, and the resources to provide young children with an environment that approaches that of the good early childhood program, then it *does* matter whether a child attends a preschool. And it matters for exactly the same reason that it matters if a parent keeps a child out of elementary school but does nothing educational at home.

The issue then is not whether preschool is important, but rather to what extent home schooling can duplicate what preschool has to offer.

Should public schools get into the business of prekindergarten education?

What I have been trying to argue throughout this [chapter] is that early childhood education is part of a continuum that includes elementary and secondary education. There is, after all, a profession of early childhood education. At many universities and colleges, students can receive degrees in early childhood education. The Bank Street School in New York City and the Eliot Pearson Department of Child Study at Tufts near Boston are but two of the best known centers for training early childhood educators. There is a professional organization—the National Association for the Education of Young Children—with a membership of more than 55,000, which offers journals, newsletters, and accreditation procedures.

Early childhood education is just that—education—not glorified babysitting. For early childhood education to function as a legitimate part of public education, however, means that professionals in public education must accept early childhood education as a distinct educational discipline. This does not mean that public education should take full responsibility for all three- and four-year-olds. Since home schooling is more feasible at the younger age levels, parents should have more freedom in this regard. In my view public schooling for three- and four-year-olds should not be mandatory.

IS PRESCHOOL CRUCIAL?

On the other hand, with more and more two-career families, fewer parents are available to provide the kind of home schooling that young children need to help them fully realize their abilities. Public school programs, along with privately supported preschool programs, can provide an educational setting for children whose parents cannot provide it at home. Some 23 states already have legislation pending to provide schooling for four-year-olds, so there is a growing recognition that early childhood education should become a legitimate part of public education.

There are dangers here, however, and that is why some of us in early childhood education have been reluctant to advocate the institutionalization of education at this level. Early childhood education is little understood by officials at higher levels of education. Consequently, the danger is that it will be perceived as little more than a downward extension of elementary education. This is already happening in preschool programs where testing, workbooks, and group drill are now imposed on four- and five-year-olds.

Early childhood education must be taken on its own terms. We do not teach the high school curriculum at the junior high level or the junior high curriculum at the elementary school level, so why in the world should we teach the elementary curriculum at the preschool level?

Yes, early childhood education should become part of public education, but on its own terms. Early childhood education has its own curriculum, its own programs of teacher training, its own methods of evaluation and classroom management.

These overlap curriculum, teacher training, evaluation, and classroom management at upper levels of schooling, but they are far from being identical.

Early childhood has been waiting in the wings of education for centuries. It is time for it to come on stage as a full-fledged member of the educational cast. The whole performance can only be enhanced by its addition.

DISCUSSION QUESTIONS

1. What are the disagreements about early childhood education programs?

2. Should early education programs be based on a universal curriculum of goals and skills, or should programs that serve different populations diversify their purposes?

3. How should programs assure that the child has choice?

4. Is early childhood education in the schools going to become a "regular" part of the educational continuum?

5. What is special about early education in the schools? How can unique features be preserved and nurtured?

12. PRESCHOOL CHILDREN IN THE PUBLIC SCHOOLS: GOOD INVESTMENT? OR BAD?

by Deborah Burnett Strother

Early childhood education has become a hot topic, with several forces working together to push the issue onto the national agenda. For example, the excellence movement has brought more stringent coursework requirements—and greater pressures on children who were already at risk of school failure. Meanwhile, as the world market grows increasingly competitive, the public recognizes that American young people must be better educated and more adaptable. Some parents, hoping to rear academic superstars, are pushing their youngsters to read and write at a very early age. Many observers are concerned about the increasing number of children who suffer the harmful effects of poverty.

But the growing number of working mothers is perhaps the strongest force pushing early childhood education onto the national agenda. In 1984-85 approximately 55 percent of women with children under the age of 15 were in the labor force, according to the U.S. Census Bureau. Nearly 25 percent of these working mothers enrolled their children in organized child-care facilities, such as nursery schools and day-care centers.[1]

Inspired by these forces and by the highly publicized positive effects of some preschool programs, business leaders and legislators. . . have begun to maintain that high-quality early education for all children is not an expense, but a necessary investment. As commission and task force reports, congressional bills, and the mass media have begun to deal with the growing need for child care, the term *child care* itself has expanded to cover a spectrum of meanings from preschool programs to custodial care.

Though the words they use may vary, legislators, business leaders, and parents agree that a need exists for more daylong programs for preschoolers. There is little consensus, however, on such issues as curriculum, funding, location of the programs, criteria for admission, teacher preparation, and teacher certification.

The Committee for Economic Development (CED) has recommended that the federal government fund broad-scale "prevention programs" for all at-risk children from birth through age 5.[2] Members of the House Select Committee on Children, Youth, and Families have maintained that "better use of the public school would expand the number of safe, affordable child-care options available to parents."[3] And the National Governors' Association recommended that states work with 4- and 5-year-old children from poor families "to help them get ready for school and to decrease the chances that they will drop out later."[4]

POLICY

Policy making in the field of early childhood education is in its infancy, and most states have little experience in setting up programs, according to Norton Grubb.[5] If the current push for early childhood education programs comes to shove, most states will have the opportunity to create an early childhood education policy from scratch. To develop an effective policy, however, policy makers must first agree on what constitutes effective programming. In order to do this, according to Grubb, they must reconcile such issues as the conflict between the goals and methodology of elementary educators and those of early childhood educators.

Grubb points out that most child-care centers and preschool programs rely on a Piagetian model, whereby children learn through their own experimentation and initiative. Most elementary teachers, by contrast, implicitly follow a behaviorist model, whereby children learn through structured interaction with the teacher and are graded on their performance. If preschool programs are placed in the public schools, some educators and parents are concerned that these programs will emphasize formal academic instruction for children as young as age 3. David Elkind has warned that formal learning programs for the very young are "risks to the child's motivation, intellectual growth, and self-

See pages 324–25 for acknowledgment and references.

esteem and could well do serious damage to the child's emerging personality."[6]

FUNDING

The federal government currently provides nearly $2 billion in relief for families that have incurred child-care expenses.[7] But two-thirds of that sum goes to families with incomes above the median, and none goes to the large number of families who lack sufficient disposable income to take advantage of the tax credits that provide the relief.

To reach such families, a variety of bills related to preschool and child-care programs have been— or are about to be—submitted to Congress. There are bills to provide tax incentives for employers who develop child-care centers in the workplace, a bill to cap the tax credit for child care (so that dollars now going to middle-income families can be diverted to low-income families to help them pay for child care), and bills to provide adult education for parents with limited parenting skills and to provide school-readiness training for their young children. Last fall the Alliance for Better Childcare, a coalition of more than 80 national organizations, proposed a bill calling for $2.5 billion, 85 percent of which would go to help low-income families pay for child care. The remaining 15 percent would pay for such services as training, the dissemination of information, and referral services. Meanwhile, the Welfare Reform Bill has new child-care provisions designed to serve women enrolled in job-training programs.

Legislators and business leaders who are pushing the child-care initiatives cite research findings on early childhood programs to support their position. However, some educators are raising important questions about this practice. Last May, at a symposium inaugurating a new early childhood education research center in Memphis, several speakers expressed concern about the speed with which legislation is being enacted, policy is being set, and programs are being created using inadequate or inappropriate research data.

Jane Stallings, head of the Department of Curriculum and Instruction at the University of Houston, talked about the growing number of state-mandated programs created without supporting research. "We are being told what should be taught with very little evidence [to back up these assertions]," she said. "So much of the legislation is aimed at raising achievement test scores. Are we evaluating what we value?"[8] Stallings urged educa-

tors to take a more active role in helping to shape those laws.

Evelyn Moore, executive director of the National Black Child Development Institute, questioned whether public school programs for 4-year-olds will adopt the methods and procedures of elementary education, which she feels have often operated to segregate black children and to label them as nonachievers. The institute she directs has published criteria designed to insure that preschool programs based in the public schools will meet the needs of black children.

Herbert Zimiles, senior research fellow with the Institute for Social Research at the University of Michigan, has warned against viewing preschool programs as a panacea for immensely complicated social problems that cannot be solved by education. Further, he believes that much of the value of preschool education depends on how expertly it is implemented, and he wonders whether the quality and value of preschool education can be maintained if it is implemented on a broad scale. He notes:

> Once regarded as a vitamin supplement painstakingly designed to serve as an enhancer of psychic growth, whose dosage was carefully prescribed by experts for different clients in a restricted age range, early education has begun to serve other purposes and has become, so to speak, an over-the-counter medication, available without prescription. And now, in order to make it universally available, we are about to put it in the drinking water.[9]

Other educators are worried that researchers may be overpromising what early childhood programs can do. In a recent policy report, Carolyn Morado said that some reformers "look to early childhood programs as a solution for complex educational and social problems that have not been solved by other means."[10] Morado warned that such an approach may lead to unrealistic expectations for some programs.

In its own recent report, the Committee for Economic Development cited researcher David Weikart's claim, made in testimony to the Select Committee on Children. Youth, and Families,[11] that every $1 spent on early prevention and intervention can save $4.75 in the costs of remedial education, welfare, and crime further down the road.[12] Yet these figures were derived from Weikart's most recent follow-up study of 98 of the original 123 children with I.Q. test scores between 60 and 90 who had been enrolled in a preschool program with a per-pupil expenditure of $6,187, a figure nearly double the cost of Head Start programs.[13]

Exemplary programs cost money. Many educators warn that it makes no sense to cite evidence regarding the educational benefits of such programs and then to enact legislation that provides inadequate funding for new programs, which must limp along with low expenditures, high pupil/teacher ratios, low teacher salaries, and inadequate teacher preparation.

THE RESEARCH

Several studies conducted during the last 20 years suggest that high-quality early childhood programs have a positive effect on children. Such programs as Head Start, the Institute for Developmental Studies at New York University, the Perry Preschool Program in Ypsilanti, Michigan, the prekindergarten program in New York State, and the Brookline Early Education Program in Massachusetts have succeeded in spurring the developmental and cognitive growth of 3- and 4-years-olds.[14] Researchers found that during the early elementary school years children who participated in the experimental preschool programs had better grades, had fewer failing grades, had fewer absences, and were less often retained than nonparticipants. The participants had greater self-confidence and self-esteem—and so did many of their parents. The participants had better-developed literacy skills, greater curiosity, and less need for special education services. They were more likely than nonparticipants to finish high school. They were more employable, less dependent on public assistance, and less likely to engage in criminal activity.

One study comparing preschool curricula found evidence that, over time, child-initiated learning can have a positive effect on social development. Lawrence Schweinhart, David Weikart, and Mary Larner compared three curricula, one of them relying on teacher-initiated learning (direct instruction) and two of them designed to foster child-initiated learning. They found that participants in the three programs did not differ significantly in I.Q. or in their achievement test scores over time. However, when the researchers interviewed 79 percent of those same children at age 15, they found fewer incidents of delinquent acts among the children who had taken part in the two programs using methods designed to foster child-initiated learning.[15]

At the Memphis symposium, David Weikart called that study "a red flag on the play—it doesn't say direct instruction should not be used on young children. It does say that, if you do prefer to use direct instruction, you'd better have a research design in place in order to assess the outcome."[16] Weikart theorizes that child-initiated learning gives children a greater sense of responsibility because it encourages them to act on their own initiative, both physically and mentally.

Despite the encouraging long-term benefits of preschool reported by Weikart and others, some researchers maintain that generalizing from studies such as these is inappropriate because the researchers followed small numbers of children (and some children dropped out of the studies along the way), because most of the children were economically disadvantaged, and because the programs in which they participated had very high per-pupil expenditures.[17] Those programs provided health and social services, in addition to a preschool curriculum—and they often provided such services to entire families, not just to program participants. The programs used curricula that adhered to principles of child development, and they employed appropriate assessment procedures. The teachers were trained in early childhood development, and they enjoyed strong administrative support. Moreover, parents played an active role in the education of their children.

Indeed, Zimiles has suggested that some of the long-term effects found by Weikart and others may reflect the degree of parental involvement in children's education, not the quality of the program per se. If some children in the group originally selected for preschool later dropped out because their families were unwilling to bring them to school, self-selection may have operated to eliminate those children whose families were least supportive. Zimiles points out that when samples are self-selected (even in part), it is difficult to interpret the meaning of research findings.

PUBLIC SCHOOL
EARLY CHILDHOOD STUDY

How involved are the public schools in preschool education, and what are the characteristics of existing programs? Researchers with the Center for Children's Policy at the Bank Street College of Education and researchers with the Center for Research on Women at Wellesley College recently investigated the involvement of public schools in the development of early childhood programs that are educationally and developmentally sound and responsive to the child-care needs of the families that use them.

The researchers surveyed and analyzed state-level

73

policy and legislation related to preschool education and child care in all the states and the District of Columbia. They surveyed 2,800 U.S. school districts with prekindergarten programs, and they examined a small sample of early childhood programs in depth to see how these programs relate to the communities they serve. (They received information on 1,700 programs, and they explored 12 programs in detail.)

The researchers found that 28 states and the District of Columbia support early childhood education through one of three funding arrangements: (1) pilot or statewide prekindergarten programs, (2) parent education programs (in lieu of direct service to prekindergarten-aged children), or (3) introduction or expansion of the Head Start program. According to Fern Marx, research director of the study at Wellesley, two-thirds of the state programs are intended to serve children at risk of school failure because they come from low-income families or suffer such problems as limited proficiency in English or lack of school readiness.[18]

Of those states offering programs, half contract directly with private agencies and half permit only public schools to provide programs, either directly or through subcontracts with other agencies (primarily private nonprofit schools or Head Start). Marx finds the acceptance of multiple systems of delivering child care exciting, because it increases the likelihood that the needs of working parents and their children will be met. However, the absence in some states of coordination of planning, services, and funding at the local level has caused Head Start programs and state prekindergarten programs to compete increasingly for students, for staff, and for space.

According to Anne Mitchell, director of the study at Bank Street College, the public school programs serve a wide variety of purposes.[19] Thirty-three percent serve special education students, 11 percent are Head Start programs, 16 percent are prekindergarten programs funded by the state, 8 percent are locally funded prekindergarten programs, 9 percent are Chapter 1 prekindergarten programs, 6.5 percent are child-care programs, 2 percent are child-care programs for teenage parents, 3 percent are preschool programs operated by high school students, 3 percent are parent education programs, and 8 percent are magnet school or summer programs.

Eighty percent of the public school programs operate only during the school year, and 60 percent of them operate three hours or less per day. (Child-care programs for the general public and some Chapter 1 programs have longer hours.) The mean class size and the mean teacher/pupil ratio are well within the limits established by high-quality programs; no public school program had classes larger than 18 or a teacher/pupil ratio greater than 1:10. Teachers in some of the early childhood programs in the public schools receive lower salaries than their counterparts in grades K-12; teachers in Head Start, child-care, and locally funded programs receive the lowest salaries.

Half of all the responding school districts in the Wellesley/Bank Street study reported that preschool teachers must be certified in early childhood education. Almost 75 percent of the districts require that preschool teachers hold bachelor's degrees; two-thirds of the districts indicated, however, that previous teaching experience is not a criterion for hiring. Nonetheless, when they were hired, slightly more than half of the preschool teachers in these districts were certified in early childhood education and had already spent at least one year teaching children younger than 5. About 20 percent of the paraprofessionals who were hired by those districts had both one year of training in early childhood education and at least one year of working with young children. Case studies from the Wellesley/Bank Street project showed that strong leadership and active parent participation are key ingredients of high-quality programs. Ninety percent of the districts reported that their early childhood programs offer parent/teacher conferences; about half said that they have parent advisory councils or boards, and a similar number reported that their programs use parent volunteers.

The researchers found great variety in teaching methods and curricula among the early childhood programs they studied. In some programs, the children received breakfast and then spent the entire school day with a given teacher. They chose their own activities, receiving help and companionship from the teacher when necessary. In other programs, the children ate breakfast with aides and had one teacher for "school," another teacher for "day care"—with little communication or coordination among the different caretakers. Some programs were divided into 15-minute periods (marked by bells), during which the teachers directed all activities. The children in these programs were rarely (if ever) allowed to engage in open-ended, creative activities. In some programs, the teachers even determined which child would jump rope, work a puzzle, or climb on the climbing frame. Where skills-based curricula were in use, the children were often given written tests to assess their mastery of the skills being taught. Most of the programs studied had adequate materials and supplies, but some of the more structured programs apparently did not make daily use of these items.

Between Promise and Practice (a book to be published in the [fall] of 1988 by the Bank Street College Center for Children's Policy) will describe in detail the schools that Mitchell and her colleagues visited. Three technical reports, describing the district survey, the state survey, and the case studies, will be available this winter.

A DUAL SYSTEM

Edward Zigler, the first director of the Office of Child Development and an early defender of the Head Start program, now a professor of psychology at Yale University, suggests a new way to use school buildings to deal with the child-care issue.[20] We should "think of two major systems within the school building," he says.

"One system is the formal educational system that we have today, and it won't change. This system will remain in the hands of educators, and they will continue to try to improve it as best they know how," Zigler explains. The second system, according to Zigler, is the child-care system, composed of a child-care center, outreach services, and a referral system.

In other words, each elementary school will contain a center equipped to provide high-quality all-day child care to 3- and 4-year-olds whose parents work outside the home. Five-year-olds will attend kindergarten for half of each school day; they will spend the remainder of the day at home (if a parent is there to oversee them) or at the child-care center (if both parents work outside the home). The child-care center will be available before and after school to serve children between the ages of 6 and 12.

Three kinds of outreach programs will also be available, Zigler predicts, because "not all families' needs are going to be met in the school building." One kind of outreach program will offer support services for new parents. A second kind of outreach program will coordinate and monitor all the local facilities that provide day care for children from birth to age 3 and will provide training and support for workers in those facilities. A third kind of outreach program will provide information and make referrals for parents who have problems related to health, education, or social services.

Zigler believes that child care, like education, should be a state-level responsibility. He recommends that parents pay for child care (with fees adjusted to their incomes) and that the federal government continue to subsidize the program (much as it does now).

Zigler would like to see the federal government support at least one pilot day-care center within the public school system in each state. He maintains that we must work child care into the very structure of the system, rather than expect the private sector and the churches to take care of the problem. The public schools are ideal places for child-care centers, in Zigler's view, because they are social institutions that are permanent, reliable, and close to home.

Zigler and Mitchell both note that close coordination between the day-care center and the host elementary school is important. When there is continuity between the two programs, the young participants will benefit. "You can run a terrific early childhood program," according to Mitchell, "but if you send the children from that program into a rigid, highly structured elementary program that differs considerably in philosophy and approach, it's bound to be a hard transition for them."

Zigler maintains that we have the knowledge to put this vision into effect immediately—if only we could gain access to school buildings. "The people we are serving with day-care centers are not teachers and principals; they are American families," he points out. "We can't allow battles to stand in the way of putting together a logical system that combines two of the basic needs of children—education and child care."

DISCUSSION QUESTIONS

1. What are the research bases for the CED and NGA proposals?

2. Can the expansion of school programs for younger children and into child care services be justified?

3. Should the public schools become the main agency for all early childhood education?

4. Are there common elements of quality and excellence that should be included in any early childhood education program?

13. DAY CARE AND THE PUBLIC SCHOOLS —NATURAL ALLIES, NATURAL ENEMIES

by Bettye M. Caldwell

My personal interest in day care began about 20 years ago at a time when any program of infant stimulation ran against the grain of theoretical ideas about proper upbringing for young children. To some extent this was true even if the mother was the "stimulator." It was especially true, however, if anyone other than the mother were the agent of stimulation and enrichment.

Our concern (Caldwell and Richmond 1964) was primarily directed to young children of poverty who were known to be growing up in somewhat chaotic family circumstances. As many of the mothers were minimally available to their children, either physically or psychologically (Caldwell et al. 1963), our interest was in developing an enrichment program that would in some way supplement the experiences available to children in their homes. Our idea was to have teachers and other specially trained caregivers work with the children for a few hours each day and introduce them to various developmental events intended to excite and stimulate them.

The idea of bringing infants together in groups was totally unacceptable at that time. The common fear was that even short-term separation of infants from their mothers would be tantamount to creating "institutional" rearing conditions. The deleterious consequences of growing up in institutional care were constantly cited in the professional literature (see Bowlby 1952) and publicized in the popular press. Our proposal to develop such a program in Syracuse, New York, was turned down, but we were offered a loophole. The Children's Bureau was willing to consider our request provided we used as subjects only those children who were already receiving some sort of substitute care and that we would not reduce in any way the daily time they spent in contact with their own mothers. In short, we could conduct our own project with children who were already in day care (see Caldwell 1971).

Our center served children from six months through five years of age. It was affiliated first with the Department of Pediatrics of the Upstate Medical Center of the State University of New York and later with the College of Home Economics of Syracuse University. Although the resources of two great universities were behind it, it operated essentially in isolation from the mainstream of either university. It also operated in isolation from the public school system into which most of the children graduated.

While my professional concern centered on preschool children, I was personally involved with the public schools, having a set of twins who entered kindergarten at precisely the time that our project was "discovered" nationally. Occasionally I would be late picking them up from school, and Syracuse winters can be very cold. There I would find two forlorn twins with icy hands and frozen cheeks. I can remember reacting with horror to their not being allowed to wait inside to be picked up; when school was out, children were expected to go home immediately. To me it seemed the most logical thing in the world to think that their elementary school could have provided some sort of extended day care. It struck me as rather ironic that while I was working hard in one part of the city to provide both care and education for other people's children, no one was concerned about providing the care needed to supplement the education mine were receiving.

Shortly thereafter I moved to Arkansas and took with me something of an obsession about the need to develop child care programs in the public school. This obsession was no longer based only on my perception of the need for such care as a service to families but also on my awareness of the need to change the public conception of what day care was or should be. Considered by many people as a service that provided only "care and protection" for low-income children, child care was actually a comprehensive service that could and did provide education, access to medical care, and social services to large numbers of children from all levels of society. It was my conviction that an alliance with public education would help to "legitimize" child care and help it gain respectability

See page 325 for acknowledgment and references.

with parents, professionals, and policymakers. Likewise, it was my hope that the provision of day care in a public school setting would make the elementary educational program more relevant to modern social realities.

NATURAL ALLIES—THE KRAMER MODEL

What developed from this obsession—with a great deal of help from Little Rock School District officials, personnel from the University of Arkansas, an interested granting agency (the Children's Bureau, shortly thereafter subsumed into the newly created Office of Child Development), and a favorable zeitgeist—was the Kramer Model. From 1969 to 1978 the project operated essentially as described here. Some of the major components are still in operation, although with slight programmatic changes and major administrative changes.

EARLY CHILDHOOD-ELEMENTARY CONTINUITY

Continuity between early childhood and elementary educational programs should be as normal and routine as continuity between 2nd and 3rd grades. In most educational settings, however, this is definitely not the case. In fact there is often a change in auspice (from private to public, or from one type of public funding, such as Head Start, to another); in location and size (from private home, church, or small-group center to large school); in educational philosophy and curriculum (from much free choice to a high degree of structure and adult control); and in training background of the personnel. Not infrequently there is distrust on the part of early childhood personnel of elementary personnel, and vice versa. Early childhood teachers often accuse elementary teachers of being concerned with subjects rather than children and of neglecting the "whole child"; elementary teachers sometimes assume and imply that their kindergarten colleagues "just play" with the children and do not "really teach" them anything.

If the transition is from anything other than a public school kindergarten, there is seldom any exchange of records. School personnel do not appear to be particularly interested in knowing much about previous educational experiences, and rarely do they send reports to teachers who previously worked with the children. Thus the new teachers receive no benefits from the insights gained by

their predecessors, and the former teachers have no opportunity to confirm or disconfirm their predictions about future educational progress of individual children.

By having both an early childhood and an elementary program in the same building—with teachers from both segments serving on all committees, attending all meetings, and sharing the same lounge—we hoped to kindle a spirit of united effort directed toward common goals. Although it took some time for this spirit to develop, it unquestionably became an important feature of the Kramer Model.

EDUCATIONAL DAY CARE

The most important component of the Kramer Model was the conversion of the entire school to an "extended day school." That is, the school officially began at 6:45 A.M. and closed at 6:00 P.M. year round. The bells rang at the same time as in all the other elementary schools within the Little Rock School District, but the program operated for the full day. The extra hours and days were funded out of the program grant. Teachers at Kramer taught for the same number of hours and total days as all other teachers in the system (although they did have the option of applying for summer and holiday work for extra pay).

Extra hours were covered by part-time and split-time staff, or, for the early childhood segment, by staggering beginning and ending hours so that at least one certified teacher was on duty at all hours. In a situation like this it is easy to let "natural" preferences work themselves out instead of conforming to statewide work hours. That is, there were always one or two early risers who preferred to begin work at 7:00 and there was always at least one person who preferred to begin work at 9:30 and stay later in the afternoon.

When day care in the public schools is discussed, concern usually is limited to children roughly in the age range of five or six to ten years. (Where kindergartens last only a half day, most working parents keep their children in a child care program until they reach 1st grade.) While this in itself is beneficial, it does not provide the range of coverage that many parents need. That is, a working mother may have children aged seven, four, and two, all of whom need day care. In many communities that can mean three child care arrangements (one school-age setting, one preschool, and one infancy program) rather than one. The elegance of the Kramer extended care arrangement was that it accommodated children from 6 months to 12 years of age in the same physical location. The convenience of this arrangement for working mothers is truly remarkable—and quite rare.

Traditional starting and ending times for public school schedules, and dates for opening in the fall and closing in the spring, are entirely anachronistic in today's world. The times and dates we now have were not arbitrarily set; they were chosen to allow the schools to dovetail with the social realities of the children and families they served. The hours allowed children to complete chores before and after school, and the dates corresponded to times when the children would be needed to help in the fields. It is unfortunate that we are so bound to custom that we have lost sight of the fact that the custom originally corresponded to demographic realities. Once we fully understand today's demographic realities, the question of whether schools should provide day care will become totally obsolete.

PUBLIC SCHOOL-UNIVERSITY COLLABORATION

Other major features of the Kramer Model include having a university professor run the school and serve as its principal; establishing an advisory board to oversee school operation consisting of university and community personnel, in addition to representatives of the Little Rock School District; and establishing special work arrangements for Kramer teachers involving both extra requirements (take a certain inservice course of work and the late-day shift) and special privileges (having an aide in the classroom) not available to other teachers in the system. Although many of the special arrangements required for Kramer went far beyond the day care situation, the same flexibility may well be necessary if a public school day care program is to be anything more than an appendage to the existing operation without any curricular or developmental relevance.

One clear but often overlooked benefit of this university-public school alliance was the constant presence in the school of student teachers and a few doctoral candidates. Not only did their presence confer status on the Kramer teachers, but their excitement about the Kramer philosophy was contagious. For example, it was not uncommon for a 5th grade teacher to complain to an early childhood teacher that a mess "your" children made at the water fountain caused "our" children to slip down. To the students, all the children

were far more likely to be perceived as "our" children, and they contributed to eliminating some of these exclusionary references.

Everything possible was done to help the students "think developmentally." For example, teachers had to spend some time with a class in each quadrant of the program—infancy, early childhood, primary (grades 1–3), and intermediate (grades 4–6). Obviously, they spent the greatest amount of time in the quadrant in which they expected or hoped to teach. Exchange times for teachers were also arranged so that intermediate teachers occasionally taught for a morning in an infancy or early childhood classroom, and vice versa. After such exchanges elementary teachers were rarely heard to complain that the early childhood teachers "had it easy" or early childhood teachers to criticize elementary teachers for not understanding and loving the children enough.

NATURAL ENEMIES

When people ask me what we learned at Kramer, I usually tell them we learned that it isn't easy. Such an arrangement makes so much sense both socially and educationally that one could logically wonder why schools are organized any other way. And yet the two domains of child care and education are also natural enemies.

CONCEPTUAL AND PHILOSOPHICAL DIFFERENCES

The first basis for the adversarial relationship between day care and education relates to the concepts out of which each service pattern has grown and, if you will, to the way in which proponents of each service want the field to be identified. Having developed largely from a social service orientation, day care has been known as a service that provides "care and protection" for children. Schools, on the other hand, provide "education." Such sharp dichotomies represent a misunderstanding of both services, for it is literally impossible to care for and protect young children without educating them, and vice versa. The domain of education already includes many services that might seem to fit more comfortably under the rubric of care and protection: school nurses, health programs, nutrition programs, hot lunches, vision and hearing screening, requirements for immunization, and so on. Likewise, during a large part of the day, every high-quality day care program will provide educational experiences that are similar if not identical to school "teaching programs" for children of comparable age. Thus it is foolish to try to distinguish between the services in terms of shibboleths such as *care* versus *education*. In order for either service to be relevant to the needs of children and families, both components must be present.

Another conceptual distinction already mentioned is that day care is believed to be largely for "poor children from problem families," whereas public education is for "all children." There are now more families with young children whose mothers work outside the home than there are families in which the mother is available fulltime as a caregiver. And because all families supplement parental care with *some* extra-family child care, we recognize that the nature of the family situation no longer defines day care—if, indeed, it ever did. There are more commonalities between the fields than there are differences.

BOTH INSTITUTIONS HELD IN LOW ESTEEM

A second reason for the animosity that we sometimes find between representatives of public education and day care is that, unfortunately, both institutions are often held in low esteem. The current clamor for "educational reform" clearly implies that somehow public education has "failed." Likewise, day care has been denounced by conservatives as "weakening the family" and by liberals as being a "wasteland" of poor quality in which children's lives could be ruined. Leaders of the day care movement have often bristled at suggestions that an alliance between the field and education would be beneficial. A typically hostile objection might be, "The schools have already ruined the older kids; let's not help them do the same thing with the little ones." Natural resistance to such a union was increased by media reports of a national surplus of elementary and secondary teachers and by the suggestion that such teachers could be diverted into the burgeoning day care field if it were part of public education and thereby comparably lucrative for teachers. Early childhood and day care personnel were legitimately offended at the implication that no special training was necessary to work with young children. However, such an attitude on the part of professional educators was no different from that often expressed by the general public and given as a reason for failing to provide higher salaries for early

childhood personnel.

The important point here is that the two fields, each of which had reason to doubt that it was held in esteem by the general public, took a stance against one another rather than forming what should have been a natural alliance. It was as though each sought to bolster its own self-esteem by asserting its independence from and superiority to the other.

MUTUAL NEED—THE BONDING AGENT

The demographic realities of modern life have made this separatism and exclusivity on the part of both day care and public education entirely obsolete. Both fields have undergone travail, and both are dealing with increasingly sophisticated consumers who legitimately advocate education that fits modern urban rather than outdated rural patterns of family living, and day care that accepts its responsibility to provide developmentally appropriate education to young children.

Representatives of both domains must learn to find strengths and assets in one another. The biggest problems many people in the child care field face are low salaries and poor working conditions. Teachers certified in early childhood who work in public schools make, on the average, $5,000 more per year (often for fewer hours and days) than certified teachers who work in child care. Likewise, the public schools are having to try to withstand the major inroads in their clientele by private schools. It is fascinating to note that the new private academies springing up all over the country are not overlooking the profit potential associated with the provision of child care. Almost without exception, such schools are providing extended day care and summer programs. Unless public schools offer comparable services, they cannot hope to hold a major share of the market. And, though we might not want to admit it, marketing is as important for public education as it is for other products and services.

The inroads into support for public education made by this increasing network of private schools have weakened the infrastructure of our educational system. Likewise, allegations of sexual abuse and concerns about maintenance of healthful conditions in child care centers have generated increased concern about the quality and benefit of such programs. One might be tempted to suggest that attempts to unite the two domains are too late; the general public now sees both services as inadequate and flawed.

But, of course, it is never too late to develop a service program that is in harmony with patterns of human need. Because a blending of day care and education can meet the needs of children for developmental guidance and the needs of parents for effective supervision of their children more conveniently than any other pattern of service, I predict that the two domains will move ever closer to one another. The resultant merger will be symbiotic for the two fields and beneficial to children, to their parents, and to society.

DISCUSSION QUESTIONS

1. How can a public school serve the day care needs of the local community?

2. What are the advantages to young children of continuity of care and education from infancy through elementary school?

3. Where did the Kramer School find additional personnel?

4. Is there a conceptual difference between *caring* for young children and *educating* young children?

5. What are the arguments *against* the Kramer School model?

14. LET CHILDREN START SCHOOL WHEN THEY'RE READY!

by Cynthia Parsons

There's not a single, solitary pedagogical justification for asking children to wait until the end of August or the first of September to start their formal schooling. Children should be enrolled as soon as they are able to learn what the school has to teach. Nor is it educationally sound to require teachers to teach groups of youngsters who have nothing in common except for the fact that they are all starting school on the same day.

These practices certainly do not serve middle- or upper-class parents, who have to provide other kinds of educational options until their children are allowed to enter school—knowing all the while that their children are marking time instead of progressing naturally with mastery of the basics. Nor does it do the U.S. school system any good to claim that it meets individual needs, when clearly it ignores such needs right from the start.

Meanwhile, numerous studies have shown that the best educational approach for the children of the poor is to begin formal schooling as early as possible. To focus on birthdates, and thus to ignore the educational needs of such children, is criminal.

Just as they walk on their own when they are ready, children should begin first grade when they are ready. Any given child should attend school full-time when three parties agree that the time is right: the child, his or her parents, and the school officials. Moreover, before any child attends school full-time, he or she should attend part-time—half days once or twice a week, perhaps. This would allow the child to adjust to school; it would also enable the parents and school officials to determine whether or not the child is ready for full-time attendance.

Conceivably, the parents, the school psychologist, the first-grade teacher, and the principal might agree that Tommy or Suzy is ready for full-time attendance—but Tommy or Suzy might disagree. Conversely, a child might plead to remain in the classroom full-time, but the parents or school officials might argue against this option because they see the child as lacking maturity or enthusiasm for school.

Finding solutions to such disagreements makes sense, educationally. But it makes no sense whatsoever to argue that children who turn 6 in February must wait until the following September to start school, while children born in October must start school a month or more before their sixth birthdays.

Then why have we established a single starting date for all first-graders—one related to birthdate but not necessarily to academic readiness? I suspect that this practice stems from primitive accounting practices of 80 to 100 years ago. State aid back in those days was based on the number of pupils in school on any given day. Some states even figured aid by half-days of attendance. Clearly, requiring all pupils to start school on the same day made the accountant's job easier.

I have more difficulty answering the next question I must pose: Why have sound scholars and sensitive parents allowed such a stupid practice to continue all these years? I do not pretend to understand why teachers, administrators, and even professors of education have agreed to be ruled by the calendar, since this forces them to ignore all the knowledge researchers have amassed about individual differences in children's development. Yet, although accounting practices have improved dramatically, the single starting date remains in place—flying in the face of every sound principle of early childhood education.

Let me restate my position once again. Any given child should attend school full-time when three parties agree that the time is right: the child, his or her parents, and the school officials.

This approach would allow primary teachers to manage family-style classrooms, in which experienced students would help the newcomers learn social and academic skills. Right from the start, youngsters who are not "natural" learners would get the individual attention they need. Teachers would quickly figure out how each child learns best and would plan instructional approaches to match those individual needs. Teachers who know how to individualize instruction would probably be thrilled to work in a setting governed by individual needs, not by the calendar.

Can you think of any justification for continuing to mandate a single, early-fall starting date for school? "We've always done it that way" will no longer suffice.

See page 325 for acknowledgment.

DISCUSSION QUESTIONS

DISCUSSION QUESTIONS
1. Is the child's chronological age the determining factor in school enrollment?
2. Do schools have any flexibility for initial school entry?

15. IT DEPENDS ON YOUR AIM

by Raymond S. Moore

Cynthia Parsons is on target when she insists that "children should be enrolled as soon as they are able to learn what the school has to teach." But I question the accuracy of her aim, unless she can tell us when youngsters are really ready for the constraints of formal schooling.

When she fires on "primitive accounting practices of 80 to 100 years ago," she picks off John Dewey, who, in 1898, insisted that *age 8* is "early enough for anything more than an incidental attention to visual and written language form."[1] She also scores a hit on Arnold Gesell, perhaps the best-known children's physician in the United States who urged his readers not to institutionalize children too early.[2]

Parsons aims straight when she accuses most educators of ignoring "all the knowledge researchers have amassed about individual differences in children's development." But she shouldn't find this flaw surprising. Few educators pay more than lip service to inconvenient facts gleaned from the work of historians or educational researchers.

For example, literacy reached its zenith *prior to* the 20th century. In that earlier time, American children attended small common schools for only a few weeks each year, with attendance beginning at some point between the ages of 8 and 12. *The remainder of their education took place at home.* And reviews by the Hewitt Research Foundation of more than 8,000 studies have failed to turn up any replicable research suggesting that *normal* children should be schooled before age 8.[3]

Whether the focus is on achievement, on behavior, on sociability, or on such other aspects of a child's development as the brain, the senses, cognition, coordination, or socialization, available evidence overwhelmingly suggests that, unless the child is handicapped or acutely deprived (a condition not necessarily linked to socioeconomic status),

he or she should be allowed to develop physically and to explore personal fantasies and intuitions until somewhere between ages 8 and 12. Our Stanford team could find no state in which early school entrance laws were founded on replicable research.[4] Except for highly specialized clinical services, even handicapped children are best taught in their homes prior to the age of 8 or 10.

William Rohwer, a faculty member at the University of California, Berkeley, has noted, "All of the learning necessary for success in high school can be accomplished in only two or three years of formal skill study." Such study, he adds, "could mean academic success for millions of school children who are doomed to failure under the traditional education system."[5]

Torsten Husén, a professor at the Institute of International Education of the University of Stockholm, agrees with Rohwer. Reporting on data from 12 countries, Husén expressed alarm at "the strong negative correlation between entry age . . . and attitude towards school."[6]

David Elkind, an authority on Piaget who teaches at Tufts University, has called attention to "a negative correlation between mental growth and formal instruction."[7] Elkind added that, to maximize mental growth, "one could legitimately argue that formal schooling ought to be delayed rather than introduced early." He suggests that we are fostering "burnout" by rushing youngsters into school too early.

Even Benjamin Bloom[8] and Glen Nimnicht,[9] early advocates of compensatory early childhood education, admit that the home is the best educational setting. The principal study supporting early childhood education, the Perry Preschool Project, has for years *focused more attention on the home* (through weekly home visits) than has the typical early childhood education program.[10]

See page 325 for acknowledgment and references.

A variety of studies in the United States and abroad confirm the fact that most children benefit educationally from one-to-one interactions with warm, responsive adults—regardless of whether or not those adults have teaching credentials or college degrees.[11] Not surprisingly, Harold McCurdy's study, sponsored by the Smithsonian Institution, found that genius derives from those situations in which children (1) spend a great deal of time with loving parents and other adults, (2) spend very little time with their peers, and (3) have the freedom to work out their own fantasies under these conditions.[12] McCurdy concluded that our public school system is a "vast experiment" that tends to "suppress the occurrence of genius."

The studies of Urie Bronfenbrenner, a professor at Cornell Univerity, suggest that, at least until grade 5 or 6, children who spend more time with their peers than with their parents become peer-dependent.[13] To the extent that children younger than 10 rely on age-mates for their values, they lose their sense of self-worth, their optimism, their respect for parents, and even their trust in peers. Bronfenbrenner warns of "the age-segregated, and thereby often amoral or antisocial, world in which our children live and grow." He adds, "Central among the institutions which . . . have encouraged these socially disruptive developments have been our schools."

Meanwhile, John Bowlby, a specialist on early childhood with the World Health Organization, contends that children who are pushed out of the home at an early age are in greater danger than many children who are beaten at home.[14] And Martin Engel, then head of the National Demonstration Center for Early Childhood Education, in Washington, D.C., declares that children sense rejection when they are schooled early.[15] Indeed, early schooling may be the most pervasive form of child abuse in the Eighties.

We all talk about parental involvement. But are we more interested in the welfare of children or in maintaining the status quo? How much more involved can parents be than when they participate in the home-schooling renaissance, which causes children to average 30 percent above the national mean on standardized tests and to demonstrate above-average behavior and sociability?[16] Such parents have included national leaders from George Washington to Sandra Day O'Connor, from Benjamin Franklin to George Washington Carver. The home-schooling movement today numbers among its participants scholars at the nation's leading universities and even Tamara McKinney, the world's top woman skier.

It seems that Parsons would shoot straighter with our children if she left them at home a little longer. History has much to teach us. It warns that state control of the family—the real issue here—presages collapse of the society, which is precisely what some sociologists predict for the United States.[17] History, research, and common sense all counsel us to avoid institutionalizing young children. Stronger families mean stronger schools, and that should be our aim.

DISCUSSION QUESTIONS

1. Should enrollment for all children be delayed until they are seven or eight years of age?

2. What are Moore's real arguments against early childhood education?

3. Are the criticisms of early school entrance justified?

4. What are some alternatives to late enrollment that will respond to Moore's concerns?

16. IN DEFENSE OF EARLY CHILDHOOD EDUCATION

by David Elkind

Young children think and learn in different ways than older children and adults. Traditional early childhood education has always taken account of these differences. It recognizes that young children learn best through the active exploration and manipulation of concrete materials. Young children are not yet ready for formal education, involving as it does the inculcation of symbolic rules. Before young children can enter the symbolic world, they need to conceptualize the concrete world which the symbols represent.

Unfortunately, this familiar approach to the teaching of young children is in danger of being forgotten in today's educational climate. Early childhood education is becoming institutionalized and is now subject to a host of social, economic, and political pressures from which it was so long immune. The fundamental differences between the modes of thinking of young children and those of older children and adults tend to be ignored. When some administrators argue, for example, that children should begin kindergarten at age four, they overlook the fact that even in kindergarten many children have trouble with symbols and symbolic rules. If formal learning is difficult for five-year-olds, it is even more so for four-year-olds.

Of course, it might be argued that young children today, thanks to television, computers, electronic toys, and the like, are more intellectually advanced than were children in previous generations.

Modern technology has accelerated the mental development of children, has it not?

Doesn't the new research on children's thinking and learning demonstrate that young children are ready and eager learners who are more capable than we have been willing to admit?

Don't the results of early intervention programs, such as Head Start, demonstrate the effectiveness of early formal instruction?

Isn't it a fact that more children than ever before come to kindergarten after a couple of years of attendance at a nursery school or day care center (or some combination of the two) where they have already been exposed to the traditional kindergarten curriculum? Don't we have to make the kindergarten curriculum more formal to accommodate these children?

These are the questions I wish to address here. Basically, my reply to each of them is "No." Young children today are no more and no less intellectually competent than they were 50 or 100 years ago. This does not mean that we should not educate young children, but that we should do so in ways that are appropriate to their unique modes of thinking and learning.

TECHNOLOGY AND MENTAL DEVELOPMENT

Does early exposure to a technology accelerate mental development, or at least increase the competence of children so exposed?

In response to the first half of the question, there is no evidence that early exposure to a technology in any way accelerates mental development. The overall effect of technology on human nature is to extend and amplify, but not alter our biological capacities. Machines extend and amplify the strength of our muscles, telephones extend and amplify our hearing, telescopes and microscopes extend and amplify our vision, and computers extend and amplify both our short-term and long-term memory.

What has to be emphasized is that such extensions and amplifications do not change our biological potential. Eyeglasses do not alter the visual system any more than a hearing aid alters the auditory system. In the same way, a computer does not alter our ability to remember any more than using an exercise machine gives us bigger muscles. Indeed, it could be argued that technology has contributed to the *decline* of some of those sensory and motor capacities that are not required to the same extent as they might be in a nontechnological society. Exercise, for example, is now an optional leisure-time activity rather than something that occurs naturally in the course of daily living.

Now for the second part of the question. If technology does not improve our sensory or motor capacities, doesn't it improve our brains and make us more sophisticated and knowledgeable than if we did not have the technology? Consider the wonders that children can see on TV: different countries, different life-styles, exotic animals, underwater and space exploration. This must have

See pages 325–26 for acknowledgment and references.

some impact on their knowledge and mental ability even if it doesn't improve their vision or hearing, isn't that so?

To be sure, there is a point here. Children today do indeed have access to more information than was true for any past generation of their age. But knowledge *about* a subject is not the same as knowledge *of* that subject. And the question really boils down to whether knowledge about leads automatically to knowledge of a subject. An analogy might be found in how children read. Learning to decode written symbols (knowledge about) does not automatically lead to comprehension (knowledge of) of the material decoded. The difference is important, because comprehension is much more central to intelligence.

The data do not support the argument that increased comprehension is a product of increased recognition or acquaintance. For example, the commendable and widely watched programs "Sesame Street" and "Electric Company" have been on the air for about 20 years. During that same period verbal SAT scores dropped some 400 points! At the same time, TV has made children and adolescents much more knowledgeable about drugs and sex than were previous generations. But this increased recognition has not decreased substance abuse and sexual activity. Quite the contrary. Substance abuse and sexual activity among the young seem to increase in direct proportion with their exposure to information regarding these activities.

True sophistication means that one comprehends and is in charge of the information in question. What children acquire through the media is at best a pseudosophistication. In short, the exposure of young people to more information than ever before does not appear to impact on the fundamental structures of intelligence.

It might still be argued, however, that the very fact that today's children are growing up with a technology such as computers makes them more familiar and competent in that technology than children who have grown up without it. Again, there is not much evidence to support this view. Consider, for example, the universality of the hand-held calculator. In the dreariest markets of the poorest countries, salespeople calculate exchange rates on these little machines as if they were mere extensions of their hands. And yet, these people did not grow up with hand calculators. Ironically, children in most advanced and technologically sophisticated countries do not use hand calculators until they are well along in their school careers.

We need to acknowledge that much of modern technology requires mental abilities that most people do not acquire until at least late childhood. Having the technology available does not necessarily help the child use it. While many mature adults learn to use computers in very little time, even when they have had little prior exposure, young children, who may be quite familiar with computers both at home and school, cannot really access these computers until they reach a level of mental ability that allows them to operate on the basis of symbolic rules.

The idea that early acquaintance with a technology is critical to competence in that technology can be shown to be fallacious on other grounds. For example, neither Steven Jobs, the founder of Apple Computer, nor Mitch Kapor, who wrote the best-selling Lotus 1-2-3 software program, grew up with computers or software, and yet both are leaders in their fields. Early exposure to a technology is neither a necessary nor a sufficient condition for proficiency in using or in advancing that technology.

In summary, the idea that the early exposure to a technology accelerates mental ability is not supported by the facts. Nor is there any factual support for the idea that children who grow up with a particular technology are necessarily more proficient with it as adults than children who have not grown up with it.

A second argument for the introduction of formal education at the preschool level is that there is new research which justifies this practice. In truth, however, we have no new data or new research about the ways in which young children think and learn!

There have been no dramatic breakthroughs in child development research in any way comparable to those that have occurred in biology or in physics. By far, the majority of today's research studies on infants and young children merely confirm what we already know: young children learn best through the active exploration and manipulation of concrete materials, not through the inculcation of symbolic rules. There is really nothing in the contemporary research literature that refutes this fundamental fact.

RESEARCH ON CHILDREN'S LEARNING

Where, then, does the idea that there is new research supporting the formal instruction of young children come from? Mostly it comes from the reinterpretation of old facts to support changing social policy. During the 1960s, the new curriculum reforms resulting from the launching of the Russian Sputnik and the large numbers of mothers entering the work force focused attention on the young child. Early childhood education, it was argued, would remedy educational deficiencies, better prepare children for science and math, and provide an intellectually stimulating environment for children in out-of-home care.

The changed perception of young children and early childhood education did not arise from any new research, but rather from a new emphasis on early childhood education as a solution to a number of difficult social problems. An example of how old facts were stretched to support the new importance of early childhood education is the work of Benjamin Bloom (1964). Bloom claimed that young children attain half of their mental abilities by the age of four! This was interpreted to mean that educational intervention should begin early to capitalize on this window of rapid intellectual growth.

Let's examine this "research." What Bloom reported was a well-known and established fact: that intelligence test scores of infants and young children are less reliable indices of later intelligence than are scores attained at later ages. By the time children reach the age of four they are sufficiently socialized and verbal so that the intelligence score attained at that age will permit us to predict, with 50 percent accuracy, the IQ score that some youngster will attain at age 17.

Bloom's statistics say nothing about mental growth or learning ability. In fact, if one examines the statement that a child has attained half of his or her intelligence by the age of four it really doesn't make any sense. Does it mean that a child has attained half of all the knowledge, skills, and values he or she will ever attain in life? Unlikely. Does it mean that the child has attained half of his or her ability to learn and adapt to new situations? Again, the idea is far-fetched.

And yet, without examining the premise, many people accepted Bloom's conclusion that educational intervention was called for at a time of rapid intellectual growth. Why? One could make the opposite case with even more vigor.

My hobby is growing small fruits and berries. One thing I learned over the years was not to prune during the growing season. To be sure, children are not plants, but there are parallels. Piaget (1952), for example, has made it clear that at times of rapid mental growth children seek out the stimuli they need to nourish their budding mental abilities. Children just learning quantity concepts will count everything in sight. To impose adult learning priorities at such times serves only to extinguish the child's spontaneous learning.

Montessori (1964) recognized the same principle. Her educational program is based on providing the materials that are appropriate to the "sensitive periods" of the child. The sensitive periods are related to the child's unfolding mental abilities and the need for materials to nourish that ability.

The work of Erik Erikson (1950) also suggests that early childhood is not the time to impose adult learning priorities. Erikson maintains that early childhood is the period during which the child needs to establish a healthy sense of initiative, and that adults can help the child by appreciating and supporting the child's need to explore, experiment, and construct. If the adults in the child's environment are too harsh in reacting to such explorations, the child's sense of guilt may overwhelm his or her sense of initiative. Such a child will move into the school years overly dependent on adult direction, and afraid to initiate activities on his/her own.

In conclusion, contemporary research only confirms what we already know about young children, namely that they think and learn differently than do older children and adults. Arguments for the early intellectual competence of young children are more political than they are empirical.

EARLY INTERVENTION PROGRAMS

What about all the research on early intervention programs that indicates their lasting and positive intellectual benefits? Or does it? Here again we find data being interpreted to support policy initiatives. Despite all the talk about the lasting effects of early intervention on intellectual prowess, the data simply do not support it. Consider the following summary of a government-sponsored evaluation of Head Start programs, submitted to Congress in August 1985:

> Children enrolled in Head Start enjoy significant immediate gains in cognitive test scores, socioeconomic test scores, and health status. In the long run, cognitive and socioemotional test scores of former Head Start students do not remain superior to those of disadvantaged children who did not attend Head Start. However, a small subset of studies finds that former Head Starters are more likely to be promoted to the next grade and are less likely to be assigned to special education classes. Head Start also has aided families by providing health, social, and educational services and by linking families with services available in the community. Finally, educational, economic, health care, social service, and other institutions have been influenced by Head Start staff to provide benefits to both Head Start and non-Head Start

families in their respective communities (McKey et al., 1985).

I single out Head Start because it is the most thoroughly researched of the early intervention programs. What is very clear from this evaluation is that there was no lasting intellectual benefit from these programs—despite the fact that a number of Head Start programs were designed to promote intellectual development and to raise children's IQs. To be sure, in specific cases with intense involvement of staff and with abundant financial resources, some intervention programs may produce lasting benefits, as in the case of the Perry Preschool Program (Berrueta-Clement et al., 1984). But such programs can hardly be taken for the norm of what most young children will be provided in early childhood intervention programs.

Again, I want to emphasize that early childhood programs can be of great benefit to both children and parents. But this benefit derives not from formal instruction but rather from the sense of security and openness to exploration and learning that sound early childhood education promotes.

PREKINDERGARTEN PREPARATION

The last argument for the introduction of formal education at the preschool level is the enhanced sophistication of children entering kindergarten today. While it is true that more than 50 percent of children below the age of five will have experienced some form of out-of-home care before they enter kindergarten, only a small fraction of them will have been exposed to an academic curriculum.

Consider the children of working parents. Only 15 percent of such parents send their children to nursery school or to day care centers. Forty percent of these children are cared for in some other person's home, and another 31 percent are cared for by someone within the parents' own home.

Children who have experienced academically oriented preschool programs comprise only a small percent of the total number of children entering kindergarten in any given year. Moreover, any advantage such youngsters enjoy—other than native ability—is likely to be short-lived. This is true because an older child will acquire the same skills and knowledge acquired by a younger child in less

time and with less effort. Indeed, despite the presumed academic sophistication of young children currently entering kindergarten, a recent review of pupils' age at kindergarten entrance suggests that readiness and maturity are still more important to success than preschool or day care experience (Uphoff and Gilmore, 1986).

To sum up, the percentage of children entering kindergarten with advanced skills as a result of exposure to academic material in a day care or nursery school setting is likely to be small, and any advantage they enjoy is likely to be short-lived. The fact that more young children in the United States than ever before are experiencing some form of out-of-home care does not in any way justify the introduction of a more rigorous or formal educational program in the kindergarten.

CONCLUSION

In this [chapter] I have argued against the introduction of formal education programs at the preschool or kindergarten level. Because young children think and learn differently than do older children and adults, this difference must be reflected in the type of education they receive. None of the arguments for formalizing the early education process really holds up against careful examination: modern technology does not accelerate mental development; research on child development does not indicate that children are brighter than in the past; intervention studies do not show lasting intellectual benefits; and children with a year or two of day care or nursery school are not in need of formal programs.

To be sure, one of the greatest needs in America today is for quality out-of-home care for all of those children who require such care. It is certainly reasonable to expect that pubic schools can help meet this need by providing programs for four-year-olds and by establishing full-day kindergartens. What is most important, however, is that such programs reflect the principles of sound early childhood education. We serve children, parents, and education best by respecting the all-important difference between early childhood education and formal education.

DISCUSSION QUESTIONS

1. Are today's children more ready for symbolic and formal educational experiences because of technology?
2. What does the research say in support of "good" early childhood education?
3. If teachers are not supposed to use formal educational practices, what is the ideal curriculum for early childhood education in the schools?

17. SYNTHESIS OF RESEARCH ON SCHOOL READINESS AND KINDERGARTEN RETENTION

by Lorrie A. Shepard and Mary Lee Smith

Every September in the United States more than three million children begin formal schooling with their first day of kindergarten. These children differ tremendously in their readiness to learn and their ability to follow directions. Many of the youngest children—those who just made the entrance-age cutoff date—seem barely ready to meet the expectations of school.

Great diversity in cognitive development and social maturity creates a teaching problem that educators are constantly trying to resolve. Should the school district change its entrance-age policy to remove the youngest children? Can these apparent differences in readiness be assessed and used to decide who should be in school and who should not? If schools are obliged to admit all students, should children who remain unready for first grade be kept in kindergarten or special transition programs for an extra year?

Current educational reforms and the desire to raise standards have intensified the problems of differential readiness. Third grade exit requirements are translated into uniform expectations for second graders, which in turn dictate absolute standards for first graders and then kindergartners. At both the state and local level, many policymakers are contemplating testing programs to determine who is prepared to begin and to leave kindergarten.

Several bodies of research inform these issues of entrance age, school readiness, and early-grades retention. In some cases common-sense impressions about what works are at odds with the accumulated evidence. What follows is a summary of relevant research and policy implications.

THE PROBLEM OF BEING YOUNGEST

Numerous researchers and reviewers have addressed the question of within-grade age effects, especially for first grade. When the children who are youngest in their grade are compared with their older classmates, they are nearly always less successful (Beattie 1970, Bigelow 1934, Carroll 1963,

Davis et al. 1980, Green and Simmons 1962, Hall 1963, Halliwell and Stein 1964, Kalk et al. 1981, King 1955). However, the achievement differences that are "statistically significant" in these studies are not necessarily very large. For example, based on sample sizes of 8,500 per grade, Davis, Trimble, and Vincent (1980) found that children who were fully six years old when they entered first grade were nine percentile points ahead of children who were only five when they started first grade.

Similarly, we also found that first graders who were in the youngest three months of their class scored on average at the 62d percentile in reading compared to the oldest three-month children who were at the 71st percentile (Shepard and Smith 1985). (In math, the difference was only 6 percentile points.) Thus, a major point to be made when we are considering practical rather than statistical significance is that achievement differences between the oldest and youngest first graders are small, on the order of 7 or 8 percentile points.

We further analyzed the age trend in first grade by ability strata (Shepard and Smith 1985). There was virtually no difference in achievement between the oldest and youngest age groups for children who were above the 75th or 50th percentile points of their respective age intervals. The overall age trend seemed to come almost entirely from the children who were below the 25th percentile of their respective age groups. Although one would not wish to draw any policy conclusions based on only one study, it should be noted that the disadvantage of achievement experienced by some younger children in relation to older classmates may more likely be a *combination* of youngness and low ability.

A second major point, looking over a number of research studies, is that even the small disadvantage of youngness eventually disappears, usually by about third grade. From analyses based on National Assessment data, Langer, Kalk, and Searls (1984) noted that the effects of being old or young in grade tended to diminish as grade level increased. For Halliwell and Stein (1964) to find achievement differences between the oldest and

See pages 326–27 for acknowledgment and references.

youngest fifth graders is the exception among research studies rather than the rule. In our own research, we found no difference in math achievement or in reading achievement between the oldest and youngest children in either the third or fourth grade (Shepard and Smith 1985). Miller and Norris (1967) found that a difference between the oldest and youngest children on readiness measures was no longer apparent at the end of second, third, or fourth grades. They attributed the lack of differences due to age to the effectiveness of an ungraded program in *individualizing* reading instruction. Their observation about individualization may have wider import. In reviewing the literature on age effects, Weinstein (1968-69) proposed that whether an initial deficit for young first graders would persist into higher grades depended on the attitudes and expectations of teachers in responding to the ability range of normal first graders.

A few studies have contributed greatly to the impression that the problem of being youngest is grave and potentially devastating. These studies note that children who are youngest in their class are more likely to repeat a grade (Langer et al. 1984, Uphoff 1985), to be referred to special education (DiPasquale et al. 1980), and to be labeled as learning disabled (Diamond 1983, Maddux 1980).

Gredler (1980) urged caution, however, in the interpretation of these later indicators since they are more susceptible to teacher biases than are achievement tests. Referral rates and retention decisions are influenced by the opinions of teachers who might either expect young children to have difficulty or decide not to retain a child who is already older. We conducted a study to see whether kindergarten teachers consider such factors as a child's age when they form judgments about the likelihood of success in first grade or the desirability of retention (Shepard and Smith 1985). In a policy-capturing experiment, 68 percent of kindergarten teachers gave some important weight to age in their recommendations for retention or promotion (with sex, physical size, social maturity, and academic skills held constant). In practice this means that a child lagging behind at the end of kindergarten might be recommended to repeat kindergarten if he were five years and nine months old. But a child with equally deficient skills who was already six years and eight months old would be passed to first grade. Clearly if teachers are more willing to hold back younger children, retention data cannot be used to evaluate the effect of youngness.

Current research in special education is also consistent with the interpretation that higher referral rates for younger children within a grade can be explained by teacher expectations and the slightly lower average achievement of the youngest children. Pugach (1985) found that children are placed in special education in mildly handicapped categories largely on the basis of teachers' referrals, and that teachers have in mind a need for one-to-one instruction or other remedial services rather than a scientific conception of handicap. In a study of learning disabled children, we found that only 43 percent were validly identified; the majority of children labeled LD had other learning needs, from very serious to extremely mild, which were generally served by additional instruction once the child was placed in special education (Shepard and Smith 1981, 1983). Given the widely acknowledged fallibility of the LD label, there is no reason to believe that children who are youngest in their grade develop real handicaps. There is, however, genuine cause for alarm that schools are so willing to affix a handicapped label to a child who is slightly behind in achievement.

In summary, the "age effect" literature does verify that children who are youngest in their first grade class are at a slight disadvantage. This is hardly surprising since an 11-month period of growth and development is a significant portion of a lifetime for six-year-olds. However, the difference between oldest and youngest children is smaller than popularly believed, only about 7 or 8 percentile points on achievement tests. Furthermore, most studies show that the age effect disappears by about third grade. Whether and how soon the age effect disappears depends on the responsiveness of the school program to individual differences. Differential referral and retention rates for children who were the youngest when they entered school are not valid indicators of the youngness problem because they are contaminated by teacher beliefs about age. However, the increased probability for younger children to be held back or placed in special education should be of concern in and of itself because these actions may have negative consequences greater than the slight achievement disadvantage that prompted them. (See reviews by Holmes and Matthews 1984, regarding the negative social-emotional effects of nonpromotion, and by MacMillan and Meyers 1979 on the elusive phenomenon of special education stigma.)

ENTRANCE-AGE POLICY

Over the past 30 years the national trend has

been slowly but surely to raise the age of entrance to kindergarten. In 1958 most states required kindergartners to be five years old by December 1 or January 1 (Educational Research Service 1958). Surveys of school districts in 1963 and 1968 reported that when the entrance age was changed, it was nearly always raised, requiring that children be a month or two older to start school (Educational Research Service 1963, 1968). In 1968 the dominant policy was a date after November 30, but 25 percent of the schools had moved to September or October 1 dates. By 1975 the percentage with September or October 1 cutoffs had increased to 35 percent (Educational Research Service 1975), although admission dates after November 30 remained the most prevalent district practice.

In 1985 a survey of states (rather than districts) revealed an even more substantial shift in policy. Now the dominant practice is to require that children be five before October 1 to start kindergarten; only 20 percent of the states (mostly in the northeast) have entrance cutoffs after November 30 (Education Commission of the States 1985). Missouri has elected to raise its entrance age a month each year so that in 1987 children must be five by July 1. In Colorado several local districts have also adopted June or July cutoffs (Management Information Services 1982). These continuations of the long-term trend into summer dates suggest that national entrance policies will not necessarily stabilize once they accommodate to the September rather than mid-year norm. Earlier and earlier cutoff dates have raised the average age of kindergartners. A child who might have been in the older half of the class in 1958 might now be one of the youngest children in some kindergarten classes.

Rhetoric surrounding decisions to raise the school entrance age has focused almost entirely on the unreadiness of the youngest children. Will moving the entrance age solve the problem of youngness? If children must be fully five before the start of kindergarten, will short-term and potentially long-term learning problems be prevented? Obviously many policymakers believe so. But for entrance-age change to be the solution, the youngness dilemma must be an absolute problem rather than a relative one. In other words, the cognitive and social demands of kindergarten must be fixed in such a way that they are consistent with what five-and-a-half-year-olds can do but are too much for children who are just barely five. Advocates seeking to raise the entrance age construe the problem in this way. All of the research evidence, however, offers a convincing case that the youngness problem is relative, not absolute.

The youngest children are at a disadvantage whether they enter school at 4.7 years of age in a district with a February cutoff, at 4.9 in a district with a December entrance age, or 5.0 in a district where September 1 is the deadline. Several authors have pointed out the absurdity of seeking an "optimal" age for first grade readiness if the children who are the "successful" group in one context are the "young-unsuccessful" group in another district only because of their relative age in comparison to their respective classmates (Gredler 1975, Weinstein 1968-69).

The relative nature of the age effect is also seen between countries. The International Study of Achievement in Mathematics (Husén 1967) found that "children with birthdays toward the end of the school year tend to do less well in all countries" (p. 228). This was true in England where the mandatory age of school entry was five and in Finland and Sweden where compulsory attendance does not begin until age seven. To contest the idea that older entrance ages would be a panacea for differential readiness, Gredler (1975, 1980) cited several studies including those by Malmquist (1958) and Jinks (1964). Speaking of younger seven-year-olds in Sweden, Malmquist lamented that large differences in intellectual development made it impossible for the same method of teaching to be effective with all the pupils. In a British study, Jinks (1964) again found that teachers praised the learning abilities of their *older* pupils, who would have been the *youngest* children in the United States.

Because the youngness problem is relative, raising the entrance age would provide only a temporary solution to the perceived problem. In a district with a September 1 cutoff, children with summer birthdays are deficient compared to their classmates. If the district responds by adopting a July 1 cut-off, in a short time normative comparisons will readjust and children with May and June birthdays will be at risk.

INDIVIDUAL DECISIONS VS. SCHOOL POLICY

States and local districts cannot solve the youngness problem by raising the entrance age because they would merely create a new youngest group. But should parents individually consider holding out of school a child who is just past the cutoff? Many parents have obviously already made this decision since there are significantly fewer children in the first month past the cutoff than in any other month (Shepard and Smith 1985). Very likely, parents believe that by waiting a year their child will have the benefit of being the oldest in the class. There are no controlled studies available on this older age group. Advocates who advise parents to keep their children at home another year cite the youngness research summarized here; they claim only good and no ill effects could come from this practice (*A Gift of Time*, 1982). In the absence of evidence, however, greater caution might be advisable Anecdotally, we know that children who are over-age for their grade are very aware of being older (Shepard and Smith 1985), but the attitudinal effects of being oldest or different have not been studied systematically. Parents should at least consider the possibility of too little challenge as well as too much challenge. Longer-term problems that we know about from the retention literature might also be considered, such as a girl reaching puberty in fourth grade or a 19-year-old young man being unwilling to finish high school.

Even if there is little research evidence about what parents should do, there is a firmer basis for saying what districts should do. Districts should *not* encourage parents to keep their young five-year-olds at home. If a district or school gives this kind of advice, the result will very likely be an increase in the heterogeneity of kindergarten and first grade classrooms because middle-class parents are more likely to follow the advice. Just as "Sesame Street" widened the gap between middle-class and poor children (Cook et al. 1975), middle-class families will be more able to know about and take advantage of this educational wisdom. In our study of kindergarten retention, many lower socioeconomic families resisted an extra year of (half day) kindergarten specifically because mothers could not afford to stay home or to pay for preschool (Shepard and Smith 1985). In one school where the youngest children were systematically asked to repeat kindergarten, all the parents of children with the highest readiness skills agreed and the parents of children with the lowest skills refused. As a consequence, the diversity of the first grade class was dramatically increased the following year.

Thus, school districts should not foster a hidden policy of encouraging parents to keep their young five-year-olds at home; the parents who are most likely to heed this advice do not necessarily have the least ready children. Teaching problems associated with great diversity in kindergartens will increase, not diminish.

ASSESSING READINESS

If a uniform entrance age cannot address the problem of differential readiness, is it possible to measure readiness directly? Can a test be used to decide who should stay out of school or who should be placed in a less-demanding kindergarten program? Numerous school readiness or screening instruments exist. Many are intended specifically to assess reading readiness, but others include a broader array of social and developmental skills relevant to a child's adjustment in school.

What should a school superintendent or state legislator—who is not interested in psychometric properties or validity coefficients—know about school readiness measures? First, there is one overriding rule for determining test validity: validity depends on how a test is used. In the case of school readiness measures, this means that some tests might be perfectly good for teachers to use in making day-to-day instructional decisions but would not be good enough (technically or in a court of law) to be used to place a child in a special school program. The more crucial the decision for an individual child, the greater are the demands for test validity evidence and due process.

Scientific knowledge underlying readiness assessment is such that none of the existing tests is sufficiently accurate to justify removing children from their normal peer group and placing them in special two-year programs. In part the lack of high correlations with later school success is caused by the instability of the very traits we are seeking to measure. Four- and five year-olds experience developmental bursts and inconsistencies that defy normative charts. In addition, the cognitive domains that can be sampled at younger ages are only moderately related to the cognitive skills demanded later by reading and other academic tasks.

Let us consider two very popular readiness batteries, the Gesell School Readiness Tests and the Metropolitan Readiness Tests. The Gesell purports to measure developmental age and is recommended by its authors for screening children into developmental or two-year kindergarten programs. Numerous reviewers have stated that the Gesell tests do not meet the standards of the American Psychological Association for validity, reliability, or normative information (e.g., Kaufman 1985, Shepard and Smith 1985); yet the tests are used in hundreds of school districts to make placement decisions. Only one study has ever been done reporting a reliability coefficient for the Gesell (Kaufman and Kaufman 1972); in that study the error of measurement was so large that a four-and-one-half developmental age score could not be reliably distinguished from a five-year-old score, but this is precisely the difference that is used to decide who should start kindergarten and who should not. One study was undertaken to evaluate the predictive validity of the Gesell (Wood et al. l984). Although the test has what sounds like a creditable agreement rate with teacher judgments (78 percent) in fact, when the children identified as "potential kindergarten failures" were examined, only *half* were accurately identified. For every potential failure accurately identified there was a successful child falsely identified. This problem of predictive inaccuracy is not unique to the Gesell but occurs with all of the readiness measures because they have moderately good but not very high predictive validities.

In an extended review of the technical properties of the Gesell tests, we found that they "lack discriminant validity from IQ tests" (Shepard and Smith 1985). Although the Gesell tests claim to measure developmental age, they essentially measure the same thing that IQ tests measure (Jensen 1969, 1980). Changing the name of what the test measures has profound policy implications. Many decision makers would be willing to hold out of school or place in a two-year track children who are "developmentally young." It is much less defensible to hold out of school children who are below average in IQ, especially since a disproportionate share of these children will come from low socio-economic backgrounds.

The Metropolitan Readiness Tests are among the technically best measures available (Ravitch 1985). The Metropolitan is not advertised, however, for the purpose of sorting children into ready and unready groups. Rather it is intended to help teachers organize instruction. For example, a kindergarten teacher might plan different activities for children who are ready to learn letter sounds than for children who cannot make auditory discriminations. If the Metropolitan were to be used to place children in special two-year programs, it would fare slightly better than the Gesell, since its predictive correlations are higher, but would still produce many identification errors.

The fact that screening programs will misidentify many children raises the question of whether it is better to catch unready children even if many of those identified will be falsely labeled. The answer depends on the benefit (or harm) of the special placement. A similar lesson was learned in the field of special education. The National Academy Panel on Selection and Placement of Students in Programs for the Mentally Retarded noted that if

special education were unambiguously a benefit, there would be no dispute over the validity of identification and placement procedures (Heller et al. 1982). The validity of readiness tests is entwined with the validity or effectiveness of special programs.

It is not possible, then, to make highly accurate assessments of school readiness. Most test publishers are careful about the claims they make for their tests, suggesting that they be used to help teachers plan instruction. If children are classified into ready and unready groups on the basis of a test, a number of identification errors will occur. How school systems should proceed knowing that readiness measures are fallible depends on the benefit of special programs.

PROVIDING AN EXTRA YEAR FOR UNREADY CHILDREN

Several options have been proposed whereby schools can provide an extra year for children who are not yet ready for the demands of first grade. In addition to the possibility of keeping children at home, the Gesell Institute has suggested that developmentally young children can attend a developmental or prekindergarten, repeat kindergarten or attend a pre-first grade class between kindergarten and first grade (*A Gift of Time* 1982). Proponents of these alternatives argue that time itself is the best cure for the problem of differential readiness. Donofrio (1977) urged that these "unfavored" children be allowed to "mark time" until they are in step psychologically with their "behavioral and maturational peers" (p. 351).

Extra-year programs are effectively like repeating kindergarten even when the curriculum is altered from one year to the next. Certainly, parents who are asked to agree to these placements struggle with the implications of "retention" regardless of whether they accept the arguments for the program (Shepard and Smith 1985). One might look to the extensive research literature on nonpromotion or grade retention to evaluate extra-year programs. The majority of parents and educators believe that grade repetition is an effective solution for academic failure and social immaturity (Byrnes and Yamamoto 1984). Yet research findings are almost uniformly negative. When retained children were compared to equally low achievers who were promoted, the socially promoted pupils were consistently ahead on both achievement and social-emotional measures (Holmes and Matthews 1984, Rose et al. 1983). Contrary to popular beliefs, repeating a grade does *not* help students gain ground academically and has a negative impact on social adjustment and self-esteem. Ironically, reviewers have also found that the practice of holding children back does not increase the homogeneity of classrooms (Bossing and Brien 1979, Haddad 1979).

Advocates of kindergarten retention are likely to dismiss the negative findings of nonpromotion research because an extra year of kindergarten is intended to prevent failure before it occurs. Many fewer studies are available on pre-first grade or prekindergarten programs. Gredler (1984) located five recent studies evaluating "transition" or pre-first grade classes. In only one of these studies (Raygor 1972) was there a benefit or achievement gain for children in the transition program. In four studies the transition-room children were no better off after an extra year than the "potential first grade failures" who were placed in the regular first grade. Bell (1972) found that transition-room children had lower self-esteem and lower self-confidence than the at-risk children who were not retained. In Raygor's study the initial benefit washed out by third grade.

May and Welch (1984) conducted a study in a school district where children were placed on the basis of the Gesell Screening Test. Children who were identified as developmentally immature were recommended to "buy a year" and spend an extra year before second grade. If their parents refused the recommendation, immature children were classified as "overplaced" and continued in the traditional grade sequence. The state achievement test at the end of third grade showed no differences between the overplaced and buy-a-year group. On the Stanford Achievement Tests given at the end of second, fourth, and sixth grades, there were likewise no differences between the two groups, one of which had had an extra year of school. More importantly, on the Stanford there were also no differences between the at-risk groups and the rest of the school district population. Thus, May and Welch concluded that the overplaced children were not suffering the learning difficulties predicted by Gesell theory, and there was no academic benefit from the buy-a-year placement.

In our study of two-year kindergarten programs, we compared children with an extra year to equally at-risk children who did not repeat (Shepard and Smith 1985). At the end of first grade the children who had repeated kindergarten were one month ahead on a standardized reading test. There were no differences between the two groups on a math achievement test nor on teacher ratings of reading

and math achievement, social maturity, learner self-concept, or attention. Parents of the two groups rated their children the same in first grade progress and relationships with peers; children who spent an extra year in kindergarten had slightly worse attitudes toward school.

Despite the promises, providing an extra year before first grade does not solve the problems it was intended to solve. Children in these programs show virtually no academic advantage over equally at-risk children who have not had the extra year. Furthermore, there is often an emotional cost associated with staying back, even when parents and teachers are very enlightened about presenting the decision to the child (Shepard and Smith 1985).

POLICY CONCLUSIONS

Children come to school with enormously different interests, aptitudes, and background experiences. They cannot be made to adapt to a uniform curriculum. The policy options, which common sense suggests, are consistently rejected by research findings. Changing the entrance age will not correct the problems of the youngest first graders because a new youngest group emerges. Children cannot be selected to stay at home or attend a two-year kindergarten on the basis of a test, because the tests are not accurate enough; too many children would be falsely diagnosed as "unready." Extra-year programs have not boosted achievement and, contrary to expectation, have hurt rather than helped self-esteem. Therefore, school districts must think again before screening children into unsuccessful programs on the basis of fallible tests.

There are other alternative solutions to the unreadiness problem but they are not so popular as simple answers—a new date, a new test, or a new grade level. As they so often do, workable solutions will depend on teachers rather than policymakers and on programs that respond to children's individual differences in readiness. In one study of extra-year programs, the biggest gains were not for the extra-year children but for the at-risk children who received extra help in the regular classroom (Leinhardt 1980). It is necessary as well to try to keep the youngness problem in perspective. The disadvantage of the youngest first graders is small, after all, only about 7 or 8 percentile points. And unless it is cast in stone by a learning disability label or grade retention, in most cases it will disappear entirely by the third grade.

DISCUSSION QUESTIONS

1. Can a child actually "fail kindergarten"?

2. Should children be matched with learning experiences by school readiness tests, age at enrollment, or other factors?

3. Does a repeat of the kindergarten year contribute to the development and educability of the child?

4. What guidance for practice can be found in the research on readiness and retention in the kindergarten?

5. Are school entrance age policies based on research, common sense, or administrative convenience?

6. What role should parents play in decisions about retention and readiness?

7. Will earlier entrance of younger children reduce or increase the problems of readiness and retention?

18. USES AND ABUSES OF DEVELOPMENTAL SCREENING AND SCHOOL READINESS TESTING

by Samuel J. Meisels

Public school involvement in early childhood education is growing rapidly, bringing with it new responsibilities for schools to identify children who may be at risk for learning problems and to place these children in appropriate educational environments. This process of identification and placement has been complicated by several basic confusions about screening and readiness tests that have resulted in young children being denied a free and appropriate public education. This exclusion is based not, as in the past, on being handicapped, coming from impoverished backgrounds, or being members of minority groups, but as a result of such labels as *young*, *developmentally immature*, or *not ready*. Moreover, these labels have been assigned on the basis of tests with unknown validity by testers who have had little training and usually no supervision.

One test that has been in widespread use nationally for identification and placement is the Gesell School Readiness Screening Test (Ilg and Ames, 1972). The purpose of this [chapter] is to analyze the uses and abuses that can be traced to the Gesell and other similar tests. I will first discuss developmental screening tests and readiness tests in general. Then I will focus on the Gesell tests, specifically addressing their validity, and

questioning their current use, given the type of information the tests were designed to produce. This [chapter] will conclude with a discussion of the implications of using readiness tests for assigning children to particular school programs.

USES AND ABUSES OF SCREENING AND READINESS TESTS

Elsewhere I have defined and analyzed the differences between developmental screening tests and readiness tests and have listed examples of each (Meisels, 1984, 1985). The two types of tests are different and were designed to accomplish different objectives. Developmental screening tests provide a brief assessment of a child's developmental abilities—abilities that are highly associated with future school success. Readiness tests are concerned with those curriculum-related skills a child has already acquired—skills that are typically prerequisite for specific instructional programs. Table 1 compares the differences between the two types of tests in terms of purpose, content, type of test, and psychometric properties.

Table 1. Contrasts Between Developmental Screening Tests and Readiness Tests

	Developmental Screening Tests	Readiness Tests
Purpose	to identify children who may need early intervention or special education services	to facilitate curriculum planning
	to identify children who might profit from a modified or individualized classroom program	to identify a child's relative preparedness to benefit from a specific academic program
Content	items that display a child's ability or potential to acquire skills	items that focus on current skill achievement, performance, and general knowledge
Type of test	norm-referenced	most are criterion-referenced; some are norm-referenced
Psychometric properties	reliability predictive validity	reliability construct validity

See pages 327–28 for acknowledgment and references.

Screening Tests

During the years, professionals have misused and abused both screening and readiness tests. The most frequent abuse of developmental screening results from using tests that have no established reliability and validity. Reliability is an indicator of a test's consistency. It measures how often identical results can be obtained with the same test. Validity is a measure of a test's accuracy. Technically, validity concerns the overall degree of justification for test interpretation and use. It tells us whether a test does what it claims to do. Because young children grow and change so rapidly from day to day and week to week, it is critical that tests used to assess these children be stable and accurate.

Tests without reliability and validity are inherently untrustworthy and should not be used to identify and place children. We do not know if such tests provide different results when administered by different testers, whether children from certain socioeconomic or ethnic backgrounds are disadvantaged by them, or whether they are strongly related to some stable, external criterion or outcome measure—such as the results of a diagnostic assessment, a systematic teacher report form, or report card grades—that permits the test results to be interpreted and the findings to be generalized.

Yet, professionals persist in using invalid and unreliable tests. In a survey of 177 school districts in New York State, Joiner (1977) found that 151 different tests or procedures were used for screening. At best, only 16 of these tests could be considered even marginally appropriate. In a recent survey in Michigan, 111 tests were being used for preschool, kindergarten, and pre-first grade programs (Michigan Department of Education, 1984). Fewer than 10 of these tests were appropriate in terms of the age group and purpose to which they were being put. What is taking place in these two states, as well as elsewhere nationwide, is a proliferation of screening tests, many developed locally, that have never been assessed in terms of reliability, validity, or other general criteria that have been established for developmental screening tests (see Meisels, 1985). In the absence of satisfying these criteria—particularly the criterion of validity—children who need special services are being overlooked; some children who are not at risk are being identified as being at risk; parents are becoming alarmed, teachers and administrators upset, and resources squandered. More than 25 states currently mandate developmental screening for 3- to 6-year-olds (Meisels, 1986). A test with known, high-level validity and reliability should always be used when this type of testing is performed. Nothing less than strict psychometric standards are acceptable for other kinds of tests, such as diagnostic assessments or school achievement tests. Using screening tests that lack validity data is an abuse of testing procedures and of the trust the community places in professional educators (see American Educational Research Association, American Psychological Association, and National Council on Measurement in Education, 1985).

Readiness Tests

Another major abuse is the substitution of readiness tests for screening tests. This substitution frequently occurs inadvertently, through confusion about the differences between screening and readiness testing. As a brief sorting device, readiness tests can be loosely considered screening tests. But, because of the type of information they yield and their lack of predictive validity, they cannot correctly be considered developmental screening tests. Readiness tests should be used to facilitate curriculum planning, not to identify children who may need special services or intervention.

One of the differences between developmental screening and readiness tests lies in the predictive relationships of these tests to such outcome measures as comprehensive developmental assessments and school performance. In general, individual readiness tests, as contrasted to multivariate reading readiness batteries that incorporate several different kinds of assessments (see Barnes, 1982; Satz and Friel, 1978), do not have a strong predictive relationship to outcome measures. Most correlations between reading success and reading readiness tests are moderate at best (Knight, 1979). Figure 1 portrays the general relationship between developmental screening, individual readiness tests, developmental assessments, and school performance. The figure portrays the conclusions from several different studies, rather than a strict quantitative representation of specific empirical findings (see Lichtenstein, 1981; Rubin, Balow, Dorle, and Rosen, 1978; Wiske, Meisels, and Tivnan, 1982). The wide, dark lines represent strong relationships, the narrower dark lines suggest moderate relations, and the broken lines indicate weak relationships.

Figure 1 suggests that readiness tests have a much weaker relationship to developmental assessments and school performance than developmental screening tests. At first glance, such a statement may seem counterintuitive because readiness tests are intended to assess readiness for a specific school

**Figure 1. Relationship of Screening and Readiness Tests
to Assessment and School Performance**

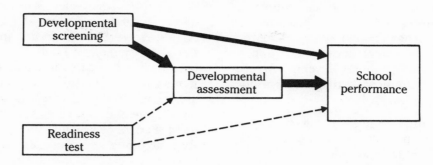

program. Nonetheless, readiness tests best describe *child entry characteristics*; they are not intended to *predict child outcomes*. Thus, children who perform poorly on readiness tests may profit proportionately more from school programs than children with higher initial skills because they have more to gain. Conversely, those with well-developed entry level skills may profit less from kindergarten than children who do poorly on readiness tests. Hence, neither the potential of those who score well nor the potential of those who score poorly is accurately assessed by single-measure readiness tests. These tests are best used by teachers for making *initial curriculum decisions about individual children*. While this function is critically important, the data from readiness tests should not be used to attempt to identify developmental problems that may affect a child's chances for school success. Mistaking readiness tests for predictive developmental screening instruments misrepresents the purpose and scope of both tests.

USES AND ABUSES OF GESELL TESTING

One of the most widely adopted tests used for both readiness and developmental screening is the Gesell School Readiness Screening Test (Ilg and Ames, 1972). Also known as the Gesell Preschool Test (Haines, Ames, and Gillespie, 1980), this test, or set of tests, is a shortened version of the Gesell Developmental Schedules—full-scale evaluations used to assess personal-social, fine motor/adaptive behavior; language and reasoning; and gross motor development of children younger than age 6. This [chapter] will focus on the Preschool Readiness Tests, not the Developmental Schedules.

In recent years the Preschool Tests have become increasingly popular. According to the Gesell Institute, thousands of public, private, and parochial schools nationwide have adopted them. In addition

to the tests, the Gesell Institute conducts week-long workshops on developmental placement. These workshops prepare kindergarten teachers and other professionals to use the Gesell test results to place children in readiness or developmental kindergartens, to recommend that the child delay entering kindergarten for a year, or to suggest conventional kindergarten placement. In other words, the Gesell *readiness* tests are explicitly presented as performing the functions of *developmental screening tests*. According to Ames, Gillespie, Haines, and Ilg (1979), "perhaps 50 percent of school failures could be prevented or cured by proper placement based on a child's behavior age" (p. 182). Claims like these are responsible for the tremendous interest that educators have shown in Gesell testing in recent years.

Nevertheless, despite their widespread popularity and the amount of time and energy expended on them, the Gesell Preschool Tests are based on an outmoded theory of child development, lack reliability and validity, and use a concept of developmental age that has never been empirically verified. The remainder of this [chapter] will be devoted to substantiating these assertions and drawing conclusions from them.

Gesell's Theory

The Gesell tests reflect a maturationist theory of development. They view behavior as a function of structure, changing in a patterned, predictable way. The stages through which most behaviors develop are considered to be highly similar from child to child.

According to this theory, behavior is almost entirely the result of maturation, and neither chronological age nor environmental intervention is considered to be highly correlated with so-called developmental age (Gesell, 1954). In other words, maturational theory links behavior with preformed, genetically determined biological structures. In the absence of unusual environmental conditions, this theory focuses on *time* as the crucial variable in behavior change, not environmental stimulation or intervention, but time to grow, mature, and endogenously develop. According to Gesell, developmental diagnosis implies prognosis (Shonkoff, 1983).

Although the importance of maturational change in development cannot be ignored, this strict Gesellian approach is at odds with research ranging from Piaget to the Perry Preschool Project. Numerous researchers have identified the ameliorative effects of environmental intervention on childhood development (see, for example, Berrueta-Clement, Schweinhart, Barnett, Epstein, and Weikart, 1984; Clarke and Clarke, 1976; Clarke-Stewart and Fein, 1983; Lazar and Darlington, 1982; Meisels and Anastasiow, 1982; and Zigler and Valentine, 1982). Modern-day researchers view maturation as only one aspect of development. Other factors include socioeconomic variables, familial factors, encounters with the physical and social environment, sex differences, and the internal regulations of new information with preexisting schemes of action. To assume, as do the Gesell theorists, that behavior is equivalent to age-related maturational growth is to confuse a description of experience with its cause. In other words, although it may be possible to describe development in terms of patterned, sequential behaviors, doing so does not imply that development occurs *because* of these behaviors. Nor does it imply that teachers and other professionals are powerless to work with children until children spontaneously achieve these behaviors (i.e., school readiness). Few teachers today would willingly accept such a passive approach to education as that which is implied by a maturationist theory. Yet, unknowingly, that is what they are doing when they subscribe to the Gesellian approach to developmental placement and readiness.

Certainly, all children are not equally ready for school when they become 4 or 5 years of age. However, identifying these differences in readiness only suggests the need for differences in curriculum planning. Other information is required before a valid judgment can be made about whether a child should attend a particular program, or should be labeled *at risk*. This is particularly true for children from linguistic or cultural groups who may be at a disadvantage because of the limitations of the tests being used.

Validity of the Gesell Tests

Although the Gesell schedules were first published in 1940 (Gesell et al.) and have been used in numerous research studies and clinical investigations, no systematic study of the validity of these tests has ever been conducted. In 1966 a subset of items covering the first 2 years of life were selected as a developmental screening test for infants—the Developmental Screening Inventory (DSI) (Knobloch, Pasamanick, and Sherard, 1966). The data that accompanied this test were insufficient to support its validity as a screening test (see McCall, 1982, for a discussion of the DSI). No other validation studies have been published. Jacqueline Haines, director of training at the Gesell Institute, confirms that the Gesell tests have not been validated. In 1984 she noted that the Gesell "documents normative responses by age. The validity of the work has been through years of experience in application. A validity study has not been completed at the present time" (personal communication, March 28, 1984).

This situation raises several problems for users of the Gesell tests. In the absence of predictive validity data, it is impossible to evaluate the claims set forth by Gesell theorists. For example, Ames and her colleagues state that "behavior develops in a patterned and highly predictable way and can be evaluated by means of simple, basic test situations" (Ames et al., 1979, p. ix). This may be true, but there is no evidence to support the position that the behavior evaluated by the Gesell Preschool Tests accurately predicts subsequent development.

A test that only "documents normative responses by age" cannot be used appropriately for prediction unless the predictive relationship has been tested and demonstrated. That is, children whose behavior is non-normative—either delayed or advanced—could, theoretically, be identified by means of the Gesell, but claims about their future performance would be purely speculative in the absence of studies that demonstrate the predictive accuracy of these normative assessments.

Another issue concerns the norms used by the Gesell tests. The original norms were developed by Gesell in 1928 and published in 1940. These norms were based on data obtained from a small, uncontrolled sample of primarily upper middle-class children and were rated by observers who were neither independent of each other nor free from potential bias. New norms have now been established for the Preschool Tests (Ames et al., 1979), but they still leave many questions unanswered. The norms are based on 640 children stratified by sex, age (eight 6-month intervals, from 2½ to 6 years), and parental occupational level. Unfortunately, nearly all of the children were Caucasian, and all lived in Connecticut. Further, no effort was made to test for the effects of differences in birth order, parental education, number of parents in the home, or prior preschool or child care experience. Also, no data are provided concerning the reliability of the standardization procedure: We do not know how many examiners participated, what the level of interobserver agreement was, whether there was intertester stability, or what the standard error of measurement was. Thus, inadequate sampling procedures, absence of validity data, inattention to issues of reliability, and sources of variance in recording performances render the entire normative foundation of the Gesell tests questionable.

Developmental Age and School Placement

One of the foremost uses of the Gesell tests is developmental placement. Ames et al. (1979) note that "of all the possible uses of the Gesell Behavior battery, its use in relation to determining the most favorable time for starting school or for subsequent promotion of students may turn out to be one of its most substantial contributions" (p. 184). According to Gesell theorists, the purpose of Gesell testing is to make examiners aware of age-related behaviors. Children's responses then show the level, or developmental age, at which they are functioning. "Regardless of either birthday age or Intelligence Quotient, in most instances a child does best in school if started and subsequently promoted on the basis of developmental age" (Ames et al., 1979, p. 6)

Clearly, the validity of the concept of developmental age hinges on the mechanism for establishing this age. Because the mechanism is the Gesell Preschool Tests—nonstandardized tests excerpted from the full-scale Gesell Developmental Schedules—the notion of developmental age is highly suspect.

Only one published study examines the predictive validity of developmental age by comparing results of kindergarten-age children on the Gesell School Readiness Screening Test with school success (Wood, Powell, and Knight, 1984). The study claims that developmental age provides a useful predictive measure of later school performance. Unfortunately, the study had major problems; the study population was small and not highly general-

izable (N = 84, all Caucasian and middle class); the outcome measure of school success (special needs status versus nonspecial needs) was undefined and unvalidated; and the study was not predictive as claimed, but at best postdictive or possibly concurrent. That is, the children were first referred for special services, then 3 months later the Gesell was administered. Because the Gesell test was given *after* the special needs designation was assigned, the study authors linearly adjusted scores back by 3 months. This circular procedure assumes the validity of the developmental age concept, which is precisely what the study was intended to prove.

In short, the use of the Gesell School Readiness Screening Test—based as it is on a set of tests with unknown validity and reliability, a theory that is outmoded and unsubstantiated, an unverified notion of developmental age, and a racially and ethnically narrow normative base—for developmental screening and class placement is empirically unjustified and professionally suspect. The Gesell tests can be used effectively as school readiness tests for initial curriculum planning for individual children, but there currently is no evidence to support more extensive application.

IMPLICATIONS FOR EARLY CHILDHOOD AND KINDERGARTEN EDUCATORS

Testing in early childhood and kindergarten should only be used to make better and more appropriate services available to the largest number of children. There are several kinds of tests that, if used as designed and intended, can assist professionals in making appropriate decisions for young children. Children who need special services can be identified by developmental screening and assessment. Children in need of modified classroom programming or individualized attention in preschool or kindergarten can be identified by readiness tests and, to a certain extent, by developmental screening inventories. Tests that exclude children from public education services or that delay their access to the educational mainstream, however, are antithetical to legal and constitutional rights to free education and equal protection. In addition, such tests and practices are incompatible with the belief systems, theoretical perspectives, and best practices of most early childhood educators.

The use of exclusionary tests suggests that children should conform to school programs, rather than schools adjusting to the needs of children. Nowhere is this reversal of the child-centered tradition more evident than in the Gesellian practice that recommends a year's delayed school entrance for children who are not ready for kindergarten. Ames and her colleagues claim that "if a 5-year-old child is still behaving like a 4- or 4½-year-old, he will in all likelihood not be ready for the work of kindergarten, regardless of what the law allows" (Ames et al., 1979, p. 6). This approach is unjustified because it is based on the assumption that the Gesell tests are valid predictors of school performance—an assumption that has not been proven. Also unproven is the assumption that all not ready or developmentally immature children develop similarly and cannot benefit from kindergarten, even if their peers who are ready can. The reality of individual differences is that even in classrooms where all the children have been certified as ready, some will be more ready than others.

Proponents of the developmental readiness concept frequently recommend that children who are immature or not ready be enrolled in *developmental* kindergartens instead of having to enter school late. These programs, also known as readiness kindergartens, usually precede a regular year of kindergarten.

Readiness kindergartens are a fast-growing phenomenon. In Michigan alone 161 school districts offered such programs during the 1983–84 school year, with 67 more districts slated to add them in the 1984–85 school year. These programs—most of which (65%) have existed for less than 5 years—served 5,700 students from 1983 to 1984 at a cost of $3,430,000 (Michigan Department of Education, 1984).

All developmental kindergartens do not subscribe to a Gesellian philosophy. Indeed, most of them are highly eclectic in approach, but they nevertheless share the same kinds of problems as Gesell-oriented programs. Specifically, these types of programs have not been systematically studied or evaluated. Among the questions that need further exploration are the following: On what basis are children placed in these programs? Are minority or poor children overrepresented in them? Are parents accorded due process in placement? What impact do these programs have on children's long-term development?

In practice, many developmental kindergartens contain a disproportionate number of younger children—those with birth dates late in the year. But the research evidence does not support this type of age grouping. Other factors in addition to simple immaturity play important roles in the explanation of school failure and learning problems (Diamond, 1983; Gredler, 1978; Maddux, Stacy, and Scott, 1981). Changing the standard of school readiness or the entry age cutoff only changes the composition of the group that is youngest or least ready—it does not eliminate it.

Many of these practices seem to result from pressures placed on kindergarten teachers to implement academically oriented programs in order to prepare children for the heavy academic emphasis seen in most first through third grades. The developmental readiness movement, as well as the widespread popularity of the Gesell tests, can be seen, in part, as well-meaning responses to these pressures, in which some children are excluded from kindergarten or enrolled in kindergarten for 2 years in order to reduce the likelihood of subsequent failure.

But this situation should cause grave professional concern. It signifies that schools are placing such institutional needs as obtaining higher achievement test scores and adopting more academically oriented early elementary curricula ahead of children's needs. To the extent that these priorities deny slowly developing or at-risk children access to public school programs, they are incompatible with child development research, contemporary social policy, and exemplary early childhood practice. Rather than label children, schools should devote their resources to helping teachers fashion individually responsive curricula that embrace a wide range of childhood abilities and readiness levels.

The National Association for the Education of Young Children's *Position Statement on Developmentally Appropriate Practice in Early Childhood Programs Serving Children Birth Through Age 8* (NAEYC, 1986) notes that high quality, developmentally appropriate programs typically include children with a range of developmental levels in a single classroom. The statement further notes that "It is the responsibility of the educational system to adjust to the developmental needs and levels of the children it serves; children should not be expected to adapt to an inappropriate system" (p. 16). Nor, it might be added, should children or their parents expect not to be served at all because children's skill levels do not conform to some external, preestablished norm or because they are being tested with an inappropriate instrument. In such situations, the schools and professionals who advocate these positions are demonstrating a failure of readiness, not the children.

Editor's Note: When Dr. Meisels's [chapter] was accepted for publication by *Young Children*, the Gesell Institute was invited to respond. These are the Institute's remarks:

THE GESELL INSTITUTE RESPONDS

As a pioneer in the field of child development and a leading architect in applying developmental understanding to the classroom, the Gesell Institute accepts its responsibilities as a leader in today's movement toward a developmentally sound, theoretically consistent use of knowledge concerning children's growth applied to school readiness.

Through extensive clinical observation, Arnold Gesell and his colleagues developed innovative observational techniques and established norms that remain the reference point for pediatric milestones, child development stages, and school readiness screening tests today (1925, 1940). When the original norms were compared to current samples in the 1970s controlled for age, sex, and socioeconomic background, the stability of the norms over time were reconfirmed (Ames, Gillespie, Haines, and Ilg, 1979; Knobloch, 1980).

Dr. Gesell was not merely a student of human behavior, but was interested in applying scientific knowledge to the creation of social environments conducive to maximizing the mental health and education of children (1930). Through their work with children in the public schools, Drs. Ilg and Ames helped to accomplish this. Drs. Ilg and Ames recognized that many children were not succeeding in school because they did not have the maturity to effectively undertake the tasks presented. They refined the clinical procedures used in their clinic so that the child's maturity level could be determined by trained educational professionals in schools. This resulted in the development of the Gesell School Readiness Screening, the Gesell School Readiness, and the Gesell Preschool Assessments.

These assessments are designed to assess a child's developmental functioning, using tasks most closely associated with maturationally related aspects of school readiness. *School readiness*, as defined by the Gesell Institute, is the capacity to simultaneously learn and cope with school environment. *School success* is defined as the ability to learn and have enough energy left over to be a competent, growing human being in all areas of living. The Gesell approach takes into account a child's emotional, social, physical, and adaptive capacities as

being of equal concern to human development as intelligence. To define school readiness as having only to do with intelligence, or as having only to do with achievement, or as having only to do with being given previous learning experiences, contradicts longstanding research and experience.

The Gesell assessments are used by schools to gain fuller developmental understanding of the child. If an assessment reveals that a child is developmentally young for kindergarten placement, for example, educational settings more consistent with that child's development can be considered. Rather than excluding a child from kindergarten, the information provided by the assessment assures that responsible recommendations for placement can be made so that the child can be included in an appropriate kind of kindergarten program at an appropriate time and pace. The Gesell assessments do not label children as at risk, handicapped, or remedial. Rather, they tell how the child is functioning on the developmental path of normalcy. Children whose developmental rate is far from that path on the Gesell assessment can be further evaluated.

Gesell readiness assessments have been predictive of school success. A longitudinal study by Ames and Ilg (1964) established a positive relationship between predictions for kindergarten readiness and school performance in the 6th grade. That the assessments measure primarily maturity and not intelligence or experience (Kaufman, 1971), is evidence of the impact maturity has on school readiness. Kaufman also reported that although test interpretation was qualitative in nature, examiners interpreted the records similarly (interrater reliability was .87). Most recently Wood (Wood, Powell, and Knight, 1984) found that developmental age was a more effective predictor of success or failure in kindergarten than chronological age. Gesell Institute is aware that many researchers want further statistical information to judge the usefulness of the assessments. This is presently one of our major thrusts. Additional statistical data pertaining to the Gesell assessment will soon be available.

A growing body of convincing evidence about the effective use of the Gesell instruments comes

See page 328 for references.

101

from schools. In diverse communities throughout the country, schools are pursing their own studies of the assessments and the concept of developmental placement. These studies are confirming the predictive ability of the assessments. Such variables as achievement, school adjustment, discipline patterns, parental and teacher satisfaction, child self-concept, retention rates, and the need for special services have all shown positive changes with use of the Gesell Screening Test and developmental placement. Schools as diverse as Broward County Schools in Florida, St. Charles Parish Schools in Louisiana, Avondale Schools in Michigan, and Oxford Central Schools in New York have all reported positive results.

Respecting the process of maturity, the process of development as it unfolds, and the individual pace of each child is what the Gesell philosophy entails. The Gesell School Readiness Screening Test, as a reflection of this philosophy, is a valuable tool for recognizing the forces of maturity in our individual students and thus is an effective means to enhance developmentally appropriate education.

Editor's Note: The following are Dr. Meisels's comments on the Gesell Institute's response:

BUT DR. MEISELS IS NOT CONVINCED

Knowing of my concerns about the Gesell School Readiness Test, a colleague recently asked me whether my doubts would be relieved by a systematic validity study that supported the Gesell Institute's claims. I replied that a carefully designed research study would eliminate many of my concerns. However, past experience casts doubt on the likelihood that such validity data can or will ever appear.

The Gesell Institute has promised statistical data for generations, as they do yet again. But all they provide are difficult-to-prove assertions about "the forces of maturity"—assertions based on faith in Dr. Gesell's admittedly pioneering efforts. It is time to move beyond the faith of the 1930s to the reason of the 1980s.

In their published response, the Institute restates its central claim that "Gesell readiness assessments have been predictive of school success" (Gesell Institute, 1987, p. 101). The burden of proof is on the Institute to support this key assertion, but the burden proves too heavy and the evidence too weak.

First, they cite Ames and Ilg (1964) as establishing a positive relationship between predictions of kindergarten readiness and school performance in the 6th grade. Yet this relationship is reported only in terms of correlations, thereby making impossible an analysis of the proportions of accurate and inaccurate predictions. Furthermore, because the highest level of agreement between predictors and outcomes was for children at the extremes of ability, the correlation reflects these extremes rather than the performance of the majority of children tested.

Second, they suggest that Kaufman (1971) confirmed that the tests measure maturity—not intelligence or experience. However, Kaufman reports that the factor structure of the Readiness Tests suggests that the tests measure intelligence and experience as well as maturity. Moreover, Shepard and Smith (1985) have shown that the Gesell tests lack discriminate validity from IQ tests. Naglieri (1985) also notes that the test items on the Preschool Test "are very similar and in some cases identical to those found in current IQ tests. . . . The major difference between the Gesell and current intelligence tests appears to be the lack of emphasis on the psychometric properties of the scale" (p. 608).

Third, the Institute cites the study by Wood, Powell, and Knight (1984) as evidence of predictive validity. Already criticized in my original article, the results presented in their study have been further analyzed by Shepard and Smith (1986). They note that only one half of the children identified as potential school failures by the School Readiness Test were accurately identified. Shepard and Smith note that for every potential failure accurately identified by the test, a successful child was falsely identified. In other words, the study by Wood, Powell, and Knight documents the predictive *inaccuracy* of the Gesell.

As the use of the Gesell tests proliferates, the

See page 328 for references.

problems associated with false predictions and false identifications continue to grow. Children are said to be *overplaced*, *developmentally young*, or simply *not ready*, when in fact the tests used to make these judgments are invalid, their norms unrepresentative, and their claims unsubstantiated. Reviews of the Gesell Preschool and School Readiness Tests have repeatedly demonstrated the limitations of the tests, concluding that the authors "ignore their responsibilities as testmakers and do not report the type of information that is mandated as essential by American Psychological Association guidelines" (Kaufman, 1985, p. 607). "The lack of emphasis on psychometric attributes of the scale leads to a potential for misuse or misinterpretation" (Naglieri, 1985, p. 608). "The test developers offer no set of cutoff scores that might be useful in making decisions about the placements, nor do they provide evidence that students who are placed according to scores on the test really benefit over the long term from such placement" (Bradley, 1985, p. 609).

The time has come for faith to give way to reason. The claims made for the Gesell should be modified, and its use as a placement and screening instrument correspondingly curtailed.

DISCUSSION QUESTIONS

1. How have screening and readiness testing been used in placing children in appropriate programs?

2. Do the present instruments actually measure the critical factors of readiness?

3. What are the specific purposes of developmental screening and readiness tests?

4. Are the Gesell assessments used appropriately to ensure proper placement and education of young children?

5. Does the empirical research support Meisels or the Gesell Institute?

19. EDUCATING YOUNG HANDICAPPED CHILDREN: WHAT CAN EARLY CHILDHOOD EDUCATION CONTRIBUTE?

by Anne H. Widerstrom

The education of children below age 5 traditionally has been the responsibility of teachers with an educational philosophy very different from that of many special educators. Most early childhood teachers come from an educational perspective strongly biased toward organizing the curriculum to allow children to develop normally and at their own pace. This child development perspective, emanating from such respected institutions as the Gesell Institute and the Bank Street College of Education, has its roots in the traditional nursery school and kindergarten, reaching back to Froebel in Germany and to Peabody and Hill in the United States (Hildebrand, 1981). Because handicapped children of preschool age previously were not the legal responsibility of the public schools and, hence, considered ineligible for educational services, they were rarely included in any public educational programs. Most services provided to these children were medical or therapeutic rather than educational in nature (Bronfenbrenner, 1961; Safford, 1978).

On the other hand, special education teachers have generally viewed their major responsibility to be the remediation of skill deficits in children who are not developing normally on their own. This goal of helping the delayed child to "catch up" has encouraged the development of highly directive teaching methods in this field. In addition, special education has a strongly clinical tradition due to its close associations with speech pathology, occupational and physical therapy, and remedial reading. This imparts to the pedagogy an emphasis on drill and teaching of specific skills which is not generally found among early childhood educators. Moreover, special education has been strongly influenced by practitioners of behavioral psychology (Axelrod, 1977; Ramp and Hopkins, 1971) whose approach to teaching and learning is individualistic (not necessarily individualized), specific-skill focused and adult-directed. Rote-learning, for example, is emphasized rather than "discovery" learning. While behavior analysis procedures have been used in some preschool programs for disadvantaged children (Baer and Wolf, 1968; Bereiter, 1972; Bushell, 1973; Risley, 1969), they have been more widely adopted in elementary and secondary special education classes (Haring and Lovitt, 1967; Kazdin and Bootzin, 1972).

The advent of public school early childhood special education programs during the last decade, therefore, produces an inevitable conflict between two very different educational philosophies. It is the intent of this [chapter] to demonstrate that this conflict need not necessarily be a bad thing and that, on the contrary, early childhood education has something important to contribute to the field of special education.

THE PROBLEM

Consider the following scenario, which was recently observed by the author in a classroom for young handicapped children. The setting is a language lesson for a group of five language-delayed 4-year-olds. They are seated around the teacher who holds several pairs of picture cards illustrating opposite concepts such as big and little, hot and cold, inside and outside.

Teacher: Point to the picture that shows the big boy, Robert. (Robert points)

Robert: Big.

Teacher: That's right. Good, Robert. He's a big boy. Now this picture shows a little mouse, right? What is the mouse?

Group: Quiet.

Teacher: That's right.
The mouse is quiet.

Teacher: Now look at this picture of the monkey. What word would we use to describe the chattering money? What do you think, Duane?

Duane: Loud?

Teacher: Loud? Well, I suppose we might say the monkey is loud. But can you think of another word? (Various suggestions are made and rejected.)

Wanda: Noisy.

See pages 328–29 for acknowledgment and references.

Teacher: Yes, Wanda, that's right. Noisy. The monkey is *noisy.* That's the word I was looking for.

This scenario will be familiar to anyone who spends much time in special education settings, for similar lessons are taught every day in most classrooms. In this case, the teacher managed to (1) maintain control of the situation in her own hands, (2) elicit what she considered to be correct information, (3) limit children's responses to one-word utterances and (4) stifle any sort of initiative or independent thinking on the part of the children. If we were to question her about her intent, she would probably be aware of 1 and 2 and quite unaware of 3 and 4.

There would appear to be two reasons why that special education teacher kept such tight control of the lesson. First, she believed that a tightly controlled, fast-paced lesson could most successfully teach the concepts she was presenting, and it gave her a situation in which progress would be accurately assessed. Second, the teacher felt more comfortable in complete control of her charges for the purpose of good management. Let us examine each of these considerations from the point of view of an early childhood educator. Here, the reader should be cautioned that we will be speaking somewhat in generalities.

Teachers of young nonhandicapped children are likely to view their role as that of facilitator. Their knowledge of child development, the influence of such theoreticians as Piaget, Montessori and Gesell, and a belief in a child-centered curriculum combine to make them sensitive to the child's communications (Kamii and Radin, 1970; Evans, 1975). They believe for the most part in responding rather than initiating, in following the child's lead and elaborating on topics in which the child expresses an interest. They do not direct activities so much as participate in them with the child, making suggestions but rarely issuing commands, listening rather than talking, accepting all of the child's contributions as valuable and worthwhile. When it comes to discipline or management, an issue often overlooked by theoreticians, early childhood teachers will usually state that they encounter few management problems if children are engaged in activities of their own choosing and appropriate to their developmental needs.

Those of us who are involved in the education of handicapped children know that methods used with nonhandicapped children are not uniformly exportable to special education classes. If that were true, special education techniques would not have needed to be developed. Teachers of handicapped

children must, for example, sometimes teach skills to children that the children may be reluctant or unable to learn on their own. Activities therefore cannot always be of the children's own choosing. It is nevertheless true that this emphasis on learning specific skills, which derives from the special education teacher's view of the child as a collection of deficits needing to be corrected, results in a highly teacher-directed curriculum not only in the individual therapy setting, where it may be appropriate, but also in group activities, where it tends to be detrimental.

The dual considerations of child initiative in learning and control of the classroom environment are areas in which traditional early childhood practices can have a beneficial influence on special education. In the following section suggestions are made for modifying special education practices both at the training level and in the instructional setting to conform with some proven good practices in early childhood special education. It is the author's belief that such practices should not be limited to mainstreamed programs or to the mildly handicapped, but that moderate and severely handicapped preschoolers can also benefit from less directive methods.

TEACHING STRATEGIES IN EARLY CHILDHOOD SPECIAL EDUCATION

The Value of Group Activities

In the special education classroom the focus tends to be on one child at a time, even when the children are in a group. Consider the following example:

A group of eight moderately delayed children are having a lesson in motor development. The room is arranged with gross motor equipment: several automobile tires to crawl through, a small trampoline to bounce on, a large ball to be rolled on. The physical therapist takes each child in turn and puts him/her through the motor sequence. The other seven sit on the sidelines awaiting their turns.

Although considered a "group" activity, this lesson is organized like individual therapy. There is little opportunity for the children to interact with each other or to learn from each other. That is because each child waits for a turn to interact with the therapist; the activity is structured so that the children as well as the adult view the motor sequence directed by the therapist as the only event of any importance taking place. Even mildly handicapped youngsters in special education settings are so accustomed to interacting only with an adult that they do not initiate many interactions with each other. In fact, such interactions are often frowned upon by adults in the interest of good classroom control.

The advantages of group activities, a mainstay of the early childhood teacher, are: (1) children are less closely supervised and so can take more initiative in experimenting, exploring, satisfying curiosity through their activity; (2) children tend to interact more with each other and not so exclusively with an adult. During peer interactions they generally have more opportunities to initiate conversations or joint activities rather than simply respond to directions.

Much literature supports the idea that children gain from informally interacting together. Perret-Clermont (1980), for example, found that children develop their ability to think logically when they exchange ideas with their peers in small groups. Examining wrong ideas together helps them to construct the correct solution. In a well-known experiment, Inhelder, Sinclair and Bovet (1974) demonstrated that children construct higher-level logic by being questioned, and not by being corrected or taught correct answers by adults. These studies confirmed Piaget's (1963) idea that social interaction among children is necessary for their development of logic. Kamii (1982), one of Piaget's major American interpreters, has stated the belief that "children of all ages would develop more rapidly...in their general abilities to think logically, if teachers would stop correcting worksheets and would instead encourage youngsters to exchange ideas honestly and to argue among themselves" (p. 250).

The Importance of Play

Play has traditionally been considered an important part of the curriculum of preschool programs. This is because play is thought to promote development in all the growth areas: intellectual, social, language and motor. (For a review of the literature on the value of play for handicapped children, see Widerstrom, 1983.) Spontaneous play is encouraged in traditional nursery school programs, for example, simply by allowing some time in the schedule each day for free play. Early childhood teachers generally do not believe that they must teach children to play, but rather that the learnings to be gained from play accrue indirectly from the experience.

Many special educators, in their zeal to narrow the developmental gap through direct teaching of skills, consider time spent in spontaneous play to be time that could be better spent working on specific deficits. Free-play sessions may not be scheduled into the preschool handicapped child's day for this reason. Nevertheless, evidence from research is clear that all children, handicapped or not, benefit developmentally from opportunities to play spontaneously (Horne and Philleo, 1976; Sylva, Bruner and Genova, 1976; Vygotsky, 1976; Widerstrom, 1983). It is not necessary for play to be a group experience, although informal play situations do provide more opportunities for children to interact with each other than do teacher-directed situations. Play can be an individual experience and still provide much benefit: the chance to experiment with toys or other objects, to practice problem-solving abilities and, most important, to perform an activity for its own sake, for the sheer pleasure of it, without worrying about attaining or failing to attain a goal.

Clearly, one important contribution that early childhood education might make to special education is a renewed awareness of the benefits to young children of spontaneous play. Programs for preschool handicapped children should include some time each day for free play, with the teacher following the child's lead as much as possible. Many young children whose handicaps fall within the mild to moderate range are capable of initiating and carrying through independently their own play activities—though they may need encouragement from an adult, especially at first, since they are accustomed to being directed. More severely impaired youngsters may not initiate play very well, or have the sensory or motor abilities to engage in typical play activities. In fact, some educators believe that such children need to be taught to play (Feitelson and Ross, 1973); Saltz, Dixon and Johnson, 1977). There is evidence to suggest that this can be done effectively, and that intellectual development increases as a result (Mindes, 1982; Mogford, 1977; Widerstrom, 1983). It should not be overlooked in the curriculum.

Teacher-Child Talk

It is probably true that all teachers, unless specifically trained, talk too much. Research studies (Amidon and Flanders, 1971) have shown that from kindergarten through graduate school teachers of all grade levels talk more than all their pupils combined, and that only 3 to 9 percent of teachers' talk reacts to or makes use of an idea expressed by a student. Preschool teachers do not seem exempt from these data.

Amidon and Flanders (1971) reported that older students (8th grade) performed better on written achievement tests in classrooms with teachers identified as "indirect"; that is, those who accepted or used students' feelings. "Direct" teachers—those who gave many directions, criticized, expressed their own ideas or gave out factual information—were not as effective in helping students to perform well on achievement tests. These studies, though not entirely appropriate in a discussion of preschool, nevertheless provide an important guideline for all teachers: less teacher talk and more child initiation and participation apparently make for better learning.

An effective program for training special education teachers to better communicate with young children by listening rather than talking and by reacting to communicative efforts initiated by the child is the INter-REactive Learning (INREAL) method (Weiss, 1981). In this model, new learnings are taught by building upon what the child already knows. The method has a strong developmental base, for each child's level of communicative competence is considered in designing teaching strategies. The child's communicative initiatives become the basis for teacher-child interaction.

The most important aspect of the INREAL model is its reactive element. The adult must react to the child's suggestions, comments or activities rather than direct the child. The method encourages the adult to respond rather than initiate, a difficult role for many teachers.

In the paragraphs below the INREAL techniques for effective teacher talk are described.

(a) *Silent Observation Understanding Listening (S.O.U.L.)*. It is interesting that INREAL's first rule for teachers is *silence*. According to Weiss (1981), the use of S.O.U.L. allows the specialist time to tune into a situation before talking with the child. At the same time it allows the child to express his or her interests without adult domination. S.O.U.L. permits the teacher to establish rapport and create an empathetic relationship.

(b) *Mirroring*. The teacher responds to the nonverbal child's movements, gestures or facial expressions by mirroring those movements as a means of establishing joint reference. Sometimes the child mirrors the adult's movements, thus completing the communicative cycle. This technique is useful in teaching the child turntaking in conversations, for example.

(c) *Self-talk*. In this activity the teacher talks out his or her own participation during parallel play with the child (in which teacher and child are engaged in the same activity). An especially effective technique for use with nonverbal children, it teaches the child topic/comment relationships. A variation of self-talk is *parallel talk*, in which the adult talks out the child's participation in the activity. The advantage of these two techniques is that they allow the adult to focus attention at the child's own level of ability and interest. Some examples of parallel talk from Weiss (1981) at increasing levels of complexity follow:

- Car's going.
- The car's going.
- The car goes along the road.
- The car you've got is broken.

In summary, the INREAL system offers teachers a method for responding to children other than directing them as more traditional special education methods dictate. It is philosophically very compatible with the indirect teaching methods used by early childhood educators.

The Comfort Index

Evidence suggests that many teachers are overly concerned about classroom control. Teachers' need to control creates problems that are shared by all teachers. Nevertheless, early childhood teachers are probably more comfortable than their special education counterparts in less structured settings. Because their background in normal child development tells them that children can learn much in an atmosphere that allows freedom of movement, spontaneous initiation of activities and informed conversations, they generally try to create a classroom environment that is open and nondirective.

The special education teacher, accustomed to direct teaching situations, feels less comfortable in an environment where he or she lacks complete control of classroom activity. Creating a classroom climate where the child is allowed more initiative might be worthy of teachers' consideration. In order to do this successfully, however, the special education teacher must feel comfortable in situations where less control is exercised over children's behavior. This means that occasionally things will happen that are unexpected and for which the teacher is unprepared. It means that the teacher must recognize the benefits to children's learning of a less teacher-controlled environment and that the trade-off for more child initiative is some increase in unacceptable child behavior.

A convenient way of viewing this dichotomy is by means of the comfort/control index. This index simply illustrates the fact that a direct relationship exists between levels of comfort and control on the part of most teachers. A high level of control usually results in a high comfort level for the teacher. If a more open classroom environment is truly to be created, the teacher must learn to be comfortable with a lower degree of classroom control. An important aim of the practicum experience during training, therefore, must be to ascertain the student teacher's comfort/control levels and to provide experiences and feedback that work toward lowering the level of control while maintaining a high comfort level. Such activities as self-observation through videotaping, teaching experiences with increasingly larger groups of children, and observations in regular early childhood educational settings are suggested means for working toward lowered control levels.

It is the author's experience that this is a slow and tedious process. A teacher who is committed to achieving a higher comfort level with lowered control must work constantly to maintain awareness of too much teacher control in the classroom. Ordinarily the goal is achieved only after much practice combined with feedback from colleagues.

In summary, it is suggested that there are four areas in which special educators can adapt effective strategies from early childhood educators. First, they could include in the curriculum group activities that foster peer interactions. Second, they could include more opportunities for free play as a regular part of the curriculum. Third, they could practice being more indirect and more reactive in their interactions with pupils. Fourth, they could adapt to a less controlled classroom atmosphere and learn to be comfortable with a lesser amount of control.

CONCLUSION

As population trends contribute to an increased number of young children under age 5, there will be an even greater need for teachers of young children in coming years. With continuing advances in medical technology, we can expect greater numbers of children born with handicaps to require special education services. It is important now for all educators of young children to pause for serious consideration of the kinds of programs we intend to provide for these youngsters. It is time to give thought to the unique characteristics of preschool children which make their educational needs so very different from the needs of older children, whether handicapped or not. It is useful for early childhood special education teachers to take time out to reflect about what they are doing in their classrooms. Finally, it is necessary for those of us committed to early childhood special education to ensure that decision-makers in our field—i.e., lawmakers, state departments of education personnel, public school administrators and parents—realize the unique educational needs of the young child and understand that young handicapped children often have more in common with their nonhandicapped peers than they have with older special needs children. Their school curriculum should reflect this fact.

DISCUSSION QUESTIONS

1. What is the fundamental difference between a remedial approach and a developmental approach?

2. Should public school programs for four-year-old ''at-risk'' students use models from special education or traditional early education?

3. Which strategies and approaches from the early education of handicapped or delayed children should be integrated into early education for all children?

4. Should special education teachers be assigned to teach younger exceptional children in the schools?

5. How can early education and special education strategies be integrated to meet the needs of all children in any classroom?

Section Four: Preschool Programs

EDITOR'S OVERVIEW

This section needs an immediate disclaimer: contemporary discussion of young children should *not* use chronological age as a line of demarcation. Since children grow in what some have called a "seamless" continuum, birth dates have relatively little to do with major decisions about their education. However, the present organization of schools clearly depends on age distinctions, and the writers have responded to these distinctions for *organizational* purposes. In particular, virtually all school programs in the United States make provision for five-year-old children: most have kindergartens. The first major change in the population to be served in recent times has to do with children who are *younger than five*. This section is therefore about children and programs divided by one year: the fours and the fives.

To begin, Scott-Jones and Baker-Ward raise questions about "preschoolers" in the public schools in relation to parents, children, and child development. Zigler presents a conditional endorsement, expecting schools to broaden their perspective and range of services to better meet the needs of the four-year-olds and their families. Futrell's concern is that a lifelong learning framework be adopted, and that children begin that journey at age four. The position statement by the Southern Association on Children Under Six is representative of the collective professional viewpoint; certain quality elements must be considered as four-year-olds move into public school programs. Dismuke samples some of the schools that are enrolling younger children, repeating some of the qualities that will most likely make the programs responsive to the needs of the children and their families. Morado summarizes characteristics of public school programs for four-year-olds sponsored by various states. Then, the National Black Child Development Institute (NBCDI) suggests ten guidelines to ensure that public school programs create a productive and effective learning environment for four-year-old Black children. And, since it is clear that the American educational system is in the process of adding one more "grade" to the educational ladder, Hymes says, "of course" four-year-olds should go to school.

Next we turn to an "old" part of public schooling in the United States: the kindergarten. With the distinction of being the only grade with a special and descriptive name, its programs that serve five-year-olds have been around for more than one hundred years. The first chapter, by Rothenberg, provides a balanced view of full-day and half-day kindergartens. Then, Robinson discusses five trends shaping the kindergarten derived from her national research. This is followed by a report on two national surveys by the Educational Research Service.

There is a considerable degree of uncertainty about how early education programs for four- and five-year-old children should be organized and delivered, as well as variation in views about the purpose and function of these programs. Most of the new programs for four-year-olds authorized by the states serve children who are educationally disadvantaged or "at risk" of reduced school success. These programs usually operate as intervention models. The kindergarten is being changed from below by these new prekindergarten classes and from above by pressure for academic performance and basic skills acquisition. The final chapter concentrates on the developmental needs of all children in this age range. The NAEYC position statement, representing a broad consensus of the profession, makes clear distinctions between educational practice that is developmentally appropriate for young children and practice that is not appropriate. These guidelines can be the core for program planning and evaluation of present early childhood education in the schools.

20. PUBLIC EDUCATION FOR PRESCHOOLERS

by Diane Scott-Jones and Lynne Baker-Ward

An issue receiving current attention is whether formal programs for preschool children should be made part of the public school system. Working parents need adequate care for children younger than school-age, and educators ask whether 3- and 4-year-olds need or would benefit from formal schooling. These two needs, that of working parents for satisfactory care arrangements for their young children and the developmental/educational needs of 3- and 4-year-olds, are pivotal in determining the desirability of public preschool education.

WILL PUBLIC EDUCATION FOR PRESCHOOLERS MEET THE NEEDS OF WORKING MOTHERS?

In the past, most women entered the labor force when their children reached the age of compulsory school attendance; the school as an institution assumed a large part of child care and supervision as well as education and socialization (Kamerman and Kahn, 1981). Today, however, many women with younger children work outside the home. Informal arrangements are not widely available because the grandmothers, aunts, and neighbors who care for children are likely to be working themselves. Kamerman and Kahn (1981) point out that the United States lags behind other industrialized countries in the formulation of explicit policy for the care of young children of working mothers. Our federal day care policy is still in the "state of suspended animation" (Levine, 1978, p. 126). A substantial number of children are left unattended during their parents' working hours (Marx, 1985). Adolescent parents who are trying to complete high school have unmet child care needs (Blank and Morgan, 1985). Affordable, high-quality care is not readily available for many single-parent families and dual-earner families. Possibilities for handling the cost of programs for these groups include sliding pay scales for parents, public funds for parents who cannot afford to pay, and funds from parents' employers. School districts, particularly those with declining enrollments, may be able

See pages 329–30 for acknowledgment and references.

to provide personnel and facilities (National School Boards Association, 1986). Some type of subsidized child care is essential to the survival of those families at or near the poverty level. Scarr (1984) ponders the contradiction in present governmental policy, which requires that tax-supported education and supervision be available for most of the work day but only for children age 5 or 6 to 18 years. Public school programs, however, may not be able to handle the needs of working parents if the programs are limited to the length of the typical school day. In addition, more than one-third of women with infants under twelve months are working (Klein, 1985). These mothers also are in need of care for their children, and public school programs for preschoolers will not meet this need.

IS EARLIER SCHOOLING BETTER FOR ALL CHILDREN?

The discussion of public education for 3- and 4-year-olds vacillates between programs for all children and programs only for poor, typically minority children, or others considered at risk. With the former view, it is expected that preschool will give all children the competitive edge they will need later to succeed. In comparisons of American and Japanese education, researchers have concluded that differences in favor of Japanese children arise in early school experiences. American kindergarten children lag behind in mathematics. Although the authors do not explicitly advocate earlier schooling for American children, they point out the importance of early academic education (Stevenson, Lee, and Stigler, 1986).

Supporting the latter view, Zigler argues against formal public preschool programs for all children, stating that "whenever the family situation permits it, the best place for a preschool child is at home" (1985, p. 9). Most family situations, however, do not permit the child to remain at home. According to Kamerman and Kahn (1981), adequate alternate care for preschool children is no longer a debatable need; it is only for children under three years that substantial questions are raised regarding the appropriate parental pattern of work and child care. Yet, Zigler (1985) asserts that public funds for preschool should be invested where they would be most cost effective—in programs for poor, handicapped, or bilingual children. Some states have moved in that direction. Recently enacted legislation in South Carolina permits the state to reimburse local school districts for half the cost of programs for 4-year-olds predicted to have academic deficiencies; Texas recently required school districts to provide programs for 4-year-olds who are non-English-speaking or from low-income families (Blank and Morgan, 1985).

Early Intervention for Poor Children

Evidence suggests that early education programs for low-income Black children have lasting positive effects on school achievement. Lazar and Darlington (1982) analyzed follow-up data for children 9 to 19 years who had attended one of 11 experimental or quasi-experimental programs. More than 90 percent of the participants were low-income Black children. Typically, children were enrolled at age 3 years and older for a period of two years or less in curricula emphasizing cognitive development. Compared to control groups, program children were significantly less likely to be placed in special education classes or to be retained in grade. Program children scored significantly higher on intelligence tests and, in some cases, achievement tests. They were more likely to express positive achievement attitudes. Lazar and Darlington concluded that a variety of good early education programs lead to measurable educational benefits for poor Black children. According to these authors, such programs should be expanded at the national, state, or local level.

The major public program for preschool children is Head Start, which includes comprehensive services as well as an educational component. Head Start is designed to serve poor children, but the majority of enrolled children are minority; 42 percent are Black, 20 percent Hispanic, 4 percent American Indian, 1 percent Asian, and 33 percent white. The enrollment of Blacks and Hispanics is twice as high as their proportion of the poverty population, whereas white enrollment is one-half their proportion of the poverty population (Washington, 1985). Only a small percentage of eligible children (13%) are actually enrolled, however. In 1985, the number of eligible children increased by one-third, whereas the programs were level-funded (Hodgkinson, 1985). In addition, Head Start hours need to be expanded in order to meet the needs of working mothers (Washington and Dyemade, 1985).

Concern has been expressed by the National Black Child Development Institute (NBCDI) regarding the wisdom of establishing programs for preschool children in the public schools. The main objection is that public schools have not done an admirable job of educating Black children. Because the public school system is judged to have failed older Black children, it may not "develop the skills and techniques necessary to nurture Black children at their most fragile and formative stage" (NBCDI, 1985, p. 3). NBCDI asserts that current proposals for public preschool programs are driven by expediency and do not give sufficient attention to child development or to the community needs, family needs, and cultural values that affect development. NBCDI discusses a number of public school practices, such as reliance on standardized tests for placement, that would be even worse for preschool Black children than for school-age Black children.

Delivery systems other than the public schools, such as churches, community organizations, private centers, and family day care homes, may be effective, according to NBCDI. Some Black-owned and operated centers currently provide excellent preschool education for Black and other minority children. Harper and Dawkins (1985) describe one exemplary center of this type that has provided service for 22 years with a relatively stable staff. These authors discuss the responsibility of Black educators for developing private multicultural preschools as alternatives to public preschools. In a later publication, NBCDI (1986) outlines criteria that public preschool programs must meet if they are to be appropriate for Black children. The criteria range from effective parent involvement to specific training for preschool teachers to regular external review by community members and child development experts.

A weakness of programs limited to poor and minority children, according to Zigler (1985), is that these groups become segregated from other children. In fact, that segregation is already occurring. Although approximately equal proportions (36%) of Black and white children are enrolled in some preschool program (Grant and Snyder, 1983), 70 percent of white but only 33 percent of Black children are in private programs. Statistics on differential enrollment in public and private programs are vividly brought to life in Lubek's (1985) study of a Black Head Start center and a white preschool. Although less than a mile apart physically, the two centers were far apart from one another in use of time, use of space, materials, activities, and patterns of interactions. The implication is not that one setting is necessarily "better" than the other. A decision must be made, however, regarding the wisdom of institutionalizing segregated and potentially unequal preschool education.

Levine (1978) emphasized the importance of "normalizing" day care—making it available to all families without any stigma of welfare, deviance, or pathology. Public schools have been the major normalizing institution for children in our society and will probably play some role in a national day care policy, but, Levine asserts, the school should not necessarily be the prime sponsor of day care—making it available to all families without any stigma of welfare, deviance, or pathology. An advocate of diversity in the solution to the day care problem, Levine (1978) describes programs in operation in five different school systems around the country. Included are school-district-operated centers with teachers paid the same salary as their public school colleagues; high-school-based centers for the children of teen parents run jointly by the school district and a private day care agency; and school-affiliated family day care programs.

Zigler (1985) suggests that schools could provide universal, but not compulsory, day care. He envisions a community school providing not only high-quality day care but also comprehensive services to families. The day care program would be staffed by licensed child development associates and would emphasize play and socialization rather than cognitive development. Hobbs et al. (1984) also express the view that child care should be available to all families through the public school system, which would be responsible for implementing the mix of school, community, and private programs best suited for the local community. Like Levine (1978), Hobbs et al. emphasize the role of the public school system as the most "regular" socializing agency reaching the largest number of families without the stigma of the welfare bureaucracy.

Critical Periods/Early Experience

A difficulty in the move toward preschool education is that educators and parents may see these few additional years of education as a panacea for many problems that arise later in children's educational centers. From a 1984 conference on day care and public schools came the recommendation that state reform efforts provide evidence that funds used for preschool education result in lower expenditures for welfare, remedial education, and prisons (National School Boards Association, 1986). Hodgkinson (1985) asserts that an expanded Head Start system would lead to savings in future services such as prisons and drug control centers. Early experience, however, can rarely be separated from *continuing* experience; to do so would require the demonstration that the early period was somehow discontinuous from the period before and afterward (Clarke, 1984). Early experience is important but not as an "inoculation" against subsequent difficulties. Both early and continuing experiences are important in children's development.

An appropriate view of early experience is important in evaluating the effects of preschool educational programs. If early experience is considered critical and the importance of all the life-span is not acknowledged, programs may promise too much and be unable to deliver. Although exaggerating the role of early experience may expedite the passage of much needed legislation for programs for young children, resources may be diverted from other programs that serve older children. In the long run, children's developmental and educational needs throughout childhood and adolescence may not be met.

Although a follow-up study of 19-year-olds who attended an exemplary preschool program found positive outcomes (Berrueta-Clement, Schweinhart, Barnett, Epstein, and Weikart, 1984), preschool education alone cannot be expected to remedy the complex, multi-faceted problems that occur later in children's lives. Further, programs being established in public schools may not incorporate important, and expensive, features of the experimental programs. In Texas, for example, programs for four-year-olds will have a staff-child ratio of 1:22 (Blank and Morgan, 1985). Proposed federal regulations (which have never been adopted) stipulate a ratio of 1:8 with a maximum group size of 16 (Scarr, 1984). Preschool education will not be viewed as successful if it promises too much for too little. The notion that the first years of a child's life are "critical" and that positive experiences during this time inoculate the child against later harmful influences leads to unrealistically high expectations for preschool education. Early experience is important, but it must be followed by later positive experiences for children to develop their potential.

FUTURE DIRECTIONS

In spite of lack of agreement regarding public education for preschoolers, a number of states and

113

school districts are moving in that direction. In North Carolina, where a higher percentage of mothers of preschoolers work than in any other state, a feasibility study concluded that the developmental needs of children and the needs of working parents result in public school responsibility for prekindergarten programs (Kahdy, 1985). Strong objections, however, were reported from private day-care providers. Others expressed reservations regarding the possible negative impact of structured programs and pressure for achievement on young children.

The Early Childhood Education Commission in New York City recently recommended that public preschool programs be made available to all 4-year-olds. Other states have allocated funds for pilot programs (National Black Child Development Institute, 1985). The National School Boards Association states in its report, *Day Care in the Public Schools* (1986), that school-based programs will become standard in many school districts. The report on education from the National Governors' Association Meeting (*Time for Results*, 1986) recommends greater access to early childhood education for low-income children, kindergarten for all 5-year-olds, and developmental programs for 3- and 4-year-olds. Some states are focusing on train-

ing parents through the public school system; Missouri recently instituted a requirement that all its local school districts hire child development specialists for programs addressed to parents of newborns and toddlers (Fiske, 1986). This strategy addresses the educational and developmental needs of young children but not parents' needs for alternate care during working hours.

In the debate on public schooling for three- and four-year-olds, values must be expressly identified. It appears that values in several related areas are not crystallized: the need for and value of women's employment outside the home, the responsibility of society for the well-being of young children, and different standards for the care of poor minority children and families than for their middle-class counterparts. Our changing and uncertain values regarding appropriate care of young children will impede progress. Effective policy probably will require consensus on some issues and flexibility to allow for diversity of values on other issues. In summary, public education for preschoolers is an idea with some merit but with a need for clarification. Before it is begun on a large scale, we must clearly specify the objectives and inherent values of such programs for young children and their families.

DISCUSSION QUESTIONS

1. Will public school programs for younger children serve important social purposes?

2. Are the needs of low income and minority children being met by current preschool programs?

3. Should future programs for young children model the cultural and socioeconomic diversity of the nation?

4. Will the addition of programs for younger children in the schools contribute to optimum development for all the children to be served?

21. SHOULD FOUR-YEAR-OLDS BE IN SCHOOL?

by Edward F. Zigler

A momentum is developing in our nation behind a movement toward universal preschool education for four-year-olds. New York City, for example, has not only made all-day kindergarten mandatory, but has established a commission to create a public school program for all four-year-olds by September 1986—a move praised in a *New York Times* editorial as "A Model for the Nation." So many positive voices have been heard endorsing preschool education for four-year-olds that it is easy to agree with Gordon Ambach, the New York State Commissioner for Education, who stated recently that it was not possible to find anyone to uphold the negative side of the issue.

In fact, there are some negative voices, and they are beginning to be heard. Herbert Zimiles, a leading thinker in the field of early childhood education, recently argued that the movement toward universal preschool education is characterized more by enthusiasm than thought. In Connecticut a study committee appointed by the commissioner of education has concluded that "under no circumstances do we believe it appropriate for all four-year-olds to be involved in a 'kindergarten-type' program within the public school." In this [chapter], I will add my voice to those who argue that universal schooling for four-year-olds requires more thought than it has so far been accorded.

The current impetus for earlier schooling has two sources. The first is the concern generated by the recent proliferation of negative evaluations of our public secondary schools. The 1983 report, *A Nation at Risk*, detailing the failures of secondary schooling in America, was soon followed by similar studies that emphasized the need for higher academic standards, more attention to basics, more rigor in teaching, and longer school days and years. Few of these reports proposed earlier schooling as a solution.

A second source of the momentum toward universal preschool education is the inappropriate generalization of the effects of a few excellent remedial programs for the economically disadvantaged. Several notable preschool intervention programs—including Head Start, the Ypsilanti-based Perry Preschool Program, the New York State pre-kindergarten program, and the Brookline Early Education Program—have succeeded in spurring the developmental and cognitive growth of low-income three- and four-year-old children. But to apply the results from these programs to all children is inappropriate for two reasons: First, the benefits of these programs were obtained *only* for economically disadvantaged children, whose needs differ from those of the middle-class children who constitute the bulk of our school population. Second, these intervention programs differ from standard school fare in a number of important ways, providing primary health and social services for both the schoolchild and the family as a whole.

These are vital differences, since many theorists believe that preschool programs are most successful when parents participate, and that the basic, noneducational needs of children and families must be met before schooling can have any effect.

Public preschool education shares few of these noneducational services and concerns, nor can they become the primary focus of the education establishment. It is an open question whether universal preschool programs will result in the kind of benefits produced by the intervention programs—benefits that may well be a consequence of services having very little to do with formal education. In fact, it was precisely those differences which I have outlined here that led many of us who were involved in the organization of the Head Start intervention program to oppose President Carter's proposal to move the program into the newly formed Department of Education, and in the end prevented its inclusion.

THE CASE FOR INTERVENTION

Preschool intervention may be particularly effective for the most economically disadvantaged children, a view supported by New York State's 1982 evaluation of its experimental preschool program. The New York study indicated that the only cognitive gains that lasted beyond the preschool period were among children whose mothers were of the lowest educational index.

See page 330 for acknowledgment and suggested reading.

This fact has not escaped educational decision makers. Almost all the states that now provide school-sponsored programs for four-year-olds limit enrollment to the disadvantaged: low-income, handicapped, and in some cases non-English-speaking youngsters. A large body of evidence indicates that there is little, if anything, to be gained by exposing middle-class children to preschool education. For example, the only advantage that Swift (1964) could find as a result of preschool education was a minimal degree of enhanced social development at school entrance, with nonparticipants reaching the same level of social adjustment in less than two years. Other researchers have found that extensive intervention programs for four-year-olds benefited lower-class children, but had no effect on other youngsters.

American schools, already under great financial pressures, must make the most efficient use possible of limited economic resources. As a long-time advocate of cost benefit analyses for all types of social programs, I feel that we can make the most effective use of limited funds by investing them in intervention programs that target children in three overlapping groups: the economically disadvantaged, the handicapped, and the bilingual. Providing such programs to all four-year-olds would spread education budgets too thin. A universal extension of preschool would not only have little effect on the more advantaged mainstream children, but would actually diminish our capacity to help those who could benefit most from early remedial care.

There is, however, one potential advantage to universal preschool education. A weakness of Head Start and similar programs is their built-in economic segregation of children. Poor children go to Head Start, while more affluent children go elsewhere. Universal preschool could better integrate children across socioeconomic lines, and would introduce equity into early childhood programs. While this might waste funding for preschool education on children who do not need it, universal preschool would guarantee its availability to children who do: Unfortunately, while we would be well-advised to promote the integration of children from diverse social and ethnic backgrounds, the cost of doing so through universal preschool education outweighs its potential benefits.

EDUCATION OR DAY CARE?

Educators in several states point to the pressure for all-day kindergarten as evidence of the value parents place on early education. I believe, however, that they have misread this demand. What many parents are expressing is less a burning desire for preschool education than their need for affordable, high-quality day care. Fifty-nine percent of the mothers of three- and four-year-olds are now employed outside their homes. Although many of these mothers have enrolled their children in child care programs that provide organized educational activities, not even the all-day kindergarten programs are able to fill adequately the day care needs of families with both parents working outside the home. Because even after-school programs at present tend to adjourn two hours before most working days end, the day care problem has not been solved but only moved back for a few hours. This token improvement could lead some parents to take fewer precautions for their children during this relatively short time, increasing rather than reducing the danger to children.

Since day care can be prohibitively expensive, it is not surprising that many families would prefer to shift the cost to the public school system. The Perry Preschool Project was estimated by its originators to cost approximately $1,500 per year per child in 1963. Given the number of three- and four-year-olds in the nation today, and adjusting the 1963 figures for inflation, the total cost of a universal program would be many billions of dollars per year. Although some advocates of universal preschool education continue to behave as though these vast sums will magically appear, fiscal reality demands that we target populations who can most benefit, and provide programs best suited to their particular needs.

We must also listen to those families who neither need nor want their young children placed in preschool. The compulsory aspect of many of the proposed early education plans has angered many parents and set them in opposition to school officials—a poor beginning to the positive home/school relationship that is vital to the educational process. Decision makers must be sensitive to the individual needs of children and parents and recognize that, whenever the family situation permits it, the best place for a preschool child is often at home.

In fact, recent studies have shown that the conversations children carry on at home may be the richest source of linguistic and cognitive enrichment for children from all but the most deprived backgrounds. Because parent and child share a common life and frame of reference, they can explore events and ideas in intimate, individualistic conversations with great personal meaning.

This is not to ignore the fact that home may be a place of abuse or neglect, a welfare hotel, or a confusing and insecure environment without adequate resources. For children in these circumstances, day care may be the best available alternative.

A TIME FOR CHILDHOOD

I concur with David Elkind (1981) and others that we are driving our young children too hard, and thereby depriving them of their most precious commodity—their childhood. The image of the four-year-old trundling off to school in designer jeans, miniature briefcase in hand, may seem cute, but going from cradle to school denies children the freedom to develop at their own pace. Children are growing up too fast today, and prematurely placing four-year-olds and five-year-olds into full-day preschool education programs will only compound this problem.

Those who argue in favor of universal preschool education ignore evidence which indicates that early schooling is inappropriate for many four-year-olds, and may even be harmful to their development. Marie Winn notes in *Children Without Childhood* that premature schooling can replace valuable play time, to the injury of the child's development. This is especially true with the present cognitive thrust in education, where there is danger of overemphasizing formal and overly structured academics. The stewardship of very young children requires a distinct form of care, suited to the rapid developmental changes and high dependency of these children, not a scaled-down school curriculum.

At the same time we must remember that while early childhood is an important and sensitive period, it is not uniquely so. In the 1960s we believed early childhood was a magic period during which minimal intervention efforts would have maximal, indelible effects on children. In the current push toward early formal education we can see the unfortunate recurrence of this idea.

Every age of a child is a magic period. We must be just as concerned for the six-year-old, the ten-year-old, and the 16-year-old as we are for the four-year-old. The proposed New York plan is especially troubling in that it includes a suggestion to add a year of education at the beginning of formal schooling, and to drop a year at the end of high school. Adolescence is itself a sensitive and fluid period in the life of the child. We must guard against shortchanging one age group in our efforts to help another.

THE EASY WAY OUT

This is not the first time that universal preschool education has been proposed. Wilson Riles, then California State Superintendent of Schools, advocated early childhood education ten years ago. Then, as now, the arguments in favor of preschool education were that it would reduce school failure, lower dropout rates, increase test scores, and produce a generation of more competent high school graduates. My interpretation of the evidence—the same as that finally reached by the State of California—is that preschool education would not achieve these results.

I'm not simply saying that universal preschool would be a waste of time and money. There is a danger in asserting that the solution to poor school and later-life performance of the disadvantaged will be solved by a year of preschool education. To repeat, we may be on the verge of falling into the overoptimistic trap that ensnared us in the midsixties, when expectations were raised that an eight-week summer program could solve all the problems of the poor. If we wish to improve the lives of the economically disadvantaged we must abandon short-term "solutions" and work for much deeper social reforms. The token nature of relying on educational innovations alone to solve the problems of poor children has been noted by historian Marvin Lazerson (1970):

> Too often discussions of educational reform appear to be a means of avoiding more complex and politically dangerous issues . . . education is . . . cheaper than new housing and new jobs. We are left with greater school responsibility while the social problems which have the greatest effect on schooling are largely ignored. The schools—in this case, preschool—are asked to do too much, and given too little support to accomplish what they are asked. (p. 84)

We simply cannot inoculate children in one year of preschool against the ravages of a life of deprivation. Even champions of early childhood education warn us not to expect too much when doing too little. Senator Daniel P. Moynihan (1984) notes that exaggerated reports of success in the field of early childhood education lead inevitably to near-nihilism when these extravagant hopes are unfulfilled: "From finding out that not everything works, we rush to the judgment that nothing works or can be made to work."

Moynihan's point that research is threatened when results are exaggerated is well taken. And just as the credibility of researchers can be damaged, so too can the credibility of educators if they insist on promising more than they can possibly deliver.

A REALISTIC SOLUTION

Educators must realize that they cannot reform the world or change the basic nature of children. The real question is how to provide the best experience during the day for a four-year-old, specifically for a child who cannot remain at home with a reliable, competent caregiver. Parents do not need children who read at age four, but they do need affordable, good-quality child care. The most cost-effective way to provide universally available—not compulsory—care would be to work with the school.

I am advocating a return to the concept of the community school as a local center for all the social services of the local neighborhood. Such a school would, in addition to other programs, provide full-day, high-quality child care for four- and even three-year-old children in the existing school facilities. Although such programs would include developmentally appropriate educational components, they would be primarily places for recreation and socialization—the real business of preschoolers.

In-school day care could also easily accommodate older children after school is dismissed. One investigator summarizes the need in this way: "We must...align the goals of programs for infants, preschoolers, and early elementary school-aged pupils so that such programs become components of an integrated, consistent plan for educating young children" (Weinberg, 1979, p. 915).

Such a program, although operating on school grounds, should not be staffed solely by teachers. Instead I propose that we staff school-based day care programs with teachers serving in a supervisory capacity, and certified Child Development Associates (CDA)—now used in our nation's Head Start project—as direct caregivers for the program's day care component. Certification of CDAs is based not on educational attainment alone, but on proven competence in meeting all the needs of young children. A recent study found that the one background characteristic of teachers that could be related to program quality was early childhood training—not years of schooling or number of degrees.

Of course, in-school day care is going to be costly, and the funding issue will have to be addressed. Federal support might be expected to subsidize costs for economically disadvantaged children. Cost containment would also be enhanced by making use of existing school facilities.

Finally, in considering the needs of three- and four-year-olds, let us not neglect the needs of five-year-olds. I believe that a full day of formal schooling is too much even for these children. Instead, I would propose a half-day kindergarten program to be followed by a half day of in-school day care for those who need it. The extra cost could be borne by parents on a sliding-fee basis, with financial assistance available to needy families. Licensed teachers would teach in the morning, and certified CDAs would care for the children in the afternoon. Again, let me emphasize that the day care element should be strictly voluntary; no parent who wanted his or her child at home after school ends at noon would be denied.

In short, we must ask ourselves what would we be buying for our children in universal preschool education programs, and at what cost? I strongly believe that a family-oriented, multiservice community school could best meet the varied needs of preschoolers and their families by providing a number of services from which families could select to suit their needs. Such services could include comprehensive intervention programs, health and nutrition components, high-quality and affordable day care, and educational opportunities, to name only a few possibilities.

Our four-year-olds do have a place in school, but it is not at a school desk.

DISCUSSION QUESTIONS

1. Is there sufficient justification for adding one more grade to the public school program in the United States—free and available public schooling for four-year-old children?
2. Why should the schools intervene?
3. Should there be a distinction between public school education and public school day care?
4. Does the public and the profession expect too much from public early education?
5. How should the education of younger children in the schools differ from the present kindergarten/primary curriculum?

22.   PUBLIC SCHOOLS AND FOUR-YEAR OLDS: A TEACHER'S VIEW

by Mary Hatwood Futrell

The process by which we determine national priorities and initiate social reforms has changed dramatically during the past decade. Today, more and more frequently, demographics dictate decisions. I make this observation, not in order to discredit demographics, but to put forth the modest claim that demography is no substitute for philosophy. As we reflect on the issue of public schooling for four-year-olds, we must be more than students of statistics. We must be students of both learning theory and cognitive development, and we must be visionaries. This philosophical dimension has been pushed to the rear of the debate on early childhood education, and that, I believe, is an unfortunate trend.

We know that between 1950 and 1985, the percentage of mothers working outside the household increased from 14 percent to 62 percent. We know that as recently as 1960, 60 percent of all American households could be described as traditional and that today that figure has dropped to 7 percent. We have precise data on divorce rates, single-parent households, and latch-key children.

The nurturing environment once provided by the home, analysts insist, is an increasing rarity. The data underlying this claim have led scores of researchers to conclude that we need "a new gray mare." The most common argument for opening the doors of our public schools to four-year-olds takes the form of resurrecting—in a most extreme form—the *in loco parentis* doctrine. Schools will become adoption agencies, and teachers will become surrogate parents.

There is more than one disturbing element in this line of argument. Most notably, it drips with disdain for today's parents. It fails to acknowledge the truly remarkable efforts that millions of parents, including single parents and parents in poverty, exert to ensure their children's healthy emotional and intellectual development. Finally, this argument defines the teacher, not as an educator who must forge partnerships *with* parents, but as a part-time police officer who protects children *from* parents. And it defines the school, not as a place of learning, but as a place of refuge.

I cannot accept a line of reasoning that takes us so far down the path toward parent-teacher and home-school antagonism. If we are to equip today's preschoolers for the information-based society that will challenge their emotional and intellectual capacities, we need to create a culture of cooperation that unites parents and teachers in a common cause.

I believe without reservation that the time has come to make public schooling available to our four-year-old population. But an adequate rationale for four-year-old schooling ought to rest on a philosophical examination of the mission of education, not on demographic data used to predict the demise of the family. And it should be rooted in a research-based understanding of the way young children grow, develop, and learn—not in a nostalgia-saturated longing for the social and familial structures of the industrial age.

THE IDEAL OF LIFELONG LEARNING

The time has come to reorient the debate on early childhood education. And at the forefront of that debate should be reflection on the ideal of lifelong learning, that is, learning that will equip students with the mental agility that the technological age demands.

For years, our nation has given lip service to that ideal. What is called for today is the recognition that we must reorganize our schools so that they facilitate attaining that ideal. School, as Ernest Boyer has noted, continues "to be identified with a certain slice of life: you get four years of play, then you go to school and learn; then you go to work and earn, then you retire." That pattern is now a parody of reality. Colleges are no longer reserved for 18- to 22-year-olds. A lifetime in a single career is almost unheard of. The president of the United States is 10 years beyond the traditional retirement age.

What do these trends tell us? They signal our

See page 330 for acknowledgment.

willingness, at last, to break free from the notion that chronology is destiny. They signal a willingness to do away with arbitrary barriers based solely on age. They signal the beginning of the end for "ageism."

IS SCHOOLING APPROPRIATE FOR FOUR-YEAR-OLDS?

But victims of ageism remain. And the most victimized population consists of pre-five-year-olds. American education excludes the very young from school on the assumption that at age five all children suddenly and simultaneously undergo a magical transformation. Does research confirm this assumption? No. Do psychological studies support this assumption? No. Do studies of affective and cognitive development tell us that all children, at precisely the same time, achieve readiness for the first formal steps toward lifelong learning? Absolutely not.

There is clearly no educational reason to deny younger children an opportunity to take those first few steps toward lifelong learning. But this does not mean that four-year-olds are ready for academic instruction in the traditional basics. Instructional programs for four-year-olds cannot be modeled on programs for kindergartners.

The research-based warnings against rushing four-year-olds into instructional activities deserve serious attention. In far too many preschool centers, noted Samual G. Sava of the National Association of Elementary School Principals and David Elkind, president of the National Association for the Education of Young People, children are asked to walk before they can crawl, to run before they can walk. The result, according to Elkind, is a child deprived of childhood, deprived of the playfulness that spurs the mind toward the inquisitiveness that is the root of critical thinking. Sava agreed. We are, he contended, "losing the developmental potential of early childhood education in a misplaced effort to mass-produce little Einsteins."

Other voices of caution have echoed Sava and Elkind. Psychologist Edward F. Zigler, the first director of the U.S. Office of Child Development, argued that "early schooling is inappropriate for many four-year-olds, and may even be harmful to their development." And Marie Winn, author of *Children Without Childhood,* contended that premature schooling can replace valuable play time, with resulting injury to the child's development.

Should we conclude from these arguments that schooling for four-year olds is an idea that should be put to rest? Not at all. The conclusion that is warranted is that we need to ensure developmentally appropriate activities for four-year-olds. Elkind himself has made this point succinctly: "Given the well-established fact that young children learn differently, the conclusion that educators must draw is a straightforward one: The education of young children must be in keeping with their unique modes of learning." In other words, we should be doing with four-year-olds precisely what we should be doing with *all* students: We should base instruction, not on the chronological age of the student, but on an assessment of each students' stage of development. Our students should not be judged by their birth certificates. And pedagogy should not bow to chronology.

Age does not define learning needs. That is the point that psychologists Sandra Scarr and Richard A. Weinberg tried to drive home when they argued that nutrition is the appropriate model or metaphor for the learning process: "It is important to feed children appropriately, not only in infancy and the preschool years, but also in later school and adolescent years to ensure that they reach their full potential."

EDUCATIONAL NEEDS OF FOUR-YEAR-OLDS

What educational nutrients are essential for four-year-olds? Play is foremost among them. Structured play—play that enlivens the imagination and exercises the intellect—is the indispensable prerequiste for the development of the critical thinking skills fundamental to academic achievement. That fact by itself suggests the content of a "curriculum" for four-year-olds. Such a curriculum would not introduce them to grammatical structure or try to make them computer literate. It would instead begin to help them develop the skills necessary for successful learning. The aim of the curriculum would be to ease the child's transition into school.

This continuity is essential. If we want to enhance the school experience for kindergartners and first-grade students, noted Bettye M. Caldwell of the University of Arkansas, "the transition between early childhood and elementary education programs should be as normal and routine as continuity between 2nd and 3rd grades."

Today, the lack of collegial exchange between early childhood education instructors and elementary teachers makes that continuity impossible. Seldom is there even a sharing of records between early childhood and elementary programs. Without this continuity, Caldwell pointed out, "the new teachers (at the elementary level) receive no benefits from the insights gained by their predecessors (at the early childhood level), and the former teachers have no opportunity to confirm or disconfirm their prediction about future educational progress of individual children." Having four-year-olds in public schools could go a long way to helping remedy this situation. The beneficiaries would be the children.

In 1984, a special task force of National Education Association (NEA) members spelled out the NEA vision of a new school environment in *An Open Letter to America on Schools, Students, and Tomorrow*. Schools, the *Open Letter* maintained, must be places that (a) discard arbitrary, age-based determinations of appropriate instruction; (b) encourage students to be active participants in learning; (c) involve parents in their children's education; (d) coordinate community resources to meet the health and social services needs of their students; and (e) promote the ideal of lifelong learning.

These are the same elements that early childhood education experts often cite as basic to successful preschool programs. These elements, in a very real sense, provide a common agenda for public school teachers and early childhood professionals, and that common agenda would ensure the development of a preschool program uniquely suited to the developmental needs of four-year-olds.

There are, of course, many battles that will need to be fought before all parents can have the option of sending their four-year-olds to early childhood programs in public schools. Financing the option of schooling for four-year-olds would be costly, but not financing it could prove more costly. The case can be made, based on studies conducted by the High/Scope Educational Research Foundation and other researchers, that budget dollars placed in quality preschool programs help children succeed in later life and actually save society money by reducing social expenditures for prisons, welfare, and unemployment.

Battles will also have to be waged over who staffs school-based early childhood programs. Early childhood professionals and teachers will have to unite and insist that these programs be staffed by professionals who are fully trained and prepared to cope with the special needs of preschool youngsters.

These battles, I believe, are well worth the effort they will take to win. Social realities have created a demand for school-based early childhood care. Let us meet that demand and treat it as an opportunity to start transforming our schools into the true lifelong centers of learning they ought to be. Chronology is not destiny. The calendar need not be a tyrant—not in our lives and not in our children's lives.

DISCUSSION QUESTIONS

1. Will public schooling for four-year-old children make the educational experience for the child better or worse?

2. Have the issues and developmental needs of younger children been seriously considered in the planning of early education programs?

3. What cautions should be observed when new programs are planned and implemented?

4. Is there sufficient professional consensus and research data to design an excellent learning experience for all younger children in the schools?

23. QUALITY FOUR-YEAR-OLD PROGRAMS IN PUBLIC SCHOOLS

Position Statement of the Southern Association on Children Under Six

The number of four-year-olds enrolled in early childhood development programs has almost doubled in the last ten years (Schweinhart, 1985). Although government funding for Head Start provides for fewer than 25 percent of the 1.5 million eligible children, the public schools of fourteen states now provide some degree of funding for programs for four-year-olds. Such action is the result of the recognition of the identified benefits of early education for all segments of the population.

Pressure for additional program availability continues to grow. The demand is based on:

• Increased awareness on the part of parents and policymakers of the long-term value of early education.

• Parents' needs for child care services (more than 50 percent of mothers of preschool aged children in work force).

• The desire of non-employed mothers for their children to have access to preschool programs (32 percent enrollment increase).

Carefully designed programs are excellent resources for fostering the development of four-year-old children. However, as public school policymakers recognize the need and rapidly increase the provision of pre-kindergarten education, **priority** must be given to the establishment of programs for four-year-olds which:

• Are based on the knowledge of and response to child development research.

• Employ only those who are professionally trained to guide the growth and development of young children.

• Focus on the specific needs and characteristics of four-year-olds and their families.

It is **imperative** that public school early childhood programs be appropriately and uniquely designed for the young children they will serve. The characteristics and appropriate experiences for such programs are stated as follows:

Given the developmental characteristics of the four-year-old and the needed learning opportunities, the Board of Directors of the Southern Association on Children Under Six proposes the following standards:

ADOPT QUALITY STANDARDS

• The administrator or building principal should have a minimum of nine semester hours of early education courses with a focus on developmental characteristics of young children and appropriate programming.

• The teacher must hold a valid early childhood certificate; training must have included work with pre-kindergarten children; the training should meet the criteria of the NAEYC guidelines adopted as NCATE Standards for programs in four-year institutions.

• The child must be age four by the same date identifying eligibility for entrance in kindergarten.

• The adult-child ratio should be 1-7, not to exceed 1-10; enrollment that exceeds ten requires the assignment of an additional responsible adult with training in early childhood education/child development.

• The session for the child should not be less than one-half day.

• The daily schedule must be flexible, include a balance of free-choice and teacher-initiated large and small group activities, and reflect the developmental needs of the whole child.

• The early childhood curriculum must be designed specifically for four-year-olds and must be appropriate for their developmental level and interests.

• The learning environment must be arranged in interest centers that provide for individual and group learning experiences.

• Materials, equipment, and supplies appropriate for a developmental curriculum must be available in sufficient quantities.

See pages 330–31 for acknowledgment and references.

- The classroom must be equipped with movable furniture of correct size, have a water supply available and restroom facilities to accommodate four-year-old children.
- The outside play area must be accessible for flexible use; be properly equipped for climbing, riding and gross motor activities; and designed for the safety of the child including fencing.
- Minimum space requirements should be based on fifty square feet per child inside and one hundred square feet per child outside.
- The program must include a parent component: education, classroom visitation, and regular conferences to support the child's educational experience.
- A process must be established to provide communication among the early childhood programs in the school; four-year-olds, kindergarten and primary grades.
- Appropriate developmental evaluation and observations must be conducted periodically to provide information for effective planning for meeting the individual needs of children.

QUALITY PROGRAMS SHOULD AVOID:

- The reassignment of upper elementary teachers who have no specialized training in early childhood education.
- The elimination of play and the opportunity for child selected activities.
- The use of watered down first grade curriculum that includes formal readiness activities, workbooks, and ditto sheets.
- The placement of children in desks or rows of chairs that inhibit an active learning environment.
- The accommodation of young children in facilities such as classroom, playground, cafeteria, and bathrooms that are designed for older children.

- The use of standardized skill tests rather than observations and informal evaluations to assess the needs of the young child.

THE ROLE FOR PUBLIC SCHOOLS IN ADVANCING APPROPRIATE EXPERIENCES FOR FOUR-YEAR-OLDS

The public school system has certain characteristics that can be of great advantage in the provision of needed high quality programs for fours. Public school programs can complement existing programs in the private sector as well as those funded for targeted populations. Parents need viable options compatible with the needs of the family group; all programs should insure effective choices.

Four-year-old programs in public schools can offer an extended support system to the child, the parent and other school age children in the family. They can provide an earlier opportunity to initiate a cooperative and beneficial relationship with the home. Many schools can accommodate a group of young children with existing space; for some, additional resources can be made available. Programs coordinated by state departments of education can set high standards through established regulations, implementation guidelines, curriculum directions, and continual opportunities for the development of staff.

Excellence in the education of four-year-old children in the public school systems of America is an available opportunity and an obtainable goal; however, the priorities must focus on actual knowledge of the real needs of the young child as stated in this position statement. The achievements of such programs can be measured in the growth and development of more positive, cooperative, productive and successful human beings.

DISCUSSION QUESTIONS

1. What essential qualities should guide the programs for four-year-olds in the schools?
2. Are the standards proposed by SACUS necessary and sufficient to assure high quality?
3. What is the research base for these standards?

24. HERE COME THE FOUR-YEAR-OLDS!

by Diane Dismuke

At South Mountain Middle School in Allentown, Pennsylvania, a four-year-old practices making the 'K' sound. In a classroom building adjacent to the Haddon Avenue Elementary School in Los Angeles, California, two- and three-year-olds listen intently as their teacher explains personal hygiene.

At Glebe Elementary School in Arlington, Virginia, three-, four-, and five-year-olds are involved in "practical life" Montessori activities.

Scenes like these are not yet common-place, but neither are they rare, as more and more school districts respond to changing public needs by creating new early childhood education programs—and expanding those already in place.

Some 3,000 of the nation's 15,000 school districts now reportedly sponsor early childhood programs. The goals of these programs vary. Some aim only to provide quality child care. Others deal with youngsters' learning problems early on. Still others focus on teaching academic readiness.

The teachers involved are almost all certificated, with degrees in early childhood education, special education, and elementary education.

NEA has long supported early childhood education that gives children effective preparation for kindergarten—as long as trained, certified teachers and aides lead the youngsters. *Early Childhood Education and Kindergarten*, an NEA resolution adopted by vote of the Representative Assembly in 1975 and last revised in 198[8], urges federal legislation to help promote and fund these efforts.

Currently, the NEA Executive Committee is preparing a report for the 1988 Representative Assembly on the feasibility of establishing neighborhood day care as an adjunct to public education.

Support for early childhood programs run by the public schools is growing on all fronts. A recent study sponsored by the Committee for Economic Development—a nonprofit organization whose trustees are mostly business executives—called for more federal dollars for "proven programs" such as Head Start and remedial reading and math programs. The study clearly demonstrated the value of these programs for disadvantaged youngsters.

In Pomona, California, 600 infants to 13-year-olds are enrolled in eight children's centers run by the unified school district. They attend approved hours between 6 a.m. and 6 p.m. each week day because their parents work or are training for jobs, or because social workers have identified these kids as being at risk for physical abuse if they stay home.

Association member Bill Ewing, Pomona's administrator of child development programs, notes that the centers are open to any child, but because fees are on a sliding scale, the centers are most advantageous to lower-income families.

Pomona's program is more than a babysitting service. With youngsters through age 4, the program seeks to advance development through "learning experiences." The curriculum—developed by High/Scope, a nonprofit educational research foundation headquartered in Ypsilanti, Michigan—allows children to choose their own daily activities within predetermined guidelines.

The Pomona program is so popular that it has a waiting list of almost 1,000. The ratio of children to adults is set by state law at 4 to 1 for infants and 8 to 1 for children up to age 4. Those adults must include one certified teacher for every 24 youngsters beyond infancy.

All but two of the Pomona centers are located on elementary school grounds. One serves infants and toddlers whose parents are still public school students themselves and works with the young parents to teach them proper child care. Another accepts mildly ill children who have a doctor's approval—a real boon for working parents.

Two other centers—one open seven days a week from 6:30 a.m. to 5 p.m., the other open Monday through Friday from 6:30 a.m to midnight—provide a safe place for parents to leave their children when they seriously need to get away for a few hours. Children in all the centers are checked regularly by school nurse practitioners.

Pomona's children's center program started in 1969, but it can trace its roots back to 1943 when Congress passed the Lanham Act, establishing federally funded child care for mothers working in defense industries. When California implemented

See page 331 for acknowledgment.

the Lanham Act, it placed the administration of a statewide child care program under the state department of education.

Ths Los Angeles unified school district sponsors a program similar to Pomona's, in operation since the 1940s.

Martha Bayer is chair of the Children's Center Committee of United Teachers–Los Angeles. Bayer, who teaches at the Haddon Avenue Center, attended the program herself as a child.

"I'm here because I believe in its benefits," she says.

Los Angeles' 90 children's centers each serve an average of 130 youngsters aged 2 to 12, from 6 a.m. to 6 p.m. every weekday. School-age children attend before and after regular classes.

"Each center has a waiting list of about 200," says Bayer. "We give preference to children who are non-English-proficient, handicapped, or recommended by protective services."

Los Angeles has its own curriculum—Foundations for Learning—that develops each child's language skills and mathematical concepts through interdisciplinary techniques like puzzles, manipulatives, and tape recordings. The youngsters are checked periodically by a nurse, a dentist, and an audiometrist.

Since the Pomona and Los Angeles programs exist primarily to provide child care, can they be considered education? David Elkind, president of the National Association for the Education of Young Children and a Tufts University professor, asserts that *all* levels of education contain some degree of child care.

"The issue is not education vs. child care but rather the proportion of the two components provided at any particular level of schooling," Elkind notes. Teachers of young children help them "acquire the fundamental concepts of space, time, number, causality, relations, and nature-concepts that form the essential data base for all later learning." And this acquisition goes hand-in-hand with learning pre-academic language and social skills, such as paying attention and taking turns, that are presupposed by formal education.

Some 23 states now have legislation pending to provide school for four-year-olds, adds Elkind—a sure sign of the growing recognition that early childhood education should become a legitimate part of public education.

In Allentown, Pennsylvania, mildly handicapped three- to five-year-olds attend Project HAPPY (an acronym for Helping Achieve Potential of Preschool Youngsters) classes for two-and-a half hours each day, four days a week. The children have been identified as likely candidates for future special education services. Most of them come from lower socioeconomic backgrounds or from families with cultural or linguistic differences.

Like most early childhood efforts, five-year-old Project HAPPY works hard to involve parents—and to make them proud of their children's classroom experiences.

"Many of the parents feel insecure—even embarrassed—by what they perceive as their own or their children's inadequacies," explains Association member Sue McNeil, a Project HAPPY teacher since 1984 and one of the program's developers. "When they feel motivated by their children's successes, we know we're making real progress."

Charlene Bembridge, whose three-year-old son Kenyatta Carter entered the program in September, notes the progress he's made in just a few months.

"Kenyatta is very active," Bembridge explains, "but the combination of structured days and individual attention he receives from Project HAPPY has changed his attitude. He now tries very hard to behave better."

Most of McNeil's students lack proper motor coordination or language proficiency. On a typical day, some children cut out sketches (being careful to follow the heavy lines drawn to guide them), others practice following directions in sequence, and still others learn social behaviors like taking turns and responding in sentences to a question.

McNeil keeps track of her students when they go on to elementary school. "When they're successful there, it means Project HAPPY is successful," she explains.

The program's benefits aren't limited to participants and their families. Child development students at the middle school that houses Project HAPPY work with the younger students to gain firsthand knowledge of what makes them thrive and learn.

In Arlington, Virginia, a 16-year-old public Montessori program enrolls some 320 three- to five-year-olds, giving preference to non-English-speaking, minority, and low-income youngsters. The 16 three-hour daily classes are offered in four different elementary schools. Each class averages 20 students. Parents of three- and four-year-olds pay a sliding tuition fee, while five-year-olds attend the program instead of traditional kindergarten. Children stay with a single teacher until they enter first grade.

"Because of this stability, we have greater flexibility in meeting a child's individual needs," explains Daena Kluegel, a Montessori teacher at

Arlington's Glebe Elementary School. "We can really get to know the needs of each child—and let new children learn from those already in the program."

The Montessori teaching method, named for the Italian physician who developed it early in this century, emphasizes individual learning. Each child concentrates on a particular skill when he or she is most ready. The teacher acts mainly as a facilitator, giving the children hands-on materials—like sandpaper letters and metal geometric shapes—to help them learn.

Arlington mother Katherine Carey credits the program with enhancing the lives of her four children—some learning disabled and others gifted.

"The method reinforced their strengths at an early age," she explains. "It recognizes a child as an individual and teaches socialization skills at the same time."

Early childhood education programs are obviously not only here to stay, but to grow and multiply.

As they spread, NEA President Mary Hatwood Futrell cautions, educators must be careful not to overlook quality.

"Early childhood professionals and teachers will have to unite and insist that these programs be staffed by professionals fully trained and prepared to cope with the special needs of the very young," Futrell noted in a recent article for *American Psychologist*, a journal of the American Psychological Association. Futrell is an enthusiastic supporter of early childhood enrichment programs.

"We should be doing with four-year-olds precisely what we should be doing with *all* students," she advises. "We should base instruction not on the chronological age of the student, but on an assessment of each student's stage of development. Our students should not be judged by their birth certificates.

"Chronology is not destiny," Futrell concludes. "The calendar need not be a tyrant. Not in our lives. Not in our children's lives."

DISCUSSION QUESTIONS

1. How have different locations met the need for providing public school programs for children younger than five?

2. What are the NBCDI guidelines for public school early education programs?

3. Will the public schools eventually provide universal programs for children younger than four years of age?

25. PREKINDERGARTEN PROGRAMS FOR FOUR-YEAR-OLDS: STATE INVOLVEMENT IN PRESCHOOL EDUCATION

by Carolyn Morado

In 15 states across the country, state departments of education, community service and community education agencies operate prekindergarten programs, and several states are moving in this direction. The programs are relatively new and signal the states' growing interest and commitment to early education. Most of the state-sponsored programs are targeted for 4-year-old children and the majority are operated by state departments of education.

While interest in state-sponsored preschool education is growing, the number of children involved remains relatively small. No state offers preschool for all its 4-year-olds. The diversity in programs is considerable. Current state practice either allows interested school districts to offer programs for 4-year-olds or sets criteria for the involvement of 4-year-olds in state-sponsored programs. In some states, prekindergarten programs are more similar to the state's kindergartens; in other states, programs more closely resemble privately sponsored programs.

Informed debate on the issue of state-sponsored prekindergarten programs must take into account the wide variation in preschool programs, definitions of children eligible to participate, funding, and program standards. This [chapter] surveys some of the practices regarding these issues in state-sponsored prekindergarten programs for 4-year-olds.

LEGISLATIVE AUTHORITY

State-sponsored prekindergarten programs are either provided for in the permissive language of a state's school code or provided by special legislative provision. In New Jersey and Pennsylvania, permissive language in each state's general school code allows school districts to provide prekindergarten programs for 4-year-olds as well as kindergarten programs for 5-year-olds.

The majority of state-sponsored prekindergarten programs, however, come from special legislation that establishes definitions and standards for the programs and provides limited funding. States that sponsored prekindergarten programs through special legislation during the 1985–86 school year included New York, Maryland, Louisiana, South Carolina, Florida, Oklahoma, California, Ohio, Texas, Illinois, Michigan, and Massachusetts. Washington has passed special legislation for prekindergarten programs that are scheduled to begin this fall. Texas is the only state requiring school districts to provide compensatory prekindergarten programs.

FUNDING

Programs are funded through regular state aid to school districts or through budget appropriations for prekindergarten programs. New Jersey and Pennsylvania fund prekindergarten programs through general education funds, and payments to districts are the same for both kindergarten and prekindergarten programs. Total funding of prekindergarten programs is difficult to calculate, however, as prekindergarten children are included with all other district students under the state aid formula, and state funding of prekindergarten does not appear as a separate budget item at either the district or state level.

In contrast, other states limit their funding through budget appropriations for programs. In these states, state funding is readily identified, and per pupil expenditures for prekindergarten programs can be calculated when the number of children to be served is specified. Typically, state support is less than $1,000 annually per child for part-day programs but may be as much as $2,700 per child.

States may require that participating school districts contribute to program funding. For example, New York requires local school districts to contribute 11 percent of the total budget in cash. Ohio requires participating school districts to use local funding to provide staff. Michigan limits state funding to 70 percent of the total program operating costs.

See page 331 for acknowledgment.

CHARACTERISTICS OF STATE-SPONSORED PROGRAMS

Most kindergarten programs are part-day programs (3 or fewer hours per day), although several states indicate a preference for full-day programs or have a long-range goal to move toward full-day programs for 4-year-olds.

Programs that operate on the basis of the general school code provisions are required to meet kindergarten standards for teacher certification and student attendance, but no special regulations apply. These programs may differ markedly from privately sponsored programs for 4-year-olds.

Special regulations for prekindergarten programs have been developed by all states that fund programs through special legislative initiatives, and regulations typically address staff qualifications, maximum class size, and staff/child ratios. Regulations may allow for fewer than 180 school days of attendance, and space and facility requirements may be outlined. Regulations typically specify criteria that are similar or identical to requirements that apply to the state's privately sponsored child care centers, preschools, and nursery schools.

Class Size

A maximum class size of 20 children is typically specified by states. Class size specifications range, however, from a low of 15 children per class to a high of 25 children.

Staff/Child Ratio

The staff/child ratio in several states is 1:10. This pattern is typical when class size is specified at 20 and both a teacher and teacher aide are assigned to each class. States which require only that a teacher be assigned to prekindergarten classes may operate programs with staff/child ratios of 1:20 or higher.

Comprehensive Services

Four states—California, New York, Maine, and Washington—require programs to provide comprehensive services similar to those provided by Head Start for prekindergarten program participants. (Head Start provides health services, opportunities for parent involvement, and social services to families as well as an education program.)

Teacher Qualifications

Some type of early childhood certification is required for teachers in the majority of the programs. While states may prefer or recommend early childhood certification for kindergarten teachers, few require such specialized training. Most prekindergarten programs, however, require specialized training beyond what is typically required for kindergarten in the states.

SELECTING CHILDREN FOR STATE-SPONSORED PROGRAMS

Most state-sponsored prekindergarten programs enroll 4-year-olds, although several states offer programs to both 3- and 4-year-olds. In several states, age is the only criterion for eligibility. States that specify additional eligibility criteria typically specify criteria intended to target children who may be at risk for school failure.

New Jersey, Pennsylvania, Oklahoma, and Ohio base eligibility solely on age. But access to programs can vary greatly, depending on selective participation of school districts, efforts to ensure geographical balance across the state, and even the location of programs within participating school districts. Maryland and Massachusetts base student eligibility on age, but each state restricts, wholly or in part, the areas or school districts in which programs may be offered.

Louisiana, South Carolina, California, New York, Maine, Florida, Texas, and Illinois target their prekindergarten programs for children designated to be vulnerable or at risk for school failure; one half of Michigan's programs are similarly targeted. States use two approaches to identify vulnerable children: Environmental or other risk conditions are used to identify potential candidates for school failure, or states screen children and select those children with apparent deficiencies.

States select vulnerable or at-risk children by using demographic and family characteristics that tend to be associated with school failure. Maryland targets its programs for low-achieving school districts by using third grade achievement data to determine eligible school districts; all 4-year-olds in participating districts are eligible without further screening. Massachusetts has specified that three quarters of its programs must be located in low-income residential areas. New York, California, Maine, Texas, and Washington base program eligibility on family income but use varying definitions of low income ranging from the federal Head Start standard of 100 percent of poverty level to family income below a specified percentage of the state median income. Children with limited English proficiency are eligible for programs in Texas and Florida.

South Carolina, Louisiana, and Illinois define their programs as compensatory programs. All children who participate in programs in these states must be individually assessed to establish that readiness deficiencies exist.

COORDINATING STATE-SPONSORED PROGRAMS WITH OTHER EARLY CHILDHOOD PROGRAMS

There appears to be growing sensitivity to the effects state-sponsored prekindergarten programs may have on programs that already exist under federal or private sponsorship. South Carolina has organized an Interagency Coordinating Council, and some states are interested in developing interagency collaboration or possibilities for agencies outside the public school system to be involved with prekindergarten programs. South Carolina, Illinois, and Michigan allow school districts to contract with agencies outside the public schools to provide prekindergarten programs. Ohio legislation provides for grants to county school boards to establish information and referral services to coordinate services for families.

The role of state education agencies in preschool education is evolving, and there is by no means a single approach to programming for 4-year-olds in the public schools. State programs reflect a diversity of educational concerns such as limited availability of federal funds for early childhood programs despite increased public interest and support, and a growing concern for children who appear to be at risk for school failure as they enter school. Public school involvement in early childhood education may offer unique opportunities for the growth of services to young children, or public school involvement may simply duplicate or replace existing community and other programs. As the role of state education agencies evolves, important considerations related to programming for all young children should continue to hold our attention and shape state involvement in education: appropriate standards, equity and equal access, meeting community needs, and continuity and coordination of services for young children.

DISCUSSION QUESTIONS

1. How are the states responding to prekindergartens in the public schools?

2. Are public preschool programs available to all children?

3. What are the common qualities of programs for four-year-olds in the states?

4. Will programs for prekindergarten children be planned for select groups of children with special needs or those who are at risk for educational problems?

5. How will states coordinate public, private, and parochial preschool programs?

26. SAFEGUARDS: GUIDELINES FOR ESTABLISHING PROGRAMS FOR FOUR-YEAR-OLDS IN THE PUBLIC SCHOOLS

by The National Black Child Development Institute

As public schools become a major provider of early childhood education and care, we can expect large numbers of Black children to use these programs for at least three reasons. First, most public schools that have begun early education programs already have large enrollments of Black children because the focus has been on "at risk" children, a large majority of whom are Black. Second, 67 percent of all Black mothers work in the labor pool; as this percentage increases, the need for child care becomes greater. Third, many Black parents want their children to have an educational advantage which they feel will result from the children's participation in early education programs. For economic reasons, their choices will be public school programs where services tend to be free or on a sliding scale.

The National Black Child Development Institute (NBCDI) has a record of support for the public schools and their teachers. As advocates for Black children, such support is mandatory—because it is here that the vast majority of Black students will be found long into the 21st Century. Still, as the public school systems add to their responsibilities the needs of yet another constituent—the very young, it is incumbent upon us to address some concerns to which this trend has given rise. These concerns emerge from past public policy in general and from trends in education which have drastically affected the lives of countless Black children. In many of our nation's cities, Blacks have inherited the failures of public policy: decrepit housing, inadequate public services, and empty municipal coffers.

In urban public schools across this nation, Blacks stand to inherit institutions and programs taxed beyond their limits. Rural and city schools alike are already struggling under the weight of their charge: to do more with less money.

We are not without sympathy for problems faced by many of our nation's public schools: underfinancing, shortages of new teachers, and the public's perception of the schools as the panacea for all unresolved social problems ranging from juvenile delinquency to teenage pregnancy. We recognize and commend individuals in various sections of the country who struggle daily for high quality programs for Black children, but they must be joined by many others to create the national imperative required to change a still inadequate educational achievement record.

For as we look at the progress of the public school system relative to Black children, the statistics are alarming. Today, 40 percent of minority youth are functionally illiterate. Black children are twice as likely to be suspended from school or to suffer corporal punishment. Eighty percent of those suspended from public schools are Black boys. Dr. Asa Hilliard, Professor of Urban Education at Georgia State University and former NBCDI Board Member, notes, "There are more Black children placed in Educable Mentally Retarded [EMR] programs than Whites nationwide." Black children make up 40 percent of EMR students, although they are only slightly more than 10 percent of the population.

The problems faced by the public education systems must be scrutinized from many different viewpoints if viable solutions are to be found. School systems need help, and advocates for children must assist by providing necessary support. The ten safeguards detailed herein offer clear and direct suggestions for ways of ensuring that early education programs in the public schools create a learning environment for Black children which is productive, effective and long lasting in positive outcomes.

THE TEN SAFEGUARDS

The First Safeguard. *Public school-based programs for Black, preschool-age children should incorporate an effective parent education program.*

The Second Safeguard. *Public school-based early childhood programs should involve parents in the decisions about the curriculum and policy.*

The Third Safeguard. *The staff of early childhood education programs should include teachers who come from the community served by the*

See page 331 for acknowledgment and references.

program and who are racially and ethnically representative of the children served.

The Fourth Safeguard. *Teachers in public school-based programs should be required to have specific training in preschool education and/or ongoing, inservice training provided by qualified staff.*

The Fifth Safeguard. *Curriculum for preschool-age children in the public schools should be culturally sensitive and appropriate to the child's age and level of development.*

The Sixth Safeguard. *Public schools which house programs for very young children should meet the same health and safety standards which apply to independent preschools and center-based child care programs.*

The Seventh Safeguard. *Public school-based ear-ly childhood programs should participate in federal and state programs which guarantee adequate nutrition to children.*

The Eighth Safeguard. *Administrators of public school-based programs for preschoolers should ensure that children entering the programs have access to appropriate health care.*

The Ninth Safeguard. *In assessing children of preschool age, the administrators of public school-based early childhood programs should not limit their assessment to, or base their program planning solely on, standardized tests.*

The Tenth Safeguard. *Public school-based early childhood programs should be subject to a regular, external review by community members and early childhood development experts.*

DISCUSSION QUESTIONS

1. What are some special considerations to assure high quality in four-year-old programs for minority group children?
2. Should minority group children have early learning experiences that differ in quality and/or quantity from programs for children of the majority?
3. Are there universal program qualities or safeguards that assure an excellent experience for all children?

27. PUBLIC SCHOOL FOR FOUR-YEAR-OLDS

by James L. Hymes, Jr.

It's about time. America has had private schools for 4-year-olds since 1922! Several states through the years—Wisconsin, Pennsylvania, Alaska, Oklahoma—have supported some public schools for 4s. And "special" 4s have benefited from massive public programs of schooling as far back as the Emergency Nursery Schools of the depression years, and in Head Start, New York State's Experimental Prekindergartens, and California's Preschool Program. America has loads of know-how about 4-year-olds and the kind of schooling that fits them. (Many other countries in the western world do too.)

The lack in the past: Almost all 4s who went to school really were "special" children. Some were "special" because their families had money and were caring and conscientious; those parents could afford to reach out for opportunities for their children. Other 4s were "special" because their families were poor. It is time now for public schools [to] open to *all* 4s, not to "special" children—open to 4s simply because they are 4, open to all whose parents want them to attend.

It's about time, but it is a bad time. Unfortunately the climate couldn't be worse for starting up a new program for young children.

The recent years have made many Americans feel that taxes are to be avoided like the plague. Spending for the private good has been touted as fine; spending for the public good (except for the military) has been considered bad. In such a mood there is the danger that America might want bargain-basement 4-year-old classes, and might be unwilling to pay what it costs to get good ones.

See page 331 for acknowledgment.

Recent years have also made many Americans uptight about education. Report after report has warned that "history will not be kind to idlers." With such sounds all around many adults have become scared. They end up pushing their children and grasping anxiously for successes in tangible, measurable areas. There is grave danger of a shortage of sympathy for the humanistic, sensitive, patient, tolerant approaches that 4s need.

There is also the danger that public schools for 4s may suddenly become the *in* thing. America has a tendency to let ideas lie dormant for years and then suddenly embrace them. New programs spurt ahead, far outdistancing the resources to make them good. This has been Head Start's fate. It was big at birth, but from the start never had adequate money for enough well-trained staff. The result: Head Start is rarely top-flight. This has been the story of our kindergartens. They mushroomed in the 1970s and 80s, expanding far faster than solid kindergarten teacher training. The result: Too many kindergartens are disaster areas where workbooks have become the teachers.

But no time is perfect. We *can* have good public schools for 4s. We are not obligated to mess up the idea. The trick is to learn from our past.

The big lesson is to recognize that trained teachers—specialists in working with young children—are the key. We should be wary of setting up more classes for 4s than we can staff with adequately paid, able specialists. In every state there are now some well-trained teachers of young children, but we must expand their number.

This is the time, right now, for 4-year teacher education institutions to develop major fields of study focusing specifically on the young child. My preference: Majors that concentrate on the under 6 years. Six years of life is a big span, and the first 6 are difficult, crucial years, a worthy field of study. But I would gladly settle for majors covering the traditional early childhood period from birth through year 8 (although learning both the rigidities of the primary school and the informality of under 6 groups is a formidable task). What none of us should settle for is so-called training or orientation that is simply an added course or two.

A second lesson is to recognize that trained teachers are wasted unless they have supports that free them to use their skills.

Teachers need right class size. With 4-year-olds, 16 ought to be tops.

Teachers of 4s need salaries equal to those of *other* public school teachers.

With 4s, teachers need an aide, paid or volunteer.

Teachers need a time schedule that makes it possible for them to talk often with parents. Without common understandings between home and school, good teaching goes down the drain.

Teachers need principals and supervisors who will respect their training and skill as specialists.

DISCUSSION QUESTIONS

1. What are the basic reasons for adding four-year-old children to the public schools?

2. What are the potential problems of universal public school programs for younger children?

3. How can program designers establish standards for staffing, scheduling, program operation, and parent involvement?

28. FULL-DAY OR HALF-DAY KINDERGARTEN?

by Dianne Rothenberg

According to educator Barry Herman (1984) and others, the majority of 5-year-olds in the United States today already are more accustomed to being away from home much of the day, more aware of the world around them, and more likely to spend a large part of the day with peers than were children of previous generations. These factors, plus the demonstrated ability of children to cope with a longer day away from home, have created a demand in many communities for full-day kindergarten programs.

This [chapter] examines how changing family patterns have affected the full-day/half-day kindergarten issue, discussing why schools are currently considering alternative scheduling and describing the advantages and disadvantages of each type of program.

CHANGES IN FAMILY PATTERNS

Among the changes occurring in American society that make full-day kindergarten attractive to families are

An increase in the number of working parents. As reported by the National Center for Education Statistics (Grant and Snyder 1983), the number of mothers of children under 6 who work outside the home increased 34 percent from 1970 to 1980. The National Commission on Working Women (1985) reports that, in 1984, 48 percent of children under 6 had mothers in the labor force.

An increase in the number of children who have had preschool or day care experience. Since the mid-1970s, the majority of children have had some kind of preschool experience, either in Head Start, day care, private preschools, or early childhood programs in the public schools. These early group experiences have provided children's first encounters with daily organized instructional and social activities before kindergarten (Herman 1984).

An increase in the influence of television and family mobility on children. These two factors have produced 5-year-olds who are more knowledgeable about their world and who are apparently more ready for a full-day school experience than the children of previous generations.

See pages 331–32 for acknowledgment and references.

Renewed interest in academic preparation for later school success. Even in families without both parents working outside the home, there is great interest in the contribution of early childhood programs (including full-day kindergarten) to later school success.

SCHOOLS AND FULL-DAY KINDERGARTEN

School systems have become interested in alternative scheduling for kindergarten partly because of the reasons listed above and partly for reasons related to finances and school space availability. Some of these reasons concern

State school funding formulas. Some states provide more state aid for all-day students, although seldom enough to completely pay the extra costs of full-day kindergarten programs. Other states allow only half-day aid; in these states, funding formulas would have to change in order for schools to benefit financially from all-day kindergarten attendance.

Busing and other transportation costs. Eliminating the need for noon bus trips and crossing guards saves the school system money.

Availability of classroom space and teachers. As school enrollment declines, some districts find that they have extra classroom space and qualified teachers available to offer full-day kindergarten.

In addition, school districts are interested in responding to parents' requests for full-day kindergarten. In New York City, for example, parents who were offered the option of full-day kindergarten responded overwhelmingly in favor of the plan ("Woes Plague New York's All-Day Kindergartens" 1983).

ADVANTAGES OF FULL-DAY PROGRAMS

Herman (1984) describes in detail the advantages of full-day kindergarten. He and others believe full-day programs provide a relaxed, unhurried school day with more time for a variety of experiences, greater opportunity for screening and assessment to detect and deal with potential learning problems, and more occasions for good quality interaction between adults and students.

While the long-term effects of full-day kindergarten are yet to be determined, Thomas Stinard's (1982) review of 10 research studies comparing half-day and full-day kindergarten indicates that students taking part in full-day programs demonstrate strong academic advantages as much as a year after the kindergarten experience. Stinard found that full-day students performed at least as well as half-day students in every study (and better in many studies) with no significant adverse effects.

A recent longitudinal study of full-day kindergarten in the Evansville-Vanderburgh, Ohio, School District indicates that fourth graders maintained the academic advantage gained during full-day kindergarten (Humphrey 1983).

Despite often-expressed fears that full-day kindergartners would experience fatigue and stress, school districts that have taken care to plan a developmentally appropriate, nonacademic curriculum with carefully paced activities have reported few problems (Evans and Marken 1983; Stinard 1982).

DISADVANTAGES OF FULL-DAY PROGRAMS

Critics of full-day kindergarten point out that such programs are expensive because they require additional teaching staff and aides to maintain an acceptable child-adult ratio. These costs may or may not be offset by transportation savings and, in some cases, additional state aid.

Other requirements of full-day kindergarten, including more classroom space, may be difficult to satisfy in districts where kindergarten or primary grade enrollment is increasing and/or where school buildings have been sold.

In addition to citing added expense and space requirements as problems, those in disagreement claim that full-day programs may become too academic, concentrating on basic skills before children are ready for them. In addition, they are concerned that half of the day's programming in an all-day kindergarten setting may become merely child care.

ADVANTAGES OF HALF-DAY PROGRAMS

Many educators still prefer half-day, everyday kindergarten. They argue that a half-day program can provide high quality educational and social experience for young children while orienting them adequately to school.

Specifically, half-day programs are viewed as providing continuity and systematic experience with less probability of stress than full-day programs. Proponents of the half-day approach believe that, given the 5-year-old's attention span, level of interest, and home ties, a half day offers ample time in school and allows more time for the young child to play and interact with adults and other children in less-structured home or child care settings (Finkelstein 1983).

DISADVANTAGES OF HALF-DAY PROGRAMS

Disadvantages of half-day programs include midday disruption for children who move from one program to another and, if busing is not provided by the school, difficulty for parents in making transportation arrangements. Even if busing is provided and the child spends the other half day at home, schools may find providing the extra trip expensive. In addition, the half-day kindergartner may have little opportunity to benefit from activities such as assemblies or field trips.

CONCLUSION

While both full-day and half-day programs have advantages and disadvantages, it is worth noting that length of the school day is only one dimension of the kindergarten experience. Other important issues include the nature of the kindergarten curriculum and the quality of teaching. In general, research suggests that, as long as the curriculum is developmentally appropriate and intellectually stimulating, either type of scheduling can provide an adequate introduction to school.

DISCUSSION QUESTIONS

1. Is half a day half as good as a full day of kindergarten?
2. Why do some schools offer full-day programs and some half-day programs?
3. Should financing or educational impact influence the decision about kindergarten scheduling?
4. Can one teacher work effectively with two groups of children during the same day?
5. What is the best schedule for the nation's kindergartens?

29. KINDERGARTEN IN AMERICA: FIVE MAJOR TRENDS

by Sandra Longfellow Robinson

On three occasions in the past 12 years, I have asked public school officials to describe kindergarten opportunities in their states. A comparison of the data from these three surveys—collected in 1974, 1981, and 1986—reveals five major trends in the education of 5-year-olds.*

First, more children are being offered the opportunity to attend public kindergarten. In 1974 only 23 states offered programs to more than 90 percent of the eligible population. By 1981, 41 states met this criterion, and in 1986, 46 states—twice as many as in 1974—provided kindergarten for nearly all children. Only Mississippi, New Hampshire, Oregon, and Vermont reported that they provide free public kindergarten for less than 90 percent of the eligible population.

However, recent changes indicate that even in some of these states more and more children will be given access to kindergarten. A recent legislative package in Mississippi mandates programs for all districts by the 1986-87 school year. In Oregon, state officials estimate that the state provides kindergarten service for 62 percent of eligible children and that private providers serve 13 percent. Approximately 25 percent of that state's 5-year-olds attend no kindergarten. Since 1974 New Hampshire has provided kindergarten to approximately one-third of eligible youngsters. In neighboring Vermont, 77 percent of 5-year-olds are offered free public kindergarten, but by 1 July 1988 all districts must provide kindergarten opportunities.

The second trend in the education of 5-year-olds in the United States is two-faceted: there is more local funding of kindergarten and more local control of kindergarten programs. Most state department officials report approximate percentages of services funded locally. In 1981 only 10 states reported that local funding exceeded 25 percent of the total. By 1986 local funds represented significant contributions in 14 states. In fact, six states (Mississippi, Montana, Nebraska, New Hampshire, Oregon, and Vermont) reported that a majority of the funding for kindergarten is provided by local districts.

The increase in local control of kindergarten programs is suggested by the fact that only 19 of 50 state officials were able to provide definite answers to questions in all six of the following

See page 332 for acknowledgment and footnote.

areas: funding, teacher education, population served, length of day, major focus of the curriculum, and compulsory nature of programs. Many state officials said that data in one or more of these categories was either unknown or unavailable to them. Decisions about birthdate deadlines for entrance to kindergarten, length of the school day, and major focus of the curriculum were frequently mentioned as local district prerogatives.

Third, more 5-year-olds are attending school for more hours each day in the 1980s than in the 1970s. While the majority of states report that half-day programs (from two to four hours) are most common, there are indications that the length of the school day is being extended. First, more state officials emphasize that a range of from two to three hours is a *minimum* requirement. Second, in 1974 only Hawaii provided a four-to six-hour day for kindergartners; in 1986 eight states (Alabama, Hawaii, North Carolina, North Dakota, Colorado, Florida, Georgia, and Tennessee) did so. Finally, in 1986, 14 states (up from eight in 1974) reported a range of from 2½- to six-hour programs when local districts supplemented state funds to provide more than the minimal requirements.

The fourth trend in the education of 5-year-olds is the tendency of states to hire teachers with more years of education. In 1974 six state officials reported that a percentage of kindergarten teachers held an associate's degree or less; in 1981 that number had fallen to four; in 1986 only Indiana reported that some kindergarten teachers had an associate's degree or less. Information in this category seems to be difficult to obtain, because a large number of respondents do not answer this item. Thus we should not infer that only one state hires teachers with less than a bachelor's degree. Twenty-eight states did indicate that the minimum requirement for kindergarten teachers was a bachelor's degree. In 11 states, more than 20 percent of kindergarten teachers had earned master's degrees. A remarkable percentage of kindergarten teachers hold master's degrees in Indiana (83%), New Mexico (80%), Kentucky (74%), Georgia (60%), Oregon (55%), Missouri (43%), and South Carolina (41%).

The final trend in kindergarten education is one that reflects both the changing nature of our society and the increasing emphasis on early education: the requirement that children begin school at age 5. In 1982 only Florida made kindergarten attendance compulsory. Four years later, seven states required children to attend kindergarten: Delaware, Florida, Kentucky, Louisiana, South Carolina, South Dakota, and Virginia. New Mexico will join this list in 1987. In some states, parents can elect to keep children at home or send them to private centers by signing waivers. Despite these options, the message is clear: early childhood education is viewed as important enough to change the traditional age for entering school.

DISCUSSION QUESTIONS

1. How have the states developed and funded kindergarten programs?
2. Which states have added kindergartens recently? Why?
3. What are the promising trends in teacher preparation?
4. Should kindergarten attendance be compulsory?

30. KINDERGARTEN PROGRAMS AND PRACTICES

Educational Research Service Staff Report

Attention focused on kindergarten programs has intensified in recent years, with factors both inside and outside education contributing to the increased interest. Discussions about the pros and cons of half-day vs. full-day programs, the most effective approach to the teaching of reading, and the appropriate goals for kindergarten involve parents and other citizens as well as professional educators. Schools must now cope with the educational and developmental needs of students with and without day care or formal preschool experience. And in addition to these societal pressures, research continues to stress the impact of early childhood education on later achievement.

Studies of kindergarten programs were conducted by the National Education Association in 1925, 1961, and 1967. Since current information was clearly needed, the Educational Research Service conducted a study of kindergarten programs and practices in April 1985. Nationwide samples of both kindergarten teachers and elementary school principals were contacted, with 1,228 principals and 1,082 teachers responding. The results of the two surveys are reported in the new ERS report *Kindergarten Programs and Practices in Public Schools* (1986). Important highlights are summarized here.

HALF-DAY VS. FULL-DAY SCHEDULES

The predominant pattern for kindergarten schedules is still half-day, with 49.1 percent of the teachers teaching both morning and afternoon sessions, 12.1 percent a morning session only, and 3.1 percent an afternoon session only. Just over one-fourth (27.7 percent) of the responding teachers work with pupils who attend a full-day every day, while 7.4 percent work with pupils on a full-day, alternate day schedule.

According to the principals, rural districts are more likely than those in other types of communities to have some type of full-day schedule, with 49.3 percent reporting either a full-day, every day or full-day, alternate day arrangement. When asked whether any change in scheduling was contemplated in their schools, 93.0 percent of the principals indicated that the present schedule would be maintained.

In general, teachers tend to prefer the type of schedule under which they are currently working. However, given the choice, there would be some shift toward full-day schedules. Of the half-day teachers, 58.5 percent would prefer to continue this schedule, while 77.1 percent of the full-day teachers selected the full-day option.

See page 332 for acknowledgment.

Preference for Teaching Schedules

Preference	Total	Current Schedule	
		Half-Day	Full-Day
Half-day, every day	45.2%	58.5%	21.6%
Full-day, every day	45.7	34.8	65.8
Full-day, alternate day . .	6.8	4.3	11.3
No response	2.2	1.4	1.3

THE KINDERGARTEN ENVIRONMENT

Full-day teachers report an average class size of 24 pupils, with half-day teachers reporting an average of 23 pupils in the morning sessions and 22 in the afternoon sessions.

About four of every ten pupils, an average of 41 percent of each class, have had a full year of day care, preschool, or nursery school experience before kindergarten. A higher proportion (51 percent) of pupils living in the Northeast have attended school before kindergarten, while 35 percent of those in Southeastern states have done so. Teachers in both the Central and Western regions report averages of 41 percent.

Almost half (48.0 percent) of the teachers report the availability of a paid teacher aide, although the person might work part time. More of the full-day teachers (57.1 percent) than the half-day teachers (43.1 percent) are assisted by a paid teacher aide. Of kindergarten teachers overall, 42.4 percent had neither a paid teacher aide, community or parent volunteers, nor a student teacher during the 1984-85 school year.

THE KINDERGARTEN PROGRAM

About six of every ten teachers (62.9 percent) characterize the focus of their kindergarten program as "preparation with a focus on academic readiness and social preparation for later schooling," while another 29.0 percent state that the focus in their program extends beyond readiness to particular academic skills and achievement. Child development rather than academic achievement is the primary focus of 5.2 percent of the kindergarten programs studied, while only 0.6 percent of the teachers classify their program as compensatory.

Both teachers who classify their kindergarten programs as "academic" and those who characterize them as "preparation" report that their daily schedules include both definite time allotments and a specific sequence for each activity, although the "academic" program teachers are more likely to do so.

Organization of the Daily Schedule

	Total	Focus of Program	
		Acad.	Prep.
Definite time allotments and sequence for each activity	60.6%	68.8%	59.0%
Activities in regular sequence; no definite time allotments	35.9	29.3	38.0
Pupils move from one activity to another with no regular sequence/time allotments	2.8	1.6	2.5
No response	0.7	0.3	0.4

Teachers were provided with a list of nine subject areas and asked whether students were organized into small groups or taught as a class. Reading is the subject most likely to be presented in small groups, with almost two-thirds (65.7 percent) of the teachers selecting this option. Music is the subject most likely to be presented to the class as a whole. Subject areas are ranked here on the basis of the percentage of kindergarten teachers stating that presentation of related material is made to small groups of students rather than to the class as a whole.

Subjects Presented to Small Groups

Topic	Percent
Reading	65.7
Mathematics	46.0
Language Arts	39.5
Art	30.4
Science	23.5
Social Studies	17.3
Health	13.6
Physical Education	13.3
Music	6.7

LEARNING GOALS

Kindergarten teachers were asked about the degree of priority that they personally believe should be placed on particular learning goals for kindergarten pupils. Although teachers in both "academic" and "preparation" programs consider language development as the most critical goal, there is some variation between the two groups as to their tendencies to classify other goals as having "high priority." In particular, the goal of academic achievement is considered a high priority by 59.2 percent of respondents teaching in "academic" programs, while only 36.1 percent of the respondents in "preparation" programs classify the goal this way. On the other hand, teachers in "preparation" programs are more concerned than teachers in the "academic" group with development of health/safety habits, physical/motor coordination, and personality. The "high priority" percentages are presented below for kindergarten teachers in general as well as those in "academic" and "preparation" programs.

"High Priority" Learning Goals

		Focus of Program	
	Total	Acad.	Prep.
Language development ..	92.8%	91.1%	93.7%
Social development	89.2	79.6	93.5
Emotional development .	82.9	74.8	86.5
Self-discipline	80.5	79.9	81.6
Development of work/ study habits	67.7	72.6	67.4
Physical coordination/ motor development...	67.1	60.2	70.5
Development of health/ safety habits	58.6	49.4	63.1
Personality development	54.3	45.5	58.6
Academic achievement ..	41.0	59.2	36.1
Artistic expression	39.5	34.1	40.4

The two groups of teachers also differ in their opinions about the appropriate approach to teaching reading/reading readiness in kindergarten. About the same proportion of each group concurs that "reading skills should be taught if readiness/ability is shown, but not stressed for other pupils" ("academic": 63.1 percent; "preparation": 61.4 percent). But 17.5 percent of teachers in "academic" programs—and only 4.0 percent of the "preparation" group—feel that reading skills should be taught to all kindergarten pupils. Almost a third (32.0 percent) of the "preparation" group agree that "all students should be *prepared* for reading, with the teaching of reading to begin in first grade"; only 15.6 percent of the "academic" group select this option. None of the "academic" group and only 0.3 percent of the "preparation" group feel that both preparation for reading and the teaching of reading skills should be excluded from the kindergarten curriculum.

PARENTS OF KINDERGARTEN PUPILS

Principals were asked about the types of activities used to involve parents in the kindergarten program. Parent/teacher conferences were reported as the most likely vehicle for encouraging parental involvement, with home visits used by one-fifth of the schools.

Activities Used to Involve Parents

Activity	Percent
Parent/teacher conference	96.4
Parent/teacher association meeting	79.5
Pre-registration programs	75.3
Parents' newsletter	71.4
Classroom observation	65.7
"Back to School" night........................	49.3
"Parent as Aide" program	41.5
Home visits...................................	20.0

Principals were also asked about the methods used to evaluate student progress or growth in *written* reports to parents, with respondents permitted to select more than one method. Used most often is a checklist of progress toward learning objectives (77.1 percent), followed by anecdotal comments (42.1 percent), ungraded—satisfactory or unsatisfactory (36.6 percent), letter grades (10.2 percent), and percentage grades (0.7 percent).

Almost two-thirds (63.9 percent) of the principals report that the results of teacher-parent conferences are taken into account when making promotion decisions at the end of the year. This factor, though, is considered less significant than either the teacher evaluation or the student's general performance in kindergarten.

PROBLEMS OF KINDERGARTEN TEACHERS

Kindergarten teachers were asked about factors that keep them from teaching kindergarten as they would like to teach it. Ranked first on the list is "lack of time for individual instruction and guidance," which 57.9 percent of the teachers consider a major problem. This is followed by "too many students per class," and "too much paperwork/lack of planning time." Full-day teachers were more concerned than their half-day counterparts about the problem of too many students per class and too much paperwork/lack of planning time, with the reverse true for "limited time for enrichment activities'' and ''lack of time for individual instruction/guidance.'' Listed here are the five factors receiving the highest ''major problem'' percentages.

Major Problems of Kindergarten Teachers

	Total	Teaching Schedule	
		Half-Day	Full-Day
Lack of time for individual instruction/ guidance	57.9%	60.9%	52.6%
Too many students per class	52.3	49.6	57.6
Too much paperwork/ lack of planning time .	39.1	36.9	43.4
Limited time for enrichment activities	38.9	46.0	25.8
Lack of teacher aides	34.4	35.9	31.8

In addition to these data, other topics in the ERS survey include use of a reading/readiness series, use of equipment in the classroom, screening and admission practices, frequency of standardized testing, retention and advancement policies, financial aid, and administration of programs. The full survey report, *Kindergarten Programs and Practices in Public Schools*, ... provides a contemporary account of current kindergarten programs and practices in the public schools.

DISCUSSION QUESTIONS

1. What are the typical patterns for kindergartens in the United States?

2. What do teachers report as the purpose of the kindergarten?

3. What is taught and how are the programs organized?

4. How are parents involved in the nation's kindergartens?

5. What are the typical problems faced by kindergarten teachers?

31. NAEYC POSITION STATEMENT ON DEVELOPMENTALLY APPROPRIATE PRACTICE IN THE PRIMARY GRADES, SERVING FIVE- THROUGH EIGHT-YEAR-OLDS

The current trend toward critical examination of our nation's educational system has recently included concerns about the quality of education provided in elementary schools (Bennett, 1986; Office of Educational Research and Improvement, 1986). Concerns have been raised because, in response to calls for "back to basics" and improved standardized test scores, many elementary schools have narrowed the curriculum and adopted instructional approaches that are incompatible with current knowledge about how young children learn and develop. Specifically, rote learning of academic skills is often emphasized rather than active, experiential learning in a meaningful context. As a result, many children are being taught academic skills but are not learning to apply those skills in context and are not developing more complex thinking skills like conceptualizing and problem solving (Bennett, 1986).

The National Association for the Education of Young Children (NAEYC), the nation's largest organization of early childhood educators, defines early childhood as the years from birth through age 8. NAEYC believes that one index of the quality of primary education is the extent to which the curriculum and instructional methods are developmentally appropriate for children 5 through 8 years of age. The purpose of this position statement is to describe both developmentally appropriate and inappropriate practices in the primary grades. This position statement reflects the most current knowledge of teaching and learning as derived from theory, research, and practice. This statement is intended for use by teachers, parents, school administrators, policymakers, and others who make decisions about primary grade educational programs.

BACKGROUND INFORMATION

Classrooms serving primary-age children are typically part of larger institutions and complex educational systems with many levels of administration and supervision. Classroom teachers may have little control over the curriculum or policies they imple-

ment. However, ensuring developmentally appropriate practice in primary education requires the efforts of the entire group of educators who are responsible for planning and implementing curriculum—teachers, curriculum supervisors, principals, and superintendents. At the same time, ensuring developmentally appropriate practice is the professional obligation of each individual educator. No professional should abdicate this responsibility in the absence of mutual understanding and support of colleagues or supervisors. This position statement is intended to support the current appropriate practices of many primary-grade programs and to help guide the decisions of administrators so that developmentally appropriate practices for primary-age children become more widely accepted, supported, and followed.

Curriculum derives from several sources: the child, the content, and the society. The curriculum in early childhood programs is typically a balance of child-centered and content-centered curriculum. For example, good preschools present rich content in a curriculum that is almost entirely child-centered. As children progress into the primary grades, the emphasis on content gradually expands as determined by the school, the local community, and the society. The challenge for curriculum planners and teachers is to ensure that the content of the curriculum is taught so as to take optimum advantage of the child's natural abilities, interests, and enthusiasm for learning.

DEVELOPMENT AND LEARNING IN PRIMARY-AGE CHILDREN

Integrated Development and Learning

In order to provide developmentally appropriate primary education, it is essential to understand the development that typically occurs during this period of life and to understand how 5- through 8-year-old children learn. We can then derive principles of appropriate practice for primary-age children. One of the most important premises of human development is that all domains of devel-

See pages 332–33 for acknowledgment and references.

opment—physical, social, emotional, and cognitive—are integrated. Development in one dimension influences and is influenced by development in other dimensions. This premise is violated when schools place a great emphasis on the cognitive domain while minimizing other aspects of children's development. Because development cannot be neatly separated into parts, failure to attend to all aspects of an individual child's development is often the root cause of a child's failure in school. For example, when a child lacks social skills and is neglected or rejected by peers, her or his ability to work cooperatively in a school setting is impaired. As interest lags, the child's learning may also be impaired, and she or he may become truant or eventually drop out (Burton, 1987). *The relevant principle of instruction is that teachers of young children must always be cognizant of "the whole child."*

Children's learning, like development, is integrated during the early years. One of the major pressures on elementary teachers has always been the need to "cover the curriculum." Frequently, they have tried to do so by tightly scheduling discrete time segments for each subject. This approach ignores the fact that young children do not need to distinguish learning by subject area. For example, they extend their knowledge of reading and writing when they work on social studies projects; they learn mathematical concepts through music and physical education (Van Deusen-Henkel and Argondizza, 1987). *The relevant principle of instruction is that throughout the primary grades the curriculum should be integrated* (Katz and Chard, in press).

Integration of curriculum is accomplished in several ways. The curriculum may be planned around themes that are selected by the children or by the teacher based on the children's interests. For example, children may be interested in the ocean because they live near it. Children may work on projects related to the ocean during which they do reading, writing, math, science, social studies, art, and music. Such projects involve sustained, cooperative effort and involvement over several days and perhaps weeks.

Integrated curriculum may also be facilitated by providing learning areas in which children plan and select their activities. For example, the classroom may include "a fully-equipped publishing center, complete with materials for writing, illustrating, typing, and binding student-made books; a science area with animals and plants for observation, and books to study; and other similar areas" (Van Deusen-Henkel and Argondizza, 1987). In such a classroom, children learn reading as they discover information about science; they learn writing as they work together on interesting projects. Such classrooms also provide opportunities for spontaneous play, recognizing that primary-age children continue to learn in all areas through unstructured play—either alone or with other children.

Physical Development

During the primary years, children's physical growth tends to slow down as compared to the extremely rapid physical growth that occurred during the first 5 years of life. Children gain greater control over their bodies and are able to sit and attend for longer periods of time. However, primary-age children are far from mature physically and need to be active. Primary-grade children are more fatigued by long periods of sitting than by running, jumping, or bicycling. Physical action is essential for these children to refine their developing skills, like batting a ball, skipping rope, or balancing on a beam. Expressing their newly acquired physical power and control also enhances their self-esteem.

Physical activity is vital for children's cognitive growth as well. When presented with an abstract concept, children need physical actions to help them grasp the concept in much the same way that adults need vivid examples and illustrations to grasp unfamiliar concepts. But unlike adults, primary-age children are almost totally dependent on first-hand experiences. *Therefore, an important principle of practice for primary-age children is that they should be engaged in active, rather than passive, activities* (Katz and Chard, in press). For example, children should manipulate real objects and learn through hands-on, direct experiences rather than be expected to sit and listen for extended periods of time.

Cognitive Development

The learning patterns of primary-age children are greatly affected by the gradual shift from preoperational to concrete operational thought, a major dimension of cognitive development during these years (Piaget, 1952; Piaget and Inhelder, 1969). Between 6 and 9 years of age, children begin to acquire the mental ability to think about and solve problems in their heads because they can then manipulate objects symbolically—no longer always having to touch or move them. This is a major cognitive achievement for children that extends their ability to solve problems. Despite this change in approach to cognitive tasks, however, primary-age children are still not capable of thinking and problem solving in the same way as adults. While they can symbolically or mentally manipulate objects, it will be some time before they can mentally manipulate symbols to, for example, solve mathematical problems such as missing addends or to grasp algebra. For this reason, primary-age children still need real things to think about. Accordingly, while children can use symbols such as words and numbers to represent objects and relations, they still need concrete reference points. *Therefore, a principle of practice for primary-age children is that the curriculum provide many developmentally appropriate materials for children to explore and think about and opportunities for interaction and communication with other children and adults. Similarly, the content of the curriculum must be relevant, engaging, and meaningful to the children themselves* (Katz and Chard, in press).

Young children construct their own knowledge from experience. In schools employing appropriate practices, young children are provided with many challenging opportunities to use and develop the thinking skills they bring with them and to identify and solve problems that interest them. In addition, appropriate schools recognize that some thinking skills, such as understanding mathematical place value and "borrowing" in subtraction, are beyond the cognitive capacity of children who are developing concrete operational thinking and so do *not* introduce these skills to most children until they are 8 or 9 years of age (Kamii, 1985).

Children in the stage of concrete operations typically attain other skills that have important implications for schooling (Elkind, 1981). Among thee is the ability to take another person's point of view, which vastly expands the child's communication skills. Primary-age children can engage in interactive conversations with adults as well as with other children and can use the power of verbal communication, including joking and teasing. Research demonstrates that engaging in conversation strengthens children's abilities to communicate, express themselves, and reason (Nelson, 1985; Wells, 1983; Wilkinson, 1984). Research also indicates that adults can help prolong and expand children's conversations by making appropriate comments (Blank, 1985). *Therefore, relevant principles of practice are that primary-age children be provided opportunities to work in small groups on projects that "provide rich content for conversation" and that teachers facilitate discussion among children by making comments and soliciting children's opinions and ideas* (Katz and Chard, in press).

Social-Emotional and Moral Development

Children of primary-grade-age are becoming intensely interested in peers. Establishing productive, positive social and working relationships with other children close to their age provides the foundation for developing a sense of social competence. Recent research provides powerful evidence that children who fail to develop minimal social competence and are rejected or neglected by their peers are at significant risk to drop out of school, to become delinquent, and to experience mental health problems in adulthood (Asher, Hymel, and Renshaw, 1984; Asher, Renshaw, and Hymel, 1982; Cowen, Pederson, Babigian, Izzo, and Trost, 1973; Gronlund and Holmlund, 1985; Parker and Asher, 1986). Research also demonstrates that adult intervention and coaching can help children develop better peer relationships (Asher and Williams, 1987; Burton, 1987). *The relevant principle of practice is that teachers recognize the importance of developing positive peer group relationships and provide opportunities and support for cooperative small group projects that not only develop cognitive ability but promote peer interaction.*

The ability to work and relate effectively with peers is only one dimension of the major social-emotional developmental task of the early school years—the development of a sense of competence. Erikson (1963) describes this major developmental challenge as the child's struggle between developing a sense of industry or feelings of inferiority. *To develop this sense of industry or a sense of competence, primary-age children need to acquire the knowledge and skills recognized by our culture as important, foremost among which are the abilities to read and write and to calculate numerically.* If children do not succeed in acquiring the competence needed to function in the world, they develop a sense of inferiority or inadequacy that may seriously inhibit future performance. The urge to master the skills of esteemed adults and older children is as powerful as the urge to stand and walk is for 1-year-olds. Yet when expectations exceed children's capabilities and children are pressured to acquire skills too far beyond their ability, their motivation to learn as well as their self-esteem may be impaired. A major cause of negative self-image for children this age is failure to succeed in school, for instance failing to learn to read "on schedule" or being assigned to the lowest ability math group.

At about age 6, most children begin to internalize moral rules of behavior and thus acquire a conscience. Children's behavior often shows that they find it difficult to live with and by their new self-monitoring and that they need adults' assistance. *Teachers and parents need to help children accept their conscience and achieve self-control.* In appropriate classrooms, teachers use positive guidance techniques, such as modeling and logical consequences, to help children learn appropriate behavior, rather than punishing, criticizing, or comparing children. In addition, teachers involve children in establishing and enforcing the few, basic rules necessary for congenial group living. Sensitive teachers ask children what they think of their work or behavior. The teacher points out how pleased the child must feel when a goal is accomplished. If achievement is lacking, the teacher empathizes with a child's feelings and solicits her or his ideas as to how to improve the situation.

Children at this age also begin to make more accurate judgments about what is true and false and to rigidly apply their newfound understanding of rules (Elkind, 1981). Their newly formed consciences are often excessively strict. For example, they may treat every little mistake as a major crime, deserving of terrible punishment. Adults help children assess mistakes realistically and find ways of correcting them. Children's developing consciences especially insist on fairness and adherence to rules. They closely observe adult infractions so it is very helpful for adults to be fair and obey rules. Sensitive teachers appeal to children's respect for fairness and rules when it comes to their interactions with others or when it is necessary to deny their requests, for example, "If I allow you to do that, I would be unfair to the others and you couldn't trust that, some other time, I wouldn't also be unfair to you" (Furman, 1980, 1987a, 1987b).

Despite their increased independence and developing consciences, 5-, 6-, 7-, and even 8-year-old children still need supervision and the support of trusted adults. As a result, children in this age group should not be expected to supervise themselves in school or after school for extended periods of time. Teachers and parents provide opportunities for children to develop independence and assume responsibility but should not expect primary-age children to display adult levels of self-control.

INDIVIDUAL DIFFERENCES AND APPROPRIATE PRACTICES

Knowledge of age-appropriate expectations is one dimension of developmentally appropriate practice, but equally important is knowledge of what is individually appropriate for the specific children in a classroom. Although universal and predictable sequences of human development appear to exist, a major premise of developmentally appropriate practice is that each child is unique and has an individual pattern and timing of growth, as well as individual personality, learning style, and family background. Children's sense of self-worth derives in large part from their experiences within the family. When children enter school, their self-esteem comes to include the school's opinion of their family. When children sense that teachers respect and value their families, and respect the particular cultural patterns by which their family lives, their own sense of self-esteem and competence is enhanced. It is developmentally appropriate to view parents as integral partners in the educational process. Teachers should communicate frequently and respectfully with parents and welcome them into the classroom. Teachers need to recognize that cultural variety is the American norm and that children's abilities are most easily demonstrated through familiar cultural forms (Hilliard, 1986).

Enormous variance exists in the timing of individual development that is within the normal range. Developmentally appropriate schools are flexible in their expectations about when and how children will acquire certain competencies. Recognition of individual differences dictates that a variety of teaching methods be used (Durkin, 1980; Katz and Chard, in press). Because children's backgrounds, experiences, socialization, and learning styles are so different, any one method is likely to succeed with some children and fail with others. *The principle of practice is that the younger the children and the more diverse their backgrounds, the wider the variety of teaching methods and materials required* (Durkin, 1980; Katz and Chard, in press; Katz, Raths, and Torres, undated).

Developmentally appropriate schools are also flexible in how they group children. Rigid adherence to chronological age/grade groupings or ability groupings is inappropriate. For this reason, some schools provide ungraded primary or several alternatives such as 2- or 3-year combination classrooms of 5-, 6-, and 7-year-olds or 6-, 7-, and 8-year-olds. Some schools recognize that many 8-year-olds are developmentally more like 9- and 10-year-olds and others more like 6- or 7-year-olds. Such combination classrooms or ungraded primary schools provide a vehicle for preserving heterogeneous groups while also providing more time for children to develop at their own pace and acquire early literacy and mathematical skills.

Most children have individual, personal interests and needs just as adults do. Most children are motivated to learn by an intense desire to make sense out of their world and to achieve the competencies desired by the culture. Children are learning all the time although they may not be learning the prescribed curriculum presented by the teacher (Elkind, 1981). For example, some children learn quickly that they are not smart (in the eyes of their teacher) or that their ideas are unimportant; other children learn that they are not effective group members. The learning that takes place in the primary grades far exceeds the knowledge and skills designated in the written curriculum. Research (Covington, 1984; Stipek, 1984) shows that unless they have a physical disability or illness or have been abused, preschool and kindergarten children are optimistic about their own powers and arrive at school confident that they will achieve. They are developing and acquiring skills so rapidly that they naturally assume that what they cannot do today will be possible tomorrow (Hills, 1986). As children get older, they begin to understand the limits of their own abilities and they also become more aware of social comparison. In the normal course of development, children compare themselves to others favorably and unfavorably. This information becomes part of their self-concept and can affect their motivation for activity. For example, children learn whether they are better at science or art or baseball and such learning influences life decisions. *Unfortunately, when schools unduly rely on competition and comparison among children, they hasten the process of children's own social comparison, lessen children's optimism about their own abilities and school in general, and stifle motivation to learn* (Hills, 1986).

During the early years, children are not only learning knowledge and skills, they are acquiring dispositions toward learning and school that could last a lifetime (Elkind, 1987; Gottfried, 1983; Katz, 1985; Katz and Chard, in press). Dispositions are "relatively enduring habits of mind and action, or tendencies to respond to events or situations," for example, curiosity, humor, or helpfulness (Katz and Chard, in press). *Longitudinal research indicates that curriculum and teaching methods should be designed so that children not only acquire knowledge and skills, but they also acquire the disposition or inclination to use them.* Compelling evidence exists asserting that overemphasis on mastery of narrowly defined reading and arithmetic skills and excessive drill and practice of skills that have been mastered threaten children's dispositions to use the skills they have acquired (Dweck, 1986; Katz and Chard, in press; Schweinhart, Weikart, and Larner, 1986; Walberg, 1984). It is as important for children to acquire the desire to read during the primary grades as it is for them to acquire the mechanics of reading. Similarly, it is as important for children to want to apply math to solve problems as it is for them to know their math facts.

The primary grades hold the potential for starting children on a course of lifelong learning. Whether schools achieve this potential for children is largely dependent on the degree to which teachers adopt principles of developmentally appropriate practice. The principles of practice described here have historical roots that include Dewey's progressive education (Biber, Murphy, Woodcock, and Black, 1942; Dewey, 1899), and the open education movement of the 1960s (Barth, 1972; Weber, 1971). Although the principles are similar in many instances to principles espoused by both those movements, this position statement does not advocate a return to practices of the past but rather builds on previous experience and reflects the knowledge acquired in the interim. Theory and research regarding effective curriculum and instruction have increased enormously in recent years and have contributed to our greater understanding of the teaching/learning process. This position statement reflects the most current knowledge of teaching and learning as derived from theory, research, and practice.

DISCUSSION QUESTIONS

1. Why is it necessary for a major professional organization to establish guidelines about appropriate practices in early childhood and the primary grades?
2. Do these recommended practices or standards restrict the innovative teacher or program?
3. What are the central principles of developmentally appropriate education?
4. Will these guidelines reduce or prevent poor quality or incorrect teaching of children in schools?

Section Five: The Curriculum for Young Children in School

EDITOR'S OVERVIEW

One of the themes that appears in many of the chapters in this book is the integrated curriculum. Several authors have argued for reducing the artificial divisions among content areas. But many specialists in the field of early childhood education find it convenient to *think about* what the child will learn as separate categories of information and skills. The ideal curriculum for young children in the schools is an integrated whole. The viewpoints that follow in this section are individual pieces of that whole; they use the traditional divisions of the instructional program for identity.

The complete answers to the questions "What should be taught and how will children learn?" are not intended to appear in these pages. Rather, the intention is to illustrate the rich diversity of theory and opinion about the early childhood curriculum in the schools. The ideal pattern for dealing with this diversity is to seek consensus on broad guidelines, support them from research, and then encourage creativity and experimentation among all teachers.

Although the acquisition of language begins at birth and never stops, the prodigious task of communicating meaning takes place at a high rate during the first years of school. The first group of authors discuss literacy as the general goal and then concentrate on writing and reading. After a long period of argument and difference of opinion about early literacy development, a coalition of important professional organizations has sought and found consensus. It is presented in the position statement of the Early Childhood and Literacy Development Committee of the International Reading Association. Jalongo and Zeigler give structure and ideas for helping children in kindergarten and first grade to write. Cunningham offers a succinct answer to the general question about

reading methods in the kindergarten, and George explains one example of using many materials to help children read. Then, Schon provides a multicultural dimension with a list of Spanish books for both Hispanic and non-Hispanic children.

Just as there are many ways to help children with their language development, so there are different viewpoints about the learning of science, mathematics, and other content areas. In the next group of chapters, Henniger shows how and what children learn about science and mathematics as they play. His focus is not on the factual content but on the more generic aspects of learning, like curiosity and motivation. Bauch and Hsu compare the 80-year-old methodology of Maria Montessori with more recent theory and research on how children actually acquire number concepts. Smith gives the reader a well-documented framework for use in thinking about and planning science experiences for young children. Brand and Fernie do the same for music as an often-neglected program element. And Dyson shows how children use drawing, talk, and dictation to communicate their ideas to themselves and others.

The final group of chapters represent examples of different ways to accomplish the general goals of early education in the schools. One of the general goals is good social interaction; suggestions for fostering this goal are provided by Rogers and Ross. Myers and Maurer choose the learning center pattern for organizing the curriculum. Hardy and Greene return us to the importance of play in the total development of the child. And Kamii, providing the justification from Piagetian theory, makes it clear that there are correct and clearly incorrect ways to organize learning during the first years of schooling.

32. JOINT STATEMENT ON LITERACY DEVELOPMENT AND PRE-FIRST GRADE

prepared by the Early Childhood and Literacy Development Committee
of the International Reading Association for ASCD, IRA, NAEYC, NAESP, NCTE

OBJECTIVES FOR A PRE-FIRST GRADE READING PROGRAM

Literacy learning begins in infancy. Reading and writing experiences at school should permit children to build upon their already existing knowledge of oral and written language. Learning should take place in a supportive environment where children can build a positive attitude toward themselves and toward language and literacy. For optimal learning, teachers should involve children actively in many meaningful, functional language experiences, including *speaking, listening, writing* and *reading*. Teachers of young children should be prepared in ways that acknowledge differences in language and cultural backgrounds and emphasize reading as an integral part of the language arts as well as of the total curriculum.

WHAT YOUNG CHILDREN KNOW ABOUT ORAL AND WRITTEN LANGUAGE BEFORE THEY COME TO SCHOOL

1. Children have had many experiences from which they are building their ideas about the functions and uses of oral language and written language.
2. Children have a command of language, have internalized many of its rules, and have conceptualized processes for learning and using language.
3. Many children can differentiate between drawing and writing.
4. Many children are reading environmental print, such as road signs, grocery labels, and fast food signs.
5. Many children associate books with reading.
6. Children's knowledge about language and communication systems is influenced by their social and cultural backgrounds.
7. Many children expect that reading and writing will be sense-making activities.

See page 333 for acknowledgment.

CONCERNS

1. Many pre-first grade children are subjected to rigid, formal pre-reading programs with inappropriate expectations and experiences for their levels of development.
2. Little attention is given to individual development or individual learning styles.
3. The pressures of accelerated programs do not allow children to be risk-takers as they experiment with language and internalized concepts about how language operates.
4. Too much attention is focused upon isolated skill development or abstract parts of the reading process, rather than upon the integration of oral language, writing and listening with reading.
5. Too little attention is placed upon reading for pleasure; therefore, children often do not associate reading with enjoyment.
6. Decisions related to reading programs are often based on political and economic considerations rather than on knowledge of how young children learn.
7. The pressure to achieve high scores on standardized tests that frequently are not appropriate for the kindergarten child has resulted in changes in the content of programs. Program content often does not attend to the child's social, emotional and intellectual development. Consequently, inappropriate activities that deny curiosity, critical thinking and creative expression occur all too frequently. Such activities foster negative attitudes toward communication skill activities.
8. As a result of declining enrollments and reduction in staff, individuals who have little or no knowledge of early childhood education are sometimes assigned to teach young children. Such teachers often select inappropriate methodologies.
9. Teachers of pre-first graders who are conducting individualized programs without depending upon commercial readers and workbooks need to articulate for parents and other members of the public what they are doing and why.

RECOMMENDATIONS

1. Build instruction on what the child already knows about oral language, reading and writing. Focus on meaningful experiences and meaningful language rather than merely on isolated skill development.

2. Respect the language the child brings to school, and use it as a base for language and literacy activities.

3. Ensure feelings of success for all children, helping them see themselves as people who can enjoy exploring oral and written language.

4. Provide reading experiences as an integrated part of the broader communication process, which includes speaking, listening and writing, as well as other communication systems such as art, math and music.

5. Encourage children's first attempts at writing without concern for the proper formation of letters or correct conventional spelling.

6. Encourage risk-taking in first attempts at reading and writing and accept what appear to be errors as part of children's natural patterns of growth and development.

7. Use materials for instruction that are familiar, such as well-known stories, because they provide the child with a sense of control and confidence.

8. Present a model for students to emulate. In the classroom, teachers should use language appropriately, listen and respond to children's talk, and engage in their own reading and writing.

9. Take time regularly to read to children from a wide variety of poetry, fiction and non-fiction.

10. Provide time regularly for children's independent reading and writing.

11. Foster children's affective and cognitive development by providing opportunities to communicate what they know, think and feel.

12. Use evaluative procedures that are developmentally and culturally appropriate for the children being assessed. The selection of evaluative measures should be based on the objectives of the instructional program and should consider each child's total development and its effect on reading performance.

13. Make parents aware of the reasons for a total language program at school and provide them with ideas for activities to carry out at home.

14. Alert parents to the limitations of formal assessments and standardized tests of pre-first graders' reading and writing skills.

15. Encourage children to be active participants in the learning process rather than passive recipients of knowledge, by using activities that allow for experimentation with talking, listening, writing and reading.

DISCUSSION QUESTIONS

1. What are the main components of a good reading program for children before first grade?

2. Why do the guidelines include beginning with oral language?

3. Why do the recommendations not include traditional reading topics such as phonetics, word attack skills, and syntax?

33. WRITING IN KINDERGARTEN AND FIRST GRADE

by Mary Renck Jalongo and Sally Zeigler

When a kindergarten teacher instructed her students to print their names on their papers, one 5-year-old asked, "But what if I can't remember how to make my name?" The teacher thought for a moment and suggested, "Look on the front of your crayon box, Angel. Your name is printed there and you can just copy it." The kindergartner brightened and began to work diligently, with her tongue turned up at the corner of her lips as a visible sign of intensive effort. After the teacher collected the girl's paper, she was surprised to see these words: "Angel Crayola Brown the Great American Crayon."

This situation illustrates two important points about early writing: that young children will write if given the opportunity and that children's early writing should be linked with their experience, imagination and art. To do otherwise makes writing a meaningless exercise.

Children's writing, particularly young children's writing, has been the focus of considerable attention in recent years (Schickendanz, 1986). The recommendations of writing research are clear, yet only a small percentage of kindergarten and 1st-grade classrooms have implemented a writing program. Some reasons why this is so include the following:

1. Much of the theory and research is in direct conflict with the traditions, curricula, methods and materials in use.

2. Few teachers are adequately prepared to initiate a writing program with 5- and 6-year-olds; thus they feel intimidated and perceive the risk of failure to be great.

3. Many educators and parents assume that because young children cannot write perfectly, they should not write at all.

4. Administrative and community support for early writing programs is often insufficient.

This [chapter] will take a very practical approach to initial writing instruction in kindergarten and 1st grade. Each of the issues outlined above will be discussed in the process.

See page 333 for acknowledgment and references.

WHY EARLY WRITING?

Young children are fascinated by words. Anyone who doubts that this is true should consider for a moment an infant's delight at discovering "Bye-Bye" or the toddler's preoccupation with the power of "No!" Donald Graves (1983), a leading authority on effective writing instruction, contends that:

> Children want to write.... They want to write the first day they attend school. This is no accident. Before they went to school, they marked up walls, pavements, newspapers, with crayons, chalk, pens, or pencils. The child's marks say "I am."
>
> "No, you aren't," say most school approaches to the teaching of writing. We ignore the child's urge to show what he knows.... Then we say, "They don't want to write. How can we motivate them?" (p. 3)

When educators are convinced that young children can be taught to write in developmentally appropriate ways, then literacy programs in preschool and 1st grade will flourish (Early Childhood and Literacy Development Committee, 1985). There are at least three important reasons for encouraging the writing efforts of young children:

1. To Know Your Students Better

Writing is a form of self-expression. If you allow children a period of time to talk, followed by time to draw and write each day, their concerns, interests and ideas will be represented in their work. When a child draws a picture for you it is not unlike those comments often heard on the playground: "Watch this. Look at me, teacher. I know how to do this—can you?" Both in play outdoors and in play with words, the child is seeking attention and approval through a display of competence. Here is what one kindergarten teacher who implemented an early writing project had to say:

> In a busy classroom, writing was often the only time I spent with one child alone. Looking into her face,

admiring her writing, being there to listen and to help allowed me to get to know each child. At writing, at sharing, and at story time, they came to know me—as a person who loved their writing and reading and books. (Von Reyn, 1985, pp. 34–35)

Role models are an important influence on early literacy. In observational studies of young children, adults who were engaged in writing behaviors such as writing a check, making a grocery list or writing a letter were often the stimulus for children's early attempts to write (Calkins, 1980). Through example, parents and teachers can make the difficult task of becoming literate seem like a worthwhile option to children. Before this can occur, adults must value those wavy lines a young child describes as "a letter I wrote" more than the child's ability to color "in the lines" (Atkins, 1984). Actually those squiggles and lines, unusual designs and arrangements, or invented letters and reversed letters are as fundamental to written language as the sounds a baby makes before learning spoken language. When a baby makes sounds, adults respond to it as conversation; when a preschooler makes marks on paper, we should respond to it as writing.

Ask yourself: How well do I know each of my students? Does the classroom create an environment for literacy, one that is full of experiences with the language arts? Am I modeling the literacy behaviors I want to see in young children?

2. To Increase Student Motivation

A mother who was concerned about her 5-year-old son's schoolwork started to chart his progress by keeping a folder for the papers he did in each subject. Within a few weeks, the folders were filled with papers. Several dittos had been repeated two or even three times. Often the purple copies were blurry or faded. Instructions were sometimes hard to follow. On one page, the wrong answer was to be crossed out while on another, the *correct* answer was marked with an X. Even labeling items correctly was sometimes difficult. On one workbook page for initial consonants, the pictured object was supposed to be a "tree"; on another, it had to be specifically named as a "pine" in order to be correct.

If a task is confusing, repetitive or boring, some of the best students will do it badly to get it over with. If a task is interesting, appropriate and challenging, most children will try to complete it. Messy work—something that teachers often complain about—may be the child's way of saying,

"I'm tired of doing this busy work, teacher. But I will try to do what you ask." Contrast this response from young children with the results of Clay's (1975) research. She found that children often made lists of numbers, letters or words that they knew without any prompting from adults. This child behavior was called "spontaneously taking inventory" of knowledge (Clay, 1975; Temple and Gillet, 1984). Far too often, there is little opportunity for children to take stock of their growth in literacy. At the end of the week, make it a practice to review all the work you have assigned to children.

Ask yourself: How many authentic opportunities for self-expression exist? Do most children complete their work? What is the quality of their work? Do I encourage children's early attempts at writing?

3. To Increase Teacher Motivation

It would be difficult to imagine a teacher who would view the job of correcting mounds of dittos and workbook papers as anything but drudgery. These papers hold no surprises, just right or wrong answers, neat or messy work. When children's original work is being reviewed, just the reverse is true. The first thing you notice about young children's drawings is that no one other than a child could have possibly done them. If *adults* try to draw or write like children, their forgeries are easy to detect because the freshness and vitality of children's work is so difficult to replicate. Even an artist as celebrated as Picasso realized this. When he was asked why his best work was done in later years he replied, "Once I drew like Raphael, but it has taken me a whole lifetime to learn to draw like children."

If teachers are cast in the role of imposing an inflexible curriculum on young children, then the very things that prompted many teachers to go into education are subverted. Most of us became educators of young children because we wanted to play a significant role in promoting children's development; we were intrigued by their thoughts, words and actions. Far too much of what teachers do today has pulled us away from those purposes (Jalongo, 1986). An early writing program puts teachers back in touch with what motivated them to become early childhood educators in the first place—an appreciation for children.

Ask yourself: When was the last time I enjoyed reviewing children's work? Does this curriculum reflect my personal philosophy of teaching? How can I rid my classroom of "busy work" and get back in touch with the child's thought and imagination?

THE KINDERGARTEN WRITING PROGRAM

Practical issues in putting an early writing program into practice include: introducing writing, monitoring progress and assessing program outcomes. Suggestions and procedural guidelines follow.

Introducing the Writing Activity

Begin by encouraging children to share ideas, thoughts, feelings and experiences (not toys or other possessions). Both research on early literacy and daily experience with children verify the "primacy of oral language." Stewig (1980) even states it in the form of an equation $1>C>P$. This "formula" means that at any given point in the sequence of language development, the child's ability to merely imitate language sounds tends to be greater than his or her ability to comprehend language. Likewise, the ability to understand what others say tends to be greater than the ability to actually produce language. Opportunities for children to practice spoken language, then, are the logical precursor of writing.

The transition from class discussion to writing and drawing can be approached in several ways:

• Make a statement such as, "It sounds as though we have lots of things to draw and write about. Now I will give you some paper so that you can draw and write." Promote the concept of a picture accompanied by writing, even if the writing is a squiggle or a collection of letters. Remember that children come to school believing they can write. To a child, writing is making marks on paper. If necessary, the teacher can demonstrate using an overhead projector or chart (Furnas, 1985).

• Distribute large pieces of paper to the children. Recycled computer paper (torn into separate sheets) enables children to have an ample supply of writing paper. Next, allow the students to select a writing utensil from among many alternatives—pencils, crayons, chalk, ball-point pens, markers, even typewriters and word processors if available. Although it is often assumed that large pencils without erasers are the best writing implement, some children can control a watercolor marker or pen better. Encourage children to experiment.

• Remember that the kindergarten teacher's role is to "Listen thoughtfully to children, extend children's language about ideas and feelings, ask questions that encourage insights and highlight contradictions, and promote and value creative, divergent responses of all children (Moyer, Egertson and Isenberg, 1987). Circulate around the room as children complete their writings and drawings.

We found that especially during the first few weeks of kindergarten, labels (Figures 1 and 2) and captions that were dictated by the child and then written by the teacher were a way to get the less confident child started (Figures 3, 4a, 4b, and 5). Although purists of the process approach to writing might take issue with this strategy, it was a useful mechanism for helping certain students "break into print." While some children were writing independently, "sounding out" the words and using invented spellings (Figures 6a and 6b), others were using simple captions (Figure 7). The particulars of learning to write vary considerably from child to child. The important thing is that young children are learning to communicate (Calkins, 1983; Calkins, 1986; Lamme, 1984).

Monitoring Children's Progress

The children's "writing" can be anything that resembles print: scribbles, invented letters, real letters, or combinations of shapes, letters or numerals. Any of these should be accepted by the teacher.

The children's work will vary considerably. Some children, like Scott, will create a detailed story (Figure 8). After reading about this 1st-grader's trip to Dinosaur World, some teachers will immediately point out that it contains errors. A better way of looking at it is to consider how much diagnostic information a teacher can obtain from this writing sample. It certainly reveals more about this boy's knowledge of language than circled answers on a worksheet. Clearly, he knows that writing is linear, that there are spaces between words, and that stories have a beginning, middle and end. Scott confidently uses phonetic spelling to tackle difficult words like *triceratops* and *brontosaurus*. He has learned to use a period at the end of the sentence, so skill in punctuation is emerging. Generally speaking, children become aware of their errors and seek correction without much adult intervention. Soon they will be asking, "Is this how you spell ———?" or saying things like, "I

Figure 1

Figure 2

Figure 3

Figure 4a

Figure 4b

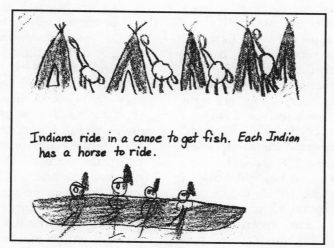

Indians ride in a canoe to get fish. Each Indian has a horse to ride.

Figure 5

The Cat I Loved

Figures 6a & 6b

This is a Dog runing after my cat.

This is a submarine in the ocean

Figure 7

Scott Happel
I won a ticket to dinusr world
I won it because I had the sam
nubrs on my ticket as the ticket
the man had. me and my mom
and dad and sisdr went on a jet.
my sisdr said the cars look so
little. then we wor ther. frist we
saw brdosois then we savv a taradl
then we saw stagasois then we saw
trisautops and then I savv it
ryanasres.

Figure 8

wrote this before I knew about ——ing'' (Bissex, 1980). Emphasizing errors has the same effect on a child as it does on an adult. If you have just prepared a cake for the first time and it is basically good, having a pastry chef critique its flavor, texture, color and appearance will only discourage you from baking. When so many things are right, why bombard a beginner with minor flaws?

Maintaining an attitude of "play with words" throughout an early writing program is important. For many 5- and 6-year-olds, "There is no planning, and there is no goal . . . writing, like play, is present tense" (Calkins, 1980, p. 209). Five- and 6-year-olds should be encouraged to play with language for some of the same reasons they are encouraged to use clay and paints. If we push young children to write "correctly" and draw representationally, their enthusiasm and originality suffer. All too soon, the young artist's fresh interpretations of trees and birds become overgrown lollipops and capital V's. An emphasis on doing things one "right" way (the adult's way) has the same adverse effects on writers. Then the proud, confident child who believed he or she could write and draw most anything refuses to try with comments such as, "I don't know how" or "It might not look right." Ideally, the writing program should build children's confidence and competence, not only in writing but also in speaking, listening and reading.

Procedural Guidelines

Writing should be an integral part of each day. If finding the time is a problem, try dispensing with any nonessential work and replacing it with writing as often as possible. After the first writing session, write down a few simple rules. If children participate in establishing these guidelines, they will be more likely to understand and follow them. If the word *conference* is used right away to describe teacher-child interaction, children will understand and use the terminology correctly.

After children have produced several stories, they can choose their favorites to publish. The child author then shares his or her book by sitting on a special story chair, reading the book aloud and showing the pictures to the group. At this point, the teacher's role is to be master of ceremonies and member of the audience. The audience applauds when the story is complete and the child takes the book home. The program continues in this way with children becoming increasingly independent writers and readers (Bromley, 1985). Note that speaking and listening skills of all the children are being developed as well. Teachers can use children's literature, group stories, field trips or mood music to stimulate other types of writing. Over the course of the school year, the children's writings and drawings produce an impressive documentation of their growth in literacy.

Program Outcomes

The writing program described here was one teacher's initial effort to become a decision-maker, to achieve greater professional autonomy and to revise the curriculum based upon knowledge of child development. Colleagues, administrators and parents were impressed, both by the quality and quantity of the children's work. The children were enthusiastic about writing too. Perhaps the best endorsement of the program came from the children themselves after an unexpected change in the daily schedule. The class was in the midst of writing when the teacher announced that it was time for recess. After an audible groan from the

---

Conferencing Guidelines

For Children	For Teachers
1. Talk quietly.	1. Kneel beside the child rather than towering above him or her.
2. Don't interrupt someone else's conference.	2. Remember that it is the child's story. Rather than giving too many suggestions, tell a child who is still thinking that you will come back later.
3. Raise your hand to let the teacher know you want a conference.	3. Encourage children to self-evaluate rather than becoming overly dependent upon the teacher's assessment.

children, the teacher said, "You will have to decide—recess or writing?" "Writing!" the class replied. If Angel had been in this class, she too could have learned to write. Unfortunately for her, she was in a classroom where the quest for simple, correct answers had overruled teachers' and students' creativity. Rollo May (1975) contends that being creative takes courage. He also views creativity as the ultimate basic:

> In our day of dedication to facts and hard-headed objectivity, we have disparaged imagination . . . art and imagination are often taken as the "frosting" of life rather than the solid food. What if imagination and art are not frosting at all, but the fountainhead of human experience? (pp. 149–150)

Literacy is basic, not because it is connected with the traditional "three R's," but because it has art and imagination at its source. If children are to become literate in the fullest sense of the word, then the connections among each child's experience, imagination, art and curriculum must be fully forged. A writing program in kindergarten and 1st grade is one important way of combining these essential elements and promoting the young child's development.

DISCUSSION QUESTIONS

1. Why have so few teachers used writing programs in early childhood education?

2. What is the role of writing in the development of self-expression?

3. How does drawing relate to a beginning writing program?

4. Why are teachers' listening skills important while helping children become creative writers?

34. HOW SHOULD READING BE TAUGHT IN KINDERGARTEN?

by Patricia M. Cunningham

The issue of reading instruction's place in kindergarten classrooms sparks immediate and often emotional response from supervisors, administrators, teachers, and parents. Those who are against reading in kindergarten argue that most five-year-olds are not ready for it and that the primary responsibility of kindergartens is to develop social, physical, conceptual, and language abilities. The advocates point out that many children *are* ready, especially those who have attended preschool programs that teach some traditional kindergarten skills.

A common compromise is to begin instruction with children who are ready and not push the others. This seemingly simple solution is difficult if not impossible to carry out in practice. First, the decision as to which kindergarten children are prepared is a complex one. Many children who can indeed begin reading are unable to complete the traditional workbook and skill sheet assignments that are part and parcel of most beginning programs. They often have six-year-old brains but five-year-old attention spans. Second, once parents realize that their child is not in a reading group, they exert tremendous pressure on teachers to begin instruction prematurely. Third, carrying out reading instuction with children who are ready leaves teachers little time and energy for planning and conducting crucial readiness activities for the other students.

A more appropriate question than, Should reading be taught in kindergarten? is, How should reading be taught in kindergarten? A whole body of research under the umbrella term, emergent literacy, shows that children who come from homes in which reading and writing are promoted and valued begin reading before they come to school. In addition to being read to, these children have "pretend reading" experiences with favorite books in which they figure out how reading works, learn to track print, and grasp some important words. They also have picked up many words such as "McDonald's" and "Pepsi" from the logo print in their environment. The other distinguishing characteristic of children who come to school ready to read is that they usually have experimented with writing by copying words and inventing spellings. The research appears clear that young children whose home experiences immerse them in reading and writing become successful school readers (Teale and Sulzby 1986).

Reading should be taught in kindergarten in a way that closely mirrors the natural reading and writing experiences fortunate children have before entering school. In classrooms in which shared reading of big books, language experience, writing with invented spellings, and word banks are a large part of daily instruction, the decision of which children are ready and which are not does not have to be made. Children who come to school lacking readiness develop it by being immersed in reading and writing. Those who come to class ready or actually reading continue their growth as they learn large numbers of words and letter-sound associations through shared reading and writing experiences. For an excellent discussion of kindergarten activities that follows this approach and further readings on this topic, see Mason and Au (1986).

DISCUSSION QUESTIONS

1. How do the differences among children influence how to approach reading in the kindergarten?

2. Is there a common-sense approach to reading with young children in kindergarten?

3. What is the influence of the home on reading readiness?

See pages 333–34 for acknowledgment and references.

35. "SUCCESS"FUL READING INSTRUCTION

by Carol J. George

Nothing succeeds like success, or so we've been told. This is apparently true in three kindergarten, three first grade, and two second grade classes at Pierce Terrace School, a K-2 school for children of military personnel stationed at Fort Jackson, South Carolina. These children, who are of many different races, abilities, and backgrounds, are taught using the Success in Reading and Writing program, one of the few eclectic approaches to teaching reading. The Success program, developed by Anne Adams and others at Duke University in the late '70s, stems from the belief that children should be taught to read and write using the materials they will rely on later in life. Reading and writing go hand in hand in the program, and children have the opportunity to do both during a daily two-hour period. The Success program relies heavily on the children's use of language and the establishment of a good experiential background before any reading or writing instruction ever starts.

This is the program's sixth year at Pierce Terrace and results have indeed been satisfying. Based on scores on the Metropolitan Achievement Test given in September and May each year, class means have risen from 1.9 to 4.0 in one second grade class, and from 2.0 to 4.2 in another. On the Comprehensive Test of Basic Skills, children in Success classes have repeatedly placed at the 70th to 80th percentile in language and reading.

Particularly impressive in these classes have been the performances of children who speak English as a second language. Some of these students, who could not score at the beginning of the year, scored at 2.5 and 4.2 at the end. The program is excellent in meeting the needs of all children, but most important, in developing in them a positive self-concept and the desire to learn.

WORKBOOK ACTIVITIES

In the Success program, 90 percent of the child's allotted reading time is spent in actual reading and writing. Because many activities found in workbooks are of dubious value in learning to read (Anderson 1985), workbooks are not used.

See page 334 for acknowledgment and references.

LANGUAGE EXERCISES

In the Success program, reading and writing go hand in hand, one reinforcing the other. Each day children are involved in the creation of some type of written composition. Language comes from the child's experiences and is used to foster writing skills while reinforcing those in reading. In the primary grades children begin the year writing short sentences or paragraphs. By the end of the year, they are composing stories of four to five paragraphs. Concepts are taught when they are needed and in a meaningful context.

MAIN CHARACTERISTICS OF SUCCESS

There are eight distinctive characteristics of the Success in Reading and Writing program.

1. There is no predetermined sequence of skills, although skills are emphasized in all modules. The timing for teaching certain skills is often generated within the moment—to extend pupils' social, psychological, and mental perspective at the optimal point in the learning process.

2. Sight words are not taught from isolated lists, but as they appear in a sentence or paragraph and in a meaningful context.

3. Verbal communication plays an important role in children's understanding. Word meanings are taught as they are volunteered by students in their own phrases or sentences.

4. Students' vocabulary is displayed on a chart, a key element of the Success program and an identifiable feature of a Success classroom.

5. Students begin with words they already know and proceed to learn words volunteered by others in the classroom or found somewhere in print. This freedom to learn to read and write an unlimited and uncontrolled vocabulary is another feature of the program.

6. Students get off to a successful start because they are not afraid of failure.

7. Small groups are formed from time to time, but never on the basis of ability levels, and are

maintained only until predetermined objectives are realized.

8. Students' positive self-concepts develop from successful endeavors in reading and writing.

By the end of the primary grades students have been exposed to a wide variety of printed materials and have composed various types of written communication. Most important, they have been given the opportunity to feel good about themselves because they have been successful.

Success is a strong program for teachers as well. It capitalizes on their expertise and ingenuity by asking them to develop a skeletal outline into a challenging and rewarding experience for students.

Administrators find the Success program cost effective. No workbooks, ditto masters, vocabulary charts, or basal readers are required since the materials needed in the program are readily available. Subscriptions to several magazines and the daily newspaper and a well-stocked library fill the bill for supplies. Monies previously spent on reading kits and materials can be used more effectively in other areas.

Success in Reading and Writing gives every child the opportunity to succeed every day. It is an exciting and challenging program for both teacher and student.

DISCUSSION QUESTIONS

1. What are the best sources and materials for helping young children become successful readers?

2. How does a success-oriented reading program affect the achievement of the children?

3. What are the critical elements of success for a kindergarten/primary grade reading program?

36. HISPANIC BOOKS/LIBROS HISPANICOS

by Isabel Schon

Hispanic children in the United States need to be exposed to a wide variety of books—in English and Spanish—that they can understand and enjoy if they are to become lifelong readers. Enough has been written recently about the importance of enjoying books with even the youngest children if we want them to learn to love reading that the fact will not be documented yet again in this [chapter]. Much has also been written over the years about the importance of including multicultural materials and experiences in *every* early childhood program to teach about diversity. Incorporating into your program materials and experiences about a culture and language specific to one of the children in your class can boost that child's self-esteem.

This [chapter] is essentially [an] annotated bibliograph[y] . . . a list of good recently published books in Spanish for young children. Through resources such as these, readers in the United States can understand and appreciate the beauty and variety of Hispanic culture and language.

GOOD CHILDREN'S BOOKS IN SPANISH

Spanish-speaking children in the United States need to be exposed to attractive, well-written books that they can read for recreational, informational, or educational purposes. Unfortunately, the selection of books in Spanish for young readers in the United States leaves much to be desired. Many books are either dull, moralistic stories that bore young children with their affected plots and saccharine characters, or uninspired "bilingual books" that pretend to teach young children to read in two languages. The following, however, are recent books for preschoolers and children in primary grades published in Spain, Mexico, and Argentina that are likely to delight young Spanish-speaking children.

El niño y el globo [The Boy and the Balloon] written and illustrated by Francisca Altamirano. 1985. Mexico City: Editorial Trillas. 12 pp. ISBN 968–24–1845–3.
Wordless picture book that shows a boy and his big blue balloon in the city, in the sky, in the country, over the ocean, over snow-capped mountains, and on a tree. The striking illustrations will attract children's attention.

Aprendiendo las figuras. [Learning Shapes]. Illustrated by Carlo A. Michelini. 1985. Madrid: Edaf. 24 pp. ISBN 84–7640–004–7.
Sturdy board pages, spiral binding, cutouts, colorful illustrations, and a rhyming text encourage children to touch and become acquainted with the principal shapes that surround them: circles, squares, and triangles. This toy book will take lots of touching by eager little hands.

La alacena [The Cupboard] (ISBN 968–39–0050–X); *El amigo* [The Friend] (ISBN 968–39–0049–6); *El bebé* [The Baby] (ISBN 968–39–0051–8); *La cobija* [The Blanket] (ISBN 968–39–0048–8); *El conejo* [The Rabbit] (ISBN 968–39–0046–1); *La escuela* [The School] (ISBN 968–39–0047–X); *El perro* [The Dog] (ISBN 968–39–0045–3) written and illustrated by John Burningham. (Serie Pre-Escolar Bilingue). 1984. Mexico City: Editorial Patria. 20 pp. each.
This charming series about a little boy's experiences at home and at school was originally published in England in 1974. Simple pastel illustrations and an easy-to read bilingual (Spanish and English) text show a curious little boy exploring a kitchen cupboard and telling about his friend Arthur, a new baby at home, his favorite blanket, his black rabbit, a neighbor's dog, and a day in school. The ingenuous illustrations and commonplace situations described should make this series of special interest to the very young. Some adults might object to the small size (6" × 6") of these publications and to the British spelling in the English text.

La casa de osito [Teddy's House] (ISBN 84–372–8001–X); *La comida de osito* [Teddy's Dinner] (ISBN 84–372–8022–8); *El jardín de osito* [Teddy's Garden] (ISBN 84–372–8003–6); *Los juguetes de osito* [Teddy's Toys] (ISBN 84–372–8000–1) written and illustrated by Michelle Cartlidge. (Libros Para Hablar). 1985. Madrid: Ediciones Altea. 14 pp. each.

See page 334 for acknowledgment and suggestions for further reading.

The very young will enjoy these attractive board books with appealing illustrations and simple vocabularies of items well known to children. A lovable teddy bear introduces children to his house, his food, his garden, and his toys.

Es navidad, Teo [It's Christmas, Teo] by Violeta Denou. 1985. Barcelona: Timum Mas. 10 pp. ISBN: 84-7176-666-3.

Colorful illustrations on sturdy cardboard pages depict happy scenes related to Christmas. This wordless picture book shows children with Santa Claus, setting up a nativity scene, talking to a wise man, opening their gifts, and removing the decorations from the Christmas tree. Hispanic Christmas celebrations are simply presented in this attractive, durable book. Other "Teo" titles are: *Teo come* [Teo Eats], *Teo juega* [Teo Plays], *Llueve, Teo* [It Is Raining, Teo], and *Los animales de Teo* [Teo's Animals].

El moño celeste [The Blue Ribbon] written and illustrated by Martha Fracchia. 1985. Buenos Aires: Editorial Plus Ultra. 26 pp. ISBN 950-21-0701-1.

Lolita is delighted with her blue ribbon tied into a bow. She wears it on her hair and sings and laughs. One day the ribbon escapes and, even though Lolita tries very hard to catch it, the ribbon disappears into the clouds. Finally Lolita finds her ribbon all dirty and wet. She washes it, puts it away for 2 days and then wears it happily again. Little girls will identify with Lolita's warm feeling about her ribbon. Engaging watercolor illustrations of Lolita and her ribbon complement the story.

El elefante [Elephant Bathes] (ISBN 84-7525-336-9); *El gorila* [Gorilla Builds] (ISBN 84-7525-331-8); *La nutria* [Otter Swims] (ISBN 84-7525-334-2); *El oso polar* [Polar Bear Leaps] (ISBN 84-7525-333-4); *El panda* [Panda Climbs] (ISBN 84-7525-335-0); *El tigre* [Tiger Runs] (ISBN 84-7525-332-6) by Derek Hall. Illustrated by John Butler. Translated by Pilar Gómez Centurión. 1986. Madrid: Ediciones Generales Anaya. 18 pp. each.

Originally published by the World Wildlife Fund in 1984, this series relates simple adventures of a young elephant, gorilla, otter, polar bear, panda, and tiger in their natural habitats. Delicate pastel illustrations and easy-to-read texts show how these young animals learn to survive with the help of their parents.

Erase una vez dos osos [There Were Two Bears] by Hanna Muschg. Illustrated by Käthi Bhend-Zaugg.

Translated from the German by Carmen Seco. 1984. Madrid: Espasa-Calpe. 77 pp. ISBN 84-239-2823-3.

Two young bears live with Mama Bear in a cave in the forest. On warm days they leave their cave to explore the forest. They learn to climb trees, fish, fight, and look for food. Upon the arrival of spring, they say good-bye to Mama to search for their own place in the forest. Gentle black-and-white line illustrations of bears in the forest exquisitely complement the text.

En casa de los abuelos [At Grandparents' House] (ISBN 84-261-2065-2); *Nuestro perro* [Our Dog] (ISBN 84-261-2066-0); *La visita* [The Visitor] (ISBN 84-261-2067-9) by Helen Oxenbury. Translated by Concepción Zendrera. (Los Libros del Chiquitin). 1984. Barcelona: Editorial Juventud. 18 pp. each.

Charming pastel illustrations and easy-to-read texts describe happy moments in the life of children. *En casa de los abuelos* tells about a little girl's weekly visits to her grandparents' house. Some readers may object to some stereotypical views of older people, such as Grandmother knitting and wearing house slippers, and Grandfather not being able to crawl out from under a table. This is, nonetheless, a warm story about a little girl and her grandparents. *Nuestro perro* shows what happens when a little boy and his mother take their dog out for a walk. *La visita* describes an embarrassing day for Mother as a result of an unexpected visitor at home.

Los abuelos [Grandparents] (Illustrated by Maria Rius, ISBN 84-342-0526-2); *Los jóvenes* [Young People] (Illustrated by Carmé Sole Vendrell, ISBN 84-342-0524-6); *Los niños* [Children] (Illustrated by Maria Rius, ISBN 84-342-0523-8); *Los padres* [Parents] (Illustrated by Carmé Sole Vendrell, ISBN 84-342-0525-4) by Josep Ma Parramón. (Las Cuatro Edades). 1985. Barcelona: Parramón Ediciones. 30 pp. each.

This series teaches children about family members. The charming illustrations of middle-class Spanish grandparents, older brothers and sisters, children, and parents in everyday activities and a simple text make this series a good introduction to the family.

Donde viven los monstruos [Where the Wild Things Are]. Written and illustrated by Maurice Sendak. Translated by Agustin Gervás. 1984. Madrid: Ediciones Alfaguara. 38 pp. ISBN 84-204-3022-6.

Sendak's award-winning *Where the Wild Things Are* has been delightfully translated for the Spanish-speaking reader. Young readers will enjoy Max's dream of going where the wild things are, ruling them, sharing their rumpus, and finally, returning home where someone loves him.

¿Qué hay detrás del árbol? [What's Behind That Tree?] by Leslie Williams. Illustrated by Carmé Sole Vendrell. Translated by Fabrici Caivano. 1985. Barcelona: Ediciones Hymsa. 24 pp. ISBN 84-7183-342-5.

A boy and a girl are curious to know what is behind a tree. They try to guess by imagining wild animals, monsters, soldiers, ballerinas, and other things. Finally, they find each other. Striking, simple illustrations add much interest to the story.

Mi primer diccionario ilustrado [My First Illustrated Dictionary] by Concepción Zendrera and Noelle Granger. 1984. Barcelona: Editorial Juventud. 24 pp. ISBN 84-261-0358-88.

One hundred and forty-eight Spanish words are included in this delightful dictionary for young children. Simple, colorful illustrations and an easy-to-understand sentence explain the meaning of each word. This is an excellent introduction to the Spanish alphabet for young children.

U.S. Dealers of Books in Spanish

Baker & Taylor
Books in Spanish
380 Edison Way
Reno, NV 89564

Bilingual Publications Co.
1966 Broadway
New York, NY 10023

French and Spanish Book Corp.
652 Olive St.
Los Angeles, CA 90014

Hispanic Books Distributors, Inc.
1870 W. Prince Rd., Suite 8
Tucson, AZ 85705

Iaconi Book Imports
3030 Pennsylvania Ave.
San Francisco, CA 94107

Lectorum Publications, Inc.
137 W. 14th St.
New York, NY 10011

Pan American Book Co.
4326 Melrose Ave.
Los Angeles, CA 90029

DISCUSSION QUESTIONS

1. Are Hispanic books only for Hispanic children?

2. Should the literature presented to young children be translated into English, even if it is about different cultures?

3. How does the use of Hispanic and other language books in early childhood classrooms relate to bilingual education programs and issues?

37. LEARNING MATHEMATICS AND SCIENCE THROUGH PLAY

by Michael L. Henniger

Quality educational opportunities in science and mathematics continue to be important priorities for children of all ages. A firm foundation in these areas is critical for many vocational options within our complex modern world. Young men and women with sound math and science understandings have many job opportunities and career choices unavailable to others.

Because of their importance, then, educators, parents and others must focus on creative ways of assisting children at all levels to have positive experiences in science and mathematics. To be successful in these areas, children must be introduced at an early age to experiences that lead to solid conceptual understandings. In addition, children need to develop positive attitudes toward, and an excitement for, mathematics and science learning. These positive experiences can be successfully built upon as children proceed through the educational system.

Childhood play provides many excellent opportunities for learning fundamental concepts and developing appropriate attitudes toward these important disciplines. Reflect for a moment upon the potential for learning inherent in a kindergarten science center. The teacher and children have collected fall seeds and leaves. The science area is organized to allow children to study, compare and contrast these treasures of nature. The play involved in collecting and analyzing these materials provides an ideal opportunity for young children to learn about nature. Through the playful exploration of meaningful materials from their local environment, children begin to build important conceptual understandings.

Consider a second situation in which preschool children are playing outdoors, taking the roles of their favorite Smurf characters. Sticks, rocks and dirt may symbolically become the ingredients of a marvelous new recipe to be shared among friends. This ability to manipulate symbols mentally in play is a necessary foundation for later learning in many academic areas. Children able to accept the arbitrariness of symbols in play are more readily able to accept the arbitrariness of the symbol systems used in mathematics and science.

Jerome Bruner (1972) effectively summarizes the value of play in learning as follows:

> Play appears to serve several centrally important functions. First it is a means of minimizing the consequences of one's actions, and of learning, therefore, in a less risky situation. . . . Second, play provides an excellent opportunity to try combinations of behavior that would, under functional pressure, never be tried. (p. 693)

By minimizing risks and opening the door to creative options, play becomes an exceedingly important vehicle for learning in science and mathematics.

The following analysis of play and its impact on science and mathematics learning is divided into two major sections. First, examples will be given of learning opportunities in science and mathematics available through children's play. The second section will deal with attitudes developed through play which are essential to effective learning in these areas.

LEARNING THROUGH PLAY

Play is a very difficult concept to define adequately, primarily because of the broad number of activities commonly called play. Take, for example, this imaginary dialogue between a mother and her son from the work of Garvey (1977):

> Tom, I want to clean this room. Go out and play.
> What do you mean, "go out and play"?
> You know what I mean.
> No, I don't.
> Well just go out and do whatever you do when you're having too much fun to come in to dinner.
> You mean toss the tennis ball against the garage? Finish painting my bike? Practice standing on my head? Tease Andy's sister? Check out the robin's eggs? (p. 2)

Although a broad, amorphous term, play is nonetheless an extremely powerful vehicle for learning. Picture the following situation with preschool children playing outdoors:

> Fifteen preschool children and two teachers are outdoors in the play yard. Four children are in the large

See pages 334–35 for acknowledgment, references, and bibliography.

sandbox playing with buckets, bottles, spoons, shovels and an assortment of wheeled toys. One of the teachers and three children are digging in the garden plot in preparation for the spring planting of seeds. Two children have discovered an ant hill and are intently watching the activity there. Near the large storage shed two more children are using colorful plastic building blocks to construct their version of a fort. Wheeled vehicles, always popular on preschool playgrounds, are being ridden by two other children in a game of "follow the leader." Finally, two children are lying on the grass, staring at the sky and talking about the "funny shapes" they see.

Upon first glance, the casual observer would suggest that these children are having great fun, but learning very little. A careful analysis of the situation, however, reveals much in the way of learning opportunities in science and mathematics. Children in the sandbox are filling and emptying containers, pouring from one to another. They are experiencing the relationships involved in measuring volume. One child is counting the number of spoonfuls of sand required to fill his container. This leads to a clearer understanding of the ordinal relationships in our number system. Two of the children are building a sand castle and are experiencing difficulties with collapsing walls. Several procedures are tried until, finally, a combination of sand and water provides the necessary consistency for durable walls. These children are practicing important problem-solving skills crucial to later learnings in science and mathematics.

The teacher and children in the garden plot are having similar learning opportunities. When a shovel of dirt uncovers two fat earthworms, the teacher and children take time to observe and discuss the life cycle and importance of worms. Some plants from last year's garden remain and children remove the seeds and sort them by size and shape. As the dead plants are removed to make room for the new garden, the teacher points out the root systems and discusses with the children how plants get the nutrients needed for healthy growth.

Fort construction provides further learning opportunities. As children select blocks of different lengths and shapes to use for walls and accessories, they discover through experience that two 12-inch blocks cover the same wall space as one 24-inch block. By laying a cylindrical solid on top of a rectangular block, the child can visually compare the surface area and volume of each. Counting opportunities abound. At the end of the play period, as children return the blocks to their storage area, children gain practice in classifying the blocks by shape.

With a little imagination, similar learning opportunities in science and mathematics can be seen in the other situations described in the playground scenario.

These and other play situations provide excellent opportunities for young children to learn about the world around them and to discover through exciting experiences many of the fundamental mathematics and science relationships necessary for later learning.

Does play also serve an important role in the mathematics and science learning opportunities of older children? Considerable evidence suggests that it does (Zammarelli and Bolton, 1977; Hartshorn and Brantley, 1973; Hutt and Bhavnani, 1972; Humphrey, 1966). Picture the following example of a 3rd-grade classroom:

> Twenty-five children, the teacher and two parent aides are busily working in a classroom organized into learning centers. After completing their required work, several children are playing together in the block corner, building an elaborate castle based on drawings from a social studies unit. This week was designated "Share a Pet" week, and the science area contains fish, a gerbil, rabbits, a dog and a cat. The games area has the ever popular chess, checkers, and Parcheesi games as well as some teacher-made games to reinforce multiplication facts. The mathematics center contains a variety of commercial manipulatives and collections of "found" objects from children's homes. In the book corner, the teacher has carefully selected and displayed several books on animals and pet care.

This enticing array of activities also provides many opportunities for learning math and science. Children in the science center are learning about the animal world through observation, discussion and hands-on experience with pets. The excitement and interest generated through play can lead children to the book area to seek further information about pets and their care. In the games corner children playing checkers and chess are thinking ahead and planning future moves. They are practicing the use of complex mental symbols and developing the ability to mentally visualize relationships. These mental manipulations are similar to those necessary for effective solutions to algebraic equations or geometric proofs in future grades. Other children, using the teacher-made games, are making the rather dull task of memorizing multiplication facts into an exciting, motivating activity. In the mathematics center itself, children are using commercial manipulatives to help them gain "concrete" understandings of complex mathematical concepts. A parent aide helps one child visualize the concept of division with the use of Cuisenaire

Rods. Another child is learning about "base 4" through the manipulation of Unifix Cubes. Playing includes a great deal of learning at this level as well!

Play is not the only avenue for learning during the preschool and elementary school years. Children can and do learn a great deal from more structured, adult-directed activities. The play experience is, rather, a unique opportunity to stimulate interest and build concrete, real-world experiences upon which more complex, abstract learnings in mathematics and science can be built. Attitudes necessary for effective learning in these areas are also enhanced through play.

ATTITUDE DEVELOPMENT IN PLAY

Play creates a valuable atmosphere for learning. By freeing the child to explore and create in a low-risk situation, the child's natural curiosity, willingness to consider varying options and motivation to learn are greatly enhanced.

Curiosity

A strong intellectual curiosity is essential for sound learning in science and mathematics. Albert Einstein (1949), in an autobiographical sketch, made the following statement:

> It is in fact nothing short of a miracle that the modern methods of instruction have not yet entirely strangled the *holy curiosity of inquiry* [emphasis added] . . . . It is a very grave mistake to think that the enjoyment of seeing and searching can be promoted by means of coercion and a sense of duty. (p. 17)

Einstein made two important points. First, children need to be curious about their world and how it works in order to be productive thinkers. Second, current methods of instruction are frequently uninteresting, unmotivating and therefore unsuccessful in stimulating curiosity.

Play, on the other hand, encourages curiosity at all levels of development. Take, for example, the young 3-year-old boy exploring with paint at the easel. Perhaps accidentally, he mixes blue and yellow paint on the paper and discovers that green paint is the result. The child's curiosity is aroused and, in an atmosphere of open exploration, he allows himself to try out a number of color combinations. His curiosity has led to important intellectual understandings at his level of development. Or consider the 11-year-old girl who sits down at

the computer to play an educational game. After several successful trials, the student becomes interested in the computer's reactions to wrong answers. To satisfy her curiosity, she playfully tries several combinations of incorrect responses. This attitude has allowed the student to learn more about the computer's operation in a playful, nonthreatening atmosphere.

Curiosity is essential to effective science and mathematics learning. In science, for example, the child who is curious about the similarities and differences in birds from various local areas is the one who will read, discuss and discover new information about birds. In mathematics, the child learning division facts may become curious about the relationship between multiplication and division. Through the use of mathematics manipulatives in play, the child can discover this important relationship. Curiosity provides the motivation to explore math and scientific phenomena for the sheer joy of learning.

Divergent Thinking

A second attitude is enhanced through play: the willingness to engage in divergent thinking. A number of researchers (Liberman, 1965; Hutt and Bhavnani, 1972; Pepler and Ross, 1981; Johnson, 1976) have provided considerable evidence that a relationship between play and divergent thinking exists.

Play provides many valuable opportunities for divergent thinking. An 8-year old girl playing with blocks may try several different combinations to see how many blocks can be stacked on top of each other without falling. The setting aside of judgments of right and wrong while playing allows her to be original and productive as she generates solutions to this problem. This same child, having gained confidence in using divergent thinking in play, can apply similar strategies to other tasks.

Children using divergent thinking in their play are researching possible solutions to specific tasks or problems. Play has been viewed as the highest form of research (Caplan and Caplan, 1974). A second quote by Albert Einstein (1954) highlights this point:

> . . . The desire to arrive at logically connected concepts is the emotional basis of this rather vague play. . . . This combinatory play seems to be the essential feature in productive thought. (pp. 25-26)

As children playfully consider the options available to them, they are enhancing their divergent thinking skills and engaging in a form of research that can lead to important new insights.

For both science and mathematics education, rote learnings are far less important than the playing around with ideas that occurs when children engage in divergent thinking. Throughout childhood, play provides daily opportunity to strengthen this important approach to learning.

Motivation to Learn

Most young preschool children are naturally inquisitive. They are eager to learn about themselves and the world around them. Tasks are approached with enthusiasm and, contrary to popular belief, young children can spend relatively long periods of time concentrating on their individual interests. Gradually, however, this motivation to learn decreases in many children and sometimes dies completely. The reasons behind this change are many and beyond the scope of this [chapter]. A partial remedy can be offered, however.

Play serves as a powerful motivator for many children. It is a vehicle for learning that provides unique opportunities to strengthen interest and motivation. One reason for this is the fact that play is freely chosen by the child. Having selected one of several available activities, the child feels more in control, more able to make decisions about the direction the play will take. No one has forced the activity upon the child and thus motivation is high.

Play is also a process-oriented activity. The end product is far less important than the process of actually playing. Failure, embarrassment and incorrect responses are infrequent in the play setting. This builds self-confidence and motivates the child to engage in further play experiences.

Play is hands-on activity where children are learning by doing. Children in the play experience are not passive observers, but rather actively engaged in moving, manipulating and exploring things in their world. Not only is this hands-on experience fun, it is also highly motivating to the play participant.

Clearly, this motivation to learn is important to any educational endeavor. Without it, the task is a slow and difficult one. The fields of mathematics and science are no exception. Students need the motivation to strike out with enthusiasm into unknown areas, seeking to learn and grow from the rich experiences presented to them. Play helps nurture this attitude in many children.

TOMORROW'S CHALLENGE

Those who wish to meet the challenges of tomorrow must be willing and able to adjust to change. Top-quality programs in science and mathematics must go beyond the standardized lecture-demonstration format and strive to nurture children to become creative problem-solvers. Jean Piaget effectively summarizes this challenge as follows:

> The principal goal of education is to create men who are capable of doing new things, not simply repeating what other generations have done ... men who are creative, inventive and discoverers. The second goal of education is to form minds which can be critical, can verify, and not accept everything they are offered. The great danger today is of slogans, collective opinions, ready-made trends of thought. We have to be able to resist individually, to criticize, to distinguish between what is proven and what is not. So we need pupils who are active, who learn early to find out by themselves, partly by their own spontaneous activity and partly through materials we set up for them. We learn early to tell what is verifiable and what is simply the first idea to come to them. (Elkind, 1981, p. 29)

Childhood play provides numerous opportunities for creative responses to challenging issues. It enables children to learn key concepts and develop essential attitudes toward learning. Its value and importance to mathematics and science learning should not be overlooked.

DISCUSSION QUESTIONS

1. Why are early experiences important to later performance in math and science?

2. What are the theoretical rationales for science and math learning through play?

3. Which attitudes can be developed and influenced while children are at play?

4. How does play relate to the learning of science and mathematics?

38. MONTESSORI: RIGHT OR WRONG ABOUT NUMBER CONCEPTS?

by Jerold P. Bauch and Huei-hsin Joyce Hsu

When Maria Montessori "invented" her method for teaching the street urchins from the slums of Rome in the early 1900s, she showed remarkable insight into children's needs and unique ways to help them learn. Montessori was truly a scientific person, earning the first medical degree granted to a woman in Italy and studying such diverse fields as pedagogy, anthropology, and psychiatry. When she was asked to develop a preschool program for the street children of Rome, she made a quantum jump forward in both instructional theory and teaching materials.

On the current early childhood education scene, both the Montessori theory and the related materials are of continuing interest. Hundreds of Montessori preschool programs are in progress across the United States, and some Montessori methods have been adapted to many other classrooms. The visitor interested in how young children learn about mathematics will immediately be drawn to the very special materials designed by Montessori and used in exactly the same way today. But was she right? Did she *really* understand how young children acquire initial number concepts?

MONTESSORI'S INSIGHT

Between 1898 and 1900, Montessori was observing and teaching young children from the insane asylums of Rome. She used a multisensory approach to "awaken their dormant senses" (Montessori 1964) and made materials that would develop a deep understanding of mathematics. In the first Montessori school, opened in 1907, children could be seen working with equipment that was designed to teach seriation, one-to-one correspondence, grouping, counting, and classification (Standing 1962). Contemporary Montessori schools are using "golden beads" when children work in base ten into the thousands; the spindle boxes for the cardinal numbers one to nine and the concept of zero; the sandpaper numerals to develop a multisensory perception of the numerals; the Seguin boards to establish the place value of ones and

tens; and number rods for the series of natural numbers one to ten.

Since Montessori was not encumbered with the developmental theories of Jean Piaget, she believed that young children could learn quite abstract concepts and operations in arithmetic at an early age. Kohlberg (1968) indicated that the most distinctive features of Montessori's theory were her emphases on classification, seriation, and one-to-one correspondence. On these points she was very close to the views presented later by Piaget. He considered number to be an example of logico-mathematical knowledge and that the concept of number was a synthesis of class and asymmetrical relations. Piaget stressed classification, seriation, and one-to-one correspondence in the construction of number concepts. He also thought that children built their concepts of number by reflective, or mental, abstraction. But Montessori believed that number concepts can be spontaneously learned and abstracted through manipulating the didactic materials in the preschool classroom. She was convinced that children could actually learn the concept of zero and do additive and multiplicative operations in the age range of three to six. Little change has taken place in the theory or the practice of Montessori education, and most Montessori preschool programs use the didactic materials in exactly the same way as suggested by Montessori eighty years ago.

WHAT WORKS AND WHAT DOESN'T?

We now have fifty years of experience with Piaget's theory and a rapidly accumulating body of specific research-based knowledge about how children actually learn mathematics. This half century of progress shows that Montessori was correct more often than not and that some of her ideas, teaching methods, and materials were not consistent with Piagetian theory. In some instances, the research base provides evidence that supports Montessori over Piaget (Hsu 1987). Since weakness in basic number facts and concepts is one of the most

See pages 335–36 for acknowledgment and references.

common problems of children who are having trouble in arithmetic (Russell and Ginsburg 1984), this [chapter] will be restricted to the basic pre-number and number concepts. Comparisons will be made among Montessori's ideas, Piagetian theory, and indicators from current empirical research.

The common number concepts that should be mastered by young children, identified in fourteen textbooks for preservice teachers (Hsu 1987), are (1) classification (sorting or grouping); (2) seriation (ordering); (3) one-to-one correspondence (matching or pairing); (4) comparison (more than, less than, and as many as); (5) rational counting; and (6) recognition and comprehension of cardinal numerals. These same concepts are part of the content of most recent textbooks for children in kindergarten.

Counting

Montessori put great faith in counting tasks with the didactic materials, but both Kohlberg (1968) and Lavatelli (1970) indicated that Piaget viewed classification and ordering as necessary mental operations in the counting process. In the Montessori model, children learn to count as they experience the meaning of the numerals in a concrete way. They count distinct red and blue sections on each number rod and then count the total units on two number rods (also a preview of addition).

Piaget did not think that this kind of counting was of much value for preoperational children because of the absence of the ability to conserve. In his perspective, counting has no meaning without the mental operations implied in a later stage of development and plays little part in the equivalence of two sets when working on one-to-one correspondence. He would certainly have criticized the place-value activities of the golden beads and other materials for this same reason. In fact, recent empirical evidence shows that preschool children in a Montessori program demonstrate an acceleration toward the stage of concrete operations (White, Yussen, and Docherty 1976; Yussen, Mathews, and Knight 1980). After children had progressed through the Montessori curriculum using the concrete materials in the prescribed ways, they outperformed children from traditional nursery schools on Piagetian seriation tasks and were also more advanced in classification (Morgan 1978; Savage 1973; White, Yussen, and Docherty 1976; Yussen, Mathews, and Knight 1980). The acquisition of classification and seriation strategies is a vital step in the progression of mathematics ability, and the Montessori method appears to have accelerated the development of these skills.

Whereas Montessori demonstrated how children learn counting with her didactic materials, Piaget thought counting was only a mechanical action until the children acquired the mental operation of number conservation. According to current research, counting precedes one-to-one correspondence in the sequence of development and is a prerequisite to understanding number conservation (Fuson, Secada, and Hall 1983; Gelman and Gallistel 1978; Kingma and Koops 1984; Russac 1978).

Concept of Zero

Montessori believed that children learn the quantity of each number from one to ten through manipulating the number rods. When they sort the forty-five spindles into trays labeled from 9 to 0 and end up with no spindles to place in the "0" tray, they will gain understanding of the zero concept. Piaget has said that children cannot understand zero in a mathematically correct way until much later in development when they have achieved formal operational thought, especially reversibility and conservation. Contrary to Piaget's views, the concept of zero as "none" or the "empty set" is commonly included in current textbooks for young children. Kraner (1978) tested children in the range of ages 3 through 6½ and found that comprehension of zero occurs between ages 5½ and 6—considerably earlier than Piaget suggested.

Control of Error

Montessori designed materials that show errors in a visible or obvious way. Among the Montessori equipment manipulated by the children is a series of knobbed cylinders that fit into holes in a long wooden block. The cylinders vary by diameter, height, or both. If a child ends up with the tallest cylinder and the shortest hole, an error is apparent. In another example, when children sort spindles into the numbered trays and have one or more left over, this mismatch indicates an obvious mistake. Most of the Montessori equipment for learning number concepts has this error-control feature, and it virtually eliminates a need for evaluation or correction by the teacher. This feature would not be consistent with Piaget's view of logico-mathematical knowledge (Kamii 1982; Kamii and DeVries 1976), in which feedback can only be perceived from the internal consistency of logic. Yet it is precisely the self-correcting nature of the Montessori materials that is so highly prized by preschool teachers and often used in programs for young children with learning delays or handicaps.

One-to-One Correspondence

Children have extensive experience with one-to-one correspondence before they arrive in preschool programs, with everything from buttoning their own clothing (one button: one button-hole) to the number of people and chairs or place settings at the dinner table. Many experiences planned for children in the Montessori curriculum are aimed at this concept. For example, children practice with different clothing fasteners on the dressing frames; they line up the pink tower next to the broad stair and compare other items to each other by length or height. In this situation it appears that everyone is on the right track. Montessori, Piaget, and most modern researchers agree that one-to-one correspondence is prerequisite to the concept of cardinal numbers (Barron 1979; Dawes 1977); is important in understanding "more than," "less than," and "as many as" relations (Kennedy 1984); and is one of the early counting principles (Brairs and Siegler 1984; Gelman and Gallistel 1978).

SUMMARY

Although some questions about young children's acquisition of number concepts are yet to be resolved, the ideas and methods first presented by Montessori eighty years ago stand up well when evaluated through the lens of current research. Considerable difference of view is evident between Montessori and Piaget about the importance of certain concepts and the level of cognitive development necessary for genuine understanding. But those teachers who use Montessori methods and materials with young children should be comforted that they are on solid ground. Textbooks for teachers, books that guide the children, and many substantial research studies support the main Montessori position. In fact, further empirical evaluation and research on Piaget's views may be in order to reconcile theory, research, and practice.

DISCUSSION QUESTIONS

1. What are some of Montessori's special approaches for learning mathematics?

2. Does the current research support Montessori methods in helping young children learn number concepts?

3. Can children learn some number concepts at an earlier age than the Piaget theory would indicate?

4. How can Montessori practices be used in any early childhood education setting? Should they be used?

39. THEORETICAL FRAMEWORK FOR PRESCHOOL SCIENCE EXPERIENCES

by Robert F. Smith

Recently I received an advertisement announcing a newsletter for early childhood educators. The brochure contained a sample science lesson you could eat—"Sink and Float: Jello." Intrigued, I read through the instructions provided. The lesson involved first graders making Jello and then adding some or all of the following ingredients: blueberries, sliced bananas, sliced peaches or strawberries, grated coconut, and crushed pineapple. Children were to observe which of these items floated and which sank. Up to this point, everything seemed pedagogically sound, but then I read further: "Some of these things will float. Some will sink. Talk about *why* things float or sink" (italics mine).

Obviously, experienced teachers will expect answers in terms of what the child can *see*, such as which objects float and which objects sink. Children may enjoy classifying objects into these two groups. Teachers should encourage children to experiment with floating and sinking and accept simple answers that refer to the object's weight, size, or shape.

Yet beginning teachers with a strong science background, using the instructions in the advertisement as a guide, might be misled by the direction, "Talk about *why*" and expect a more sophisticated explanation from the children. The cause-effect relationships, however, that cause some objects to sink and others to float (buoyancy and displacement concepts) are beyond the intellectual capabilities of preschoolers and most primary grade students (Ward, 1978; Wolfinger, 1982).

Another example of inappropriate science for 3-, 4-, and 5-year-olds would be to expect them to understand concepts such as *air is almost everywhere; air is real—it takes up space;* or *air presses on everything from all sides* (Harlan, 1984). Because air is invisible, such concepts are not understood by the young child (Kamii and DeVries, 1978). Iatridis (1981), in designing a science curriculum for 4s and 5s, eliminated air as a topic at the suggestion of both science and early childhood educators.

Some experiences with air *are* appropriate for preschoolers. They can *feel* air as they try to blow up a balloon; they can *feel* air on their faces as they release it from the balloon; they can *feel* air (wind) on their faces on a windy day. They can also *observe* the effects of wind, for example, papers or leaves blowing, or sailboats moving across water.

Many new and inexperienced teachers depend on the literature (journals, magazines, curriculum guides, newsletters) for appropriate science activities. Some teachers take it for granted that what they find in these resources is developmentally or pedagogically sound. This is not always the case, as the examples I have cited demonstrate.

A theoretical framework for a preschool science curriculum, with illustrative experiences, can help preschool teachers develop their ability to let—or make—appropriate science experiences happen in their classrooms. In addition, such a framework can help teachers evaluate activities or experiences suggested in the literature in terms of developmental appropriateness for 3-, 4-, and 5-year-olds.

A THEORETICAL FRAMEWORK

A theoretical framework can be developed by integrating research that examines how children construct knowledge and how appropriate science experiences contribute to children's ability to construct knowledge or learn about their world.

The most significant research about the construction of knowledge was done by Piaget (1929; 1954; 1973). Kamii and DeVries (1978) and Forman and Kuschner (1983) discuss the theoretical significance of Piagetian constructivism and its implications for early childhood education. More specifically, Howe (1975) and Smith (1981) discuss the implication of Piagetian theory for early childhood *science* education.

For Piaget, *the foundation upon which all intellectual development takes place is physical knowledge, knowledge that comes from objects. This includes information about the properties of objects (their shape, size, textures, color, odor), as well as knowledge about how objects react to*

See page 336 for acknowledgment and references.

different actions on them (they roll, bounce, sink, slide, dry up). Children construct physical knowledge by acting on objects—feeling, testing, smelling, seeing, and hearing them. They cause objects to move—throwing, banging, blowing, pushing, and pulling them, and they observe changes that take place in objects when they are heated, cooled, mixed together, or changed in some other way. As physical knowledge develops, children become better able to establish relationships (comparing, classifying, ordering) between and among the objects they act upon. Such relationships (logicomathematical knowledge according to Piaget) are essential for the emergence of logical, flexible thought processes.

Informal experiences (for example, at the water table, or in the animal center, sandbox, or block corner) allow children to explore objects freely and discover their properties, what they are made of, and how they react when acted on in various ways. Iatridis (1981) found that children exposed to specific science experiences using carefully selected materials "increased their self-directed discovery (active, child-initiated exploration rather than aimless handling of materials) and verbalized curiosity" (p. 26). Such behaviors, that is, active exploration initiated by children themselves and increased verbalization, contribute to the child's construction of knowledge. Educators and researchers have long advocated the importance of experiences in preschool science education that promote

the development of these behaviors (Flavell, 1963; Greenberg, 1975; Hawkins, 1965; Hochman and Greenwald, 1963).

A theoretical framework for a preschool science curriculum integrates the child's construction of knowledge with science-related experiences and promotes active, child-initiated action on objects and observations of changes.

Using such a framework, criteria have been developed (see Table 1) that can be used to determine whether the science experiences suggested for preschoolers are developmentally appropriate. They can also be used by teachers to develop their own preschool science curriculum.

The teacher's role in implementing such a curriculum is a challenging one:

1. Teachers should be aware of daily experiences that might involve science, for example, painting (Lasky and Mukerji, 1980), cooking (Wanamaker, Hearn, and Richarz, 1979), or playing with musical instruments (McDonald, 1979). Such an awareness enables the teacher to capitalize on the children's involvement with a science experience, either by leaving them alone to pursue their own curiosities or initiatives (Kamii and DeVries, 1978), or by encouraging them to observe more closely, ask questions, and compare and classify what they are acting on, or to make their own discoveries (Iatridis, 1981).

2. To encourage and facilitate children's explorations with science-related phenomena, a variety

Table 1. Criteria for Developmentally Appropriate Science Experiences (ages 3 to 5)

Are the materials selected those that
- children will naturally gravitate to for play?
- provide opportunities for the development of perceptual abilities through total involvement of the senses (perception of color, size, shape, texture, hardness, sound, etc.)?
- encourage self-directed problem solving and experimentation?
- children can act upon—cause to move—or that encourage children's observations of changes?

Do the experiences that evolve from children's play with the materials
- provide opportunities for the teacher to "extend the child's learning by asking questions or making suggestions that stimulate children's thinking" (NAEYC, 1986, p. 10)?
- allow for additional materials to be introduced gradually to extend children's explorations and discoveries?
- allow for differences in ability, development, and learning style?
- allow children to freely interact with other children and adults?
- encourage children to observe, compare, classify, predict, communicate?
- allow for the integration of other curriculum areas?

of equipment and materials should be made available (Holt, 1977). Kamii and Devries (1978) suggest principles for planning physical knowledge activities that are applicable and that involve children with materials related to science experiences. The way in which materials are introduced to young children can maximize their initiative. The teacher can put out materials that children will naturally gravitate toward. For example, a variety of musical instruments can be displayed to encourage children's explorations with sound. Or the teacher can present specific materials and ask children to think of different things they could do with these materials. One set of such material might initially include an inclined plane and different-sized balls or other round objects. Objects that are not round or toy trucks and cars of different sizes can gradually be added to the collection when the teacher feels it is the right moment "to enter the child's world" (Forman and Kuschner, 1983).

3. In guiding children's experiences in science, teachers should remember that "meaningful learning is an active, self-regulated process" (Forman and Kuschner, 1983, p. 123). Any attempt to shape the child's behavior according to predetermined objectives may interfere with this self-regulation. Forman and Kuschner (1983) clearly describe when and how teachers can begin appropriate learning encounters with young children and set forth the following special requirements: skillful techniques for observing children's behavior, a broad child development knowledge base with which to interpret observed behaviors, good entry techniques, and sensitive timing.

ILLUSTRATIVE EXPERIENCES FOR 3- AND 4-YEAR-OLDS

Developmentally appropriate experiences that illustrate how teachers can let or make science happen in the preschool include the following:

Paints

Young children love to paint; they enjoy experimenting with color and can be quite creative in their artistic expression. Teachers can use experiences with painting to heighten children's awareness of colors and color changes. As children become familiar with the primary and secondary colors through painting activities (naming or labeling colors is not necessary at this time), color

matching and sorting on the basis of visual comparisons can gradually be introduced. "Visual comparisons remain the principal concept for young children to master" (McIntyre, 1981a, p. 40). As the children use different colors in their paintings, the teacher can encourage them to match the colors of their paints to the clothes they are wearing or to other objects in the room. Further opportunities for developing color perception can be made available through additional materials or experiences (Lasky and Mukerji, 1980; McIntyre, 1981a; Neuman, 1978; Schools Council, 1973b).

During their painting activities, children may mix paints together and produce a new or different color. Teachers should help children focus on this color change; the observation that a change has taken place, however, is more important at this stage than what combination of colors produced the change. Children can even be encouraged, through the teacher's example, to experiment by mixing different paints together to discover what happens. An activity that allows children to combine colors (mixing food colors in water or mixing paints), is an excellent example of observing changes in objects, a type of physical knowledge activity described by Kamii and DeVries (1978) in which observation is primary and the child's action is secondary.

Tactile experiences can also evolve from children's painting. Their dried, finished products may be lumpy or bumpy in some spots and smooth in others. Having children carefully feel their dried paintings enhances their sense of touch and begins to focus their attention on different kinds of surfaces. Appropriate language—smooth, rough, bumpy, scratchy—can be introduced by the teacher. Thus, an added dimension of an object's properties, that of roughness or smoothness, begins to become part of the child's developing knowledge. Zeitler (1972) found that a small sample of 3-year-olds did not mention texture (roughness or smoothness) of an object as one of its properties. More informal experiences, similar to those described here, can encourage 3- and 4-year-olds to focus on texture.

Sounds

"Listening to, making, and sharing sounds with others are enjoyable activities for young children and provide a base for simple generalizations and understandings related to the science of sound" (McIntyre, 1981b, p. 34). Thus, classrooms for preschoolers should include a sound corner where a variety of musical instruments are available for the children to play with. At first, only a few instruments should be displayed for exploration. As children become familiar with the sounds these instruments make, others can be added. As children freely explore each instrument, they rely on their sense of hearing—they begin to discriminate between the sounds each different instrument makes. They are also actively involved in producing their own sounds; they experiment by plucking, banging, tapping, striking, or shaking. Children as young as 3-years-old begin to see that action or movement is necessary in order to have sound.

When children become familiar with each of the different instruments, games can be introduced to help them develop their perception of sound. The teacher can select one instrument at a time, hide it from the children's view, and make a sound with it; the children can guess which instrument the teacher is playing. To help children make discriminations, the teacher can make sounds with two instruments simultaneously; the children have to guess what both instruments are. Children can also play these guessing games with each other, and tape recordings can be made of the instrument sounds for children to identify. To learn a child does not always need teaching.

Children should have greater opportunity to listen to and identify ordinary sounds in the classroom. For example, voices, moving chairs, splashing water, footsteps, tumbling blocks, and cars or trucks rolling across the floor. They can also listen for sounds outside the classroom. The teacher plays a key role in helping children focus their listening on specific sounds and in introducing appropriate vocabulary: "the *chirp* of a bird, the *thump* of a heartbeat, the *crunch* of footsteps on gravel" (Schools Council, 1972a, p. 31). Children can be asked to talk about the sounds they like and dislike, they can imitate sounds of familiar objects and show that they have associated specific sounds with specific objects, and everyday events in the classroom can be used to help children identify loud and soft sounds.

Foods

Cooking activities are an integral part of the preschool curriculum and provide a unique opportunity to engage children in developing sight, touch, taste, and smell. Foods, fruits and vegetables in particular, vary in color, texture, taste, smell, size, and shape. All these properties can be explored by the children during snack time or a special cooking activity (Christenberry and Stevens, 1984; Parent Nursery School, 1974; Wanamaker et al., 1979). Three- and 4-year-olds tend to focus on taste because this is the most desirable property of a particular food. The teacher's role, however, is not only to provide the children with enjoyable tasting experiences; she or he can also intervene by helping the children focus on other properties of a food. Appropriate questions might include: "How does it feel?"; "Can you find another fruit that feels the same (or different)?"; "Can you find something on the table the same shape as your orange?"; or "Which smell do you like the best?"

The shape of a particular fruit can be used to explore the movement of round objects. Children can roll an apple or orange across various surfaces; they can compare the action of the apple with that of a pear or banana ("Which fruit rolls best?" "Can you find other objects in the room that roll like your apple?").

In addition to offering children opportunities to act on individual foods—to feel, taste, and smell—experiences with cooking also give children chances to observe changes taking place: corn seeds changing to popcorn, cream turning to butter, apples changing into applesauce. Making applesauce in two different ways enables children not only to observe changes taking place, but also to observe and compare different textures and tastes. Children can first cook apples to make applesauce; they can also grind raw apples, with the teacher's assistance, with a small food mill. They then can compare textures and tastes of cooked and raw applesauce.

CONSTRUCTING LOGICAL RELATIONSHIPS

These examples of science experiences suitable for 3- and 4-year-olds are only a small sampling of what can be incorporated into a science curriculum for them. Other experiences could include: water play (Kamii and DeVries, 1978); discoveries with sand (Hill, 1977); science using toys (Hirsch, 1984; Schools Council, 1972b); investigating themselves (Holt, 1977; Schools Council, 1973a); and investigating animals (McIntyre, 1984). Only selected specialists are referenced here, but many fine nursery educators have been encouraging activities like these for years.

As preschoolers construct physical knowledge, they will be better equipped to begin constructing logical relationships between and among the objects they have already encountered. Such relationships include classifying objects on the basis of a common property (size, shape, color, texture, taste); ordering objects according to a common property (size, weight, length); and comparing objects (shorter-longer, darker-lighter, smoother-rougher, thicker-thinner).

An activity that involves the movement of objects (Kamii and DeVries, 1978) clearly illustrates how these relationships begin to emerge. The teacher presents each child with a straw and shows them a box containing several of each of the following items: tissues, popsicle sticks, straws, empty cans (frozen orange juice, coffee), marbles, and small blocks. She or he then asks, "Can you find something that you can blow across the floor?" (p. 6). As the children look at each object in terms of its blowability, they begin to think, "at some vague, intuitive level" (p. 7), about each object's weight, shape, or both. Consideration of these objects' properties at this time depends on previous knowledge constructed through action and observation. As children experiment to find an answer to the question, they begin to construct logicomathematical relationships. For example, children might group the objects according to the "things that *never* move (a block)" and "things

that *always* move (a tissue, marble, straw, and popsicle stick)" (p. 7). The same objects could also be categorized according to whether they slide or roll.

CONCLUSION

A theoretical framework, then, that evolves both from research and experiences with young children, enables preschool teachers to provide appropriate environment and science experiences to help children learn about their world. New and inexperienced teachers can use this framework as a guide for developing their own science curriculum and also as a criterion for evaluating those activities suggested in the literature. In fact, such a framework serves to heighten teachers' awareness that science is not necessarily a separate curriculum area: "Science in the infant [early childhood] classroom is very much interwoven into the activities that normally go on there, it is indistinguishable as a separate entity...." (Schools Council, 1972a, p. 2).

DISCUSSION QUESTIONS

1. Why is it important that early science experiences be concrete and specific to the child's ability to observe and manipulate?

2. What are some of the *inappropriate* science teaching practices?

3. How do the theories of cognitive development provide guidance for teaching science to young children?

4. What are the criteria for planning or evaluating science experiences for young children?

5. How can the teacher integrate the curriculum content areas for science learning?

6. What are some broad concepts about science that should be part of the early childhood curriculum?

40. MUSIC IN THE EARLY CHILDHOOD CURRICULUM

by Manny Brand and David E. Fernie

Young children love exploring their world, a world that very much includes sound and music. Not only do these ever-present aural stimuli ignite the same curiosity within the child as a new toy or a leaping frog, but children seek to actively explore and understand their musical environment. Traditionally, children's natural sensitivity to and interest in sounds, voice qualities and musical instruments justify music in the early childhood curriculum. There are many other reasons, however, why music is so important during these early years.

Today, music is an ever-present companion for children. In addition to the radio and the record player, music is heard on television and in elevators and supermarkets. Many young children even have their own cassette tape recorders and are able to take their music wherever they go. While music pervades their environment, it is important that children do more than just "bathe" in this musical milieu.

The value of a favorable music curriculum for children 2 to 8 years of age cannot be overemphasized, since these years represent the optimum opportunity for influencing an individual's musical potential. Recent research shows that music aptitude develops during these early years (Miller, 1980). This, of course, does not mean that children over the age of 8 or 9 cannot learn music. Love of music, performance skills and music achievement can all be developed at any age; but a child's musicality can best be influenced during the early years.

Formerly, music psychologists generally agreed that music aptitude was hereditary. They believed that environmental factors, including music activities and instruction, had absolutely no effect on music aptitude. Today, however, most music psychologists acknowledge that music aptitude is only partly innate. Regardless of the level of music aptitude one is born with, that level will never be realized in achievement without positive musical experiences during the early years (Gordon, 1979). Early childhood, then, is a critical period for music aptitude, just as it is for the promotion of cognitive development and the acquisition of language.

Thus, not only are early informal and formal environmental influences in music essential, but the real challenge is to integrate the content of music in ways that are consistent with children's developmental levels and interests. By promoting activities that turn children's interest to active and directed involvement with music, we help children to learn about the variety and the elements of music and to develop musical skills. To accomplish these goals, we advocate an emphasis on vocal development, instrumental skills and music appreciation in Early Childhood curricula.

VOCAL DEVELOPMENT

Singing is the most personal, natural and earliest form of musical activity. Children have been using their voices from the moment of birth, experimenting with vocal sounds. They express cries of pain and coos of pleasure, and they "play" with vocal timbres by manipulating the tongue, lips and vocal cords. These sounds are the precursors of singing.

Children's initial song repertoire consists of the little melodies they create during their play. The observant teacher can begin by imitating these songs, thus highlighting children's actions. The teacher may also make up melodic phrases depicting classroom events and concerns. For example, the teacher can communicate about children's appearances, clothing and physical features through song. Even suggestions and directions can be easily sung. In turn, children will invent further singing responses. During play activities such as painting and block-building, children can sing and thus continue to build their singing voices in a very natural way (Andress et al., 1973).

Young children also enjoy songs selected from various song books. For instance, Mother Goose songs and songs about animals are early favorites. Teachers may also want to select several available children's books that combine illustrations, text and songs, such as *A Mouse in My House* (Houston, 1972). Songs that appeal to children usually have a simple and repetitive melody, a steady

See pages 336–37 for acknowledgment and references.

rhythm and a limited melodic range. Generally, very young children are most comfortable staying in a five-note range (e.g., *d* to *a*). This range is soon expanded to an octave (e.g., *b* to *b*). Typically, 8-year-old children can sing with a slightly wider range.

Before introducing a song to children, the teacher should obviously like the song, be able to sing it comfortably, and plan its introduction. Haines and Gerber (1980) offer several ways of introducing a new song, such as showing pictures of animals or objects featured in the song or asking children to find new or "silly" words in the song. After focusing the children's interest in the song, the teacher should sing or play a recording of part or all of the song (depending on the age of the children). Next, the starting pitch needs to be established. The teacher should cue the children by singing on pitch, "one, two, ready, sing," in the tempo of the song. Young children enjoy repeating a song, particularly if movement or gesture is added or if a few simple rhythm instruments are used to accompany the song.

The primary purpose of singing is to enable young children to sing their own melodies and those of others, and to use the voice in expressive ways (Andress, 1980). In addition, singing activities obviously expand children's song repertoire, and enable them to perform with the most personal instrument: the voice.

INSTRUMENTAL SKILLS

Many music educators believe that music education for young children should begin with an emphasis on the discovery of sounds (Zimmerman, 1971; Biasini, Thomas and Pogonowsky, 1972). This process of discovering environmental and body sounds is in keeping with children's natural learning style of exploring and experimenting, and generally precedes the use of actual musical instruments. Young children might be encouraged to locate and/or produce interesting and different sounds from non-musical sources, such as those made by clicking tongues and squeaking closet doors.

Some Early Childhood teachers have created music activity centers that provide planned sound-explorations. Andress (1980) describes several successful music activity centers. Take, for example, the sound box. This plywood or cardboard box has a lid, floor and entry way, and measures approximately four feet per slide. Inside the box, there is a removable sound wall, which can be changed to emphasize a variety of sounds. One panel might be covered with several different sandpaper textures. Various car-shaped blocks, some covered with sandpaper, are used by the child to produce a variety of "scratchy" and "swishy" sounds. By changing sound panels, children can easily explore high and low, short and long, fast and slow, or unusual sounds.

Locating and producing these sounds are preliminary steps to music learning; for, if music learning is to take place, the teacher must actively focus children's attention on the unique properties of sounds. When the teachers asks which sounds are high or low in pitch, long or short, loud or soft, the children are moving beyond mere sound awareness and toward an understanding of musical concepts. The characteristics of music—pitch, duration and volume—are the basis of all music, and attention to these components provides an excellent foundation for music learning.

Once a child has the opportunity to learn about musical characteristics through nonconventional sounds, classroom instruments are introduced. Classroom instruments usually refer to rhythm instruments such as cymbals, tambourines, triangles, maracas, woodblocks, sandpaper blocks, claves, rhythm sticks, bells and drums. Others range from the relatively expensive Orff instruments (e.g., high quality xylophones) to the inexpensive homemade variety (e.g., beans in an orange juice can). All are important in the Early Childhood music program.

These classroom instruments can be used in many ways. Initially, the children should freely experiment with the instruments while the teacher helps them find the different ways to make sounds and to use the instruments. Encourage the children to share and demonstrate what they have discovered about their instruments. Children enjoy using these instruments to keep the beat while the teacher sings or plays a song. These musical activities sensitize children to the steady beat or rhythm which is characteristic of so many kinds of music.

Follow-up activities might include having small groups of children assigned to play different parts or phrases of a song. Additionally, the teacher may want to have a child "compose" a simple rhythm to accompany a favorite song. Throughout all of these activities, it is important that the teacher encourage the children to analyze which rhythms are fast, slow or best fit the mood of a particular song. This concept of matching children's rhythmic creations to the style, mood and tempo of familiar songs is another important musical goal.

In addition to classroom instruments, young children can be given the opportunity to play standard musical instruments such as violin and piano. These piano and violin lessons for nursery school children emphasize the development of correct playing technique and the playing of simple nursery rhyme songs by ear. The most well-known approach is the Suzuki method of instruction, which incorporates carefully programmed learning sequences and an emphasis on imitation accompanied by frequent reinforcement (Zimmerman, 1971). Parental involvement is one of the cornerstones of the Suzuki approach, and parents are encouraged to surround their child with music beginning at birth. Actual lessons on miniature violins can begin at the age of 3 or 4.

Playing instruments is another effective way of introducing the joy of music to young children. Discovering the world of sound and achieving success in performance can provide a lasting involvement and genuine love of music.

MUSIC APPRECIATION

Music appreciation denotes enjoyment and understanding of music. Young children's active involvement with songs and musical instruments will contribute greatly to this goal. Unfortunately, music appreciation has not been emphasized in the early years because many have equated music appreciation with passive listening for sustained periods of time. In contrast, we believe that when a variety of music is experienced in developmentally appropriate ways, the goal of music appreciation can be successfully promoted in Early Childhood programs.

An appropriate approach to music appreciation seeks to actively involve the young child. For example, music can be played, then followed by movement activities and/or dramatization of actions evoked by the mood of the music. The teacher's role in promoting the foundations of music appreciation is also an active one. Initially, a few of the teacher's favorite recordings should be brought to the classroom and played. This effort is relatively simple, since no vocal or instrumental skills on the teacher's part are involved. Children will benefit from repeated listening and become familiar with these teacher-favorites. The teacher can easily comment on the enjoyment and meaning which these selections hold for him or her.

Teachers have traditionally used music to accompany activities from vigorous marching to peaceful waterplay, and authors have suggested appropriate selections for a wide variety of activities (see Nye, 1979). Yet this music serves as more than accompaniment to non-musical activities. It can signal, focus and heighten activities for young children. While evoking physical and emotional responses in children, the teacher is modeling the enjoyment that one can obtain from music.

The teacher's role in stimulating music appreciation, however, is more complex than merely dropping a needle or pushing a button at various times of the day. Since the goal is also to expand children's preferences, the repertoire should not reflect any one person's notion of "good" music, as it is likely to be both subjective and somewhat limited. In the attempt to present a variety of music, one should consider popular, classical, jazz, ethnic and even electronic music. Parents, other teachers and perhaps even the children can be sources for suggesting selections of diverse music. Children's music appreciation can be broadened as new selections are gradually introduced to complement those already familiar to them. Once children find music that evokes feeling and enjoyment, other important responses will follow. In the words of Rachel Carson (1960), "Once our emotions have been aroused, then we wish for knowledge about the object of our emotional response. Once found, it has lasting meaning" (p. 45).

Teachers can best promote children's understanding of vocal and instrumental music by being aware of the musical elements that children find salient. For example, McDonald (1979) suggests that children respond to music that is either highly rhythmic or highly melodic. Zimmerman (1971) supplements this view, contending that "the perception of loudness develops first, followed by pitch and rhythm, with perception of harmony developing last" (p. 28). Some guidance in selecting instrumental music is provided by Fullard (1976). This research found that children do recognize the timbre or tone color of instruments, and can discriminate between them on this basis. This suggests that music with variations in tempo and dynamics, performed by small ensembles with different timbres, may be appropriate to the preschooler's intellectual and discriminatory abilities. Since much vocal music is sung by a single performer, teacher-made cassette tapes featuring performers with different voice timbres might be enjoyed by young children. Room could be left for children to record their own singing voices on the tapes.

Records and tapes are somewhat abstract and removed from music performances. Music listening, therefore, can be made more concrete by using community resources that are often available to teachers and children. Musically skilled parents and high school students will often be willing to perform for, and involve, the receptive and somewhat awed young audiences. Trips to band and orchestral concerts can reinforce the pleasures of both performing and listening to music. These "real" experiences with music can inform children about the relationship between recorded and live music, and make them further aware of the diversity and very personal nature of music.

In conclusion, we have stressed the importance of music in Early Childhood curricula and suggested an appropriate approach to accomplish this goal. A focus on music appreciation, as well as on vocal and instrumental skills, can help young children establish a continuing involvement with the world of music. By both extending and directing their natural musical interests, children can experience the music of others and express themselves through this most enjoyable medium.

DISCUSSION QUESTIONS

1. What is the value of music in the early childhood education curriculum?

2. What is the role of singing in the musical development of young children?

3. How should the teacher plan the singing part of the early music experience?

4. What are appropriate instrumental skills for young children?

5. How can the teacher stimulate and develop music appreciation in young children?

41. APPRECIATE THE DRAWING AND DICTATING OF YOUNG CHILDREN

by Anne Haas Dyson

"Draw a picture and then we'll write a story about it." And so begins one of the most common early childhood activities, an activity that might result in children's first school reading texts (Veatch, Sawicki, Elliott, Barnette, and Blakey, 1973) or their first writing journals. Throughout the century, this is the way children whose teachers have primarily focused on the *language experience* approach have been learning to read, write and even spell, in classrooms around the country. This activity has received increased attention lately, as interest in early literacy has grown. Even preschool teachers are urged to give their young students journals in which to draw, dictate, and write (Rich, 1985).

Despite the value teachers have long placed on this activity, we have not looked carefully at the varied ways young children approach it. After all, this is an open-ended task; there are no parts to be assembled as in a puzzle: "[T]he blank sheet and salient edges of the page provide an immense number of potential 'degrees of freedom' which have to be reduced to workable order" (Freeman, 1977 p. 4). Children come up with their own puzzle parts, their own problems to solve. The solutions to those problems are reflected in their pictures and their texts.

Listen, for example, to a small group of kindergartners at work:

Jesse, Aron, Maggie, and Reuben are sitting together drawing. The boys stop their own work to study Maggie's drawing. She has just made three horses and two cows on a hill. The cows have udders. But in one case, the udders are long and angular and thus look like an extra pair of legs (see Figure 1).

> *Maggie:* "See, that one looks sort of scared? That one. That one." Points to the animal described above.
> *Jesse:* "That's not even a horsie!"
> *Maggie:* "That's a cow."

The children begin pointing to each animal, labeling them as *horsie* or *cow*. Maggie says that she isn't sure what the "scared" one is.

See pages 337–38 for acknowledgment and references.

> *Reuben:* "How many horses?"
> *Maggie:* "Horsie, horsie, fifteen-legged horsie..." Points to the questionable one which she had originally skipped. "...horsie, cow."
> *Aron:* "No, a six-legged horsie."

Later Maggie dictates:

> This is four horses.
> And one of them is a cow.

Maggie has now accounted for all the animals, but then she adds:

> And one of them is a six-legged cow. The end.

The efforts of Maggie and her peers illustrate how children use drawing, talk, and dictation to create order. In the course of drawing and talking, Maggie solved varied conceptual problems, including the drawn parts needed to represent the animals, the features distinguishing the category of *horse* from the category *cow*, and the number of horses and cows. The most puzzling piece of Maggie's drawing finally slipped into place with the coining of a new name, *a six-legged cow*.

Children's drawing and independent writing are valuable parts of the early childhood curriculum in their own right, but it is the linking of drawing and dictation that is of interest here.

CHILDREN AS MEANING MAKERS

Symbols: Tools for Order

During the early childhood years, children work to make their world a more orderly place. To organize and make sense of their experiences, children use the tools provided by symbols. For example, as children learn language, they learn about the objects, people, and events surrounding them—vague perceptions take form as they are put into words (Brown, 1973; Nelson, 1973; Vygotsky, 1962). Similarly, as children draw, they learn about the visual qualities of objects and also about the graphic properties of line, color, and shape (Smith, 1979). A child, for example, experiments

Figure 1. Maggie's horses and cows.

with paints and brush and discovers the possiblility of a wavy line. "Water," says the child, as previous experiences with water and the present experience with paints come together. A line that can symbolize water is discovered and the fluid qualities of water become salient as well.

Drawing: A "Literacy" Activity

Both drawing and language provide children with opportunities to reflect upon, organize, and share experiences. During the preschool and early school years, children become able to talk, not only about current activities, but also about past experiences and possible future ones (Bloom, 1975: Wells, 1981). They begin to tell stories as well (Applebee, 1978; Leondar, 1977; Stein, 1979); based on their experiences, children select significant events and organize them into plots with beginnings, middles, and ends.

Similarly, children's drawings become more complex during these years. After exploring lines and shapes, children begin to form basic objects—people, houses, trees; by 5 or 6 years, children combine these symbols into orderly scenes (Brittain, 1979; Smith, 1983).

Educators and researchers tend to talk about each kind of symbol separately. But when young children sit together around a work table, the teacher will most likely see drawing, talking, movement, and quite possibly singing and writing as well (Dyson, 1981; Korzenik, 1977). Recently the link between drawing and writing has received special attention, as interest has grown in young children as readers and writers (Gundlach, 1981; Lamme and Childers, 1983; Zalusky, 1983). Young children themselves make clear this link, as they claim to "write houses and stuff" (Dyson,

1982). Some kindergarten teachers in fact refer to children's drawing as "writing," seeing drawing as "the communication of thoughts rather than the production of pleasing visual images" (Hipple, 1985, p. 255; see also Newkirk and Atwell, 1982).

From this perspective, drawing is important primarily because it helps children plan and organize their dictated or written text. The interest is in children's developing ability to communicate a message independently from the pictures. Teachers might thus evaluate children's texts by asking whether they sound "written" as opposed to "spoken" (King, 1980). For example, is a child's word choice and arrangement clear? (Consider the ambiguous "He's shooting him" vs. "The large monster is attacking the small monster.") Is the text organized like a story? (Does it have a beginning, a middle, and an end?)

We quite naturally want to take advantage of the link between drawing and written language. But it seems important to acknowledge that, although drawing and writing are both ways of representing experience, they each have unique ways of capturing that experience and that, further, each is governed by the goals of the producer, the child, whose purposes may not match those of the teacher.

The Developing Symbolizer: The Child in Charge

Each symbolic material, be it modeling clay, language, paint or music, highlights different features of objects and events and is governed by a unique set of rules for structuring meaning (Golomb, 1974; Smith, 1979; Wolf and Gardner, 1981). As the opening discussion among Maggie, Jesse, and their peers illustrates, the drawing event

179

highlighted the visual qualities of animals to a degree that might not have arisen if, for example, Maggie were telling about a recent experience at a farm. When children draw, they are not simply communicating about their experiences; they are solving visual problems as well. The problems they solve influence the nature of the texts they create.

Further, children do not all use these materials in the same way. As children mature and gain experience, they learn new and more complex ways of manipulating paints, clay, language, and other symbolic material; but children *choose* from their repertoires the strategies that will help them reach their goals (Franklin, 1973). We must always ask, then, what is the child trying to do?

For example, children have different ways of using drawing. Wolf and Gardner (1979) note that some children, referred to as *patterners,* may be primarily interested in exploring the graphic qualities of colors or paint; these children may draw a design rather than represent anything in particular, or they may work toward depicting a scene. Other children, *dramatists,* seem much more interested in the talking than in the drawing; the drawing may simply serve as a prop for the talked-about experience.

THE CHILDREN AND THEIR CLASSROOM

The drawing and language samples shared in this [chapter] are taken from a participant observation study in a public school kindergarten in the western United States. The 18 class members, 7 girls and 11 boys, came from neighborhoods across this urban community and were of Anglo, Asian, Black, Hispanic, and mixed ethnicity.

The literacy curriculum centered on "journals" (construction paper books of approximately 13 drawing/writing products each). The children drew several times a week, dictating a story to their teacher and then copying part of it.

I observed in this classroom an average of twice a week for a 5-month period (January through May 1985). I audiotaped the children's spontaneous talk during journal time and their dictations, took notes on their drawing behaviors and photocopied their completed products. In addition, their teacher saved every other journal completed by each child, so I was able to view samples of the children's work done during the school year.

The following sections illustrate what the children did during journal time and, on the basis of those behaviors, suggest the purposes guiding their efforts. Samples of the children's work are drawn from across the school year. Two kindergartners introduced earlier, Maggie and Jesse, are highlighted, as their behaviors reflect the range observed, capture the general trends noted, and convey the mood, the spirit of their classroom. As we observe their work, keep in mind that the children are 5- and 6-year-olds; their ways of making sense of this task may be quite different from those of younger children.

THE CHILDREN'S INTENTIONS DURING JOURNAL TIME

Exploring and Refining the Graphic Medium

At the beginning of the school year, the children used lines and shapes to represent simple objects (houses, people). But, on occasion, they arranged dots, lines, and shapes in nonrepresentational ways. Like his peers, Jesse gave straightforward descriptions for his "stories":

> The story is about two circles.
> The two circles are in the water. (9/10/84)

> This is my dots and colors.
> I make them with my markers.
> I like them. (10/10/84)

> This is two different colors.
> These two different colors I like.
> They are purple and orange. (10/12/84)

Not only did children explore basic graphic elements, they worked to combine these elements into basic forms. For the month of October, for example, Jesse repeatedly drew a house, apparently directing his energy at solving the visual and motor problems it posed. His first houses were simply patches of color or rectangular shapes. Next came a triangular house (see Figure 2) and houses formed by pasting squares of paper together in varied arrangements. Finally, Jesse formed a house by putting a small triangle on top of a square; his basic symbol for a house was now set (see Figure 3).

Throughout this "house hunting" period, Jesse dictated a set text or a variation of that text.

> This is my house.
> I live in it.
> I just moved in.

Interestingly, Jesse had not moved during the year nor was a move planned. This seemed to be a text of convenience; his energy was directed toward his house.

Figure 2.   Jesse's triangular house.

Figure 3.   Jesse's final symbol for a house.

Figure 4.   Maggie's flowers and hearts.

In the opening months of school, Jesse's peer, Maggie, concentrated on hearts, flowers, and butterflies (see Figure 4). Although, like Jesse's house, the drawn objects became more refined, her text remained a simple descriptive statement:

> Two butterflies are flying around. (9/12/84)

> These are some flowers growing.
> There are some hearts keeping them company. (9/17/84).

> The hearts and flowers are growing and growing. (9/17/84)

> These are hearts and moons and lightning. (9/21/84)

Depicting a Scene

As the year progressed, the children as a group tended to create detailed scenes combining objects and figures that captured their attention in different arrangements. Maggie, for example, kept her interest in hearts, butterflies, and flowers; they now turned up in scenes with other figures and objects (see Figure 5). As her pictures became more elaborate, so did her texts:

> This is under the ocean and there is a whale with black lipstick on.
> And there's a flower lady under water.
> And there's insect butterflies.
> And there's a couple of stars and a moon
> and a rainbow and a sun. (11/6/84)

> This is a girl. She's playing in her garden and picking some flowers. And she's about to pick one more. That one more is the only tulip. The end. [One cloud in the sky is shaped like a heart.] (5/2/85)

The persistency of Maggie's interest in hearts and flowers is not atypical. Observers of young children's drawing have commented on children's repetition. Like adult artists, children explore particular themes (Gardner, 1980; Lindstrom, 1970; Smith, 1983). Similar repetition has been noted in a variety of media (Gardner, Wolf and Smith, 1982), including writing (Graves, 1983). Although repetition may at times prevent the child from exploring new ideas, it is generally an avenue to experimentation and growth (Gardner, Wolf and Smith, 1982), as illustrated by Maggie's increasingly more complex work.

Because for young children drawing is a frequent lead-in to composing, observers of young writers have suggested that, as children's drawings are elaborated, so are their texts (Graves, 1983; Zalusky, 1983). Although this was true for many children in the room, it was not true for all.

Playing a Story

By January, Jesse showed little interest in producing well-detailed scenes of figures and objects. Rather, he concentrated on what might be called two-dimensional dramatic play—on dramatizing action-packed adventures, as did Wolf and Gardner's dramatists.

Although Jesse was capable of drawing basic forms for people, vehicles, and houses, he seldom did so from January through April. His pieces, in fact, looked like those of a child still in the prerepresentational stage of drawing. In his efforts to play out an action, he did not labor over each object. He used simple patches of color to stand for places and objects (castles, spaceships), as he had first used patches to stand for houses. He seldom depicted the characters carrying out actions. Rather, he concentrated on the actions themselves, as his earlier occurring dots and strokes of color created bomb explosions and destructions by monsters.

For example, in producing Figure 6, Jesse dramatized a time bomb exploding on the moon. Jesse makes a small mark on his paper. Listen to a section of his talk:

> There's a time bomb. The time bomb's right here.

Jesse now begins writing numbers on his papers, accidentally making two ones, then turning the second into a zero.

> 10, 9, 8, 7, 6, 5, 4, 3, uh, 3, 2, 1.
> No, I don't need that 1.
> Zero. [loudly] Kerplooh.

He now makes dots all over his paper. "What are you doing, Jess?" ask two peers intently watching. Jesse replies:

> Now look how many moons are around the moon.

Jesse then makes an airplane sound and connects the dots. Later he dictates the following text:

> This is a time bomb.
> The time bomb is on a light.
> And it blowed up a light.

Jesse's text summarized, rather than relived, the basic drama that unfolded during his drawing and talking.

Coordinating Text and Picture

By the last months of the school year, the children as a group made more elaborate pictures and, also, appeared aware of the need to organize coherent messages about those pictures. Paul, for

Figure 5.   Maggie's garden scene.

Figure 6.   Jesse's time bomb explosion.

example, claimed to have eliminated one possible journal topic because of the difficulty of coming up with a text about it:

Reuben (to Paul): "Why do you always write about—make monsters?"
Paul: I make houses too. But I don't like to work in my journal making houses.
Author: Why?
Paul: I don't know. Because I don't know what to say about them.

In the event described in the opening of this [chapter], which took place in May, we saw Maggie and her peers work to make the visual image and language cooperate. Their efforts finally came together in the term six-legged cow—Maggie had something to say.

In May, Jesse faced similar coordinating problems. By then, he had begun to draw recognizable houses and people again, weaving them together into stories. Consider, for example, the production of Figure 7.

Jesse has already drawn a person (originally identified as his "friend"), a rainbow, and a house. To this point, these objects have not been related to each other in his accompanying talk. Jesse next draws a boot, remarking:

He [the man] lost his boot right here.

Now, the man and the boot are thematically connected. After drawing rain and smoke, which seems appropriate for a picture containing a boot, Jesse narrates this story:

And then he saw a boot and grabbed it and walked in [to his house].

Jesse then makes a line from the person's foot to the boot, crosses out the boot, and continues the line into the house.

Now it's [the boot's] not there any more.

Then Jesse dictates his story, which does not convey the entire narrative related during the drawing:

A man's walking home.
And he saw a boot.

Perhaps the clear image of the man in his picture, who obviously is not inside the house, led

Figure 7. **Jesse's lost boot picture.**

him to a dictation that also does not place the man inside the house.

Like Maggie's dictation about the cows and horses, Jesse's text hides the problem solving, the coordination of picture and talk, that resulted in this seemingly simple text.

ACKNOWLEDGING THE OPEN-ENDEDNESS OF OPEN-ENDED TASKS

A plain piece of paper and a box of crayons are simple tools, but with them children can pose for themselves complex tasks. As Brittain (1979, p. 19) writes, a child's drawing is "a challenge which is manifest on the paper." The children in the observed class explored the nature of the graphic medium, constructed a figure, depicted a scene or played out a story, and, at times, negotiated between talk and picture. The children's dictations were most often records of the experience of drawing, rather than records of past incidents.

Over the course of the year, as the children worked in their journals, they were learning about drawing, about the basic elements of literature, and about written language itself. As the year progressed, many children in the room began arranging their drawn symbols into scenes that reflected their interests and experiences. In addition, through their talking and drawing, the children were busy "inventing worlds" (Winner, 1982). They built scenes from a cast of *characters*; the characters were often engaged in *actions* and, in the latter half of the year, increasingly placed in *settings*. Thus, the children were organizing the basic stuff of which literature is made.

Finally, through dictation, the children were also learning about the nature of written symbols. The children appeared to progressively adapt their dictations to written language (see Sulzby, 1982, for a study of this phenomenon). For example, by May they more often paused after each clause, sometimes backing up and repeating a clause word by word for their scribe; they frequently observed as their dictations were transcribed and spontaneously attempted to read their texts themselves.

Despite this obvious literacy learning, the children's behaviors suggest cautions for those who assess and foster literacy growth. First, researchers and teachers *analyzing* children's texts must be aware of children's purposes. As noted earlier, adults may evaluate these texts for their quality as "stories." But children pose varied problems for

themselves during drawing and talking. So, if a child is not concerned with telling a story while drawing, that child may not dictate a story. For example, judging Jesse's ability to use conventional story grammar or explicit language by analyzing his "house" composition or Maggie's by studying her "cow" piece would seem strange—the children would be evaluated for tasks they did not complete (Newman, Griffin, and Cole, 1984). One might better judge those abilities by having children read wordless picture books or simply dictate stories on particular topics rather than on their own drawings (Sulzby, 1985; Magee and Sutton-Smith, 1983).

Second, the teachers must also be sensitive to children's purposes when *responding to* their efforts. For, as we talk to children, we help them reflect upon their goals and articulate their plans and strategies (Smith, 1983). We must, then, be sensitive to what those goals are. For example, in responding to Jesse's house composition, attempts to discuss his moving experiences would not seem as helpful as talking to him about his strategies for actually making the house. On the other hand, his "bomb" picture would seem an appropriate occasion for discussing the depicted imaginative experience.

Finally, the diversity of the children's behaviors also has implications for planning literacy programs for young children. A variety of text-producing experiences is needed to encourage a variety of kinds of text from different children. For example, Vivian Paley (1981) describes the imaginative stories her children dictated when those stories were acted out, as were "every other kind of printed word—fairy tales, storybooks, poems, and songs" (p. 12). These stories presented Paley with opportunities to help children think logically about themselves, their world, and, of course, their stories. Using another technique, Sylvia Ashton-Warner (1963) was able to elicit powerful personal narratives by writing special "key" words for children, like *kids*, *love*, and *ghost*, words that carry "their own illustrations in the mind" (p. 39). And, as many educators have recently discussed, children need regular opportunities to be writers, rather than dictators—to take pen in hand and explore the connection between meaning and print (Dyson, 1981, 1985).

In sum, whether composing with lines or language, children invent symbols for figures, objects, and events (Smith, 1983); engage in the thinking processes of organizing and abstracting as they work to portray their concepts (Brittain, 1979); and communicate their ideas to themselves and others. Depending upon their skill in each medium, their personal style, and their perception of the current task, the goals guiding individual children will vary. We must remember, then, that the plans we make for children are not necessarily the tasks they set for themselves. To accurately assess their performance, respond supportively to their efforts, and provide a range of literacy experiences, we must appreciate this diversity. And, like the children, we must take the time to observe, listen, and ask, "What are you doing, Jess?"

DISCUSSION QUESTIONS

1. How do drawing and talking relate to literacy development?

2. What is the role of symbols in language learning?

3. How can the use of journals enrich and expand the early childhood learning experience?

4. What are the appropriate teacher roles to encourage and maximize children's abilities to communicate?

5. How should teachers use open-ended questions and good listening skills to help children develop their literacy skills?

42. ENCOURAGING POSITIVE SOCIAL INTERACTION AMONG YOUNG CHILDREN

by Dwight L. Rogers and Dorene Doerre Ross

Some children easily find friends and convince peers to accept their ideas. Others find it difficult to relate to playmates, share materials, protect their rights, and deal with problems without causing conflict. In most classrooms there are a few isolates—children who are rejected by their peers. Many of these isolates are unable to enter into and negotiate social interactions. This [chapter] will explore two questions: Why is it important to help isolate-children develop more effective social skills and what can adults do to encourage children's positive social interactions?

FUTURE IMPLICATIONS

Bremm and Erickson (1977) note that children who are unable to identify and follow the rules of the social group not only disrupt interactions but are apt to be judged socially and intellectually incompetent. Children who are socially competent during their school years tend to "be tracked higher; [and] advised toward higher ranked curricula, post-secondary programs and jobs" (p. 159).

In addition to children's academic and career potential, early social adjustment in the peer group seems to predict adult social adjustment. Based on several longitudinal studies, Roff, Sells, and Golden (1972) conclude that the inability to form satisfactory peer relationships in the primary grades is associated with poor conduct evaluations in the military and with future delinquency. Similarly, Cowen, Pederson, Babijian, Izzo, and Trost (1973) found that poor peer relationships in third grade are the best predictor of future emotional and mental health problems.

While most of these studies have included elementary children, "we know very little about the effects of preschool social experiences on adjustment in kindergarten, the primary grades or beyond" (Moore, 1981, p. 107). Because the importance of elementary children's effective social interaction is so well established, it seems probable

that social competence during the preschool years also predicts future adjustment because it is during the early years that children develop social skills. How, then, can adults facilitate positive social interaction among preschool and primary children?

VALUES OF PEER INTERACTION

Although children need adult guidance to promote prosocial development, they also need opportunities to interact with peers with minimal adult intervention. Charlesworth and Hartup (1967) confirm this point in a study of social reinforcement among preschool children. They found that positive peer social reinforcement is more likely to occur during free play activities (e.g., blocks, dramatic play) than during adult structured or project-oriented activities (e.g., music, art, or table games).

Rubin (1972) found a significant correlation between the frequency of kindergarten children's contact with peers and the development of empathy skills (an important element of social competence).

Through peer interactions, children are confronted with real social problems. Honig (1982) argues that children benefit from opportunities to provide sympathy and help to peers in real "situations of distress or misfortune." Peer interactions provide concentrated experience in situations where children get natural and realistic feedback about the attitudes of others and areas of conflict (Wilkinson and Dollaghan, 1979; Denzin, 1977). In these situations, children continually try, modify, and discard behaviors as they develop their style and ability in social situations (Wilkinson and Dollaghan, 1979).

As children interact and experiment with social interaction strategies, they are more likely to imitate the positive social behavior of peers than the negative social behavior. Vaughn and Waters (1980) found that the behaviors of the most social-

See pages 338–39 for acknowledgment and references.

ly competent children are watched and imitated by their preschool peers more often than the behaviors of less socially competent children. Similarly, children who play with altruistic peers display significantly more altruism than those who do not have such models (Hartup and Coates, 1967).

Peer interaction also encourages prosocial behavior because positive responses to children's prosocial behavior reinforce that behavior (Charlesworth and Hartup, 1967; Moore, 1981). Moore also states that highly aggressive children are negatively reinforced when they are resisted and avoided. Such peer interactions give highly aggressive children "the message that their companions would like them to change" (p. 106).

Ways to Ensure Peer Interaction

Clearly, peer interaction provides children with the impetus to change, the opportunity to observe and model competent behavior, and reinforcement for prosocial interactions. In order to provide sufficient opportunities for peer interaction to occur, teachers must allocate time and space for process-oriented activities and play with minimal adult supervision. Only then will children, and not the adults, control the social interactions. Adults can anticipate some potentially troublesome situations and structure activities to avoid them (see Stone, 1978).

The development of empathy and other positive social interactions will be encouraged when children engage in activities such as block play, water and sand play, dramatic play, or similar activities with limited adult intervention. Teachers can circulate among the groups during these free play times, commenting about and asking questions pertinent to the children's play. The teacher's role is to show interest in—rather than to control—their play.

As Mead (1930) noted, individuals also grow through conflict, frustration, and the confrontation of problems. Children who are given the opportunity to resolve their own problems can test the validity and worth of the developing social skills and attitudes.

Hill (1982) summarizes the importance of activities with minimal adult supervision:

The inevitable conflicts that arise in social interaction provide important occasions for learning about other people's needs, wants, etc. . . . In early childhood classrooms, too much adult intervention might reduce the number of potential learning situations. (p. 9)

OBSERVE SOCIAL COMPETENCE

The first step in helping children become more successful in their social interactions is to observe them. Adults can identify children who are passive, aggressive, isolated, or effective in their social interactions.

During the primary grades, unpopular children are more likely to try to exert control over others (Putallaz and Gottman, 1981). Their demands usually lead to negative responses from others (Leiter, 1977). Dirk uses an assertive/aggressive style, with predictable results.

Dirk has a strong desire to be "the boss." Each time another child suggests an idea or states a desire, a disagreement occurs as Dirk reasserts his authority. . . . Dirk consistently gets his way but [his kindergarten] teacher notices many conflicts and disagreements centering around him. While Dirk has a few friends . . . he is not considered a highly desirable playmate by most of the children. (Ross and Rogers, 1982, pp. 26–27)

Other children, like Nellie, seem to say or do the wrong thing and are consistently excluded from play situations.

Few children seem to want to play with Nellie. . . . Her repeated attempts to enter the play of others are frequently rejected. When . . . children allow Nellie into their play, she is often excluded again within a few minutes. She seems unable to match her desires and behavior to the . . . group. By suggesting the wrong thing or by trying to alter the course of play inappropriately, she inadvertently alienates herself from the other children. Nellie constantly looks to the teacher for help in gaining entrance and acceptance in play situations. (Ross and Rogers, 1982, pp. 22–27)

Children who are social isolates are also a concern. These children seldom initiate contact or respond to the overtures of others, and thus seldom interact with their peers.

By observing children who are highly competent social negotiators like Kyle, teachers can identify strategies children use to maintain successful social relationships.

Everyone seems to enjoy playing with Kyle. He is able to suggest ideas to guide the direction of a play episode and yet also can smooth over potential disagreements. Kyle seems to understand and be able to meet the needs and interests of other children while at the same time fulfilling his own needs. The teacher seldom needs to intervene in a play group where Kyle is a participant. (Ross and Rogers, 1982, pp. 25-26)

Once these strategies are identified, children like Dirk and Nellie can be helped to adopt them in their play.

Sociometric measures can help validate observations and provide additional information about the children in the group. "Sociometric measures avoid the problems with assessing social competence from an adult's point of view by eliciting playmate preferences or nominations for each [child]" (Vaughn and Waters, 1981, p. 276).

One sociometric measure asks children to "assign pictures of each of their classmates to one of three faces according to how much they liked to play with that person: a happy face, a neutral face, and a sad face" (Asher, Singleton, Tinsley, and Hymel, 1979, p. 444). The scores derived from this measure are more reliable than the common technique of asking children to name the children whom they consider to be their most and least preferred playmates.

After making observations and using sociometric measures, teachers can evaluate the information, determine which social skills are lacking, and decide upon the most appropriate intervention for each child.

ELEMENTS OF SOCIAL SKILLS

Several skills have been identified as elements of effective social interaction for preschool and elementary children.

- *Ability to assess what is happening in a social situation.* The child must be able to determine the focus of the interactions and be sensitive to the problems encountered in that situation (Bremm and Erickson, 1977; Putallaz and Gottman, 1981; Spirak and Shure, 1974).

- *Skill to perceive and correctly interpret the actions and needs of the children* in the group at play (Bremm and Erickson, 1977; Hill, 1982; Mussen and Eisenberg-Berg, 1977).

- *Ability to imagine possible courses of action and select the most appropriate one* (Bremm and Erickson, 1977; Spivak and Shure, 1974)

Spivak and Shure also found that children who were able to generate a wide variety of possible solutions were more likely to solve the problem in a prosocial manner. They stress that the child must be sensitive to the possible consequences of an action in order to select the most appropriate solution. Further, the most appropriate solution seems to be one that will be perceived positively by other children (Gottman, Gonso, and Rasamussen, 1975; Asher, Oden and Gottman, 1977). We also found that the most competent children are able to select a strategy to meet both the needs of the children in the group and their own

needs simultaneously. Less effective children frequently use a variety of strategies to try to meet their own needs but are unable to predict the reaction of the children in the group (Ross and Rogers, 1982; Putallaz and Gottman, 1981). Unpopular children are more likely to try to alter the action and conversation of the group toward themselves rather than to determine a way to integrate their actions and conversation.

This kindergarten play episode illustrates the importance of these elements of effective social interaction.

> Dirk, Nathan and Sabrina were working together to build a slide out of large hollow blocks. Nellie was nearby building an independent structure. When the slide was completed, Dirk selected an H-shaped block and used it as a raft to slide down the slide. Nathan also grabbed a raft and Dirk called to Sabrina to get one too. Nellie, hoping to join their play, said "I'll get in behind Sabrina." Dirk emphatically told her to get her own. Nellie continued to try to join the play . . . in a variety of ways. . . . She suggested they all build a house. This idea was emphatically rejected. . . . She also . . . told the teacher several times and tried to use the teacher's authority. "The teacher says to let me on there." Finally, she . . . got the teacher and successfully joined the play. However, when she sat on the slide refusing to go down, she was soon excluded from play again. (Ross and Rogers, 1982, pp. 26-27)

As was often the case, Nellie was unable to determine the focus of the other children's play and unable to take into account their interests. Although she used a wide variety of strategies to enter the play, she was unable to predict the children's reactions and thus did not select a strategy that would be successful.

WAYS TO HELP CHILDREN

Increase Group Play

Encouraging group play is especially effective in helping children who are social isolates learn how to interact with others. Teachers can stimulate interaction by directing the child to a group of children with similar play interests or by playing with the child and gradually involving other children as well (Smilansky, 1971; Christie, 1982). Information gleaned from observations about the child's play interests will be valuable in determining the type of activity most likely to engage the isolate.

Smilansky offers several strategies to help children think of possible connections between their play and that of others. For example, the teacher might encourage a child playing alone with a car to join nearby children pretending to be gas station attendants by asking her "Does your car need gas?" If the child does not try to enter the group, the teacher might try more direct strategies. By making a statement such as "I go to the gas station for a fill-up every week," the teacher can clarify the behavior expected. "Your gas gauge is on empty. Before your car runs out of gas, why don't you go to the gas station?" further elaborates on the suggestion.

Some children may still be reluctant to join the group. If it seems appropriate, the teacher may establish contact between the children by commenting to the group, "The driver of this red car needs to fill up with gas." Or the teacher may model the appropriate dialogue for the social isolate by taking another car and saying to the group, "I need to fill my car with gas before I run out."

Teachers can also promote positive social behavior by grouping children who have inappropriate social skills with more socially competent children, since we know that children model effective behaviors of their peers (Hartup and Coates, 1967; Moore, 1981; Vaughn and Waters, 1980).

For example, a teacher might group an overly assertive/aggressive child such as Dirk with an equally strong yet prosocial child like Kyle. Most likely, less socially competent children's familiar strategies will be ineffective in such a group. At the same time, the more competent children provide a model for more effective strategies.

Through this sensitive structuring of the play by using questions and suggestions, most children will begin to interact with others. Such interventions must be enthusiastic, natural, and timed so that they do not disrupt, but rather add to, children's play. If reluctance is expressed by any of the children, the teacher should respect the children's wishes and find other times to help the isolate child establish a tie with another group. Patience will be needed, too, as children's progress in social skills is gradual and depends upon their frequent use.

Build Communication Skills

Children who have difficulty assessing situations and interpreting the needs and actions of others can be encouraged to refine their communication skills through several techniques.

Putallaz and Gottman (1981) suggest teaching children to ask questions as they approach a group at play in order to determine the group's interest.

For example, children might ask "What are you playing?" "Who are you pretending to be?" or "What are you building?" Once familiar with the group's intentions and play direction, a child is able to make more accurate judgments about how to integrate personal desires into the group perspective.

A similar, but less intrusive, strategy is to suggest that children observe briefly before attempting to enter the group.

Young children who reflect on their own feelings develop a greater understanding of the feelings of others (Hughes, Tingle, and Sawin, 1981; Hill, 1983). When children can consider the listeners' perspectives they will be less likely to work at cross purposes with the others in the group (Asher, Oden, and Gottman, 1977). Adults who encourage children to talk with them about their problems, feelings, and desires thus help those children improve their communication skills and sensitivity to others (Schacter, Kirshner, Klips, Friedricks, and Sanders, 1974).

For example, a teacher might help upset children to clarify their feelings by saying "You look very sad. Can you tell me what happened?"

A logical next step is for teachers to encourage children to express desires, provide explanations, and resolve arguments through discussion with other children, without teacher intervention.

Children also may need help in deciding which behaviors will be perceived positively by their peers. Coaching children is advocated by Asher, Oden, and Gottman (1977). In coaching, the adult advises the children on how to have fun during play and then offers the opportunity to put it into practice. For example, during the episode about Nellie, the teacher might have suggested she try using a different block as a raft to enter the play of others. She also might have said, "Everyone likes to slide down, so when it's your turn, slide down quickly. Then you'll get another turn very soon and everyone will have fun."

Putallaz and Gottman (1981) suggest a similar strategy. They advocate helping children to talk about rules or social norms during disagreements to justify their positions. This strategy, they found, is used by popular children. For example, a child attempting to enter the block area where the other children have already said he cannot play, might be encouraged to state the classroom rule, "There are only three people in here and four are allowed to play."

Other strategies to help children improve their perspective-taking skills and decide upon the most appropriate behaviors are role-playing and structured discussion (Krogh, 1982). Both strategies help children explore the possible consequences of alternative solutions and thus improve their reasoning ability. By helping children understand how others might perceive their actions, these two strategies help children make decisions about appropriate and inappropriate behavior.

When a problem occurs during play, teachers might guide children toward more appropriate behavior choices by using reflective discipline (Hill, 1982). This technique helps children think about their feelings and the feelings and intentions of others. The teacher asks questions designed to provide the child with information leading to a better understanding of the consequences of her or his acts. For example, if Alison hit Kevin with a block, the teacher might ask, "How do you think Kevin felt when you hit him? What could you say to get him to give your block back?"

For children with poor communication skills, the teacher may need to intervene in interaction problems before they become major conflicts. Often the adult's presence lends needed support. For example, the teacher might walk with the child to a group, bend down, and speak for the child by saying "Sam has something he wants to say to you." This may be sufficient for Sam to express his desires and encourage the others to welcome him into their play.

Other children may need the teacher to provide verbal reasoning to help them negotiate social interactions (Asher, Oden, and Gottman, 1977).

In the above example, the teacher might need to extend her participation for the nonverbal child by suggesting, "Sam, how can you tell Michael and Marshall that you want to play? Can you remind them that three can play in the block corner?"

SUMMARY

All adults who work with young children know that social development is an integral part of the early childhood curriculum. This component is essential if children are to become socially competent adults. Current research indicates that these strategies will encourage positive social interaction among children.

• Provide activities in which children interact with minimal adult supervision such as blocks, water, sand, and dramatic play.

• Observe, assess, and group children so that those who are effective social negotiators can interact with children whose skills are less refined.

• Help children learn to ask questions, observe a group before entering, improve their communication skills, and talk about their feelings and desires. Pointing out effective behaviors or suggesting ideas may be needed for some children.

Each of these strategies will offer children opportunities to develop social skills in a natural context in which they receive immediate feedback about their behavior.

DISCUSSION QUESTIONS

1. Should social interaction be a goal of the early education program?

2. How do children differ on social interaction skills?

3. Is peer interaction important for all children?

4. What should teachers do to encourage positive peer interaction?

5. What is the role of teacher observation?

6. Which social skills are of the most importance to young children?

43. TEACHING WITH LESS TALKING: LEARNING CENTERS IN THE KINDERGARTEN

by Barbara Kimes Myers and Karen Maurer

Randy had come to school early to help his teacher set up the new learning center so he knows all about the plastic eggs. He lifts one, trying to recall if it feels like the egg he had put four pennies in earlier—or maybe the five-penny egg. He studies the direction card, sees the picture of an ear, and tries listening to the sound of four pennies—or maybe five. Finally, he opens the egg and counts. Aha! Five it is. Carefully he closes all the eggs and lines them up, each on its own mat, the way he found them. He takes a green card from the egg-math center to the record keeping station, stamps it with the date, and slips it into the cubby labeled *Randy*. He moves on to the blocks where Martin and Deseree build garages for their cars.

Maria and Jonathan share their exploration. "Mine doesn't have anything in it!" complains Maria.

"That's zero," Jonathan explains. "Let's put all the money in one egg. Then they'll all be zero except mine."

He counts the contents of his plastic egg with all the pennies in it, goes to find his teacher, and, knowing she is interested in important discoveries, announces that he has found an egg with 14 pennies in it!

Randy, Martin, Deseree, Jonathan, and Maria are active learners in a kindergarten where their teacher uses carefully planned learning centers. Their teacher feels that learning centers are one method of teaching that allows for developmental theory and educational practice to be integrated. She believes that learning centers permit her to meet individual needs of children while enabling her to structure their learning environment.

In the example, Randy's teacher, like other kindergarten teachers who use learning centers, structures the learning environment not by strict scheduling and insistence upon children remaining seated, but by the arrangement of space, equipment, and materials through which children are free to move, choose, and busy themselves. Rather than instructing the entire group of children, Randy's teacher invites them to become involved in learning centers so that she is freed to interact with small groups or individual children. A learning center approach is consistent with what leading early childhood professionals have defined as *developmentally appropriate practice* since before the turn of the century, because it allows teachers to consider both the age appropriateness and the individual appropriateness of learning experiences (NAEYC, 1986). The terms *learning center* and *developmentally appropriate* are variations of the same concepts phrased slightly differently for almost 100 years.

LEARNING THROUGH PROJECTS IS NOT A NEW NOTION

Learning centers have long been an integral part of the educational scene. Their roots can be found in the work of educators like Pestalozzi, who believed that children learn through direct interaction with other children and their environment; Dewey, with his emphasis on learning through doing and the "organic connection between education and personal experience" (Dewey, 1966, p. 25); and Montessori, with her deep conviction that the young child learns through tasks and carefully prepared teaching materials. The *open education* movement in the 60s and early 70s was another step toward opening the schoolroom and the schedule to make room for educational projects, committee work, and learning activities meaningful to children, in contrast to giving them, in a fixed sequence, printed material prepared *for* them.

More recently, Day (1983) described three essential characteristics of this teaching strategy. According to Day, as well as to the many other educators who have written on the subject, a learning center approach for young children provides an intentional strategy for the active involvement of children, experience-based learning, and individualization in relation to children's developmental abilities, interests, and learning styles. Building from Day, we have suggested that curriculum taught through learning centers be termed *responsive curriculum*

See page 339 for acknowledgment and references.

(Myers and Maurer, 1986). Nimnicht used a term almost like this in his 1964 "new nursery school," made well-known in the book by the same name (Nimnicht, McAfee, and Meier, 1968); the school's curriculum was called the *responsive environment*.

A learning center style curriculum can be viewed as *responsive* for two reasons. First, the curriculum is designed for a specific group of individuals and therefore meets them where they are developmentally and experientially. Second, the curriculum responds to children at the same time it also builds upon the teacher's (responder's) previous experiences with young children; formal teacher training; beliefs about appropriate teachers' roles within particular educational settings; and individual skills, values, and interests.

Kindergarten teachers are expected to either develop their own curriculum, work with colleagues to plan a curriculum that fits within a specific school setting (often such a curriculum is part of a K–6 or K–8 continuum), or use a prescribed curriculum. In any of these situations, learning centers can offer responsive possibilities for teaching a complex mixture of skills, subject content, and character traits as long as the teacher is knowledgeable about age-appropriate curriculum for children in a specific kindergarten group; is attentive to the developmental levels, interests, learning styles, and needs of the individual children in the group; and has a great deal to say about the development and expansion of the prescribed curriculum. Obviously, if prescribed curriculum is simply divided among a number of learning centers and each child is expected to do it all—as is often the case in kindergarten classrooms—much of the value of learning centers is lost.

Many teachers hesitate to use learning centers. Such teachers are at either end of a continuum—one pole representing those fearing chaos in the classroom, the other representing those not wanting to intrude on children's spontaneous play. Persons at both ends of the spectrum can be reassured by observing a kindergarten teacher skilled in using learning centers. Those fearing chaos will see children busy with learning center activities and invested in their own learning. Those not wanting to be too directive will see how more *intentional planning* (a Lucy Sprague Mitchell term) facilitates spontaneous play and provides a rich variety of carefully structured activities consistent with the social, emotional, cognitive, and physical development of young children. For both sets of teachers learning new ways of doing things can be anxiety producing because it always involves some risk taking and is not easy. The most important resources for persons wanting to incorporate learning centers into their kindergarten practice are a strong, viable network of early childhood professionals and a strong personal disposition to learn (even when learning brings change).

LEARNING CENTERS INVITE CHILDREN

Spodek (1985) stresses that although kindergarten teachers intentionally structure the activities presented in each center, "it is the children who carry the activity forward, and in the final analysis, determine its content" (pp. 217–218).

Learning centers invite children to assume responsibility for their own learning through implicit or explicit contracts. (Sometimes children are required to record their own work as Randy did in the example.) Children of varying ages and with different interests and learning styles can benefit from centers. A center is set up in a defined space (i.e., table, floor, mat, packing box, wall, play area), may have defined or open-ended educational objectives, and either is self-directing or has instructions included within the center. (All instructions included [within] the center need to be understood by a kindergarten-age child. They should have pictures, agreed-upon symbols, examples, and sometimes words if there are children in the group who can read.)

Learning centers do not need continuous adult supervision, but some children may need help making what the teacher views as good choices or they may want to share a discovery or display some work. A teacher may want to have a morning planning session with the class to discuss the choices for the day and give background or demonstrate techniques to be used in a new center.

DECISIONS TO BE MADE BY ADULTS

Before setting up learning centers, teachers have to make a number of decisions about the size and structure of the classroom and how learning centers can best fit into the overall scheme: adult-child ratios; skills, interests, and abilities of staff members; length of school day; characteristics of the children; available resources; parents' and school personnel's expectation of kindergarten teachers; teachers' assumptions about how children learn; and teachers' values. Some of the questions that need to be addressed include:

• Will centers be offered all day, every day; part of the day; or only some days of the week?

(Our choice is to offer centers for a large block or blocks of time every day at approximately the same time. This allows children to plan ahead, make choices, and become involved in activities. It allows teachers to initially structure learning centers throughout the room and gradually add centers, remove centers, or modify centers during the year. The centers themselves do not often change; the activities available in some of them do.)

• What classroom features offer potential settings for centers? Teachers can make creative use of walls, floors, chalkboards, tables, and nooks and crannies.

• Should there be limits on the number of children using any specific centers? If so, how will this be determined, and how will children know what the limits are? Learning centers should be planned so there is opportunity for children to work individually or in small groups of various numbers. The size of a small group of children at any center is determined by the amount of materials available, the educational objectives of the center, physical space considerations, and the need to avoid overstimulating confusion. Signs with stick figures and numbers can indicate the number of children who can use a specific center.

• What kinds of centers will provide a workable balance in terms of content? This will depend on the characteristics of the children and staff.

• How free should movement be in and out of the centers? (Our choice is that children move at their own paces guided by the teacher. This allows for more individualization within the program.)

• Must every child use every center? Each day? Each week?

• How will children know what to do in each center? Some centers will have directions built into their structure. Others will need direction cards. When a new center is added or a center is modified the teacher needs to help children understand rules related to that specific center.

• Is it important that a record be kept of each child's center work? If so, what is the most efficient way to keep records?

Our answers to the question listed have evolved from the context of our own experiences. A unique blend of values, assumptions, and resources will shape each teacher's responses.

TYPES OF LEARNING CENTERS

Learning centers may be described as *self-directing/self-correcting*; *self-directing/open-ended*; or *teacher-instructed/exploratory*. The first type allows teachers to set up an activity for a prescribed purpose. The latter two types allow teachers to set up activities for children of varying ages, learning abilities, and experience levels, and allow the child to determine the outcome.

It has been our experience that often early childhood personnel follow the elementary and secondary educators' model of dividing the curriculum into subject areas such as language arts, social science, mathematics, science, creative arts. When an educational strategy includes learning centers and an academic subject model is used, the subject areas overlap and are integrated. Although we will now focus on language arts centers, the academic areas of mathematics, science, social studies, and the creative arts could also have been used as examples, as well as other terms within a different curriculum-naming framework (i.e., large muscle, small muscle, cognitive). Ideas for activities to be included in centers can come from other teachers, conference workshops, age-appropriate activity recipe books, curriculum guides, observations of children's activities, and parents' suggestions.

Self-Directing/Self-Correcting Learning Centers

Self-directing/self-correcting centers have obvious and prescribed uses; the material tells the learner whether a given action is correct or incorrect. Puzzles and other toys with parts that fit together in one specific way are self-directing/self-correcting. Battery-operated matching games and computer-assisted instruction programs also fall into this category, as do many Montessori materials. See Table 1 for examples of self-directing/self-correcting centers.

Any educational catalog or supply store sells learning games like these. Games can be made by cutting, pasting, and laminating workbook and ditto sheet exercises.

Self-Directing/Open-Ended Learning Centers

Self-directing/open-ended learning centers allow for a variety of learning outcomes, including some that teachers may not initially consider appropriate. A unit block or hollow block center is self-directing because the blocks invite building and the creative possibilities are limited only by the children's experience and imagination. An egg carton with objects to place in the hollows may motivate children to drop one object in each hollow for a one-to-one correspondence, to put two in each, to count, to sort, or to pretend that the

Table 1. Self-Directing/Self-Correcting Centers

Educational objectives	Defined space	Materials
1. auditory discrimination, preparation for paper and pencil matching	rug samples or carpet squares	direction cards with correct match illustrated on back, object pairs that can be matched by some criterion (e.g., initial sound, rhyme), lengths of yarn
2. auditory discrimination, verbal interaction and cooperation when two or more children work together	table	boxes labeled with upper- and lower-case letters, pictures on individual cards to be sorted into boxes according to the same initial sound (same center may be varied so that sorting is by final sound or by rhyme)
3. understanding and audio discrimination of rhyme to sharpen audio discrimination, opportunity for verbal interaction and cooperation when children work together	table, rug	a puzzle having pairs of rhyming objects

hollows are nests and all rounded objects are eggs. Table 2 gives several examples of self-directing/open-ended centers.

All activity and play areas suited to preschool classrooms for 3- and 4-year-olds are also appropriate for 5s.

Teacher-Instructed/Exploratory Learning Centers

Teacher-instructed/exploratory centers can provide opportunities for children to further explore techniques or concepts that have been presented earlier in a teacher-directed activity. Following a teacher-presented experiment in which a cork, a rock, a coin, and a piece of wood are tested to see whether each will sink or float, children may extend the possibilities beyond the initial four items. Children might work from a larger prepared set or create their own set of items to test. The presentation thus becomes a model for the children's free exploration. In the presentation the teacher may want to model attitudes, words, and behaviors that she believes are desirable for the children to incorporate into their explorations, but the critical factor is that the children redesign the experiment by extending the set of objects tested.

As part of such a science center on floating and sinking, a teacher may want to demonstrate how to record findings on a group or individual chart: by placing the object on a chart in the float column or the sink column; by drawing the object in the appropriate column; or by cutting out a picture and gluing it in the proper column. Later in the year some children may choose to write the names of the floating and sinking objects on the chart.

Examples of teacher-instructed/exploratory centers are provided in Table 3.

The purpose of the three types of centers and the several examples of each one can be made clear to children with a minimum of direction from the teacher. For instance in the object-matching example given under self-directing/self-correcting learning centers, one set of objects can be lined up in a vertical column on a small rug with the matching set loosely clustered on a second small rug. This center also has a directions card presented along with a picture of an ear and several matching sets shown (e.g., dog matches door, sun matches sock—yarn connecting the two). The directions card may also show some stick figures and a numeral if the teacher wishes to limit the number of children who may use the center at one time. Children will argue, correct, and teach each other. The center is made self-correcting by having the acceptable matches shown on the reverse of the card.

Because children using self-directing/open-ended or teacher-instructed/exploratory learning centers may respond in a variety of ways, the outcomes of these centers often depend on the sophistication of the learner. The type of center offered at any specific time may depend on the teacher's perception of children's specific needs. For example, Victor's teacher planned to use a self-directing/open-ended center:

Victor, a child in a kindergarten/child care setting, was close to being able to write his name. He worked the soft green dough clay with obvious enjoyment, rolling long snakes that he shaped to the strokes of the letters his teacher had printed on a large sheet of construction paper. An observant parent helped watch him complete the *r*, handed him a marker, and remarked encourag-

Table 2. Self-Directing / Open-Ended Centers

Educational objectives	Defined space	Materials
1. audio discrimination, listening pleasure, motivation for children to practice rhyming or making up stories of their own	table	tape recorder, headsets, audio tape with recordings of stories written in rhyme
2. representation of experiences and feelings with oral and written language	tables near display of children's paintings	12'' × 18'' paper, pencils, markers (This center will need a couple of parent volunteers or older students from the 5th or 6th grade who can write down the children's dictations about their pictures. Children who are writing independently with conventional or invented spelling, of course, write their own stories.)
3. visual discrimination, practice in formation of letters	table	rubber stamp letters, ink pad, pencils and paper
4. opportunity for oral language and verbal and nonverbal cooperation, representation of experience through pretend play	family living center	child-sized furniture, clothes for dress up, other props for dramatic play

Table 3. Teacher-Instructed / Exploratory Centers

Educational objectives	Defined space	Materials
1. practice in rhyming, audio discrimination, exploring and sharing own ideas	table	tape recorder, headsets, teacher-made audio tapes of rhymes with time on the tape for children to add their own examples
2. idea that experience can be represented in visual form, opportunity for children to explore and share feelings and experiences with others, expansion of vocabulary as children mix paints in various colors and tones	tables or easel	tempera paint (the three primary colors, black, and white), 12'' x 18'' paper, ½-inch wide brushes (teacher initiates the activity with conversation about sensory memories related to a common experience the children have recently had)
3. concept of writing as meaningful marks on paper and of stories as something that can be written down	table next to bulletin board where children's original stories are displayed as well as library display of picture books (teachers have previously written the children's original stories with them)	magazine pictures mounted on 12''x 18'' sheets of unlined paper, pencils or felt-tipped markers, stapler (for those who may want to make a book)

ingly, "I think you're ready to write your name." He did, again and again! Then, it was lunchtime and as he marched triumphantly down the hall to his child care room, Victor could be heard chanting softly, "I thought I could, I thought I could, I thought I could."

Obviously, Victor was influenced by *The Little Engine That Could*, as well as by his good feelings about writing his name. The responsive open-endedness of the center allowed for the adult's suggestion as well as for Victor's input.

Just as each child is unique, so is each teacher. The teacher's own skills, values, and interests will color the structure and use of learning centers. Instruction may be more heavily weighted in one area of the curriculum if the teacher has specific skills related to academic subjects such as math and science or development areas such as language acquisition. Teachers who fear chaos may initially use more self-directing/self-correcting activities. Teachers concerned about excessive intrusion into children's play may initially plan for more self-directing/open-ended centers—educational play areas, such as those we see in early childhood programs for *younger* children.

Some researchers in the field of early childhood education (Berlak and Berlak, 1981; Bussis, Chittenden, and Amarel, 1976; Halliwell, 1980; King, 1976; King, 1978; Myers, 1984) have found that teachers teach both a surface or explicit curriculum that is clearly articulated and a more hidden or implicit curriculum. The former generally includes the kind of activities a teacher would describe in her plan book, but the latter is taught through the arrangement of time, space, and materials as well as interpersonal relations and interactions. Teachers with strong educational philosophies of any kind

know this. Researchers have further shown that by reflecting on the events of their own classrooms, any teacher can make implicit curriculum more explicit. Often, although not always, the explicit curriculum includes academic skills and subject content, while the implicit curriculum involves the development of character traits or personal attributes. Selecting the appropriate type of learning center allows teachers to help children develop certain character traits or personal attributes, in addition to learning skills and subjects.

Setting up effective learning centers, some of which will serve only one or two children and others of which will serve various size groups, is initially time consuming. But once the environment is structured and children learn the uses and limits for each center, teachers can concentrate on working with small groups or individuals as needs arise. When the teachers' active participation is not necessary, they can spend time observing students so that better informed curriculum decisions can be made. Gradually, new centers will be added, some centers removed, and others modified. When one, two, or several children are helped to understand how a new or modified center is to be used, they can help other children learn.

Angela Andrews, an exemplary kindergarten teacher and teacher educator skilled in the use of learning centers, tells those who compliment her on her kindergarten practice, "Thank you, I worked hard to learn to do this."

Teaching a reponsive curriculum through learning centers requires knowledge, skill, and a lot of thought. It is hard work, but seeing young children vibrant and deeply involved in the process of learning is a tremendously rewarding experience.

DISCUSSION QUESTIONS

1. Are children learning while the teacher is not "teaching"?

2. What is the justification for learning through projects and learning centers?

3. How do adult decisions and child interest fit together in good learning center environments?

4. What are the characteristics of the various types of learning centers?

5. Do learning centers increase the individualization of instruction in the classroom?

44. INFLUENCES FROM THE PAST: PLAY IN THE EARLY CHILDHOOD CURRICULUM

by Margie L. Hardy and Laurie J. Greene

Throughout the course of history, the role of children's play has been influenced by the zeitgeist of the time, causing it to have varying definitions and purposes. More recently, proponents of the back to the basics movement, which is characterized by rigor in the curriculum and competency testing, tend to view play as unimportant. It is necessary, therefore, for us to examine the purpose of education. Is our main concern to produce high test scores or are we committed to the child's development, well-being, and means through which he learns most effectively, including play? Identifying play as the child's work and exploring the roots of play and its recurrence through history can help strengthen its role in the early childhood curriculum.

In order to identify play as the child's work, it is necessary to understand what is meant by the term, play. Definitions characterizing play vary according to the educational purpose and historical setting of which it was a part.

According to Glickman, during the late 1800s play was viewed as an imitation of adults and a release of surplus energy. During the progressive era, play was viewed as important in problem solving and socialization. In the era following World War II, play was viewed as nonproductive and frivolous. A more contemporary definition reveals play as intrinsic, enjoyable, and an active base for language, cognitive, motor, and social development (Yawkey and Pellegrini, 1984).

Part of the confusion concerning the meaning of play arises from the separation between work and play with the belief that while work is good, play is somehow questionable, if not sinful or bad, according to Frank (Hartley and Goldenson, 1963). Athey states the division between work and play as useful and useless activity parallels the view of the preschool as less important than formal education (Yawkey and Pellegrini, 1984). Piaget (1962) wrote, "But the main reason for the difficulty lies perhaps in the fact that there has been a tendency to consider play as an isolated function... whereas play is in reality one of the aspects of any activity." Kamii (1985) notes that some educators make a distinction between work and play by including worksheets in "work" and games in "play." Some educators concede that children do need to play, but the need is relegated to recess or playground activities. It is further observed that when group games are allowed in the classroom they are usually reserved for "after the children have finished their work" (Kamii, 1985). Kamii further feels that although work and play become differentiated as the child grows older, the differentiation is never complete because work and play can share common elements including enjoyment, learning, intrinsic motivation, and a sense of accomplishment.

Piaget provides a cognitive view of play from his studies which reveal that children come to understand and master their environment according to their age and stage of development (Butler, Gotts and Quisenberry, 1978). During infancy, Piaget relates play in its initial stages to assimilation or the integration of new experiences or environmental information into the child's already existing cognitive structure. Even though no new cognitive structure is produced during assimilation, the child repeats an action for the sheer joy it brings. Symbolic assimilation is referred to as the source of make believe play while functional assimilation is the source of practice play. On the other hand, accommodation forces the infant to develop new cognitive structures. Hence, Piaget classifies play and imitation as representative of two poles of intellectual thought. Play is defined as a continuation of assimilation, while imitation is defined as a continuation of accommodation (Butler, Gotts and Quisenberry, 1978).

In further consideration of a definition of play, Lawrence Frank declares,

> Play is the way the child learns what no one can teach him. It is the way he explores and orients himself to the actual world of space and time, of things, animals, structures and people. Through play, he learns to live in our symbolic world of meanings and values, of progressive striving for deferred goals, at the same time exploring and experimenting and learning in his own individualized way. (Hartley and Goldenson, 1963)

Over one hundred years earlier, Froebel declared

See page 339 for acknowledgment and references.

that, "Play is the highest phase of child development...for it is self active representation of the inner from inner necessity and impulse" (Hailmann, 1887).

Since play has been considered the crux of the preschool experience for much of this century, it is important to understand something of its historical background in order to make decisions about its inclusion in today's early childhood curriculum. Glickman states that play, as an educational enterprise, has its roots in the French Revolution, especially in the writings of Rousseau (Yawkey and Pellegrini, 1984). The ancient Greeks also saw value in play. Plato wrote ". . . the play of children have the mightiest influence on the maintenance or nonmaintenance of laws" (Hailmann, 1887). Plato also wrote that education for children should be a sort of amusement (Braun and Edwards, 1972). Paralleling the view that instruction should be rendered as amusement was Quintillian, a Roman, who advocated learning through use of games and imitation. Play assumed a greater role of imitation in preparing children for their future role in society during the Middle Ages.

A forerunner of the "child-centered" philosophy of education was Erasmus, who believed that work, meaning study, should begin by way of play. Play was viewed as a release from work or learning by some educators of the Reformation including Martin Luther (Hailmann, 1887).

During the Early Modern Period, physical exercise and games for health purposes were emphasized by such spokesmen as Comenius and Locke. Locke believed that a sound body should be cultivated as well as a sound mind. He further believed that freedom of play and activity would reveal natural temperaments and levels of development.

During the 18th century, amid the aristocratic society of France, Rousseau advocated following nature's way in his book, *Emile* (1762). Rousseau believed that the child needed to be active in a natural environment. Rousseau believed children learn through sensory experience. Hence he reiterated Comenius' earlier belief that everything must be related through sense impression if possible. By allowing the child to demonstrate his own interest and follow it, a foundation for learning could begin to be constructed where the child was free to explore, act and question. According to Glickman, Rousseau advocated play as an educational enterprise and he believed that through changes in the education of society's youth, changes would follow in the society (Yawkey and Pellegrini, 1984).

Influenced by the educational ideas of Rousseau, Pestolozzi applied Rousseau's view of the child as an active explorer of nature and practiced a teaching methodology based on sense impression. He favored the use of free play and movement in the learning process. Pestolozzi's teaching method was aimed at strengthening the child's own faculties, thus enabling him to think for himself.

Froebel, who studied with Pestolozzi and read Rousseau's writings, went beyond the methods and theory of play. He derived a new conception of childhood, meaning that it was not merely preparation for adulthood, but that it was of value itself. Froebel developed instructional materials along with guides for teachers and encouraged the organization of the environment (Yawkey and Pellegrini, 1984).

The plays and occupations which Froebel used in the curriculum encouraged activity. Imitation was a significant development which arose from free activity. Even though play mainly consisted of activity in the early stages, later it assumed a more definite purpose because representation of the thing to be represented in the activity was sought.

Froebel felt that physical and sensory training were important and that the way a child revealed his nature was dependent on the kinds of play and occupations which he chose. Hence, Froebel wrote, "The educator should not regard the manifestations of children's activity as external and isolated, but always affecting or arising from their inner life" (Hailmann, 1887). Parents were urged to cultivate the spontaneous play of the child.

"Although Froebel understood the role of play in the development of the child, he never actually worked out a system of classification on play as play" (Butler, Gotts, and Quisenberry, 1978). However, three successive stages are identified by Piaget in the evolution of children's play including practice, symbolism and rules. Practice play begins in the first months of a child's life, and symbolic play occurs in the second year with games and rules primarily belonging to the third stage (ages 7-11). Piaget's description of the development of intelligence parallels the successive stages of play (Butler, Gotts, and Quisenberry, 1978).

The research of Piaget, Bloom, and others recognized the importance of the early years to later cognitive development. As a result, Athey states that many of the worklike activities of the elementary school were pushed downward into the early childhood grades. This was the opposite of the extension of play into the elementary grades (Yawkey and Pellegrini, 1984).

Because the back to the basics movement stresses that more time be spent on direct instruction in reading, writing and arithmetic, replacing a more informal activity-centered curriculum, it is important to examine our purpose and goal for education.

Piaget once stated,

> The principal goal of education is to create men who are capable of doing new things, not simply of repeating what other generations have done . . . The second goal of education is to form minds which can be critical, can verify and not accept everything they are offered . . . So we need pupils who are active, who learn early to find out by themselves, partly by their own spontaneous activity and partly through materials we set up for them . . . (Munsinger, 1975)

In the past, early childhood educators have supported a variety of interpretations of play. These interpretations intended to help the child develop either physically, cognitively, socially or emotionally. Throughout history, society's definition of play has been a critical factor. By knowing the roots of play and how it is identified as the child's work, our commitment to the child's development and well-being is strengthened. And we have also learned that play is important and has a necessary role in the early childhood curriculum.

DISCUSSION QUESTIONS

1. What is the meaning of play in the early childhood curriculum?

2. How has play been defined and justified in the historical literature?

3. Is there time in the current school program for play?

4. How can play be explained and justified to parents?

45. LEADING PRIMARY EDUCATION TOWARD EXCELLENCE: BEYOND WORKSHEETS AND DRILL

by Constance Kamii

It is almost impossible today to talk with teachers of young children, especially those in the primary grades, without hearing some complaints about having to produce higher test scores. Most teachers trained in the child development tradition believe, for example, that some of their children are not yet ready to learn how to read. Yet these teachers feel compelled to give phonics lessons simply because they are expected to produce acceptable test scores, and this pressure is working downward even to some classrooms of 4-year-old children. In arithmetic, too, many teachers believe that first graders cannot possibly understand missing addends (the $\Box$ in $4 + \Box = 6$) and place value (the fact that the first 3 in 33 means 30, while the second 3 means 3). Yet, they feel compelled to teach this content simply because it is on the achievement test.

Education is an amazing profession in which professionals can be forced to do things against their conscience. Physicians are not forced to give treatments that only make the symptoms disappear, but many teachers give phonics lessons and worksheets, knowing perfectly well that the imposition of the 3 R's may make children dislike school and lose confidence in their own ability to figure things out. Why is it that such harmful practices are going on in early childhood education from coast to coast?

One explanation is that administrators in education, who have the power to make decisions, are ignorant of child development. Many of them are politically motivated and go along with the pressure to produce higher test scores. While these statements may be true, they do not fully explain why those of us within the profession who believe in child development are not winning the battle against those who believe in force-feeding the 3 R's. I would like to offer an additional explanation of why we are not winning the battle and then propose some suggestions about what we might do to lead primary education forward toward excellence rather than backwards to worksheets and drill.

See page 339 for acknowledgment and references.

COMMON SENSE NOTIONS OF INSTRUCTION AND DEVELOPMENT

Let me clarify first what is generally understood by the term *development*. To most people, development means a long-term process of unfolding or maturation from inside the child, like the unfolding of a flower that develops out of a bud. Child development is a loosely related field in psychology consisting of a variety of theories about the child that are not directly applicable to education. For example, Sigmund and Anna Freud are big names in child development, and so are Erik Erikson and Jane Loevinger. But their theories cannot be applied to instruction because they do not deal with children's cognitive development, and social and emotional development is only indirectly related to the 3 R's and other academic subjects. The work of Arnold Gesell and L. S. Vygotsky comes closer to education because it deals with children's cognitive development. However, their ideas are too diverse to unite into a theory of instruction, and each is too sketchy to select one of them for curriculum development.

When early childhood educators speak of child development, they are referring not to descriptive or explanatory theories but to a philosophy or an approach to education. This philosophy may be excellent, but it represents an intuitive leap from psychological theories to educational practices, without precise theoretical links between the two. In medicine, the objective of the practitioner is always defined in relation to scientific explanation, and if the cause of a disease is not known, physicians know that the cause is not yet known.

In early childhood education, however, if we look in any textbook written in the child development tradition, we do not find objectives based on a precise explanatory theory. We find, instead, vague and broad goals such as emotional, social, and intellectual development and more specific objectives defined along traditional subjects such as language arts, math, and science. With these objectives defined without any foundation in a precise, scientific, explanatory theory, it is not surprising to find a variety of activities—all without precise theoretical links to an explanatory theory—such as pretend play, painting, block building, water play, and games. It is these activities that seem softheaded and worthless to the traditionalists who believe that education consists of the 3 R's, lessons, exercises, and/or drills. When the pressure is on to use worksheets, furthermore, advocates of play can usually not defend play's educational value.

For centuries, education has been based on mere common sense, trial and error, and opinions called philosophies, such as Rousseau's and Dewey's philosophies. When some educators attempted to introduce a scientific foundation into the profession, they found associationism, behaviorism, and psychometric tests. Behaviorism, a more intense and systematic version of associationism, is a scientific theory that has been confirmed all over the world. Psychometric tests yield numbers and printouts that give the impression of being scientific. If we want to win the battle against the force-feeding of the 3 R's and worksheets, we have to have a scientific theory that is powerful enough to disprove associationism, behaviorism, and the desirability of psychometric tests.

I would like to back up and focus more sharply on common sense. According to common sense, teaching consists of *telling* or *presenting* knowledge, and learning takes place by the *internalization* of what is taught. When proponents of child development methods speak of unfolding from the inside, or maturation, these ideas appear in an almost mutually exclusive relationship with the common-sense notion of instruction as can be seen in Figure 1. To people who think in common-sensical and either-or terms, this relationship implies that the development approach necessitates giving up instruction, which is exactly what they want to intensify in going back to basics. Behavior-

ism, associationism, and psychometric tests are compatible with common sense because they grew out of common sense. This is why I put A for associationism inside the circle on the left. Behaviorism, shown with the B within associationism, is an intensified version of associationism that breaks "correct" behaviors, or answers, down to small components and sequences them to ensure better internalization. Psychometric tests approach evaluation in a similar way, by focusing on "correct" behaviors, or answers, thereby reinforcing the common-sense notion that the child who has acquired more knowledge is the one who can give more correct answers. Now that the common-sense notion of teaching has thus been buttressed by behaviorism, associationism, and psychometric tests, it is even harder for the Educational Establishment to accept the child development philosophy.

Developmentalists, however, are convinced that there is a process of unfolding from inside the child, and that the force-feeding of isolated skills with worksheets is inappropriate for young children. But we need to go beyond saying that worksheets are developmentally inappropriate and explain precisely and scientifically **why** these are inappropriate. We must also go beyond criticizing the undesirable, and advance alternative ways to replace what we criticize. I would now like to show how Piaget's theory can help us accomplish both of these tasks.

Constructivism and the Curriculum

Reading and Writing

Let me give an example from Ferreiro's (Ferreiro and Teberosky, 1982) research in reading and writing to show the kind of precise scientific explanation that is possible to present against associationists and behaviorists. Ferreiro was a collaborator of Piaget in Geneva until she returned to her native land, Argentina, where she did her research in Spanish. She interviewed 4- to 6-year-old children before they received any instruction in school in reading and writing. She asked them, for example, to write their own name, the name of a friend or a member of their family, and words such as *mamá*, *papá*, *oso* (bear), *sapo* (toad), and *pato* (duck).

She found developmental levels among these children who had not received any instruction in school. At the first and lowest level, the children wrote essentially the same squiggles for everything.

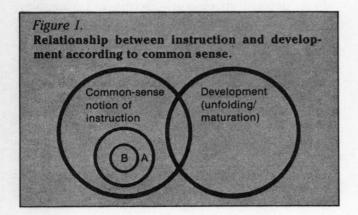

Figure 1.
Relationship between instruction and development according to common sense.

Common-sense notion of instruction

Development (unfolding/maturation)

B A

Here is an example:

mamá 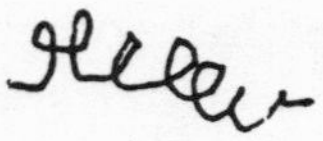

papá 

oso 

Interestingly, at this level, the child often thought that a big animal like a bear had to be written with bigger squiggles or with more squiggles than a small animal like a duck!

At the second level, the child believed that to read different things, there had to be objective differences in the writing. When they had a limited repertoire of letters consisting of only four letters, for instance, they wrote different words such as the following by varying the order of the same four letters:

mamá 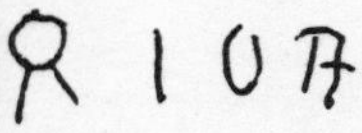 oso 

papá 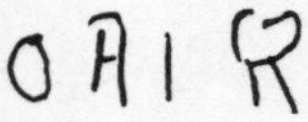 sapo 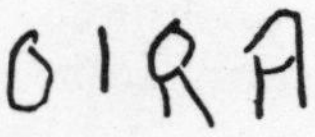

The third level, called the syllabic hypothesis level, is a major achievement because the child thinks that each "letter" stands for one syllable. One child wrote as follows:

sapo 

oso 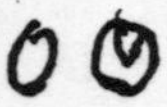

patito 

This syllabic level is a major achievement because for the first time children make correspondences between the parts they write and the parts they utter.

At the fourth level, called the alphabetic hypothesis level, the child's analysis goes beyond syllables as can be seen in the follow examples:

pato PAO

Susana SANA

I simplified all these levels for purposes of clarity, and further details can be found in Ferreiro and Teberosky's book entitled *Literacy before Schooling*. I hope you can see that the conventional alphabetic writing comes next, at the fifth level, and that the children who can benefit most from phonics lessons are those who are already at this high developmental level. Some children learn despite the poor methods!

These levels illustrate what to me is the most important point of Piaget's theory, namely constructivism. No one teaches children that if they write *mamá* with four letters, they can write *papá* simply by changing the order of the same letters. Yet, children construct, or invent this way of writing when it occurs to them that each word has to look different. The syllabic hypothesis at the next level is also wrong, but it represents enormous progress over the previous level. Such progress is never picked up by achievement tests. For tests, the only thing that counts is correct answers, but according to Piaget children develop by constructing one level after another being "wrong."

Arithmetic

I would now like to go on to the teaching of arithmetic to illustrate constructivism in another area of the curriculum. A typical worksheet gets children to write *3* next to a picture of three cookies and *4* next to a picture of four bottles. Children who can do these worksheets already know how to do them, and do not learn number concepts by completing them. Those who cannot do them, on the other hand, will not learn number concepts by filling out worksheets. Number is something children construct by thinking, in their heads, and not by pushing pencils.

I would like to clarify children's construction of number by discussing a Piagetian task (Inhelder and Piaget, 1963). The child is given a glass, and the researcher takes an identical glass. The adult then asks the child to drop a bead into his glass each time she drops one into hers. After about six beads have thus been dropped in each glass with one-to-one correspondence, the adult says, "Let's stop now, and I want you to watch what I am going to do." The researcher then drops one bead into her glass and suggests, "Let's get going again." Each person drops about six more beads into his or her glass with one-to-one correspondence, and the child is asked whether the two people have the same amount, or the child has more, or the adult has more.

Four-year-olds usually say that the two glasses have the same amount, and when asked "How do you know?" they explain, "Because I can see they both have the same." Upon being asked to describe how the beads were dropped, they can usually give all the empirical facts correctly ("... Then you told me to stop, and you put one in your glass.... Only you put an extra one in your glass, and I watched 'cause you told me to wait.... Then we got going again...").

By age five or six, however, the majority of children can deduce logically that the experimenter has one more. When we asked them what will happen "if we continued to drop beads in the same way [one-to-one correspondence] all afternoon," only some of them reply that the adult will always have one more. Others make empirical statements such as "I don't know because we haven't done it yet" or "We don't have enough beads to keep going all afternoon."

The logical nature of number can be clarified by understanding the distinction Piaget made among three kinds of knowledge according to their ultimate sources: physical knowledge, logico-mathematical knowledge, and social (conventional) knowledge. *Physical knowledge* is knowledge of objects in external reality. The color and weight of a bead are examples of physical properties that are *in* objects in external reality, and can be known by observation. The knowledge that a bead will go down when we let go of it is also an example of physical, empirical knowledge.

Logico-mathematical knowledge, on the other hand, consists of relationships constructed by each individual. For instance, when we are presented with a red bead and a blue one, and think that they are different, this difference is an example of logico-mathematical knowledge. The beads are indeed observable, but the difference between them is not. The difference is a *relationship* created mentally by the individual who puts the two objects into this relationship. The difference is neither *in* the red bead nor *in* the blue one, and if a person did not put the objects into this relationship, the difference would not exist for that person. Other examples of relationships the individual can create between the two beads are "similar," "the same in weight," and "two."

The ultimate source of *social knowledge* is con-

ventions made by people. Examples of social knowledge are the fact that Christmas comes on December 25, that a bead is called *bead*, and that grown-ups sometimes greet each other by shaking hands.

You can see that the spoken words "one, two, three, four..." and written numerals belong to social knowledge and representation, which are the most superficial parts of arithmetic. The underlying number concepts belong to logico mathematical knowledge, which has its source in each child's head. The bad news from Piaget's theory is that **number concepts are not teachable,** as they can be constructed only by children, through their own mental activity. The good news, however, is that **we don't have to teach number concepts because children will construct them on their own.**

It is amazing to me that all of math education is based on the empiricist, wrong assumption that number is something that has to be learned by internalization from the environment. Piaget (Piaget and Szeminska, 1941) showed more than 40 years ago that number concepts are constructed by each child, but math education is still going on as if Piaget had never published The *Child's Conception of Number* and many other subsequent volumes.

Based on his theory, I did an experiment in first grade arithmetic. We eliminated all traditional instruction from first grade arithmetic including worksheets and used instead two kinds of activities that emphasized thinking: (a) situations in daily living such as the counting of votes and (b) group games such as dice and card games. I will not go into the details of this study, since a book was recently published entitled *Young Children Reinvent Arithmetic* (Kamii, 1985). I would simply like to make one point from this research, that **worksheets are harmful for first graders' development of arithmetic while play is highly beneficial.**

One of my reasons for saying that worksheets are harmful is that they require children to write answers, and having to write interferes with the possibility of remembering combinations such as "3, 2, 5" and "4, 2, 6." Children can remember sums better when they are free to concentrate on these combinations, without having to write the answers.

My second reason for saying that worksheets are harmful is that they teach children to count mechanically when they don't know a sum. In extending my research into second and third grades, I am amazed that the great majority of traditionally taught second graders are still counting on fingers to do sums such as 5 + 6, and this need to count persists in the third grade. The first graders I had worked with used their heads instead and said, "5 + 5 = 10; so 5 + 6 has to be 11," but the children who had been taught with worksheets in first grade had become counting machines. Since they were required to write answers to satisfy the teacher, they used the most mechanical, surest, deadly technique they were taught to be able to write the correct answer. Children who had thus mindlessly engaged in counting, repeated the same mechanical procedure if 7 + 2 was followed immediately by 2 + 7, or 6 + 4 was followed immediately by 7 + 4.

GOING BEYOND COMMON SENSE

I would like to return to Figure 1 to point out that constructivist teaching is not maturationist. Piaget clearly differentiated maturation, which is a biological process like the baby's becoming able to walk, from the construction of knowledge through children's own mental activity. While people are passive in biological maturation, they are mentally very active when they construct knowledge. A more precise way to talk about this mental activity is to say that children construct knowledge by putting things into relationships. For example, children are mentally very active when they construct the knowledge that 2 + 3 gives the same result as 4 + 1.

Knowledge is constructed through an active mental process that is far from the maturationist view represented by the Gesellian school. If you believe in maturation, you will wait for the child to mature. If you believe in construction, however, you will promote activities that stimulate the constructive process such as board games with dice in the first grade.

You must have noted that Piaget's scientific theory about how children learn is very different from behaviorism, which is another scientific theory about how children learn. Why is it that two scientific theories can be so diametrically opposed?

The answer is that the same relationship can be found in every other scientific field such as astronomy. While the heliocentric theory disproved the geocentric theory, according to which the sun revolved around the earth, the new theory did not eliminate the old one. The new theory went beyond the old one by encompassing it as can be seen in Figure 2. The proof is that even today, we still talk about the sunrise and sunset, even though no one believes in the geocentric theory anymore.

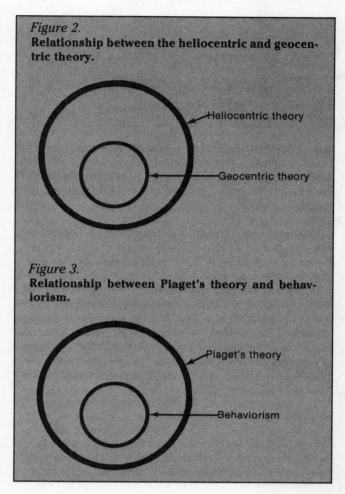

Figure 2.
Relationship between the heliocentric and geocentric theory.

Heliocentric theory
Geocentric theory

Figure 3.
Relationship between Piaget's theory and behaviorism.

Piaget's theory
Behaviorism

It is still true that the sun rises and sets, when we limit ourselves to a certain perspective.

The relationship between Piaget's theory and behaviorism is similar as can be seen in Figure 3. Piaget's theory went beyond behaviorism by encompassing it. Therefore, his theory can explain the phenomena explained by behaviorism, but the converse is not true. Piaget explained conditioning as an instance of organisms' adaptation to the environment. Worms, rats, and dogs, as well as human beings, adapt to rewards and punishments. But human beings are more complicated than dogs, and behaviorism cannot explain human knowledge.

Piaget's constructivism thus did not eliminate behaviorism. This is why behaviorism remains scientifically true as long as we limit ourselves to surface, observable behaviors. If we view learning only as a change in behavior, we can define our objectives behaviorally and use rewards and/or punishments to modify it. The results of such teaching are often higher test scores because psychometric tests in early childhood education are made to evaluate surface skills such as children's ability to count and to recognize numerals. But this kind of teaching is like trying to cure a patient's illness by giving aspirin. Aspirin works on symptoms, but not on the underlying cause of the illness. Many children who can write 8 next to a picture of eight ice cream cones continue to believe that eight chips spread out are more than eight chips pushed close together.

I would like to say one more thing about Piaget's theory in relation to behaviorism and associationism. All sciences begin by studying surface, observable, and limited phenomena, and by explaining them with mere common sense. In astronomy, the geocentric theory came first and was a surface, common-sensical interpretation of the apparent movement of the sun. It is not surprising that psychologists, too, began by studying behavior, which is observable and easier to study than complicated phenomena such as human knowledge and morality. Teaching by telling and rewards and/or punishments makes good common sense, but the time has come for educators to go beyond mere common sense. It is very hard to give up common sense, and this is why it took humanity about 150 years to accept the heliocentric theory (Taylor, 1949).

I hate to say this, but I think educators' acceptance of behaviorism, associationism, and/or psychometric tests constitutes progress in our profession. I say *progress* because it was a big step forward for education to go beyond the primitive stage of making decisions based only on tradition, common sense, and opinions called philosophies. Other professions such as medicine, engineering, and architecture have long had a scientific foundation, but education was entirely in a prescientific stage until it accepted associationism, behaviorism, and psychometric tests.

One of the major points of constructivism, as I said earlier, is that each child has to develop by going through one level after another of being "wrong." Science, too, develops by going through one level after another of being "wrong." The geocentric theory was wrong, but it was a necessary stage without which the heliocentric theory could not have been invented. The heliocentric theory was thus a great achievement, but Kepler later proved Copernicus wrong when he found the planets to move in elliptical orbits rather than circular ones.

Behaviorism was likewise a necessary stage in the history of psychology, and many psychologists are already saying that behaviorism is dead. I have seen many people change from behaviorism and associationism to Piaget's theory as I did, but I have never heard of a Piagetian who later became a behaviorist. Psychometric tests, too, are a stage that psychology is bound to go beyond. Speaking of intelligence tests, Piaget (1965) said 20 years ago, "either we shall one day find good tests, or else intelligence tests will go into history as an example of a fruitful error" (p. 150).

I have no doubt about the eventual victory of the developmental point of view simply because science does not stand still and human intelligence does not stay permanently satisfied with low-level knowledge. But victory will not happen all by itself, without considerable efforts on our part.

As I said earlier, I have not found in a single book written in the child development tradition any rigorous conceptualization of educational objectives based on a scientific, explanatory theory. Physicians know whether their objective is to alleviate only the symptom or to remove the cause of a disease. But educators do not define their objectives with such scientific rigor. We must first be clear about how children construct knowledge because without an explanatory theory about how children construct knowledge, it is impossible to conceptualize specific objectives in relation to long-range goals. [For a clarification of this point, the reader is referred to Kamii (1984).]

I cannot insist enough on the importance of defining objectives based on precise scientific knowledge of how children construct knowledge. In arithmetic, for example, place value is taught not only in first grade but also in second grade, third grade, fourth grade, fifth grade, and sixth grade! It is amazing to me that no one in the Educational Establishment has noticed that there must be something profoundly wrong if the same thing has to be taught every single year in the first six grades. Place value ought to be outlawed in the first two grades, along with missing addends, because it is cognitively impossible for most young children to understand them.

Only after defining valid objectives based on children's development does it make sense to debate whether play is superior to worksheets to achieve these goals. Some kinds of play are more educational than others, and the same kind of play, such as the card game of War, is educational only at a certain level of intellectual development. I will not go into the details of these activities, since these have already been published in *Physical Knowledge in Preschool Education* (Kamii and DeVries, 1978), *Group Games in Early Education* (Kamii and DeVries, 1980), *Number in Preschool and Kindergarten* (Kamii, 1982), and *Young Children Reinvent Arithmetic* (Kamii, 1985).

The philosophy of child development may be correct, but we must go beyond philosophies or opinions if we want to stop being dictated to by other philosophies or opinions. I, therefore, plead for educators to construct the next stage of our profession from within by studying Piaget's theory about how human beings construct knowledge and moral values. It is easy to complain about the naiveté of behavioral objectives and the evils of achievement tests. But we must be willing to go beyond complaining and study children's construction of knowledge in the same rigorous way physicians study physiology and pathology, and engineers study physics and mathematics. Rather than being on the defensive and complaining about the pressure downward from the primary grades, we ought to be leading primary education toward excellence based on precise knowledge of cognitive and moral development.

The public knows that today's medicine and engineering are not what they were 30 or 40 years ago because it knows that science does not stand still. While the public does not tell physicians and engineers to go back to the basics of 40 years ago, it proudly tells us to go back to . . . I don't even know when. The reason is that politicians and the public honestly believe that there is no more to education than common sense, and that their common sense is as good as educators' common sense. As long as we continue to teach with worksheets, the public will continue to think of education as an unskilled job because any adult of normal intelligence can give and correct worksheets, with or without a teaching certificate.

The recommendations often espoused for "excellence" are based on mere common sense. It is not by lengthening the school day or the school year, giving more homework, pushing the 3 R's down to kindergarten, and increasing the requirements for high school graduation, that we are going to produce a generation who has the knowledge and originality to build a better world in ways that humanity has not yet imagined.

I am aware that scientific rigor alone will not stop legislators or the Educational Establishment from imposing its quick and simple solutions. But if all the teachers in America knew only parts of ten books by Piaget, the Establishment could not get away with their ignorance anymore.

I am also aware that education will always remain an art, in spite of my insistence on science. As Piaget (1965) said, the practice of medicine, too, is an art, but an art based on scientific knowledge rather than on mere common sense or intuition.

Reform is obviously needed in teacher education and colleges of education, too. Although change is painfully slow in colleges of education, the fact is that not a single course is taught today in educational psychology without some discussion of Piaget's theory. This is an improvement, considering that when I got my Ph.D. 20 years ago, I did not get even 2 minutes of graduate school devoted to Piaget's theory. The theory is usually badly taught and misunderstood, but professors of education, too, must go through one level after another of being wrong.

I apologize for all the negative statements I made about the child development philosophy, and would like to hear about any disagreement anyone may have. I honestly believe that educators must construct the next stage of our own profession from within if we are to stop being dictated by politicians and the public and by the old pendulum that keeps gong back to what did not work before. Back to basics is bound to fail because it is based on wrong, outdated assumptions about how human beings construct knowledge. Whether education will then go forward or backward on another bandwagon depends on us and our willingness to be scientifically more rigorous, both about how we define our objectives and about how we try to achieve these objectives.

DISCUSSION QUESTIONS

1. What is known about child development that can guide the teacher away from incorrect practices in the classroom?
2. How does the initial experience and behavior of the child help the teacher in planning learning experiences?
3. Are worksheets really harmful to children in the first grade? Which practices are better?
4. What is the relationship between Piaget's theory and behaviorism?
5. How does the theory of constructivism influence the curriculum and teaching practices for early childhood education?

Section Six: Evidence and Evaluation

EDITOR'S OVERVIEW

Although evaluation and research are far more sophisticated than answering the questions "What did you do?" and "What did you get?" the 1980s have become the decade of reliance on solid evaluation to justify good early education. As the chapters in this section point out, the evidential framework is growing. We have dependable insight into the developmental, educational, and economic outcomes from carefully designed program efforts. Even the best early childhood program in the schools cannot survive very long or confirm its value without comprehensive and systematic evaluation.

Powell clarifies the question of difference among program models and summarizes the effects of these models on the children. The studies do not identify the ultimate model, nor do they end the discussion of one approach over another. At best,

they produce questions that are yet to be answered. In the next two chapters, Schweinhart and Weikart, and Schweinhart et al. come to a somewhat different point in their review of the research evidence: that good programs work. These two chapters represent the evaluation research on several experimental programs and include a detailed analysis of the authors' own Perry Preschool model. Then, the purpose, practice, and personnel of evaluation are the subjects of Sponseller and Fink's discussion of evaluation in early childhood education.

The body of evidence is improving, and the science and art of evaluation are growing rapidly. Both the expert and the practitioner have equivalent obligations to know what they are doing, how to evaluate it, and how to communicate the results to the profession and the general public.

46. EFFECTS OF PROGRAM MODELS AND TEACHING PRACTICES

by Douglas R. Powell

During the last several years there has been an important shift in the public debate about early childhood education. Questions about the overall effectiveness of preschool programs are being replaced by an interest in the effectiveness of certain types of programs and teaching practices. This is not a new question, yet it is increasingly a critical one as growing numbers of programs emphasize basic academic skills and public schools become more involved in the education of 4-year-olds.

The early education field is characterized by a wide range of teaching approaches. A major difference is between didactic, teacher-directed approaches and child-centered or discovery approaches where children initiate or select activities. Program differences also exist regarding the amount of teacher contact with groups of children versus individual children. In addition, teachers vary in how often they present information versus ask questions, and in the amount of positive versus negative reinforcement of child behaviors. These and related program differences reflect diverse assumptions about how children learn and the role of teachers in guiding or structuring the learning process.

This [chapter] reviews findings of selected studies on the effects of different types of preschool programs and teaching practices on children. It includes recent research on the long-term effects of model early childhood programs and on the nature and consequences of teacher behaviors. Most of the research has involved children from predominantly low-income Black families and hence the findings cannot be generalized to other population groups.

SCOPE OF MAJOR STUDIES

In the late 1960s, several researchers initiated major studies comparing different preschool curriculum models. The aim was to determine whether one approach was superior in terms of child outcome. Fortunately, investigators have collected follow-up data on children who were enrolled in these preschool programs, permitting an examination of how children who experienced different types of early education function in later years. A brief description of these studies follows.

The Louisville Experiment, initiated by Louise Miller and her colleagues (1983b) in the Head Start program in Louisville, Kentucky, compared four preschool programs. Two programs used didactic instructional methods with small groups of children. One of these programs was the direct instruction model developed by Bereiter and Englemann (1966). This model is also known as the DISTAR program. In direct instruction, teachers use a patterned drill procedure to elicit responses, in unison, from children. The pace is rapid and repetitive. The curriculum is organized into reading, language, and arithmetic.

The other didactic program in the Louisville Experiment was DARCEE, developed by Susan Gray (see Gray, Ramsey, and Klaus, 1982). It emphasizes remediation of linguistic and conceptual deficiencies and the development of attitudes related to academic achievement (e.g., delayed gratification). Formal instruction in language is a major part of the program.

The two other programs in the Louisville Experiment did not entail group instruction. One was a Montessori (1964) program that emphasizes developing the senses, conceptual development, competence in daily activities, and character development. The child decides which activities to pursue. The other non-didactic program was a traditional nursery school that focuses on social and emotional development. Consistent with the child development point of view (Hymes, 1968), this program emphasizes development in all areas at each child's pace. The largest single portion of the school day is occupied by free play, a time when children engage in whatever activities they choose.

The Louisville Experiment included an initial sample of 214 four-year-old children in the four program models plus a control group of 34 children. Children were randomly assigned to programs by school. The study involved four each direct instruction, DARCEE, and traditional classrooms, and two Montessori classrooms (14 total). The short-term effects (through second grade) are

See page 340 for acknowledgment and references.

reported in Miller and Dyer (1975), and the long-term effects are reported in Miller and Bizzell (1983a, 1983b).

The High/Scope Curriculum Comparison Study (Schweinhart, Weikart, and Larner, 1986) was developed by David Weikart in Ypsilanti, Michigan to compare three program models: direct instruction (DISTAR), the High/Scope model, and a traditional child-centered nursery school. The High/Scope model uses an open-framework approach where teacher and child plan and initiate activities and actively work together. It is known as the High/Scope Cognitively Oriented Preschool Curriculum (Hohmann, Banet, and Weikart, 1979). Parents of each child in all program models received a home visit from the teacher every 2 weeks. Initially the study involved 68 three- and four-year-old children from low-income families; 65 percent were Black. Children were randomly assigned to program models. Study details and a follow up of the children at 10 years of age are reported in Weikart, Epstein, Schweinhart, and Bond (1978). A follow up at 15 years of age is reported in Schweinhart et al. (1986).

In this [chapter], discussion of the long-term effects found in the Louisville and High/Scope studies will be supplemented by findings from curriculum comparison studies by Karnes and her colleagues (Karnes, Shwedel, and Williams, 1983) involving preschool children, and by Stallings (1975) involving Follow Through classrooms in first and third grades. This [chapter] also draws on additional research reports on the long-term effects of the direct instruction model.

A major limitation of curriculum comparison studies is that they confound content, activities, and materials with teaching techniques. Some teaching practices are necessarily related to program goals and content. For instance, if a program goal is to teach numbers, it seems inappropriate for a teacher to ask a child to elaborate on the correct answer to the question, ''What comes after three?'' (Miller, Bugbee, and Hybertson, 1985). This confounding makes it difficult to determine whether program content, teaching technique, or some other program dimension is related to child outcome.

To avoid this problem, Miller et al. (1985) conducted a study where both content (e.g., language) and global teaching method (e.g., small group instruction) were controlled in order to determine whether specific teaching techniques (e.g., amount of reinforcement) were related to child outcome. This 1-year study involved eight Head Start classrooms where teachers used the

PeabodyLanguage Development Program (Dunn, Horton, and Smith, 1968) in a standardized manner. The sample included 111 four-year-old children from low-income, predominantly Black families. The research is referred to in this [chapter] as the Preschool Dimensions Study. This study by Miller and colleagues should not be confused with the Louisville Experiment; they are different investigations.

SUMMARY OF FINDINGS

Findings of the follow-up studies do not support the idea that different types of well-implemented preschool programs have similar effects on children. The data suggest that the kind of preschool program attended by low-income children may affect them through their middle-school and early teenage years. In particular, the results raise questions about the effects of didactic approaches to early education. They also indicate that program effects vary by sex of child.

Long-Term Studies

Follow-up data from the Louisville Experiment show that by eighth grade, boys who had been enrolled in a nondidactic preschool program (Montessori or traditional) were superior in school achievement to boys who had been enrolled in a didactic preschool program (direct instruction or DARCEE). Nondidactic boys had a 12-month advantage in reading and a 10-month advantage in math compared to didactic boys. In sixth and seventh grade, the reading and math scores of nondidactic boys were also superior to the scores of didactic boys. By eighth grade, didactic girls performed better in reading than nondidactic girls but not in earlier years and not in math at any year beyond second grade.

There were also differences in IQ scores. During the period from prekindergarten to eighth grade, the boys who had been in a didactic preschool program lost 9.2 points while the boys formerly in a nondidactic preschool program lost 3.1 points. Both didactic and nondidactic girls lost 11.8 points from the end of prekindergarten to the end of eighth grade (Miller and Bizzell, 1983a). There was a greater IQ decrease for direct instruction children than for the other program groups. Boys formerly enrolled in the Montessori preschool program performed significantly higher than all other groups in math and reading in sixth, seventh, and eighth grade. This was not the case for girls. DARCEE boys performed significantly lower in reading in sixth, seventh, and eighth grade than boys in the other three programs combined. They also scored lower in sixth-grade math (Miller and Bizzell, 1983a). By 10th grade, the superior performance of Montessori boys in achievement tests had continued. They performed above national norms academically and were in the normal IQ range. In preschool, Montessori boys started at the same IQ levels as DARCEE boys, but by 10th grade the Montessori boys were 15.3 points above the DARCEE boys (Miller and Bizzell cited in Stallings and Stipek, 1986). The IQ scores of Montessori girls increased at the end of preschool and then dropped dramatically.

While additional research is needed to confirm and elaborate upon these findings, the results of the Louisville Experiment cannot be dismissed as chance. The research was well designed and executed, with random assignment and no indication of selective attrition of children. The original sample was large, and 60 percent to 65 percent were secured for the follow up. Also, longitudinal research by Karnes et al. (1983) indicates there were a higher percentage of high school graduates, higher school success ratings, and a lower grade-retention rate among former Montessori preschool children compared to children who were enrolled in four other model preschool programs.

Results of the High/Scope Curriculum Comparison Study indicate that at age 15 (ninth grade), children who had attended the direct instruction (DISTAR) program engaged in twice as many delinquent acts as the children who had been in the High/Scope and traditional preschool programs. The delinquent behavior included 5 times as many acts of property violence. This juvenile delinquency pattern, however, was no worse than that of control group in the Perry Preschool study. The DISTAR children participated less often in sports and held fewer appointments to a school office or job. Also, in response to the question, "How does your family feel you're doing?," a greater percentage of DISTAR children expressed a negative impression ("poorly") than children enrolled in the High/Scope (0%) and traditional (6%) preschool program. These social behavior outcomes are based on self-reported data. School achievement scores and IQ performance were not reported for the sample at 15 years of age. Follow-up data at earlier points (4 through 10 years) indicate no significant differences by curriculum model in IQ and achievement scores (Weikart et al., 1978). Schweinhart et al. (1986) caution that the High/Scope study is not definitive. Although an impressive 79 percent of the original children

were included at 15 years of age in the follow up, the sample is relatively small.

Didactic preschool programs may not sustain higher IQs and achievement scores unless they are followed by a similar program in kindergarten and elementary school. Children who entered a nondidactic program after attending a direct instruction preschool program did not perform well on achievement tests in the Louisville Experiment (Miller and Dyer, 1975). Similarly, Becker and Gersten (1982) found that without continued involvement in the direct instruction Follow Through program, most children demonstrated losses when compared to a standardized sample. Another study found that fifth graders who had been in a DISTAR program for 4 years had significantly higher achievement scores than comparison children (Meyer, Gersten, and Gutkin, 1984). Meyer (1984) examined three direct instruction Follow Through classrooms for 3 to 4 years, and found superior reading and math performance in ninth grade when contrasted to a comparison group.

Short-Term Studies

Short-term studies provide additional data on the effects of different program approaches and teaching practices. Stallings's (1975) study of first-and-third-grade Follow Through classrooms found higher scores in reading and mathematics among children in highly controlled classrooms where teachers used systematic instruction and a high rate of positive reinforcement. In flexible classrooms where there was more exploratory material and children had more choice, children scored higher on a test of nonverbal perceptual problem solving, showed greater willingness to work independently, and had lower absence rates (perhaps an indicator of attitude toward school). Also, children from more flexible classrooms took responsibility for their own successes but not for their failures. Children in the highly structured classrooms took responsibility for their failures but attributed their successes to the teachers or some other outside force. Similarly, a 2-year study of elementary schoolchildren by Fry and Addington (1984) found that children in open classrooms had higher scores in social problem solving and self-esteem than children in more closed, traditional classrooms.

In a study of 13 Head Start classrooms, Huston-Stein, Friedrich-Cofer, and Susman (1977) found that children in classrooms with a high level of teacher-directed activities engaged in less prosocial behavior with peers and less imaginative play, and were less aggressive than children in classrooms with a lower level of adult control. Children in the high-structure classes were more attentive in circle time and helped to clean up more after free play, but did not show more independent task persistence. In an observational study of free play periods in preschool classrooms by Fagot (1973), children who engaged in a high amount of task-relevant behavior had teachers who gave fewer directions, criticized less, and responded more to questions.

As noted earlier, a problem with curriculum comparison studies is that they cannot identify relevant program dimensions. For example, when positive child outcomes are produced by a structured academic preschool program such as direct instruction, is it because of academic content or a teacher technique such as drill? In the Preschool Dimensions Study, where content and global methods were held constant across eight classrooms, Miller et al. (1985) found that didactic teaching (drill) was negatively related to boys' auditory and visual receptive skills but positively associated with verbal expression. The researchers questioned the use of didactic methods to improve boys' expressive abilities, noting there are likely to be alternative methods that may not have a negative impact on important receptive skills.

The types of questions asked and the information provided by teachers also relate to child behavior. In a preschool program that used teacher questioning to enhance children's representational thinking, children showed significantly greater competence in tasks that required prediction than children in a traditional nursery school program. Also, parents of children in the inquiry program reported their children had more hobbies and interests, and were more curious compared to parent reports of children in a traditional nursery group (Sigel, 1979).

Smothergill, Olson, and Moore (1971) compared two teaching practices with nursery school children. In one group, teachers used an elaborative style by giving detailed task information and encouraging child comment and involvement. In the other group, teachers used a nonelaborative style, giving only necessary task information and not encouraging child involvement. Children in the elaboratively taught group performed better from pre- to posttests on a verbal similarities task and on a storytelling task.

Naturally occurring teacher-child interactions in free play situations were used by Hart and Risley (1975) for incidental teaching of language skills. Teachers responded to child interests by emphasizing compound sentences. The children's unprompted use of compound sentences increased, first in those directed to teachers and then to other children. The incidental teaching approach also seemed to stimulate spontaneous variety in speech.

PRESCHOOL EXPERIENCES AND SEX OF CHILD

In addition to the sex differences in program outcome noted previously, it appears that boys and girls may have different day-to-day experiences in the same classroom. In three separate classroom observation studies, Fagot (1973) found that teachers appeared to instruct girls more than boys. They answered girls' questions more often, and gave girls more favorable comments. Similarly, in all four of the preschool models examined in the Louisville Experiment, girls received more instructional contact than boys (Biber, Miller, and Dyer, 1972).

A number of differences in teacher behavior were related to sex of the child in the Preschool Dimensions Study (Miller et al., 1985). Girls received twice as much drill from teachers as boys. Moreover, it appeared that when boys were uninterested in group work they received individual instruction; girls in the same situations were reprimanded. Positive reinforcement from the teacher was associated with boys' volunteering and offering opinions, but with girls' peer interactions. Also, girls who volunteered more and asked more questions received relatively more negative than positive reinforcement. The data suggest that this child behavior pattern probably was viewed by teachers as disruptive even though it was task-related.

More research is needed on factors surrounding teacher behaviors in relation to sex of children. Are teachers responding to sex differences already present in the children, or are they responding to their own preconceived biases toward the sexes (Fagot, 1973)?

Variations in child behavior in a preschool program were associated with different child outcomes in the Preschool Dimensions Study (Miller et al., 1985). Further, relationships between child behavior and child outcome varied by sex of child. One of the most striking findings dealt with the effects of participation in group work. For boys, group participation was related to higher scores in divergent thinking and logic, but for girls group participation was related to lower scores in logic and curiosity.

INTERPRETATIONS AND IMPLICATIONS

Taken together or separately, these studies do not provide a solid empirical base for advocating one program or teaching method over another. However, they do raise crucial questions about the effects of didactic versus nondidactic approaches, and the experiences of boys versus girls in early education programs.

Why would the nondidactic Montessori program prove to be beneficial for low-income boys but not girls? Why would there be a tendency for girls but not boys to benefit from didactic direct instruction and DARCEE programs? Miller and Bizzell (1983a) have speculated that because girls mature faster than boys, girls may be more ready to process information gained through observation and verbal instruction in a didactic preschool group setting. Boys may need more hands-on manipulation of materials such as provided by the Montessori approach. The individually paced, self-correcting, cognitive materials of the Montessori program may be a good match for 4-year-old boys' cognitive receptivity (see Stallings and Stipek, 1986).

There is the strong suggestion that didactic preschool programs may not produce positive long-term results unless they are followed by similar didactic programs in elementary school. Moreover, the High/Scope study shows negative results in the social behavior of 15-year-olds who attended a didactic direct instruction preschool. It appears that the direct instruction (DISTAR) program did not actually harm the children's social development, because there is no evidence that the direct instruction program children engaged in more delinquency than they would have if they had not attended the preschool program. Yet children enrolled in two nondidactic preschool programs (traditional nursery and High/Scope models) had lower rates of juvenile delinquency and other social behavior problems. Schweinhart et al. (1986) speculate that the presence of social behavior goals and child-initiated learning activities in the nondidactic programs may account for the differences.

We must use caution in our assumptions about why various preschool curricula might yield different results. The dimensions of a preschool classroom that relate most strongly to child outcomes are not always the ones that discriminate between programs. For instance, Soar and Soar (1972) found the amount of teacher talk (versus child talk) in a classroom was related to complex-abstract cognitive growth (e.g., word meanings) in children, yet the dimension of teacher versus child talk did not differentiate programs. We need more

research such as the Preschool Dimensions Study (Miller et al., 1985) to identify the specific aspects of programs that relate to child behavior and outcomes.

The findings of the studies reviewed here challenge the idea that any theoretically coherent, well-implemented preschool program can have positive effects on children. This was the influential 1978 message of the High/Scope Curriculum Comparison Study (Weikart et al.), and subsequent investigations indicated that different types of programs achieved similar results (Lazar and Darlington, 1982; Karnes et al., 1983). Now there is persuasive evidence to the contrary.

Teachers should be sensitive to how they approach girls versus boys. For instance, if praise is given to boys for one type of behavior and to girls for another, as the findings suggest, teachers should examine carefully the determinants of their own behavior. At a maximum, perhaps different teaching strategies should be used with low-income boys versus girls. The group participation which had positive benefits for boys but negative outcomes for girls in the Preschool Dimensions Study raises questions about the appropriateness of using the same method for both sexes. The Lousiville Experiment findings raise similar questions.

There is a profound need for research on program approaches and teaching practices with children from families other than those with low incomes. Very little of the research reviewed here can be applied to children from middle-class families, regardless of race. This is a serious limitation in the field today. Equally limiting is the narrow range of outcome areas generally considered in program evaluations. Considerably more attention needs to be given to social competence (Zigler and Trickett, 1978), and to attitudinal factors such as a child's disposition to learn (Katz, 1985) and desire to read, write, and think critically (Willert and Kamii, 1985).

Both practitioners and researchers need to consider the contributions of child characteristics and classroom behaviors to child outcomes. In the Preschool Dimensions Study, child behaviors were stronger predictors of child outcome than teacher behaviors. We need to examine two-way processes in the child-teacher/program relationship. For instance, in one study, high-arousal children appeared to be ill-suited for an open classroom environment (Koester and Farley, 1982). Instead of searching for *the* best approach to early childhood education, our energies should focus on finding the best match between child and program.

DISCUSSION QUESTIONS

1. Are there essential differences among the various models for early education programs?

2. What were the findings of the major comparative studies on program models?

3. Do differences in program models produce immediate and long-range effects that are also different from program to program?

4. How does gender interact with type of program model? Are some programs more effective with girls? with boys?

5. Should future curriculum development take the best parts of several models, or should professionals be seeking a generic model that is more effective?

47. EVIDENCE THAT GOOD EARLY CHILDHOOD PROGRAMS WORK

by Lawrence J. Schweinhart and David P. Weikart

In the early 1960s, many leading educators and social scientists expressed hopes that preschool education programs for poor children could help break the cycle of poverty. They assumed that a chain of cause and effect linked family poverty to the scholastic failure of children and to their subsequent poverty as adults.

These educators and social scientists speculated that preschool education would enhance the intelligence of poor children. This theory received support from early reports that several experimental preschool programs were in fact raising I.Q.s.[1]

However, two well-publicized events in 1969 undermined the popular credibility of the scientific basis for claims about the beneficial effects of preschool education for poor children. The first was a negative evaluation, by the Westinghouse Learning Corporation and Ohio University, of the first years of Head Start; the second was Arthur Jensen's article in the *Harvard Educational Review*, in which he argued that "compensatory education has been tried and it apparently has failed."[2]

As the years passed, however, evidence of the effectiveness of preschool began to mount. Evidence from several evaluations demonstrated that good preschool programs have both short- and long-term positive effects on low-income youngsters. Many studies bear on these issues, but we will consider only seven of these evaluations here. The ones we chose, though not perfect, are among the most scientifically rigorous, and reviewing them provides a clear picture of the long-term effectiveness of early childhood education, as well as an overview of some of the problems that researchers face in conducting such studies.

SEVEN STUDIES

The seven studies listed in Table 1 have followed subjects at least to age 9 and at most to age 21. They have been conducted in locales that represent a cross section of America's urban communities, in both northern and southern states,
though all were conducted in areas east of the Mississippi River. Six of the seven studies evaluated programs that operated in a single location.

These seven studies and most of the other recent research on the effects of early childhood education have focused on children living in poverty. The concern of the 1960s for righting the wrongs of poverty was closely tied to the struggle of blacks to obtain civil rights. Thus the response to this concern tended to focus on the needs of the black population, combining compensatory education programs with new policies to insure equal rights in voting, housing, employment, and education. It is not surprising, then, that in most of the studies reviewed here, at least 90 percent of the subjects are black.[3]

The size of the samples and any special characteristics of the populations are listed in Table 2. The sample sizes varied from a low of 40 in the Milwaukee Study to 2,058 in the New York Prekindergarten Program. The Perry Preschool Project focused on children whose tested I.Q.s at age 3 were between 60 and 90.* The Milwaukee Study focused on children whose mothers had tested I.Q.s of 75 or below. The Harlem Study focused exclusively on males. The New York Prekindergarten Program was open to the public in selected school districts, so the sample more nearly represents the racial mix of low-income families in the population at large.

Attrition is a major threat to the validity of longitudinal studies. As more subjects are lost, both internal and external validity are at risk. The investigators who carried out these seven studies fared well in locating subjects for their follow-up studies: they found at least 71 percent of the original subjects. The Perry Preschool Project found 100 percent of its original subjects and interviewed 98 percent of them. The median percentage of subjects located in the follow-ups was 80 percent. Moreover, differential attrition across groups within the subject populations was not large enough to constitute a major problem.

Four of the seven studies used the standard

See pages 340–41 for acknowledgment, footnote, references, and recent reports on the seven studies.

Table 1. The Seven Studies

Study	Year Study Began	Place	Age of Subjects At Last Report
Early Training Project	1962	Murfreesboro, Tenn.	21
Perry Preschool Project	1962	Ypsilanti, Mich.	19
Mother-Child Home Program	1965	Long Island, N.Y.	9-13
Harlem Study	1966	New York, N.Y.	13
Rome Head Start Program	1966	Rome, Ga.	20
Milwaukee Study	1968	Milwaukee, Wis.	10
New York Pre-K Program	1975	New York State	9

experimental design; their treatment and control groups were selected from the same population by procedures designed to insure equivalent groups. In ther study of the Early Training Project and in the Milwaukee Study, students were randomly assigned to groups. In the Harlem Study, treatment groups were selected by applying the same sample selection procedures to children born in different months. By chance, one of the two experimental groups had an average I.Q. at age 3 that was six points higher than the average I.Q. of the control group at age 2 years and eight months. This difference was controlled for in the analysis of group differences.

Three of the seven studies use a quasi-experimental design; their treatment and control groups were selected from different populations. One such study, that of the Rome Head Start Program, began in 1966 by identifying all first-graders in the Rome, Georgia, public schools who qualified for federal funds for the economically disadvantaged. Some of these students had attended Head Start and some had not. In the absence of data to the contrary, we cannot rule out the possibility that Head Start participants and nonparticipants in this study differed in important ways before the study began. Because of such doubts, this study cannot stand alone. However, in combination with other studies, it bears examination because of its extraordinary duration.

In the study of the Mother-Child Home Program—a quasi-experimental effort for the years reviewed here—treatment was offered to all willing participants within a given geographic area. This group was then compared to a demographically similar control group in a nearby geographic area. The groups thus selected were generally equivalent on important background factors, though some risk of unmeasured group differences may affect the outcomes of the study.

The third quasi-experimental study, that of the New York Prekindergarten Program, compared two control groups to an experimental group of approximately 1,800 youngsters who took part in the program in 1966. The control group for comparisons of test scores consisted of 87 children on the program's waiting list. This group may or may not have differed from the program participants, depending on the original procedures for selecting participants. For comparisons of scholastic placement, the control group consisted of both the waiting-list group and a group of 171 children of slightly higher socioeconomic status who came from neighboring school districts. Thus some between-group differences certainly exist, but they tend to favor the control group. For example, mothers in the treatment group reported 10.9 years of schooling while control-group mothers from other districts reported 12.0 years of schooling.

The seven programs varied in size, design, and presumably cost. The Milwaukee program was the most extensive, providing full-time, year-round developmental child care for children ranging in age from a few months to 6 years. It also provided an educational and vocational program for mothers. The Perry Preschool Project provided one home visit per week and a morning classroom program five days a week for two school years (at ages 3 and 4). Its classroom component was equivalent in scope to the one-year programs of the New York Prekindergarten Program for 4-year-olds and the Rome Head Start Program for 5-year-olds. The latter two programs also included several home visits during the school year and offered parents the chance to become involved in the classrooms. The Early Training Project featured part-time classroom experiences five days a week in the summer and weekly home visits during the school year for either three years (for children starting at age 3) or two years (for children starting at age 4). The

Table 2. Design Information

Study	Selection Procedure	Special Sample Characteristics*	Original Sample Size	Subjects Included in Most Recent Follow-up %
Experimental Design				
Early Training Project	Random assignment	——	90	80
Harlem Study	Selections from same population	Boys only	315	81
Milwaukee Study	Random assignment	Mothers' I.Q.s 75 and below	40	80
Perry Preschool Project	Assignment of matched pairs	Children's I.Q.s 60-90	123	98
Quasi-experimental Design				
Mother-Child Home Program	Assignment by site	——	250	74
New York Pre-K Program	Some assignment by site	42% white; 42% black; 16% other	2,058	75
Rome Head Start Program	Self-selection	Blacks and whites	218	71

*All samples were selected on the basis of family poverty. Unless otherwise noted, 90% or more of the subjects are black.

Mother-Child Home Program consisted of twice weekly home visits for one to two years, and the Harlem Study provided one-to-one sessions between a child and a tutor twice weekly for eight months.

In reviewing the findings of these studies, we will also mention corroborating findings from the Consortium for Longitudinal Studies. The Consortium was an association of a dozen educators and psychologists, each of whom had initiated a longitudinal study of an early childhood program during the 1960s and had agreed to collaborate in a follow-up assessment during the late 1970s. The Consortium was formed in 1975 by Irving Lazar of Cornell University and Edith Grotberg of the U.S. Administration for Children, Youth, and Families. As investigators for the Perry Preschool Project, we belonged to the Consortium, and our review of the seven studies in this [chapter] is the better for our experience with that group. The Consortium based its conclusions on careful review of the methodology of each longitudinal study, and we maintain that tradition here.[4]

FINDINGS

The documented effects of early childhood education may be organized according to the major outcomes for participants at each period of their lives. These outcomes and the ages at which they occurred are: improved intellectual performance during early childhood; better scholastic placement and improved scholastic achievement during the elementary school years; and, during adolescence, a lower rate of delinquency and higher rates of both graduation from high school and employment at age 19.

Early childhood. The best-documented preschool effect is an immediate improvement in intellectual performance as represented by intelligence test scores. Of the studies reviewed here, the six that collected such data all attest to the immediate positive effect of early childhood education on I.Q. Four studies reported a maximum effect of between one-half and one standard deviation (16 points on the Stanford-Binet test); however, statistically significant group differences disappeared by age 8. The intensive Milwaukee Study had a maximum effect of two standard deviations; the difference when the children were last tested (at age 10) was still greater than one standard deviation.

Two other studies in the Consortium for Longitudinal Studies reported effects on I.Q. of about half a standard deviation, which disappeared by age 8. Craig Ramey and his colleagues recently reviewed 11 experimental studies that included I.Q. data on children between the ages of 1 and 6; eight of these studies had data on children between the ages of 1 and 3. In every study, the average I.Q. of children who participated in preschool was as good as or better than the average I.Q. of children in control groups. I.Q. differences ranged from zero in two studies to 21 points in one; the median difference was six points. Of the eight studies with I.Q. data for children between the ages of 1 and 3, six showed I.Q. differences of up to half a standard deviation, and two showed I.Q. differences between one-half and one standard deviation.[5]

Elementary school years. In the studies we are reviewing, every single comparison of scholastic placement was favorable to the group that had received early childhood education (Table 3). In four of the five studies that included data on special education placements, the rate of such placements was usually reduced by half. In the Perry Preschool Project, the overall figure for special education placements (by student-years rather than by students, as reported here) was reduced by half. Two studies report statistically significant reductions in retentions as well. The Harlem Study could not obtain data on placements in special education.

The staff of the Consortium for Longitudinal Studies reported similar findings on scholastic placement. Moreover, their technique of pooling probability estimates confirms the improbability of obtaining all the findings in Table 3 purely by chance.

Avoiding placement in special education programs was one of the major financial benefits of preschool education to emerge from the cost-benefit analysis of the Perry Preschool Project. The strength and consistency of the finding that participants avoided such placements in these other studies argue persuasively that these other preschool programs, too, would show a favorable cost-benefit ratio.

Most of the experimentally derived evidence for the positive impact of preschool on scholastic achievement comes from the study of the Perry Preschool Project, which found differences consis-

tently favoring the preschool group over the control group at ages 7, 8, 9, 10, 11, 14, and 19. Of the other studies reviewed here, only that of the Early Training Project had sufficient data on achievement (from 70 percent or more of the subjects) to enable conclusions to be drawn. This study found some positive effects at age 8, but no effects at ages 7, 10, or 11.

The Consortium for Longitudinal Studies analyzed achievement test scores across seven of its studies. The pooled analysis found statistically significant positive effects of preschool on arithmetic scores at ages 10, 11, and 12, but not at age 13. In reading, the Consortium analysis found statistically significant positive effects of preschool at age 10 only.

Adolescence. The studies of the Perry Preschool Project and the Rome Head Start Program are the only preschool studies we know of that have collected information on delinquency or crime—either from police and court records or from self-reports. Neither study found a difference between participants and nonparticipants in the number of persons referred to juvenile court. But the study of the Perry Preschool program did find reduced delinquency among participants—documented by self-reports at age 15[6] and by official records of either total number of arrests or referrals to juvenile court.

Both the Perry Preschool Project and the Early Training Project collected information on rates of teenage pregnancy. The Perry Project reported 64 teenage pregnancies per 100 females who had attended preschool and 117 teenage pregnancies per 100 females who had not attended preschool. The Early Training Project found that 38 percent of the females in the study reported a pregnancy, with no between-group differences. The Early Training Project did find that after pregnancy and childbirth, 88 percent of the females who had gone to preschool were likely to complete high school, while only 30 percent of the females who had not gone to preschool were likely to return to school after pregnancy and childbirth.

In three of the studies reviewed here, youngsters who had attended a preschool program were less likely to drop out of high school than were their peers who had not attended preschool. Table 3 shows that the dropout rates of those who attended preschool as opposed to those who did not were 17 percent lower in the Rome Head Start Program, 21 percent lower in the Early Training Project, and 18 percent lower in the Perry Preschool Project. As far as we know, the Perry Project is the only study of the effects of preschool that includes data on

Table 3. Findings For Scholastic Placement

Study	Program Group %	Control Group %	p*
Rome Head Start (age 20)			
Placed in special education	11	25	.019
Retained in grade	51	63	—
Dropped out of high school	50	67	.042
Perry Preschool (age 19)			
Placed in special education	37	50	—
Retained in grade	35	40	—
Dropped out of high school	33	51	.034
Early Training (age 18)			
Placed in special education	3	29	.004
Retained in grade	53	69	—
Dropped out of high school	22	43	.079
Harlem (age 13)			
Placed in special education	No data	No data	No data
Retained in grade	24	45	.006
Dropped out of high school	No data	No data	No data
New York Pre-K (age 9)			
Placed in special education	2	5	.006
Retained in grade	16	21	.019
Dropped out of high school	No data	No data	No data
Mother-Child Home (age 9)			
Placed in special education	14	39	.005
Retained in grade	13	19	—
Dropped out of high school	No data	No data	No data
Milwaukee	No data	No data	No data

*Two-tailed p-values are presented if less than .1.

employment after graduation, reporting an employment rate at age 19 of 50 percent for the preschool group and 32 percent for the nonpreschool group.

From our review of these seven studies and from the data collected by the Consortium for Longitudinal Studies, we feel safe in concluding that *good* early childhood programs are a wise investment of public funds that can benefit children, their families, and all citizens and taxpayers. To what extent is the U.S. making this investment today?

During the past 30 years, the federal government has provided the lion's share of funding for early childhood programs for children from low-income families. For prekindergartners, this funding has taken two forms: the Head Start Program and subsidized child care. Head Start has maintained a modest but steady growth since it began in 1965. Federal funding for child care—now provided primarily through the Social Services Block Grant and the Child Care Food Program—has had its ups and downs, but it is still substan-

tial. The federal government annually provides about a billion dollars each for Head Start and subsidized child care.

Compensatory education, during the past three decades, has essentially been delivered by Title I of the Elementary and Secondary Education Act of 1965, now Chapter 1 of President Reagan's Education Consolidation and Improvement Act of 1981. In deciding who participates in Chapter 1 programs, school districts must give priority to children enrolled in kindergarten through grade 12. Thus only a small portion of Chapter 1 funding has found its way to programs serving very young children. During the 1981-82 school year, Chapter 1 funds served a total of 4,866,108 students; only 332,355 of them (7 percent) were in kindergarten or prekindergarten programs.

However, there are good reasons for state and local school administrators to use whatever Chapter 1 funds they can for prekindergarten programs for children at risk of scholastic failure. The cost-benefit analysis of the Perry Preschool Project showed that school systems recoup their investment in a one-year prekindergarten program by the time the participants graduate from high school.

But the federal government is only a minor source of education funding in general. Well over 90 percent of funding for education comes from state and local sources. Furthermore, state and local governments bear the largest burden of paying for juvenile delinquency, teenage pregnancy, and welfare assistance. Therefore, state and local governments stand to profit the most from investment in good early childhood programs for children from low-income families.

California leads the nation in funding for early childhood education and child care, spending $277 million in 1984-85. No other state even comes close. New York spends only $155 million on early childhood programs, with $141 million of that sum coming from the Federal Social Services Block Grant. However, the New York Prekindergarten Program has received a good evaluation, and both the staunch support of that program by Gov. Mario Cuomo and State Education Commissioner Gordon Ambach and the recent increase in funding for that program (from $10 million to $14 million) are largely due to the positive research results. In South Carolina, Gov. Richard Riley made expanded child development programs an integral part of his education reform package with funding for early childhood programs slated to rise to about $11 million. Texas has authorized $50 million for early childhood programs in the coming years, and Missouri recently passed comprehensive legislation on early childhood education. Funding legislation for early childhood programs is now pending in more than a dozen states.

Yet, despite compelling research findings and despite the recent actions of a number of states, there are still not enough good early childhood programs for children from low-income families. We must all do something about that.

DISCUSSION QUESTIONS

Questions for this chapter and Chapter 48 are combined; they appear at the end of Chapter 48 on page 225.

48. THE PROMISE OF EARLY CHILDHOOD EDUCATION

by Lawrence J. Schweinhart, John R. Berrueta-Clement, W. Steven Barnett,
Ann S. Epstein, and David P. Weikart

One out of every five children in the United States lives in poverty.[1] Only 39 percent of the 4-year-olds in families that are below the poverty line attend preschool programs.[2] Yet recent longitudinal studies of early childhood programs—such as the Perry Preschool Study that we are reporting here—have shown that good preschool programs can have a beneficial effect on the lives of children reared in poverty.[3]

The federal government invests about a billion and a half dollars annually in early childhood programs for poor children through Head Start, federally funded child-care services, education programs for the disadvantaged, and incentive grants for handicapped children.[4] Several states invest in early childhood programs independently of the federal government, and even more states are considering doing so. New York and South Carolina have substantially increased their funding of early childhood programs, and Texas has begun a new program. Local agencies and school districts also provide early childhood programs, though no national statistics have been compiled. A recent survey by the Michigan Department of Education found that one-third of that state's school districts offer prekindergarten programs.[5]

The past two decades have seen an increasing number of reports of longitudinal evaluations of early childhood programs for poor children. Such research was originally based on the hypothesis that human intelligence could be improved during the early years. However, as the years have passed, the research has broadened its conceptual framework and considered program effects other than test scores and success in school.

In addition, theorizing about human development has moved beyond questions of whether such personal traits as intelligence are inherited or are products of experience. The focus today is on the unfolding relationship between an individual's genetic make-up and environmental opportunities. Still, all that we can observe and measure is a person's performance in a given setting. Thus the effects of the Perry Preschool Program reported here may be seen as a sequence of performances in various settings, at various times, and in various domains of life.

THE PERRY PRESCHOOL STUDY

The Perry Preschool Study examined the lives of 123 youths born between 1958 and 1962. The students were divided into five waves: Wave Zero, 4-year-olds selected in 1962; Wave One, 3-year-olds selected in 1962; Wave Two, 3-year-olds selected in 1963; Wave Three, 3-year-olds selected in 1964; and Wave Four, 3-year-olds selected in 1965.

Each wave was divided into a preschool group and a nonpreschool group. The Wave Zero preschool group attended preschool for one year; the other four preschool groups attended preschool for two years. For purposes of analysis, we generally combine the waves to form a larger sample. Our most recent longitudinal analysis was conducted using data collected when the subjects were 19 years old, an age reached by Wave Zero in 1977 and by Wave Four in 1981.

The children selected for the study lived in the attendance area of the Perry Elementary School, a neighborhood located on the south side of Ypsilanti, Michigan, that has been populated primarily by low-income black families for some time. Children of preschool age were identified by means of a school census of families with youngsters already attending the school, by referrals from neighborhood groups, and by door-to-door canvassing.

Once the preschool-age children had been identified, the socioeconomic levels of their families were assessed on the basis of the parents' education, the level of employment of the head of the household, and the ratio of rooms in the home to persons in the household. Children from families below a specified socioeconomic level were given the Stanford-Binet Intelligence Test. Those whose scores were between 60 and 90 and who exhibited no evidence of an organic handicap were selected for the study.

Families whose children participated in the study were considerably less well-off than the average American family, according to comparisons with data from the 1970 U.S. Census. The parents of participants had a median 9.4 years of schooling— only .4 years less than the national average for blacks in 1970, but 2.6 years less than the national average for the entire population. Fewer than one

See pages 341–42 for acknowledgment and references.

in five of the parents had completed high school. Forty-seven percent of the children in the study lived in single-parent families, although only 14 percent of all American families in 1970 were headed by a single adult.[6]

The scientific strength of this study—its ability to identify preschool effects 20 years later—is primarily due to an experimental design that randomly assigned subjects to treatment and control groups. Neither teachers nor parents had any say in who was assigned to the program and who was not.

Each year, children in the incoming wave were put in pairs according to their Stanford-Binet test scores; the members of each pair were assigned to different groups. Then, pairs of similarly ranked children were exchanged between the two groups to equate within-group ratios of boys to girls and to adjust the average socioeconomic level of the two groups. Finally, a toss of a coin determined the group assigned to the preschool condition and the group assigned to the nonpreschool condition.

We made few exceptions in this assignment procedure. In Waves Two, Three, and Four, any siblings were assigned to the same group as their older siblings in order to maintain the independence of the groups. Between three and six children with single parents employed outside the home were transferred from the preschool group to the nonpreschool group because they were unable to participate in the classroom and/or home-visit components of the preschool program.

Using these procedures, 58 children were assigned to the preschool group and 65 to the nonpreschool group. Once children were assigned to the groups, none of the families withdrew from the program.

Group comparisons on background characteristics provide added assurance that the effects we found can be attributed to the preschool program. When they entered the project, our two subject groups showed no statistically significant differences ($p < .1$) on the following background characteristics: ratio of boys to girls, child's age and I.Q. at entry, family socioeconomic level, father's presence or absence, parents' scholastic achievement, family welfare status, father's level of employment, household density, family size, and birth order.[7] Because several children whose single parents worked outside the home had been reassigned from the preschool group to the nonpreschool group, there was a statistically significant difference between the groups on maternal employment—9 percent maternal employment in the preschool group versus 31 percent in the nonpreschool group. Statistical analyses indicate that the maternal employment rate had no effect on the pattern of findings.[8]

THE PRESCHOOL PROGRAM

The program to which the 58 children in the preschool group were assigned was an organized educational program directed at the intellectual and social development of young children. Each year, teams of four teachers, who had received extensive inservice training staffed the program. The children took part in the program for two school years, at ages 3 and 4, except in the case of Wave Zero, which included only 4-year-olds, who took part in the program for only one year.

The school year lasted for 7½ months, from October to May. Classes were conducted 2½ hours each morning, Monday through Friday; the teacher/child ratio was one adult for every five or six children. Teachers made home visits to each mother and child for 1½ hours weekly. *The Cognitively Oriented Curriculum*[9] describes the course of daily activities.

Except for participation in the preschool program, both groups received the same treatment. All 123 children in the study were interviewed and tested in exactly the same way regardless of which group they were in. Testers, interviewers, and subsequent teachers were not informed about the group membership of the children. Any knowledge they did acquire about preschool attendance may be considered a natural extension of the experimental treatment.

ANALYZING THE DATA

The major sources of data in the Perry Preschool Study were an interview at age 19, reports from primary and secondary schools, police and court records, and records of social service agencies. The outcome variables of this study may be divided into three domains of measurement: scholastic success, socioeconomic success, and social responsibility.

Attrition in the study sample was minimal. The median rate of missing data across all measures was only 5 percent. The interview at age 19 was administered to all but two study participants, and school records were located for all but 11. These low rates of missing data generally mean that attrition does not affect either the representativeness of the sample or the validity of group comparisons.

The findings for the subjects at age 19 are displayed in Table 1. In the area of scholastic success, members of the preschool group stayed in school longer, scored better on tests of functional competence, were less often classified as mentally retarded, and spent fewer years in special education classes. In the area of social responsibility, members of the preschool group were arrested less often than members of the nonpreschool group, and the females had fewer pregnancies as teenagers. In the area of socioeconomic success, nearly twice as many members of the preschool group were employed, and only half as many were receiving welfare.

A cost-benefit analysis of the program and its effects indicated that the money that society invested in the preschool program was money well spent. The return on the initial investment was 3½ times the cost of two years of preschool and seven times the cost of one year (based on an analysis of outcomes for pupils in Wave Zero only). The major benefits to society were in the form of reduced costs of later education and increased earnings, both actual and predicted. Other benefits included decreased costs for welfare assistance and crime. The economic benefits obtained by the end of high school were sufficient to justify public investment in one year of preschool for children at risk of failure.

Table 2 summarizes the costs and benefits of the program; all entries are in constant dollars discounted at 3 percent. Discounting takes into account the fact that it is better to receive an amount of money today than a year from today (much like the interest that would accrue on a bank deposit held for a certain interval). The 3 percent rate was chosen because it is the long-term economic growth rate for the nation.

The per-pupil costs of the Perry Preschool Program were relatively high, but no higher than the costs for many early childhood special education programs. The figures reported are upper-bound estimates of the full costs to society; some of these expenses, such as the cost of the building, would not be borne by a sponsoring agency. Furthermore, the program was an innovation when it began, with the emphasis on quality and effectiveness rather than on efficiency.

Our analysis does suggest certain ways that the program could have been made more efficient—for example, by limiting the program to one year instead of two. Table 2 shows that both one and two years of preschool are good investments, but the benefits of one year are about the same as the benefits of two years. Since two years cost about twice as much, there is little economic justification for investing in the second year of preschool. On the other hand, note that only 13 of the children in this study attended preschool for only one year, while 45 attended for two years. Thus we can be

Table 1. Major Effects of the Perry Preschool Program at Age 19

Category	N	Preschool Group (%)	Nonpreschool Group (%)	p*
Schooling Success				
High school graduation (or equivalent)	121	67	49	.034
College or vocational training	121	38	21	.029
Functional competence (average or above-average score)	109	61	38	.025
Ever classified as mentally retarded	112	15	35	.014
Percentage of years in special education	112	16	28	.039
Social Responsibility				
Ever detained or arrested	121	31	51	.022
Teen pregnancies	49	64	117	.084
Socioeconomic Success				
Employed	121	50	32	.032
Receiving welfare assistance	121	18	32	.044

*Two-tailed probability of chance occurrence.

Table 2. Summary of Costs and Benefits*

	Benefit or Cost**	
	One Year Preschool	Two Years Preschool
Measured		
Preschool program	−$ 4,818	−$ 9,289
Child care	290	572
Education, K-12	5,113	4,964
Earnings, ages 16-19	642	623
Welfare at age 19	55	53
Crime through age 20	1,233	1,197
Predicted		
College	−704	−684
Earnings after age 19	23,813	23,121
Crime after age 20	1,871	1,816
Welfare after age 19	1,438	1,396
Net Benefit†	$28,933	$23,769
Benefit/Cost Ratio	7.01	3.56

*Entries are present values in constant 1981 dollars, discounted at 3% annually.
**Costs are indicated as negative amounts.
†Column sums differ from net benefits because of rounding.

considerably more confident about the findings for two years than we can about the findings for one year.

However, the findings of the Perry Preschool Study and similar studies should not be construed as an endorsement of *all* early childhood programs. There is no intrinsic value in a young child's leaving home for a few hours a day to join another adult and a group of children. Unless the content of a program is carefully defined, a preschool is just another place for a child to be.

Such thinking has led us to conclude that quality is essential in early childhood programs if they are to have long-term benefits. We have developed a definition of quality in preschool programs that is based on research and on our experience in running such programs. Quality in early childhood programs calls for parent involvement, programmatic leadership by supervisors and directors, competent and genuinely enthusiastic teachers, an articulated curriculum of proven effectiveness, a sound inservice training program, and the feedback provided by program evaluation. If a program has these features, we believe it is a good one that will produce lasting effects.

The Perry Preschool Program was a developmental program that helped children to plan, to carry out their plans, and to take responsibility for problem solving. It did not simply follow either of the two most common approaches to early childhood education. First, it was not simply unguided play for children, with the teacher merely keeping them from harming themselves or their classmates. Second, it was not a narrowly focused academic program, and there was no academic drill. The focus was not on letters, numbers, shapes, and colors. Unfortunately, these things often become the focus of early childhood education, when they should properly be viewed as no more than means to an end.

A good early childhood program, we believe, teaches children two things: how to be good learners and how to work with adults who are not members of their families. These are the real basic skills to be imparted by early childhood education. If children do not become learners, open to their experiences, and if they don't learn to work with adults other than family members, then they will never have more than limited access to reading, writing, and arithmetic.

Two conclusions can be drawn from our research. The first, we have detailed here: a good preschool program helps children overcome the effects of poverty to some extent. But preschool and poverty are merely the specific experiences explored here. The more general conclusion of our study is that early childhood education has a lasting impact on adult life. Easy rhetoric, now documented as fact. The quality of life of today's young children has profound consequences for tomorrow's adults. For better or worse, that is the promise of early childhood education.

DISCUSSION QUESTIONS

1. What are the main effects of excellent early education programs over time?

2. Can we generalize these findings to all early childhood education programs?

3. What are the critical qualities of the "good" programs?

4. Do the results of the longitudinal studies justify the cost/effort of the early intervention programs?

5. Are the research findings sufficient to justify major quality improvements and expansion of good programs for all children?

6. How can these research findings be used by the classroom teacher?

7. What are the policy and program evaluation implications of these research findings?

49. EARLY CHILDHOOD EVALUATION: WHAT? WHO? WHY?

by Doris Bergen Sponseller and Joel Fink

Evaluation has always been a component of educational practice. In early times, however, the questions asked were concerned primarily with individual student performance rather than with program effectiveness. Further, how well students learned was seen as a function of their ability, not of the effectiveness of the education environment. In early childhood education programs, children were usually evaluated in terms of their social and emotional adjustment. The value of accepted educational practice in the traditional early childhood settings was not examined.

With the advent of federal financial support and active promotion of early childhood education as a means to increase children's academic learning potential, the focus of evaluation shifted to program effectiveness. How well students learned was seen as a function of their educational environment, rather than of their individual abilities. Developers of early childhood programs were required to evaluate their activities in order to obtain and to continue to receive public funding. In order to identify effective educational environments, comparisons were made both among various planned programs and between these programs and naturally occurring child rearing settings. While different evaluation approaches have been used, there is general agreement that evaluation has not produced the clear results expected and promised. Numerous writers have suggested that there are major problems with current evaluation practices (e.g., Glick, 1968; Circirelli et al., 1970; Bentley et al., 1974; House and Hutchins, 1978; Takanishi, 1979). Inadequacies of design and measurement methodology, incongruities between goals and measures, inappropriate analysis procedures, simplistic or politically motivated conclusions, and deleterious policy implications have been exhaustively discussed.

In response to these problems, alternatives to current practice have been suggested, including a stress on developmental models (Takanishi, 1979); classroom rather than child assessment (Zimiles, 1977); naturalistic inquiry (Guba, 1978); synthesis of research evidence (Pillemer and Light, 1980), clinical supervision approaches (Goldhammer,

1969); and responsive evaluations using case studies (Stake, 1975, 1978).

Three basic questions about evaluation are raised and discussed here: (1) What is to be evaluated? (2) Who is to do the evaluating? (3) For what purpose is the evaluation to be conducted? We feel that if early childhood educators clarify their positions on these questions, they will be more able to develop appropriate evaluation strategies. For each of these questions, two major alternative answers will be presented, and a statement will be offered of what we view as desirable responses. Evaluators' consideration of these responses may point to more useful future evaluation strategies.

Although these three questions may seem to be ones that would be routinely addressed, this is seldom done explicitly. Studies have been conducted in which conflicting values of early childhood educators, program evaluators, and government representatives have been incorporated in the same evaluation design. Unless these conflicting views are highlighted, and addressed, the evaluation activities can be confusing and unsatisfactory to those involved.

WHAT IS TO BE EVALUATED?: PRODUCT AND PROCESS EVALUATIONS

Product evaluation emphasizes measuring children's performance as the major method of assessment. The assumption that well-designed product measures can best demonstrate effectiveness of program has been generally accepted. The products most commonly measured are students' intellectual or academic performance. Further, this linking of measurement of children's outcomes performance with program worth has suggested implications for policy decisions. Early childhood educators believe that if evidence of successful products is not clearly demonstrated, public support for early childhood programs may be affected.

There has been criticism of product-centered evaluation. For example, Takanishi (1979) has questioned whether short-term product measurement is appropriate when a developmental per-

See page 342 for acknowledgment and references.

spective might predict that behavior changes would become evident only over a longer term. She also asserts that measured performance may not reflect competence.

Early childhood educators have consistently reminded evaluators that processes are as important as products and that products unrelated to intellectual or academic success have value. For example, in the Head Start program, where process goals such as parent participation, staff development and community mobilization are identified, program success may be demonstrated, even if the measures of children's products do not reflect academic gains. In addition, experiences provided for children may be intrinsically worthwhile processes if they are congruent with positive child development. They can also lead to desirable social outcomes. Program quality may thus be determined by carefully observing and describing the processes within the program setting, as well as by measuring a range of products.

Takanishi (1979) states that a perspective which focuses on a number of levels of child, adult, and program development can give greater richness and depth to evaluation. Whether products or processes are the major focus of evaluation or whether a combination of both are used should be decided within the context of overall program goals. Decisions should not be based on the ease or difficulty of measurement, but on articulated quality standards defined by a consensus of early childhood educators and community representatives.

Even evaluators who have successfully demonstrated long-term academic effects of early childhood programs have concluded that policy decisions are only minimally influenced by evidence of children's academic success (Lazar, 1980). Perhaps this realization will encourage evaluators to broaden their perspectives in deciding on content of evaluation and on whether product or process measures are needed. The dimensions identified as crucial to program quality are what should be evaluated.

WHO IS TO DO THE EVALUATING?: EXTERNAL AND STAFF EVALUATION

Because the essence of evaluation is judgment, measurement compared to standards, the appropriateness of the evaluators who are selected is a crucial issue. Evaluation practice has stressed that objectivity is most likely to be preserved if outside evaluators collect and analyze the data. Subjectivity may result from staff biases in the measures select-

ed; staff variations in methods of collection that decrease reliability; and staff specification of measurement targets that increase possibilities for obtaining favorable results. In addition to stress on the use of outside evaluation to achieve objectivity, there has also been an emphasis on quantitative measures that are adaptable to statistical analysis, rather than qualitative measures which provide indepth descriptions.

A common complaint of early childhood educators has been that outside evaluators do not always have a perspective that enables them to make judgments which adequately reflect program quality. When evaluators come into settings with predetermined goals and an evaluation design which may be insensitive to local conditions, essential elements may not be measured. Across-program model comparisons have often been criticized because individual setting variables substantially affect the basic model. Pillemer and Light (1980) have suggested synthesizing data from many studies in order to examine internal variations in similar program models.

A major evaluation alternative has been to have each program evaluated individually with evaluation done by program staff. Some programs have had staff members collect data using more objective norm-referenced measures. Others have developed criterion-referenced measures closely tied to specific program goals. These staff evaluator methods may be superior precisely because they emphasize self-identified goals, measures and targets. Without an outside validation of staff-conducted measures, however, internal evaluation may not be objective.

There are approaches that build upon the strengths of both external and staff evaluation, and are designed to control for subjectivity and bias even though they use program staff in the evaluation process and collect qualitative data. (Scriven, 1972, has pointed out that objective data may be qualitative as well as quantitative.) One such approach is Goldhammer's (1969) clinical supervision model which avoids the imposition by external observers of the objects for evaluation. Staff members are asked to clearly identify the teaching and learning behavior to be emphasized. The evaluator then carefully observes and records these observations. Finally, during a post-observation conference, the evaluator systematically shares the observations and documents these with recorded evidence. This clinical supervision model retains the objectivity of external evaluation while requiring staff to direct the process. An important product of this approach is a renewed professional commitment by staff to program improvement.

Guba (1978) recommends using an outside evaluator who takes a phenomenological perspective, observing goals, relevant processes and products, and identified problems through the perspective of staff members. This method of naturalistic inquiry requires balanced discussions with all relevant participants and the use of procedures to cross-check and confirm information.

Each of these evaluation models preserves objectivity because reliable and confirmable information is collected. The emphasis on multiple evaluators may well enhance objectivity, since this prevents the superficial understandings of external evaluators and the unconscious biases of the staff from influencing the judgments made. An evaluation approach which involves participants in the evaluation and which looks at variations as well as similarities in programs may provide the most useful approach to the question of who should evaluate.

FOR WHAT PURPOSE IS THE EVALUATION CONDUCTED?: SUMMATIVE AND FORMATIVE EVALUATION

The emphasis in educational evaluation has most commonly been on summative approaches, assessing how well a program has done its work *after* it is supposedly completed. This results from a need to compare programs in order to select those which best promote children's learning in a cost-effective way. In many cases, formative evaluation which would give ongoing feedback and lead to program changes was limited so as not to confound outcome data.

On the other hand, early childhood educators have often felt threatened about these measurements because of the tie between summative evaluations and funding decisions. In those cases where summative evaluations were routinely collected with few guidelines and with no stated relationship to funding decisions, they were often perceived as *pro forma* efforts. Results were sent to state or federal agencies to be filed and forgotten.

More attention needs to be devoted to formative evaluation to promote program quality. Formative evaluation with its planned and continuing review of data, its promotion of systematic changes and staff skill development, and its monitoring of the effects of these changes can be of great value in achieving the goals of early childhood education

programs. These programs are dynamic, with constant staffing reassignments, curriculum additions and deletions, changes in the composition of the children's groups, and movement in program locations. Dynamic programs create measurement problems for summative evaluation approaches. A formative evaluation approach which can assist in the management of change and in adjusting to change may not only prevent destructive effects, but also enhance program quality.

Finally, the acceptance of the legitimacy and desirability of formative evaluation makes it more plausible to recommend an emphasis on evaluating processes and on involving staff in evaluation activities. Conversely, so long as only summative evaluations are considered legitimate, there is likely to be undesirably strong emphasis on products and external evaluation to the exclusion of concern with process objectives and staff involvement. A cyclical model which includes formative and summative data collection periods can serve multiple purposes. Once the purposes have been clearly identified, an appropriate balance between formative and summative approaches can be planned.

ALTERNATIVE STRATEGIES FOR EVALUATION

Although many of the evaluation studies which were conducted in the past 15 years have been flawed, they have demonstrated that learning ability was enhanced in the majority of programs at least over the short term and that long-term positive effects also are evident for some programs (e.g., Lazar, 1977). The cost-effectiveness of early childhood education also has been given support by evaluation results (Weber et al., 1978).

Throughout this period, the evaluation strategies employed have most commonly presumed that only products should be measured, that evaluation should be conducted by external evaluators, and that it should be summative. Perhaps these emphases have been a result of pressures imposed by public funding sources.

We are currently in a period of low public support for early childhood education and of an easing of outside pressures to evaluate. Perhaps this time can be productively used by evaluators to modify their past responses to the questions raised in this [chapter]. New consideration can be given to evaluation approaches that (1) include a greater emphasis on educational processes and on a wider variety of products, (2) protect objectivity while also increasing staff participation, and (3) offer useful information to guide the task of program design and modification.

Evaluation approaches which use naturalistic inquiry or case study methods, which are adapted from the clinical supervision model, and which synthesize data from a number of programs with attention to differences as well as to similarities of results need to be pursued further. Hopefully, as early childhood educators reflect on the three questions raised in this [chapter], alternative evaluation strategies will receive the careful examination which they merit.

DISCUSSION QUESTIONS

1. What are the problems associated with evaluating early education programs?

2. How should evaluation be conducted? What should be evaluated? How should the results be used?

3. Are outside evaluators necessary for a quality evaluation? Why?

4. Have evaluation results been used effectively in program revision and improvement? in policy decisions?

5. Are program effects on the children the ultimate evaluative criteria, or are there other purposes for evaluation of early educational programs?

Section Seven: Electronic Technology for Early Childhood Programs

EDITOR'S OVERVIEW

As the computer and other electronic technologies transform the way people work, they are also having an influence on the way we teach and on the way children learn. This is a period of transition from initial introduction to a better picture about what computers can and cannot do for early childhood education.

Anselmo and Zinck give a classroom-eye view of computer use with young children while reminding readers that computers cannot replace some of the traditional, concrete learning experiences. More of the critical questions are presented by Clements, with answers to the questions derived from the research literature. Then, Buckleitner and Hohmann raise the question of priorities in the use of computers in early education, with special attention to financial considerations.

The costs, the benefits, the effects, and the influence on teaching and learning are persistent areas of concern when computers and electronic technologies are introduced into the schools. The challenge to the profession is to determine optimum applications, to identify limitations, and to blend these technological tools into the stream of instructional methods for teaching young children.

50. COMPUTERS FOR YOUNG CHILDREN? PERHAPS

by Sandra Anselmo and R. Ann Zinck

The popular press and professional journals are filled with accounts of the prowess of young children with computers. Television commercials depict good parents guiding toddlers' pudgy fingers to computer keys as a first step to success. In advertising their services, some child care centers prominently mention the availability of computers.

In contrast to what is said and implied in the media, we are not awed by computers, nor do we assume they are essential for early childhood classrooms. Rather, this [chapter] will take a more balanced look at the possible value of computers for young children.

HOW WE BEGAN

Many early childhood educators became interested in computers because of the potential for creative thinking and interaction. Papert (1980) raised hopes that the use of computers could add another dimension to children's problem-solving skills. This possibility seemed timely when the National Assessment of Educational Progress (1983) confirmed that problem-solving skills among American children were declining. Children seemed better able to do rote computation than to search for meaning and think out implications.

While Papert (1980) and Turkle (1984) stirred our interest in computers for young children, we still had many questions. Even though we were experienced with home computers and with curriculum development, we were hesitant to generalize from blocks, scissors, and crayons to computers. If computers were added to early childhood classrooms, what software and instructional approaches should be used? What could computers add to classrooms that was not already being handled without electronics?

To help answer our questions, we placed an Apple IIe™ computer in one preschool and one kindergarten classroom in a private, nonprofit school. The Rainbow School was chosen because it has a well-articulated curriculum based on the development of thinking skills (Anselmo, Rollins, and Schuckman, 1986), and because the teachers were enthusiastic about the project.

To learn about computers, the teachers enrolled in a university course on LOGO in the classroom. When they were ready, computers were added as another interest area in classrooms already rich with activity choices. Two chairs were placed in front of each computer to encourage children's interactions. Children were shown individually and in groups how to use the hardware and then were allowed to use the computers freely. Children were shown how to use software only as they had questions.

Teachers were available to assist children if asked, but they consciously avoided extended individual sessions. They also met regularly with us to evaluate software and test it with young children, and assisted us in collecting information on the reactions of children, parents, and teachers.

SOFTWARE TO ENCOURAGE THINKING SKILLS

Software, like all other materials in the classroom, must be evaluated in the context of developmentally appropriate curriculum goals (NAEYC, 1986a, 1986b). Computers are controlled by software, so it is essential to select programs that are consistent with the principles of good early childhood education. Children must already have a broad background of concrete experiences before they can find meaning in the more abstract computer activities.

Our curriculum emphasis is on the process of helping young children develop their thinking skills. Without neglecting content, our priority is to help children learn to use and trust their abilities to receive information, remember it, make decisions, and solve problems. We thus searched for software that would enhance children's thinking skills in comprehension, memory, evaluation, and creativity.

New software is being released daily, and programs are subject to change. Therefore, although we mention the names of some programs we found suitable for our purposes, readers are cautioned to evaluate any software thoroughly before purchasing it.

See page 342 for acknowledgment and references.

Comprehension

Comprehension is the ability to be aware of and to understand information. Young children use this skill when they smell, taste, and touch food; when they listen to stories; and when they put puzzles together. Comprehension is an essential aspect of all learning.

One aspect of comprehension is *visual closure*, the process of mentally completing a picture, word, or other figure from information gained by only seeing a part of it. Visual closure skills are used in reading: Good readers look quickly at whole words or groups of words, rather than at individual letters. Two computer games, Guess Who? on *Ernie's Quiz* (Children's Television Workshop, 1981a), and Instant Zoo (Children's Television Workshop, 1981b), seem to help children improve visual closure. In these games, children use scattered visual clues to determine what figure is partially pictured on the monitor. As children watch, more segments are gradually filled in on the screen.

Similar activities can be conducted without computers (Anselmo, 1983), but the process is cumbersome and involves drawing several pictures of the object.

Another aspect of comprehension is the ability to complete mazes by using *visual tracking*, a skill also used in reading as children follow the lines of print. *Peanuts Maze Marathon* (1984) provides a variety of colorful mazes for children to solve by manipulating the movement of an object on the screen. This program can build on children's experiences in constructing mazes or obstacle courses with blocks, for example.

Memory

Memory is the ability to store information so it can be used at a later time. Well-developed memory skills are essential for virtually every aspect of life.

The third part of *Facemaker* (1982) contains an appealing computer memory game for children who can recall the labels assigned and identify initial letters of words. Children create a face, program expressions on the face, and then play the game with those expressions. For example, the face might smile and stick out its tongue. The child types *S* and then *T* to indicate the sequence has been remembered. A three-part sequence is then presented. Children who are unsuccessful are given another two-part sequence.

A program like this is not a substitute for memory games using concrete objects such as the memory tray or memory book (Anselmo, Rollins, and Schuckman, 1986), nor is it appropriate for children who have yet to develop the necessary language skills. However, this sophisticated game allows older children to challenge their memories without teacher assistance.

Evaluation

Evaluation is the ability to make decisions. Young children evaluate when they decide what to wear in the morning, when they find a way to enter into play with a group of children, or when they help a child in distress.

Gertrude's Secrets (1982) gives children an opportunity to classify—one aspect of evaluation. Gertrude, a goose, has many rooms in which she tries to group items by color and shape. Children help Gertrude classify using two or more attributes.

Evaluation skills are also used in *Estimation* (1983). For example, one part of Bug Tracks asks children to estimate which of two trails is longer, which may aid in the development of the concept of conservation of length. Choo Choo gives children control of sound, speed, and visibility as they estimate the location of a train in a tunnel.

Another game that uses evaluation skills is Layer Cake on *Mix and Match* (Children's Television Workshop, 1981c). Children try to move cakes of three sizes from one spindle to one of two others without crushing the smaller cakes. Planning and strategy are used by successful players.

Programs such as these can be matched with children's abilities and interests to supplement other activities designed to help children solve real problems, both concrete and interpersonal.

Creativity

Creativity is the ability to use divergent thinking to solve problems. Children use creativity when they make up new words and motions to a favorite song, when they propose how to divide an apple among three children, and when they add a new role for a child joining them in dramatic play.

Creativity may well be the thinking skill that the computer most enhances. The capabilities of the LOGO language make it possible for older preschoolers and kindergarten children to program the computer. According to Papert (1980), children who program computers are active participants in their learning. For example, they might program the movement of the turtle using *Draw* (undated) as an introduction to Apple™ LOGO (1983). Papert contrasts this more interactive, problem-solving use of computers with their inappropriate use as electronic workbooks.

Another way the computer can encourage creativity is with word processing programs such as *Kidwriter* (1984). Most young children will need teacher assistance to record their stories, although older children may use the stories to develop some word-recall and keyboard skills.

POTENTIAL VALUES OF COMPUTERS

The distinctive thinking patterns of young children have been extensively described (Piaget and Inhelder, 1969; Thomas, 1985). In the context of our understanding of young children's development, we observed children's use of computers. Our observations have led us to four general conclusions about the use of computers with preschool and kindergarten children:

- Computers can be interactive.
- Age is a relevant variable.
- Children prefer action.
- Nonreaders may be encouraged to read.

Computers Can Be Interactive

Computer use seems to provide a vehicle for two types of interaction: child-computer and child-child. Child-computer interaction depends to a great extent on the software. Some software requires children to choose one response, which is then corrected. In contrast, the software described here requires more child involvement. *Gertrude's Secrets* (1982) allows children to use information on the screen to construct classification systems. Children receive feedback, and if they desire, modify the classification.

Child-child interaction at the computer seems to depend on the arrangement of the environment as well as on the selection of software. As indicated earlier, two chairs were placed at each computer. Other children were drawn to the vicinity because we placed related concrete materials (beads, parquetry blocks, geoboards) on adjacent tables. This enabled children to discuss problems and assist each other with possible solutions. Some programs also are designed for, or lend themselves better to, participation by more than one child.

Age Is a Relevant Variable

Before adding computers to classrooms, we wondered whether computer use might prevent some children from participating in hands-on experiences scheduled at the same time. We need not have worried. We found almost no computer use by 3-year-olds, moderate use by 4-year-olds, and enthusiastic use by nearly all of the kindergarten children. Three-year-olds did not choose time at the computer when the alternatives included block building, digging in sand, and stuffing mail in boxes at the classroom post office.

Why are younger children less interested in computers? The answer lies in an understanding of child development. Piaget has described the preoperational stage, from 2 to 7 years, in which hands-on experiences are important as children construct their own understanding of the world. In the middle of this period—around age 4—children begin to use an intuitive, prelogical form of thought. And around this age is when children began to express interest in computers.

Papert (1980) suggested that computers may be a vehicle for making certain concepts "simple and concrete" (p. 7) for intuitive thinkers. Computers may serve as a transition from actual objects to mental representations.

Teacher presence seems to be a second factor regarding the age of children and their interest in computers. As children mature and have more experience in group settings, they become more independent. In the setting we created, teachers were not regularly near the computers. For 3-year-olds, the lack of the reassuring presence of a teacher, and the compelling sensual satisfactions found in sand and water play, may have been a factor in their lack of interest.

Children Prefer Action

Just as in other aspects of their play, children like action with computers, and they do not necessarily choose to follow the rules of games. They watch what happens when they press new keys, and they purposely may try to squash the cakes in Layer Cake. One of the strengths young children bring to computer use is their fearless experimentation!

Children's search for action was made clear by their reaction to *Draw*, which was used to introduce LOGO. Children conducted interesting explorations of turtle graphics until we began to add other software. After that, *Draw* was used only occasionally. Why were the supposedly popular turtle graphics less appealing? First, *Draw* is visually unexciting, and it pales in comparison with the color and graphics in other software. Secondly, it is not a very powerful program. It lacks the repeat, nesting, and procedural functions of LOGO, so children can only create line drawings. Perhaps some of the older children could have benefited from systematic instruction in the more flexible LOGO.

As we watched children use the computer, we were curious to know what they were thinking. When asked "What are you doing?" and "What are you learning?" we frequently received a puzzled look and occasionally heard action-oriented responses such as "Moving this from here to here," or "To move this thing."

While the children in these groups are generally quite verbal, their lack of response might result from a perceived lack of continuity between computer use and the rest of their lives. They were often the first in their families to use computers, or if not, the youngest to do so. Perhaps teachers should take more opportunities to talk with children about the similarities and differences between activities on the computer and off, about the meaning of those activities, and about children's reactions.

Children's preference for action also leads us to recommend that, just as with foods, only nutritious choices should be offered in software. Midway through the year, someone slipped a copy of the arcade game *Frogger* into our carefully selected collection of disks. The game became an instant hit. Although we will not make a case that playing such games is harmful, we believe that children's time is precious and should be spent on growth-enhancing activities whenever possible. We are responsible for choosing software that fits within our curriculum goals.

Nonreaders Encouraged to Read

We planned to create visuals with pictorial prompts so the software could be used by the nonreading majority of the children in the groups. Before these plans could be implemented, we found them to be unnecessary. Children mastered keyboard letter-matching tasks after a few weeks. Within 2 months, most children were easily able to select options from menus and read prompts related to the operation of particular programs. These children were reading! In most cases, they had little or no outside assistance.

Even among different programs, the framework for using the computer is often similar (use of menus, prompts for return and space bar, escape key). Within this meaningful context, children became adept at reading the language they needed to control a new environment.

As children gained reading skill, they tended to help each other. For instance, one day we asked two children if they could read a particular prompt. They responded "No." After being told once what the prompt meant, they were able to read the screen and follow through with the appropriate action the next time the prompt appeared. When one of the children left the computer, the remaining child immediately taught the next child what the prompt meant.

In addition to meaningfulness, motivation seems to explain the success of previously nonreading children who learned to read computer terminology. Four- and 5-year-old preschoolers chose to spend an average 22 minutes at the computer, while 5- and 6-year-old kindergartners spent 29 minutes—an indication of substantial interest and involvement.

CONCLUSIONS

We were pleased to find an array of interesting software that emphasized the four thinking skills we encourage in our process-oriented curriculum. Readers are urged to identify the skills they wish to promote, and then evaluate software based on its appropriateness for young children.

For those interested in using computers with 3-year-olds, we recommend substantial amounts of adult feedback, guidance, and encouragement. To build in more tactile experiences, a Koala Pad or add-on keyboard with fewer and larger keys might be helpful.

Teachers working with 4-year-olds will also want to schedule more individual or small group interaction, both with the computer and in other activities.

Some 4-year-olds and many kindergarten children can be successful, independent computer users for sustained periods of time. While this high level of interest may be a positive feature, there is some danger that the time spent with computers could detract from other valuable learning experiences, especially in part-day programs. We encourage teachers to monitor usage to ensure a balance in children's self-directed activities.

Do we recommend purchasing computers for preschool and kindergarten classrooms? Our strongest positive response is. "Perhaps . . . depending on the circumstances." We believe that the pleasure and success young children experience with computers is proportional to the foundation of pleasure and success they have already built by comprehending, remembering, evaluating, and creating with tangible objects and familiar people. It is important that children already have sufficient self-confidence to take risks and to experiment with computers, developing what Erikson (1982) calls a sense of initiative.

A good environment for young children includes many experiences that involve sight, sound, touch, taste, and smell: adult-child and child-child conversation, children's literature, block construction, opportunities to manipulate objects, creative art, sand and water exploration, and a host of other age-appropriate activities. Computers can supplement, but do not substitute for, experiences in which children can discover with all their senses.

Only after a sound, basic program has been developed should preschools and kindergarten teachers consider buying a computer. First should come blocks, sand and water tables, art materials, books, and all of the other proven elements of a good program for young children.

The research reported in this [chapter] was supported by the McDaniel Educational Opportunity Fund. We also appreciate the interest and assistance of Rita Schuckman and Pamela Rollins, directors of Rainbow School, in carrying out this project.

DISCUSSION QUESTIONS

1. What happens when computers are introduced into the early childhood education classroom?

2. Is the software adequate for use with young children?

3. What can children learn from computers in the classroom?

4. Do some software programs stimulate higher-order thinking?

5. At what age or developmental level can children best be introduced to computers for instruction?

51. COMPUTERS AND YOUNG CHILDREN: A REVIEW OF RESEARCH

by Douglas H. Clements

Although questions of the use and effectiveness of computers in education are raised at all levels, these questions are debated most passionately about the early childhood ages (birth through 8). Are young children physically and cognitively ready to use computers? Will such use inhibit their social development? Can computers help build skills or develop problem-solving ability? Which is preferable? Research has not answered these questions definitively. However, in just a few short years since a similar review was published (Brady and Hill, 1984), there has been a substantial increase in what we know about young children's use of computers.

YOUNG CHILDREN USING COMPUTERS

Are Computers Developmentally Appropriate for Young Children?

This is perhaps the first question early childhood educators should ask about computers. An expressed concern is that children must reach the stage of concrete operations before they are ready to work with computers (e.g., Brady and Hill, 1984). Recent research, however, has found that preschoolers are more competent than has been thought and can, under certain conditions, exhibit thinking traditionally considered concrete. Rohwer, Ammon, and Crammer (1974) put it this way: "Children do not universally wake up on their seventh birthdays . . . to find that they have arrived at the period of concrete operations" (p. 172).

A related concern is that computer use demands the ability to work with symbols (i.e., that *computers* are not concrete). This ignores, however, that much activity in which young children engage *is* symbolic. They communicate with gestures and language, and they employ symbols in their play and art. Thus, it appears that preschool children might benefit from using computer programs.

But should they? Isn't this "rushing" them? One answer is that computers are no more danger-

ous than books or pencils—all could be used to push a child to read or write too soon. However, they can also be used to provide developmentally appropriate experiences. Watson, Nida, and Shade (1986) suggest that the dilemma best be handled by allowing children to select and work with activities at their own level. If so permitted, how do children react to this new technological learning device?

Children's Interactions with Computers

Children approach computers with comfort and confidence and appear to enjoy exploring this new medium (Binder and Ledger, 1985). Even preschoolers can work cooperatively with minimal instruction and supervision if they initially have adult support (Rosengren, Gross, Abrams, and Perlmutter, 1985; Shade, Nida, Lipinski, and Watson, 1986). However, adults play a significant role in successful computer use. Children are more attentive, more interested, and less frustrated when an adult is present (Binder and Ledger, 1985; Shade et al., 1986). Thus, teachers may wish to make the computer one of many choices, placed where they can supervise and assist children.

Using the standard keyboard is not a problem for young children, and is often superior to other devices, such as a joystick. Indeed, typing appears to be a source of motivation and sense of competence for many (Borgh and Dickson, 1986b; Lipinski, Nida, Shade, and Watson, 1986; Muller and Perlmutter, 1985; Swigger and Campbell, 1981). Preschool children can successfully use age-appropriate software requiring that they press only a few single keys. They can turn the computer on and off, remove and replace diskettes properly, follow instructions from a picture menu, and talk meaningfully about their computer activity (Watson, Chadwick, and Brinkley, 1986).

A computer center may vary from being among the most popular free-time activity to being chosen slightly less frequently than many other areas (Picard and Giuli, 1985). Such differences may be

See pages 343–44 for acknowledgment and references.

due to the physical setup, the teacher interventions, and especially the computer programs (software) used. For example, children prefer programs that are animated, problem-solving-oriented, and interactive—that give them a feeling of control over the computer (Shade et al., 1986; Sherman, Divine, and Johnson, 1985; Sivin, Lee, and Vollmer, 1985). In most cases, 3- to 5-year-old children apparently spend approximately the same amount of time playing in the computer center as drawing, talking, or playing in the block or art centers (e.g., Hoover and Austin, 1986; Picard and Giuli, 1985). The attraction outlives the novelty effect. However, play in other important centers, such as blocks, is not decreased by the presence of a computer. Thus, the computer is an interesting, but not engrossing, activity for young children (Lipinski et al., 1986).

Characteristics of Children

Do any characteristics distinguish preschoolers most interested in using computers? They tend to be older and to exhibit significantly higher levels of cognitive maturity. They manifest higher levels of representational competence and vocabulary development and display more organized and abstract forms of free play behavior. They do not differ from less interested peers in creativity, estimates of social maturity, or social cognitive ability. Thus, there may be important cognitive underpinnings of computer involvement by preschoolers (Hoover and Austin, 1986; Johnson, 1985).

How Young?

Although older children may be more interested in using computers, there is little evidence that computers should not be introduced to younger children. No major differences have been found between the way computers are used by younger and older preschoolers (Beeson and Williams, 1985), although 3-year-olds take longer to acclimate to the keyboard than 5-year-olds (Sivin et al., 1985). Some research suggests that 3 years of age and older be selected as an appropriate time for introducing a child to discovery-oriented software. However, even 2-year-olds might be introduced to simple, single-keystroke software, mainly for developing positive attitudes. The crux is appropriately designed software (Shade and Watson, in press). If computers are seen as a general educational tool, perhaps no one is too young. Noting that handicapped infants are at high risk for learned helpless-

ness, Brinker (1984) sought ways to use computers to help them exert control over their environment. Infants wore ribbons attached to switches. Their arm or leg movements sent different signals to a computer, which was programmed to turn on a tape recording of the mother's voice or of music, show a picture, activate a toy, or the like. These activities built motivation to control such events and increased the infants' smiling and vocalizing.

Equity: Girls and Boys

A consistent finding is that as early as the later elementary school years, boys have more access to computers, own more computers, and use computers more frequently and with more control (Lieberman, 1985; Picard and Giuli, 1985). Is this imbalance present in early childhood? There are some similar signs. For example, a pair of studies found that, although children 5 years or older used computers similarly, boys younger than 5 used the computer more than did girls the same age (Beeson and Williams, 1985). In addition, two studies, one at the preschool and one at the primary level, have found that boys are more interested in creative problem-solving programs—in exploring their control over the computer—whereas girls tend to stay within the dictates of established drill and practice programs (Shrock, Matthias, Anastasoff, Vensel, and Shaw, 1985; Swigger, Campbell, and Swigger, 1983). However, other studies have not revealed such differences (e.g., Sherman et al., 1985), and the vast majority report that girls and boys do not differ in the amount or type of computer use (Hess and McGarvey, in press; Hoover and Austin, 1986; Johnson, 1985; Lipinski et al, 1986; Muller and Perlmutter, 1985; Shade et al., 1986; Swigger and Campbell, 1981; Swigger et al., 1983). Considering the traditional heavy dominance of computer use by males, these researchers have suggested that the early years are the ideal time to introduce students to computers. "Imagine what it might mean in the life of young girls to have positive, early experiences with computers before society convinces them that 'computers are for boys'" (Watson, Nida, and Shade, 1986, p. 313).

SOCIAL/EMOTIONAL DEVELOPMENT

First grader Darius never talked aloud, was slow to complete his work, and had been placed in a socialization group to draw him out of his shell.

When the computer arrived, Darius spent nearly 90 minutes with the machine the first day. Immediately thereafter, his teacher noticed that he was completing seatwork without prompting. Then he would slide his seat over to the computer and watch others program in Logo. A bit later, he stood beside the computer, talking and making suggestions. When others had difficulties, he was quick to show them the solution. Soon, others started getting help with Logo from him. In brief, Darius moved up to the high reading group, skipping the third preprimer. He began completing twice as much work per day as he had previously. He participated eagerly during class discussions and—as a crowning achievement—was given a 10-minute "time out" because he wouldn't stop talking (St. Paul Public Schools, 1985)! Such episodes are strikingly inconsistent with the negative vision of isolated children working with computers.

In retrospect, the early concern that computers would stifle playful social interaction appears overstated. Children would either have to be forced or mesmerized into solitary use of computers for long periods. Actually, young children prefer social use of computers, and rarely work alone (e.g., Lipinski et al., 1986; Rosengren et al., 1985; Swigger et al., 1983; Swigger and Swigger, 1984). The addition of a computer center does not disrupt ongoing play activities; many studies have found that computers encouraged social interaction (Binder and Ledger, 1985; Rosengren et al., 1985). As we shall observe repeatedly, people affect how computers are used more than computers affect people. For example, Fein, Campbell, and Schwartz (1984) compared young children's social and cognitive behaviors when computers were in or out of the classroom. As usual, the computers were not disruptive. Interestingly, several specific effects varied as a function of classroom and teachers. For example, in the computer's presence, dramatic play decreased in one classroom and increased in the other, because only the teacher in the latter classroom made interesting changes in the dramatic play center. Other factors, such as the ratio of computers to children, may also influence social behaviors. Lipinski et al. (1986) found that only with a 1:22 ratio (and no teacher present) was there any aggressive behavior, along with a sex difference favoring boys. With a ratio of 1:12, there was no such behavior and the sex difference favored girls. Thus, they suggest that a 1:10 ratio might ideally encourage computer use, cooperation, and equal access to girls and boys. With

these caveats in mind, let us see specifically what kinds of social behavior occur in computer environments.

Interaction and Cooperation

Although there is agreement that computers do not isolate children, there is some disagreement as to whether computers promote interaction more than other activities or to approximately the same degree. For instance, Lipinski et al. (1986) reported that social interactions are similar to interactions in other play areas; others have found that, in comparison to other areas, computers facilitate social interaction and cooperation (Clements and Nastasi, 1985; Muhlstein and Croft 1986; Miller and Perlmutter, 1985), friendship formation (Swigger and Swigger, 1984), and group constructive play (Hoover and Austin, 1986). Considering the nature of both computer and noncomputer activities can resolve the discrepancy. Preschoolers' social interactions may be no different in computer learning centers from those in other centers such as blocks or art. However, computers may stimulate interaction *more* than noncomputer activities. Interactive behavior should not be viewed as a unitary phenomenon. Computer activities may facilitate interactive problem solving, but not interactive play (Fein et al., 1984). Finally, computer use should not be viewed as a unitary activity. Relatively simple software cannot be expected to engender interactions similar to those promoted by cognitively richer computer programs.

Teaching and Helping

A frequent report is that children help and teach each other while working on the computer. For example, Shade et al. (1986) traced the development of 4-year-olds from positioning for a turn to assisting one another. Several other reports confirm that children spontaneously and effectively teach and help each other in computer environments (e.g., Borgh and Dickson; 1986b; Paris and Morris, 1985; Wright and Samaras, 1986). Kull (1986) observed first graders engaging in a considerable amount of peer tutoring often modeled on their teachers' strategies (therefore using a guided questioning approach). Not surprisingly, these actions were most successful when such assistance was requested (Paris and Morris, 1985)!

Social and Cognitive Interaction

In sum, computers appear to facilitate certain prosocial behaviors. Although they may not do so to a greater degree than other worthwhile learning centers, computer contexts appear to have one unique benefit: They facilitate both social and cognitive interactions. Hoover and Austin (1986) found that computers produced a more advanced cognitive type of play and concluded that this technology represents another way for children to learn, both socially and cognitively. In another study, the computer was the only activity that resulted in high levels of both language development and cooperative play (Muhlstein and Croft, 1986). Finally, Logo programming has been found to increase both prosocial and higher-order thinking behaviors (Clements and Nastasi, 1985; Clements, 1986). Thus, *computers may represent an environment in which both social and cognitive interactions simultaneously are encouraged, each to the benefit of the other.* As we shall see, research on the cognitive influences of computer use supports this claim.

Attitudes

Researchers frequently observe young children commenting positively about their computer work (e.g., "I did it. I did it. I made it work"; Shade et al., 1986). When asked, girls and boys alike express favorable attitudes toward the computer (Shrock et al., 1985). How valid are these findings?

Observing 5-year-olds, Hyson (1985) found that, in comparison to television watching, computer use produces far more active, positive, and emotionally varied facial expressions and more smiling. Also, children working at a computer speak more often either to each other or to observers. They are far more animated and display more varied and complex expressions. It appears, then, that the computer enhances both communication and self-confidence.

Of course, the type of software used influences these behaviors. In one study, a drawing program tended to elicit more indicators of concentration, planning, and social engagement than a face construction and counting program (Hyson, 1985). In a similar vein, Borgh and Dickson (1986b) found that children's verbal statements are strongly affected by the characteristics of the software. Programs with definite correct answers elicit verbalizations about correctness and winning, but also encourage peer teaching; open-ended programs elicit more wondering and hypothesizing (i.e., stimulate imagination).

Often used in an open-ended manner, Logo programming has potential to engender positive attitudes, especially persistence. Strand, Gilstad, McCollum, and Genishi (1986) showed that preschool students competently managed their Logo environment and evidenced enthusiasm and confidence. Kindergarten children sustained their attention on Logo tasks for substantial time periods, even when they had the option to choose other activities in lieu of programming. Clements and Nastasi (1985) found that primary grade children in a Logo environment exhibited a greater frequency of several behaviors indicating motivation to actively control their environment, including engaging in self-directed explorations and showing pleasure at discovery. Logo has been found particularly effective in increasing disabled children's engagement in learning (Weir, 1987). One researcher recorded the following statement of a boy persisting in the face of several setbacks on his Logo project: "He turns to me and very seriously says 'I say, never give up!'" (Carmichael, Burnett, Higginson, Moore, and Pollard, 1985, p. 286).

Properly used, Computer-Assisted Instruction (CAI) might provide similar benefits, at least for primary grade children. One study found students to be more task oriented, even during regular instruction, than those in a control group. This suggests that experiences with the computer transfer to regular classroom group activity. Students' attitudes toward learning were also positively affected (Silfen and Howes, 1984).

Not all results have been positive, however. For example, one group of preschoolers' interest in using the computer declined (Goodwin, Goodwin, Nansel, and Helm, 1986). It may be significant that the experimental treatment was short, solitary, and inflexible. In comparison, other studies report that children verbalize considerable curiosity, interest, enthusiasm, and sense of personal control after direct involvement with computers (e.g., Wright and Samaras, 1986). Thus, most, but not all, studies have reported increases in positive attitudes after computer use, especially when children work in groups, write on the computer, or program in Logo (cf. Lieberman, 1985). This is promising, especially as the motivational advantages of good computer software—challenge, curiosity, control and fantasy—are compellingly consonant with the type of experiences desired for young children.

LANGUAGE

Language Development

Not surprisingly, increases in social interaction and positive attitudes help generate increased language use. Preschoolers' language activity, measured as words spoken per minute, was almost twice as high at the computer as at any of the other activities: dough clay, blocks, art, or games (Muhlstein and Croft, 1986). Research with Logo indicates that it engenders interaction and language rich with emotion, humor, and imagination (Genishi, McCollum, and Strand, 1985). Reports such as these help allay the fear that computers will deemphasize play and fantasy. When children are in control, they create fantasy in computer programs beyond the producers' imaginations. For example, two children humanized the lines they were constructing with a computer drawing program. When the line went off screen, they declared, "It's sleeping." When it reappeared, they said "It woke up." Another boy pretended the cursor erasing was a termite eating wood (Wright and Samaras, 1986).

Prereading and Reading

As early as 1972, Atkinson and Fletcher taught first graders to read with computer programs emphasizing letter recognition and recall, sight words, spelling, phonics, and sentence and word meanings. Since then, it has been demonstrated that about 10 minutes work with CAI per day significantly benefits primary grade children's reading skill development (e.g., Ragosta, Holland, and Jamison, 1981; Silfen and Howes, 1984). Similarly, preschoolers can develop such reading readiness abilities as visual discrimination and letter naming (e.g., Swigger and Campbell, 1981). As always, however, results are not guaranteed. For example, three 20-minute sessions with simple readiness software had no effect on preschoolers' prereading concepts in one study (Goodwin et al., 1986). In a different study, however, placing computers and appropriate software in kindergartners' classrooms for several months significantly facilitated their acquisition of school readiness and reading readiness skills. When supplemented by concurrent computing activities outside of school (each child in one class also received a computer to use at home), academic gains were even greater (Hess and McGarvey, in press).

A specific program that has had substantial success in kindergartens is Writing to Read. Children work with computers, typewriters, and tape recorders in both preparatory activities and story writing using a simplified phonetic alphabet. Kindergartners effectively learned to read and write better than those in comparison groups, with no deleterious effects on spelling (Murphy and Appel, 1984).

Computers can make a special contribution to special needs children. After 6 weeks of reading instruction using a microcomputer, 3- to 6-year-old deaf children demonstrated a significant improvement in word recognition and identification (Prinz, Nelson, and Stedt, 1982). Taking advantage of young children's cognitive readiness regardless of their primary mode of communication, the program allowed them to press a word (say, "flower") and see a picture of a flower, the word, and a graphic representation of a manual sign.

Writing

Why is writing skill so scarce? One reason may lie in its tedium; another in its lack of power. For young children especially, spoken language provides them control over their environment. Their written language is anemic in comparison. But certain computer environments can infuse writing with control and power. The written word can create animated pictures and stories that can be heard. They can also reduce the tedium of writing. Little or no research has been conducted with the most innovative writing programs, but we do know something about using computers as word processors, often incorporating speech, with young children.

First, we know that the benefit of using computers is in providing scaffolding, or necessary support, for young writers (Clements, 1987; Rosegrant, 1986). Used in construction, scaffolds serve as supports, lifting up workers so they can achieve something that otherwise would not be possible. Educational scaffolds support children, helping them achieve otherwise impossible personal communicative tasks. Computer scaffolds allow children to maintain a sense of competence: "I did it by myself." Importantly, scaffolding allows the child—right from the beginning—to use written language for a purpose: communication. Children can experiment with letters and words without being distracted by the fine motor aspects of handwriting.

If encouraged to use such scaffolding, children

write more, are less worried about making mistakes, take increased pride in their writing because text looks better, have fewer fine motor control problems, and are more willing to take risks and revise (Clements, 1987; Phenix and Hannan, 1984). Borgh and Dickson (1986a) have reported that a talking version of a word processor significantly increased the amount of editing children performed on their compositions, although it did not significantly affect length or quality. It may be that the spoken feedback fostered an awareness of the need to edit ("When the computer talks it sorta sounds like someone else is reading it to me and that way if it doesn't sound quite right . . . I can change it"; Borgh and Dickson, 1986a, p. 15). Beginning writers learn to name letters, sound out words, invent spelling, express ideas, and write simple sentences (Rosegrant, 1985). Perhaps more importantly, young children learn to use the computer as a tool for exploration and experimentation. For example, one 4-year-old repeatedly scrambled the letters of her name to assess the effects on pronunciation. Another confused "b" and "d" and continued to experiment on her own (note her initial choices: ded dird dlue, for dead, bird, and blue). A group of kindergartners discovered—on their own—"magic letters" that caused their word processor to pronounce a word rather than separate letters (these were, of course, vowels; Hofmann, 1986).

Speech is not always the appropriate presentation. Deaf children as young as 3 to 5 years have improved their writing, reading, and general communication skills by composing with a special keyboard that included animation of color pictures and representations of signs from American Sign Language (Prinz, Pemberton, and Nelson, 1985). This represented a true communicative context for these children.

Benefits do not always accrue, however (Clements, 1987), and, like all computer applications, word processors can be misused. For instance, in one study parents were involved in teaching their own children to compose with word processors. The computer became a "tool" or a "trauma," depending on how it was used (Rosegrant, 1986). For example, Jessica wrote a letter to one of her grandmothers, mailing it when she got home. Several days later, her other grandmother called, jestingly "demanding" her own letter. During the next session, Jessica loaded in the old computer letter, typed the second grandmother's name over the first, added a quick personalized "P.S." and promptly mailed out the "new" letter! The mother joked, "My mother just got a form letter from

her own grandchild!" She was, however, quite pleased with (and supportive of) her child's intelligent use of the tool.

On the other hand, Jane had to write 13 thank you letters—all virtually identical—following her birthday party. She, too, thought of using the same basic "file," altered appropriately. Her mother refused to let her take that shortcut, forcing her to type the exact same letter 13 times. Needless to say, Jane's impressions of writing, the use of the computer as a tool, and the experience as a whole were traumatic, unlike Jessica's. As a tool, the computer is used to facilitate communication, print frequent drafts, and explore and experiment. The teacher is a supportive mentor. As a trauma, the computer is used to help you be more accurate and print only when the composition is "correct." The teacher is a critic. Word processors will not support children's writing without corresponding support from the teacher.

MATHEMATICS AND PROBLEM SOLVING

The most dramatic gains in the use of CAI have been in mathematics for *primary* grade children, especially in compensatory education (Niemiec and Walberg, 1984; Ragosta et al., 1981). Again, 10 minutes per day proved sufficient for significant gains; 20 minutes was even better. Properly chosen, computer games may also be effective. Kraus (1981) reported that second graders with an average of one hour of interaction with a computer game per 2-week period responded correctly to twice as many items on an addition facts speed test as students in a control group with no computer experience.

Younger children may benefit as well. Three-year-olds learned sorting from a computer task as easily as from a concrete doll task (Brinkley and Watson, undated). Reports of gains in such skills as counting have also been reported for kindergartners (Hungate, 1982). Similarly, kindergartners in a computer group scored higher on numeral recognition tasks than those taught by a teacher (McCollister, Burts, Wright and Hildreth, 1986). There was some indication, however, that instruction by a teacher was more effective for children just beginning to recognize numerals; but the opposite was true for more able children. This recalls the finding that children more interested in using computers had greater representational competence, and has implications for use of this type of drill and practice program. Children should not work with such programs until they understand the concepts; then, practice may be of real benefit.

Studies have explored the potential of computer graphics for developing spatial and geometric abilities. For example, one found that a computerized and a teacher-directed program for learning about shapes were equally beneficial for kindergartners (von Stein, 1982). Perhaps more promising, however, is a different approach to developing such abilities.

Working with preschoolers, Forman (1986b) found that certain graphics programs offer a new, dynamic way of drawing and exploring geometric concepts. For example, a *boxes* function allows children to draw rectangles by stretching an electronic "rubber band." Using this stretching process gives children a different perspective on geometric figures. The *area fill* function, which fills closed regions with color, prompts children to reflect on topological features such as closure as the consequences of *actions* rather than merely as characteristics of static shapes. The power of such drawing tools lies in the possibility that children will internalize the functions, thus constructing new mental tools.

Other engaging situations Forman (1986a) has explored include computerized "kinetic print," or symbols that move. For example, he found that children 3 to 5 years old think more about process in a computer Smurf program (Paint and Play Workshop) and more about content in a three-dimensional doll house. Children had to reflect more because choices must be more deliberate in the computer medium. Ideas for using miniature real objects seemed to flow from the physical manipulation of those objects, whereas ideas for use of the computer objects come full-blown from premeditation, often announced to others. Thus the computer may promote planfulness, possibly at the cost of playfulness. The computer also allowed and encouraged creative thinking, such as adding a *2* to a chair (leading to laughter about how *2* can be one arm of a chair) or cloning a single bed into a bunk bed.

Children had to be explicit about the "locations" to which they would move. The increased distance between their own action and the manipulation of the objects increased the need to reflect on their performance. This distance also contributes to benefits children derive from watching a replay of their actions (in effect, a cartoon the children created that could be viewed repeatedly). Replay is a powerful tool to help the children think about the future when constructing the

present action on the computer. In a sense, these children are "both watching an action and watching themselves watching it later" (Forman, 1985, p. 33). Computers can help present children with representations of their own past trials and errors. These representations can be observed and edited. "Let children play with kinetic print replays of their own performance" (Forman, 1985, p. 33).

Teachers who expect computer drawing tools

to help children draw more realistic pictures probably will be disappointed. Teachers who expect Paint and Play Workshops to generate emotionally rich stories probably will not be satisfied. On the other hand, teachers who see these media as new systems of cause and effect relations, logic relations, and spatial relations will make hundreds of interesting observations and will invent hundreds of games that children will find educational. (Forman, 1986b, p. 73)

Logo programming is another rich environment that can elicit reflection on mathematics and problem solving. Classroom observations have demonstrated that students do use certain mathematical notions in Logo programming, such as notions of inverse operation. First grader Ryan wanted to turn the turtle to point into his rectangle. He asked the teacher, "What's half of 90?" After she responded, he typed RT 45. "Oh, I went the wrong way." He said nothing, eyes on the screen. "Try LEFT 90," he said at last. This inverse operation produced exactly the desired effect (Kull, 1986). Kull maintains that such behaviors illustrate what Piaget called the "spontaneous mathematical intelligence of the young child" (Kull, 1986, p. 113).

Other studies have indicated that programming in Logo increases problem-solving abilities in kindergartners (Degelman, Free, Scarlato, Blackburn, and Golden, 1986) and special needs preschoolers (Lehrer, Harckham, Archer, and Pruzek, 1986). Several studies have reported increases in both preschoolers' and primary grade children's ability to monitor their comprehension (i.e., realize when they don't understand; Clements, 1986; Miller and Emihovich, 1986). This may reflect the prevalence of "debugging" in Logo programming. It is essential to note that a critical element in each of these successful efforts was an active role of the teacher—encouraging, questioning, prompting, modeling, and, in general, mediating children's interaction with the computer. This scaffolding led children to reflect on their own thinking behaviors and bring problem-solving processes to an explicit level of awareness. Logo does induce high quality instruction, even from fairly naive and inexperienced adults. However, "the importance of Logo is that it provides an unusually rich problem space within which children can confront important ideas; it does not guarantee that the confrontation will occur'' (Fein, 1985, p. 22).

Such problem solving often has social roots, and computer environments appear to have the potential to facilitate social, as well as cognitive, problem-solving behaviors. Primary grade children working with Logo exhibit similar amounts of conflict as those working with CAI programs. However, they resolve these conflicts more frequently. Logo children also evince more high-level problem-solving behaviors (e.g., determining the nature of problems and selecting strategies to solve them; Clements and Nastasi, in press). Computers stimulate the social interaction of preschoolers to the benefit of their problem solving (Muller and Perlmutter, 1985). The children are also more persistent and effective at solving problems (Perlmutter, Behrend, and Muller, undated). This is true mostly for 5-year-olds, rather than 4-year-olds, however. Younger preschoolers' problem solving may be disrupted by social interaction. For them, the cognitive demands of simultaneously solving a challenging problem and managing social relations may be too taxing. They may also find it too difficult to take the perspective of their partner.

CONCLUSION

We now know that computers are neither panacean nor pernicious. Young children do not need computers any more than they "need" any of many potentially valuable learning centers. There is, however, nothing to lose and potentially rich benefits to acquire through informed use of computers with young children. Informed, because inappropriate or insipid uses will have little or no benefit. Effectiveness depends critically on the quality of the software, the amount of time it is used, and the way in which it is used. Research needs to evolve beyond simply assessing, for example, the effects of computers on social behaviors. We need guidance on effective programs to use and effective ways to use them. Even in this process, we should avoid inflexible conclusions; the field is changing too radically. Acceptance of a certain level or type of either hardware or software, without consideration of advances, or rejection of it for its shortcomings, would be unfortunate. This review can reflect only what is. Teachers should be proactive in determining what could and should be. They know that the gold is to develop problem solvers, not programmers; communicators, not word processors; fulfilled children, not early achievers. The strength of quality computer applications is not that they replace the teacher, but that they allow the teacher to focus on the human parts of teaching, as shown by a Writing to Read letter from a first grader to her teacher (Wallace, 1985, p. 23):

I liket the tipe riter Best of all
and I like to work with you.
And I likt lisoning to the story's
But best I like working with you.

DISCUSSION QUESTIONS

1. Do the age, gender, and other characteristics of the child influence the effectiveness of computers in the classroom?

2. Do computers enhance or delay social development?

3. How can children learn from each other using computers?

4. Does computer-based instruction influence language development? How?

5. Do computers improve the educational opportunities for handicapped or developmentally delayed children?

6. What are the effects of computer-based instruction on thinking and problem solving?

52. TECHNOLOGICAL PRIORITIES IN THE EDUCATION OF YOUNG CHILDREN

by Warren W. Buckleitner and Charles F. Hohmann

Can we find ways to use technology to help improve the learning experiences we offer young children? Should technology be a priority? These questions have been addressed by a healthy body of researchers and practitioners in early childhood, among them Clements (1985), Cuffaro (1984) and Tan (1985). We believe the answer to both questions is *yes*, but we also feel it is essential to first examine overall priorities in early childhood education and then see how technology fits in.

QUALITY AND INITIATIVE: TOP PRIORITIES FOR EARLY CHILDHOOD PROGRAMS

Quality is essential in delivering effective early education. This is the principal conclusion of several long-term studies of early childhood programs (Lazar et al., 1982), including the longitudinal study of the Perry Preschool Project. The Perry study (Berrueta-Clement et al., 1984), which followed 123 disadvantaged children for more than 25 years, showed that quality preschool experience increases the overall quality of children's lives and saves society money in the long run. The positive benefits for children include less retention and special education, higher rates of high school graduation and subsequent college enrollment, increased employment and higher lifetime earnings. Society benefits from quality preschool education through reduced welfare costs, lower crime rates and fewer teenage pregnancies. But the Perry reports go beyond highlighting these findings. They define the characteristics of quality early childhood programs as having:

• Class size no greater than 20 and one teacher or aide per 10 children.
• Qualified staff implementing a validated curriculum model and planning, teaching, and evaluating as a team.
• Administrative leadership in curriculum and curriculum-related inservice training.
• Parents working as partners with teachers in the child's education.

These characteristics thus become priorities for effective programs.

The High/Scope Curriculum Demonstration Project Study (Schweinhart, Weikart and Larner, 1986) indicates that certain learning styles are priorities too. The study examined the effects of three distinctly different curriculum approaches. The results were surprising. Nineteen years after preschool, children who had participated in programs featuring many child-initiated activities reported only one-fifth as many acts of property damage and one-half as many acts of drug abuse as those who had participated in highly teacher-controlled programs. As teens, the preschool initiators participated in more sports and extracurricular school activities than the highly directed youngsters. In addition, the former were viewed in a more positive light by their families than the latter. A fundamental priority of early childhood programs, then, is the encouragement and support of children's initiative in assuming responsibility for their own learning activities.

Quality and child initiative are top priorities in the education of young children—the *sine qua non* of effective early learning. Within this context, a school provides a safe, stimulating educational environment, managed by adults who allow children to make decisions about what they will do and how they will do it. It also provides children experiences that facilitate emotional development.

AN EXAMPLE OF TECHNOLOGY INFLUENCING THE EDUCATION OF YOUNG CHILDREN— THE MICROCOMPUTER

Many types of technology have had both direct and indirect effects on the lives of American children. Television is a good example. Only in the last five years, however, has the microcomputer started to play a more direct role in the daily classroom routine of children. Computers—and the peripherals they can accommodate such as voice synthesizers, touch screens and printers—are pre-

See page 345 for acknowledgment and references.

senting tempting instructional options for educating young children. Almost overnight, they have become commonplace in classrooms. According to reports from the 1985 National Survey: Institutional Uses of School Computers (Becker, 1986), the proportion of U.S. elementary schools having five or more computers in the building jumped from 7 percent in 1983 to 54 percent in 1985.

In 1978, High/Scope began to explore the use of computers with young children (ages 3-7 years). Since that time, High/Scope has been carefully integrating computer technology into its preschool and kindergarten curriculum. This curriculum undergoes continuing development at the High/Scope demonstration school in Ypsilanti, Michigan, where a visitor can see children using computers as routinely as they use blocks and art materials.

1. Computers in the Learning Environment

When computers are used in the learning environment, we have found them to be a powerful learning device that facilitates cognitive development and positive social interaction without harm to young children. Computers in the High/Scope classroom can be found in an activity center similar in function to the block area, the art center and the dress-up area. Along with other experiences, they are offered to children as a free-choice activity. Computers are also used in small-group instructional activities, transported on a cart from the computer area. These computer small-group activities employ teaching techniques like those used in typical non-computer small-group activities—starting with concrete materials, then moving the activity to the computer (Hohmann, 1986). A counting program, for example, would begin with each child counting real objects such as corks or inch-cubes before continuation of the concept in the computer context.

Computers are also used at "circle time": teachers type children's dictation for a group story that is later printed, illustrated by children and sent home as a personal storybook to be read with parents. Experimentation has taught us that children do best with computer activities if they are first introduced, through manipulative materials, to the concept they will pursue at the computer and to the physical act of operating the keys that make the program work.

Moving, counting, measuring, sanding, mixing, comparing, tasting, feeling, climbing and spinning are all components of the "active learning" at the heart of a typical day in the High/Scope school. The computer is added to this environment in

support of the curriculum goals—not as a goal in itself. Searching for good software that supports these curriculum goals is essential to the computer's success in the classroom. Good software allows children to experiment, exercise control, solve problems and learn through their own initiative. Carefully screening over 200 pieces of early childhood software on three types of computers has helped us find software that supports many of the school's curriculum objectives and lives up to our "Hallmarks of Quality Software" (Buckleitner, 1986). We have found age-appropriate software on language, classification, seriation, number and spatial concepts, enabling us to introduce new computer activities at the rate of one per week throughout the school year. The search for good software and input devices that decrease keyboard dependence is an ongoing priority. The computer doesn't do everything well by any means; it can't provide emotional support, for example. But by facilitating certain classroom tasks, the computer can release teachers to focus on extending children's thinking, providing varied activities, resolving disputes and offering affection.

2. Use of Computers by Teachers

Just as technology is leading to greater efficiency in grocery stores and banks, it is playing a role in professionalizing the work of the teacher. Given high quality software and the opportunity to explore, teachers can discover on their own the advantages and limits of a computer system. In addition to its application to young children's learning, the computer can help teachers write and revise letters; print posters, signs and greeting cards; and keep children's records. Software packages such as *Appleworks* (1983, Apple Computer, Inc.), *Print Shop* (1984, Broderbund Software) and *Magic Slate* (1985, Sunburst Communications) can greatly aid these processes. Although such use of technology is not a direct educational priority, it can improve the working climate for early childhood professionals, leading to positive spin-offs that eventually affect the profession as a whole.

COST FACTORS OF TECHNOLOGY USE IN PRESCHOOL—THE COST BENEFIT QUESTION

Even though the price of computers has dropped tremendously in the past five years, a computer system with at least 64K, a disk drive and color monitor, the minimum for early childhood computer activities, will cost between $500 and $1000. A service contract (an amortized approximation of average maintenance costs) can add another $80 per year. In addition, at least $350 must be budgeted for software to provide a meaningful range of computer learning experiences for one center or classroom. Staff training in computer operation, including released time to try out computers and software, is still another cost factor in using computers.

Do the benefits of computer use in preschool warrant these expenses? Too little is currently known about the specific benefits of computer learning to address this question adequately. The priority of using the computer with young children must be worked out without benefit of such data. Even without answering the cost/benefit question, the equity issue is clear. The significant cost of computers means that poorer populations consume their resources on higher priorities, without specific assistance in this area.

THE BOTTOM LINE FOR PRIORITIES— WHERE DOLLARS HAVE BEEN SPENT FOR TECHNOLOGY

At the preschool level, almost half the nation's programs with 20 or more children enrolled have microcomputers, with nearly three-fourths used for educational and recreational activities (*Report on Preschool Programs*, June 25, 1985). This means that more than a third of preschools with 20 or more children use a computer in the classroom. Having a computer is already a priority in many preschool programs.

At the elementary and secondary levels, the number of computers in use quadrupled from about 250,000 to over one million between spring 1983 and spring 1985. The typical computer-using elementary school went from two computers in use to six. During the 1984-85 school year, approximately 15 million students and 500,000 teachers used computers as part of their schools' instructional programs (Becker, 1986).

CONCLUSIONS ABOUT OUR CURRENT TECHNOLOGICAL PRIORITIES

For lack of a single benefit equation, the calculation of priorities for computer use must vary from program to program. But as humans, unaided by computers, we are reasonably good at making judgments when information is limited. Here are a few conclusions that have guided our priorities in the use of computers. First of all, computers can be integrated quite naturally into the daily routine of programs that emphasize "active learning" through concrete experiences and exploration. They function as an aid for promoting certain types of reasoning, problem-solving and exploration. We have found that computers:

- *Inspire practice* of important skills by providing varied and lively formats, by allowing children to choose activities and by providing automatic pacing and feedback.
- *Stimulate thinking* with tasks that have simple but meaningful consequences on the computer; e.g., sorting colored shapes.
- *Help children use symbols* by giving letters, numerals, words and sentences the power to make things happen.

In short, we have found the microcomputer to be an educational asset when integrated into a developmental program in a way that supports the curriculum goals. Major effort needs to be directed toward identifying the contributions computers can make to children's learning and to early childhood educators' work. Moreover, new materials and systems to aid children's learning need to be developed. There's plenty for all to do. We believe that careful application of technology can improve the quality of the programs we offer young children: our foremost priority.

DISCUSSION QUESTIONS

1. Is new technology necessary to improve early childhood education programs?

2. What are the positive effects of using computers with young children? Are there negative effects?

3. How can the teacher take advantage of computer technology?

4. Will the costs of new technology be justified in the possible effects on children and the program?

5. Will new technology increase or reduce equity in early childhood education programs across SES and other child characteristics.

Section Eight: Parents and Community Involvement

EDITOR'S OVERVIEW

For many children, early childhood education in the schools will be their first out-of-home educational experience. For others, it is a transition from some form of day care to the school experience. But for all children, the relationship between home and school is an important linkage to make and enrich. The family is a great source of knowledge about the child, and has already had a huge influence on the child's overall development. Since most parents are relatively unprepared to create optimal learning experiences for their young children, they need the support and interaction that can come from active participation in the work of the school. And since the school and the home exist in a broader context, the educational value of the community must also be considered.

Zorn starts the section with a description of how one school system involved parents in decisions about early childhood education in the schools. Comer's contribution further explains the reasons for better relationships between home and school. Probably the most critical form of parent involvement is through face-to-face conferences between parents and teachers. Bjorklund and Burger give extensive guidelines for conducting conferences with professional effectiveness and personal consideration. A quite different use of technology is described by Bauch, with a model using computers and telephones for better school/home interaction. Next, Shapiro and Doiron examine the influence of the home on the child's literacy, helping teachers make the home/school connections around language development. Then, Ross and Bondy give teachers directions for helping parents think about beginning reading, one of the most frequent parental questions.

53. IN DESIGNING A PRESCHOOL PROGRAM, WE WENT STRAIGHT TO THE SOURCE: PARENTS

by Robert L. Zorn

When we asked parents last spring how interested they might be in a preschool/day-care program run by our school system, we expected a nibble or two. But we received an overwhelmingly positive response, and that turned out to be just the first of many surprises we've had in developing the program, which opened in the Poland (Ohio) Schools (K–12; enr.: 2,300) this past September.

Ohio statutes, like those in many states, do not permit school systems to spend tax dollars on preschool or day-care programs. The laws do, however, allow school systems to operate such programs where fees make them self-supporting. So our preliminary survey was designed simply to find out how many parents might be attracted to a preschool/day-care program run by the school and paid for by the parents using it. Because we sent out letters only to parents of children already enrolled in our school system, we didn't find out how much community interest there really was, but we did identify 60 possible enrollees. This was encouraging enough for us to go on to some planning.

We proposed a pilot program to demonstrate that people wanted preschool/day-care services and that those services could be self-sustaining. The program would be housed in a centrally located elementary school that we had closed in 1985 and subsequently reopened as a continuing education center. We figured a preschool would fit nicely into this operation, which already served youngsters as well as senior citizens. What's more, there were empty classrooms available.

We next sent a second letter to parents laying out options and fees, and after their responses confirmed their interest, we offered our final plan. The day-care program would operate five days a week (including school holidays), September through May, and both the preschool and the day-care programs would include morning and afternoon snacks. Here are the program choices we gave parents:

• *Two-day Preschool:* 3, 4, or 5-year-olds, Tuesday and Thursday from 9 to 11:30 a.m., when the Poland Schools are in session, $32 per month.

Additional hours, $1.25 per hour.

• *Three-day Preschool:* 3, 4, or 5-year-olds, Monday, Wednesday, and Friday from 9 a.m. to 11:30 a.m., when the Poland Schools are in session, $45 per month. Additional hours, $1.25 per hour.

• *Half-day Day Care:* 3, 4, or 5-year-olds, Monday through Friday from 7:30 a.m. to 12:30 p.m. or 12:30 to 5:30 p.m., $6 per day or $30 per week.

• *Full-day Day Care:* 3, 4, or 5-year-olds, Monday through Friday from 7:30 a.m. to 5:30 p.m., $11 per day or $55 per week. This includes preschoolers.

Of course, we didn't come by these fees easily. We looked at how much local private schools and day-care centers charged for similar services, and then we worked backward from the number of youngsters we figured we would enroll versus the likely costs of the program. (For financial details, see . . . pages 251–52.)

GOALS AND SERVICES

Our coordinator/teacher put together brochures explaining what parents and children could look for in the Poland Schools Preschool and Day-care Program. We emphasized the relaxed and casual atmosphere we hoped to create and the teacher-directed activities—both quiet and active—in which students would participate. Because these early childhood programs were to be integrated with our regular school curriculum, we planned with care. Our aims: to stimulate children's interest in areas such as art, music, health, and science and to help the children develop motor skills, cognitive vocabularies, basic mathematical skills, and positive ideas about themselves.

We quickly found school system sponsorship made the programs especially attractive to many parents. The school system's expertise and its accountability made a strong appeal, and so did linking the preschool programs to the rest of the school curriculum. As it happened, we also were

See page 345 for acknowledgment.

250

able to provide services that would have been difficult if not impossible for private preschool and day-care programs to offer. Well-equipped play areas belonging to the former elementary school were available, for example. So were school buses for field trips. And we could offer students enrolled in the all-day programs hot lunches at school lunch prices.

Some parents of preschoolers who had older children taking part in a K–5 latchkey program also held at the continuing education center enjoyed an additional convenience: one-stop child pickup at the end of the day.

What would we do if we were beginning again? We'd be prepared for a lot more interest than we expected. Instead of the 60 students we planned for, we got 90. Next year, we might be using the entire first floor of the continuing education center. We also would be prepared to be more flexible in our offerings. School people are used to doing things the way they do them. So when we made our original proposal, we assumed that all the children would attend five days a week. The parents educated us to *their* needs by telling us they wanted more flexibility—which is why we offered both two-day and three-day weeks. And if we had it to do over again, we would start out offering day care on a year-round basis instead of 40 weeks per year (in fact, we made that change after the program started last fall).

These changes have been easy to take care of, and I'm confident everybody agrees the programs are a big success. Parents tell us they feel relaxed about leaving their young children in school-sponsored programs. And taxpayers are impressed that the schools have been able to add an important service without increasing taxes. We are pleased because child care is a big problem for many people, yet it's one the public schools should be able to help with.

I don't need to tell you that schools tend to be conservative and slow to change—and insofar as those qualities keep them from running headlong into ditches, they're useful. But schools also need to be responsive to the important needs of the communities they serve. In Poland, we're happy that we saw such a need and responded.

HERE'S WHERE THE MONEY GOES

In figuring how much to charge parents for a proposed preschool/day-care program in Poland (Ohio) schools, . . . we recognized the fees had to be in line with the realities of what it would cost to run the program.

Our first assumption was that we would enroll 60 youngsters, based on what parents told us when we surveyed them. That led us to project the following revenues:

- *Two-day Preschool:* Fifteen kids paying $32 per month for nine months came to $4,320.
- *Three-day Preschool:* Fifteen kids paying $45 per month for nine months came to $6,075.
- *Half-day Day Care:* Seven youngsters paying $30 per week for 40 weeks came to $8,400.
- *Full-day Day Care:* Seven youngsters paying $55 per week for 40 weeks came to $15,400.

Total projected receipts for parental fees, then, came to $34,195 for the 40-week 1987–88 school year beginning September 1, 1987.

Next, we estimated the costs. To run the program, we calculated we would need one coordinator/teacher and three part-time aides: The coordinator/teacher would work from 8:30 a.m. to 3 p.m.; the teacher, from 7:30 a.m. to noon; the first aide, from 8:30 a.m. to 12:30 p.m.; and the second aide, from 12:30 to 5:30 p.m.

We wouldn't have been able to offer the program at all if we'd had to pay the staff according to scale. Fortunately, the local collective bargaining agent agreed to unusual conditions as a sign of its support for our experiment: Staff members in the preschool/day care program would be noncontract and receive limited benefits, and their employment would depend on adequate enrollment.

Given these conditions, we anticipated these salaries: The coordinator would earn $7.50 an hour for 35 hours a week, for a total of $262.50 a week; the teacher would earn $7.13 an hour for 17.5 hours a week, for a total of $124.78 a week; the aides would earn $3.50 an hour for 65 hours a week, for a total of $227.50 a week; and retirement and workers' compensation contributions would total $90 a week.

The weekly total, then, was to be $704.78, or a 36-week total of $25,372.08.

Because the day-care program—unlike the preschool—would run during four weeks of school vacation between September and May, we calculated that program would involve additional salary costs of $1,782.56, bringing the total costs for a 40-week day-care and 36-week preschool program to $27,154.64.

For snacks, we estimated the following costs:

- *Two-day Preschool:* Fifty cents for each of 15 students attending two days a week for 36 weeks came to $540.

• *Three-day Preschool:* Fifty cents for each of 15 students attending three days a week for 36 weeks came to $810.

• *Half-day Day Care:* Fifty cents for each of seven students attending five days a week for 40 weeks came to $700.

• *Full-day Day Care:* Fifty cents for each of seven students having two snacks a day for five days a week for 40 weeks came to $1,400.

The total for snacks, then, was $3,450.

Then we added that total to the personnel costs ($27,154.64) for a program total of $30,604.64, against receipts of $34,195. The difference of $3,590.36 we would use to pay the school board for utilities and maintenance at the center. At $90 per week for our 40-week session ($3,600), we would have just enough to cover these operating expenses. In other words, our program would be self-supporting, as the law required.

DISCUSSION QUESTIONS

1. How can a school system implement an early childhood education program that is responsive to parents?

2. Should parents be given choices and input into the early education program in the schools?

3. What are the financial implications of various program and schedule options?

54. IS 'PARENTING' ESSENTIAL TO GOOD TEACHING?

by James P. Comer, M.D.

The idea that teachers are "parent surrogates" for their students doesn't sit well with many people, though most find the notion of teachers as child developers less troublesome. But when we consider the fact that good child rearing and child development practices promote academic learning, the notion of teacher as parent surrogate becomes logical. In fact, many of the techniques and conditions required for successful parenting in families are also required for successful teaching in schools.

All adults involved with children either help or thwart children's growth and development—whether we like it, intend it, or not. The effort to limit the role of the teacher and the school to academics is one of the primary reasons America's great experiment in education—the effort to educate more than the intellectual elite and economically privileged—has been less successful than it might have been. This limitation has been one of the reasons that so many students drop out and only about 20 percent actually thrive in our schools.

Teaching and learning are too often considered mechanical processes. This view, reinforced by the emergence and growth of technology, sees student minds as computers. Teachers input information; students process the input and respond.

Despite the lessons of John Dewey, Maria Montessori, Lucy Sprague Mitchell, and others who have recognized the importance of feelings and relationships in fostering student growth and development, this mechanical view of the learning process has prevailed. It was reinforced by the educational reform movement of the 1920s and '30s—and the resulting changes in educational standards, school organization and functioning, and teacher training.

The cognitive sciences and experimental and quantitative research gained acceptance and prestige during the 1950s—to the detriment of the affective sciences and clinical, field, and qualitative research. This development contributed to the widespread perception of learning as a mechanical cognitive function—as opposed to a cognitive *and* affective process that involves relationships and development.

In 1957, the Russians sent Sputnik into space—and the United States panicked. Our schools tried to do even more of what they were already doing—teachers teaching and students learning in a mechanical fashion. But gradually, study by study, a new theme emerged. Teachers, parents, and students alike began pointing to the importance of the quality of relationships among everybody involved in the educational enterprise. Those most intimately involved in our schools were telling us that these relationships received little attention—and as a result are often not conducive to student learning and development.

"*They* don't care" is the number one complaint heard from student dropouts. Teachers complain about behavior problems and the lack of student motivation. Parents complain that they feel unwanted by schools—except when they're needed to control their children. These are all relationship issues.

THE 'GOOD OLD DAYS'

Nonetheless, school reform reports over the past few years have reemphasized the same issues addressed in the 1920s and '30s—educational standards, school organization and functioning, and teacher training. More than half a century later, educational reform is still paying little attention to relationships, to the role of the affect in learning.

Our public schools are under mounting pressure. The U.S. economy, and our standard of living as a nation, will deteriorate unless the majority of students receive an adequate education. And that education must do more than enable students to earn "acceptable" scores on standardized tests. The schools must prepare students to be responsible family members and citizens of their communities and our society.

Educational policymakers must learn the lessons of the past. Many students will not be motivated to learn, to master academic material, while troublesome underlying relationship feelings and conditions are at play. Our schools cannot provide educational excellence until the policymakers make it possible for teachers and school people to again serve as parent surrogates.

Prior to the mid-1950s, most teachers were

See pages 345–46 for acknowledgment and suggestions for further reading.

PARENTS AND COMMUNITY INVOLVEMENT

parent surrogates without ever being fully aware of it. Before this time, transportation was slow, television nonexistent. There was only modest movement of people and ideas in and out of communities. Teachers were an integral part of the community in which they lived and worked. They went to the same churches or synagogues as their students. They shopped in the same stores or used the same post office. Some walked to school hand in hand with their students. They sometimes engaged in play and leisure time activities with the families of their students.

As a result of the limitations on travel and communication, parents, teachers, religious leaders, and other adult authority figures were the "source of all truth" for children in their early developmental years. These significant adults generally held a consensus about what was right and wrong, good and bad.

A set of attitudes, values, and ways dominated individual communities and were generally accepted by children and adults alike. This situation limited change and free expression. At the same time, it made the environment very predictable, provided children with a sense of belonging and place—even when "your place" was not acceptable by today's standards. All of these conditions created a local sense of community—of which the school was a natural part. This allowed for a transfer of authority from home to school in a way that permitted parents and teachers to support children's growth and development.

When I was in elementary school in the 1940s, I went on a shopping expedition to the A&P store every Friday with my parents and siblings. I can't remember a week that we did not encounter someone from the school—the custodian, principal, teacher, school clerk. There was always an exchange of information about how we were doing in school, what was expected of us, and what to do if we didn't meet those expectations. The positive relationship between my parents and school people—and the probability of a weekly report—made it difficult for me to do anything short of live up to the expressed expectations.

Learning at home that prepares children for school initially takes place through imitation of, identification with, and internalization of the attitudes, values, and ways of parents, family, and selected friends, kin, and social institutions. A positive relationship between home and school allows children to imitate, identify with, and internalize the attitudes, values, and ways of school people. This makes it possible for school people to counsel, guide, and motivate students to grow

along all the crucial developmental pathways—social-interactive, psycho-emotional, moral, speech and language, intellectual-cognitive-academic.

I don't remember much from the college algebra course I took in high school. But the teacher was also the dean of students, and he once adjudicated a student election in a way that was fair despite a great deal of pressure to do otherwise. His behavior was a model of fairness and integrity that lives with me today. Modern technology has replaced typesetting by hand. But my print shop teacher remains important to me because in casual conversation with several of us he pointed out that most of us will never be Einsteins, Franklin Roosevelts, or Joe Louises; that the important thing in our lives was to prepare ourselves to be able to take care of self and family in a responsible way.

I haven't had much use for high school Latin over the years. And as mischievous teens we were amused that our teacher appeared to be on familiar terms with Julius Caesar, Marc Anthony, and other figures of ancient Rome. But I was also motivated to learn Latin—despite the fact that it was a dead language—because of our teacher's enthusiasm for the subject. When I complained about the slowness of the democratic process in dealing with obvious injustices, my government teacher said, "The wheels of democracy grind slowly, but they grind." His observation alerted me to the complexity of human systems and contributed to my eventually becoming a student of behavior and social systems.

The ways my teachers worked and interacted with us were very much like the ways of concerned parents. The attention they gave to our nonacademic thoughts, fears, concerns, and problems did not detract from teaching the basics. In fact, it was their concern, interest, and enthusiasm that motivated many of us to learn the academic material—often when it had no intrinsic or obvious value, interest, or even benefit, other than a grade. Cognitive skills were honed and the confidence and discipline to learn were gained because of positive relationships—first with parents, then with teachers in school.

SOCIETAL TRANSITION

After the 1940s, our society began to change very rapidly and dramatically. Today airplanes move people in half a day from coast to coast and continent to continent—distances that took weeks and months to travel less than a hundred years ago. Work is less often local, and play is less often

254

communal. Modern roads, cars, and rapid transportation allow people to live long distances from where they work. These conditions decrease the interactions among, as well as the power and influence of, parents, teachers, religious leaders, and other local authority figures. There's a concomitant decrease in the predictability of the environment and children's sense of trust, belonging, and place.

Television now brings attitudes, values, and ways from around the world directly to children without the censorship or sanctions of the important adults around them. Sometimes what they observe is in conflict with what their parents are trying to teach them. Children can listen to differences of opinion about what is right and wrong on almost every newscast. There is less of a single truth and way to understand and behave agreed on by important adult authority figures.

There are now many truths in competition with each other. And television bombards young people with more information than ever before. Human shortcomings and frailties are revealed to children at very early ages. "Dynasty," "Dallas," and other television programs present young people with the "nitty gritty" of adult life, including appropriate and inappropriate sexual expression. And some children, because of working or careless parents, are able to watch "Debbie Does Dallas" and other pornographic films.

Nonetheless, children are no more mature than they were 40 years ago—even if they appear to be because they have more information. Our children's exposure to a complex world increases their need for adult guidance and support to integrate the information into their developing psyches. Children need adults to help them learn what, when, and how to act on the information they receive, and develop the controls to do so appropriately.

THE SCHOOLS ADJUST . . .

Children need more adult guidance than in the past—but for many reasons they receive less. Families with two working parents are now the norm instead of the exception—and children spend less time with their parents. There's more family stress, conflict, and divorce. There are more young, single parents with inadequate incomes rearing children. There is less extended family, social network, and community support for parents and children.

And our children don't receive adult guidance and support in the schools. School organization and management are designed to facilitate a focus on academic content rather than to promote desirable staff-student interactions and adequate student growth and development. The organization is usually hierarchical and departmentalized. Management is usually authoritarian and top-down in execution. Teachers and administrators are not trained to appreciate the way school organization and management impact the behavior of staff, parents, and students.

Most teachers and administrators who work well with students and promote their development do so on the basis of intuitive knowledge and skills, not through knowledge they gained in applied child development courses in their pre-service or in-service training. There aren't many such courses. All of these conditions make it difficult for school people to serve as parent surrogates—to help their students learn to manage a more complex age and school environment, to help them succeed and stay in school.

Education theorists and policymakers ignored the changes in communities, relationships, and behavior brought about by science and technology after World War II. The schools adjusted to societal changes by concentrating almost exclusively on the new academic demands. Policymakers also ignored the fact that schools would now be expected to educate children who in the past usually dropped out, but still found a place in the labor force.

Those children who are provided with a good developmental experience prior to school, whose parents' attitudes, values, and ways are similar to those of the school, and whose parents make a conscious effort to support the activities of the school, are the children most likely to succeed in school. This was as true 40 years ago as it is today. But young people who didn't succeed in school 40 years ago could leave. They could find a job that would enable them to take care of themselves and their families, feel rewarded for doing so, and be motivated to be responsible family members and citizens of their communities and the society.

Today when young people drop out of school, they are usually embarking on a downhill course in life, with reduced chances of meeting their adult responsibilities. In short, a higher level of academic achievement and social development is required to carry out adult tasks today than has ever been required before in the history of the world.

Because of the complexity of today's world, all students need more support from school people than in the past. But a disproportionate number of the children who will not do well in school are from low-income families, families under excessive stress, or families with lifestyles very different from the expectations of the school. And a disproportionate number of these families are from the minority groups that have had the most traumatic experiences in this country—Native Americans, Hispanics, and Blacks. These groups differ from others in that they have experienced the most cultural discontinuity and destruction of their organizing and stabilizing institutions and practices, as well as forced exclusion from education and other developmental opportunities.

After the 1940s, education increasingly became the ticket of admission to living wage jobs. Minorities, greatly undereducated prior to that time, were increasingly closed out of primary job market opportunities and locked into the lowest level of the work force. Minorities had always been relegated to the bottom of the occupational ladder in this country. But through the first half of this century, many minority families in rural areas, with strong religious and cultural support systems, functioned reasonably well despite low incomes.

By the mid-1950s, rural minority families were being pushed off the land and into urban centers by technological and economic developments. These families, which had previously functioned reasonably well, began to function less well. They came under social stress of all kinds and became increasingly unable to give their children the kind of preschool experiences that would allow them to achieve well in school. These children need the teacher-as-parent surrogate—in alliance with their own parents—more than any other group of children. Unfortunately, due to our history and culture, these are the children least likely to receive parenting in the schools.

HOW SCHOOLS FAIL

Differences between home and school—whether of class, race, income, or culture—always create potential conflict. Today, because the school is no longer a natural part of the community, the alliance between home and school must be forged if it is to exist at all. And wherever there is a disparity of power between groups who must relate to each other to achieve a goal, the group with the most power must make the greatest effort to overcome the real and potential obstacles to creating a desirable relationship. The effort must be made with good will and skill in order to avoid condescension and other attitudes that will only exacerbate the conflict.

Children who have not received an adequate developmental experience prior to school—for whatever reasons—often present themselves in ways that cause school people to view them as willfully "bad" and of limited ability. A common response is to punish such youngsters or to have low expectations for them. But because societal conditions today don't provide the kind of absolute authority schools had in the past, students often fight back in acting-out or disruptive ways. The staff often then makes an even stronger effort to control the behavior without responding to the underlying problems with relationships and development of the children. This makes the situation worse. In addition, school staff—like all of us—want to be successful in their work. Children who don't appear to be ready, motivated, or trying to learn make it difficult for school staff to experience success.

School staff and students are often unable to develop the kind of relationships that will allow emotional attachment and bonding, imitation, identification, and internalization of the attitudes, values, and ways of the school that are necessary to promote adequate academic learning. Many students withdraw, lose confidence, or adjust in other ways that limit their academic performance. In turn, staff attitudes about the behavior and ability of the students are confirmed. Teachers are then less likely to be positive parent surrogates. These negative interactions lead to a spectrum of conditions from controlled and quiet but academically underachieving schools, to chaotic and academically underachieving schools.

Parents are often asked to get involved in meaningful ways with schools only after their children are in trouble or not learning well. Because they don't have natural interactions with school staff, parents are often suspicious and distrustful before there are problems and convinced that their feelings were justified after problems arise. Some parents have difficult memories and ambivalent feelings about schools themselves. And those under great stress, with their own personal problems and failures, often view the school problems of their children as yet another failure. Thus, many parents stay away from schools or interact with school people in angry, defensive, and confrontational ways.

NEGATIVE RELATIONS

School staff—doing their best and not appreciated—often respond in understandably defensive ways. Staff people sometimes say and feel, "The parents don't care." They offer in evidence the fact that the parents don't keep appointments or attend school functions—while at the same time they blame the school for their children's problems. In fact, most parents do care—but they have difficulty interacting with the school.

When parents are unhappy, and students are not behaving or learning adequately, conflict often develops among school staff. The social workers, psychologists, and special education teachers are expected to "fix" the children's problems—but often feel those problems are created or exacerbated by the classroom teachers. Some teachers want to have more influence in the management of the school in order to address problems. Others simply want the administrator to get tough and do his or her job—punishing the badness out of the kids.

The negative cycle intensifies. Disappointment and conflict consume energy and get in the way of gratifying professional experiences. Hopelessness and despair can lead to apathy, poor staff performance, and criticism from within and without the school. Additional problems based on racial, class, cultural, and economic differences often arise.

The traditional organization of schools doesn't allow the staff to work together to overcome problems. Departmentalization in middle and high schools further separates and fragments staffs. Even in schools that serve students from better educated families under less economic stress—but where students still need guidance and support—the school organization makes it difficult for staff to develop desirable relationships with students, to serve as parent surrogates.

We cannot turn back the clock and return to "the good old days." In fact, it's necessary to keep in mind that many students from all socio-economic groups didn't achieve to the level of their academic potential in the good old days. But we can reorganize schools so that staff can support social and emotional growth—and in turn, academic learning.

A reasonable consensus is needed to accomplish the schools' mission. This consensus can't be mandated as it was in the past—it doesn't exist in our schools or our communities. A mechanism must be created through which school building leadership can create desirable relationships and develop a consensus consistent with school system goals that will allow staff and parents to support the development of students—and involve students in their own self-development and learning.

In my initial intervention research work in two schools in New Haven, Connecticut, we observed many of the most severe problems described above.

We realized that no single group—parents, teachers, administrators, students—was at fault. We recognized that no single intervention—curriculum change, behavior modification method, physical environment improvement—would make a significant and sustained difference.

The problem was that the schools were addressing new problems and opportunities in old and now ineffective ways. The interaction between home and school, among school staff, and between staff and students created a climate that made it difficult for the staff to form an alliance with parents and serve as parent surrogates.

We created a governance and management group, led by the principal, made up of representatives of the key adult groups in the school—teachers, pupil personnel staff, teacher assistants, and parents. This group encouraged the interaction between critical authority figures—the kind of interaction that took place in yesterday's communities in natural ways. This mechanism decreased distrust and alienation between home and school. Parents and staff realized their mutual interest and developed a sense of program ownership and responsibility, along with the principal. Effective communication and planning became possible.

The governance and management group eventually developed a comprehensive building plan that focused on creating a desirable climate of social relationships in both the entire school and the academic program. The objectives and strategies of the plan dictated the kind of staff development that took place at the building level. And systematic assessment of the outcomes in both the behavioral and academic areas allowed the group, with the support of the entire staff and parent community, to modify the school program as indicated.

We also brought the social worker, psychologist, special education teacher, and other support staff together as a group. They continued to provide service to individual children and families. But the emphasis was shifted from responding to problem behaviors to preventing them. A member of this group served on the governance and management team and helped team members, and the entire staff, think of children as underdeveloped, under stress, or with skills that work outside of school, but not in school. They helped the staff see children as having modifiable behaviors—not as being simply bad, "dumb," or of limited intelligence.

SCHOOL AS COMMUNITY

The staff responded by helping the children

modify undesirable behaviors—as good parents do. They received parental support because the parents were involved in the program to help establish a good school climate. Pot luck suppers, fashion shows, book fairs, workshops by teachers for parents, and a variety of other academic and social projects restored the trust between home and school. These activities created an alliance that permitted both staff and parents to parent. The program brought the parents into the school during good times rather than bad.

The decreased behavior problems in the school led to decreased conflict among school staff. The more desirable interaction between staff and students increased parent and community support of the schools. This in turn increased staff energy, hope for student success, and for professional success for themselves. There was more time for teaching and planning. In such an environment, teacher-student attachment and bonding, imitation, identification, and internalization of school ways by students could take place.

Eventually it became possible to tailor the co-curricular activities—arts, athletics, social skills—and the academic curriculum of the school to the specific needs of the children. The schools went from being the lowest achieving in the city to within the top five with no change in the 99 percent Black, almost all poor make-up of the student population. Staff and parents, planning together, were able to develop a number of programs that worked in a changed climate of interaction that probably would not have worked in a climate in which the emphasis was on teaching academic material with no attention to the quality of relationships. Teachers were able to discourage undesirable behavior and encourage desirable behavior, and to respond to the thoughts, fears, concerns, and problems of the students much in the way of parents.

One of the single parents from the school called her 10-year-old son's teacher because the child had left home upset, it was very late, and he hadn't returned. The teacher went to the school and found the child huddled at the front door in the dark and the cold. The teacher started his search at the school because he knew it had come to mean support and security to the youngster. While the school does not want to take over the role of the parent, creating a climate that permits such strong positive feelings allows the staff to influence positive student behavior and motivate academic learning.

We're taking the same general intervention approach in a New Haven middle and high school as we took in the elementary schools. Our work at the secondary level is too recent to report results. But it's also possible to create activities related to the curriculum and student learning that bring staff, parents, and students together in ways that support the growth of middle and high school students. The specific ways this can occur must be developed at the building level because each school is different, with different needs and opportunities, assets, and problems.

Positive outcomes are possible in certain instances without changing the traditional organization of the schools. Creative and charismatic leaders can create desirable home-school relationships, and some gifted teachers are able to help children grow and develop even in difficult school situations. But such positive situations often "fall apart" when the unusual leader or gifted teacher leaves. And many more students can be helped to develop when the school climate permits all of the adults interacting with the children to serve as successful parent surrogates.

Our society has changed—so have our schools. But by focusing solely on academic changes, the schools have ignored the affective domain—the crucial relationships that students need to grow and learn. We remain mired in a mechanical approach to learning. It's one that has never served our children well—and in today's world dooms many of our students to failure.

DISCUSSION QUESTIONS

1. Why is a positive relationship between school and home important to today's programs?
2. Are there lessons and practices from the past that can be used to improve home/school relationships in the present?
3. Do children under "social stress" need special support from teachers and parents during their first school experiences?
4. What are some barriers to positive relationships between teachers and parents?
5. How can new interactions and partnerships be established between parents and teachers? What are the potential outcomes?

55. MAKING CONFERENCES WORK FOR PARENTS, TEACHERS, AND CHILDREN

by Gail Bjorklund and Christine Burger

Communication with parents is an essential part of any good early childhood education program. Parents want and need to know about their child from the school's perspective. At the same time, the school benefits from the input of parents as teachers seek to develop a more comprehensive understanding of a child's behavior. Parent-teacher conferences are an important part of this communication process. Both parent and teacher possess valuable information about the child's abilities, interests, likes, dislikes, and needs. This information must be shared in a positive manner so that the best interests of the child can be served (Morrison, 1978; Nedler and McAfee, 1979).

Conducting successful parent-teacher conferences is a difficult task. What strategies can teachers use to conduct conferences that will result in better teaching and better parenting? This [chapter] will offer guidelines and a model strategy, all based on the experiences of early childhood professionals, to help you conduct more productive parent-teacher conferences.

GUIDELINES FOR CONFERENCES

Advance Preparations

Teachers should view preparing for parent-teacher conferences as an ongoing process. Preparation should begin before the child enters the program and continue until the child leaves. Teachers should collect samples of children's art and record anecdotes of typical behaviors to share with parents. This will help set the stage for meaningful dialogue with the parents. In most early childhood programs there are opportunities for daily contact with parents. If you take advantage of these, you can get to know the family better each day and anticipate what parents might like to discuss in a more formal setting.

Once you know the families, you will be more confident about adjusting to the many individual differences among parents (Hymes, 1974). Parents' attitudes may range from comfortable to skeptical, depending upon their background and experience (Nedler and McAfee, 1979). When you expect this

See page 346 for acknowledgment and references.

variation in how parents will approach the conference, you will feel better equipped to handle any situation which might arise.

You can help parents prepare for the conference, too. In addition to an announcement and general information about the conference, provide each parent with concrete information about your goals for the conference and suggest things for them to think about before you meet.

Take time to create a proper conference setting. If your meeting is to be a productive, comfortable, two-way interaction, you will need to ensure privacy (Berger, 1981). Teachers need to be sensitive to the hidden messages that barriers, such as a desk between parents and teacher, can imply (Chinn, Winn, and Walters, 1978). A good arrangement is to sit in adult-size furniture around a low table so the child's work and any other items can be displayed and discussed. Proper lighting, ventilation, and temperature are also necessary to help you focus your attention on the child.

When You Talk with Parents

When conducting the conference, you should strive to

1. help the parent feel relaxed, comfortable, and wanted, since the school is "teacher territory,"

2. communicate with parents on their level, without educational jargon,

3. accentuate the positive attributes of the child, and

4. provide specific suggestions for ways parents can help their children at home.

Effective communication is crucial to the success of a parent-teacher conference. Reflective or active listening will encourage information sharing and discourage confrontation between you and the parent. To be an active listener, you must pay attention to both the stated and implied feelings of the parent and respond in a reflective way so as to set the stage for further communication. An active listener makes "an empathetic response that speaks verbally and physically to the specific feelings of the speaker'' (Chinn, Winn, and Walters, 1978, p. 84).

For example, if the parent of a 3-year-old states, ''I just don't see where Matthew is learning very much in this group,'' an active listener might respond with an understanding, reflective statement like, ''You're concerned that Matthew is not making as much progress as you expected.'' This active-listening statement will encourage the parent to elaborate on why the child's progress has been disappointing: ''We really thought that by now he would be able to say his ABCs and write his own name.''

A quick, closed, or negative response by the teacher, on the other hand, will stop productive communication. A teacher comment such as an incredulous ''You're dissatisfied with our curriculum?'' or a patronizing ''Oh, no, he really is a very bright child,'' or a defensive ''I find that hard to believe when . . . !'' will immediately limit the parents' willingness to continue the discussion.

Berger (1981) recommends that in any parent-teacher conference the teacher speak no more than 50 percent of the time. This allows you half of the conference time to get to know the parent and child better.

After the Parents Leave

The conference is far from over when the parents leave. ''The parent-teacher conference is only as good as the follow-up and follow-through that occur after the conference'' (Morrison, 1978, p. 163). Immediately after the parents leave, write a careful record of the conference; include in it suggestions that were made and questions that were raised. If a response from you is expected, be sure to follow up immediately. Depending on the family, an acceptable follow-up might include referrals to other resources, scheduling another conference, a telephone call, a home visit, a written report, an informal note to the parents, an evaluation form asking for suggestions about conference format, and informal daily chats with parents.

Why is follow-up so important? Following through with parents can be advantageous because it allows you to

1. acknowledge to the parents that you genuinely care,

2. clarify issues or problems,

3. encourage children and parents to continue to do their best,

4. offer opportunities to extend classroom learnings at home, and

5. plan programs to serve parents and children. (Morrison, 1978)

These guidelines highlight the importance of using parent-teacher conferences to resolve issues, search for answers, decide on goals, determine mutual strategies, and form a team on behalf of the young child. We have developed a strategy that will help ensure that these goals are accomplished.

A STRATEGY FOR A SUCCESSFUL CONFERENCE

George Mason University's Project for the Study of Young Children in Fairfax, Virginia, has developed a coordinated strategy for conducting parent-teacher conferences. This strategy seeks to help teachers initiate effective conference techniques within a sequential framework and it can readily be adapted to a variety of settings for young children.

As you look over the outline of this strategy, it is essential that you consider the role of all possible conference participants—not only parents and teachers, but also administrators, teacher assistants, associate teachers, and children. In most programs the administrator assumes responsibility for implementing the strategy, and a committee representing the other groups could offer assistance.

Phase 1: Set the Stage

At the beginning of the school year, or whenever it seems appropriate for your program, the director (or other designated staff member) should lead a discussion about the conference strategy with all of the staff and the parents. For staff, topics covered can include

• a brief overview of when and how conferences will occur throughout the year,

• a detailed examination of the developmental curriculum goals—their meaning, examples of behaviors in each, and sample activities which best address the goals (see Table 1), and

• a discussion of alternative techniques to use in order to observe each child prior to the first conference.

Also during this phase, parents should gather as a group so the director can explain the developmental curriculum goals of the program. Parents should be encouraged to think about how these goals pertain to their child and which goals are most important to them.

Table 1

Project for the Study of Young Children
Developmental goals

Social and emotional goals:

1. to become increasingly autonomous
2. to use initiative in pursuing curiosities
3. to have confidence in one's ability to solve problems
4. to feel secure in relationships with adults
5. to enjoy playing with other children and alone
6. to begin to coordinate different points of view by cooperating and re- solving conflicts
7. to cope with fears, anxieties, and frustrations constructively
8. to demonstrate persistence in completing a task

Cognitive goals:

1. to express ideas through language and symbolic representations in effec- tive and varied ways
2. to put ideas or objects into relationships, noting similarities and differ- ences
3. to come up with interesting and creative ideas, problems, and questions

Physical goals:

1. to build awareness of one's body in space
2. to coordinate fine and gross motor skills

These developmental goal statements are the key to this initial phase. Adapted from Kamii and DeVries (1973), they are based on Piagetian theory and phrased in a way that respects individual differences. You can easily translate these goals into curriculum content to promote several aspects of development simultaneously. In our project, we emphasize the social and emotional goals, and provide a foundation for growth in the other areas.

Phase 2: Set Priorities at a Planning Conference

Shortly after the initial meeting, the parents, head teacher, and project director meet in a plan- ning conference. To prepare for this conference *parents* will

• examine the developmental curriculum goals and select between two and four priority goals for their child based upon the child's strengths or areas of need.
• complete the Minnesota Child Development Inventory if their child is between 2½- and 3½-

years-old (Ireton and Thwing, 1974), or the Min- nesota Preschool Inventory if their child is between 3½- and 5-years-old (Ireton and Thwing, 1979). Parents should submit these materials to the direc- tor 1 week prior to the planning conference.

In preparation for the planning conference, *teach- ers* will

• organize their observations and select some representative anecdotes.
• select two to four priority goals for each child.

The *director* will

• score the Minnesota Child Development In- ventory or Minnesota Preschool Inventory and write a brief summary for each child.
• offer help and advice to teachers as they select their priority goals. The director might make a focused classroom observation of selected children or give teachers release time so they can observe the children without interference.

The results of the Minnesota Inventories are recorded in a profile format which parents can readily understand. We have found that these instruments accurately depict a child's development, but we do not use these or any other standardized test as the sole indicator of a child's progress or development. We use the profile in conjunction with anecdotal records and work samples to draw a more complete and accurate picture of individual children.

The planning conference begins with casual, positive comments and proceeds to a brief summary of the conference format by the conference leader. Ask parents to share the priority goals they have selected for their child. As the parents discuss these, the teacher can comment upon the goals by relating anecdotes of classroom behavior which clarify, support, or alter the goals. This provides a transition into a discussion of the priority goals selected by the teacher and the determination of mutually agreed upon goals. The director may also use the results of the Minnesota profiles to further delineate meaningful and appropriate goals for each child. Participants can also discuss how the priority goals might be addressed both at school and at home.

The 20 minutes allotted for this conference is very effective in focusing discussion on developing a joint educational plan, since many of the ideas have been prepared prior to the conference. Parents report that this advance planning makes them feel less apprehensive about the conference. They also indicate that they are impressed by the attention given to their opinions and concerns. Staff, too, have found that the focus on goals gives structure and direction to the conference while allowing for flexibility to meet the needs of families and children.

Phase 3: Observe at Regular Intervals

Throughout the year, each child's progress regarding all of the educational goals is observed and recorded. Special attention is given to the priority goals selected by parents and staff. The curriculum is built around these same developmental goals, with each 2-week period focusing on a few of the goals as priorities. These planned learning experiences enable teachers to center their observations on the children whose priority goals match those of the curriculum. Teachers document growth through anecdotal records, checklists, rating scales, and behavior frequency tallying.

Teachers in our program formally record children's progress on all developmental goals in January. Conferences with parents are called in situations where changes in behavior are dramatic or where concerns arise. Programs that operate year-round will probably want to gather and review this information about every 3 or 4 months.

Phase 4: Involve the Child in the Progress Conference

Starting in April, our project holds progress conferences: the parents, teacher, assistant teacher, and child all meet together. After this much time in the program, everyone has had ample opportunity to establish solid relationships and to discuss concerns without the child's presence. Thus, much of the groundwork necessary for success has taken place long before the progress conference.

Prior to the conference, the teacher should send a progress report to the parents which summarizes the growth seen during the year and describes the child's behavior in each of the developmental areas (Table 2). At the same time, the families should receive a guide sheet emphasizing that this conference will focus on the strengths and accomplishments of the child. In addition, the guide sheet should list three topics the family will discuss at the conference and suggest that they talk about these in advance:

1. What do you like best about school?
2. Who are some of the special friends you like to play with at school?
3. Are there any things you would like to do more at school?

The teacher begins the progress conference by sharing examples of the child's growth through anecdotes which describe some of the child's best skills or characteristics. This leads into a discussion of the three questions with the child. This portion of the conference gives each child a special opportunity to share ideas with people who are important to them. Children also hear good things about themselves, which contributes to their self-image.

When we introduced the progress conference into our program, teachers and parents expressed reservations and apprehensions about the child's presence: "What if my child doesn't talk?" or "What if negative behaviors need to be discussed?" However, our experiences with this format have been positive. The children have a chance to participate in a conference (possibly the only chance they will ever have in their school careers). The parents are able to comment on the varied and sometimes unexpected answers they get to the three questions on the guide sheet. And

Table 2

Project for the Study of Young Children Progress report	
Developmental objectives	**Progress notes**
Social and emotional areas: 　　Growth in a child's sense of autonomy, initiative, and confidence—characteristics which make a child feel good about her or himself—are a child's ability to relate well with other children as well as adults are vital tasks during the preschool years. Children also need to grow in their ability to cope with fears and frustrations and to show persistence in completing a task.	
Cognitive area: 　　Developing a child's thinking processes during the pre-school years involves coming up with interesting ideas, pursuing problems and questions, putting ideas or objects into relationships, and expressing ideas in a variety of ways. Children learn through active interaction with their environment.	
Physical area: 　　Physical aspects of growth provide a child with an awareness of one's body in space and how one's body moves and the effects of these movements on the environment. Children also need opportunities to build small and large muscle coordination.	

teachers enjoy the sense of positive closure this three-way conference brings to the year. All-year programs might schedule progress conferences in the summer, especially for children who will be leaving to attend other schools.

CONCLUSION

Conferences offer a rich opportunity to build communication and understanding between the home and school. Their value to parents, staff, and children depends on the active participation of each person involved. Successful conferences lay the foundation for high quality programs for young children. The model outlined here can be adapted for use in any good early childhood program.

DISCUSSION QUESTIONS

1. What should a teacher do to prepare for parent/teacher conferences?

2. What are appropriate goals for conferences?

3. Why is follow up after the conference important?

4. How should the teacher guide the conference?

5. What are the recommended states or phases of successful conferences between teachers and parents?

56. INNOVATION IN PARENT INVOLVEMENT: USING HIGH TECH TO CONNECT PARENTS AND TEACHERS

by Jerold P. Bauch

When busy parents and busy teachers try to communicate, they face several barriers. First, their schedules seldom match. When parents want to hear about their child's day, the teachers are at home and trying to relax. When teachers need to communicate with parents, they are at work or not available. Second, parents have to think about only one teacher; teachers have to think about many parents and try to communicate with each of them. These repetitive interactions are very time-consuming. Third, teachers have complete and specific information about the child's learning and development. Parents have very little information about the curriculum and the child's daily program; this knowledge sometimes has been inaccessible to parents, yet they cannot actively participate in their child's learning and development without it.

During the first years of schooling, fundamental changes take place in parents as well as in their developing children. For first-time parents, initial contacts with the school will establish their perceptions about continued involvement. If parents do not begin to grow in partnership with their child's teachers, it is unlikely that they will form these partnerships during later school years. On the other hand, if parents have rich and frequent information about their child's first learning experiences, they are more likely to understand their teaching roles at home and to comprehend the nature and practice of early education at school. Early childhood education is a critical stage for parents, too. If they are actively involved, they will form "attachments" that will enable them to make vital contributions to the learning process.

The field of early childhood education has a solid and long history of involving parents in the child's schooling. For example, Froebel, Rousseau, and Pestalozzi each recognized the important role of parents. They also knew that the school could help parents grow with the role, and suggested that parent education be a part of the educational program. When the national PTA was formed in 1896, a model of partnerships was forged between parents and teachers. The early education revolution of the 1960s provided new access to education for children of the nation's poor; the most common element of all the new programs was active involvement of parents. In fact, federally funded early childhood programs were judged not in compliance if they could not demonstrate that parents were involved.

Since the 1960s many new approaches have been tried. Home visitors taught parents in their own homes. Classrooms with observation rooms were built so that parents could observe their children at school. Some parents attended parenting classes; others served as aides in the classroom. In a few communities, classrooms on wheels were brought into the neighborhood so that early education was closer to home. But in virtually all cases, parents were expected to bear considerable responsibility for their children's education. Not many of the innovations in early childhood parent involvement have endured as widespread and routine practices, however. Most were very personnel intensive, took a great deal of time and energy to sustain, and required supplementary funding for operating expenses. The federal mandates concerning parent involvement have been reduced, yet the needs of parents remain exactly as they have been for many years. Parents want to know what is going on with their children at school, and they want the information to be frequent and accurate. They also do not want to spend large blocks of time receiving small bits of information, but want to reserve their precious "quality time" for interaction where it counts—in direct support of the child's learning.

The circumstances and distance between the home and school of the "good old days" have become even more intense, as economics, gender equity, changing family patterns and social concerns make home/school communication more difficult. Day care, by its very definition, means that parents are busy elsewhere while the child is being cared for. Single parents faced with economic pressures have much more competition for their time than in the past. Teachers and school personnel also face new demands on their time, from extensive paperwork to expanding professional responsibility. The need for convenient, quick, frequent, meaningful, and useful communication between school and home is serious. One response to this need is the application of new technology to link the parents of the young child with the educational program.

When parents send their child to "school" for the first time, the very reactions that are well known among children also are experienced by the parents. Parents suffer from separation anxiety, a fear of the unknown, the uncertainty about the people and experiences at the new place, and a major lack of information that could quell these concerns. Fortunately, a major new innovation in parent involvement has appeared on the scene; it uses computer and telephone technology to build stronger relationships between home and school. Now, any early childhood program can give parents *daily, accurate, and relevant information and it takes the teacher only five extra minutes per day!* Telephone answering machines give the parents this daily access, so news about the child's day is only a phone call away. The administrator or teachers in any early childhood program can also reach the parents with the same ease, using computer-based calling to send information from school to home over the telephone. These two technical systems are the essential components of a high-tech parent involvement model that has been developed at the Betty Phillips Center for Parenthood Education, a project of Peabody College at Vanderbilt University in Nashville, Tennessee.

The model uses a sophisticated new computer-calling system named Compu-Call to deliver information to homes. Someone at the school just records a message, sets the time for calls to be placed, and goes home. At the designated time, the computer makes the call and delivers the message in the natural voice of the sender. It will also keep records of the calls completed, which can be reviewed and printed out the next day. When the phone rings at home, a greeting message is heard to prepare the parent for the main information. If someone other than the parent answers, there is time for the parent to come to the phone before the main message is delivered. The message for families who prefer languages other than English can be delivered in their preferred language. (The message must be translated and recorded in the preferred language at the school.)

For direct access to information about the child's daily experience, the parent has a direct phone number to the classroom. Each teacher has an answering machine, and uses the announcement feature to let parents know about the program. For example, at the end of the school day the teacher writes a short script and records the message. When parents call the number, they hear:

> Today in math, the children in Ms. Hampton's group were working on counting up to ten with the Cuisenaire rods. You could help by asking your child to count objects at home; if the child touches each item when saying the number, he/she develops the concept of 1:1 correspondence. In art we painted with red, yellow, and blue, and children are learning to identify these colors. Our next science unit is on green plants, and we will be planting bean seeds. A good weekend project would be to have your child help with any planting or gardening around the house. Please leave your name and number if you want me to call you back. Call again tomorrow.

Every parent can call the classroom number and hear the teacher describe the program for that day, and can follow up on the suggestions with the child at home. The continuity between school learning and home learning is greatly enhanced, enabling parents to become real partners with the teacher. Easy access to daily information can also strengthen the parents' interest in the school program and establish a long-term pattern of active participation.

Using computers and answering machines is not intended to replace all other forms of parent involvement, but only to increase the ease of routine communication. The use of this technological model can double or triple the contact between school and home, and it takes no more than five extra minutes per day! Busy teachers and busy parents need not be out of touch—they are only a phone call apart.

DISCUSSION QUESTIONS

1. How do time and scheduling reduce the opportunities for teachers and parents to interact?

2. What is the historical rationale for parent/teacher relationships?

3. How can new technology improve the communication between school and home?

4. What is the potential for parent involvement when parents have accurate, daily information about their child's school experiences?

57. LITERACY ENVIRONMENTS: BRIDGING THE GAP BETWEEN HOME AND SCHOOL

by Jon Shapiro and Ray Doiron

For many years educators believed that children about to start school knew very little about reading and writing. Hence, the job of the teacher was to get children "ready" and then begin the teaching of reading. Writing was usually taught after many reading skills were mastered. Research has now shown, however, that literacy skills begin to emerge at a much earlier age, well before school starts. This [chapter] will examine the major preconditions for literacy that are rooted in the home environment and then discuss some of the implications of this home literacy environment for schools.

Research into the roots of literacy arose in an attempt to determine the best environment in which children can learn to read and write. A link was made between children's oral language development and a similar development of all the language strands (Holdaway, 1979). Support for this view was found in longitudinal studies that examined the emerging reading and writing of preschool children (Bissex, 1980; Chomsky, 1972).

Wells (1985) found that children's experiences using story in decontextualized ways developed skills necessary in reading and writing development. Goodman (1980) described the importance of print awareness and how children begin to act on literate forms within their environment. A great body of research has examined the many aspects of literacy behavior in the home and how it relates to later literacy acquisition. Several conditions have been reported as being prerequisite to literacy development. The major ones to be discussed in this [chapter] are: (1) oral language development, (2) hypothesis construction and testing, (3) experiences with the tools of literacy, (4) modeling of literacy skills, (5) the use of decontextualized language and (6) a developing sense of story. A brief elaboration on each of these conditions within the home literacy environment will lead to a discussion of several implications for schools.

ORAL LANGUAGE DEVELOPMENT

One of the greatest accomplishments of the young child is fluency in oral language. Children develop a tremendous amount of language from birth until school entry. Oral language develops in the social setting of the home without formal instruction and because of the basic need to communicate with the important adults in one's life (Goodman, 1980). Children develop oral language skills through their natural efforts to understand the world around them. They are active participants in private explorations of their home, as well as in the interactions with their parents. Parents allow attempts at words and encourage children to say a word after them. Parents attribute meaning to utterances that seem close to the real world.

Cazden (1983) outlined several ways adults assist language development. The first one, scaffolding, consists of vertical constructions for building new information or retelling past events. Proto-conversations, peak-a-boo routines and picture book reading all provide opportunities for parents to build scaffolds for their children. A second technique, often combined with scaffolding, is modeling, in which the child not only imitates the model but strives to acquire its underlying structure. An example would be an adult coaching a child in a narrative accounting by detailing all the steps they use to do something or by telling a story about the things the child did. The third and most obvious form of assistance comes in the form of direct instruction. An adult models an utterance and asks the child to repeat it. Adults also use direct instruction to teach the interpersonal uses of language, such as politeness, or to teach vocabulary.

Inherent in the adult's use of language, and developed within the child, is an understanding that language is functional. Children learn to use language to communicate their needs, desires, demands, fears, pleasures and affections. Children learn that language contains a message they can interpret and act upon. Children find their attempts at oral language are nurtured and encouraged by adults who believe the child can talk. Even the most remote attempt is praised, and the child is encouraged to get closer and closer to the real world. Parents attribute intent and meaning to

See pages 346–47 for acknowledgment and references.

children's utterances and provide strong supportive feedback to the child.

Oral language develops in a natural, supportive and interactive environment where strong models and lots of encouragement guarantee success. Children are receptive, motivated and active in the whole development of their oral language.

HYPOTHESIS CONSTRUCTION AND TESTING

The ideal home environment can be described as "safe" or risk-free. Children are encouraged to explore their environment and to ask questions about everything they come into contact with. They are provided enriching experiences that allow new information to be gathered, as well as opportunities for language to grow. Parents go out of their way to provide chances for their children to work out their understandings of the world around them. They take precautions to ensure that no harm comes to the children. The materials or experiences they provide for the children always have a built-in success rate. Children approach their play as a great adventure into new and exciting worlds never before seen.

While engaged in their play, children direct their own activities. They decide what goes with what, what should be done next and when it is time to stop. Research into the ways children approach literacy events in the home implies that children are actually in control of highly sophisticated processes that guide their learning (Bissex, 1984). Bissex suggests that children act as their own teachers and carry on inner and outer dialogues as they negotiate their way through new information and already established structures. Holdaway (1979) found that children corrected themselves as they tried to reconstruct familiar stories. When they make their literacy decisions, even very young children seem well aware of what they know and don't know (Harste et al., 1981). Read's (1971) extensive work with children's use of invented spelling presents children as actively involved in their own learning—forming hypotheses which they test and reformulate to come up with rules they apply consistently to their spelling.

The environment where this hypothesis-testing is nurtured must reflect an accepting, supportive and stimulating relationship between parents and children. Within this environment there exists a respect for children's ability to direct their learning. Bissex (1984) tells us children assume there is order in the world and set out to reconstruct it by

establishing rules by which they can understand it. These rules are revised as new information and various experiences are made available to the child. The fact that children have demonstrated their ability to abstract, hypothesize, construct and revise has serious implications for the manner in which we deliver instruction in our schools.

MODELING OF LITERACY SKILLS

As children learn, they search through their environment for examples of what they want to know. Aware of the consistent use of a behavior in their environment, children are likely to seek out the same sorts of behavior. Given that children are active participants in their own learning, it is not surprising that it should be considered important for children to see adults involved in the use of literacy skills. Most parents could cite lots of examples of their own children caught in the act of imitating some characteristic of the parents. Children assume that the people who have provided all of their needs since birth are prime examples of how to deal with the world around them.

Holdaway (1979) drew attention to the importance of modeling when he noted how children will open books and immediately shift inflection in their voice into the one they often heard from parents reading stories aloud. Harste et al. (1984) noticed children wanting to engage in writing activities after they saw their parents making a list, filling out a check or writing a letter. Parents who recognize these events as ones that teach children about literacy skills are also recognizing the importance of allowing these fledgling attempts to take place within an environment of support and encouragement.

Shirley Brice-Heath (1985) presented a comparison of the ways preschool children and adults interacted in two communities of differing sociocultural milieus. Both communities provided examples of how important it is for parents not only to talk about literacy and about the form and content of the materials in order to give them importance, but also to be active users of their own literacy skills. Children must see parents reading and writing in purposeful and enjoyable situations, not just as promoters of literacy skills. Children must see models of the skills, as well as have opportunities to participate in literacy events.

One of the most important ways parents model literacy skills is by reading to their children. Bissex (1980) says that reading to children provides them with a sense of what reading is all about. Teale (1984) sees reading to children as important in establishing that print is meaningful. Oral reading to children provides experiences with the functions and uses of written language, as well as nurturing a positive attitude toward reading. Of all the activities characteristic of literate family homes, the most important one found by Wells (1985) was the sharing of stories. Wells also concluded that homes in which reading and writing were naturally occurring daily events gave children a particular advantage when they started school.

It appears then that preschool children need to see adults frequently as participants in purposeful literacy events. Children then attribute an importance to these activities and use them as a model for their own development of these skills.

EXPERIENCE WITH THE TOOLS OF LITERACY

Consistent with the provision of purposeful and functional models for children developing literacy skills is the ease of access children have to pencils, paper, books and other materials needed to become literate. Children will not learn how to read and write easily if their experiences with the tools of literacy have been limited.

Reading to children is recognized as a strong support for the emergence of literacy (Teale, 1984; Wells, 1985). Literate homes go further and allow children to handle, manipulate and "read" these books themselves. Children are then able to pretend to read by modeling the reading behavior and become practitioners themselves of reading skill. Children who receive books as gifts or who buy books themselves are again establishing a significance for books in their lives. Trips to the library, where children are encouraged to select their own books and become regular users of the library, are a concrete way parents can provide the materials of literacy.

Along with many experiences with the handling of books, parents need to provide children with the materials of writing. Harste et al. (1984), Bissex (1980) and Chomsky (1971) found it useful when they provided letters, markers, crayons and other materials which their subjects were free to use in literacy events. Many parents engage in daily activities that demonstrate what writing is all about, such as drawing up a shopping list, writing checks to pay bills, or writing a note for someone and posting it in the kitchen.

USE OF DECONTEXTUALIZED LANGUAGE

As children's language grows in size and sophistication, it becomes possible for a language about language to begin to develop. One of the characteristics of literate people is their ability to talk about language. Brice-Heath (1985) recognized how some people carry in their language an ability to talk about language and to analyze language as a system of bits and pieces in patterns. This analysis requires us not only to recognize patterns in print, but also to talk about words, letters and sentences metalinguistically. Parents who talk about rhyming words, the alphabet, fairy tales, fables and poetry are building into children's language the vocabulary and concepts necessary to abstract language from its immediate context and to talk about what it is made up of and how it works.

Catherine Snow (1983) refers to adult literacy as "the ultimate decontextualized skill": a skill that develops from the highly contextualized experiences of early oral language development into the more decontextualized experiences of book reading and the telling of oral narratives in play experiences. Initially children treat reading as a highly contextualized skill by reading words contained in the popular logos within their environment or by reading their own names. Children must gain experiences that allow them to establish distance between themselves and the message they want to send. Such experiences as retelling past events provide opportunity to use language to relate things not part of the child's immediate experience. Home environments that engage in the use of decontextualized language are providing a major experience that children need if they are to read. In teaching reading schools often begin with very contextualized experiences with print, but children without a strong decontextualized base or the means to make the transition may soon develop problems with the more decontextualized reading of the intermediate program (Snow 1983).

A DEVELOPING SENSE OF STORY

Closely linked to using decontextualized language, yet unique because of its influence from literature and its role in a child's imaginative play, is children's developing sense of story. Hardy (1977) defines narrative as the "primary act of the mind" that enables us to understand the world around us. Research indicates that children engage in various "storying" activities. They create fictions based on actual experiences, as well as imagine new situations in which they play out their evolving understanding of the world (Wells, 1986). Children use language to create the context of the stories, and they use that language as a narrative tool to create their story.

Arising from this private or "inner" narrative comes a willingness to share in the narratives of others, which we call stories. In addition to creating their own stories, children listen to the stories of others either told or read to them. Story becomes a way to communicate one's own narratives, as well as a way to share in the narratives of others. Applebee (1978, 1980) details children's developing "sense of story," which he says begins with the very personal experiences of the child such as a visit to grandparents or a trip to the zoo. Gradually character development, actions and settings become removed from that experience and narrative structures become more tightly controlled.

Since literature contains perfect examples of the narratives of others, it plays a significant role in the child's developing "sense of story." In an attempt to determine what preschool activities related to later literacy development, Wells (1985) reported that the activity of looking at and talking about books helps a child develop new vocabulary, as well as providing practice at answering display questions. More important, by listening to stories read aloud, children gain experience with the organization of written language and its characteristic rhythms and structures. Also, children experience language as it is used to create new experiences removed from the context of their everyday lives. They learn to escape the "big bad wolf" or to sail away "to where the wild things are."

By school age, children are experienced users of narrative (Applebee, 1980). Their own inner storying is active within their play; they create stories to establish order in the world; they have listened to many stories read by adults; and they are heightening their ability to use language in its decontextualized forms. Their "sense of story" is firmly established.

FROM THE HOME INTO SCHOOL: BRIDGING THE GAP

No one of these six major prerequisites for literacy development has been identified as the single most important. All six work together and contribute differently to literacy development. Children begin this development soon after they are born and continue pursuing literacy activities of increasing difficulty. Upon school entry, many children undergo a major shift in their method of learning. Before school entry, they proceed at their own rate and within the supportive environment of their home. In school, they must often adjust their rate of learning by speeding up or slowing down to match the speed set by school. Before entering school, children determined many of their learning goals and now they must throw out their own goals or readjust them to match the goals set for them by the school. Parents had full control over their children's learning environment, and now they must turn over most of that control to authorities operating in their child's best interests. These distinctive differences between the home and school environments have left the child outside of the discussion of what methods best suit how children learn.

This [chapter] began by exploring six of the major conditions within literate homes that research has identified as prerequisite for literacy development. The outlining of these conditions contains obvious messages for parents who want to enhance their home literacy environment and make it more conducive to emerging literacy skills. What then must schools do differently to reflect the knowledge that literacy is an emerging skill, developing from birth and continuing to grow on into adulthood?

First, schools must recognize and applaud the home as the foundation of the child's learning. This recognition should include awareness of the achievements of the child prior to school entry.

Second, schools must establish a bridge between the home literacy environment and the school literacy environment, including instruction. Presently, the gap between home and school—especially in terms of language related to instruction (Wells, 1985; Downing, 1970) and verbal mediation of learning (Juliebo, 1985)—is often quite wide. When the gap is wide, children are forced to develop new strategies for learning in what is not always a risk-free and nurturing environment.

In an effort to close the gap between home and school environments, kindergarten and primary grade teachers need to create classrooms that reflect many of the positive qualities of the home literacy environment. These classrooms would recognize and reflect the following beliefs, actions and environment:

• Children acquire language socially; therefore, if language is to grow children must have frequent interaction with peers and teachers.

• Children enter school with a great deal of language; therefore, their oral language should be linked to written forms of language.

• Children are just emerging into proficiency with decontextualized uses of language; therefore, they require rich language experiences that heighten their oral language and focus on the decontextualized nature of language.

• Children enter school with knowledge of both reading and writing; therefore, instructional schemes should expand and extend this knowledge by developing reading and writing simultaneously.

• Children learn by doing; therefore, they need opportunities to observe literacy in action, take part in literacy events, and construct and test their own hypotheses related to reading and writing.

• Children need to experience the richness and power of the written word; therefore, a literature program utilizing the best examples of written discourse the culture has to offer should be implemented.

• Children are influenced by the significant models in their lives; therefore, teachers should extend the modeling role of the parents by appearing as active users of reading and writing skills.

• Children's comprehension development and skills mastery are affected by their attending behavior, which is a product of motivation; therefore, classrooms should respond to the interests of children and provide opportunities for them to direct their own learning.

• Children's new learning is built upon previously established foundations; therefore, teachers must identify children's abilities and strengths so that new instruction is appropriate.

• Children learn when risks of failure are minimal; therefore, the classroom must nurture and develop the "safe" and supportive environment of the home.

Finally, schools must recognize that the bridge built between the home literacy environment and the school literacy environment cannot be a one-way path. Parent involvement must be allowed and supported, and parents' understandings extended. After all, parental involvement and knowledge are resources for the child's continued success in learning to read and write.

DISCUSSION QUESTIONS

1. How does the home environment contribute to the preconditions of literacy?

2. What are the ways adults influence early language development?

3. What characteristics of an optimal home situation will improve literacy?

4. How can parents model the literacy skills they want to foster in their children?

5. What are the features of decontextualized language?

6. How can the schools influence the home literacy experience and improve initial school literacy success?

58. COMMUNICATING WITH PARENTS ABOUT BEGINNING READING INSTRUCTION

by Dorene D. Ross and Elizabeth Bondy

Parents of youngsters in early childhood settings typically have many concerns and questions about their children. Does Mary have friends? Does Jason pay attention? Does Sara eat all of her lunch? Invariably, they have questions about learning to read. To many parents, reading success is an indication of their child's competence and of their competence as parents. They want their children to succeed and as a result they may come to you with questions or concerns about reading instruction. This is more likely to happen if your reading program differs from the one the parent or an older child experienced.

There are several ways to deal with parent concerns. One way is to wait for parents to ask questions. If you don't have any parents who express concern, this is by far the easiest path; generally, however, it is better to communicate with parents before they come to you with questions. You might send a letter home at the beginning of the year, explaining your reading program and the kinds of strategies you will be using. A sample letter appears at the end of this [chapter]; you may want to adapt it to suit you and your classroom.

Another strategy that has worked for many teachers is to send home a regular newsletter. How often you send a newsletter will depend on your schedule and your needs. For most teachers, two to four times a month works well. A newsletter need not be elaborate; its main purpose is to tell parents what you have been doing in the classroom. You can also include the words to songs and fingerplays you have been teaching the children. Suggestions can be added for parents who wish to work at home with their children on the things you have been teaching in school. A sample newsletter used by one kindergarten teacher is also included in this [chapter].

Early communication with parents usually convinces them that you have a sound beginning reading program. Occasionally, however, a parent will come in with a question. The remainder of this [chapter] lists some questions that parents may ask and provides information that may be useful in answering them. A theme unites the answers: children become skilled, enthusiastic readers through varied, ongoing positive experiences with print. Teachers who use this approach emphasize reading and writing for meaning and the development of oral language competence, and de-emphasize instruction in the formal elements of reading such as pencil-and-paper drill on reading skills. The approach is consistent with the developmental needs and abilities of young children (Elkind, 1986) and with research about the development of competence in reading (Anderson et al., 1985; Goodman, 1984; Teale, 1982).

1. *My child knows all the letters of the alphabet, but his kindergarten teacher is not teaching him to read. Why?*
Children need to know many things before they are ready to read. While it is useful for children to learn the names and sounds of the letters of the alphabet, many other types of knowledge and experience are necessary if they are to become successful readers. For example, research about successful readers indicates that all of the following information is necessary for success in reading:

• Understanding that speech can be written down
• Recognizing the special vocabulary and sentence structures of print
• Becoming familiar with a variety of types of literature (folk tales, poetry, mysteries, etc.)
• Knowing that reading is useful and pleasurable
• Developing a rich background of knowledge about the world
• Knowing that the print and not the pictures tells the story
• Knowing that the order of letters in words is important
• Knowing front and back, top and bottom of book
• Knowing that one reads from left to right
• Having a clear concept of the special language of reading, such as "word," "letter" and "sentence"

See page 347 for acknowledgment and references.

• Expecting that what one reads will make sense. (Anderson et al., 1985; Allington, 1983; Bussis, 1982; Roney, 1984; Taylor, 1977)

It is important that children develop a firm grounding in all of these background experiences. Too much emphasis on letters and letter sounds can encourage children to focus on reading words rather than understanding the meaning of the story. Successful readers are more concerned with understanding the story than with reading any particular word. It is likely that your child's teacher is providing experiences that will develop fundamental background knowledge.

2. *My daughter's friend brings home reading papers from kindergarten. She is already in a workbook and seems to do five or six little letter papers every day. Will my daughter fall behind because she is not doing any of this in school?*

Drill on letters, a frequent focus in workbooks for beginning readers, may not be the most fruitful approach to raising skilled, avid readers. Most reading researchers have expressed concern about the overemphasis on written drill of reading skills and the lack of time devoted to meaningful reading activities (Anderson et al., 1985; Cazden, 1978; Durkin, 1978-79; Strange, 1978). Individual symbols (letters) frequently are meaningless to young children and may confuse them about the reading process. Furthermore, children faced with letter drill may develop inaccurate concepts of reading (Bondy, 1984) which lead them to dislike and avoid books. Your child is probably not missing out on important reading experiences. Check with the teacher and find out if your daughter is getting the following experiences in school:

• The teacher reads to children at least daily.
• The teacher leads children in songs and fingerplays.
• The teacher writes down what children say on charts and on their papers.
• The teacher provides a variety of experiences for children to help them learn about the world.
• The teacher provides many books in the classroom and time for children to explore them.
• The teacher encourages children to write without insisting on correct spelling and letter formation.
• The teacher brings environmental print to the children's attention (e.g., lunch menu, signs, memos).

3. *My child seems to waste a lot of time playing in the housekeeping center. Wouldn't this time be better spent in learning how to read?*

As your child plays in the housekeeping center, he/she practices a number of behaviors associated with reading and writing: newspapers are read, shopping lists composed, bedtime stories read, notes written, and mail sent and received. Less obvious reading-related behaviors also occur: using symbols, sequencing events and resolving conflicts through clarification and compromise (Pellegrini and Galda, 1985). Additionally, play helps children (1) increase their vocabulary and knowledge of concepts, (2) lengthen their attention span, (3) develop a better understanding of causal relationships and (4) develop knowledge of the difference between reality and fantasy (Sponseller, 1982). Each of these abilities is important in the development of competence in reading. Far from a waste of time, play actually provides children with opportunities to practice and elaborate literacy skills. You can facilitate this productive play by contributing print-related materials to your child's play area, such as magazines, junk mail and note pads.

4. *What are some materials I should buy and activities I should do to help my child learn to read?*

Actually, very few things need to be purchased. Your child needs to see, hear, write and talk about print. Opportunities for these experiences abound in the natural course of your day together. Make a point of sharing the print you encounter. Involve your child in your own literacy experiences: making shopping lists, locating a favorite television show in the guide, cooking, reading and writing postcards and letters, identifying road signs. It isn't necessary to buy special materials to provide these experiences. If your supply of paper and writing implements is low, you might replenish it since experimenting with writing is related closely to reading development (Butler and Turbill, 1984).

In addition, if your child does not have a library card, now is the time to apply for one. In doing so, you are giving the child access to unlimited pleasurable encounters with books. You need not buy word or letter flashcards, as these break meaningful print into meaningless pieces. Your child will have plenty of opportunities to learn individual letters and words when encountering them in meaningful contexts.

In summary, you don't have to buy special materials to help your child learn to read. Providing access to print and talking about print experiences are what really count. Also, make sure your child sees you reading and writing. Modeling is a powerful teacher! No matter how important you may say reading is, your child will not get the message if you do not find time to read yourself.

5. *My child wants to hear the same story over and over again. This is so boring! What should I do about it?*

Holdaway (Park, 1982) explained that a child's experience with a favorite book passes through three phases. First, the child is introduced to the book and may participate as it is being read. Second, the child demands many repetitions of the book. Third, the child "reads" the book independently and does other activities related to it such as drawing and "writing." Children who have these experiences "develop a complex range of attitudes, concepts and skills" that Holdaway (1984) calls the "literacy set." According to Holdaway, "Such children are all set up for reading and writing—they are ready to go" (p. 49).

Because hearing a book read over and over again is part of the process by which children become readers, it is important that you provide this experience for your child. It is also important, however, that parents as well as children enjoy their reading experiences together. A strategy that works for some parents is to read a book two or three times at one sitting and then to encourage the child to choose a different book. Additionally, it is important for children to be exposed to a variety of literature. You can accomplish this by taking your child to the library regularly.

6. *My child is pretending to read. She has memorized some stories and "reads" them. Should I tell my child she is not really reading?*

Although, to you, your child is not "really reading," she is in fact practicing reading behavior as Holdaway explained (see question 5). The behavior you describe is a positive and significant step along the road to proficient reading. Encourage your child. Help her believe she is reading, for she is. With repeated exposure to print and opportunities to practice reading, your child will gradually become more proficient at reading independently. Don't rush her, and continue reading to her and writing together.

7. *My son is beginning to read and reads to me every night. What should I do when he cannot read a word or misreads a word?*

It is important that home reading be a pleasurable activity. If your son cannot read a word, encourage him to guess, using all available clues, or to skip the word and come back to it later. If, after trying these alternatives, he is still unable to read the word and it is important to the story's meaning, simply tell him the word. It is more important for the beginning reader to get the meaning of the story than to read every word accurately (Smith, 1973). The tedious "sounding out" of words disrupts the flow of a story and can make reading boring and frustrating. The most important thing you can do for your son is to make sure he enjoys your nightly reading activities and understands what he reads.

Good readers focus on understanding what they read and keep track of how well they understand what they are reading (Davey, 1983). You can help your child develop this ability, called self-monitoring, by withholding immediate feedback when a mistake is made during oral reading (Smith, 1973). Instead, when your child misreads a word, resulting in a sentence that does not make sense, let your child finish the sentence and see if he corrects himself. If not, say to your child, "Did that make sense?" Usually, this is all that is needed for the child to detect his error. If the child is unable to self-correct, repeat the sentence as he reads it. He may then be able to hear the mistake. By using this feedback strategy, you will encourage your child to read for meaning and to monitor his understanding as he reads.

In addition to listening to him read, make sure you continue to read to your child. For oral reading, select books that are a little too difficult for him to read independently. You will both enjoy the time together and it will help him in his efforts to become a successful reader.

If teachers want parental support of their efforts in the classroom, they must help parents understand the nature and purpose of classroom practices. In the case of beginning reading instruction, teachers must provide parents with some insight into the reading process and the ways in which young children learn. The abused practice of drill on isolated reading skills is based on an inaccurate view of reading (Bussis, 1982); no set of essential subskills or processes has yet been identified (Rosenshine, 1980). The strategies that have been discussed represent a more holistic approach, one that focuses on familiarizing the young child with the nature of the language and print in the immediate environment. These strategies are consistent with the way young children learn in general and the way they become readers. Furthermore, children who have pleasurable, meaningful experiences with reading are more likely to become avid readers than those faced with confusing drills.

When children spend more time reading and engaging in meaningful writing, however, they will do fewer ditto and workbook pages. These papers, which are sent home, are frequently the parents' main contact with the school. We all know what children say when asked what they do in school:

"Nothin'" or "We just played all day." When children make such comments and don't bring home as many papers as the parents had expected, parents may become concerned. Teachers must be prepared to help parents understand the complexity of the reading task and the nature of good reading instruction. This essential role of the teacher is one that cannot be neglected if we expect to provide children with the best reading instruction possible.

Sample Letter to Parents

Dear Parents:

I want to take this opportunity to welcome you and your child to our class. Each new school year is exciting and challenging for me and I am looking forward to getting to know you and your child. I hope you will come and visit with us from time to time. If your schedule makes it possible, we'd love to have you work in the classroom on a regular basis. If not, I hope you can join us for field trips, occasionally for lunch, or for a visit when you have a day off. You are always welcome, so please stop in.

Because reading plays such a large role in our classroom, I'd like to take this opportunity to describe our reading program. The major focus of our program is to help children love reading, to see reading as useful and to develop the knowledge and experience they need to become successful readers. While we will be working, of course, on the names and sounds of the letters of the alphabet, that is only a small part of our program. The children also will be learning the following information which is necessary for success in reading:

— Understanding that speech can be written down
— Developing familiarity with many different types of stories
— Learning the patterns of spoken and written language
— Learning that reading is fun
— Learning that we can learn things through reading
— Developing a rich background of knowledge about the world.

It is very important that children develop a firm foundation in all these background experiences if they are to become competent readers. Consequently, I will do the following things during the school year to help your child develop the necessary skills and knowledge:

— Spend time daily reading to children in large and small group situations.
— Provide time for children to go to the library, look at books and share books with their friends.
— Record information on classroom charts and the blackboard. We do a lot of singing and finger-plays. Recording familiar information on charts helps children begin to learn to read words and phrases.
— Take dictation from children. By recording what your child says, he/she learns that reading is just "talk written down." Reading then becomes more familiar and children begin learning words and phrases.
— Provide time for children to write and draw independently. Writing and reading are connected. Children who enjoy writing also enjoy reading.
— Provide practice in learning letters, sounds and words.

Your child will bring home papers that emphasize drill on some reading skills, but this is not the major focus of our reading program. Research in reading indicates that overemphasis on skills can be counterproductive in helping children learn to read and can lead to negative attitudes toward reading. As we work on reading at school, you can help by reading to your child at home. Providing 15 minutes of reading time daily can make a big difference.

I hope you will feel free to call me or stop by and see me if you have questions about any aspect of our kindergarten program. I'll look forward to meeting you and talking with you.

Sincerely,
Your child's
kindergarten teacher

Sample Parent Newsletter

KINDERGARTEN CORNER

ABOUT OUR WEEK:

In Language Arts we:
— sang and read "Here We Go Round the Mulberry Bush"
— made up and illustrated new verses for our classroom Mulberry book
— read a recipe and made potato latkes
— read books about Hanukah and Christmas celebrations
— drew and labeled pictures showing how each of us celebrates the holidays.

In Math we:
— talked about putting things together in a group and reasons for putting things together in a group
— grouped various kinds of beans
— grouped various kinds of macaroni
— sorted a collection of buttons
— put blocks or assorted shapes and colors into one of two circles.

For our Winter Holiday unit we:
— talked about Hanukah
— made dreidles (tops used in a traditional Jewish game)
— made latkes (potato pancakes, a traditional Hanukah food).

ABOUT YOUR CHILD:

NEXT WEEK WE WILL:
— make holiday placemats for our family and friends
— begin writing in journals by drawing and labeling things we will give to others for the holidays
— make a Christmas carol book
— review classification, pattern making and comparison activities
— talk about families and how our holiday celebrations are similar or different.

ANNOUNCEMENTS:
— Our Winter Holiday party will be next Friday, Dec. 20 at 1:00. We are expecting a surprise visitor!
— Our room mother will be contacting you to find out what you can send in for the party.
— Don't forget the Holiday program tonight at 7:30. See you there!

HOME ACTIVITIES:
— Have your child help you sort and fold the laundry to practice putting things into groups.
— Read traditional holiday books with your child.
— Let your child make wrapping paper for holiday presents.
— Help your child make Christmas or Hanukah cards for special people.
— Help your child write thank-you notes after the holidays.

HAVE A SAFE AND HAPPY HOLIDAY

DISCUSSION QUESTIONS

1. What do parents want to know about their child's reading experience and performance?

2. What are the characteristics of successful readers?

3. What are the inappropriate and appropriate early reading experiences for young children?

4. How does play relate to initial reading experience?

5. Why should teachers provide extensive information about the beginning reading program?

Section Nine: Child Behavior and Discipline

EDITOR'S OVERVIEW

Children who are out of control or disruptive in the classroom cannot gain the maximum impact of the educational experience. Young children, in the school setting for the first time, are not likely to behave perfectly at all times. But there are good ways and bad ways for helping children control themselves and focus their attention on the learning experiences provided for them. The selections presented in this section reflect a definite bias, but it is a bias held by most clear-thinking professionals who work with young children.

Cryan's important presentation of the position paper of the Association for Childhood Education International (ACEI) on corporal punishment leaves no room for ambiguity; it says, "No corporal punishment!" Next, Bauch gives a special point of view that uses a cognitive approach to the management of behavior in the classroom. Then, the social and moral problems associated with corporal punishment enumerated by Meier make a connection with the last chapter. To carry a humane concern for children's welfare one step further, Meddin and Rosen make definite suggestions for dealing with child abuse and neglect.

59. THE BANNING OF CORPORAL PUNISHMENT: IN CHILD CARE, SCHOOL AND OTHER EDUCATIVE SETTINGS IN THE UNITED STATES

by John R. Cryan

Nearly 100 years ago the American public became outraged over several much-publicized cases of child abuse. Organizations were formed to combat abuse and protect children. Subsequently, and for nearly 50 years, child welfare issues received widespread publicity. One of those issues was the use of corporal punishment as a form of school discipline. Opposition to this method was strong. Educators writing at the turn of the century disapproved of corporal punishment and seemed to think that its use was rare. No longer feeling the need for corporal punishment to maintain order, schools abandoned it in favor of more humane discipline. By the mid-1920s the issue of corporal punishment disappeared. Along with other progressive social issues, it remained dead for four decades (Hiner, 1979).

Today we are again experiencing a major child welfare movement. Once again children's rights, health and safety are at issue. And once again child-advocate groups are condemning corporal punishment.

One such group, the Association for Childhood Education International (ACEI), passed the following resolution at a business meeting of its 1985 Annual Study Conference in San Antonio, Texas. In doing so, ACEI joined parents, teachers, doctors, lawyers, psychologists, social workers and 14 major national organizations in the effort to ban corporal punishment.

• Whereas the United States is one of a scant few of relatively developed countries in which children can lawfully be beaten, and
• Whereas effective September 1, 1985, only eight states (Massachusetts, New Jersey, Hawaii, Maine, Rhode Island, New Hampshire, Vermont, and New York) forbid teachers and other school employees to hit or hurt children in their care, and
• Whereas many major cities including New York, Philadelphia, Chicago and Seattle have banned the practice of corporal punishment in schools, and

• Whereas there is a resurgence in some quarters of a call for a return to the "old-fashioned" discipline in the schools, and
• Whereas ACEI is committed to the belief that child care and educative settings should be models of appropriate behavior toward the young, and
• Whereas there is considerable psychological and medical evidence that corporal punishment impairs the development of children into socially responsible adults and interferes with the process of learning, and
• Whereas better methods of discipline are available, and
• Whereas reported cases of child abuse are alarmingly on the rise in the United States (60,000 physical abuse cases alone in 1983), and
• Whereas the National Education Association is the *lone* education organization among other major national organizations opposing corporal punishment (American Medical Association, National Association for the Advancement of Colored People, American Academy of Pediatrics, Mental Health Association, Children's Defense Fund, American Psychological Association, National Association of Social Workers and League Against Child Abuse).
• *Be it therefore resolved that ACEI publish a written statement (position paper) speaking against corporal punishment in child care and educative or school settings with the understanding that as a part of this statement there will be support for specific alternative disciplinary practices likely to foster self-controlled individuals and a democratic citizenry.*

Why is it necessary to campaign against the corporal punishment of children in a country where the Constitution protects every adult—even convicted criminals—from physical violence and cruel or unusual punishment?

Why is it necessary to campaign against corporal punishment of children in a country where virtually every state forbids physical abuse of any animal

See pages 347–48 for acknowledgment and references.

or child?

Because the fact is that, although the issue of corporal punishment of children in schools died 50 years ago, the hitting did not stop.

Because the national average of those children in schools receiving corporal punishment is estimated at 3.5 percent of the population in schools.

Because in a country where democracy and human rights are its cornerstone, 42 of its 50 states allow or specifically endorse the use of corporal punishment as a means of disciplining children in schools.

Corporal punishment is ". . . an officially sanctioned form of institutionalized child abuse in the United States" (Hyman and Wise, 1979, pp. 4–5).

The remainder of this [chapter] will attempt to present evidence in support of ACEI's position that *the barbaric practice of corporal punishment in child care, school and other educative settings must be BANNED.* Suggestions will be made regarding solutions to this problem.

DEFINITION

"Punishment," according to *Webster's Dictionary*, comes from the same Latin root *poen* as do the words "penalty" and "pain" and means "to impose a penalty for some fault," "to inflict a penalty in retribution" or "to deal with harshly." The word "corporal" derives from the Latin word *corpus*, meaning "body." So we have a legal definition taken from *Black's Law Dictionary* (1968) that corporal punishment is "physical punishment as distinguished from pecuniary punishment or a fine; any kind of punishment of or inflicted on the body, such as whipping or the pillory." And, we have an education definition: "the infliction of pain by a teacher or other educational official upon the body of the student as a penalty for doing something which has been disapproved of by the punisher" (Hyman and Wise, 1979, p. 4). As the NEA notes (1972), pain may be inflicted by not only beating the child but also by: (a) confining the child in a small, uncomfortable space; (b) forcing the child to stand for a long period of time or (c) forcing the child to eat obnoxious substances. These and a host of other refinements fit the definition.

Interestingly, these types of practices were abolished in the U.S. Navy in 1850 and in the schools of Luxembourg, Holland, Austria, France, Finland, Sweden, Denmark, Belgium, Cyprus, Japan, Ecuador, Iceland, Italy, Jordan, Qatar, Mauritius, Norway, Israel, The Philippines, Portugal and all

Communist bloc countries (Hyman and Wise, 1979).

How is it that such practices are forbidden in only eight states in the United States? A brief look at the religious, historical and legal perspectives will help explain the resistance to change.

RELIGIOUS PERSPECTIVE

The Bible is often quoted to provide the rationale for corporal punishment. Solomon's familiar admonition "Spare the rod and spoil the child" may be found in the early scriptures. In *Proverbs* we read: "Foolishness is bound in the heart of a child; but the rod of correction shall drive it from him. . . . Withhold not correction from the child; for if thou beatest him with the rod, he shall not die. Thou shalt beat him with the rod and shalt deliver his soul from hell."

Add to these biblical sanctions the traditional Christian concept of children born into sin and it becomes clear why it was thought that God sanctioned the molding of children's character through severe punishment. School teachers of colonial days, for example, viewed children as "wild and satanic—needing to have the devil beaten out of them" (Williams, 1979, p. 30).

But reading the Bible one verse at a time will enable finding justification for nearly any activity. *Proverbs* recommends, "The mouth of the just bringeth forth wisdom, but the forward tongue shall be cut out." It was common punishment in the past to cut out tongues of "sassy children" but we no longer follow that practice. We are more enlightened today and reject the use of Bible verses as commandments.

HISTORICAL PERSPECTIVE

Schooling in the "good old days" was not exactly what we would like to remember. The following passage was written in 1870:

Wanting elbow room, the chair would be quickly thrust on one side, and Master John Todd was to be seen dragging his struggling suppliant to the flogging ground in the center of the room. Having placed his left foot upon the end of a bench, with a patent jerk peculiar to himself, he would have the boy completely horsed across his knee, with his left elbow on the back of his neck to keep him securely on.... Having his victim thus completely at his command .:., once more to the staring crew would be exhibited the dexterity of master and strap.... Moving in quick time, the fifteen inches of bridle rein would be seen ... leaving on "the

place beneath'' a fiery streak at every slash.
    "Does it hurt?"
    "Oh yes, Master! Oh don't Master!"
    "Then I'll make it hurt thee more.... Thou shan't want a warming pan tonight." (Watson, 1870, p. 290)

William Channing (1851) describes the discipline in his dame school as enforced by means of the Dame's long round stick, which stood next to her soft easy chair like a "watchful sleepless being of ancient mythology" (Channing, 1851, p. 23).

Elizabeth Montgomery (1867) describes the practices of a girls' school. Girls were forced to wear a necklace of sharp Jamestown weed-burs if they permitted their heads to fall forward. If they slighted their work, the usual punishment was to wear a morocco spider on the back confined to the shoulders by a belt.

The nonconformist was forced to suffer severe consequences. Manning (1979) lists the following contingencies implemented over 100 years ago in a North Carolina school: "For boys and girls playing together, four lashes; for failing to bow at the entrance of strangers, three lashes; for blotting copy book, two lashes; for scuffling, four lashes; for calling each other names, three lashes" (Manning, 1979, p. 52).

These examples typify colonial and later schooling which was at best dull; mostly involved drill, repetition and recitation; and had clearly defined behavioral expectations that remained static for many years. Unmistakable is the mix of belief in punishment as a necessary part of pedagogy with religious philosophy focusing on morality and character development (Hyman and Lally, 1981).

LEGAL PERSPECTIVE

For about as long as the Bible has been used to rationalize corporal punishment in American schools so has the concept of *in loco parentis* (in place of parents). Derived from English law, this concept ascribed responsibility to the teacher to act as a parent in the absence of parents. This notion made sense in England when the wealthy who hired tutors for their children could fire them easily for unsatisfactory performance. Education then was voluntary and personal. The parent voluntarily committed the child to the authority of the teacher, who usually spent the entire day with the child in a small class or school, thereby developing an approximation of the parent-child relationship. In today's school bureaucracy education is no longer voluntary, parents have little if any opportunity to choose among teachers or schools,

teachers instruct children only part of the day, and few opportunities exist for teachers to form close relationships with children in large classes or schools. Moreover, the school-child relationship is intermittent, with different adults involved at different times of the day and year, very often at superficial levels.

The courts have failed to reach common interpretation of the *in loco parentis* concept as it pertains to the hitting of school children. In *Baker v. Owens* (1975) the state's right to use corporal punishment to maintain law and order in the classroom was affirmed, thereby invalidating the *in loco parentis* concept. In *Glaser v. Marietta* (1972) the court came to the opposite conclusion. The Supreme Court in *Ingraham v. Wright* (1977) refused to deny teachers the right to hit children, stating that there is nothing in the U.S. Constitution that forbids it. Yet four years later a West Virginia District Court in *Hall v. Tawney* (1981) ruled that children may not be denied substantive due process; that is, the child's punishment may not be in excess of the minimum necessary to protect the state's interest in maintaining order in the school.

In the absence of court support it becomes obvious that, if children's rights to freedom from excessive corporal punishment are to be assured, states and school boards will have to ban the practice. Until then the *in loco parentis* concept will stand as the rationale for all manner of knocking children about. One has to wonder why schools do not use this same concept to:

> Authorize medical intervention as a parent would.
> Order incarceration of an incorrigible child.
> Take responsibility for feeding, clothing, and housing a child as parents do. (Maurer, 1981)

Corporal punishment is an antiquated approach to children's discipline in both school and home. It seems ingrained in the minds of some parents, teachers and school administrators that children must be "disciplined" and that hitting them to make them more disciplined is a right and responsibility.

USE OF CORPORAL PUNISHMENT

Not too long ago *Time* captioned a picture, "As a teaching tool, the hickory stick ranks with such pedagogical fossils as the dunce cap and McGuffy's Readers" (Maurer, 1981). The assumption was that we have made progress. The truth is that the hickory stick has been replaced by other even more fearsome weapons such as belts, canes and paddles. Paddles are the most formidable and are frequently drilled with welt-raising holes. This is progress?

Just how much paddling takes place in American schools is difficult to know because there is no systematic reporting of individual incidents. One can get some sense of it, however, by looking at individual research studies and federal and state government records.

Hapkiewicz (1975) reports that it took "65 beatings a day to sustain a school of 400" in Boston in 1850 and that there were 11,768 children physically punished in Boston in 1889. The California State Assembly-mandated survey of corporal punishment in 1972-73 revealed 46,022 instances of corporal punishment. Los Angeles and 80 other school districts failed to report for that study (Maurer, 1981). Corcoran (1975) reports Vermont State Department of Education statistics for 1974-75. During that school year there may have been as many as one out of every 379 children punished, 60 percent of whom were in grades K-4.

The Office of Civil Rights in the Department of Education first began keeping records on the number of paddlings in 1976. In that year there were 1,521,896 punishments (Maurer, 1984). Three years later the figure stood at more than 1,000,000 in 77,000 schools (Van Dyke, 1984) and by 1982 had been reduced to 792,556 (Maurer, 1984).

Although the trend seems to show a significant reduction in the amount of paddling year by year, one still has to be concerned about its widespread use (Hyman and D'Alessandro, 1984). Rose (1984) reports that, based upon a random survey of 324 principals in 18 states from all 9 census districts, virtually every region in the country supports paddling of students in every grade. The national average is about 3.5 percent of students paddled in a year, ranging from 0 percent in four states to a high of 12.6 percent in one state (Maurer, 1984).

MEDICAL EFFECTS

A fine line of distinction may be drawn between discipline and child abuse. It differs from family to family and school to school. In the majority of corporal punishment incidents, the abuses children experience are minor injuries such as soreness and redness of the skin. Few require medical treatment, but the potential exists to cause other injuries such as hematomas, ruptured blood vessels, massive fat emboli, sciatic nerve damage, muscle damage and brain hemorrhage (Hyman, 1978). When one con-

siders that forms of punishment other than paddling are reported to include striking students with sticks, ropes, fists or belts; choking; throwing them against walls or desks; sticking them with pins; dragging them by the hair or arm; tying them to chairs; forcing them to do strenuous exercise; forcing them to remain in uncomfortable positions, such as standing on their toes; and confining them in closets, school vaults, storerooms or boxes, it becomes very clear how punishment is at variance with accurate information about the vulnerability of children's bodies (National Committee for the Prevention of Child Abuse, 1983). Adults plainly underestimate the amount of force they are capable of producing. Sometimes children are injured during even the mildest punishment when they jerk away and the blow lands off target, or when they fall against the sharp edge of some object. Eyes, ears and brains may be permanently damaged as a result of paddling. Whiplash injuries may result from shaking. Injuries from blows to the chest and abdomen are life threatening. Bones are easily fractured and even the slightest whack may produce a jolt to the brain through the bony spinal column and spinal cord, resulting in significant swelling or bleeding (Taylor and Maurer, 1985). A thorough analysis of the medical effects of physical punishment is found in Taylor and Maurer (1985).

Psychiatric News (1982) states that the psychological effects may be as harmful as the physical effects. These include:

a. Lost of self-esteem
b. Increased anxiety and fear
c. Impairment of ego functioning
d. Feelings of helplessness and humiliation
e. Stifled relationship with others
f. Aggression and destruction at home and at school
g. Self-destructive behavior, often culminating in suicidal gestures
h. Limited attention span and hyperactivity in school, leading to deficient academic performance. (*Psychiatric News*, 1982)

RESEARCH FINDINGS

In the face of evidence that corporal punishment is widespread in the schools (Rose, 1984), that 83 percent of American parents spank their children (*Reader's Digest*, 1986), and that physical and mental harm to the child being punished is likely, what does research on corporal punishment tell us?

Ethics in research obviously do not permit researchers to manipulate punishment directly (inflicting pain deliberately) and then measure the effects. Further, it is nearly impossible for researchers to time school visits to observe paddling or its antecedents. Medical research is hampered because only the most severe injuries come to the attention of medical personnel. Linking developmental impairments to single causes is all but impossible because of the intertwined nature of physical and psychological injury during punishment (Taylor and Maurer, 1985). Therefore, what scant research does exist is based upon correlational or retrospective studies and inferential commentaries from related research (Hyman and Wise, 1979).

Bongiovanni (1977) produced an exhaustive review of empirical research on punishment as it relates to corporal punishment in schools. He concluded that ''corporal punishment is ineffective in producing durable behavior change; it is potentially harmful to students, school personnel, and property; it is highly impractical in light of the control required for maximal effectiveness'' (Bongiovanni, 1977, p. 35).

Lamberth (1979) reviewed research on the effects of punishment on academic achievement. His attempt was mainly to update the findings of the popular Rosenshine and Furst (1971) study that revealed a negative relationship between teacher criticism and students' school achievement. His conclusion supports Rosenshine and Furst (1971) and states that extreme forms of punishment are counterproductive to learning.

Maurer and Wallerstein (n.d.) report a series of findings relative to the influence of school corporal punishment on crime:

   a. Violent criminals were often abused and beaten in early youth.
   b. There is a direct relationship between severe corporal punishment in early childhood and delinquency later in the life cycle.
   c. Young male drivers who had oppressive school experiences were inclined toward ''speeding, recklessness, lawlessness and defiance of authority.''
   d. For identical offenses those 18-year-olds of the *Philadelphia Birth Cohort Study* who were severely punished were more likely to be in prison than those who were lightly punished, or not at all.
   e. High corporal punishment schools are also high on vandalism.
   f. The more a child is beaten in youth the more likely he or she is to become a lawbreaker.
   g. The single most important correlate of juvenile delinquency is severe parental punishment.
   h. When comparing school corporal punishments in the 50 states with the crime rate as measured by prison admissions in those states, the correlation is 0.66.

In a separate publication they relate two other findings (Maurer and Wallerstein, 1983):

   a. There is a negative correlation of −0.54 between the extent of school corporal punishment and the proportion of high school graduates.
   b. Physical punishment in the home significantly reduces school achievement among junior high school students in Illinois.

CONCLUSION AND ALTERNATIVES

The position of the Association for Childhood Education International with respect to corporal punishment comes through clearly in its 1985 resolution: *Corporal punishment must be BANNED in child care, school and other educative settings.* It is a barbaric practice that:

• Is unnecessary.
• Preempts better means of communicating with a child.
• Teaches by example that the infliction of pain on others is permissible.
• Increases aggressiveness in the child.
• Develops deviousness; the trick is to not get caught.
• Is dangerous in that it escalates into battering.
• Reduces the ability to concentrate on intellectual tasks.
• Can cause sexual aberrations.
• Damages the punisher in that it narrows his options, tunnels his vision and tarnishes his image as a scholar.
• Is inconsistent with any view of the child as a person worthy of respect. (Adapted with permission from statement of purposes of the Committee To End Violence Against the Next Generation, Inc., 977 Keeler Ave., Berkeley, CA 94708. In *The Last Resort*, Fall 1985, p. 28.)

Corporal punishment is rejected by professionals who are either directly or indirectly involved with the care and education of children. It is rejected by the American Medical Association, the American Bar Association, the National Association for the Advancement of Colored People, the Americans for Democratic Action and the American Public Health Association. It is rejected by religious groups such as the Society of Friends (Quakers), Unitarian Universalists and Presbyterians.

C. Everett Koop, M.D., Surgeon General of the United States, convened a Workshop on Violence. He presented the recommendations of that workshop to the Senate Subcommittee on Children, Families, Drugs and Alcoholism in October 1985. In part, he said that the Working Group on Child Abuse Prevention recommends that the U.S. ''Conduct a massive campaign to reduce the public acceptance of violence and to protect children against all forms of violence including physical punishment ('No Hitter Day' is one of the many possible techniques—enlist the media's help)'' and ''Abolish corporal punishment of children in all forms'' (Maurer, 1985-86, p. 1).

The only warranted conclusion based upon medical evidence, research findings and expert professional judgment is to STOP HITTING CHILDREN.

What then are the alternatives? *We must first resist the temptation to use punishment as the automatic solution to behavior problems.* Americans tend to see punishment and discipline as synonymous (Hyman and D'Alessandro, 1984). *Second, we must view discipline as motivated by a set of internal controls, not by the fear of harm. Third, we must recognize and demonstrate respect for individual rights. Fourth, our systems of discipline must center upon the desire to understand the causes and motives of misbehavior.*

To improve and promote effective discipline in schools without resorting to corporal punishment will require at least the following:

• The improvement of school climate with the support for that improvement by *all* school personnel.

• The increased competence of staffs through extensive inservice training to help educators see the theory-practice link.

• The improvement of teacher training by focusing the training on techniques to motivate students and effectively handle discipline problems.

• The early identification of potential problem children and follow-up counseling aimed at preventing discipline problems.

• The use of other strategies such as ''time-out,'' ''in-school suspension,'' ''peer/cross-age counseling'' and ''Latchkey (after school) programs.'' (See Hyman and D'Alessandro, 1984, and Maurer, 1984, for elaboration on these strategies.)

Schools, teachers, administrators and parents can learn positive techniques for changing behavior, building good character and developing good citizenry. More difficult for them to learn, however, is how to guide children through internal motivation while resisting the urge to model control by authority.

DISCUSSION QUESTIONS

1. What is the official position of ACEI on punishment?

2. What are the reasons for eliminating corporal punishment from the schools?

3. How have the historical antecedents influenced present attitudes and practices?

4. What is the legal situation concerning punishment in the schools?

5. Does punishment work? What does research say about the effects of punishment?

6. What are some acceptable alternatives to punishment?

60. A COGNITIVE APPROACH TO BEHAVIOR MANAGEMENT

by Jerold P. Bauch

The Cognitive Curriculum for Young Children* is now being implemented in over 60 classrooms across the United States and Canada (Weatherford, 1986). This curriculum model is currently found in Head Start programs, public and private schools and in classrooms for children who are developmentally delayed or at risk. The program model centers on developing children's thinking skills. Teachers intentionally structure learning opportunities to focus children's attention on what they are learning while they are learning. The curriculum is sequentially organized in terms of specific cognitive or thought processes. Teachers emphasize how children use these basic thought process skills over and over again in their daily routines and activities.

Every grouping of young children includes potential sources of disruptive behavior needing behavior management by the teacher. At least eight states added public school programs for children younger than five years of age last year. The classroom mix of children with a wide variety of home and social experiences and developmental levels may also seem to increase the "discipline" problems; the new combinations of children in many classrooms may accentuate a need for really effective management techniques.

A NEW COGNITIVE APPROACH

New research on how children learn and how teachers can create optimum learning environments has also produced important new insights about behavior management. The Cognitive Curriculum for Young Children (CCYC) (Haywood, Brooks, and Burns, 1986a) is one of the newest approaches for teaching young children. In this curriculum, considerable emphasis is placed on behavior management, and the program gives teachers some new insight about the solution to behavior problems.

The CCYC asks teachers to view disruptive behavior as a problem needing a solution and an opportunity to facilitate the development of self-control. Its theory about behavior management is that young children can and should be taught to assume control of their behavior in the classroom.

In this cognitive model, this learning takes place within the formal curriculum and in the hundreds of unplanned incidents that occur. The CCYC formal curriculum is currently composed of seven units, two of which concentrate on behavior and self-control: self-regulation and role-taking (Haywood, Brooks, and Burns, 1986b). The very beginning classroom experiences in the first unit on self-regulation are organized around the behavior of the individual child. For example, many traditional games, such as "Simon Says," "Ring Around the Rosie," and "London Bridge," are used to show how following the rules makes the game go smoother.

As children begin to control their own behavior, they move into two "content" units and then return to the fourth unit, Role-Taking. In this unit, children learn to think about their behavior in its social context and are helped to change their perspective when faced with conflict. Games like "I Spy" and discussion activities about "things I like or dislike" give the teacher a chance to demonstrate how other children might feel or react. Teachers then use these concrete experiences as examples when a disruption occurs, often using phrases like "How did you feel when..." or "If we have to wait for you, then..." to help a child consider others as well as his or her own actions. The CCYC believes experiences in role-taking and perspective-taking give children cognitive reasons for controlling their own behavior and help them move toward a higher level of self-control. The goal in each of these two units is to help children identify a particular problem and participate in its solution.

PRINCIPLES OF CCYC BEHAVIOR MANAGEMENT

Mediation Teaching

The primary function of parents and teachers of young children is to help them understand and interpret their world. Good teachers are good explainers, and the heart of the CCYC is on the

See page 348 for acknowledgment, footnotes, and references.

process of helping children understand. The entire CCYC curriculum model is guided by six principles of **mediational teaching style**: the ways in which teachers influence and explain things to children (Feuerstein, Rand, Hoffman, and Miller, 1980). Applied to behavior management, the principles are:

1. There is a great emphasis on the thinking **process**; children learn to **think** about their behaviors.

2. Discipline problems are dilemmas needing solutions, and teachers use a **problem-solving** approach.

3. Children can learn general **strategies** for dealing with behavior that apply in many situations.

4. The model assumes that **children are capable** of learning how to behave in acceptable and productive ways.

5. The primary role of the teacher is to **facilitate** children's learning about behavior, not to control their behavior from the outside.

6. The specific behavior problem and the way the problem (and others like it) have been solved are **shared** with other children so that everyone can learn from the incident.

The Cognitive Method

Teachers in CCYC-based classrooms apply six criteria of mediated learning when teaching children how to solve their own behavior problems. These criteria are:

1. **Intentionality**. Teachers organize the curriculum to provide opportunities for children to make changes in the way they think about their behavior. Consequently, group games like "Duck, Duck Goose" or "Doggie, Doggie Who's Got the Bone" are selected because (1) they demonstrate the principle of rules, and (2) allow teachers to explain reasons behind rules. Teachers intentionally plan activities that allow children to practice rules.**

2. **Transcendence**. Teachers try to make solutions to immediate behavior problems generic and applicable to similar problems. Teachers continuously "bridge" backwards to earlier situations where a similar problem occurred or explain to children what to do if faced with this same situation at a future time.

3. **Meaning and purpose**. Teachers explain why a particular solution is being used, and how it will help all of the children to become better learners

and classroom participants. Because rules help organize behavior, teachers emphasize why rules are necessary, how rules help to keep us safe, have more fun, learn more, and get along better.

4. **Feelings of competence**. Teachers mediate the process of problem-solving by giving feedback to children about their behavior that is objective and very specific. In this way, children learn to discriminate between the correct and incorrect elements of behavior and, therefore, are more in control because they understand the impact of their behavior upon others. Teachers in the CCYC classroom seldom use "I like the way..." statements, but are more likely to say, "When you slide your chair over, it makes more room for Charles and now you both can see." This kind of statement explains the cause and effect relationships in children's behavior.

5. **Regulation of behavior**. Teachers should help children bring their behavior under self-control while explaining (mediating) the process. If a child takes paper shapes from another child's set, the teacher may combine both groups of shapes and count: "One for you and one for Charles." This helps demonstrate fair and equitable division of materials and, with further discussion, can explain why each child will need enough squares, triangles and rectangles to complete the activity.

6. **Sharing**. Solutions to behavior problems are viewed as learning opportunities not only for the children involved but for everyone. Therefore, solutions to behavior problems are described and communicated. Roles and responsibilities are defined so that the solution-seeking process is understood by all. At the beginning of the school year, teachers may even stop an ongoing activity to "teach" a solution to the whole group before continuing the lesson.

APPLICATIONS IN THE CLASSROOM

The curriculum units of the CCYC model organize the classroom content within these principles and criteria of behavior management. Curriculum activities include games where the teacher points out the rules and the need for rules. Rules for self-regulation are then generalized to other classroom performances, and games with more complex rules are introduced. At every point, teachers explain the reasons for rules; as a result, children should begin to apply rules when problems arise. Usually, reminding a child about one of these rules is enough intervention to help a child solve his/her own problem.

For example, in the self-regulation unit there are about 25 lessons to help children acquire self-control. The long-range goal, of course, is to make control intrinsic. The first several lessons use games that most children know or can learn quickly. Each of the lessons states the **cognitive functions** that are to be learned, e.g., thinking about one's behavior or using precise language. The teacher is provided with a detailed **main activity** within the curriculum guide and several ideas for variations. The curriculum guide has pictures or other materials when needed. There is information on **bridging and generalization**, so that teachers can help children see the immediate and long-range applications of these cognitive functions to other situations. The curriculum guide ends each activity with a stated **minimal level of mastery** to make evaluation and monitoring of progress easier. The following example describes this process.

> In a small-group activity, children are working with individual sets of ten small wooden cubes. Curtis takes several blocks from Karen's set.
> 1. Let the child know why the behavior is a problem. "Curtis, everyone needs 10 blocks for this game."
> 2. Encourage the child to take another perspective by highlighting Karen's point of view. "Karen won't be able to play unless she has 10, and she wants to play, too. How do you think she will feel?"
> 3. Ask the child what the more appropriate behavior would be. "How many blocks should each child have? What could we do to make sure everyone has the same number of blocks?"
> 4. Discuss with the child (versus telling) possible rules that might apply and then, together, select an appropriate rule. "Curtis, what rules might help solve this problem?" (Wait for a response.) "What if we used a rule that says: Everyone works with their own materials?"
> 5. Seek agreement on a reasonable rule, and remind children about the rule if a similar situation reoccurs (bridging). "I will make sure that everyone has ten blocks; we will each use our own blocks for the game."

A key understanding in a mediational approach to behavior management is that children **should think** about behavior problems as just another classroom problem to be solved. Disruptive behavior is removed from its emotional context and treated with intelligence and reason.

What is different about the cognitive approach in the CCYC model is that desirable behavior is taught as the basic content of the curriculum. Teachers select and plan activities that systematically teach children how to perform and behave in the classroom so children learn what they're learning while they're learning. Children are active participants in solutions to behavior problems in exactly the same way they are involved in solving learning problems. Strategies and rules then become part of their self-regulating behavior.

DISCUSSION QUESTIONS

1. How does contemporary cognitive theory provide a fresh way of viewing discipline and behavior management in the classroom?

2. What are the principles of the cognitive method for helping children acquire self-control?

3. Does thinking about behavior result in more permanent control and behavior in the classroom?

4. How can positive classroom management be taught in the curriculum?

61. CORPORAL PUNISHMENT IN THE SCHOOLS

by John H. Meier

I just encountered an interesting paradox. On one side of an official school district memorandum were suggested guidelines for administering corporal punishment in the schools and on the other side the criteria for child abuse, including the new legal requirements for educators to report suspected child abuse. The paper-thin line between corporal punishment and child abuse is obviously an exquisitely fine one to draw. Consequently, many teachers continue to teach to the tune of a hickory stick.

Another paradox: On April 19, 1977, shortly after several professional symposia and hearings declared corporal punishment to be generally counterproductive, the U.S. Supreme Court decided that children are not protected under the Eighth Amendment to the Constitution, which forbids the use of cruel and unusual punishment (Ingraham v. Wright, 1977). This was in spite of testimony presented in opposition to the Court's finding by such authorities as Harvard's distinguished Professor of Psychology, B. F. Skinner. Dr. Skinner's pioneering work in the shaping of animal and human behavior led him to assert that, although punishment does momentarily stop undesirable behavior, it is recommended only as a last resort and is not nearly so effective as systematically reinforcing or rewarding desirable behavior.

A University of California Professor, Harold Hodgkinson, then Director of the U.S. National Institute of Education, cited impressive statistics showing a high positive correlation between the use of corporal punishment in high schools and the extent and severity of vandalism therein. Although a correlation does not prove a cause-effect relationship, it was repeatedly pointed out that violence begets violence.

Other authorities from a variety of disciplines cited shocking examples of brutality, including the use of electric shock apparatus, for disciplining students. Opponents even exhibited gruesome instruments such as 4-foot-long, 8-inch-wide paddles, facetiously referred to as ''Boards of Education,'' with holes drilled in them to reduce air resistance and to produce painful welts that would prevent child-assault victims from sitting for a week or longer to remind them and others of their transgressions. Irwin Hyman, a school psychology specialist at Temple University, leads a growing movement to abolish corporal punishment in the schools; members believe such brutality to be the United States' officially sanctioned brand of child abuse.

During the United States Bicentennial Year, I was serving as Director of the U.S. Office of Child Development and Chief of the U.S. Children's Bureau, the latter being a 60-year-old agency responsible for determining the best interests of the nation's children and youth. My testimony addressed the abusive, inhumane and brutal aspects of such violence in both school and home at a time when Sweden was outlawing corporal punishment in the home, having already banned it in the schools. It was pointed out that the public schools are the only public institutions in the U.S. (including prisons) which permit and even encourage corporal punishment for a variety of misdeeds.

Since the National Center for Child Abuse and Neglect was an important part of the U.S. Children's Bureau, I had ready access to the history of U.S. child abuse legislation. I was, however, already sensitized to the current concerns because of my familiarity with the public consciousness-raising American Humane Association and my experience as a former member of the University of Colorado Medical School's Pediatrics Department, whose chairman, Dr. C. Henry Kempe, was instrumental in alerting the medical community to the plight of the battered child in the early 1960s.

Moreover, my wife, a lay therapist in the Denver treatment program, had informed me of the many pernicious emotional and sexual concomitants of the more dramatic and visible physical damage suffered by these abused children: Often, corporal punishment was the sole means parents relied upon to discipline their children because that was all their own parents had used.

This same approach is characteristic of many school personnel who truly do not know any better means of discipline than swatting, pinching, hairpulling or the verbal sadism of humiliating, ridiculing and indeed destroying the budding self-

See page 348 for acknowledgment.

concepts of the children entrusted to them. Rather than being this battlefield for the use of sophisticated physical and psychic weaponry, the schools should instead encourage the most advanced and effective methods of child management. Most states now require all school personnel to report suspected child abuse and neglect. These new laws, then, should result in a marked increase in early detection and reporting of child abuse within the home, school and other institutions. This legislation should also help to prevent a great deal of senseless corporal punishment and encourage the substitution of constructive alternatives.

Until the past decade, however, there was virtually no place to solicit help for an abused child, except to call the local Humane Society, whose primary concern is the prevention of cruelty to animals. Another paradox is the alacrity with which persons will report suspected or witnessed cruelty to cats, dogs and other animals but the hesitancy with which they will report a neighbor whom they suspect of child abuse. As one bumper sticker puts it, "People are not for hitting—and children are people too." Another sticker advises, "Children are to be seen and not hurt."

Only recently has the Judeo-Christian legal system begun to acknowledge formally the rights of children and to treat them as human beings rather than as property or chattels. The recent adoption of model child abuse legislation by most states and the widespread public awareness campaigns launched by public and private sector organizations, including IOI's Children's Village, U.S.A., has unveiled the tip of an ugly iceberg. Child-rearing infractions hidden behind closed domestic doors have been revealed to public scrutiny to promote the best interests of children. Although it is agreed that a man's home is his castle, it is not agreeable that his children (or spouse) should be tortured in the dungeon. It is sobering to review the case histories of scores of battered children and to realize that so many of them started out to receive well-intentioned spankings that degenerated to incredible acts of brutal assault and battery.

Ironically, when battered children who survive are removed from their homes and placed in the care of foster or group homes, they are guaranteed a whole series of rights by public laws, enforced by the state licensing agency, including the right "Not to be subjected to corporal punishment, humiliation, mental abuse, withholding of monetary allowances or punitive interference connected with the daily functions of living, such as eating or sleeping" (California Administrative Code, Title 22, 8034).

Paradoxically, the punishment for truancy in many school systems is suspension or expulsion. Judging from statistics about "Children Out of School in America," marshaled most cogently by the Children's Defense League, I wonder whether we are dealing with dropouts, pushouts or "punish-outs." The delinquency data also reveal that much of the vandalism in schools is committed by those who have been driven out of school, often for trivial or capricious reasons. Adah Mauer, a pioneer in the Berkeley-based movement to end violence against the next generation, including the elimination of corporal punishment in the schools, speaks of a David Copperfield syndrome as the classic example of beating the dickens out of children, who in turn predictably employ similar techniques for intimidating the weaker people in their world.

Equal rights are for all human beings. For schools to remain training institutions that sanction violent techniques for dealing with children's behavior or learning problems only perpetuates and exacerbates the same societal tragedies of institutional and domestic violence that the schools are allegedly attempting to eradicate. The recent demand by some Los Angeles teachers for permission to use corporal punishment in the schools, regardless of the legal precautions and parental permissions involved, is alarming. It ominously underscores a vindictive and inhumane mentality predisposed to using violent solutions to problems. Educational institutions should be, however, exemplars of gentle, humane and more effective alternatives for facilitating optimum human development.

Must we continue to nurture our next generation, including our future leaders, on the curdled milk of humankind's unkindness? Contrary to the above indications, most parents and teachers do love children very much, but all too often they do not love them very well. Those of us in education, however, must stop violating the educational process by employing corporal punishment as an inducement to learning since it lessens what the victim learns and simply tells the student what not to do. Let those educators who live by the maxim "spare the rod and spoil the child" reinterpret the *rod* to mean a unit of measurement or a standard. Rather than using the hickory stick whenever children misbehave, adults can set reasonable limits of behavior and "catch children being good," rewarding them for desirable behavior until it becomes rewarding in itself.

Ironically, education has become preoccupied with corporal punishment, whereas its efforts should be focused upon eliciting the pleasure of discovery and mastery of new ideas and skills by the mind and developing a positive concept of competence and compassion within the psyche. If we continue to teach violence in the schools and if our students continue to learn "never force anything—just get a bigger hammer," someday, when they grow up and run our world, they may then teach us a lesson or two, with a violent vengeance.

DISCUSSION QUESTIONS

1. Does the law enable or restrict the use of corporal punishment in schools?
2. If a teacher uses corporal punishment, is the teacher subject to child abuse charges?
3. Does severe punishment produce the desired result? What are the negative consequences?
4. Do children have a right to a violence-free childhood? How can this right be assured?

62. CHILD ABUSE AND NEGLECT: PREVENTION AND REPORTING

by Barbara J. Meddin and Anita L. Rosen

Each year nearly 12 million children in the United States are reported to be abused or neglected. Even more alarming is the possibility that more than 2 million other cases are not reported to the agencies whose responsibility it is to protect children from further abuse (U.S. Department of Health and Human Services, 1981).

Most of these situations are treatable, however, and a great deal of harm to children is preventable (Kempe and Helfer, 1972). Because teachers are often the only adults who regularly see the child outside of the immediate family, teachers are often the first to observe children who have been or are at risk for abuse and/or neglect (McCaffrey and Tewey, 1978).

Teachers of young children are an essential part of the professional team that can prevent abuse and neglect. What steps can you as a teacher take to be alert to potential abuse or neglect? If indeed you believe a child has been harmed or is at risk of harm, how should it be reported?

WHAT IS CHILD ABUSE AND/OR NEGLECT?

Child abuse and/or neglect is any action or inaction that results in the harm or potential risk of harm to a child. Includes

- physical abuse (cuts, welts, bruises, burns);
- sexual abuse (molestation, exploitation, intercourse);
- physical neglect (medical or educational neglect, and inadequate supervision, food, clothing, or shelter);
- emotional abuse (actions that result in significant harm to the child's intellectual, emotional, or social development or functioning); and
- emotional neglect (inaction by the adult to meet the child's needs for nurture and support).

Every state mandates that *suspected* cases of child abuse be reported by professionals such as

teachers (Education Commission of the States, 1976). In Illinois, for example, professionals who do not report are subject to loss of their license to practice the profession. Those who report suspected cases are protected by law from any personal or civil liability growing out of that report (Illinois Public Law, 1979).

Teachers are not expected to know for sure whether a child has been harmed as a result of abuse and/or neglect. It is up to the child welfare or child protection agency to confirm the existence of abuse or neglect. Neither is the teacher expected to take custody of the child. The child protection agency or the police decide what action needs to be taken to protect the child.

Only about 13 percent of all child abuse reports are made by teachers or other school personnel (The American Humane Association, 1983). It appears that teachers are reluctant to report suspected cases, especially when physical neglect or emotional abuse and neglect are involved. Some teachers may feel they should not interfere with family relationships or childrearing techniques, and thus do not report cases where children are at risk (Underhill, 1974). However, it is both a legal and ethical responsibility for teachers to combine their knowledge of child development and their observation skills to identify children in need of protection.

INDICATORS OF ABUSE AND NEGLECT

Physical manifestations, child or adult behaviors, and environmental situations may indicate a child has [been abused] or may be at risk of abuse or neglect. The factors that most often can be observed by teachers will be discussed here.

Child Characteristics

Many of the characteristics described here occur in contexts other than abusive situations. Rarely does the presence or absence of a single factor

See pages 348–49 for acknowledgment and references.

signal child abuse. A pattern of these factors and behaviors will more likely indicate harm or risk to the child.

Teachers of young children often observe bruises or wounds on children that are in various stages of healing. This indicates the injuries occurred at different times, and may have been inflicted on a regular basis. Physical abuse can be suspected, for example, if injuries appear a day or so after a holiday or long weekend (bruises take a day to show up). Injuries that occur on multiple planes of the body or that leave a mark that looks like a hand or tool should also be considered nonaccidental.

Children naturally use their hands to protect themselves. Usually when a child falls, the hands go out to stop the fall and protect the face. Children's hands, knees, or foreheads are usually injured when they attempt to break their fall. If children report their injuries were caused by a fall, but the injuries do not include these areas, you should be suspicious.

When children fall, they also are most likely to fall on one side or plane of the body. Therefore, multiple injuries, such as a head injury coupled with a bruise to the ribs or buttocks, should be considered suspicious because more than one plane of the body is involved.

For example, a first grade teacher noticed that a child in her class returned from the Christmas holiday with bruises on the right side of her face and on the back of her left arm. Although the child said she had fallen, the teacher contacted the state child welfare agency. The child's mother initially contended the girl had been roughhousing with her brothers. Further investigation revealed that she had been hit twice by her grandfather who had been visiting and allegedly could not tolerate the girl's loud noises.

Burns often leave clues as to their origin. Oval burns may be caused by a cigarette. Stocking or doughnut-shaped burns may indicate that the child was put into a hot substance. Any burn that leaves an imprint of an item, such as an electric stove burner on a child's hand, may indicate that the injury was not accidental. The natural response of children is to withdraw when a body part comes in contact with a hot object; thus only a small section of skin is usually burned if the burn is accidental.

School-age children who come to school early and leave late may be indicating they have a reason not to go home. Likewise, young children who say they have been harmed should be believed. Rarely do children make up reports of abuse.

Older children may also discuss harmful events with classmates. Help children feel comfortable enough to confide in you because of your shared concern for a child. Susan, age 8, told a friend she had been molested by her father. The classmate confided in the teacher, who made a report. Susan had indeed been molested. Through counseling for the family, the molestation stopped.

Children who take food from others may be suffering from neglect. One agency investigated a case where a preschool child constantly took food from other children's lunches. The child was receiving one-half of a peanut butter sandwich a day at home and needed the additional food for survival.

Another common sign of neglect is children who come to school inappropriately dressed for the weather. The child who wears sandals in the winter or who doesn't wear a coat on a cold snowy day meets the definition of neglect and can be seen as at risk of harm.

Young children cannot be expected to sit still for long periods. However, some children who have trouble sitting may be experiencing discomfort in their genital areas as a result of sexual abuse. Children whose knowledge of the sexual act is much more sophisticated than that of peers or for their level of development may also be indicating they have been sexually abused. For example, a child might engage in inappropriate sex play with dolls or with other children in the dramatic play area or at recess.

Radical behavior changes in children, or regressive behavior, should be viewed as a possible indicator of abuse or neglect. For example, children who suddenly become extremely hostile or withdrawn should be considered to be possible victims of abuse or neglect. Regression often indicates that children are attempting to protect themselves or to cope with the situation. Typical of such a behavior change might be the 5-year-old child who develops toileting problems. Likewise, the child who strives to do everything exactly right, or fears doing anything wrong, may be trying to avoid incurring the anger of adults.

Another behavior that is a possible clue to abuse or neglect is the child who always stays in the background of activities. This child usually watches intently to see what adults are doing—possibly to keep out of the way of adults in order to prevent being harmed.

Children who are abused frequently expect such abuse from all adults. Do you know children who cower when you lift your hand in the air? Are there children in your group who hide broken crayons rather than asking for tape to repair them? Discussion, stories written by children, drawings, or sharing time may also reveal episodes of abuse and neglect.

It is important to stress that teachers should be alert to a *pattern* of characteristics and behaviors that indicate child abuse or neglect.

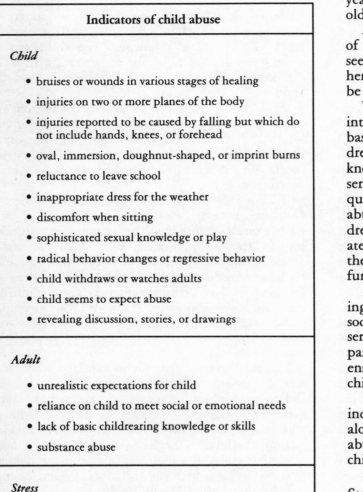

Indicators of child abuse
Child
• bruises or wounds in various stages of healing
• injuries on two or more planes of the body
• injuries reported to be caused by falling but which do not include hands, knees, or forehead
• oval, immersion, doughnut-shaped, or imprint burns
• reluctance to leave school
• inappropriate dress for the weather
• discomfort when sitting
• sophisticated sexual knowledge or play
• radical behavior changes or regressive behavior
• child withdraws or watches adults
• child seems to expect abuse
• revealing discussion, stories, or drawings
Adult
• unrealistic expectations for child
• reliance on child to meet social or emotional needs
• lack of basic childrearing knowledge or skills
• substance abuse
Stress
• positive or negative changes—moving, new baby, unemployment, divorce

ADULT CHARACTERISTICS

Parent (or other prime caregiver) behavior may also give clues that children are at risk of harm. Most preschool program staff see parents twice a day, and occasionally during parent conferences or home visits as well. Teachers of primary-age children have fewer occasions to observe parents, but can still be aware of parent behaviors through responses to notes, questionnaires, or phone calls.

There are a number of indicators of an adult's inability or unwillingness to care for and protect children. The parent who has unrealistic expectations for the child can be seen as placing the child at risk. For example, a parent may believe a 6-month-old child can be toilet trained, or that a 5-year-old should be able to read, or that an 8-year-old should always act like a lady.

Adults who look to their children to meet some of their own social or emotional needs can also be seen as a high-risk parent. The teenager who keeps her baby to have someone to love her is likely to be very disappointed!

Whenever possible, observe the parent and child interacting with one another. Parents who lack basic childrearing knowledge or skills place children at risk. For instance, a parent who doesn't know about nutrition or health care, or who has a serious physical illness, may be unable to adequately care for a child. Parents who are substance abusers—either drugs or alcohol—place their children at risk. Because most parents don't deliberately harm their children, all the parents with these types of problems need support to help them function in healthier ways with their children.

At the same time, when teachers observe parenting styles, they must be aware of and sensitive to social and cultural differences. Child protection services are not designed to impose middle-class parenting standards on everyone, but are aimed at ensuring a *minimum* standard of care for all children so they are free from harm.

While none of the above factors automatically indicates child abuse, the presence of any of them, along with other clues or patterns of suspected abuse, may indicate harm or potential harm for children.

Stress in the Environment

Adult stress can often be the cause of one-time or chronic harm to children. Therefore, whenever a family is under stress, the likelihood that abuse or neglect may occur is increased. The source of stress can be either positive or negative—a move, the birth of a new baby, unemployment, death, inadequate housing, divorce. Any stressor can affect parents' ability to care for their children and to maintain their own self-control.

Once again, however, stress should be considered as just one indicator that may produce a potentially dangerous situation for children.

PREVENTING ABUSE AND NEGLECT

Teachers of young children have many opportunities to aid in the prevention of child abuse and neglect. Certainly each teacher is a role model for parents. Many of your actions, such as your way of greeting children when they return from an illness or vacation, your methods for handling misbehavior, and your expectations for children, can help parents see positive ways to guide children.

For teachers who are not in contact with children's parents every day, it is more difficult to serve as a role model. However, you can talk with parents often by phone, hold discussion groups about common concerns such as discipline or early reading, and encourage parents to visit your classroom.

Once you are familiar with the clues that indicate children and families may be at risk, you can spot potential problems early. If a family is going to move, for example, you can talk with them about how to make a more comfortable transition for their children into their new school (Jalongo, 1985).

If you sense a potential danger to the child, you can help the family link up with appropriate supports, such as counseling services or material assistance, before their need becomes overwhelming and children are harmed.

WHAT HAPPENS WHEN A REPORT IS MADE?

In most states, one child welfare agency receives and investigates reports of suspected child abuse or neglect. The main purpose of the agency is to protect children from harm or from further harm, not to punish parents. These agencies work on the assumption that the best context for childrearing is in the child's own home (Kadushin, 1978).

When abuse or neglect is a reality, children will not necessarily be removed from their parents. The agency will strive to take the appropriate action to protect the child at home in the short run, while working with the parents to solve the problem for the future. All services are aimed at enhancing the parents' ability to care for and protect their children.

Before calling your local child protection agency, review the policy and procedures established for your program or school. These policies may help you determine when it is best to report, may support you in making the report, and may stipulate channels for reporting. The report should always be made in accordance with those policies and procedures, and should be done factually and without emotion.

Depending upon the state, a report is made either to a central or a local field office of the child welfare agency. That agency must begin its investigation by contact with the child, the child's family, and the alleged perpetrator of the harm. This contact is usually initiated within 24 hours, but can begin immediately if it appears the child is currently in danger.

While the family will not be told who initiated the action, the agency may ask for your name, address, and phone number when you make the report. This identification is necessary in case the agency needs to get back to you for further information.

Program directors and principals should offer in-service training to teachers to keep them abreast of the state's reporting law, the specific practices of the state child welfare agency, and the school's policy and procedures. Familiarity with the procedure, and the implicit support for reporting suspected abuse, can help teachers to follow through with their responsibility.

Filing a report of suspected child abuse begins a process through which the child welfare agency determines whether or not the child has actually been harmed or is at risk of harm from abuse or neglect. When harm has occurred, then the agency works to protect the child and help the family protect the child. The emphasis is always on treatment, not punishment. Teachers are an important part of a multidisciplinary team to help prevent and treat victims of abuse and neglect.

While teachers may hesitate to report suspected cases of abuse or neglect for fear of straining the parent-teacher relationship, that fear is often unfounded (Jirsa, 1981). Most parents love their children and are concerned about their welfare. Abuse and neglect rarely occur as a result of deliberate intent to harm a child. Rather, it occurs when a parent temporarily lacks control or judgment, or lacks the knowledge or resources to adequately care for the child. After their initial and appropriate anger at the intervention of the agency, most parents feel a sense of relief that the problem has been identified, and they are usually very willing to work toward a solution.

In cases where only the potential for abuse or neglect exists, the link with the child welfare agency can provide parents with the resources or referrals needed to create a more effective home environment.

Like teachers, child welfare professionals' first allegiance is to the child. Teachers of young children are in a unique position to both report and help prevent child abuse and neglect through their daily contact with children and families.

When in doubt, report. Only then can we all work together to intervene on behalf of the child, work toward solutions, and enhance the quality of life for children and families.

When in doubt, report.

Steps to take in reporting suspected child abuse or neglect.

1. Carefully observe children and parents for any patterns of circumstances or behaviors that may indicate an abusive, neglectful, or potentially harmful situation.

2. Review the policies and procedures for your program or school so you can make the report in accordance with them.

3. Call

_____

_____

_____

_____

to report your concerns.*

Fill in with local numbers, clip out, and place near your program's phone.

DISCUSSION QUESTIONS

1. What is the nature of child abuse and neglect in our society?

2. How can teachers know if a child is being abused or neglected?

3. What are the obligations of the teacher for reporting?

4. How can the school program reduce and prevent abuse?

Section Ten: The Future

EDITOR'S OVERVIEW

It is always risky to speculate or even attempt to forecast the future. This is particularly true about early childhood education in the schools, since the field is influenced by forces from within the profession and shaped by many external pressures and trends. So we step lightly by presenting a few reasoned views.

First, Isenberg describes the social pressures on the children and families of today that will influence the children entering schools tomorrow. Next, Day and Drake take us into a setting that represents much of what should be included in school programs for younger students. Then, Hodges brings the reader through the last 30 years—a time of rapid change for the human race—as he describes the important events and dynamic precedents that set the stage for today and tomorrow. Keliher reminds us that going back into history is not the preferred path where the future of our children is concerned. And Riles shows how California has attempted to move forward in a state-wide commitment to better schools through early education. Finally, Boyer urges readers to face some present realities and to solve social problems with his hypothetical "Basic School," where policy produces excellent education in response to present and future social needs.

It might also be noted that some of the previous sections in this publication anticipate that more children younger than five will attend the public schools, that the schools will have to expand the range of services and opportunities for these children and their families, and that teaching younger children ought to be qualitatively and perhaps quantitatively different from the standard elementary offering.

63. SOCIETAL INFLUENCES ON CHILDREN

by Joan Isenberg

Today's youth live in a fast-paced, changing world characterized by social pressures that push them to grow up too fast. They are pressured to adapt to changing family patterns, to achieve academically at early ages, and to participate and compete in sports and specialized skills. Moreover, they are pressured to cope with adult information in the media before they have mastered the problems of childhood. Such pressure places increased responsibility and stress on children while simultaneously redefining the essence of childhood itself (Berns, 1985; Postman, 1985; Damon, 1983; Suransky, 1982; Elkind, 1981).

Both educators and psychologists are expressing concern over the impact of these changes on children. In examining the pressures of contemporary society, Elkind (1981) labels today's child "the hurried child," pushed by adults to succeed too soon, thereby increasing the likelihood of failure. Others (Winn, 1983; Postman, 1982) contend that the media have contributed to the disappearance of childhood through "adultification" of children in television, films, and literature. And Suransky (1982) believes the very concept of childhood is eroding through the institutionalization of early learning environments that deprive children of their right to discover, create and invent by imposing preschool curricula unrelated to their development and interests.

Because children are shaped and molded largely by the expectations of the institutions society creates for them, the social context in which they grow deeply affects their development. Erikson's (1963) theory of studying individuals in their social contexts illustrates the importance of children's interactions and interrelationships with critical agents in their social environment. Within these agents of the family, school, peer group and media, children acquire social skills and behaviors enabling them to participate in society. Recent changes in the patterns of these settings, however, push children out of childhood too fast and threaten their basic social needs at all ages and stages of development.

To best understand how today's youth are influenced by these societal agents, this [chapter] will identify children's basic social needs, describe the social pressures affecting those needs and provide suggestions for balancing social priorities for children.

CHILDREN'S SOCIAL NEEDS

Despite the fact that children have their own unique personalities, all children have basic social needs that must be adequately met to develop a healthy sense of self (Erikson, 1963; Bronfenbrenner, 1979). Such needs form the necessary and basic conditions for children from birth through the elementary years and enable them to better meet the lifelong challenges of productive social interaction. Figure 1 outlines the critical ages and conditions for developing children's needs and their subsequent personality outcome.

SOCIAL PRESSURES AFFECTING CHILDREN'S NEEDS

Family

As the United States has moved toward urbanization, industrialization and the information age, significant changes have occurred in the structure and function of families (Bronfenbrenner, 1985a; Elkind, 1984; Umansky, 1983). We have witnessed a rise in single-parent homes, divorce, blended families and working mothers, as well as a decline in extended family homes and the birth rate. Today, approximately 20 percent of our youth live in single-parent families. Moreover, each year more than one million children experience divorce in their families (National Center for Health Statistics, 1983; Wallerstein and Kelley, 1980). Yet while the structure of families may have changed, the needs of children are still the same. The family remains their primary socializing agent.

Consequences

The dissolution of the family places additional pressure on children to adjust. Many of these

See pages 349–50 for acknowledgment and references.

Figure 1—Social Needs

Need	Critical Age	Necessary Conditions	Personality Outcome
Love, Security, Stability	Infancy	Parents and caretakers provide consistent, regular and predictable care.	Develop strong sense of trust and belief in security of world. Foundation for self-confidence.
Independence	Toddlerhood	Parents and caretakers provide encouragement, freedom and choices for children to practice newly developed skills.	Grow self-confident and develop autonomy as they begin to find their own personality and self-will.
Responsibility	Preschool	All family members provide opportunities and encouragement for children to self-initiate exploration and discovery of their environment through projects, role-playing and taking time to answer "why" questions.	Develop sense of purpose, goal-directedness, willingness to try new things.
Competence and Success	Elementary School	Family, neighborhood and school provide opportunities for children to learn how things work and become competent and productive "tool-users" in their society.	Develop self-esteem and sense of self. Sense of competence and order.

children experience pressure to mature and assume increased adult responsibility (Berns, 1985; Elkind, 1981; Hetherington, 1979).

Preschool children, the most vulnerable to divorce, often do not understand the reasons given and have a strong need to identify with the absent parent. Consequently, they often feel guilty and responsible for the divorce and think that the parent left because they were bad. Elementary children may be very frightened, experience an acute sense of shame and display anger at one or both parents. They may engage in acting-out behavior (stealing, cheating) or develop physical symptoms (headaches, stomachaches). Early adolescents also feel anger and depression and may act out sexually or quickly assume adult roles and responsibilities (Wallerstein and Kelley, 1976). No matter what the age, children experiencing divorce often face additional challenges along with the usual tasks of growing up. Their ability to resolve these tasks depends, in part, on their own resilience and, in part, on parental handling of the separation issues (Papalia and Olds, 1986).

In addition to family changes precipitated by single parenting, the increase in women in the labor force has contributed to the pressure on children to grow up too early. A major problem for working mothers—and, therefore, children—is the availability of adequate child care. The lack of adequate child care has given rise to a group of unsupervised children, commonly referred to as "latchkey" children. At least 7-10 million children between the ages of 7 and 13 are left unattended after school (Seligson et al., 1983). These children spend part of each day alone and take responsibility for themselves. Such lack of supervision may lead to physical or psychological harm, contribute to delinquency, or produce feelings of abandonment and fear through lack of adult contact and security (Galambos and Gabarino, 1983; Herzog and Sudia, 1973). As the number of working mothers increases, the need for adequate child care also increases. Without adequate supervision, "latchkey" children are placed at risk.

297

Because the family is the child's first introduction to societal living, it has primary responsibility for children's socialization. How children learn to relate within the family context strongly affects their developing values, personalities and basic social needs.

Schooling

In addition to affecting the family, societal changes have affected the shape of early education. Today's parents are pushing their children to learn as much as they can earlier than ever (Spodek, 1986; *Newsweek*, 1983; Elkind, 1981). Anxious parents, influenced by mass media, believe that the earlier children begin learning academics, the more successful their school and life experience will be. Publishers are producing popular books such as *Teach Your Child To Read in 20 Minutes a Day* (Fox, 1986) and *Teach Your Child To Read in 60 Days* (Ledson, 1985), better baby videos and "teach your child at home kits." All focus on developing children's intelligence at the expense of their personal and social adjustment. Advertisements promote anxiety in parents, which is then imparted to children: "And by the time they are 2 or 3 years old, another miracle can occur—if you allow it to. They can begin reading" (Moncure, 1985).

Today public kindergarten is available in every state. Moreover, increases in availability of preschool experiences have made the world of schooling available to children earlier (Spodek, 1986). Unfortunately, in many cases elementary school criteria and programming are being applied to programs for young children (Elkind, 1986; Suransky, 1982). Pressure to provide more formal learning and more rigorous academic content has resulted in refocusing early education: from meeting children's developmental needs in an environment generally free of social pressures to pressuring children to prepare for elementary school and later life. The notion of the "competent infant" fits into our changing lifestyles, along with the idea that children today are more sophisticated and advanced because of the nature of their experiences (Hunt, 1961; Bloom, 1964; Bruner, 1960). New importance has been attached to children's intellectual developments as children are placed in high-pressure academic programs for "their own good" (Elkind, 1986).

Consequences

The pressure for early academic achievement has been criticized by child development experts not only because there is no research base to support it but also because it may impede development of other equally important skills (Spodek, 1986; Elkind, 1986; Seefeldt, 1985). Some argue that formal instruction at early ages makes unnecessary demands on children and places them in unnatural learning modes. Others argue that undue emphasis on early formal learning has the potential to diminish children's long-term motivation to learn by interfering with the natural development of their need for self-directed learning. It places children at intellectual risk by interfering with their developing reflective abstraction and at social risk by forcing them to rely on "adults for approval and . . . social comparison for self-appraisal" (Elkind, 1986, p. 636).

Pressure for academic achievement can encourage school failure. Maturity, one factor of development virtually ignored in past years, is now the subject of considerable attention. According to Friesen (1984), there is the "possibility that much of the failure in our schools is the result of overplacement, and that we might reduce the rate of failure by finding a better match between a youngster's grade assignment and his or her developmental age" (p. 14). Research supports the proposition that overplacement can be a significant cause of school failure.

"There is, of course, no evidence to support the value of such early pushing. There is, however, considerable evidence that children are showing more and more serious stress symptoms than ever before" (Elkind, 1984, p. viii). Attempting to force children at early ages to learn specific academic material or develop specific skills may produce a negative attitude toward learning in general, with serious long-term effects evidenced in increased dropout rates and a high rate of cheating (Harris, 1986; Elkind, 1982).

Peers

Peer groups provide yet another critical agent of socialization. Historically, children have relied primarily on informal peer groups, formed and maintained by themselves, to develop social roles and cooperative interests. Today, however, more and more children are engaged in formal group activities, organized and maintained by adults. Activity markers such as organized sports, beauty contests, graduations and specialized arts training—once reserved for the teen years—are rapidly being pushed down to younger and younger children. Elkind (1984) suggests that much of this "premature structuring" stems from parental need rather than concern and understanding for the child. Children pushed too soon into formal and adult organized groups often raise questions in adolescence: "Why am I doing this? Who am I doing this for? When seeking answers to these questions, children revolt in many ways when the answer is for the parent. Delinquency, school dropouts, drugs, alcohol and refusal to perform are some of the behaviors evidenced by children forced to achieve too early" (Elkind, 1982, pp. 178-179). The shift of these activity markers from adolescence to childhood creates unnecessary stress for children, causing them to develop parts of their personality and leaving other parts undeveloped (Elkind, 1984).

Consequences

Unsuccessful children pushed by parents into sports or specialized activities become discouraged and humiliated by not meeting parental expectations and may even end up hating the activity itself. Although the range of pressure is great, some feel rejected by both parents and peers for not achieving (McElroy, 1982).

The notion of competition carries with it negative aspects. Psychological damage can occur when adults stress competition over learning skills and view their children's victories, losses and performances as indicators of their personal successes or shortcomings.

Television

Because television-watching occupies more time than any other single activity except sleeping (Bee, 1985; Gerbner and Gross, 1978; Stein and Friedrich, 1975), it acts as a powerful socializing influence. By the end of high school, the average American child has watched over 20,000 hours of television, more than the number of hours spent in school (Comstock, 1975).

Television programs provide the same information to everyone, regardless of age (Postman, 1985). Information about violence, sexual activity, aggression, and physical and mental abuse is readily available and erodes the dividing line between childhood and adulthood. It places

> ...children and adults in the same symbolic world.... All the secrets that a print culture kept from children—about sex, violence, death and human aberration—are at once revealed by media that do not and cannot exclude any audience. Thus, the media forced the entire culture out of the closet. And out of the cradle. (Postman, 1981, p. 68)

Consequences

The content of prime-time television programming and advertising can cause children to increase their aggressive behavior in the short term (NIMH, 1982) and become desensitized to violence later in life (Thomas, 1982). Viewing violent content through images, characters and plots—whether on prime-time TV, cartoons, MTV or the nightly news—discourages children from cooperating to resolve problems because they come to accept what they see as appropriate behavior (Papalia and Olds, 1986; NIMH, 1982).

Advertisements, on the other hand, glorify instant gratification both explicitly and implicitly. New products and new fads constantly bombard viewers. Advertising directed explicitly at young children can create resentment when parents refuse to purchase products; for older children, it can create unrealistic fantasies that certain products will make them more popular.

Postman (1985) argues that children view one million commercials before age 18 at a rate of 1,000 per week, most of them perpetuating a youth culture, sex and materials as a way of solving problems instantaneously. Elkind (1981) suggests that by treating children as consumers before they are wage earners, children are pressured into a kind of "hucksterism," causing "adults to treat them as more grown-up than they are" and to assume they are able to see through the deceptions of advertising and to make informed choices (p. 79).

Thus, television programming and advertising continue to erode the dividing line between childhood and adulthood by opening secrets once only available to adults, eliminating the innocence of childhood, reducing the concept of childhood, and making the adult's and child's world homogeneous (Postman, 1985, p. 292). In a world where children view adult programming and advertising, how well are our youth being nurtured? Indeed, "the children of the 80's are growing up too fast, too soon. They are being pressured to take on the physical, emotional and social trappings of adulthood before they are prepared to deal with them" (Elkind, 1981, p. xii).

BALANCING PRIORITIES FOR CHILDREN

Pushing children to grow up too early affects the very core of the social fabric that develops, sustains and connects healthy, competent children. There is an urgent need to re-weave the unravelling social fabric of significant social influences (Bronfenbrenner, 1985a, p. 10). This can be accomplished by attending to the following critical agents of socialization at the family, school and policy levels.

Family

Balance concern for academic achievement with equal concern for developing feelings of competence, confidence and self-worth.

Children's successful adjustment to family life affects their ability to adjust to the outside world. The quality of parent/child relationships is built from the means of communication used. As the structure of families changes, there is greater need for positive communication about issues that affect children's self-respect and self-regard. Through empathic listening, talking, and responding—setting realistic and honest expectations and talking about fears—families can build a strong foundation for children's positive feelings about themselves.

One context for this communication is the *family meeting*, which provides opportunities for parents and children to talk about concerns, make decisions and suggest ways to solve problems. Children can assume responsibility as family members as well as have a time for "hurried lives" to engage in constructive "family time."

Balance the need for structured and professionalized activity with opportunities for play.

Probably the least understood childhood need is the need for play. Play is vital to children's intellectual, social and physical development and is "seen as a primary mode for a child who is involved in becoming" (Suransky, 1982, p. 12). Families contribute to children's optimal development by assuring opportunities for children to generate their own play with peers. In so doing, "they are fulfilling a fundamental human activity of intentionality and purposiveness" (Suransky, 1982, p. 173). Denying children the right to play denies them their primary means of learning about themselves and their world. Lack of adequate opportunities to engage in genuine play is evident in our hurried children today (Elkind, 1981, p. 193).

Help children become critical TV-viewers.

Children can develop proper TV-viewing habits with simple guidelines. Adults can view programs with children and talk with them about what they see. In viewing TV, adults should notice those behaviors children can imitate; for example, TV characters who model caring behaviors and programs that depict women as being competent. Moreover, adults should talk to children about the programs and note the differences between make-believe and reality. They should discuss alternate ways to solve problems they see on TV, as well as the effect of commercials.

School

Establish balanced curricula that meet children's needs.

Teachers, administrators and parents must be informed about what children are expected to learn and how they learn best. They need to set high but realistic expectations for children and encourage them to do their best work without pressuring them to perform beyond their level. We need to employ sensitive teachers who promote children's abilities and who recognize the power of their pedagogic task.

Provide inservice support for teachers and administrators about school and community resources.

Schools must take responsibility for educating school personnel about realistic expectations for children and changing family patterns. School counselors must be able to support teachers and help children and families through the varied transitions of schooling and family patterns. In providing this stability and support, counselors must understand current literature and research on the changing fabric of societal institutions.

Provide courses, workshops and training sessions for parents and educators.

Both colleges and communities must provide parenting courses and teaching courses in response to the stresses of contemporary society. Educating parents about parenting is no longer a luxury; it is an imperative.

Policy

Advocate for quality and appropriate child care.

Families with children must demand high-quality child care that takes into account the needs of children and their families. Whether the care occurs in or out of the home, children's social patterns and behaviors continue to form in these settings. Young children need settings that integrate play naturally, encourage their active exploration and foster a sense of trust and security. They also need caregivers who enjoy working with young children, understand their growth and development, have realistic expectations for their behavior and are responsive to parents.

School-age children need safe and supervised care in which they are involved in activities appropriate to their stage of development. They also need teachers who understand them, their families and their needs.

Parents and community members must be advocates for quality, comprehensive child care settings. An informed community must develop appropriate programs for children, its most vulnerable group.

CONCLUSION

Pressured by each of the critical socializing agents in their lives, today's children are experiencing shortened childhoods. The sources and consequences of such pressures are clear. Also clear is the urgent need to direct our efforts toward balancing priorities for children at the family, school and policy levels.

DISCUSSION QUESTIONS

1. What are the universal social needs of children?
2. How can the institutions of society, including the school, help to meet these social needs?
3. Can good early education programs compensate for negative changes in family structure and operation?
4. Do early childhood education programs in the schools reduce the pressures and problems for children or do they contribute to these negative influences?
5. Can the teachers, parents, and policymakers achieve balance in future programs that will improve the development and learning potential for young children? How can this be achieved?

64. DEVELOPMENTAL AND EXPERIENTIAL PROGRAMS: THE KEY TO QUALITY EDUCATION AND CARE OF YOUNG CHILDREN

by Barbara Day and Kay N. Drake

At the heart of the educational process lies the child. No advances in policy, no acquisitions of new equipment have their desired effect unless they are in harmony with the nature of the child, unless they are fundamentally acceptable to him.

Knowledge of the manner in which children develop, therefore, is of prime importance, both in avoiding educationally harmful practices and in introducing effective ones (Plowden et al. 1966).

Given the well-established fact that young children learn differently, the conclusion that educators must draw is a straightforward one: the education of young children must be in keeping with their unique modes of learning (Elkind 1986).

The Plowden Report and the Elkind statement, written 20 years apart, succinctly summarize the rationale for developmental early childhood education programs. The reality of such programs . . . is a complex learning environment designed to support the intellectual development of the young child.

The basic philosophy for developmental early childhood education is built on two beliefs: that each child is unique and needs a flexible program to develop as an individual and that interaction, understanding, and cooperation in a group are fundamental requirements of society. Developmental programs allow for a flexible and varied curriculum designed to meet a broad range of developmental, socioeconomic, and cultural needs (Leeper et al. 1984).

ASPECTS OF A DEVELOPMENTAL PROGRAM

Four major areas should be considered when planning a quality developmental program. The first involves children's opportunities to practice developmental tasks (Tryon and Lilienthal 1950), including gaining appropriate dependence-independence patterns, establishing healthy patterns for giving and receiving affection, developing a con-

science, encouraging physical growth, and creating communication opportunities that enhance the child's use and understanding of symbols.

The second major area concerns teachers and staff. The teachers' knowledge of the physical, social, and cognitive development of children is essential, as is the interaction between teachers and students. Phyfe-Perkins (1981) showed that where teachers participated more with the children and were less directive, the children exhibited higher levels of cognitive play, task involvement, and verbal interaction.

Third, academics have an important place in the quality program. Children between the ages of two and seven are in the concrete stage of cognitive development. They learn from concrete experiences. Thus stories, dictating to the teacher, and counting can be used creatively to expose children to reading, writing, and mathematics. First and second graders also need to continue to learn through concrete experiences as they make the transition into primary school.

The fourth major area considered in planning a quality program is the physical setting. Developmental classrooms are designed to encourage children to be independent and to have hands-on learning experiences. Learning centers for math, science, reading, writing, art, cooking, listening, and so on can engage children in experiences that allow them to use their hands, eyes, ears, and minds. Through them children learn about themselves and the world around them.

ORGANIZATION AND MANAGEMENT

Consideration also must be given to curriculum organization and classroom management (Day and Drake 1983). Curriculum organization is made up of three components—learning centers, skills groups, and units of study—that are organized to teach specific topics such as self-concept or animal habitats.

See page 350 for acknowledgment and references.

Classroom management components include color coding, which is the systematic use of color to organize games, books, and activities to help young children manage a multitask environment; contracts, which are pictorial (later written) plans for the child's day to ensure that each child stays on task; and external and internal methods of discipline. External discipline refers to how the classroom environment influences the child's behavior. Internal discipline refers to the child's own ability to behave in appropriate ways. Clear expectations, consistent use of rules, and frequent feedback are techniques educators can use to help a young child develop internal discipline.

EFFECTIVENESS

We recently conducted a study using the Wasik-Day Open and Traditional Learning Environments and Children's Classroom Behavior Instrument. We found that children had an on-task behavior rate of 92 percent when their classrooms featured eight or more learning centers, were multiaged (five- and six-year-old children were grouped together), and used contracts (Day and Drake 1983). Because of their exceptional on-task behavior, the children in the developmental classrooms actually received 120 more hours of schooling (20 more school days) over the entire school year than did children whose classrooms did not include learning centers or contracts.

Our intent was to investigate the relationship between various types of early childhood classroom environments and the on-task behavior rates generated by the children in each program. For this purpose the classroom environment was defined in terms of the number of simultaneous activity segments operating at any one time (Wilson 1983).

We observed 18 kindergarten and first-grade classrooms and categorized them into five different organizational patterns.

Type 1. Six-year-old children in classrooms that operated for most of the school day with only one or two simultaneous activities.

Type 2. Five-year-old children in classrooms that operated multiple activity segments (including eight or more learning centers) for the first hour of the school day, then operated only one or two simultaneous activities for the rest of the day.

Type 3. Six-year-old children in classrooms that operated multiple activity segments during the morning. The afternoon included only one or two simultaneous activity segments.

Type 4. Five-year-old children in classrooms that had multiple activity segments operating all day.

Type 5. Five- and six-year-old children in classrooms that operated multiple activity segments all day and used written contracts as a management technique.

Children in Type 5 classrooms were grouped in five-year-old kindergarten programs (Type 5a), six-year-old first grade programs (Type 5b), and multiaged five- and six-year-old programs (Type 5c).

Table 1 shows the on-task behavior rates generated by each type of classroom.

Types 1, 2, and 3, which had little or no simultaneous activity, had similar on-task behavior rates of approximately 78 percent. Small positive changes in on-task behavior were produced by Type 4 classrooms (82 percent). Type 5 classrooms, however, generated on-task behavior rates as high as 92 percent.

These results suggest that a complex early childhood environment featuring learning centers in conjunction with an appropriate management system can achieve rates of on-task behavior higher than those achieved in less complex classrooms that rely on large- and small-group instruction and seatwork assignments.

Additionally, five- and six-year-olds had higher on-task behavior rates when working in learning centers than when engaged in seatwork activities. This suggests that young children need classrooms that feature a variety of learning experiences.

We noted a particularly interesting example of the interaction between the developmental readiness of children for an activity and the on-task behavior rates generated by that activity. Five-year-olds had on-task rates of 29 percent, and six-year-olds had an on-task rate of 93 percent. Reading centers, as they are typically designed in early childhood classrooms, often do not involve five-year-old children, most of whom are nonreaders. There appears to be a need to reorganize reading centers for five-year-olds to include stimuli other than print. For example, books with tape recordings of their content might interest five-year-olds more than books alone.

Table 2 presents interesting contrasts in how time is actually spent in kindergarten and first-grade classrooms. The typical first-grade day in this study is clearly structured differently from the typical kindergarten day.

Life is a spectrum of all types of overlapping skills and activities. A developmental teaching approach helps the child to see how new skills could fit into a broader realm of experience, thus provid-

Table 1
Percentage of On-Task Behavior by Classroom Type

Type	Activities	Time	Contract	On-Task Behavior
1	1–2	——	no	79%
2	multiple	1 hr/day	no	79%
3	multiple	½ day	no	78%
4	multiple	all day	no	82%
5a	multiple	all day	yes	85%
5b	multiple	all day	yes	87%
5c	multiple	all day	yes	92%

Table 2
Percentage of Time by Place

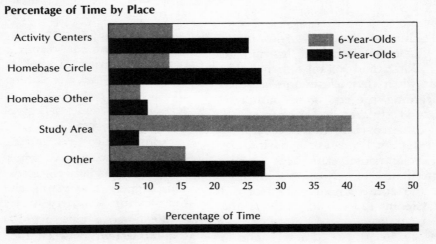

ing a reason for learning. This method, involving center-oriented, simultaneous activity segments within the learning environment, is one of the most effective approaches to total child development.

DISCUSSION QUESTIONS

1. Are there some fundamental factors that must be present in future early education programs?

2. How does the developmentally appropriate classroom operate? What is the role of the teacher?

3. How do children respond to a well-planned classroom program and schedule? What are the results?

65. UPON WHAT CAN WE BUILD OUR CHILDREN'S EDUCATIONAL FUTURE?

by Walter Hodges

Twenty-five years ago changes in the perceptions of early childhood development were beginning to influence the types of programs available for preschool and primary children. At least three major sets of beliefs—maturationism, behaviorism, and cognitivism—were being used to guide the development of these new programs. Many believe that these different sets of beliefs lead to incompatible programs. Maturationists believe in the primacy of the child and the child's ability to learn and develop given an appropriate but non-coercive environment. Behaviorists believe that many children need the systematic input from well-designed teaching programs in order to master the skills necessary for survival in the schools and in society. The cognitivists believe that children build their own intelligence based on their interactions with a richly furnished world while guided by knowledgeable adults.

In 1965, early childhood educators holding one or the other of these various views were beginning to confront one another. It was a time when new ideas of child development, child care, and early childhood education were being tested in the crucible of public programs, seriously debated in professional societies, and vehemently argued among early childhood practitioners and leaders. From then till now, public programs have been stringently tested, professionally debated, and argued extensively, albeit sometimes acrimoniously. Due to such acrimony, the field has often been divided and unable to serve children as well as could have been done with fewer polemics.

The thesis here, however, is that these differences among points-of-view, while often destructive, have, nevertheless, produced a rich body of understanding about different approaches to early childhood. It is possible that this knowledge could be used to generate a second or third wave of truly sophisticated approaches to the interrelated problems of child-rearing, child care, and child education similar to those which were developed in the late sixties. Such new waves are certainly needed.

While celebrating the past is justified for the point to which it has brought us, it is also useful to chronicle these past 25 years by calling to mind some of the landmark events that mark the evolution of modern early childhood education.

A good place to start is 1961. J. McV. Hunt (1961) published his very important challenge to the hereditarians in *Intelligence and Experience*. He argued that experience had not been given its just place in the theories of human development and incorporated a readable interpretation of the work of Jean Piaget reviving the argument about what is most important—heredity or environment.

In that same year, 1961, a national survey of Aid to Families with Dependent Children revealed an average annual per person income of $408. Did these children go to school? Yes, they did, but probably for no longer than they were forced to do so. Susan Gray's Early Training Project was beginning in Tennessee (Gray, Ramsey, and Klaus, 1980) and David Weikart was initiating the Perry Preschool Project in Michigan (Weikart and Schweinhart, 1980). Bereiter and Engelmann (1966) were also developing their direct instruction model with 4- and 5-year-old children at the University of Illinois.

In 1962, Michael Harrington published *The Other America*, a book that captured the growing awareness that poverty in America was not a trivial, isolated problem but rather a large-scale, serious concern as well as a threat to all of us.

In 1963, a friend of education was lost when John Kennedy was assassinated but the Report of the President's Panel on Mental Retardation presented a new look at the relation of poverty to retardation. At Indiana, the Experimental Preschool Project—A Diagnostically Based Curriculum for Preschool Children was begun (Hodges, McCandless, and Spicker, 1971). Studies were published questioning the efficacy of special classes for mildly retarded young children (Dunn, 1960).

Then a bill that fostered a revolution in early childhood passed Congress—the Economic Opportunity Act of 1964—out of which came Head Start and, later, Follow Through, two programs for preschool and primary children still operating in 1986. Unfortunately, as far as one can surmise,

See pages 350–51 for acknowledgment and references.

305

these two programs have yet to be fully appreciated for the knowledge they have revealed concerning how best to encourage young children's growth.

During this period, (1) the Montessori method was being rediscovered; (2) early prevention was being recognized as better than later remedial efforts; (3) achievement in academic and cognitive areas was coming to take precedence over social adjustment and general socialization in the preschool; (4) intelligence was now thought to be modifiable; (5) development was believed to be more seriously subject to environmental influences; (6) parents were becoming more educationally visible; and (7) poverty and intelligence were linked in a powerful inverse relationship.

Furious action broke loose on several fronts at once in 1965. The war in Vietnam escalated tremendously, the War on Poverty here in the states expanded, and the battles for civil rights raged in places like Watts and Selma.

A major front for the war on poverty—Head Start—began in the summer of '65 for preschool children from low-income homes. A second major front was the passage of Public Law 89-10, The Elementary and Secondary Education Act of 1965, which marked the beginning of compensatory education. Heber (1978), at the University of Wisconsin, began a massive intervention project with high-risk infants and their mothers which became known as the Milwaukee Project and Phyllis Levenstein began a much more modest, but important, intervention through her Mother-Child Home Program of Verbal Interaction (Madden, O'Hara, and Levenstein, 1984).

In 1966, the whole early childhood movement got another boost from an unexpected source when the Coleman Report on *Equality of Educational Opportunity* (Coleman et al., 1966) was published. Its emphasis on family variables made it apparent that the family part of the educational equation accounts for more variance than most people had been willing to admit. Early childhood educators were not surprised. They had recognized and capitalized on this phenomenon for years.

Other major events marked the year: (1) the President appointed a Multidisciplinary Task Force on Early Childhood Development chaired by J. McV. Hunt, to decide what to do next. (2) Harold Skeels published a monograph entitled *Adult Status of Children with Contrasting Life Experiences* (Skeels, 1966). This monograph reported dramatic evidence that massive intervention in the lives of young children who were at risk for mental retardation can lead to great changes in life chances.

(3) Bereiter and Englemann published their book on *Teaching Disadvantaged Children in the Preschool* (1966) in which they advocated the direct teaching of basic school readiness skills. (4) Maya Pines' book on the *Revolution in Learning: The Years from Birth to Six* (1966) described the revolution taking place in early education where the "new mind-builders" were using "pressure cooker," talking-typewriter, and other "new" methods in attempts to halt the downward spiral of children's intellectual development. And, finally, (5) the Educational Policies Commission of the NEA published a small pamphlet entitled *Universal Opportunity for Early Childhood Education* in which it was proposed that four-year-olds be given the opportunity for early schooling.

In 1966, the battle among those who advocated various solutions to the problem of children at risk in education was made public through these and other books, pamphlets, articles, and speeches. Behaviorists, maturationists, and cognitivists were in conflict. Some thought the pressure cookers too hot for children. Others thought the child-centered approach was negligent of the needs of children at risk. Still others thought it impossible to implement the often abstruse ideas of Piaget in preschool programs.

In 1967, Follow Through and the Parent-Child Centers were authorized. "Open education" was introduced to this country by Joseph Featherstone (1967) and this idea added more heat to the differences among those who would cook under pressure and those who would use a simmering technique. B. F. Skinner (1968) published *The Technology of Teaching*, which further expanded the role of behaviorism in early education. In Arkansas, the first Office of Child Development in the nation was established.

In 1968, the bubble of enthusiasm for Head Start was burst when studies indicated that it was extremely difficult to distinguish the academic performance of children who had been in Head Start from similar children who had not been. But Follow Through was starting just because Head Start had been deemed a "failure." Follow Through became an experiment in primary (K-3) education for children at risk. For the first time in the history of education in this country, differences among philosophies of education were made explicit in a variety of models of early childhood education—Direct Instruction, Cognitive Curricula, Behavior Analysis Classroom, Reponsive Environments, Open Education, Bank Street, Parent Education, Behavior Oriented Prescriptive Teaching, and others were all sent to the field to be implemented by real teachers, with real children, in the real context of local school districts. The model builders had to convince others to do the model, train them in doing it, monitor their progress, and collect research data at the same time. Needless to say, these tasks were enormous and, perhaps, unrealistic, in retrospect. But everyone wanted to show that their model was the one which could solve the problem.

Arthur Jensen's (1969) article entitled "How Much Can We Boost IQ and Scholastic Achievement?" opened with the catchy phrase: "Compensatory education has been tried and it has failed." And now the arguments shifted from among those advocating different approaches to early childhood education to the battle against those who said that the approach made no difference since children at risk were that way because of their genetic inheritance. The heredity-environment issue is on the table again.

In 1969, the Office of Child Development in the Department of Health, Education, and Welfare was opened and Head Start was transferred from the Office of Economic Opportunity to the Office of Child Development while Follow Through was moved to the Office of Education. In spite of these major moves at the federal level, the idea of legislation in support of comprehensive child care was never implemented. Congressman John Brademas and Senator Walter Mondale offered many child care bills in the late 1960s. They finally succeeded with Congress in 1971 only to be frustrated by President Nixon's veto on the grounds that such support of child care was anti-family and thus in some sense anti-American.

In early childhood, the 1970s were less exciting by comparison to the 1960s, but many battles were still being fought: (1) for public kindergartens; (2) for more quality child care; (3) for better prepared child care workers; (4) for better quality Head Start programs.

From 1973 to 1977, several major projects were completed and reviewed in the literature: the Child Development Associate credentialing process was begun; Sheldon White (1973) and his colleagues prepared a massive and discouraging report on *Federal Programs for Young Children*; the disappointing Head Start Planned Variation experiment results were published in several papers; Urie Bronfenbrenner (1974) published a famous monograph entitled *Is Early Intervention Effective?* wherein he proposed a system of child education based on his understanding of the research literature; The National Day Care Study was commissioned; J. McV. Hunt (1975) published his "Re-

flections on a Decade of Early Intervention"; the confusing Follow Through Planned Variation experiment (Stebbins et al., 1977) results were published; and, most important, the Developmental Continuity Longitudinal Studies (Consortium, 1978) of follow-ups of children in the experimental preschool programs of the 1960s and the monographs documenting the follow-up of Weikart's Perry Preschool Project (Berrueta-Clement et al., 1984) children (then in their teens, now in their 20s) appeared. Children in most of the experimental preschool projects seemed to be doing slightly better than their stay-at-home counterparts. At least fewer of them were behind in grade placement or in special education. And, for some, their achievement in school was somewhat improved. Still, there was no cure for the problem of progressive achievement decrements among high risk children.

Since 1977, the world of early childhood education has been less volatile although young children are still at risk. The topics of concern seem to have shifted: child abuse, child pornography, latchkey children, single-parent families, parenting, industry supported child care, family day care, and day care scandals wherein children have been found to be sexually molested by adult caregivers, and a handful of other problems and programs have been given much of the popular press time devoted to children and families.

It wasn't until 1984 that Weikart and his colleagues were able to persuade the major print and video media that there is still a problem of children at risk for educational disability in this country and that there are programs which work and which are designed to reduce the risk. These programs have spanned the range of programs developed during the 1960s and 1970s—but not all programs are equally successful. Quality counts for a great deal. And quality is usually embodied in people. But quality people need quality training, quality materials, quality environments, and effective support from directors, leaders, parents and community.

The diversity and resulting conflicts of these 25 years have been difficult and wearing. Polarizations have separated people whose goals were the same. There have been intelligent, compassionate, and caring people on both ends and in the middle. The downside is that we have not used our resources as well as we might have. The benefit is that those programs which have survived have sharpened their approach. They have gotten both more theoretical and more practical, which is just what should happen, since good theory leads to good practice. In some ways, early childhood has become more professional, especially in the sense that early childhood work is based on the theory that is known. In other ways, some of the narrowness characteristic of the early Montessori movement has been retained. Some early childhood professionals have not been open to those who propose programs from alternative perspectives. That is not professional; it is suicidal.

Early childhood education as a profession is at a point where a carefully planned integration of approaches is possible—not probable—just possible. Piaget, as interpreted by Kamii and DeVries (1978), suggests three different types of knowledge or ways of knowing—social, physical, and logical-formal. Social knowledge is that which we gain by being told. It is embedded in the culture. These are societal conventions—"This group of letters makes a word. We call that word 'cat.' Cat refers to a particular type of animal and I will show you some examples of animals to which we apply the appellation of 'cat.' " This is, of course, much too simple, but the point is clear. Such social knowledge is often taught best by direct instruction.

Physical knowledge can be taught directly, too, but not by telling. Physical knowledge is that which is gained by seeing, feeling, hearing, feeding, cleaning behind, being scratched by, and loving through cuddling and other machinations (i.e., hands-on experiences). One may even argue that such physical knowledge must precede the social knowledge that this thing we have seen, felt, and so on is a "cat." Either way, it is no longer reasonable to argue that there is only one way to skin the cat (of learning and teaching) as many in early childhood education are wont to do.

Logical-formal knowledge can be taught directly, too, but, again, not by telling, even though in colleges, universities, high schools, elementary schools, and yes, even preschools we pretend that when we have told, someone has understood (i.e., learned). There is much to be learned from the "experimental" learning and teaching as exemplified in the programs of Weikart, or DeVries, or Foreman and others who have translated Piagetian theory into activities for young (and not so young)

children. There is also much to learn from a wide array of other theoretically based programs from the behaviorists, from the maturationists, and from the direct learning and teaching models to the interpersonal skills models. It is too early to cease experimenting with these models since the solutions to our problems of educating those at risk are not yet manifest.

Where good people diverge so dramatically in their solutions to problems there is probably some merit in each of their approaches. The problem is to determine just what it is in each of the solutions that makes a difference and then, where possible, to blend the forces of each.

Since there are known differences in the kinds of things children learn, and there are different approaches to learning among us, a reversion to the overall position of the Gestalt psychologists, i.e., behavior is a function of the person and the environment, is required. The formula can be modified to fit early childhood teaching and learning as follows: (a) a teaching strategy must change according to (b) the child and (c) the content, skill, or attitude to be learned. In most instances, social learning is taught by direct instruction with no apology necessary. Physical knowledge is a contact sport, learned by exploration. And logical-mathematical knowledge is taught by experiment, guidance, and telling. Thus, we become neither behaviorist, maturationist, nor cognitivist, but rather a theoretical realist, whose purpose is not to convince others of the "way," but to help children acquire the wide array of tools that competent learners use. These tools are not limited to memorization, copying, questioning, observing, experimenting, or exploring, but include all of these skills and more.

And since this [chapter] was to celebrate the past, it is possible to propose an agenda for the next 25 years—the continuation of the search for ever more effective ways to help children construct, acquire, and accept the kinds of tools that they need to live a decent life built on the ability to care for themselves and their families, to love and to laugh, and to learn.

DISCUSSION QUESTIONS

1. What are the implications of the recent past for the future of early childhood education in the schools?
2. Has all the action of the past 25 years produced new knowledge and insight about early education?
3. Have the inappropriate and ineffective practices been eliminated? What universal themes have emerged?
4. Will programs in the future be significant improvements over the experiments and trials of the past?
5. What can the teacher do to make progressive changes in programs for young children for the future?

66. BACK TO BASICS OR FORWARD TO FUNDAMENTALS?

by Alice V. Keliher

Once again we are hearing that four-letter word—BACK! Do the proponents of Back to Basics think their appeal is new?

In 1933, I protested, "We also confront a general move on the part of an uncomprehending lay public aided and abetted by reactionaries . . . to retrench to the three R's" (p. 278).

In 1954, I warned, "Actually the 'three R's' are *W* (writing, *A* (arithmetic), and *R* (reading). . . . Sadly enough . . . these letters spell WAR"—the cause of many dropouts. But they also spell the RAW materials of learning when used with meaningful experiences.

Again in 1962, I scolded, "Imagine the members of a community who honestly thought it was best for the children to go BACK to the McGuffey Readers (1836) in an age when the movement in every important field is *FORWARD*" (p. 62).

Also that year I tried to get people to see how real learning takes place.

The world is so full of a number of things that there should be no difficulty in maintaining a rich, vital, active, challenging environment in every classroom. World news, activities in space, new scientific materials for home and school. . . . Add to these TV programs about exciting ideas and events from near and far parts of the world, fun and facts from 1700 new books written for children and youth each year. . . . The possibilities are limited only by the imaginations of teacher and children.

But some school people (and parents) say, "Yes, all this richness of experience is available, but we don't have time *left over* for it." Left over from what? The three R's? This is truly upsidedown thinking. The three R's (the RAW materials) are best learned and remembered through rich, meaningful experiences. (pp. 1–8)

So here we are again, facing the same old cry—BACK to Basics. Take our children back to the "good old days."

Why these recurrent cycles? The dates mentioned here were years of profound anxieties—the Great Depression with its hunger and unemployment, the Russian success with Sputnik, the McCarthy witch hunts, the Korean "police action" with its thousands of deaths, the proliferation of atomic devices, and now today, more hunger, unemployment, feelings of helplessness and mal-

See page 351 for acknowledgment and references.

aise. These concerns contribute to underlying periods of anxiety. There are too many uncontrollables, we feel. We wake in the gray hours of the morning and cannot get back to sleep. *Something* is wrong but what can we do about it? Where can we find certainty? Maybe the "good old days" were safer, more secure, more predictable?

BACK TO WHAT?

So, let's take our children BACK to those good old days. Let's make them conform to the old ways of doing things. Let's have the children read the same books, do the same math workbooks, memorize the same spelling words, obey the same strict rules of discipline, even wear the same uniforms. And the state legislators will follow right along and mandate that children must pass the same proficiency tests from first grade up.

What if these anxiety-ridden parents, teachers, or legislators suddenly sought to go back to basics in medicine and public health? Suppose they wanted to go back to the 1800s. In the 20th century alone we would miss metallic radium (1910), insulin (1921), penicillin (1928), polio vaccine (1955), and many other public health victories.

In those same years of the 20th century, a great deal of fundamental research about child development, growth, and learning has taken place. Just as no sensible person would want to bypass the burgeoning medical knowledge of the 20th century, none should ignore the wealth of information we now possess about children and youth.

Instead of BACK to basics we should hoist the banner FORWARD to fundamentals: Today's children will be the adults of the 21st, not the 18th, century! We owe them the kind of education that will prepare them for the years *ahead*, not the years *behind*.

FORWARD TO FUNDAMENTALS

What would take us ahead to fundamentals? The first fundamental is that *each child in unique*. Each child possesses different abilities, interests, talents, and ways of learning, and each child has her or his own pace. This is the immutable law of nature. Parents who have more than one child know this is so. Every research study confirms it.

The second fundamental is that *each child has a range of differences within*. An average mental age or an average IQ tells little. A high mental age score may be the result of excellent math skills, but only moderate language ability. Some children may have a lopsided mind, with very special ability in one field—music, science, mechanics, electronics—but not necessarily in others. Taylor, a researcher in creativity, said,

> The brain which underlies the mind is far too complex to hope that all of its intellectual activities can be represented by only a single score or by only a handful of dimensions. In fact it might be considered an insult to the brain and human mind to do so. (1961)

The third fundamental is that *learning that lasts is embedded in meaningful experiences*. Hess once said, "The meaning of deprivation is the deprivation of meaning" (1965). In the wonderful French film *Passion for Life*, the harried schoolboy trying to do well on his oral exam blurted out, "What I understood, I remember!"

Children who have followed their mail through the post office, who have greeted new giraffes at the zoo, and who have experienced farm life, will certainly find meaning in reading material portraying these areas of life. If children help count the money for a picnic, it they keep the class accounts for milk money, if they help turn in daily attendance records, they are learning that arithmetic has substance they can understand and use.

Feeling is also embedded in learning. Success is a great supporter of effort. Fun gives a lift to a job to be done. Happiness sets the glands to work. Confidence moves things steps ahead. Learnings underwritten by these feelings will endure and find their use in the years ahead.

The fourth fundamental is *a good teacher*. A person who likes people, especially children, is interested in them, intrigued by their ways of doing things, likes to watch them grow in mind and body, and enjoys their emerging accomplishments. A good teacher knows about the rough edges of growth, that children need help and guidance—that this is one reason for teachers. Early each year this good teacher takes all the time needed to get to know each child as an individual—listens carefully to her or his dreams, hopes, fears, and sizes up areas of strength and weakness, makes notes of these, and plans ways to meet the individual child's needs. This teacher uses ways of teaching that are truly diagnostic.

This wise teacher is sensitive to needs and values. The school day has peak experiences with rich feelings and deep meanings. There are moments of rare beauty in sharing poetry, music, dance, literature, dramatics. Time schedules are flexible to permit fleeting moments of high value to be enjoyed. Children are helped to know that some parts of life are more important than others. Time is the servant, not the master, in this teacher's day. Children feel good about seeing this teacher each day. So do parents.

The fifth fundamental is the *relationship between parents and teachers*. Real partnership comes when parent and teacher recognize that each has a role—vital but different—and that together they can accomplish more than just twice as much. They give the child the security of feeling that these important people in their lives are pulling together.

So let us resolve to help parents and children prepare for the *real and changing demands* of what is left of the 20th century and what may lie ahead in the 21st. Surely the one certainty for the years ahead is *change*. Let's build the fortitude to live with it.

DISCUSSION QUESTIONS

1. What is the most promising direction for the future?

2. Is history the best source of guidance for planning excellent programs for young children in the schools?

3. What are the fundamental qualities that must be present in any future program?

4. How can early childhood professionals provide a high-quality education now that will equip the child for effective living in the uncertain future?

67. THE FUTURE OF EDUCATION

by Wilson Riles

When asked about the future of public education in America, as I frequently am, I recall a story of a young lawyer being interviewed for a high-level position in a major corporation. "How much is two plus two?" asked the Chief Executive Officer in an obvious attempt to determine how the young applicant would handle a simple problem.

After getting up and locking the office door from the inside, the lawyer re-seated himself and leaning close to the CEO queried, "How much would you like it to be?"

There is an old saying among more cynical politicians that a democracy reflects the worst government a people will tolerate. This maxim may be applied to schools. When parents and the general public demand standards of excellence in their schools, and when they are willing to back that demand with full support *of* and involvement *in* their schools, then educators will know that nothing less than the best is acceptable. If, however, demands are minimal and scant support is provided, the future of public education will be dismal indeed. In short, it is we who determine the future of the schools.

Unfortunately, some uninformed individuals condemn public education as just one more expensive, failed and flawed governmental intrusion into private choice. They accept the charge of failure without examining the contrary evidence. They rush to find private sector alternatives—alternatives they propose to subsidize with public funds.

A BRIGHT FUTURE
FOR PUBLIC EDUCATION

The public school system is not, however, a failed or fatally flawed idea whose time has passed. In truth, the future of public education has never been brighter.

In the United States, schools now provide more education for a greater percentage of the population than ever before and the percentage of young people in school has increased dramatically. As recently as 1950, less than half of the youth graduated from high school; only 10 percent of blacks graduated. Slightly more than a quarter of a

See page 351 for acknowledgment.

century later, over 80 percent of the youth complete the 12th grade; the high school graduation rates for blacks have increased eightfold. The number of students who attend college, moreover, has doubled: not only the affluent, but the poor as well, are finding the doors of higher education open. Unquestionably, progress toward providing equality of access to public schools has enhanced the prospect of upward mobility in society.

Although increased numbers of children are being educated, the quality of educational attainment has not dropped. I say this notwithstanding much of the current rhetoric that would have us believe otherwise. Students today (including those less motivated who would have dropped out had they gone to school in an earlier era) score better on the identical reading tests given their counterparts in the 1940s.

I am always reminded of Will Rogers when I hear people bemoaning the diminution of quality in education. Rogers said, "Schools ain't what they used to be and they never wuz." Thousands of youngsters in previous generations were forced out of school because they did not fit into the system. Thousands more left because they fell behind, and few schools had programs designed to overcome their deficiencies. Still others, by the thousands, failed to complete even one year of high school because early in their lives teachers and administrators conveyed the message that little was expected of them.

We need only look at public school systems across the United States to know that the reasons for school failure are now recognized and are in the process of being eliminated. Schools are continuously adapting to the needs of society for socially and technologically literate citizens. America is still welcoming millions of immigrants lacking the basic skills required to function in an industrial or post-industrial society and, through the alchemy of the public school system, turning these immigrants into productive members of society.

Not all problems are solved. Not all reasons for failure have been eliminated. Not every school offers the quality of education we feel to be the right of each child. Beyond a doubt, however, changes are occurring—changes that will bring us closer to the goal of quality education with equality of access for every child.

To support the contention that public school systems are improving, I would like to cite a few of the outstanding shifts in school operation in California and the benefits accrued from those changes.

CALIFORNIA, A CASE IN POINT

Perhaps the most important new development in California's schools over the past decade is *parent involvement*. Since parents are the first and most continuous teachers of their children, they should have a place in the decision-making processes involving the education of their children. Ten years ago, they rarely had such a place; now they do.

The movement began in California in 1966 when the state pioneered in parent participation. We required schools with state or federal compensatory education programs to establish advisory committees composed of parents of disadvantaged children to advise the district's board of education. The federal government followed in our footsteps three or four years later with similar requirements. We expanded advisory committees by encouraging parents to volunteer as tutors and classroom aides. Bridging the moat that once surrounded the fortress called *the school*, we made the schools part of the community.

From this beginning, parent involvement expanded to include the parents of all children: first under Early Childhood Education (ECE) and now under the School Improvement Program (SIP). Over 60 percent of our schools have councils on which parents participate as equal partners with teachers in determining student needs and devising instructional strategies to meet them. Throughout the state, approximately 40,000 parents and community members currently serve on school site councils, and about 200,000 volunteers assist in the actual implementation of school improvement programs.

I lead my discussion of important changes in public education with parent involvement because I am convinced that parents are truly concerned about their children's growth and development, both preschool and in-school. They also usually know more about their children's needs than anyone else. When parents are involved and informed of the importance of appropriate "home start" activities for their children before they attend school, these children, in turn, succeed more readily in school. Children do better in school when

parents share responsibility for goal-setting in the schools their children attend.

Those critics who say that parents have no voice and no choice in the education their children receive simply have not been inside the rapidly evolving parent involvement movement, an important component of the success of California's school improvement program. Other states are moving in a similar direction.

The second most important development in making the future of public education bright is the renewed emphasis on *improving education in the early years*. In California we started our reform of public education nearly a decade ago with our ECE Program covering the primary years.

Briefly, for both philosophical and practical reasons we started where the children start. Philosophically, we were convinced that quality early childhood education addresses the critical years of a child's growth and development—the years before age 8, when 80 percent of that development takes place. Practically, we were convinced of two things:

• First, that programs for the disadvantaged, particularly ESEA Title I programs, penalized success because of the way they were funded (if children do well, funds are taken away). Further, they depended on the goodwill of the majority for meeting minority needs.

• Second, that children who failed to leave the 3rd grade with a solid foundation in the basic skills often did not recover from that failure regardless of extensive remediation received in the upper grades. It is simply more economical and more effective to give children the best start possible.

Our ECE Program reflected those practical considerations. Funding rewarded success. As each district started programs in limited numbers of schools, expansion to all schools was contingent upon the success of those first programs. No school lost funds because children learned. Programs were not limited to the disadvantaged minority. ECE covered all children in the school's primary grades—majority and minority, advantaged and disadvantaged. Success depended upon meeting every child's needs. All parents had an equal stake and voice in working as partners with teachers and administrators to plan and implement programs that focused on the learning needs of each child.

Achievement test results now reflect the wisdom of our decision to begin reforms by concentrating on early years education. Test scores for the primary grades have been increasing each year since the program's inception in 1973. Test scores at the 6th-grade level have likewise been increasing each year for the past five years, reflecting the sound foundation acquired in the K–3 grades. And for the past two years scores at the 12th-grade level have reversed the previous decline and are now moving up. Starting reform where the children start affects the entire system.

The success of our systemwide improvement efforts is based on the following principles:

- Parent involvement at the school-site level
- Inclusion of all children
- Focus on individual needs
- Identification of strengths and weaknesses of current programs
- Planned activities that build on strengths and correct weaknesses
- Evaluation of results
- Modification of activities that are not effective.

The School Improvement Program has fewer pupil restrictions but greater demands for formal school planning and parent involvement than the traditional programs experienced by previous generations of students. SIP schools reflect the working partnership between parents and teachers achieved by the establishment of school site councils that have legal program responsibility and ability to evaluate and remedy ineffective educational efforts.

Today's SIP schools reflect the public school system's capability of self-renewal. They respond to community values; they give parents that voice and choice they thought were available only in private schools. They demonstrate the old axiom: when people care enough to demand the very best, the very best is what they will attain.

The changes achieved in our public school system have stemmed from Californians' concern for public education. Californians have formed coalitions of diverse interest groups to lobby for legislative authority and funding for programs designed to make public schools better for all children. They have banded together to resist ballot measures that would erode school support. They have shown, year after year, that they would permit neither media criticism nor dwindling resources to kill the institution that made America a great nation. Because of the faith and the confidence of these concerned citizens, I know that the future of public education has never had brighter prospects.

IMPORTANT ISSUES

But I am all too aware that the criticism, deserved or not, will not diminish. Voucher systems, tuition tax measures and similar proposals to provide government subsidy to private schools are essentially proposals to eliminate public oversight of publicly supported education.

I strongly believe in a dual system of education, public and private. I think it would be wrong to weaken either. However, since public money has to be followed by regulation to ensure accountability, the ability of private schools to be masters of their own destiny would be impaired. No longer would they be able to innovate freely, to establish their own rules for admission or exclusion, and to teach particular moral and spiritual values.

Public schools, because they are public, provide youngsters with a common core of experience and education. Separating students into diverse private schools would only encourage schools to be socially, racially and philosophically isolated.

Both voucher schemes and tuition tax credits are costly endeavors. They would substantially reduce the amount of revenue available to support public education at a time when school support is barely adequate.

Moreover, I sense no real groundswell in the United States supportive of either tuition tax credits or educational vouchers. These ideas are being promoted by a few academic theorists and a few legislators. In fact, the only experiment with educational vouchers, undertaken in the Alum Rock district in California, proved a total failure. Furthermore, in instances where voucher system schemes have been placed before voters, the proposals have been overwhelmingly defeated. This occurred in Michigan and, most recently, in the District of Columbia where voters turned down a voucher proposal by a vote of 9 to 1. Even those parents with children in private or parochial schools voted 4 to 1 against the proposal. In California, a two-year effort by a group to raise money and secure signatures for a ballot proposal on vouchers was recently abandoned due to lack of citizen support.

I am optimistic about the future of public education because I believe that most parents want a strong, responsive, quality public education system for their children.

And in the end it will be exactly what they really want it to be.

DISCUSSION QUESTIONS

1. Is a comprehensive early education program essential to the future of the public schools in America?

2. How can school systems make changes to meet the dynamic needs of children and their families?

3. How did California respond to the need for early education in the schools?

4. What elements of success should be used in other situations to plan excellent early education programs?

68. EARLY SCHOOLING AND THE NATION'S FUTURE

by Ernest L. Boyer

For almost four years education has been high on the nation's agenda. Thirty governors have named school reform commissions, and legislators have enacted programs. The corporate sector has adopted schools. College presidents have spoken out for public education, and colleges and universities have raised graduation requirements. Districts have raised teacher salaries at twice the inflation rate. And public attitude toward teachers has turned around dramatically.

During these years, we've had more constructive action on behalf of public education than during any comparable period in recent memory. Still, I see a dark lining to the silver cloud. "Advantaged" schools are getting better, but many others—especially those in our major cities—remain deeply troubled institutions. These schools differ not just in degree, but in *kind*. The social pathologies that surround them are so great and the problems so complex that current efforts are inadequate to their needs.

EDUCATION AND POVERTY

Twenty years ago, this nation launched a crusade to improve urban education. The centerpiece of the plan was desegregation. Elaborate "remedies" were designed, and agonizing battles were fought out in the courts and sometimes in the streets. The crusade of the 1960s, which today is but a faded memory, has not been followed with new ideas, but with disillusionment and neglect.

In some city high schools on any given day, at least four out of ten students are absent. In Philadelphia the dropout rate is 38 percent; and in Boston it's 43 percent. Almost half of the Mexican-American and Puerto Rican students who enroll in our public high schools drop out before they receive a diploma. How are we to achieve excellence when students aren't even in the building?

In Chicago over half of the students failed to graduate in 1984, and only a third of those who did were reading at the twelfth-grade level. Last year, in the Cleveland Public Schools, there was not a single semifinalist in the National Merit Scholarship competition. Boston and Detroit each had only one high school with semifinalists.

What's disturbing about these statistics is that they show how little the school reform movement is confronting the core of our educational dilemma. An enormous gap separates rhetoric and results. The breakup of the home, communities wrenched by crime, poverty, and loss of good teachers threaten to overwhelm our most troubled schools. To require a failing student in an urban ghetto to take another unit in math or foreign language without offering a better environment or better teaching is like raising a hurdle for someone who has already stumbled without providing more coaching. And the problems are increasing.

By the year 2000 in America, one of every three public school pupils will be nonwhite. Approaching the educational system is a group of children who will be poorer and more ethnically and linguistically diverse, children who will have more handicaps that surely will affect their schooling. Unless we deepen our commitment, the crisis in urban education will increase. The gap will widen between the haves and the have-nots. Within our

See page 351 for acknowledgment.

major cities we will be left with an educational Third World. In these schools, the battle of American education will be won or lost. If urban schools do not become a national priority, the promise of excellence will remain sadly unfulfilled.

There are no panaceas. If there were obvious answers to the problems of urban education, we would have found them long ago. If failure is not to become a way of life for many urban youths, we must recognize that poverty and schooling are connected. What we see as poor academic performance may be related to events that precede schooling and even birth itself.

HUNGER AND BRAIN DEVELOPMENT

The growing fetus requires a diet rich in protein, vitamins, and minerals, and yet most poor mothers do not have adequate nutrition. Furthermore, the human brain grows most rapidly during the first year of life, and yet 40 percent of all persons in America today classified as poor are children. Malnutrition affects almost a half-million children in this nation.

The implications for schooling are dramatic. A major report by the Physicians Task Force on Hunger in America revealed that children who are deprived of adequate nutrition during the critical years of brain growth risk "cognitive deficits," which obviously restrict later learning. A recent Louisiana study compared poor children who had received food supplements during the first year of life and whose mothers had received nutritional support during pregnancy with children who were denied good nutrition. Those in the first group showed higher IQ, longer attention span, and better grades in school.

It is ironic that at the very time when better schools are being pushed, funds for federal child nutrition programs are restricted. Babies and poor health may appear to be disconnected from the school reform agenda, but the evidence to the contrary is overwhelming. Our educational problems cannot be divorced from the problems of the poor. If good schooling is our goal, all mothers and young children must have good nutrition.

LANGUAGE AND THE BASIC SCHOOL

We must give top priority to early education, especially to language. I propose that every school district, certainly those with high dropout rates, organize what might be called the Basic School, a unit that would include kindergarten through grade three.

The Basic School would make language—the sending and receiving of messages that makes us truly human—central. Language is imprinted in the genes, and by the time children march off to school, they are already linguistically empowered with a vocabulary of several thousand words. Any child who can speak and listen, I believe, can also be taught to read and write.

The goal of the Basic School would be to assure that every child reads with understanding, writes with clarity, and speaks and listens effectively. In a school saturated with rich language, children, from their first entry, would be speaking, writing, talking about words, listening to stories, and building a vocabulary. If a child is not linguistically empowered in the early years, it is almost impossible to compensate for the failure later on. It's like playing tennis with a broken racquet.

Further, the Basic School would blur rigid grade levels in the early years. It's foolish for teachers to fret over the curious question of whether to "fail" a student in grade one or two. Some children develop more slowly than others, and whether a student is in first grade or second grade is inconsequential. What is important is not the age, but each child's linguistic progress. The school would ensure that students would read and write with confidence and handle math accurately before they move to the next level, at which the focus would be on the core of common learning. This is the only way to assure that students in the upper grades will succeed academically.

CLASS SIZE AND RESULTS

In the Basic School, class size is also crucial. Primary school teachers sometimes have 30 or more students in a single class. Even under the best conditions these teachers can give only a minute or two to each child per hour. This is simply not enough. The State of Indiana recently compared the achievements of first-graders in large classes with those in classes with fewer than 20 students. The evidence was overwhelming: small classes bring more academic gains. Thus, this nation should move quickly to implement the recommendation of the recent report of the National Governors' Association, *Time for Results*, which advises one teacher for every 15 students in kindergarten through grade three.

Smaller classes mean more money, and recent polls show that Americans are willing to spend more for education if they feel the investment will pay off. Further, it's my own conviction that a good Basic School would reduce the cost of high school special and remedial education, which is expanding at an alarming rate. On the other hand, the recent High Scope study of the long-term impact of quality early education concluded that for every dollar invested, the payoff is more than four to one.

WORK AND THE SCHOOL CALENDAR

If we are to reorder national education priorities, we also must adjust the school schedule to changing family and work patterns. This national challenge goes far beyond the crisis of the poor. When today's school calendar was set almost a century ago, with nine months of study and three months off, over 90 percent of all school-age children were living on a farm with two parents, working hard, and staying home in the summer to tend the crops. The school calendar mirrored national work and family patterns.

Today, the world has turned upside down. Less than 3 percent of today's families are on farms. In most households both parents work away from home. Moreover, nearly one in five families is headed by a woman, two-thirds of whom work outside the home. About half the children now in first grade will have lived in one-parent homes by the time they graduate from high school.

I'm convinced that the school schedule needs to match both family and work patterns as it did 100 years ago. Already, because of the number of working parents, over 40 percent of the nation's children are in prekindergarten programs.

Increasingly schools will be called upon to provide prekindergarten sessions to serve young children who need care outside the home. In fact, the nation's governors, in their new report, urge states to provide quality early education for at-risk four-year-olds and "where possible" for three-year-olds as well. This recommendation touches real life.

Today, one out of ten children comes home to an empty house or apartment. And as this "latch-key" problem grows, schools should operate on a longer day, offering after-hour programs such as special studies in science, computers, music, or athletics, for example. I'm also convinced that we should lengthen the school calendar. A three-month summer recess is anachronistic now, especially at a time when most parents work outside the home year-round. Rather, we need an optional summer term for children, not for babysitting but

for learning. We cannot magically turn off children's needs when school is out.

THE EXTENDED SCHOOL

I see emerging prekindergarten programs, after-hour workshops, and summer sessions to fit what families and children need today. The danger is that affluent families will find their own summer camps, private lessons, and youth clubs, for example, while poor children will be allowed to drift.

In 1983, 53 percent of upper- and middle-income families had their preschool children in special programs, but only 29 percent of at-risk three- and four-year-olds were enrolled. If we are to narrow this gap, new enrichment programs— which I will call an Extended School—should be an option for all students, not just the privileged few. Families who can pay for these extra services should pay for them—at fees that will make the activities self-supporting.

For those who cannot afford the cost, I urge a state-financed plan that would give poor families a certificate of eligibility, linked to the federal Chapter 1 guidelines, to be redeemed at the preschool, after-school, or summer program of their choice. Several states provide a precedent for this procedure. New Jersey, Pennsylvania, and South Carolina have state-financed enrichment programs, in which the eligibility is based on Chapter 1. While these projects focus on remediation, the procedures could be applied to the Extended School as well.

Furthermore, financing this enrichment program jointly, through parent payment and through the state, would relieve local budgets and assure equity in public school financing. For the core school program, however, current funding patterns would be kept in place.

A school district that chose not to conduct enrichment programs internally could contract with a college, a youth club, local artists, or computer centers, for example. Most important, the enrichment programs would provide the option for children from all social and economic backgrounds, and perhaps from both public and private schools, to participate together.

LEARNING ABOUT INTELLIGENCE

In the days ahead it is urgently important that we find out more about how children learn. The attention we are giving to education has done little to teach us about learning, and we are still ignorant about how to measure the results. We have good schools and good teachers; but my optimism about the future of schooling is based on the conviction that, in the days ahead, we will become more knowledgeable about learning and about how we can assess the potential of all children.

The most exciting work, in my opinion, is being done by Howard Gardner at Harvard. Gardner, in his provocative and insightful book, *Frames of Mind*, reminds us that children not only have verbal intelligence, but they also have logical, mathematical, spatial, bodily, and personal intelligence. I suspect they have intuitive and social intelligence as well.

Gardner suggests that we should find ways to understand the many dimensions of intelligence in our children. Regrettably, paper-and-pencil tests focus on a limited range of verbal and computational skills, representing a meager sampling of selected words and numbers.

We need yardsticks to assure that our $140 billion annual investment in public schools is paying off. Tests are useful in providing a barome-ter of how well schools are doing, but our tests do not come close enough to individual children or provide teachers with sufficient information. By reducing students to numbers we may be telling children that they are failures before they've had a chance to discover what they might become.

If our goal is to educate all children, we must broaden our definition of "potential." We also must honor the full range of talent that contributes to our civility and, perhaps, to our survival, too. To achieve excellence in education we must confront the problems of poor children, give priority to early education, affirm the centrality of language, provide enrichment programs that reflect the changing work and family patterns of the nation, and learn more about how children learn.

As we move toward a new century, we must answer an urgent question: Will America continue to believe in education for all children, or will it separate winners from losers, educate them accordingly, and in so doing become a more divided nation?

DISCUSSION QUESTIONS

1. Is early childhood education an effective tool to address problems of poverty, health, and families?

2. What are the negative consequences to children, families, and society if comprehensive early education efforts are not implemented?

3. Does excellent early childhood education make a durable and continuing contribution to the child?

4. Can early childhood education programs contribute to the transformation of society?

ACKNOWLEDGMENTS, FOOTNOTES, AND REFERENCES

Section One: Historical Perspectives of Early Childhood Education

1. **Early Childhood Education's Past as Prologue: Roots of Contemporary Concerns, by Bernard Spodek, pp. 10–13.**
Young Children, July 1985, pp. 3–7. Copyright © 1985 by the National Association for the Education of Young Children. Reprinted with permission.

Clark, B. (1970). *The distinctive college: Antioch, Reed and Swarthmore,* Chicago: Aldine.

Kaestle, C.F., and Vinovskis, M.A. (1978). From apron strings to ABCs: Parents, children and schooling in nineteenth-century Massachusetts. In J. Demos, and S.S. Boocock (Eds.), *Turning points: Historical and sociological essays on the family. American Journal of Sociology Supplement, 84.*

May, D., and Vinovskis, M.A. (1977). A ray of millenial light: Early education and social reform in the infant school movement in Massachusetts, 1826–1840. In T. Harevan (Ed.), *Family and kin in urban communities, 1700-1930* (pp. 62–99). New York: New Viewpoints.

Mittenthal, S. (1982, November 11). A trend to more serious preschool subjects. *The New York Times*, p. C1.

Ross, E.D. (1976). *The kindergarten crusade.* Athens, OH: Ohio University Press.

Spodek, B. (1982). The kindergarten: A retrospective and contemporary view. In L. Katz (Ed.), *Currrent topics in early childhood education* (Vol. 4. pp. 173–191). Norwood, NJ: Ablex.

Strickland, C.E. (1982). Paths not taken: Seminal models of early childhood education in Jacksonian America. In B. Spodek (Ed.), *Handbook of research in early childhood education* (pp. 321–340). New York: Free Press.

Zigler, E., and Anderson, K. (1979). An idea whose time had come: The intellectual and political climate. In E. Zigler and J. Valentine (Eds.), *Project Head Start: A legacy of the war on poverty* (pp. 3–19). New York: Free Press.

2. **The European Roots of Early Childhood Education in North America, by Gary Woodill, pp. 14–22.**
International Journal of Early Childhood Education, vol. 18, no. 1, 1986, pp. 6–21. Copyright © 1986 by the *International Journal of Early Childhood Education*. Reprinted with permission.

Anderson, K. (1985). Commodity exchange and subordination: Montagnais-Naskapi and Huron women. *Signs: Journal of Women in Culture and Society,* 11(1), 48–62.

Aries, P. (1962). *Centuries of childhood: A social history of family life.* New York: Knopf.

Bagnell, K. (1980). *The little immigrants.* Toronto: MacMillan.

Braun, S. and Edwards, E. (1972). *History and theory of early childhood education.* Worthington, Ohio: Charles A. Jones.

Corbett, B. (1968). *The public school kindergarten in Ontario, 1883 to 1967.* Doctoral Thesis. Toronto: University of Toronto.

Cremin, L. (1970). *American education: The colonial experience, 1607-1783.* New York: Harper and Row.

Cubberly, E. (1920). *The history of education.* Boston: Houghton Mifflin.

Deasy, D. (1978). *Education under six.* London: Croom Helm.

deMause, L. (1974). *The history of childhood.* New York: The Psychohistory Press.

Elkind, D. (1970). The case for the academic preschool: Fact or fiction? *Young Children,* 25, 132–139.

Elkind, D. (1976). *Child development and education: A Piagetian perspective.* New York: Oxford University Press.

Evans, B. and Waites, B. (1981). *IQ and mental testing: An unnatural science and its social history.* Atlantic Highlands, New Jersey: Humanities Press.

Fein, G. and Clarke-Stewart, A. (1973). *Day care in context.* New York: John Wiley.

Kamin, L. (1974). *The science and politics of I.Q.* New York: John Wiley.

Kuhn, T. (1967). *The structure of scientific revolutions.*

Chicago: University of Chicago Press.

Kurtz, J. (1976). *John Frederic Oberlin.* Boulder, Colorado: Westview Press.

Munroe, W. (1907). *History of the Pestalozzian movement in the United States.* Syracuse, N.Y.: C. W. Bardeen.

Omwake, E. (1971). Preschool programs in historical perspective. *Interchange,* 2(2), 27–40.

Osborn, D. K. (1980). *Early childhood education in historical perspective.* Athens, GA: Education Associates.

Pollock, L. (1984). *Forgotten children: Parent-child relations from 1500 to 1900.* Cambridge University Press.

Postman, N. (1982). *The disappearance of childhood.* New York: Dell Publishing.

Quiney, L. (1982). *A Canadian orphanage in the nineteenth century: The orphan's home of the City of Ottawa, 1864-1893.* Master's Thesis. Toronto: University of Toronto.

Rooke, P. and Schnell, R. L. (1983). *Discarding the asylum: From Child Rescue to the Welfare State in English-Canada (1800-1950).* Lanham, MD: University Press of America.

Ross, E. (1976). *The kindergarten crusade: The establishment of preschool education in the United States.* Athens, Ohio: Ohio University Press.

Schulz, P. (1978). Day care in Canada: 1850–1962. In Kathleen Gallagher Ross (Ed.), *Good day care.* Toronto: Women's Press.

Shapiro, M. (1983). *Child's garden: The kindergarten movement from Froebel to Dewey.* University Park, PA: Pennsylvania State University Press.

Steinfels, M. (1973). *Who's minding the children: The history and politics of day care in America.* New York: Simon and Shuster.

Vandewalker, N. (1971). *The kindergarten in American edu-*

cation. New York: Arno Press.

Weber, E. (1969). *The kindergarten: Its encounter with educational thought in America*. New York: Teachers' College Press.

Weber, E. (1970). *Early childhood education: Perspectives on change*. Worthington, Ohio: Charles A. Jones.

Young, R. (1932). *Comenius in England*. London: Oxford University Press (Reprinted by Arno Press, New York, 1971).

3. A Mini-History of Early Childhood Education, by Blythe F. Hinitz, pp. 23–24.

Young World, vol. 19, Winter-Spring 1981. Copyright © by the New Jersey Association for the Education of Young Children. Reprinted with permission.

For Further Reading on the History of Early Childhood Education

Braun and Edwards. *History and Theory of Early Childhood Education*. Worthington, Ohio: Charles A. Jones Publishing Company, 1972.

Greenleaf, Barbara. *Children Through the Ages*. New York: Barnes and Noble, 1978.

Grotberg, Edith. *200 Years of Children*. Washington, D.C.: U.S. Department of Health, Education and Welfare, 1977.

Osborn, D. Keith. *Early Childhood Education in Historical Perspective*. Athens, Georgia: Education Associates, 1975.

Snyder, Agnes. *Dauntless Women in Childhood Education*. Washington, D.C.: Association for Childhood Education International, 1972.

Weber, Evelyn. *The Kindergarten, Its Encounter with Educational Thought in America*. New York: Teachers College Press, 1969.

Early Childhood Texts with Excellent Chapters on the History of Early Education

Maxim, George. *The Very Young: Guiding Children from Infancy through the Early Years*. Belmont, Calif.: Wadsworth Publishing Company, 1980.

Morrison, George S. *Early Childhood Education Today*, 2d Edition. Columbus, Ohio: Charles Merrill Publishing Company, 1980.

Seefeldt, Carol. *Teaching Young Children*. Englewood Cliffs, N.J.: Prentice-Hall, 1980.

4. The Kindergarten in Historical Perspective, by S. Dianne Lawler and Jerold P. Bauch, pp. 25–28.

Bartolini, L., and Wasem, L. *The Kindergarten Curriculum*. Illinois State Board of Education. Springfield: Illinois State Board of Education, 1985. ED 260 832.

Belgrad, S. "Teacher and Parent Roles in the Development of Kindergarten Curriculum." *Illinois School Research and Development* 20 (1984): 7–8.

Bloom, B. *All Our Children Learning*. New York: McGraw Hill, 1981.

Cruikshank, S. "The All-Day Kindergarten Curriculum: What Does 'More' Mean?" *Early Years* 16 (1986): 33–35.

Davis, H. "Reading Pressures in the Kindergarten." *Childhood Education* 57 (1980): 76–79.

Elkind, D. *The Hurried Child*. New York: Addison-Wesley, 1981.

Elkind, D. *Miseducation: Preschoolers at Risk*. New York: Knopf, 1987.

Etheridge, G. "Should Education for the Young Child Focus on the Whole Child or on Specific Skills?" *Tennessee Educational Leadership* 13 (1986): 23–25.

Federlein, A. "Kindergarten—to Read or Not to Read." *Eastern Educational Journal* 16 (1984): 23–25.

Gullo, D.; Bersani, C.; Bayless, K.; and Clements, D. "All-Day Kindergarten Makes a Difference: The Effects of Three Kindergarten Schedules on Academic Achievement and Classroom Social Behaviors." Paper presented at the Annual Conference of the National Association for Education of Young Children, New Orleans, 1985.

Hewes, D. "Compensatory Early Childhood Education: Froebelian Origins and Outcomes." Bethesda, Md.: ERIC Document Reproduction Service, 1985. ED 264 980.

Hewes, D. "Looking Backward: Fascinating Facts About ECE in the 1800's." *National Association of Early Childhood Teacher Educators Bulletin* 26 (1987): 9–19.

Lawler, D. "A Comparative Study of Kindergarten and First-Grade Teachers' Use of Instructional Time." Doctoral dissertation, Vanderbilt University, Nashville, Tennessee, 1987.

Lazerson, M. *Origins of the Urban School: Public Education in Massachusetts, 1870–1915*. Cambridge: Harvard University Press, 1971.

Naron, N. "The Need for Full-Day Kindergarten." *Educational Leadership* 38 (1981): 306–9.

Ransbury, M. "Friedrich Froebel, 1782–1982." *Childhood Education* 59 (1982): 104–5.

Seefeldt, C. "Tomorrow's Kindergarten: Pleasure or Pressure." *Principal* 64 (1985): 12–15.

Sheehy, E. *The 5s and 6s Go to School*. New York: Henry Holt, 1954.

Snyder, A. *Dauntless Women in Early Childhood Education, 1856–1931*. Washington, D.C.: Association for Early Childhood Education International, 1972.

Spodek, B. "The Kindergarten: A Retrospective and Contemporary View." Bethesda, Md.: ERIC Document Reproduction Service, 1981. ED 206 375.

Vandewalker, N. *The Kindergarten in American Education*. New York: Macmillan, 1908.

Washington, V. "Trends in Early Childhood Education." *Dimensions* 16 (1988): 4–7.

Webber, D. "How Are Today's Children Different from Yesterday's?" *Tennessee Educational Leadership* 13 (1986): 13–16.

Webster, N. "The 5s and 6s Go to School Revisited." *Childhood Education* 45 (1984): 325–30.

Werner, L. "A View of Today's Kindergarten Across the United States." *Illinois School Research and Development* 20 (1984): 1–2.

Section Two: Policy Decisions About Present and Future Issues

5. Policy Options for Preschool Programs, by Lawrence J. Schweinhart, Jeffrey J. Koshel, and Anne Bridgman, pp. 30–35.
Phi Delta Kappan, vol. 68, no. 7, March 1987, pp. 524–29. Copyright © 1987 by Lawrence J. Schweinhart. Reprinted with permission.

1. For more detail on the issues treated in this [chapter] and for a description of the early childhood initiatives in specific states, see Lawrence J. Schweinhart and Jeffrey J. Koshel, *Policy Options for Preschool Programs* (Ypsilanti, Mich.: High/Scope Early Childhood Policy Papers, No. 5, published in collaboration with the National Governors' Association, 1986).

2. *Investing in Our Children* (New York: Research and Policy Committee of the Committee for Economic Development, 1985).

3. This editorial appears in a collection of material titled *The American Millstone* (Chicago: Contemporary Books, Inc., 1986), p. 297.

4. *The Crisis in Infant and Toddler Care* (Washington, D.C.: Ad Hoc Day Care Coalition, 1985).

5. Lawrence J. Schweinhart and David P. Weikart, *Young Children Grow Up: The Effects of the Perry Preschool Program on Youths Through Age 15* (Ypsilanti, Mich.: High/Scope Press, 1980).

6. John R. Berrueta-Clement, Lawrence J. Schweinhart, W. Steven Barnett, Ann S. Epstein, and David P. Weikart, *Changed Lives: The Effects of the Perry Preschool Program on Youths Through Age 19* (Ypsilanti, Mich.: High/Scope Press, 1984).

7. *Meeting the National Mandate: Chicago's Government-Funded Kindergarten Programs, Fiscal 1984* (Chicago: Department of Research and Evaluation, Chicago Public Schools, 1985).

8. *Draft Statement on Compensation and Affordability* (Washington, D.C.: National Association for the Education of Young Children, 1986); and Craig Coelen et al., *Day Care Centers in the U.S.: A National Profile, 1976-77* (Cambridge, Mass.: Final Report of the National Day Care Study, Vol. III, Abt Associates, 1978).

9. *Analysis of the FY 1987 Federal Budget for Children* (Washington, D.C: Children's Defense Fund, 1986), p. 355.

10. Unpublished data from the Bureau of Labor Statistics, U.S. Department of Labor, based on the March 1985 Current Population Survey.

11. Richard Ruopp, Jeffrey Travers, Frederick Glantz, and Craig Coelen, *Children at the Center: Summary Findings and Their Implications* (Cambridge, Mass.: Final Report of the National Day Care Study, Vol. I, Abt Associates, 1979).

12. James L. Hymes, Jr., *Early Childhood Education: The Year in Review: A Look at 1985* (Carmel, Calif.: Hacienda Press, 1986)

13. Lawrence J. Schweinhart, David P. Weikart, and Mary B. Larner, "Consequences of Three Preschool Curriculum Models on Youths Through Age 15," *Early Childhood Research Quarterly* (Norwood, N.Y.: Ablex Publishing Corporation, 1986).

14. Hymes, *Early Childhood Education: The Year in Review....*

15. Of the 452,300 children who were served by Head Start in 1985, at least 90% (407,070) met poverty guidelines. But those 407,070 children accounted for only 24% of the 1,702,000 preschoolers who were living in poverty in the U.S., according to a 1984 Current Population Survey.

6. Early Childhood Development Programs: A Public Investment Opportunity, by Lawrence J. Schweinhart and David P. Weikart, pp. 36–43.
Educational Leadership, vol. 44, no. 3, November 1986, pp. 4–12. Reprinted with permission of the Association for Supervision and Curriculum Development and Lawrence J. Schweinhart and David P. Weikart. Copyright © 1986 by the Association for Supervision and Curriculum Development. All rights reserved.

Barnett, W. Steven. *The Perry Preschool Program and Its Long-Term Effects: A Benefit-Cost Analysis.* High/Scope Early Childhood Policy Papers, No. 2, Ypsilanti, Mich.: High/Scope Press, 1985.

Berrueta-Clement, John R., Lawrence J. Schweinhart, W. Steven Barnett, Ann S. Epstein, and David P. Weikart. *Changed Lives: The Effects of the Perry Preschool Program on Youths through Age 19.* (Monographs of the High/Scope Educational Research Foundation, 8.) Ypsilanti, Mich.: High/Scope Press, 1984.

Congressional Research Service and Congressional Budget Office. *Children in Poverty.* Washington, D.C.: U.S. Government Printing Office, 1985.

Consortium for Longitudinal Studies. *As the Twig Is Bent ...Lasting Effects of Preschool Programs.* Hillsdale, N.J.: Lawrence Erlbaum Associates, 1983.

Education Commission of the States, National Assessment of Educational Progress. *The Third National Mathematics Assessment: Results, Trends, and Issues.* Denver: Education Commission of the States, 1983.

Elliott, D. S., S. S. Ageton, and R. J. Canter. "An Integrated Theoretical Perspective on Delinquent Behavior." *Journal of Research in Crime and Delinquency* 16 (January 1979).

Epstein, Ann S., Gwen Morgan, Nancy Curry, Richard C. Endsley, Marilyn R. Bradbard, and Hakim M. Rashid. *Quality in Early Childhood Programs: Four Perspectives.* (High/Scope Early Childhood Policy Papers, No. 3.) Ypsilanti, Mich.: High/Scope Press, 1985.

Guttmacher Institute. *Teenage Pregnancy: The Problem That Hasn't Gone Away.* New York: Guttmacher, 1981.

Hill, Martha S., and Michael Ponza. "Poverty and Welfare Dependence Across Generations." *Economic Outlook USA.* Institute for Social Research (Summer 1983): 61.

Hohmann, Mary, Bernard Banet, and David P. Weikart. *Young Children in Action: A Manual for Preschool Educators.* Ypsilanti, Mich.: High/Scope Press, 1979.

Hymes, James L., Jr. *Early Childhood Education: The Year in Review: A Look at 1985.* Carmel, Calif.: Hacienda Press, 1986.

Lazar, Irving, Richard Darlington, Harry Murray, Jacqueline Royce, and Ann Snipper. "Lasting Effects of Early Education.'' (Monographs of the Society for Research in Child Development, 47) (1-2, Serial No. 194, 1982).

Loeber, Rolf, and T. Dishion. ''Early Predictors of Male Delinquency: A Review.'' *Psychological Bulletin* 94, 1 (1983).

McKey, Ruth H., L. Condelli, H. Ganson, B. Barrett, C. McConkey, and M. Plantz. *The Impact of Head Start on Children, Families and Communities* (Final Report of the Head Start Evaluation, Synthesis and Utilization Project). Washington, D.C.: CSR, Inc., 1985.

Meisels, Samuel J. *Developmental Screening in Early Childhood: A Guide.* Rev. ed. Washington, D.C.: National Association for the Education of Young Children, 1985.

National Center for Education Statistics. *The Condition of Education: 1985 Edition.* Washington, D.C.: U.S. Government Printing Office, 1985.

National Center for Education Statistics. *Preprimary Enrollment 1980.* Washington, D.C.: National Center for Education Statistics, 1982.

National Center for Education Statistics. *Two Years in High School: The Status of 1980 Sophomores in 1982.* Washington, D.C.: National Center for Education Statistics, 1983.

Pierson, Donald E., Deborah Klein Walker, and Terrence Tivnan. ''A School-Based Program from Infancy to Kindergarten for Children and Their Parents.'' *The Personnel and Guidance Journal* (April 1984): 448-455.

Roopnarine, Jaipaul L. and James E. Johnson, eds. *Educational Models for Young Children.* Columbus, Ohio: Charles E. Merrill Co., in press.

Ruopp, Richard, Jeff Travers, F. Glantz, and Craig Coelen. *Children at the Center: Summary Findings and Their Implications* (Final Report of the National Day Care Study, Volume 1). Cambridge, Mass.: Abt Associates, 1979.

Schweinhart, Lawrence J., *Early Childhood Development Programs in the Eighties: The National Picture.* (High/Scope Early Childhood Policy Papers, No. 1) Ypsilanti, Mich.: High/Scope Press, 1985.

Schweinhart, Lawrence J., and David P. Weikart. *Young Children Grow Up: The Effects of the Perry Preschool Program on Youths Through Age 15.* (Monographs of the High/Scope Educational Research Foundation, 7.) Ypsilanti, Mich.: High/Scope Press, 1980.

Schweinhart, Lawrence J., David P. Weikart, and Mary B. Larner. ''Consequences of Three Preschool Curriculum Models through Age 15.'' *Early Childhood Research Quarterly* 1. 1 (1986): 15-45.

U.S. Bureau of the Census. *Child Care Arrangements of Working Mothers: June 1982* (Current Population Reports, Series P-23, No. 129). Washington, D.C.: U.S. Government Printing Office, 1983.

U.S. Bureau of the Census. *Money Income and Poverty Status of Families and Persons in the United States: 1983.* (Current Population Reports. Series P60, No. 145.) Washington, D.C.: U.S. Government Printing Office, 1984.

U.S. Bureau of the Census. *School Enrollment—Social and Economic Characteristics of Students: October 1984 (Advance Report.)* (Current Population Reports, Series P-20, No. 404.) Washington, D.C.: U.S. Government Printing Office, 1985.

Weikart, David P., Ann S. Epstein, Lawrence J. Schweinhart, and James T. Bond. *The Ypsilanti Preschool Curriculum Demonstration Project: Preschool Years and Longitudinal Results.* (Monographs of the High/Scope Educational Research Foundation, 4.) Ypsilanti, Mich.: High/Scope Press, 1978.

7. Quality: The Key to Successful Programs, by Daniel S. Cheever, Jr., and Anne E. Ryder, pp. 44-47.
Principal, vol. 65, no. 5, May 1986, pp. 18-21. Copyright © 1986, National Association of Elementary School Principals. All rights reserved.

Section Three: Issues, Trends, and Directions

8. Trends in Early Childhood Education—Part I: Demographics, by Valora Washington, pp. 51-55.
Dimensions, January 1988, pp. 4-7. © 1988, Southern Association on Children Under Six, Little Rock, Arkansas. Reprinted with permission.

AAAS (American Association for the Advancement of Science). (1982). *Children: An Invisible Constituency.* Washington, D.C.: AAAS.

Baltes, P. and Brim, O. *Lifespan Development and Behavior, Vols. 1-4.* (1978-82). New York: Academic Press.

Berrueta-Clement, J., Schweinhart, L. J., Barnett, W. S., Epstein, A. S., and Weikart, D. P. (1984). *Changed Lives. The Effects of the Perry Preschool Program on Youths Through Age 19.* Ypsilanti, Michigan: High Scope Educational Research Foundation.

CDF (Children's Defense Fund). (1982). *America's Children and Their Families: Key Facts.* Washington, D.C.: CDF.

CDF (Children's Defense Fund). (1985). *Black and White Children in America.* Washington, D.C.: CDF.

Cole, O. J. and Washington, V. (In Press). Head Start: A critical analysis of the assessment of the effects of Head Start on minority children. *Journal of Negro Education.*

Cunningham, C. E. and Osborn, D. K. (1979, March). An historical examination of blacks in early childhood education. *Young Children,* 34, 20-29.

Elder, G. H., Jr. (1979). Historical change in life patterns and personality. In P. Baltes and O. Brim. *Life Span Development and Behavior, Vol. 2.* New York: Academic Press.

Feistritzer, C. E. (1985, July 16). A new baby boomlet hits the schools. *The Washington Post,* Cl.

Hale, J. (1982). *Black Children: Their Roots, Culture and Learning Styles.* Provo, Utah: Brigham Young University Press.

Hartman, K. (1977, March). How do I teach in a future shocked world? *Young Children,* 32, 32-36.

Jones, E. and Prescott, E. (1982, May). Day care: Short- or long-term solution? *The Annals of the American Academy of Political and Social Science,* 461, 91-101.

Laosa, L. M. (1984). Social policies toward children of diverse ethnic, racial, and language groups in the United States. In H. W. Stevenson and A. E. Siegel (Eds.) *Child Development Research and Social Policy.* Chicago: The University of Chicago Press, 1-109.

Machado, J. M. and Meyer, H. C. (1984). *Early Childhood Practicum Guide.* Albany, N.Y.: Delmar Publishers.

ACKNOWLEDGMENTS, FOOTNOTES, AND REFERENCES

McNett, I. (1983). *Demographic Imperatives: Implications for Educational Policy*. Washington, D.C.: American Council on Education.

NEA (National Education Association). (1985). *Estimates of School Statistics, 1985*. Stock No. 3100–8–00, P.O. Box 509, West Haven, CT.: NEA Professional Library.

Ornstein, A. C. (1982). What are we teaching in the 1980's? *Young Children, 38*, (1), 12–17.

U.S. Department of Commerce, Bureau of the Census. (1976). *Statistical Abstracts of the United States*. Washington, D.C.: U.S. Government Printing Office, 6.

U.S. Department of Health and Human Services, Office of Human Development Services. (1980). *The Status of Children, Youth and Families, 1979*. Washington, D.C.: U.S.

Government Printing Office, 5.

Washington, V. (1976). Learning racial identity. In R. C. Granger and J. C. Young (Eds.). *Demythologizing the Inner City Child* (PP 85-98). Washington, D.C.: National Association for the Education of Young Children.

Washington, V. (1982). Implementing multicultural education: Elementary teachers' attitudes and professional practice. *Peabody Journal of Education, 59* (3), 190–200.

Washington, V. (1985). Social policy, cultural diversity and the obscurity of Black children. *Journal of Educational Equity and Leadership*. (In Press).

Washington, V., and Oyemade, U. J. (1984). Employer-sponsored child care: A movement or a mirage? *Journal of Home Economics, 76* (4), 11–19.

9. Trends in Early Childhood Education—Part II: Instruction, by Valora Washington, pp. 56–59.
Dimensions, April 1988, pp. 4–7. © 1988, Southern Association on Children Under Six, Little Rock, Arkansas. Reprinted with permission.

Ade, W. (1982, March). Professionalism and its implications for the field of early childhood education. *Young Children, 37* (3) 25–32.

Almy, M. (1975). *The Early Childhood Educator at Work*. New York: McGraw-Hill.

Almy, M. (1982). An early childhood education care research agenda. Paper presented at the Annual Conference of the National Association of the Education of Young Children. Washington, D.C.

Almy, M. (1985, July) Letter to the editor. *Young Children, 40* (5), 2, 20.

Ames, L. B. and Chase, J. A. (1980). *Don't Push Your Preschooler*. New York: Harper and Row.

Atkin, M. J. (1980). The government in the classroom. *Daedelus, 109*(3) 85–87.

Barbour, A. and the Editors. (1984, October). Computing in America's classrooms. *Electronic Learning, 4*(2), 29–44; 100.

Berkman, D. (1972). The myth of educational technology. *The Educational Forum, 36*(14), 451–460.

Blank, H. (1985, May) Early childhood and the public schools: An essential partnership. *Young Children, 40*(4), 52–55.

Bracey, G. W. (1985, Jan.). Computer, computer, who's got the computer? *Phi Delta Kappan, 66*(5), 376–377.

Bronfenbrenner, U. (1979). *The Ecology of Human Development*. Cambridge, Mass.: Harvard University Press.

Brookover, W. B. (1985). Can we make schools effective for minority students? *Journal of Negro Education 54*(3), 257–268.

Caldwell, B. (1984, March). What is quality child care? *Young Children, 39*(3), 3–13.

CDF (Children's Defense Fund). (1982). *America's Children and Their Families: Key Facts*. Washington, D.C.: CDF.

CDF (Children's Defense Fund). (1985). *Black and White Children in America*. Washington, D.C.: CDF.

Elkind, D. (1970). The case for the academic preschool: Fact or Fiction? *Young Children, 25* (3), 132–140.

Elkind, D. (1981, July). Child development and early childhood education: Where do we stand today? *Young Children, 36*(5), 2–9.

Elkind, D. (1982). *The Hurried Child: Growing Up Too Fast, Too Soon*. Addison-Wesley Publishing Co., Inc.

Haiman, P. E. (1984, Nov.). There is more to early childhood education than cognitive development. *Young Children, 40*(1) 8.

Hostetler, L. and Klugman, E. (1982, September). Early childhood job titles: one step toward professional status. *Young Children, 37*(6), 13–22.

Hyson, M. C. (1982, Jan.). Playing with kids all day: Job stress and early childhood education. *Young Children, 37*(2), 25–32.

Joffe, C. (1977). *Friendly Intruders*. Berkeley, Calif.: University of California Press.

Joyce, B. R., Bush, R. N., and McKibbin, M. D. (1981). *Information and Opinion from the California Staff Development Study*. Sacramento: California State Department of Education.

Joyce, B. and Clift, R. (1984). The Phoenix Agenda: Essential reform in teacher education. *Educational Researcher, 13*(4), 5–18.

Katz, L. (1977). *Talks with Teachers*. Washington, D.C.: National Association for the Education of Young Children.

Leeper, S. H., Witherspoon, R. L., and Day, B. (1984). *Good Schools for Young Children. 5th Edition*. N.Y.: Macmillan Publishing Co.

Lezotte, L. W. and Bancroft, B. A. (1985). School improvement based on effective schools research: A promising approach for economically disadvantaged and minority students. *Journal of Negro Education, 54*(3), 301–312.

Lightfoot, S. (1978). *Worlds Apart*. New York: Basic Books.

Machado, J. M. and Meyer, H. C. (1984). *Early Childhood Practicum Guide*. Albany, N.Y.: Delmar Publishers.

May, D. and Vinovskis, M. A. (1977). A ray of millenial light: Early education and social reform in the infant school movement in Massachusetts, 1826-1840. In T. Hareven (Ed.), *Family and Kin in Urban Communities, 1700-1930* (pp. 62-99). New York: New Viewpoints.

McPhail, I. P. (1985). Computer inequities in school uses of microcomputers: policy implications. *Journal of Negro Education, 54*(1), 3–13.

Mittenthal, S. (1982, Nov. 11). A trend to more serious preschool subjects. *The New York Times*, Cl.

Morrison, G. S. (1984). *Early Childhood Education Today*. 3rd edition. Columbus, Ohio: Charles E. Merrill Publishing Company.

Morse, S. (1985, August 27). All-day kindergarten gaining popularity amid debate. *The Washington Post*, C5.

Moursund, D. (1981). *Teachers' Guide to Computers in the Elementary School*. Eugene, Oregon: International Council for Computers in Education.

NAEYC (National Association for the Education of Young Children). (1984, November). NAEYC Position Statement on Nomenclature, Salaries, Benefits, and the Status of the Early Childhood Profession. *Young Children, 40*, 52–59.

Nimnicht, G. (1981, September). Back to the basics: More loving, tender care for young children. *Young Children, 36* (6), 4–11.

Ornstein, A. C. (1982). What are we teaching in the 1980's? *Young Children, 38*(1), 12–17.

Phillips, D., Editor. (1984). Continuity of care. A guide for social programs. *International Journal of Mental Health, 12* (4), 1–86.

Pipho, C. (1985, June). The excellence movement: On ice for the summer? *Phi Delta Kappan, 66*(10), 669–670.

Postman, N. (1982). *The Disappearance of Childhood*. N.Y.: Delacorte Press.

Reingold, F. (1985, Feb.) Sorting out the equity issues.

Electronic Learning, 4(5), 33–37.

Sava, S. G. (1985, March). Signs of life. *Young Children, 40* (3), 9–10.

Schlecty, P. C. and Vance, V. S. (1982). The distribution of academic ability in the teaching force: Policy implications. *Phi Delta Kappan, 64*(1), 22–27.

School Tech News. (1984, Oct.) "Writing to Read" rel. Wins high praise, 2(2), 1.

Silen, J. G. (1985). Authority as knowledge: A problem of professionalization. *Young Children, 40*(3), 41–46.

Sizemore, B. A. (1985). Pitfalls and promises of effective schools research. *Journal of Negro Education, 54*(3), 269–288.

Stevens, J. H. and King, E. W. (1976). *Administering Early Childhood Education Programs*. Boston: Little, Brown and Co.

Tucker, A. and Mautz, R. B. (1984). Solving the teacher education problem: A university-wide obligation. *Educational Record*, Vol. 65(2), 34–37.

Williams, L. R. (1985). Review of Handbook of research in early childhood education. Bernard Spoder, Ed. *Teachers College Record, 86*(1), 251–253.

Zigler, E. and Valentine, J. (Eds.) (1979). *Project Head Start: A Legacy of the War on Poverty*. New York: Free Press.

10. Early Childhood Education: Issues and Trends, by Paula Jorde, pp. 60–64.
The Educational Forum, vol. 50, no. 2, Winter 1986, pp. 171–81. Copyright 1986 by Kappa Delta Pi, an International Honor Society in Education. Reprinted with permission.

1. Burton White, The First Three Years of Life (Englewood Cliffs, N.J.: Prentice-Hall, 1975); J. McV. Hunt, *Intelligence and Experience* (New York: Ronald Press, 1961); Benjamin Bloom, *Stability and Change in Human Characteristics* (New York: Wiley, 1964); F.D. Horowitz, ed., *Review of Child Development Research* (Chicago: University of Chicago Press, 1975); John Berrueta-Clement, Lawrence Schweinhart, William Barnett, Ann Epstein, and David Weikart, *Changed Lives* (Ypsilanti, Michigan: High/Scope Research Foundation, 1984).

2. Urie Bronfenbrenner, "The Changing Family in a Changing World: America First?" *Peabody Journal of Education* 61 (Spring 1984): 52–70; Ellen Galinsky *The New Extended Family* (Boston: Houghton Mifflin, 1977); Kenneth Keniston, *All Our Children: The American Family under Pressure* (New York: Harcourt Brace Jovanovich, 1978).

3. Greta Fein and Allison Clarke-Stewart, *Day Care in Context* (New York; John Wiley and Sons, 1973); Urie Bronfenbrenner, *The Ecology of Human Development* (Cambridge, Mass: Harvard University Press, 1979).

4. Edward Zigler and Edmund Gordon, *Day Care: Scientific and Social Policy Issues* (Boston: Auburn House, 1982).

5. Sheila B. Kamerman, *Child Care: Options for the 80's* (New York: The Association of Junior Leagues, 1982).

6. Robert Halpern, "Assuring Quality Early Childhood Services," *Child Welfare* 61 (June 1982): 325–340.

7. Helen Blank, *Child Care: The States' Response* (Washington, D.C.: Children's Defense Fund, 1984).

8. Ibid.

9. Sharon Kagan and Roger Neugebauer, "What's Ahead: Directors Speak about the Future of Child Care," *Child Care Information Exchange* (January 1984): 15–18; "What Price Day Care?" *Newsweek* (September 10, 1984): 14–21; "Chal-

lenges of the 80's," *U.S. News and World Report* (October 15, 1979): 45–80; M. Cetron and T. O'Toole, *Encounters with the Future: A Forecast of Life into the Twenty-First Century* (New York: McGraw-Hill, 1982); Lawrence J. Schweinhart, *Early Childhood Development Programs in the Eighties: The National Picture* (Ypsilanti, Michigan: High/Scope Press, 1985).

10. Marce Verzaro-Lawrence, Denise LeBlanc, and Charles Hennon, "Industry-Related Day Care: Trends and Options," *Young Children* (January 1982): 4–10; Dana Friedman, *Encouraging Employer Support To Working Parents* (New York Center for Public Advocacy Research, 1981); Kathleen Perry, *Employers and Child Care: Establishing Services Through the Workplace* (Washington, D.C.: U.S. Department of Labor, Women's Bureau, 1982).

11. "Day Care," *Newsweek*, p. 20.

12. S. Fosburg, *Family Day Care in the United States* (Washington, D.C.: U.S. Department of Health and Public Services, 1981).

13. Helen Blank, "Early Childhood Education and the Public Schools," *Young Children* (May 1985): 52–55.

14. Eileen Linder, Mary Mattis, and J. Rogers, *When Churches Mind the Children* (Ypsilanti, Michigan: High/Scope Press, 1983).

15. Ibid.

16. "Day Care," *Newsweek*.

17. Blank, *Child Care*.

18. Bettye Caldwell and Asa Hilliard, III, *What is Quality Child Care?* (Washington, D.C.: National Association for the Education of Young Children, 1985).

19. Jane Stallings and Mary Wilcox, "Quality of Day Care: Can It Be Measured?" in *Child Care and Public Policy*, eds., Philip Robins and Samuel Weiner (New York: Lexington

Books, 1978).

20. National Association for the Education of Young Children, *Accreditation Criteria and Procedures* (Washington, D.C.: National Association for the Education of Young Children, 1984).

21. David Elkind, *The Hurried Child* (Reading, Mass.: Addison-Wesley, 1981); Mary Miller, *Childstress* (Garden City, N.Y.: Doubleday, 1982); Neil Postman, *The Disappearance of Childhood* (New York: Delacorte, 1982).

22. Richard Roupp, *Children at the Center* (Cambridge, Mass.: Abt, 1979).

23. Paula Jorde, *Avoiding Burnout in Early Childhood Education* (Washington, D.C.: Acropolis, 1982).

24. U.S. Department of Labor, *Occupational Projections and Training Data* (Washington, D.C.: U.S. Government Printing Office, 1984); "Wanted: Experienced Teachers," *Child Care Employee News* (Fall 1984): 2.

11. Educating the Very Young: A Call for Clear Thinking, by David Elkind, pp. 65–70.

NEA Today, vol. 6, no. 6, January 1988, pp. 22–27. Copyright © 1988 by the National Education Association of the United States.

*This is true only when the initiative for reading instruction comes from the adult, not from the child. Children who spontaneously evidence an interest in reading (i.e., have a structural imperative for it) should of course be helped when they ask for assistance and be encouraged by the provision of ample, appropriate books and of unhurried time to explore them.

**A number, as a true unit, is like every other number in the sense that it is a number, yet different from every other number in its order of enumeration. *Three* is like all other numbers in that it is a number, but different from all others in that it is the only number that comes after *two* and before *four*.

Early Schooling: The National Debate. Sharon Lynn Kagan and Edward Zigler. Yale University Press, 1987.

Early childhood education experts discuss political, practical, social, economic, and philosophical issues involved in providing out-of-home programs. They also review and evaluate related research.

Engaging the Minds of Young Children: The Project Approach. Lillian G. Katz and S. Chard. Ablex, forthcoming.

A comprehensive discussion of teaching practices and strategies relating to young children. Solidly grounded in research and experience, this text provides up-to-date material for teachers in training as well as those who work with young children in noneducational settings.

Miseducation: Preschoolers at Risk. David Elkind. Knopf, 1987.

Education is not always beneficial. This book deals with the tendency of today's parents and schools to miseducate young children. After dealing with the parental, historical, and social dynamics responsible for this widespread miseducation, the book deals with the risks of miseducation and provides guidelines for healthy education.

12. Preschool Children in the Public Schools: Good Investment? Or Bad? by Deborah Burnett Strother, pp. 71–75.

Phi Delta Kappan, December 1987, pp. 304–8. © 1987, Phi Delta Kappan, Inc.

1. U.S Bureau of the Census, *Who's Minding the Kids?* (Washington, D.C.: Current Population Reports, Household Economic Studies, Series P-70, No. 9, 1987). The figures cited were calculated from this and other sources by Amaru Bachu, a statistician with the U.S. Bureau of the Census.

2. *Children in Need: Investment Strategies for the Educationally Disadvantaged* (New York: Committee for Economic Development, 1987).

3. Select Committee on Children, Youth, and Families, U.S. House of Representatives, 98th Congress, Second Session, *Families and Child Care: Improving the Options* (Washington, D.C.: U.S. Government Printing Office, 1984), p. xviii.

4. *Time for Results: The Governors' 1991 Report on Education* (Washington, D.C.: National Governors' Association, 1986), p. 3.

5. W. Norton Grubb, "Young Children Face the States: Issues and Options for Early Childhood Programs," Center for Policy Research in Education (CPRE) Note Series, sponsored by the U.S. Department of Education in conjunction with the Eagleton Institute of Politics at Rutgers University, the Rand Corporation, and the University of Wisconsin-Madison, May 1987.

6. David Elkind, "Formal Education and Early Childhood Education: An Essential Difference." *Phi Delta Kappan*, May 1986, pp. 631–36.

7. Select Committee, p. viii.

8. Remarks by Jane Stallings at a symposium hosted by the College of Education of Memphis State University and the Barbara K. Lipman Early Childhood Research Institute, 22–23 May 1987.

9. Herbert Zimiles, "Rethinking the Role of Research: New Issues and Lingering Doubts in an Era of Expanding Preschool Education," *Early Childhood Research Quarterly*, vol. 1, 1986, pp. 189–206.

10. Carolyn Morado, "Prekindergarten Programs for 4-Year-Olds: Some Key Issues," *Young Children*, July 1986, p. 62.

11. "Prevention Strategies for Healthy Babies and Healthy Children," 30 June 1983.

12. *Children in Need . . .*, p. 6

13. Grubb, p. 47.

14. See, for example, Lawrence J. Schweinhart and David P. Weikart, "Evidence That Good Early Childhood Programs Work," *Phi Delta Kappan*, April 1985, pp. 545–53; Consortium for Longitudinal Studies, *As the Twig Is Bent . . . Lasting Effects of Preschool Programs* (Hillsdale, N.J.: Erlbaum, 1983); and Donald E. Pierson, Deborah Klein Walker, and Terrence Tivnan. "A School-Based Program from Infancy to Kindergarten for Children and Their Parents," *Personnel and Guidance Journal*, April 1984, pp. 448–55.

15. Lawrence J. Schweinhart, David P. Weikart, and Mary B. Larner, "Consequences of Three Preschool Curriculum Models Through Age 15." *Early Childhood Research Quarterly*, vol. 1. 1986, pp. 15–45.

16. Remarks by David Weikart at a symposium hosted by the

College of Education of Memphis State University and the Barbara K. Lipman Early Childhood Research Institute, 22–23 May 1987.

17. See, for example, Edward F. Zigler, "Formal Schooling for Four-Year-Olds? No." *American Psychologist*, March 1987, pp. 254–60.

18. Telephone conversation with Fern Marx. 10 September 1987.

19. Telephone conversation with Anne Mitchell. 10 September 1987.

20. Telephone conversation with Edward Zigler. 15 September 1987.

13. Day Care and the Public Schools—Natural Allies, Natural Enemies, by Bettye M. Caldwell, pp. 76–80.

Educational Leadership, vol. 43, no. 5, February 1986, pp. 34–39. Reprinted with permission of the Association for Supervision and Curriculum Development and Bettye M. Caldwell. Copyright © 1986 by the Association for Supervision and Curriculum Development. All rights reserved.

Bowlby, J. *Maternal Care and Mental Health*. Geneva, Switzerland: World Health Organization, 1952.

Caldwell, B. M. "Impact of Interest in Early Cognitive Stimulation." In *Perspectives in Psychopathology*, edited by H. Rie. 293–334. Chicago: Aldine-Atherton, 1971.

Caldwell, B. M., L. Hersher. E. Lipton, J. B. Richmond, G.

Stern, E. Eddy, R. Drachman, and A. Rothman. "Mother-Infant Interaction in Monomatric and Polymatric Families." *American Journal of Orthopsychiatry 33* (1963): 653–664.

Caldwell, B. M., and J. B. Richmond, "Programmed Day Care for the Very Young Child: A Preliminary Report." *Journal of Marriage and the Family 26* (1964): 481–488.

14. Let Children Start School When They're Ready! by Cynthia Parsons, pp. 81–82.

Phi Delta Kappan, September 1985, pp. 61–62. © 1985, Phi Delta Kappan, Inc.

15. It Depends on Your Aim, by Raymond S. Moore, pp. 82–83.

Phi Delta Kappan, September 1985, pp. 62–64. © 1985, Phi Delta Kappan, Inc.

1. John Dewey, "The Primary Education Fetish," *Forum*, vol. 25, 1898, pp. 314-28.

2. Arnold Gesell, *The Normal Child and Primary Education* (New York: Ginn, 1912).

3. Raymond S. Moore, *School Can Wait* (Provo, Ut.: Brigham Young University Press, 1979).

4. Pascual D. Forgione and Raymond S. Moore, *The Rationales for Early Childhood Education Policy Making*, prepared for the U.S. Office of Economic Opportunity under Research Grant No. 50079-G/73/01 (Washougal, Wash.: Hewitt Research Foundation, 1975).

5. William D. Rohwer, Jr., "Prime Time for Education: Early Childhood or Adolescence?" *Harvard Educational Review*, vol. 41, 1971, pp. 316–41.

6. Torsten Husén, letter to Raymond S. Moore 23 November 1972.

7. David Elkind, "The Case for the Academic Pre-School: Fact or Fiction?" *Young Children*, vol. 25, 1970, pp. 180–88.

8. Benjamin S. Bloom, *All Our Children Learning* (Washington, D.C.: McGraw-Hill, 1980).

9. Glen P. Nimnicht, as quoted in Betty Hannah Hoffman, "Do You Know How to Play with Your Child?" *Woman's Day*, August 1972, pp. 46, 118–20.

10. Lawrence J. Schweinhart, letter to Raymond S. Moore, 28 April 1981.

11. Egon Mermelstein and Lee S. Shulman, "Lack of Formal Schooling and the Acquisition of Conversation," *Child Development*, vol. 38, 1967, pp. 39–52; Harold M. Skeels et al., "A Study of Environmental Stimulation: An Orphanage Preschool Project," *University of Iowa Studies in Child Welfare*, vol. 15, no. 4 (Iowa City: University of Iowa Press, 1938); and Marcel Geber, "The Psycho-Motor Development of African Children in the First Year, and the Influence of Maternal Behavior," *Journal of Social Psychology*, vol. 47, 1958, pp. 185–95.

12. Harold G. McCurdy, "The Childhood Pattern of Genius," *Horizon*, vol. 2, 1960, pp. 33–38.

13. Urie Bronfenbrenner, *Two Worlds of Childhood: U.S. and USSR* (New York: Simon & Schuster, 1970), pp. 97–101.

14. John Bowlby, *Maternal Care and Mental Health* (New York: Schocken Books, 1967), pp. 68–69.

15. Martin Engel, "The Care and Feeding of Children for Fun and Profit: Some Thoughts on Day Care," unpublished manuscript, National Demonstration Center in Early Childhood Education, Washington, D.C., n.d.

16. J'aime Adams, "Home Schooling: An Idea Whose Time Has Returned," *Human Events*, 15 September 1984, pp. 12–14, 19; and John Whitehead and Wendell Bird, *Home Education and Constitutional Liberties* (Westchester, Ill.: Crossway, 1984), p. 17.

17. Carle Zimmerman, *Family and Civilization* (New York: Harper, 1947).

16. In Defense of Early Childhood Education, by David Elkind, pp. 84–87.

Principal, vol. 65, no. 5, May 1986, pp. 6–9. Copyright 1986, National Association of Elementary School Principals. All rights reserved.

Berrueta-Clement, J. R.; Schweinhart, L. J.; Barnett, W. S.; Epstein, A. S.; and Weikart, D. P. *Changed Lives: The Effects of the Perry Preschool Program on Youths Through Age 19*. Monographs of the High/Scope Educational Research Foundation, No. 8. Ypsilanti: High Scope Press, 1984.

Bloom, B. *Stability and Change in Human Characteristics*. New York: John Wiley & Sons, Inc., 1964.

Erikson, E. *Childhood and Society*. New York: WW Norton & Co., Inc., 1950.

McKey, R. H.; Condelli, L.; Ganson, H.; Barrett, B.; McConkey, C.; and Plantz, M. *The Impact of Head Start on Children, Families and Communities*. Final Report of the Head Start Evaluation, Synthesis and Utilization Project. Washington, D.C.: CSR, Inc., June 1985.

Montessori, M. *Spontaneous Activity in Education*. Cambridge: Robert Bentley, Inc., 1964.

Piaget, J. *The Origins of Intelligence in Children*. New York: International Universities Press, 1952.

Uphoff, J. K., and Gilmore, J. "Pupil Age at School Entrance: How Many Are Ready for Success." *Young Children* (January 1986): 11–16.

17. Synthesis of Research on School Readiness and Kindergarten Retention, by Lorrie A. Shepard and Mary Lee Smith, pp. 88–94.

Educational Leadership, vol. 44, no. 3, November 1986, pp. 78–86. Reprinted with permission of the Association for Supervision and Curriculum Development and Lorrie A. Shepard and Mary Lee Smith. Copyright © 1986 by the Association for Supervision and Curriculum Development. All rights reserved.

Beattie, C. "Entrance Age to Kindergarten and First Grade: Its Effect on Cognitive and Affective Development of Students." 1970. (ERIC No. ED 133 050.)

Bell, M. "A Study of the Readiness Room Program in Small School District in Suburban Detroit, Michigan." Doctoral diss., Wayne State University, 1972.

Bigelow, E. B. "School Progress of Underage Children." *Elementary School Journal* 25 (1934): 186–192.

Bossing, L., and P. Brien. *A Review of the Elementary School Promotion Retention Dilemma*. Murray, Ky.: Murray State University, 1979. (ERIC No. ED 212 362.)

Byrnes, D., and K. Yammamoto. "Grade Repetition: Views of Parents, Teachers and Principals." Logan: Utah State University, 1984.

Carroll, M. L. "Academic Achievement and Adjustment of Underrage and Overage Third Graders." *Journal of Educational Research* 56 (1963): 415–419.

Cook, T. D., H. Appleton, R. F. Conner, A. Shaffer, G. Tomkin, and S. J. Weber. *"Sesame Street" Revisited*. New York: Russell Sage Foundation, 1975.

Davis, B. G., C. S. Trimble, and D. R. Vincent "Does Age of Entrance Affect School Achievement?" *Elementary School Journal* 80 (1980): 133–143.

Diamond, G. H. "The Birthdate Effect—A Maturational Effect." *Journal of Learning Disabilities* 16 (1983): 161–164.

DiPasquale, G. W., A. D. Moule, and R. W. Flewelling. "The Birthdate Effect." *Journal of Learning Disabilities* 13 (1980): 234–238.

Donofrio, A. F. "Grade Repetition: Therapy of Choice." *Journal of Learning Disabilities* 10 (1977): 349–351.

Education Commission of the States. November 1985. *State Characteristics: Kindergartens*. Denver, Colo.

Educational Research Service, 1985. *Admission Policies for Kindergarten and First Grade*, Circular No. 3. Arlington, Va.

Educational Research Service, 1963. *Entrance-Age Policies and Exceptions*, Circular No. 3. Arlington, Va.

Educational Research Service. 1968. *Entrance-Age Policies*, Circular No. 5. Arlington Va.

Educational Research Service, 1975. *Kindergarten and First Grade Minimum Entrance Age Policies*, Circular No. 5. Arlington, Va.

A Gift of Time. New Haven, Conn.: Gesell Institute of Human Development, 1982.

Gredler, G. R. "Ethical and Legal Dilemmas in the Assessment of Readiness of Children for School." In *Ethical and Legal Factors in the Practice of School Psychology*, edited by G. R. Gredler. Harrisburg, Pa.: State Department of Education, 1975.

Gredler, G. R. "The Birthdate Effect: Fact or Artifact?" *Journal of Learning Disabilities* 13 (1980): 239–242.

Gredler, G. R. "Transition Classes: A Viable Alternative for the At-Risk Child?" *Psychology in the Schools* 21 (1984): 463–470.

Green, D. R., and S. V. Simmons. "Chronological Age and School Entrance." *Elementary School Journal* 63 (1962): 41–47.

Haddad, W. D. *Educational and Economic Effects of Promotion and Repetition Practices*. Washington, D.C.: The World Bank 1979. (ERIC No. ED 195 003.)

Hall, R. V. "Does Entrance Age Affect Achievement?" *Elementary School Journal* 64 (1963): 391–396.

Halliwell, J. W., and B. W. Stein. "A Comparison of the Achievement of Early and Late Starters in Reading Related and Non-Reading Related Areas in Fourth and Fifth Grades." *Elementary English* 41 (1964): 631–639.

Heller, K. A., W. H. Holtzman, and S. Messick, eds. *Placing Children in Special Education: A Strategy for Equity*. Washington, D.C.: National Academy Press, 1982.

Holmes, C. T., and K. M. Matthews. "The Effects of Nonpromotion on Elementary and Junior High School Pupils: A Meta-Analysis." *Review of Educational Research* 54 (1984): 225–236.

Husén, T., ed. *International Study of Achievement in Mathematics, Vol. 1*. Stockholm: Almquist & Wiksell, 1967.

Jensen, A. R. "Understanding Readiness: An Occasional Paper." Urbana, Ill.: ERIC Clearinghouse on Early Childhood Education, 1969. (ERIC No. ED 032 117.)

Jensen, A. R. *Bias in Mental Testing*. New York: The Free Press, 1980.

Jinks, P. C. "An Investigation Into the Effect of Date of Birth on Subsequent School Performance." *Educational Research* 6 (1964): 220–225.

Kalk, J. M., P. Langer, and D. Searls. *Trends in Achievement as a Function of Age of Admission* (Report No. AY-AA-51). Denver: National Assessment of Educational Progress, Education Commission of the States, December 1981.

Kaufman, N. L. "Review of the Gesell Pre-school Test" In *The Ninth Mental Measurements Yearbook, Vol. I*, edited by J. V. Mitchell. Lincoln, Nebr.: Buros Institute of Mental Measurements, 1985.

Kaufman, A. S., and N. L. Kaufman. "Tests Built from Piaget's and Gesell's Tasks as Predictors of First-Grade Achievement." *Child Development* 43 (1972): 521–535.

King, I. B. "Effect of Age of Entrance Into Grade 1 Upon Achievement in the Elementary School." *Elementary School Journal* 55 (1955): 331-336.

Langer, P., J. M. Kalk, and D. T. Searls, "Age of Admission and Trends in Achievement: A Comparison of Blacks and Caucasians." *American Educational Research Journal* 21 (1984): 61-78.

Leinhardt, G. "Transition Rooms: Promoting Maturation or Reducing Education?" *Journal of Educational Psychology* 72 (1980): 55-61.

MacMillan, D. L., and C. E. Meyers. "Educational Labeling of Handicapped Learners." In *Review of Research in Education, Vol. 7*, edited by D. C. Berliner. Washington, D.C.: American Educational Research Association. 1979.

Maddux, C. D. "First-Grade Entry Age in a Sample of Children Labeled Learning Disabled." *Learning Disability Quarterly* 3 (1980): 79-83.

Malmquist, E. *Factors Related to Reading Disabilities in the First Grade of the Elementary School.* Stockholm: Almquist & Wiksell, 1958.

Management Information Services. "Entrance Age Requirements for Kindergarten and First Grade." (Two-page memo.) Aurora, Colo.: Denver Area Superintendent's Council, 1982.

May, D. C., and E. L. Welch. "The Effects of Developmental Placement and Early Retention on Children's Later Scores on Standardized Tests." *Psychology in the Schools* 21 (1984): 381-385.

Miller, W., and R. C. Norris. "Entrance Age and School Success." *Journal of School Psychology* 6 (1967): 47-60.

Pugach, M. C. "The Limitations of Federal Special Education Policy: The Role of Classroom Teachers in Determining Who Is Handicapped." *Journal of Special Education* 19 (1985): 123-137.

Ravitch, M. M. "Review of Metropolitan Readiness Tests, 1976 Edition." In *The Ninth Mental Measurements Yearbook, Vol. 1*, edited by J. V. Mitchell. Lincoln, Nebr.: Buros Institute of Mental Measurements, 1985.

Raygor, B. "A Five-Year Follow-Up Study Comparing the School Achievement and School Adjustment of Children Retained in Kindergarten and Children Placed in a Transition Class." Doctoral diss., University of Minnesota, 1972.

Rose, J. S., F. J. Medway, V. L. Cantrell and S. H. Marus. "A Fresh Look at the Retention-Promotion Controversy." *Journal of School Psychology* 21 (1983): 201-211.

Shepard, L. A., and M. L. Smith. "An Evaluation of the Identification of Learning Disabled Students in Colorado." *Learning Disability Quarterly* 6 (1983): 115-127.

Shepard, L. A., and M. L. Smith. *Boulder Valley Kindergarten Study: Retention Practices and Retention Effects.* Boulder. Colo.: Valley Public Schools, March 1985.

Shepard, L. A., and M. L. Smith with A. Davis, G. V. Glass, A. Riley, and C. Vojir. *Evaluation of the Identification of Perceptual-Communicative Disorders in Colorado.* Boulder: Laboratory of Educational Research, University of Colorado, February, 1981.

Uphoff, J. K. "Pupil Chronological Age as a Factor in School Failure." Paper presented at the annual conference of the Association for Supervision and Curriculum Development, Chicago, March 1985.

Weinstein, L. "School Entrance Age and Adjustment." *Journal of School Psychology* 7 (1968-69): 20-28.

Wood, C., S. Powell, and R. C. Knight. "Predicting School Readiness: The Validity of Developmental Age." *Journal of Learning Disabilities* 17 (1984): 8-11.

18. Uses and Abuses of Developmental Screening and School Readiness Testing, by Samuel J. Meisels, pp. 95-103.

Young Children, vol. 42, no. 2, January 1987, pp. 4-9. Copyright © 1987 by the National Association for the Education of Young Children. Reprinted with permission.

Dr. Meisels's Original Chapter

American Educational Research Association, American Psychological Association, and National Council on Measurement in Education (1985). *Standards for educational and psychological testing.* Washington, DC: American Psychological Association.

Ames, L. B., Gillespie, C., Haines, J., and Ilg, F. (1979). *The Gesell Institute's child from one to six.* New York: Harper & Row.

Barnes, K. E. (1982). *Preschool screening: The measurement and prediction of children-at-risk.* Springfield, IL: Thomas.

Berrueta-Clement, J. R., Schweinhart, L. J., Barnett, W. S., Epstein, A. S., and Weikart, D. P. (1984). *Changed lives: The effects of the Perry Preschool Program on youths through age 19.* Ypsilanti, MI: High/Scope.

Clarke, A. M., and Clarke, A. D. B. (1976). *Early experience: Myth and evidence.* New York: Free Press.

Clarke-Stewart, A. K., and Fein, G. G. (1983). Early childhood programs. In M. M. Haith and J. J. Campos (Eds.), *Infancy and developmental psychobiology* (pp. 917-999). New York: Wiley.

Diamond, G. H. (1983). The birthdate effect—A maturational effect? *Journal of Learning Disabilities, 16*, 161-164.

Gesell, A. (1954). The ontogenesis of infant behavior. In L. Carmichael (Ed.), *Manual of child psychology* (pp. 335-373).

New York: Wiley.

Gesell, A. et al. (1940). *The first five years of life.* New York: Harper & Row.

Gredler, G. P. (1978). A look at some important factors in assessing readiness for school. *Journal of Learning Disabilities, 11*, 284-290.

Haines, J., Ames, L. B., and Gillespie, C. (1980). *The Gesell Preschool Test manual.* Lumberville, PA: Modern Learning Press.

Ilg, F. L., and Ames, L. B. (1972). *School readiness.* New York: Harper & Row.

Joiner, L. M. (1977). *A technical analysis of the variation in screening instruments and programs in New York State.* New York: City University of New York, New York Center for Advanced Study in Education (ERIC Document Reproduction Service No. ED 154 596).

Knight, L. N. (1979). Readiness. In J. E. Alexander (Ed.), *Teaching reading.* Boston: Little, Brown.

Knobloch, H., Pasamanick, P. H., and Sherard, E. S. (1966). A Developmental Screening Inventory for infants. *Pediatrics, 38*, 1095-1108.

Lazar, I., and Darlington, R. (Eds.). (1982). Lasting effects of early education: A report from the Consortium for Longitudinal Studies. *Monographs of the Society for Research in Child Development,* 47 (2-3, Serial No. 195).

Lichtenstein, R. (1981). Comparative validity of two preschool screening tests: Correlational and classificational approaches. *Journal of Learning Disabilities, 14,* 68–72.

Maddux, C. D., Stacy, D., and Scott, M. (1981). School entry age in a group of gifted children. *Gifted Child Quarterly, 25,* 180–184.

McCall, R. B. (1982). A hard look at stimulating and predicting development: The cases of bonding and screening. *Pediatrics in Review, 3,* 205–212.

Meisels, S. J. (1984). Prediction, prevention and developmental screening in the EPSDT program. In H. W. Stevenson and A. E. Siegel (Eds.), *Child development research and social policy.* Chicago: University of Chicago Press.

Meisels, S. J. (1985). *Developmental screening in early childhood: A guide* (rev. ed.). Washington, DC: NAEYC.

Meisels, S. J. (1986). [National survey of early childhood special education policies and practices]. Unpublished raw data.

Meisels, S. J., and Anastasiow, N. J. (1982). The risks of prediction: Relationships between etiology, handicapping conditions, and developmental outcomes. In S. Moore and C. Cooper (Eds.), *The young child: Reviews of research* (Vol. 3). Washington, DC: NAEYC.

Michigan Department of Education. (1984). Superintendent's Study Group on Early Childhood Education. Lansing, MI: Author.

NAEYC. (1985). *Position statement on developmentally appropriate practice in early childhood programs serving children from birth through age 8.* Washington, DC: NAEYC.

Rubin, R. A., Balow, B., Dorle, J., and Rosen M. (1978). Preschool prediction of low achievement in basic school skills. *Journal of Learning Disabilities, 11,* 664–667.

Satz, P., and Friel, J. (1978). Predictive validity of an abbreviated screening battery. *Journal of Learning Disabilities, 11,* 347–351.

Shonkoff, J. (1983). The limitations of normative assessments of high-risk infants. *Topics in Early Childhood Special Education, 3,* 29–43.

Wiske, M. S., Meisels, S. J., and Tivnan, T. (1982). The Early Screening Inventory: A study of early childhood developmental screening. In N. J. Anastasiow, W. K. Frankenburg, and A. Fandel (Eds.), *Identification of high risk children.* Baltimore: University Park Press.

Wood, C., Powell, S., and Knight, R. C. (1984). Predicting school readiness: The validity of developmental age. *Journal of Learning Disabilities, 17,* 8–11.

Zigler, E., and Valentine, J. (1979). *Project Head Start: A legacy of the War on Poverty.* New York: Free Press.

Gesell Institute's Response

Ames, L. B., Gillespie, C., Haines, J., and Ilg, F. (1979). *The child from one to six.* London: Hamish Hamilton.

Ames, L. B., and Ilg, F. L. (1964). Gesell behavior tests as predictive of later grade placement. *Perceptual and Motor Skills, 19,* 719–722.

Gesell, A. (1925). *The mental growth of the preschool child.* New York: Macmillan.

Gesell, A. (1930). *The guidance of mental growth in infant and child.* New York: Macmillan.

Gesell, A., et al (1940). *The first five years of life.* New York:

Harper & Row.

Kaufman, A. (1971). Piaget and Gesell: A psychometric analysis of tests built from their tasks. *Child Development, 42,* 1341–1360.

Knobloch, H. (1980). *Manual of developmental diagnosis.* New York: Harper & Row.

Wood, C., Powell, S., and Knight, R. C. (1984). Predicting school readiness: The validity of developmental age. *Journal of Learning Disabilities, 17,* 8–11.

Dr. Meisels's Response

Ames, L. B., and Ilg, F. L. (1964). Gesell behavior tests as predictive of later grade placement. *Perceptual and Motor Skills, 19,* 719–722.

Bradley, R. H. (1985). Review of Gesell School Readiness Tests. In J. Mitchell, Jr. (Ed.), *The ninth mental measurements yearbook* (Vol. I). Lincoln, NE: The University of Nebraska Press.

Gesell Institute (1987). The Gesell Institute responds. *Young Children, 42* (2).

Kaufman, A. (1971). Piaget and Gesell: A psychometric analysis of tests built from their tasks. *Child Development, 42,* 1341–1360.

Kaufman, N. L. (1985). Review of Gesell Preschool Test. In J. Mitchell, Jr. (Ed.), *The ninth mental measurements yearbook*

(Vol. I). Lincoln, NE: The University of Nebraska Press.

Naglieri, J. A. (1985). Review of Gesell Preschool Tests. In J. Mitchell, Jr. (Ed.), *The ninth mental measurements yearbook* (Vol. I). Lincoln, NE: The University of Nebraska Press.

Shepard, L. A., and Smith, M. L. (1985). *Boulder Valley Kindergarten Study: Retention practices and retention effects.* Boulder, CO: Boulder Valley Public Schools.

Shepard, L. A., and Smith, M. L. (1986). School readiness and kindergarten retention: A policy analysis. *Educational Leadership, 44* (3), 78–86.

Wood, C., Powell, S., and Knight, R. C. (1984). Predicting school readiness: The validity of developmental age. *Journal of Learning Disabilities, 17,* 8–11.

19. Educating Young Handicapped Children: What Can Early Childhood Education Contribute? by Anne H. Widerstrom, pp. 104–8.
Childhood Education, vol. 63, no. 2, December 1986, pp. 78–83. Reprinted by permission of Anne H. Widerstrom and the Association for Childhood Education International, 11141 Georgia Avenue, Suite 200, Wheaton, MD. Copyright © 1986 by the Association.

Amidon, E. J., and Flanders, N. A. (1971). *The role of the teacher in the classroom*. Minneapolis: Association for Productive Teaching.

Axelrod, J. (1977). *Behavior modification for the classroom teacher*. New York: McGraw-Hill.

Baer, D., and Wolf, M. (1968). The reinforcement contingency in preschool and remedial education. In R. Hess and R. Bear (Eds.), *Early education* (pp. 119–129). Chicago: Aldine.

Bereiter, C. (1972). An academic preschool for disadvantaged children: Conclusions for evaluating studies. In J. Stanley (Ed.), *Preschool programs for the disadvantaged*. Baltimore: Johns Hopkins.

Bronfenbrenner, U. (1961). The changing American child: A speculative analysis. *Journal of Social Issues, 17*, 6–18.

Bushell, D., Jr. (1973). The behavior analysis classroom. In B. Spodek (Ed.), *Early childhood education* (pp. 163–175. Englewood Cliffs, NJ: Prentice-Hall.

Evans, E. D. (1975). *Contemporary influences in early childhood education*. New York: Holt.

Feitelson, D., and Ross, G. S. (1974). The neglected factor—Play. *Human Development, 16*, 202–223.

Haring, N., and Lovitt, T. (1967). Operant methodology and education technology in special education. In N. Haring and R. Schiefelbusch (Eds.), *Methods in special education* (pp. 12–48). New York: McGraw-Hill.

Hildebrand, V. (1981). *Introduction to early childhood education* (3rd ed.). New York: Macmillan.

Horne, B. M., and Philleo, L. L. (1976). A comparative study of the spontaneous play activities of normal and mentally defective children. In J. S. Bruner, A. Jolly and K. Sylva (Eds.), *Play: Its role in development and evolution* (pp. 512–520). New York: Basic Books.

Inhelder, B., Sinclair, H., and Bovet, M. (1974). *Learning and the development of cognition*. Cambridge, MA: Harvard University Press.

Kamii, C. (1982). Encouraging thinking in mathematics. *Phi Delta Kappan, 64*(4), 247–251.

Kamii, C., and Radin, N. A. (1970). A framework for preschool curriculum based on Piagetian concepts. In I. J. Athey and D. O. Rubadean (Eds.), *Educational implications of Piaget's theory* (pp. 89–100). Waltham, MA: Ginn-Blaisdell.

Kazdin, A., and Bootzin, R. (1972). The token economy: An evaluative review. *Journal of Applied Behavior Analysis, 5*, 343–372.

Mindes, G. (1982). Social and cognitive aspects of play in young handicapped children. *Topics in Early Childhood Education, 2*(3), 39–52.

Mogford, K. (1977). The play of handicapped children. In B. Tizard and D. Harvey (Eds.), *Biology of play* (pp. 170–184). Philadelphia: Lippincott.

Perret-Clermont, A. (1980). *Social interaction and cognitive development in children*. London: Academic Press.

Piaget, J. (1963). *The psychology of intelligence*. Patterson, NJ: Littlefield, Adams.

Ramp, E. A., and Hopkins, B. L. (Eds.). (1971). *A new direction for education: Behavior analysis*. Lawrence, KS: Dept. of Human Development, University of Kansas.

Risley, T. (1969). *Juniper gardens nursery school project*. Lawrence, KS: Department of Human Development, University of Kansas.

Safford, P. L. (1978). *Teaching young children with special needs*. St. Louis: Mosby.

Saltz, E., Dixon, D., and Johnson, J. (1977). Training disadvantaged preschoolers on various fantasy activities: Effects on cognitive functioning and impulse control. *Child Development, 48*, 367–380.

Sylva, K., Bruner, J. S., and Genova, P. (1976). The role of play in the problem solving of children 3-5 years old. In J. S. Bruner, A. Jolly, and K. Sylva (Eds.), *Play: Its role in development and evolution* (pp. 244–260). New York: Basic Books.

Vygotsky, S. (1976). Play and its role in the mental development of the child. In J. S. Bruner, A. Jolly, and K. Sylva (Eds.), *Play: Its role in development and evolution* (pp. 537–554). New York: Basic Books.

Weiss, R. (1981). INREAL intervention for language handicapped and bilingual children. *Journal of the Division for Early Childhood, 4*, 24–27.

Widerstrom, A. H. (1983). How important is play for handicapped children? *Childhood Education, 60*(1), 39–50.

Section Four: Preschool Programs

20. Public Education for Preschoolers, by Diane Scott-Jones and Lynne Baker-Ward, pp. 111–14.
  Tennessee's Children, vol. 29, no. 1, Fall 1987, pp. 10–14. Copyright © 1987 by Diane Scott-Jones and Lynne Baker-Ward. Reprinted with permission.

Berrueta-Clement, J. R., Schweinhart, L. J., Barnett, W. S., Epstein, A. S., and Weikart, D. P. (1984). *Changed lives: The effects of the Perry Preschool Program on youths through age 19*. Ypsilanti, MI: High/Scope Press.

Blank, H., and Morgan, G. (1985). Early childhood and the public schools: An essential partnership. *Young Children, 40*(4), 52-55.

Clarke, A. M. (1984). Early experience and cognitive development. *Review of Research in Education, 11*, 125-157.

Fiske, E. B. (1986, April 27). Preschool education stressed as more mothers work. *Raleigh News & Observer*.

Grant, W. V., and Snyder, T. D. (1983). *Digest of Education Statistics*. Washington, DC: U.S. Government Printing Office.

Hobbs, N., Dokecki, P. R., Hoover-Dempsey, K. V., Moroney, R. M., Shayne, M. W., and Weeks, K. H. (1984). *Strengthening families*. San Francisco: Jossey-Bass.

Hodgkinson, H. L. (1985). *All one system: Demographics of education, kindergarten through graduate school*. Washington, DC: Institute for Educational Leadership.

Kahdy, G. A. (May 1985). *Prekindergarten programs in the public schools of North Carolina*. Report to the State Superintendent of Schools.

Kamerman, S. B., and Kahn, A. J. (1981). *Child care, family benefits, and working parents: A study in comparative policy*. New York: Columbia University Press.

Klein, R. (1985). Caregiving arrangements by employed women with children under one year of age. *Developmental Psychology, 21,* 403-406.

Lazar, I., and Darlington, R. (1982). Lasting effects of early education: A report from the consortium for longitudinal studies. *Monographs of the Society for Research in Child Development, 47* (2-3, Serial No. 195).

Levine, J. A. (1978). *Day care and the public schools: Profiles of five communities.* Newton, MA: Education Development Center.

Lubek, S. (1985). *Sandbox society: Early education in Black and white America—a comparative ethnography.* Philadelphia: Falmer Press.

National Black Child Development Institute (1985). *Child care in the public schools: Incubator for inequality.* Washington, DC: Author.

National Black Child Development Institute (1986). Growing national trend toward child care in public schools may spell disaster for Black children. *The Black Child Advocate, 13,* 7-8.

National School Boards Association (1986). *Day care in the public schools* (Leadership Reports vol. 1). Alexandria, VA: Author.

Scarr, S. (1984). *Mother care/Other care.* New York: Basic Books.

Stevenson, H. W., Lee, S. Y., and Stigler, J. W. (1986). Mathematics achievement of Chinese, Japanese, and American children. *Science, 231,* 693-699.

Time for Results. (1986). Report of the National Governors' Association Meeting, Hilton Head, SC.

Washington, V., and Oyemade, U. J. (1985). Changing family trends: Head Start must respond. *Young Children, 40*(6), 12-19.

Zigler, E. (1985, August). *Formal schooling for 4-year-olds? No.* Paper presented at the meeting of the American Psychological Association, Los Angeles.

21. Should Four-Year-Olds Be in School? by Edward F. Zigler, pp. 115–18.
Principal, vol. 65, no. 5, May 1986, pp. 11–14. Copyright © 1986, National Association of Elementary School Principals. All rights reserved.

Ambach, G. "Public School for Four-Year-Olds: Yes or No?" Paper presented at the American Association of School Administrators, March 1985, in New York.

Bronfenbrenner, U. "Is Early Intervention Effective?" In *Handbook of Evaluation Research*, edited by M. Guttentag and E. L. Struening, vol. 2. Beverly Hills, Calif.: Sage Publications Inc., 1974.

Darlington, R. B.; Royce, V. M.; Snipper, A. S.; Murray, A. W.; and Lazar, I. "Preschool Programs and Later School Competence of Children from Low-Income Families." *Science* 208 (1980): 202–204.

Elkind, D. *The Hurried Child.* Reading, Mass.: Addison-Wesley Publishing Co., Inc., 1981.

Irvine, D. J.; Flint, D. L.; Hick, T. L.; Horan, M. D.; and Kikuk, S. E. *Evaluation of the New York State Experimental Preschool Program: Final Report.* Albany, N.Y.: The State Education Department, 1982.

Kagan, S. L., ed. "Four-Year-Olds—Who is Responsible?" Unpublished report presented to the Connecticut Board of Education, 1985, by the Committee on Four-Year-Olds, Their Families, and the Public Schools.

Lazar, I., and Darlington, R. *Lasting Effects of Early Education: A Report from the Consortium for Longitudinal Studies.* Monographs of the Society for Research in Child Development, 47 (2–3, Series No. 195), 1982.

Lazerson, M. "Social Reform and Early Childhood Education: Some Historical Perspectives." *Urban Education* 5 (1982): 84–102.

Moynihan, D. P. "On the Present Discontent." Paper presented at the convocation for the 140th anniversary of the School of Education, 1984, at the State University of New York, Albany.

Swift, J. W. "Effects of Early Group Experience: The Nursery School and Day Nursery." In *Review of Child Development Research*, vol. 1, edited by M. L. Hoffman and L. W. Hoffman. New York: Russell Sage Foundation, 1964.

Tizard, B., and Hughes, M. *Young Children Learning.* Cambridge: Harvard University Press, 1984.

Weinberg, R. "Early Childhood Education and Intervention: Establishing an American Tradition." *American Psychologist* 34 (1979): 912–916.

Winn, M. *Children without Childhood.* New York: Penguin Books, 1983.

Zigler, E., and Berman, W. "Discerning the Future of Early Childhood Intervention." *American Psychologist* 38 (1983): 894–906.

Zimiles, H. "The Role of Research in an Era of Expanding Preschool Education." Revised version of an address, "Four-Year-Olds in the Public Schools: What Research Does and Does Not Tell Us." Paper presented at the meeting of the American Educational Research Association, April 1985, in Chicago, Ill.

22. Public Schools and Four-Year-Olds: A Teacher's View, by Mary Hatwood Futrell, pp. 119–21.
American Psychologist, vol. 42, no. 3, March 1987, pp. 251–53. Copyright 1987 by the American Psychological Association. Reprinted by permission of the publisher.

23. Quality Four-Year-Old Programs in Public Schools, Position Statement of the Southern Association on Children Under Six, pp. 122–23.
Dimensions, April 1986, pp. 29–30. © 1986, Southern Association on Children Under Six, Little Rock, Arkansas. Reprinted with permission.

Bronfenbrenner, U. (1985). "The three worlds of childhood." *Principal*, May, 1985.

Dowd, J. L. and Finkelstein, J. M. (1985). "A two-year kindergarten that works." *Principal*, May, 1985.

Hymes, J. L., Jr. (1981). *Teaching the child under six,* third edition. Columbus, Ohio: Charles E. Merrill Publishing.

Halpem, R. (1981). "Assuring quality early childhood service: The challenge ahead." A conference report. High/Scope Foundation.

Maryland Committee for Children, Inc. (1985). *Programs for four-year-olds*. Maryland.

National Council for Accreditation of Teacher Education. "Curriculum standards for teacher training programs." NAEYC Guidelines.

Roupp, R., Travers, J., Glanz, F. E., and Coeles, C. (1979).

Children at the center: Summary findings and their implications. (Vol. 1) Cambridge, MA: Abt Associates.

Schweinhart, L. J. and Weikart, D. P. (1981). "Early childhood development programs in the eighties: The national picture." High/Scope Foundation.

Swick, K. J. and Castle, K. (Eds.) (1985). *Acting on what we know: Developing effective programs for young children*. Little Rock, AR: SACUS.

24. Here Come the Four-Year-Olds! by Diane Dismuke, pp. 124–26.
NEA Today, vol. 6, no. 5, December 1987, pp. 4–5. Copyright © 1987 by the National Education Association of the United States.

25. Prekindergarten Programs for Four-Year-Olds: State Involvement in Preschool Education, by Carolyn Morado, pp. 127–29.
Young Children, vol. 41, no. 6, September 1986, pp. 69–71. Copyright © 1986 by the National Association for the Education of Young Children. Reprinted with permission.

26. Safeguards: Guidelines for Establishing Programs for Four-Year-Olds in the Public Schools, by The National Black Child Development Institute, pp. 130–31.
Pages iii–2. Copyright 1987, The National Black Child Development Institute, Washington, D.C. Reprinted with permission.

Coleman, Madeleine, ed. *Black Children Just Keep on Growing: Alternative Curriculum Models for Young Black Children*. Washington, DC: Black Child Development Institute, 1977.

Hale, Janice. "Black Children: Their Roots, Culture, and Learning Styles." In *Understanding the Multicultural Experience in Early Childhood Education*. Eds. Olivia N. Saracho and Bernard Spodek. Washington, DC: National Association for the Education of Young Children, 1983.

Hale, Janice. *Black Children: Their Roots, Culture, and Learning Styles*. Provo, UT: Brigham Young University Press, 1982.

Honig, Alice S. *Parent Involvement in Early Childhood Education*. Washington, DC: National Association for the Education of Young Children, 1975.

Hymes, James L. "Public Schools for Four Year Olds." *Notes and Comments*, Fall 1986.

Levine, James A. *Day Care and the Public Schools: Profiles of*

Five Communities. Newton, MA: Education Development Center, Inc., 1978.

Moore, Evelyn K. "Day Care: A Black Perspective." In *Day Care: Scientific and Social Policy Issues*. Eds. Edward F. Zigler and Edmund W. Gordon. Boston: Auburn House Publishing Co., 1982.

National Association for the Education of Young Children. "NAEYC Position Statement on Developmentally Appropriate Practice in Programs for Four and Five Year Olds." June, 1986.

National Black Child Development Institute. *Beyond the Stereotypes: A Guide to Resources for Black Girls and Young Women*. Washington, DC: National Black Child Development Institute, 1986.

National Black Child Development Institute. *Child Care in the Public Schools: Incubator for Inequality?* Washington, DC: National Black Child Development Institute, 1985.

ABOUT NBCDI

The National Black Child Development Institute was established in 1970 to improve the quality of life for Black children and youth. A national, nonprofit, charitable, and educational organization, NBCDI focuses on the issues of health, education, child welfare, and child care. NBCDI is composed of dedicated volunteers who help to educate their communities about national, state, and local issues facing Black children and youth. NBCDI's public education component is implemented through [its] quarterly newsletter, periodic updates, publications, and the annual conference.

NBCDI's affiliate network serves as a catalyst for change on the local level. Affiliates engage in a variety of program activities beneficial to Black children and youth. For example, they have addressed the issue of competency testing, tutored children and youth, and provided leadership training through conferences and workshops. Membership in NBCDI is open to all interested persons.

27. Public School for Four-Year-Olds, by James L. Hymes, Jr., pp. 131–32.
Young Children, vol. 42, no. 2, January 1987, p. 51. Copyright © 1987 by the National Association for the Education of Young Children. Reprinted with permission.

28. Full-Day or Half-Day Kindergarten? by Dianne Rothenberg, pp. 133–34.
ERIC Digest, 1984. ERIC Clearinghouse on Elementary and Early Childhood Education, University of Illinois, Urbana, Illinois.

Evans, Ellis D., and Dan Marken. *Longitudinal Follow-up Comparison of Conventional and Extended-Day Public School Kindergarten Programs*, 1983. PS 014 383; Ed number to be assigned.

Finkelstein, Judith M. *Results of Midwestern University Professors' Study: Kindergarten Scheduling*. ED 248 979.

Grant, W. Vance, and Thomas D. Snyder. *Digest of Education Statistics 1983-84*. Washington, DC: National Center for

Education Statistics, 1983.

Herman, Barry E. *The Case for the All-Day Kindergarten. Fastback 205.* Bloomington, IN: Phi Delta Kappa Educational Foundation, 1984. ED 243 592.

Humphrey, Jack W. *A Longitudinal Study of the Effectiveness of Full-Day Kindergarten,* 1983. ED 247 014.

National Commission on Working Women. "Working Moth-ers and Their Families: A Fact Sheet." *Women at Work: News about the 80%,* Winter 1985, 5.

Stinard, Thomas A. *Synopsis of Research on Kindergarten Scheduling: Half-Day, Everyday; Full-Day, Alternate Day; and Full-Day, Everyday,* 1982. ED 219 151.

"Woes Plague New York's All-Day Kindergartens." *New York Times,* 13 October 1983, p. 47.

29. Kindergarten in America: Five Major Trends, by Sandra Longfellow Robinson, pp. 135–36.

Phi Delta Kappan, vol. 68, no. 7, March 1987, pp. 529–30. © 1987, Phi Delta Kappan, Inc.

*The data collected in 1974 are reported in Edward H. Robinson and Sandra L. Robinson, "Early Childhood Education: Practice Outpaces Theory," *Phi Delta Kappan,* April 1975, pp. 566–68. The data collected in 1981 are reported in Sandra L. Robinson, "An Update on the Status of Early Childhood Education in the United States," *Phi Delta Kappan,* October 1983, p. 140; and Sandra L. Robinson, "Educational Opportunities for Young Children in America," *Childhood Education,* September/October 1982, pp. 42–45.

30. Kindergarten Programs and Practices, Educational Research Service Staff Report, pp. 136–39.

ERS Spectrum, Spring 1986, pp. 22–25, vol. 4, no. 2, Educational Research Service, Arlington, Virginia.

31. NAEYC Position Statement on Developmentally Appropriate Practice in the Primary Grades, Serving Five-Through Eight-Year-Olds, pp. 140–44.

Young Children, vol. 43, no. 2, January 1988, pp. 64–68, 81. Copyright © 1988 by the National Association for the Education of Young Children. Reprinted with permission.

Asher, S., Hymel, S., and Renshaw, P. (1984). Loneliness in children. *Child Development, 55,* 1456–1464.

Asher, S., Renshaw, P., and Hymel, S. (1982). Peer relations and the development of social skills. In S. Moore and C. Cooper (Eds.), *The young child: Reviews of research* (Vol. 3, pp. 137–158). Washington, DC: NAEYC.

Asher, S. R., and Williams, G. A. (1987). Helping children without friends in home and school contexts. In *Children's social development: Information for teachers and parents* (pp. 1–26). Urbana, IL: ERIC Clearinghouse on Elementary and Early Childhood Education.

Barth, R. S. (1972). *Open education and the American schools.* New York: Agathon Press.

Bennett, W. (1986). *First lessons: A report on elementary education in America.* Washington, DC: U.S. Government Printing Office.

Biber, B., Murphy, L. B., Woodcock, L., Black, I. (1942). *Child life in school: A study of a seven-year-old group.* New York: Dutton.

Blank, M. (1985). Classroom discourse: The neglected topic of the topic. In M. Clark (Ed.), *Helping communication in early education* (pp. 13–20). Education Review Occasional Publication No. 11.

Burton, C. B. (1987). Children's peer relationships. In *Children's social development: Information for teachers and parents* (pp. 27–34). Urbana, IL: ERIC Clearinghouse on Elementary and Early Childhood Education.

Covington, M. V. (1984). The motive for self-worth. In R. Ames and C. Ames (Eds.), *Research on motivation in education: Vol. 1. Student motivation* (pp. 78–113). New York: Academic.

Cowen, E., Pederson, A., Babigian, M., Izzo, L., and Trost, M. (1973). Long-term follow-up of early detected vulnerable children. *Journal of Consulting and Clinical Psychology, 41,* 438–446.

Dewey, J. (1899). *School and society.* New York: The University of Chicago Press.

Durkin, D. (1980). *Teaching young children to read.* Boston: Allyn & Bacon.

Dweck, C. (1986). Motivational processes affecting learning. *American Psychologist, 41,* 1040–1048.

Elkind, D. (1981). *Children and adolescents: Interpretive essays on Jean Piaget.* New York: Oxford University Press.

Elkind, D. (1987). *Miseducation: Preschoolers at risk.* New York: Knopf.

Erikson, E. (1963). *Childhood and society.* New York: Norton.

Furman, E. (1980). Early latency: Normal and pathological aspects. In S. Greenspan and G. Pollock (Eds.), *The course of life: Vol. 2. Latency, adolescence and youth* (pp. 1–32). Washington, DC: National Institute of Mental Health, U.S. Department of Health and Human Services.

Furman, E. (1987a). *Helping young children grow: I never knew parents did so much.* Madison, CT: International Universities Press.

Furman, E. (1987b). *The teacher's guide to helping young children grow.* Madison, CT: International Universities Press.

Gottfried, A. (1983). Intrinsic motivation in young children. *Young Children, 39*(1), 64–73.

Gronlund, N., and Holmlund, W. (1985). The value of elementary school sociometric status scores for predicting pupils' adjustment in high school. *Educational Administration and Supervision, 44,* 225–260.

Hilliard, A. (1986). Standardized testing in early childhood programs. Unpublished paper.

Hills, T. (1986). *Classroom motivation: Helping students want to learn and achieve in school.* Trenton: New Jersey Department of Education.

Kamii, C. (1985). Leading primary education toward excellence: Beyond worksheets and drill. *Young Children, 40*(6), 3–9.

Katz, L. (1985). Dispositions in early childhood education. *ERIC/EECE Bulletin, 18*(2), 1, 3.

Katz, L., and Chard, S. (in press). *Engaging the minds of young children: The project approach.* Norwood, NJ: Ablex.

Katz, L., Raths, J., and Torres, R. (undated). *A place called kindergarten.* Urbana, IL: ERIC Clearinghouse on Elementary and Early Childhood Education.

Nelson, K. (1985). *Making sense: The acquisition of shared meaning*. New York: Academic.

Office of Educational Research and Improvement. (1986). *Becoming a nation of readers: Implications for teachers.* Washington, DC: U.S. Department of Education.

Parker, J., and Asher, S. (1986, March). *Predicting later outcomes from peer rejection: Studies of school drop out, delinquency, and adult psychopathology*. Paper presented at the annual conference of the American Educational Research Association, San Francisco. In press: *Psychological Bulletin.*

Piaget, J. (1952). *The child's conception of number*. London: Routledge & Kegan Paul.

Piaget, J., and Inhelder, B. (1969). *The psychology of the child*. New York: Basic.

Schweinhart, L., Weikart, D., and Larner, M. (1986). Consequences of three preschool curriculum models through age 15. *Early Childhood Research Quarterly, 1*(1), 15–46.

Stipek, D. (1984). The development of achievement motivation. In R. Ames and C. Ames (Eds.), *Research on motivation in education: Vol. 1. Student motivation* (pp. 145–174). New York: Academic.

Van Deusen-Henkel, J., and Argondizza, M. (1987). Early elementary education: Curriculum planning for the primary grades. In *A framework for curriculum design: People, process, and product*. Augusta, ME: Division of Curriculum, Maine Department of Educational and Cultural Services.

Walberg, H. (1985). Improving the productivity of America's schools. *Educational Leadership, 41*(8), 19–30.

Weber, L. (1971). *The British Infant School and informal education*. Englewood Cliffs, NJ: Prentice-Hall.

Wells, G. (1983). Talking with children: The complementary roles of parents and teachers. In M. Donaldson, R. Grieve, and C. Pratt (Eds.), *Early childhood development and education* (pp. 127–150). New York: Guilford.

Wilkinson, L. (1984). Research currents: Peer group talk in elementary school. *Language Arts, 61*(2), 164–169.

Section Five: The Curriculum for Young Children in School

32. Joint Statement on Literacy Development and Pre-First Grade, prepared by the Early Childhood and Literacy Development Committee of the International Reading Association for ASCD, IRA, NAEYC, NAESP, NCTE, pp. 147–48.

The Reading Teacher, vol. 39, no. 8, April 1986, pp. 819–21. Copyright 1986 by the International Reading Association. Reprinted with permission of the International Reading Association.

33. Writing in Kindergarten and First Grade, by Mary Renck Jalongo and Sally Zeigler, pp. 149–55.

Childhood Education, vol. 64, no. 2, December 1987, pp. 97–104. Reprinted by permission of Mary Renck Jalongo and Sally Zeigler and the Association for Childhood Education International, 11141 Georgia Avenue, Suite 200, Wheaton, MD. Copyright 1987 by the Association.

Atkins, C. (1984). Writing: Doing something constructive. *Young Children, 40*, 3–7.

Bissex, G. (1980). *Gyns at work: A child learns to write and read*. Cambridge, MA: Harvard University.

Bromley, K. D. (1985). SSW: Sustained spontaneous writing. *Childhood Education, 62*(1), 23–29.

Calkins, L. M. (1980). Children learn the writer's craft. *Language Arts, 57*(2), 207–213.

Calkins, L. M. (1983). *Lessons from a child*. Portsmouth, NH: Heinemann.

Calkins, L. M. (1985). I am one who writes. *American Educator, 9*(3), 26–29, 42, 44.

Calkins, L. M. (1986). *The art of teaching writing*. Portsmouth, NH: Heinemann.

Clay, M. (1975). *What did I write?* Portsmouth, NH: Heinemann.

Early Childhood and Literacy Development Committee (1985). *Literacy development and pre-first grade*. Newark, DE: International Reading Association.

Furnas, A. (1985). Watch me. In J. Hansen, T. Newkirk, and D. H. Graves (Eds.), *Breaking ground: Teachers relate reading and writing in the elementary school*. Portsmouth, NH: Heinemann.

Graves, D. H. (1983). *Writing: Teachers and children at work*. Portsmouth, NH: Heinemann.

Holdaway, D. (1979). *The foundations of literacy*. New York: Ashton/Scholastic.

Jalongo, M. R. (1986). Decisions that affect teachers' professional development. *Childhood Education, 62*(5), 351–356.

Lamme, L. L. (1984). *Growing up writing*. Honesdale, PA: Highlights for Children.

May, R. (1975). *The courage to create*. New York: Norton.

Moyer, J., Egertson, H., and Isenberg, J. (1987). The child-centered kindergarten, ACEI position paper. *Childhood Education 63*(4), 235–242.

Schickendanz, J. A. (1986). *More than ABCs: The early stages of reading and writing*. Washington, DC: National Association for the Education of Young Children.

Stewig, J. W. (1980). *Children and literature*. Boston: Houghton-Mifflin.

Temple, C., and Gillet, J. W. (1984). *Language arts: Learning processes and teaching practices*. Boston: Little, Brown.

Von Reyn, J. (1985). Learning together: A teacher's first year teaching reading and writing. In J. Hansen, T. Newkirk, and D. H. Graves (Eds.), *Breaking ground: Teachers relate reading and writing in the elementary school*. Portsmouth, NH: Heinemann.

34. How Should Reading Be Taught in Kindergarten? by Patricia M. Cunningham, p. 156.

Educational Leadership, vol. 45, no. 1, September 1987, p. 83. Reprinted with permission of the Association for Supervision and Curriculum Development and Patricia M. Cunningham. Copyright © 1987 by the Association for Supervision and Curriculum Development. All rights reserved.

Mason, J. M., and K. H. Au. "Reading in Kindergarten." In *Reading Instruction for Today*. Glenview, Ill.: Scott Foresman, 1986.

Teale, W., and E. Sulzby, eds. *Emergent Literacy: Writing and Reading*. Norwood, N.J.: Ablex, 1986.

35. "Success"ful Reading Instruction, by Carol J. George, pp. 157–58.

Educational Leadership, vol. 44, no. 3, November 1986, pp. 62–63. Reprinted with permission of the Association for Supervision and Curriculum Development and Carol J. George. Copyright © 1986 by the Association for Supervision and Curriculum Development. All rights reserved.

Anderson, Richard. Condensed comments from interview. "We Can Become a Nation of Readers!" *Instructor* 95 (Nov.-Dec. 1985): 30-36.

Success in Reading and Writing, Teachers' Editions, K-6. Glenview, Ill: Good Year Books, Scott Foresman and Company, 1978 (first grade), 1980 (K).

36. Hispanic Books/Libros Hispanicos, by Isabel Schon, pp. 159–61.

Young Children, vol. 43, no. 5, May 1988, pp. 81–85. Copyright © 1988 by the National Association for the Education of Young Children. Reprinted with permission.

Cardenas, B., and Cardenas, J. (1973). Bright-eyed, bilingual, brown, and beautiful. *Today's Education, 62*(2), 49–51.

Cazden, C. B., Bryant, B. H., and Tillman, M. A. (1981). Making it and going home: The attitudes of Black people toward language education. In C. B. Cazden (Ed.), *Language in early childhood education* (rev. ed., pp. 97–106). Washington, DC: NAEYC.

Clemens, S. G. (1988). A Dr. Martin Luther King, Jr. curriculum: Playing the dream. *Young Children, 43*(2), 6–11, 59–63.

Connell, D. R. (1987). The first 30 years were the fairest: Notes from the kindergarten and ungraded primary (K–1–2). *Young Children, 42*(5), 30–39.

Escobedo, T. H. (1979). Mexican-American children and culture. *Texas Child Care Quarterly, 3*(2), 8–14.

Escobedo, T. H. (1983). *Early childhood bilingual education: A Hispanic perspective*. New York: Teachers College Press, Columbia University.

Fassler, J., and Janis, M. G. (1983). Books, children, and peace. *Young Children, 38*(6), 21–30.

Gingras, R. C. (1983). Early childhood bilingualism: Some considerations from second-language acquisition research. In O. N. Saracho and B. Spodek (Eds.), *Understanding the multicultural experience in early childhood education* (pp. 67–74). Washington, DC: NAEYC.

Gonzalez-Mena, J. (1981). English as a second language for preschool children. In C. B. Cazden (Ed.), *Language in early childhood education* (rev. ed., pp. 127–132). Washington, DC: NAEYC.

Hale-Benson, J. (1986). *Black children: Their roots, culture, and learning styles* (rev. ed.). Baltimore: Johns Hopkins University Press.

International Reading Association. (1985). *Literacy develop-ment and pre-first grade*. Newark, DE: Author.

Kontos, S. (1986). What preschool children know about reading and how they learn it. *Young Children, 42*(1), 58–66.

Laosa, L. M. (1977). Socialization, education, and continuity: The implications of the sociocultural context. *Young Children, 32*(5), 21–27.

Morris, J. B. (1983). Classroom methods and materials. In O. N. Saracho and B. Spodek (Eds.) *Understanding the multicultural experience in early childhood education* (pp. 77–90). Washington, DC: NAEYC.

Phillips, C. B. (1988). Nurturing diversity for today's children and tomorrow's leaders. *Young Children, 43*(2), 42–47.

Rashid, H. M. (1984). Promoting biculturalism in young African-American children. *Young Children, 39*(2), 12–23.

Saracho, O. N., and Hancock, F. M. (1983). Mexican-American culture. In O. N. Saracho and B. Spodek (Eds.), *Understanding the multicultural experience in early childhood education* (pp. 3–15). Washington, DC: NAEYC.

Saville-Troike, M. (1973). *Bilingual children: A resource document*. Arlington, VA: Center for Applied Linguistics.

Schickedanz, J. (1983). *Helping young children learn about reading*. Washington, DC: NAEYC.

Schickedanz, J. (1986). *More than the ABCs: The early stages of reading and writing*. Washington, DC: NAEYC.

Stone, J. C. (Ed.) (1971). *Five heritages: Teaching multicultural perspectives*. New York: Van Nostrand-Reinhold.

Teale, W. H. (1984). Reading to young children: Its significance for literacy development. In H. Goelman, A. Oberg, and F. Smith (Eds.), *Awakening to literacy* (pp. 110–121). Portsmouth, NH: Heinemann.

Wardle, F. (1987). Are you sensitive to interracial children's special identity needs? *Young Children, 42*(2), 53–59.

37. Learning Mathematics and Science Through Play, by Michael L. Henniger, pp. 162–65.

Childhood Education, vol. 63, no. 3, February 1987, pp. 167–71. Reprinted by permission of Michael L. Henniger and the Association for Childhood Education International, 11141 Georgia Avenue, Suite 200, Wheaton, MD. Copyright © 1987 by the Association.

Bruner, J. S. (1972). The nature and uses of immaturity. *American Psychologist 27*(8), 687-708.

Caplan, F., and Caplan, T. (1974). *The power of play*. New York: Anchor Press.

Einstein, A. (1954). *Ideas and opinions*. New York: Crown Publishers.

———. (1949) Autobiographical notes. In P. A. Schilpp (Ed.), *Albert Einstein: Philosopher scientist*. Evanston, IL: The Library of Living Philosophers.

Elkind, D. (1981*). Children and adolescents* (3rd ed). New York: Oxford University Press

Garvey, C. (1977). *Play*. Cambridge, MA: Harvard University Press.

Hartshorn, E., and Brantley, J. (1973). Effects of dramatic

play on classroom problem-solving ability. *Journal of Educational Research*: 66(6), 243-246.

Humphrey, J. (1966). An exploratory study of active games in learning of number concepts by first grade boys and girls. *Perceptual and Motor Skills, 23,* 341-342.

Hutt, C., and Bhavnani, R. (1972). Predictions from play. *Nature,* 237(5351), 171-172.

Johnson, J.E. (1976). Relations of divergent thinking and intelligence test scores with social and non-social make-believe play of preschool children. *Child Development,* 47(4), 1200-

1203.

Lieberman, J. (1965). Playfulness and divergent thinking: An investigation of their relationship at the kindergarten level. *Journal of Genetic Psychology,* 107(2), 219-224.

Pepler, D., and Ross, H. (1981). The effects of play on convergent and divergent problem solving. *Child Development,* 52(4), 1201-1210.

Zammarelli, J., and Bolton, N. (1977). The effects of play on mathematical concept formation, *British Journal of Educational Psychology,* 47(1), 155-161.

Bibliography

Bruner, J., Jolly, A., and Sylva, K. (Eds.). (1976). *Play: Its role in development and evolution.* New York: Basic Books.

Dansky, J. L. (1980). Make-believe: A mediator of the relationship between play and associative fluency. *Child Development, 51(2),* 576-579.

Fink, R. S. (1976). The role of imaginative play in cognitive development. *Psychological Reports, 39(3),* 895-906.

Frost, J., and Sunderlin, S. (1985). *When children play: Proceedings of the international conference on play and play environments.* Wheaton, MD: ACEI.

Ghiselin, B. (Ed.). (1952). *The creative process.* Berkeley: University of California Press.

Golomb, C., and Cornelius, C. (1977). Symbolic play and its cognitive significance. *Developmental Psychology, 13(3),* 246-252.

Harter, S. (1975). Developmental differences in the manifestations of mastery motivation on problem-solving tasks. *Child Development, 46(2),* 370-378.

Li, A. K. (1978). Effects of play on novel responses in kindergarten children. *The Alberta Journal of Educational Research, 23,* 31-36.

McKee, J. S. (Ed). (1986). *Play: Working partner of growth.* Wheaton, MD: ACEI.

Rosen, C. (1974). The effects of sociodramatic play on problem-solving behavior among culturally disadvantaged preschool children. *Child Development, 45(4),* 920-927.

Saltz, E., Dixon, D., and Johnson, J. (1977). Training disadvantaged preschoolers on various fantasy activities: Effects on cognitive function and impulse control. *Child Development, 48(2),* 367-380.

Severeide, R. C., and Pizzini, E. L. (1984). The role of play in science. *Science and Children, 21(8),* 58-61.

Singer, J. L. (Ed). (1973). *The child's world of make-believe.* New York: Academic Press.

Smilansky, S. (1968). *The effects of sociodramatic play on disadvantaged preschool children.* New York: Wiley.

Smith, P. K., and Dutton, S. (1979). Play and training in direct and innovative problem-solving. *Child Development, 50(3),* 830-836.

Yawkey, T. (1980). More on play as intelligence in children. *Journal of Creative Behavior, 13(4),* 247-256.

38. Montessori: Right or Wrong About Number Concepts? by Jerold P. Bauch and Huei-hsin Joyce Hsu, pp. 166–68.
Arithmetic Teacher, vol. 35, no. 6, February 1988, pp. 8–11. Copyright 1988 by the National Council of Teachers of Mathematics. Reprinted with permission.

Barron, Linda. *Mathematics Experiences for the Early Childhood Years.* Columbus, Ohio: Charles E. Merrill Publishing Co., 1979.

Briars, Diane, and Robert S. Siegler, "A Featural Analysis of Preschoolers' Counting Knowledge." *Developmental Psychology* 20 (July 1984):607-18.

Dawes, Cynthia G. *Early Maths.* New York: Longman, 1977.

Fuson, Karen C., Walter G. Secada, and James W. Hall. "Matching, Counting, and Conservation of Numerical Equivalence." *Child Development* 54 (February 1983): 91-97.

Gelman, Rochel, and C. R. Gallistel. *The Child's Understanding of Number.* Cambridge, Mass.: Harvard University Press, 1978.

Hsu, Huei-hsin Joyce. "*An Integrated Model for Learning Number Concepts at the Preschool Level in Taiwan.*" Ph.D. diss., Peabody College of Vanderbilt University, 1987.

Kamii, Constance. *Number in Preschool and Kindergarten: Educational Implications of Piaget's Theory.* Washington, D.C.: National Association for the Education of Young Children, 1982.

Kamii, Constance, and Rheta DeVries. *Piaget, Children, and Number: Applying Piaget's Theory of the Teaching of Elementary Number.* Washington, D.C.: National Association for the Education of Young Children, 1976.

Kennedy, Leonard M. *Guiding Children's Learning of Mathematics.* 4th ed. Belmont, Calif.: Wadsworth Publishing Co., 1984.

Kingma, Johannes, and Willem Koops. "Consequences of Task Variation in Cardination Research." *Genetic Psychology Monographs* 109 (February 1984):77-94.

Kohlberg, Lawrence. "Montessori with the Culturally Disadvantaged: A Cognitive-developmental Interpretation and Some Research Findings." In *Early Education: Current Theory, Research, and Action,* edited by Robert D. Hess and Roberta M. Bear, pp. 105-18. Chicago, Ill.: Aldine Publishing Co., 1968.

Kraner, Robert E. "An Acquisition Age of Quantitative Concepts of Children from Three to Six Years Old." *Journal of Experimental Education* 46 (Winter 1978):52-59.

Lavatelli, Celia S. *Piaget's Theory Applied to an Early Childhood Curriculum.* Boston, Mass.: American Science and Engineering, 1970.

Montessori, Maria. *The Montessori Method.* Translated by Anne E. George. Cambridge, Mass.: Robert Bentley, 1964.

Morgan, Susanna M. "A Comparative Assessment of Some Aspects of the Development of the Concept of Number and Arithmetical Skills in Montessori and Traditional Preschools." *Dissertation Abstracts International* 39B (December 1978):2966.

ACKNOWLEDGMENTS, FOOTNOTES, AND REFERENCES

Russac, R. J. "The Relation between Two Strategies of Cardinal Number: Correspondence and Counting." *Child Development* 49 (September 1978):728–35.

Russell, Robert L., and Herbert P. Ginsburg. "Cognitive Analysis of the Children's Mathematics Difficulties." *Cognition and Instruction* 1 (Spring 1984):217–44.

Savage, Carol J. H. "A Comparison of a Montessori and a Traditional Preschool Curricula." *Dissertation Abstracts International* 34A (December 1973):3041-42.

Standing, E. Mortimer. *Maria Montessori: Her Life and Work.* New York: New American Library, 1962.

White, Jacqueline M., Steven R. Yussen, and Edward M. Docherty. "Performance of Montessori and Traditionally Schooled Nursery Children on Tasks of Seriation, Classification, and Conservation." *Contemporary Educational Psychology* 1 (October 1976):356–68.

Yussen, Steven R., Samuel Matthews, and Jacqueline W. Knight. "Performance of Montessori and Traditionally Schooled Nursery Children on Social Cognitive Tasks and Memory Problems." *Contemporary Educational Psychology* 5 (April 1980):124–37.

39. Theoretical Framework for Preschool Science Experiences, by Robert F. Smith, pp. 169–73.

© 1987, Robert F. Smith. *Young Children*, January 1987, pp. 34–40.

Christenberry, M., and Stevens, B. (1984). *Can Piaget cook?* Atlanta: Humanics Limited.

Flavell, J. H. (1963). *Developmental psychology of Jean Piaget.* New York: Van Nostrand.

Forman, G. E., and Kuschner, D. S. (1983). *The child's construction of knowledge: Piaget for teaching children.* Washington, DC: NAEYC.

Greenberg, P. (1975). *Bridge-to-reading comprehensive preschool curriculum: Discovery science.* Washington, DC: Acropolis.

Harlan, J. (1984). *Science experiences for the early childhood years.* Columbus, OH: Merrill.

Hawkins, D. (1965). Messing about in science. *Science and Children, 2,* 5–9.

Hill, D. (1977). *Mud, sand, and water.* Washington, DC: NAEYC.

Hirsch, E. S. (1984). *The block book* (rev. ed.). Washington, DC: NAEYC.

Hochman, V., and Greenwald, M. (1963). *Science experiences in early childhood.* New York: Bank Street College of Education.

Holt, B-G. (1977). *Science with young children.* Washington, DC: NAEYC.

Howe, A. (1975). A rationale for science in early childhood education. *Science Education, 59,* 95–101.

Iatridis, M. (1981). Teaching science to preschoolers. *Science and Children,* 19(2), 25–27.

Kamii, C., and DeVries, R. (1978). *Physical knowledge in preschool education: Implications of Piaget's theory.* Englewood Cliffs, NJ: Prentice-Hall.

Laskey, L., and Mukerji, R. (1980). *Art: Basic for young children.* Washington, DC: NAEYC.

McIntyre, M. (1981a). Color awareness. *Science and Children* 18(7), 40–41.

McIntyre, M. (1981b). The sounds of music. *Science and Children* 18(5), 34–35.

McIntyre, M. (1984). *Early childhood and science.* Washington, DC: National Science Teachers' Association.

National Association for the Education of Young Children. (1986). NAEYC postion statement on developmentally appropriate practice in early childhood programs serving children from birth through age 8. *Young Children,* 41(6), pp. 3–19.

Neuman, D. B. (1978). *Experiences in science for young children.* Albany, NY: Delmar.

Parents Nursery School. (1974). *Kids are natural cooks.* Boston: Houghton Mifflin.

Piaget, J. (1929). *The child's conception of the world.* New York: Harcourt & Brace.

Piaget, J. (1954). *The construction of reality in the child.* New York: Basic.

Piaget, J. (1973). *To understand is to invent: The future of education.* New York: Grossman.

Schools Council. (1972a). *Early experiences.* London: Macdonald Educational Ltd.

Schools Council. (1972b). *Science from toys.* London: Macdonald Educational, Ltd.

Schools Council. (1973a). *Ourselves.* Milwaukee, WI: Macdonald-Raintree.

Schools Council. (1973b). *Coloured things.* London: Macdonald Educational Ltd.

Smith, R. F. (1981). Early childhood science education: A Piagetian perspective. *Young Children* 36(2), 3–10.

Wanamaker, N., Hearn, K., and Richarz, S. (1979). *More than graham crackers: Nutrition education and food preparation with young children.* Washington, DC: NAEYC.

Ward, A. (1978). The clay boat project: Floating and sinking studies with infants. *School Science Review* 59, 626–633.

Wolfinger, D. M. (1982). Effect of science teaching on the young child's concept of Piagetian physical causality: Animism and dynamism. *Journal of Research in Science Teaching* 19, 595–602.

Zeitler, W. R. (1972). A study of observational skill development in children of age three. *Science Education* 56, 79–84.

40. Music in the Early Childhood Curriculum, by Manny Brand and David E. Fernie, pp. 174–77.

Childhood Education, vol. 59, no. 5, May/June 1983, pp. 321–26. Reprinted by permission of Manny Brand and David E. Fernie and the Association for Childhood Education International, 11141 Georgia Avenue, Suite 200, Wheaton, MD. Copyright © 1983 by the Association.

Andress, Barbara. *Music Experiences in Early Childhood.* New York: Holt, Rinehart and Winston, 1980.

Andress, Barbara, et al. *Music in Early Childhood.* Washington, DC: Music Educators National Conference, 1973.

Bayless, Kathleen M., and Marjorie E. Ramsey. *Music: A Way of Life for the Young Child:* 2nd Ed. St. Louis, MO: C. V.

Mosby Co., 1982.

Biasini, Americole; Ronald Thomas, and Lenore Pogonowsky. *MMCP Interaction: Early Childhood Music Curriculum.* Bardonia, NY: Media Materials, 1972.

Carson, Rachel. *The Sea Around Us.* New York: New American Library, 1960.

Fullard, William. "Operant Training of Aural Music Discrimination with Preschool Children." *Journal of Research in Music Education* (1967): 201–09.

Gordon, Edwin. *Primary Measures of Music Audiation: Test Manual.* Chicago: G. I. A. Publication, 1979.

Haines, B. Joan, and Linda Gerber. *Leading Your Child to Music: A Resource Book for Teachers.* Columbus, OH: Charles

E. Merrill, 1980.

Houston, John. *A Mouse on My House.* Reading, MA: Addison-Wesley, 1972.

MacDonald, Dorothy. *Music in Our Lives: The Early Years.* Washington, DC: National Association for the Education of Young Children, 1979.

Miller, Samuel. "Edwin Gordon, Music Psychologist for Our Time: A Critique." *Southwestern Musician* (1981): 20-22.

Nye, Venice. *Music for Young Children.* Dubuque IA: William C. Brown, 1979.

Zimmerman, Marilyn. *Musical Characteristics of Children.* Washington, DC: Music Educators National Conference, 1971.

41. Appreciate the Drawing and Dictating of Young Children, by Anne Haas Dyson, pp. 178–86.

Young Children, vol. 43, no. 3, March 1988, pp. 25–32. Copyright © 1988 by the National Association for the Education of Young Children. Reprinted with permission.

Applebee, A. (1978). *The child's concept of story.* Chicago: University of Chicago Press.

Ashton-Warner, S. (1963). *Teacher.* New York: Simon and Schuster.

Bloom, L. (1975). Language development review. In F. D. Horowitz (Ed.), *Review of child development research* (Vol. 4, pp. 245-304). Chicago: University of Chicago Press.

Brittain, W. L. (1979). *Creativity, art, and the young child.* New York: Macmillan.

Brown, R. (1973). *A first language: The early stages.* Cambridge, MA: Harvard University Press.

Dyson, A. H. (1981). Oral language: The rooting system for learning to write. *Language Arts, 58,* 776-784.

Dyson, A. H. (1982). The emergence of visible language: Interrelationships between drawing and early writing. *Visible Language, 6,* 360-381.

Dyson, A. H. (1985). Puzzles, paints, and pencils: Writing emerges. *Educational Horizons, 64,* 13-16.

Franklin, M. (1973). Nonverbal representation in young children: A cognitive perspective. *Young Children, 29*(1), 33-52.

Freeman, N. (1977). How young children try to plan drawings. In G. Butterworth (Ed.), *The child's representation of the world* (pp. 3-30). New York: Plenum.

Gardner, H. (1980). *Artful scribbles.* New York: Basic.

Gardner, H., Wolf, D., and Smith, A. (1982). Max and Mollie: Individual differences in early artistic symbolization. In H. Gardner (Ed.), *Art, mind, and brain: A cognitive approach to creativity* (pp. 110-127). New York: Basic.

Golomb, C. (1974). *Young children's sculpture and drawing.* Cambridge, MA: Harvard University Press.

Graves, D. (1983). *Writing: Teachers and children at work.* Exeter, NH: Heinemann.

Gundlach, R. A. (1981). On the nature and development of children's writing. In C. H. Frederiksen and J. F. Dominic (Eds.), *Writing: The nature, development and teaching of written communication, Vol. 2. Writing: Process, development and communication* (pp. 133-152). Hillsdale, NJ: Erlbaum.

Hipple, M. L. (1985). Journal writing in kindergarten. *Language Arts, 62,* 255-261.

King, M. (1980). Learning how to mean in written language. *Theory Into Practice, 19,* 163-169.

Korzenik, D. (1977). Saying it with pictures. In D. Perkins

and B. Leondar (Eds.), *The arts and cognition* (pp. 192-207). Baltimore: Johns Hopkins University Press.

Lamme, L. L., and Childers, N. M. (1983). The composing processes of three young children. *Research in the Teaching of English, 17,* 32-50.

Leondar, B. (1977). Hatching plots: Genesis of storymaking. In D. Perkins and B. Leondar (Eds.), *The arts and cognition* (pp.172-191). Baltimore: Johns Hopkins University Press.

Lindstrom, M. (1970). *Children's art.* Berkeley and Los Angeles: University of California Press.

Magee, M. A., and Sutton-Smith, B. (1983). The art of storytelling: How do children learn it? *Young Children, 38*(4), 4-12.

Nelson, K. (1973). Structure and strategy in learning to talk. *Monographs of the Society for Research in Child Development, 38*(1-2, Serial No. 149).

Newkirk, T., and Atwell, N. (Eds.)., (1982). *Understanding writing.* The Northeast Regional Exchange, 101 Mill Rd., Chelmsford, MA 01824.

Newman, D., Griffin, P., and Cole, M. (1984). Social constraints in laboratory and classroom tasks. In B. Rogoff and J. Lave (Eds.), *Everyday cognition* (pp.172-193). Cambridge, MA: Harvard University Press.

Paley, V. (1981). *Wally's stories.* Cambridge, MA: Harvard University Press.

Rich, S. J. (1985). The writing suitcase. *Young Children, 40*(5), 42-44.

Smith, N. R., (1979). Developmental origins of structural variation in symbol form. In N. R. Smith and M. B. Franklin (Eds.), *Symbolic functioning in childhood* (pp. 11-26). Hillsdale, NJ: Erlbaum.

Smith, N. R., (1983). *Experience and art.* New York: Teachers College Press, Columbia University.

Stein, N. (1979, April). The concept of a story: A psycholinguistic analysis. In R. Bracewell (Chair), *Recent approaches to writing research: An evaluation and forecast.* Symposium conducted at the meeting of the American Educational Research Association, San Francisco.

Sulzby, E. (1982). Oral and written language mode adaptations in stories by kindergarten children. *Journal of Reading Behavior, 14,* 51-59.

Sulzby, E. (1985). Children's emergent reading of favorite storybooks: A developmental study. *Reading Research Quarter-*

ly, 20, 458-481.

Veatch, J., Sawicki, F., Elliott, G., Barnette, E., and Blakey, J. (1973). *Key words to reading: The language experience approach begins.* Columbus, OH: Merrill.

Vygotsky, L. S. (1962). *Thought and language.* Cambridge, MA: M.I.T. Press.

Wells, G. (1981). *Language at home and at school: Vol. 1. Learning through interaction: The study of language development.* Cambridge, England: Cambridge University Press.

Winner, E. (1982). *Invented worlds: The psychology of the arts.* Cambridge, MA: Harvard University Press.

Wolf, D., and Gardner, H. (1979). Style and sequence in early symbolic play. In N. Smith and M. B. Franklin (Eds.), *Symbolic functioning in childhood* (pp. 117-138). Hillsdale, NJ: Erlbaum.

Wolf, D., and Gardner, H. (1981). On the structure of early symbolization. In R. L. Schiefelbusch (Ed.), *Early language: Acquisition and intervention* (pp. 289-320). Baltimore: University Park Press.

Zalusky, V. (1983). Relationships: What did I write? What did I draw? In W. Frawley (Ed.), *Linguistics and literacy* (pp.91-124)). New York: Plenum.

42. Encouraging Positive Social Interaction Among Young Children, by Dwight L. Rogers and Dorene Doerre Ross, pp. 187–91.

Young Children, vol. 41, no. 3, March 1986, pp. 12–17. Copyright © 1986 by the National Association for the Education of Young Children. Reprinted with permission.

Asher, S. R., Oden, S. L., and Gottman, J. M. (1977). Children's friendships in school settings. In L. G. Katz (Ed)., *Current topics in early childhood education* (Vol. 1). Norwood, NJ: Ablex.

Asher, S. R., Singleton, L. L., Tinsley, B.R., and Hymel, S. (1979). A reliable sociometric measure for preschool children. *Developmental Psychology, 15*(4), 443-444.

Bremm, D. W., and Erickson, F. (1977). Relationships among verbal and non-verbal classroom behaviors. *Theory Into Practice, 16*(3), 153–161.

Charlesworth, R., and Hartup, W. W. (1967). Positive social reinforcement in the nursery school peer group. *Child Development, 38*(4), 993–1002.

Christie, J. F. (1982, May). Sociodramatic play training. *Young Children, 37*(4) 25-32).

Cowen, E. L., Pederson, A., Babijian, H., Izzo, L. D., and Trost, M. A. (1973). Long-term follow-up of early detected vulnerable children. *Journal of Consulting and Clinical Psychology, 41,* 438–446.

Denzin, N. K. (1977). *Childhood socialization.* San Francisco: Jossey Bass.

Gottman J., Gonso, J., and Rasamussen, B. (1975). Social interaction, social competence, and friendship in children. *Child Development, 46*(3), 709–718.

Hartup, W. W. and Coates, B. (1967). Imitation of a peer as a function of reinforcement from the peer group and rewardingness of the model. *Child Development, 38*(4). 1003–1016.

Hill, T. C. (1982, November). *Promoting empathy in the preschool: An important part of the curriculum.* Paper presented at the annual meeting of the National Association for the Education of Young Children, Washington, DC.

Hill, T. C. (1983, April). *The effect of self reflection on preschool children's empathetic understanding and prosocial behavior.* Paper presented at the annual meeting of the Society for Research in Child Development, Detroit.

Honig, A. S. (1982, July). Research in review: Prosocial development in children *Young Children. 37*(5), 51-62.

Hughes R., Tingle, B. A., and Sawin, D. B. (1981). Development of empathic understanding. *Child Development, 52,* 122-128.

Krogh, S. L. (1982, November). *Encouraging positive justice reasoning and perspective taking skills.* Paper presented at the annual meeting of the National Association of Early Childhood Teacher Educators, Washington, DC.

Leiter, M. P. (1977). A study in reciprocity in preschool play groups. *Child Development, 48*(4), 1288–1295.

Mead, G. H. (1930). The philosophies of Royce, James, and Dewey in their American setting. *International Journal of Ethics, 40,* 211–231.

Moore, S. G. (1981). Unique contributions of peers to socialization in early childhood. *Theory Into Practice, 20,* 105–108.

Mussen, P., and Eisenberg-Berg, N. (1977). Roots of caring, sharing and helping. San Francisco: W. H. Freeman.

Putallaz, M., and Gottman, J. M. (1981). An introductional model of children's entry into peer groups. *Child Development, 52*(3), 986–994.

Roff, M., Sells. S. B., and Golden, J. M. (1972). *Social adjustment and personality development in children.* Minneapolis: University of Minnesota Press.

Ross, D. D. and Rogers, D. L. (1982, November). *Block play and social development: What do children learn as they play?* Paper presented at the annual meeting of the National Association for the Education of Young Children, Washington, DC.

Rubin, K. H. (1972). Relationship between egocentric communication and popularity among peers. *Developmental Psychology, 7*(3), p. 364.

Schacter, F. F., Kirshner, K., Klips, B., Friedricks, M., and Sanders, K. (1974). Everyday preschool interpersonal speech usage. *Monographs of the Society for Research in Child Development, 39*(3) 1–88.

Smilansky, S. (1971). Can adults facilitate play in children?: Theoretical and practical considerations. In S. Arnaud (Ed.), *Play: The child strives for reality.* Washington, DC: National Association for the Education of Young Children.

Spivak, G., and Shure, M. B. (1974). *Social adjustment of children.* Washington, DC: Jossey Bass.

Stone, G. S. (1981). *A guide to discipline* (rev. ed.). Washington, DC: National Association for the Education of Young Children.

Vaughn, B. E., and Waters, E. (1980). Social organization among preschool peers: Dominance, attention, and sociometric correlates. In D. R. Omark, F. F. Strayer, and D. G. Freeman (Eds.), *Dominance relations: Ethological perspectives on human conflict.* New York: Garland Press.

Vaughn, B.E., and Waters, E. (1981). Attention structures, sociometric status, and dominance: Interrelations, behavior correlates, and relationships to social competence. *Developmental Psychology 17*(3), 275–288.

Wilkinson, L. C., and Dollaghan, C. (1979). Peer communi-cation in first grade reading groups. *Theory Into Practice, 18,* 267–274.

43. Teaching with Less Talking: Learning Centers in the Kindergarten, by Barbara Kimes Myers and Karen Maurer, pp. 192–97.

Young Children, vol. 42, no. 5, July 1987, pp. 20–27. Copyright © 1987 by the National Association for the Education of Young Children. Reprinted with permission.

Berlak, A., and Berlak, H. (1981). *Dilemmas of schooling.* London: Methuen.

Bussis, A. M., Chittenden, E. A., and Amarel, M. (1976). *Beyond surface curriculum: An interview study of teachers' understandings.* Boulder: Westview.

Day, B. (1983). *Early childhood education: Creative learning activities.* New York: Macmillan.

Dewey, J. (1966). *Experience and education.* New York: Collier.

Halliwell, G. L. (1980). *Kindergarten teachers and curriculum construct systems.* Unpublished master's thesis, University of Illinois, Urbana.

King, N. (1976). *The hidden curriculum and the socialization of kindergarten children.* Unpublished doctoral dissertation, University of Wisconsin, Madison.

King, R. (1978). *All things bright and beautiful.* New York: Wiley.

Myers, B. (1984). *An analysis of one early childhood teacher's beliefs about the events of her classroom.* Paper presented at the annual meeting of American Education Research Association, New Orleans, LA.

Myers, B., and Maurer, K. (1986). *Childspace in the kindergarten curriculum.* Paper presented at the Illinois Kindergarten Conference, St. Charles, IL.

National Association for the Education of Young Children. (1986). Position statement on developmentally appropriate practice in early childhood programs serving children from birth to age 8. *Young Children, 41*(6), 3-19.

Nimnicht, G., McAfee, O., and Meier, J. (1968). *The new nursery school.* General Learning Corporation, 250 James St., Morristown, NJ 07960.

Spodek, B. (1985). *Teaching in the early years.* Englewood Cliffs, NJ: Prentice-Hall.

44. Influences from the Past: Play in the Early Childhood Curriculum, by Margie L. Hardy and Laurie J. Greene, pp. 198–200.

Dimensions, vol. 14, no. 3, April 1986, pp. 8–10. © 1986, Southern Association on Children Under Six, Little Rock, Arkansas. Reprinted with permission.

Braun, S. J., and Edwards, E. P. (1972). *History and theory of early childhood education.* Belmont, CA: Wadsworth.

Butler, A. L., Gotts, E. E. and Quisenberry, N. L. (1978). *Play as development.* Columbus, OH: Merrill.

Hailmann, W. N. (1887). *The education of man.* New York: D. Appleton (original work published in 1826).

Hartley, R. E., and Goldenson, R. M. (1963). *The complete book of children's play* (2nd ed.). New York: T. Y. Crowell.

Kamii, C. K. (1985). *Young children reinvent arithmetic: Implications of Piaget's theory.* New York: Teachers College Press.

Munsinger, H. (1975). *Fundamentals of child development* (2nd ed.). New York: Holt, Rinehart & Winston.

Piaget, J. (1962). *Play, dreams and imitation in childhood.* New York: Norton.

Yawkey, T. D. and Pellegrini, A. D. (Ed.) (1984). *Child's play: Developmental and applied.* Hillsdale, NJ: Lawrence Erlbaum.

45. Leading Primary Education Toward Excellence: Beyond Worksheets and Drill, by Constance Kamii, pp. 201-7.
Young Children, vol. 40, no. 6, September 1985, pp. 3–9. Copyright 1985 by Constance Kamii. Reprinted with permission.

Ferreiro, E., and Teberosky, A. (1982). *Literacy before schooling.* Exeter, NH: Heinemann.

Inhelder, B., and Piaget, J. (1963). De l'itération des actions à la récurrence élémentaire. (From the iteration of actions to elementary recurrence). In P. Gréco, B. Inhelder, B. Matalon, and J. Piaget (Eds.), *La formation des raisonnements recurrentiels* (Etudes d'epistemologie genetique, XVIII). *(The formation of reasoning by recurrence.)* Paris: Presses Universitaires de France.

Kamii, C. (1982). *Number in preschool and kindergarten.* Washington, DC: National Association for the Education of Young Children.

Kamii, C. (1984). Autonomy: The aim of education envisioned by Piaget. *Phi Delta Kappan*, 65, 410–415.

Kamii, C. (1985). *Young children reinvent arithmetic.* New York: Teachers College Press, Columbia University.

Kamii, C., and DeVries, R. (1978). *Physical knowledge in preschool education.* Englewood Cliffs, NJ: Prentice-Hall.

Kamii, C., and DeVries, R. (1980). *Group games in early education.* Washington, DC: National Association for the Education of Young Children.

Piaget, J. (1972). *Science of education and the psychology of the child* (rev. ed.). New York: Viking. (Original work published 1965)

Piaget, J., and Szeminska, A. (1965). *The child's conception of number* (rev. ed.). New York: Norton. (Original work published 1941)

Taylor, F. S. (1949). *A short history of science and scientific thought.* New York: Norton.

Section Six: Evidence and Evaluation

46. Effects of Program Models and Teaching Practices, by Douglas R. Powell, pp. 210–15.
Young Children, vol. 41, no. 6, September 1986, pp. 60–67. Copyright © 1986 by the National Association for the Education of Young Children. Reprinted with permission.

Becker, W. C., and Gersten, R. (1982). A follow up of Follow Through: The later effects of the direct instruction model on children in fifth and sixth grades. *American Educational Research Journal, 19*, 75-92.

Bereiter, C., and Englemann, S. (1966). *Teaching the disadvantaged child in the peschool.* Englewood Cliffs, NJ: Prentice-Hall.

Biber, H., Miller, L. B., and Dyer, J. L. (1972). Feminization in preschool, *Develpmental Psychology, 1,* 86.

Dunn, L. M., Horton, K. B., and Smith, J. O. (1968). *Peabody Language Development Kits for Level P.* Circle Pines, MN: American Guidance Service.

Fagot, B. (1973). Influence of teacher behavior in the preschool. *Developmental Psychology, 9,* 198-206.

Fry, P. S., and Addington, J. (1984). Comparison of social problem solving of children from open and traditional classrooms: A two-year longitudinal study. *Journal of Educational Psychology, 76,* 318-329.

Gray, S. W., Ramsey, B. K., and Klaus, R. A. (1982). *From 3 to 20: The Early Training Project.* Baltimore: University Park Press.

Hart, B., and Risley, T. B. (1975). Incidental teaching of language in the preschool. *Journal of Applied Behavioral Analysis, 4,*. 411–420.

Hohmann, M., Banet, B., and Wiekart, D. P. (1979). *Young children in action: A manual for preschool educators.* Ypsilanti, MI: High/Scope Press.

Huston-Stein, A., Friedrich-Cofer, L., Susman, E. (1977). The relation of classroom structure to social behavior, imaginative play, and self-regulation of economically disadvantaged children. *Child Development, 48,* 908-916.

Hymes, J. L. (1968). *Teaching the child under six.* Columbus, OH: Merrill.

Karnes, M. B., Shwedel, A. M., and Williams, M. B. (1983). A comparison of five approaches for educating young children from low-income homes. In Consortium for Longitudinal Studies, *As the twig is bent. . . . Lasting effects of preschool programs* (pp. 133-170). Hillsdale, NJ: Erlbaum.

Katz, L. (1985). Dispositions in early childhood education. *ERIC/EECE Bulletin, 18,* 1-3.

Koester, L. S., and Farley, F. H. (1982). Psychophysiological characteristics and school performance of children in open and traditional classrooms. *Journal of Education Psychology, 2,* 254-263.

Lazar, I., and Darlington, R. (1982). Lasting effects of early education: A report from the Consortium for Longitudinal Studies. *Monographs of the Society for Research in Child Development, 47* (2-3, Serial No. 195).

Meyer, L. (1984). Long-term academic effects of direct instruction Follow Through. *Elementary School Journal, 4,* 380-394.

Meyer, L., Gersten, R., and Gutkin, J. (1984). Direct instruction: A Project Follow Through success story. *Elementary School Journal, 2,* 241-252.

Miller, L. B., and Dyer, J. L. (1975). Four preschool programs: Their dimensions and effects. *Monographs of the Society for Research in Child Development, 40* (5-6, Serial No. 162).

Miller, L. B., and Bizzell, R. P. (1983a). Long-term effects of four preschool programs; 6th, 7th, and 8th grades. *Child Development, 54,* 725-741.

Miller, L. B., and Bizzell, R. P. (1983b). The Louisville Experiment: A comparison of four programs. In Consortium for Longitudinal Studies, *As the twig is bent. . . . Lasting effects of preschool programs* (pp. 171-199). Hillsdale, NJ: Erlbaum.

Miller, L. B., Bugbee, M. R., and Hybertson, D. W. (1985). Dimensions of preschool: The effects of individual experience. In I. E. Sigel (Ed.), *Advances in applied developmental psychology* (Vol. 1, pp. 25-90). Norwood, NJ: Ablex.

Montessori, M. (1964). *The Montessori method.* New York: Schocken.

Schweinhart, L. J., Weikart, D. P., and Larner. M. B. (1986). Consequences of three preschool curriculum models through age 15. *Early Childhood Research Quarterly, 1,* 15-45.

Sigel, I. E. (1979). On becoming a thinker: A psychoeducational model, *Educational Psychologist, 14,* 70-79.

Smothergill, N. L., Olson, F., and Moore, S. G. (1971). The effects of manipulation of teacher communication style in the preschool. *Child Development, 42,* 1229-1239.

Soar, R. S., and Soar, R. M. (1972). An empirical analysis of selected Follow Through programs: An example of a process approach to evaluation in early childhood education. In I. Gordon (Ed.), *71st yearbook of the National Society for the Study of Education: Part 2.* Chicago: University of Chicago Press.

Stallings, J. (1975). Implementation and child effects of teaching practices in Follow Through classrooms. *Monographs of the Society for Research in Child Development, 40* (7-8, Serial No. 163).

Stallings, J. A., and Stipek, D. (1986). Research on early childhood and elementary school teaching programs. In M.C. Wittrock (Ed.), *Handbook of research on teaching* (3rd ed., pp. 727-753). New York: Macmillan.

Weikart, D. P., Epstein, A. S., Schweinhart, L. J., and Bond, J. T. (1978). *The Ypsilanti Preschool Curriculum Demonstration Project: Preschool years and longitudinal results.* Monograph of the High/Scope Educational Research Foundation, 4. Ypsilanti, MI: High/Scope Press.

Willert, M. K., and Kamii, C. (1985). Reading in kindergarten: Direct versus indirect teaching. *Young Children, 40,* 3-9.

Zigler, E., and Trickett, P. K. (1978). IQ, social competence, and evaluation of early childhood intervention programs. *American Psychologist, 33,* 789-799.

47. Evidence That Good Early Childhood Programs Work, by Lawrence J. Schweinhart and David P. Weikart, pp. 216–21.
Phi Delta Kappan, vol. 66, no. 8, April 1985. Copyright 1985 by Lawrence J. Schweinhart. Reprinted with permission.

*The data for the Perry Preschool Project are included in the tables, but we will limit our discussion here. For a more detailed description of the evaluation of the Perry Preschool Project, see "The Promise of Early Childhood Education," by Lawrence J. Schweinhart, John R. Berrueta-Clement, W. Steven Barnett, Ann S. Epstein, and David P. Weikart, pp. 222–25.

1. Rupert A. Klaus and Susan W. Gray, *The Early Training Project for Disadvantaged Children: A Report After Five Years* (Chicago: University of Chicago Press, Society for Research in Child Development, Monograph No. 120, 1968); and David P. Weikart, ed., *Preschool Intervention: Preliminary Results of the Perry Preschool Project* (Ann Arbor, Mich.: Campus Publishers, 1967).

2. Westinghouse Learning Corporation, *The Impact of Head Start: An Evaluation of the Effect of Head Start on Children's Cognitive and Affective Development, Vols. I–II* (Athens: Ohio University, 1969); and Arthur R. Jensen, "How Much Can We Boost I.Q. and Scholastic Achievement?," *Harvard Educational Review,* February 1969, pp. 1–123.

3. This focus on early childhood education for low-income blacks has left its mark. In 1980, for 3- and 4-year-olds in families with annual incomes under $15,000, the preschool enrollment figures were 37 percent for black children but only 25% for white children. See Gerald Kahn, *School Enrollment of 3- and 4-Year-Olds by Race/Ethnic Category* (Washington, D.C.: National Center for Education Statistics, 1982), p. 13.

4. Irving Lazar, Richard Darlington, Harry Murray, Jacqueline Royce, and Ann Snipper, *Lasting Effects of Early Education* (Chicago: Society for Research in Child Development, Monograph No. 194, 1982). The investigators of the Early Training Project, the Harlem Study, and the Mother-Child Home Program also belonged to the Consortium.

5. Craig T. Ramey, Donna M. Bryant, and Tanya M. Suarez, "Preschool Compensatory Education and the Modifiability of Intelligence: A Critical Review," in Douglas Detterman, ed., *Current Topics in Human Intelligence* (Norwood, N.J.: Ablex, 1984).

6. Lawrence J. Schweinhart and David P. Weikart, *Young Children Grow Up: The Effects of the Perry Preschool Program on Youths Through Age 15* (Ypsilanti, Mich.: High/Scope Press, 1980).

RECENT REPORTS ON THE SEVEN STUDIES

Early Training Project. Susan W. Gray, Barbara K. Ramsey, and Rupert A. Klaus, *From 3 to 20—The Early Training Project* (Baltimore: University Park Press, 1982).

Perry Preschool Project. John R. Berrueta-Clement, Lawrence J. Schweinhart, W. Steven Barnett, Ann S. Epstein, and David P. Weikart, *Changed Lives: The Effects of the Perry Preschool Program on Youths Through Age 19* (Ypsilanti, Mich.: High/Scope Press, 1984).

Mother-Child Home Program. Phyllis Levenstein, John O'Hara, and John Madden, "The Mother-Child Home Program of the Verbal Interaction Project," in Consortium for Longitudinal Studies, *As the Twig Is Bent...Lasting Effects of Preschool Programs* (Hillsdale, N.J.: Erlbaum, 1983), pp. 237-64.

Harlem Study. Francis H. Palmer, "The Harlem Study: Effects by Type of Training, Age of Training, and Social Class," in *As the Twig Is Bent...*, pp. 201-36.

Rome Head Start Program. Eleanor Monroe and M. S. McDonald, "A Follow-up Study of the 1966 Head Start Program," Rome City Schools, Rome, Ga., 1981.

Milwaukee Study. Howard L. Garber and Rick Heber, "The Efficacy of Early Intervention with Family Rehabilitation," in Michael J. Begab, H. Carl Haywood, and Howard L. Garber, eds., *Psychosocial Influences in Retarded Performance, Vol. II: Strategies for Improving Competence* (Baltimore: University Park Press, 1981), pp. 71-88.

New York Prekindergarten Program. David J. Irvine, "Evaluation of the New York State Experimental Prekindergarten Program," paper presented at the annual meeting of the American Educational Research Association, New York, N.Y., 1982.

48. The Promise of Early Childhood Education, by Lawrence J. Schweinhart, John R. Berrueta-Clement, W. Steven Barnett, Ann S. Epstein, and David P. Weikart, pp. 222–25.
Phi Delta Kappan, vol. 66, no. 8, April 1985. Copyright 1985 by Lawrence J. Schweinhart. Reprinted with permission.

1. U.S. Bureau of the Census, *Current Population Reports,* Series P60, No. 133, Tables 1, 2.

2. Martin Chorvinsky, *Preprimary Enrollment 1980* (Washington, D.C.: National Center for Education Statistics, 1982).

3. These findings are more fully described in our monograph, *Changed Lives: The Effects of the Perry Preschool Program on Youths Through Age 19* (Ypsilanti, Mich.: High/Scope Press, 1984). A four-year grant from the U.S. Department of Education provided funding for the most recent phase of the research. The Levi-Strauss Foundation and the Rosenberg Foundation of San Francisco provided matching grants for the economic analysis and for a dissemination project. The views expressed in this article are solely those of the authors and do not necessarily reflect the official positions of the funding agencies.

4. Report by the Congressional Research Service of the Library of Congress to the House Select Committee on Children, Youth, and Families, *Federal Programs Affecting Children* (Washington, D.C.: U.S. Government Printing Office, 1983).

5. *Superintendent's Early Childhood Study Group Report* (Lansing: Michigan Department of Education, September 1984).

6. Lawrence J. Schweinhart and David P. Weikart, *Young Children Grow Up: The Effects of the Perry Preschool Program on Youths Through Age 15* (Ypsilanti, Mich.: High/Scope Press, 1980), pp. 17-19.

7. Ibid., pp. 21-24.

8. *Changed Lives...*, pp. 181-86.

9. David P. Weikart, Linda Rogers, Carolyn Adcock, and Donna McClelland, *The Cognitively Oriented Curriculum: A Framework for Preschool Teachers* (Urbana: University of Illinois, 1971). The curriculum has continued to evolve since then; its current status is described in Mary Hohmann, Bernard Banet, and David P. Weikart, *Young Children in Action: A Manual for Preschool Educators* (Ypsilanti, Mich.: High/Scope Press, 1979).

10. David J. Irvine, "Evaluation of the New York State Experimental Prekindergarten Program," paper presented at the annual meeting of the American Educational Research Association, New York, N.Y., 1982.

49. Early Childhood Evaluation: What? Who? Why? by Doris Bergen Sponseller and Joel Fink, pp. 226–29.
Studies in Educational Evaluation, vol. 8, 1983, pp. 209–14. Copyright 1983 by the Pergamon Press, Inc. Reprinted with permission.

Bentley, R. J., Washington, E. D., and Young, J. C. Judging the educational progress of young children: Some cautions. In J. McCarthy and C. May (Eds.), *Providing the best for young children*. Washington, DC: National Association for the Education of Young Children, 1974.

Cicirelli, V. H., Evans, J. W., and Schiller, J. S. The impact of Head Start: A reply to the report analysis. *Harvard Educational Review*, 1970, *40*, 105–129.

Glick, J. Some problems in the evaluation of preschool intervention programs. In R. D. Hess and R. M. Bear (Eds.), *Early education*. Chicago: Aldine, 1968.

Guba, E. G. Toward a methodology of naturalistic inquiry in educational evaluation. *CSE Monograph Series in Evaluation*, 1978, *8*, University of California, Los Angeles.

Goldhammer, R. *Clinical supervision*. New York: Holt, Rinehart, and Winston, 1969.

House, E. R., Glass, G. V., McLean, L. D., and Walker, D. F. No simple answer: Critique of the follow through evaluation. *Harvard Educational Review*, 1978, 48, 128–160.

Lazar, I., et al. *The persistence of preschool effects. A longterm follow-up of 14 infant and preschool experiments*. Washington, DC: U.S. Government Printing Office, 1977.

Lazar, I. Social research and social policy: Reflections of relationships. In R. Haskins and J. J. Gallagher (Eds.), *Care and education of young children in America*. Norwood, NJ: Ablex, 1980.

Pillemer, D. B., and Light, R. J. Synthesizing outcomes: How to use research evidence from many studies. *Harvard Educational Review*, 1980, *50*(2), 176–195.

Scriven, M. Objectivity and subjectivity in educational research. In L. G. Thomas (Ed.), *Philosophical redirection of educational research* (71st Yearbook, Part I). Chicago: National Society for the Study of Education, University of Chicago Press, 1972.

Stake, R. E. Program evaluation, particularly responsive evaluation (Occasional Paper No. 5). Kalamazoo: The Evaluation Center, Western Michigan University, 1975.

Takanishi, R. Evaluation of early childhood programs: Toward a developmental perspective. In L. Katz (Ed.), *Current topics in early childhood education* (Vol. 2). Norwood, NJ: Ablex, 1979.

Weber, C. U., Foster, P. W., and Weikart, D. P. *An economic analysis of the Ypsilanti Perry Preschool Project*. Ypsilanti, MI: High/Scope, 1978.

Zimiles, H. A. A radical and regressive solution to the problem of evaluation. In L. G. Katz (Ed.), *Current topics in early childhood education* (Vol. 1). Norwood, NJ: Ablex, 1977.

Section Seven: Electronic Technology for Early Childhood Programs

50. Computers for Young Children? Perhaps, by Sandra Anselmo and R. Ann Zinck, pp. 232–36.
Young Children, vol. 42, no. 3, March 1987, pp. 22–27. Copyright © 1987 by the National Association for the Education of Young Children. Reprinted with permission.

Anselmo, S. (1983). Activities to enhance thinking skills: Visual closure. *Day Care and Early Education*, *11*(1), 36-37.

Anselmo, S., Rollins, P., and Schuckman, R. (1986). *R is for rainbow: Developing young children's thinking skills through the alphabet*. Menlo Park, CA: Addison-Wesley.

Apple™ LOGO. (1983). Cupertino, CA: Apple Computer.

Children's Television Workshop. (1981a). *Ernie's quiz*. Cupertino, CA: Apple Computer.

Children's Television Workshop (1981b). *Instant zoo*. Cupertino, CA: Apple Computer.

Children's Television Workshop (1981c). *Mix and match*. Cupertino, CA: Apple Computer.

Draw. (Undated. Developed by an unknown person).

Erikson, E. H. (1982). *The life cycle completed*. New York: Norton.

Estimation. (1983). Lawrence Hall of Science. University of California, Berkeley, CA 94720.

Facemaker. (1982). Spinnaker, 215 First St., Cambridge, MA 02142.

Gertrude's secrets. (1982). Learning Company, 4370 Alpine Rd., Portola Valley, CA 94025.

Kidwriter. (1984). Spinnaker, 215 First St., Cambridge, MA 02142.

NAEYC. (1986a). Position statement on developmentally appropriate practice in early childhood programs serving children from birth through age 8. *Young Children*, 41(6), 3–19.

NAEYC. (1986b). Position statement on developmentally appropriate practice in programs for 4- and 5-year-olds. *Young Children*, 41(6), 20–29.

National Assessment of Educational Progress. (1983). *The third national mathematics assessment: Results, trends, issues*. (Research Rep. No. 13-MA-01). Denver, CO: The Education Commission of the States.

Papert, D. (1980). *Mindstorms: Children, computers and powerful ideas*. New York: Basic.

Peanuts maze marathon. (1984). New York: Random House.

Piaget, J., and Inhelder, B. (1969). *The psychology of the child*. New York: Basic.

Thomas, R. M. (1985). *Comparing theories of child development* (2nd ed.). Belmont, CA: Wadsworth.

Turkle, S. (1984). *The second self: Computers and the human spirit*. New York: Simon & Schuster.

51. Computers and Young Children: A Review of Research, by Douglas H. Clements, pp. 237–44.
Young Children, vol. 43, no. 1, November 1987, pp. 34–44. Copyright © 1987 by the National Association for the Education of Young Children. Reprinted with permission.

Atkinson, R. C., and Fletcher, J. D. (1972). Teaching children to read with a computer. *The Reading Teacher, 25*, 319–327.

Beeson, B. S., and Williams, R. A. (1985). The effects of gender and age on preschool children's choice of the computer as a child-selected activity. *Journal of the American Society for Information Science, 36*, 339–341.

Binder, S. L., and Ledger, B. (1985). *Preschool computer project report.* Oakville, Ontario, Canada: Sheridan College.

Borgh, K., and Dickson, W. P. (1986a, April). *The effects on children's writing of adding speech synthesis to a word processor.* Paper presented at the annual meeting of the American Educational Research Association, San Francisco.

Borgh, K., and Dickson, W. P. (1986b). Two preschoolers sharing one microcomputer: Creating prosocial behavior with hardware and software. In P. F. Campbell and G. G. Fein (Eds.), *Young children and microcomputers* (pp. 37–44). Reston Publishing, 11480 Sunset Hills Rd., Reston, VA 22090.

Brady, E. H., and Hill, S. (1984). Research in review. Young children and microcomputers. Research issues and directions. *Young Children, 39*(3), 49–61.

Brinker, R. P. (1984). The microcomputer as perceptual tool: Searching for systematic learning strategies with handicapped infants. In R. E. Bennett and C. A. Maher (Eds.), *Micropcomputers and exceptional children* (pp. 21–36). New York: Haworth.

Brinkley, V. M., and Watson, J. A. (undated). *Effects of microworld training experience on sorting tasks by young children.* Manuscript submitted for publication.

Carmichael, H. W., Burnett, J. D., Higginson, W. C., Moore, B. G., and Pollard, P. J. (1985). *Computers, children and classrooms: A multisite evaluation of the creative use of microcomputers by elementary school children.* Toronto, Ontario, Canada: Ministry of Education.

Clements, D. H. (1986). Effects of Logo and CAI environments on cognition and creativity. *Journal of Educational Psychology, 78*, 309–318.

Clements, D. H. (1987). Computers and literacy. In J. L. Vacca, R. T. Vacca, and M. K. Gove (Eds.), *Reading and learning to read* (pp. 338–372). Boston: Little, Brown.

Clements, D. H., and Nastasi, B. K. (1985). Effects of computer environments on social-emotional development: Logo and computer-assisted instruction. *Computers in the Schools* 2(2-3), 11–31.

Clements, D. H., and Nastasi, B. K. (in press). Social and cognitive interactions in educational computer environments. *American Educational Research Journal.*

Degelman, D., Free, J. U., Scarlato, M., Blackburn, J. M., and Golden, T. (1986). Concept learning in preschool children: Effects of a short-term Logo experience. *Journal of Educational Computing Research, 2*, 199–205.

Fein, G. G. (1985, April). *Logo instruction: A constructivist view.* Paper presented at the annual meeting of the American Educational Research Association, Chicago, IL.

Fein, G. G., Campbell, P. F., and Schwartz, S. S. (1984). *Microcomputers in the preschool: Effects on cognitive and social behavior.* Manuscript submitted for publication.

Forman, G. (1985). The value of kinetic print in computer graphics for young children. In E. L. Klein (Ed.), *Children and computers* (pp. 19–34). San Francisco: Jossey-Bass.

Forman, G. (1986a). Computer graphics as a medium for enhancing reflective thinking in young children. In J. Bishop, J. Lochhead, and D. N. Perkins (Eds.), *Thinking* (pp. 131–137). Hillsdale, NJ: Erlbaum.

Forman, G. (1986b). Observations of young children solving problems with computers and robots. *Journal of Research in Childhood Education, 1*, 60–74.

Genishi, C., McCollum, P., and Strand, E. (1985). Research currents: The interactional richness of children's computer use. *Language Arts, 62*, 526–532.

Goodwin, L. D., Goodwin, W. L., Nansel, A., and Helm, C. P. (1986). Cognitive and affective effects of various types of microcomputer use by preschoolers. *American Educational Research Journal, 23*, 348–356.

Hess, R., and McGarvey, L. (in press). School-relevant effects of educational uses of microcomputers in kindergarten classrooms and homes. *Journal of Educational Computer Research.*

Hofmann, R. (1986). Microcomputers, productive thinking, and children. In P. F. Campbell and G. G. Fein (Eds.), *Young children and microcomputers* (pp. 87–101). Reston Publishing, 11480 Sunset Hills Rd., Reston, Va 22090.

Hoover, J., and Austin, A. M. (1986, April). *A comparison of traditional preschool and computer play from a social/cognitive perspective.* Paper presented at the annual meeting of the American Educational Research Association, San Francisco. (ERIC Document Reproduction Service No. ED 270 220)

Hungate, H. (1982, January). Computers in the kindergarten. *The Computing Teacher,* pp. 15–18.

Hyson, M. C. (1985). Emotions and the microcomputer. An exploratory study of young children's responses. *Computers in Human Behavior, 1*, 143–152.

Johnson, J. E. (1985). Characteristics of preschoolers interested in microcomputers. *Journal of Educational Research, 78*, 299–305.

Kraus, W. H. (1981). Using a computer game to reinforce skills in addition basic facts in second grade. *Journal for Research in Mathematics Education, 12*, 152–155.

Kull, J. A. (1986). Learning and Logo. In P. F. Campbell and G. G. Fein (Eds.), *Young children and microcomputers* (pp. 103–130). Reston Publishing, 11480 Sunset Hills Rd., Reston, VA 22090.

Lehrer, R., Harckham, L. D., Archer, P., and Pruzek, R. M. (1986). Microcomputer-based instruction in special education. *Journal of Educational Computing Research, 2*, 337–355.

Lieberman, D. (1985). Research on children and microcomputers. A review of utilization and effects studies. In M. Chen and W. Paisley (Eds.), *Children and microcomputers: Research on the newest medium* (pp. 59–83). Beverly Hills: Sage.

Lipinski, J. M., Nida, R. E., Shade, D. D., and Watson, J. A. (1986). The effects of microcomputers on young children: An examination of free-play choices, sex differences, and social interactions. *Journal of Educational Computing Research, 2*, 147–168.

McCollister, T. S., Burts, D. C., Wright, V. L., and Hildreth,

G. J. (1986). Effects of computer-assisted instruction and teacher-assisted instruction on arithmetic task achievement scores of kindergarten children. *Journal of Educational Research, 80*, 121–125.

Miller, G. E., and Emihovich, C. (1986). The effects of mediated programming instruction on preschool children's self-monitoring. *Journal of Educational Computing Research, 2*, 283–297.

Muhlstein, E. A., and Croft, D. J. (1986). *Using the microcomputer to enhance language experiences and the development of cooperative play among preschool children.* Unpublished manuscript, De Anza College, Cupertino, CA. (ERIC Document Reproduction Service No. ED 269 004)

Muller, A. A., and Perlmutter, M. (1985). Preschool children's problem-solving interactions at computers and jigsaw puzzles. *Journal of Applied Developmental Psychology, 6*, 173–186.

Murphy, R. T., and Appel, L. R. (1984). *Evaluation of Writing to Read.* Princeton, NJ: Educational Testing Service.

Niemiec, R. P., and Walberg, H. J. (1984). Computers and achievement in the elementary schools. *Journal of Educational Computing Research, 1*, 435–440.

Paris, C. L., and Morris, S. K. (1985, March). *The computer in the early childhood classroom: Peer helping and peer teaching.* Paper presented at the Microworld for Young Children Conference, College Park, MD. (ERIC Document Reproduction Service No. ED 257 555).

Perlmutter, M., Behrend, S., and Muller, A. (undated). *Social influence on preschool children's problem solving at a computer.* Unpublished manuscript, University of Michigan, Ann Arbor.

Phenix, J., and Hannan, E. (1984). Word processing in the grade one classroom. *Language Arts, 61*, 804–812.

Picard, A. J., and Giuli, C. (1985). *Computers as a free-time activity in grades K–4: A two year study of attitudes and usage.* Unpublished manuscript, University of Hawaii, Honolulu.

Prinz, P., Nelson, K., and Stedt, J. (1982). Early reading in young deaf children using microcomputer technology. *American Annals of the Deaf, 127*, 529–535.

Prinz, P. M., Pemberton, E., and Nelson, K. E. (1985). The ALPHA interactive microcomputer system for teaching reading, writing, and communication skills to hearing-impaired children. *American Annals of the Deaf, 130*, 444–461.

Ragosta, M., Holland, P., and Jamison, D. (1981). *Computer-assisted instruction and compensatory education: The ETS/LAUSD study.* Princeton, NJ: Educational Testing Service.

Rohwer, W. D., Ammon, P. R., and Crammer, P. (1974). *Understanding intellectual development.* Hinsdale, IL: Dryden.

Rosegrant, T. J. (1985, April). *Using a microcomputer to assist children in their efforts to acquire beginning literacy.* Paper presented at the annual meeting of the American Educational Research Association, Chicago.

Rosegrant, T. J. (1986, April). *Adult-child communication in writing.* Paper presented at the annual meeting of the American Educational Research Association, San Francisco.

Rosengren, K. S., Gross, D., Abrams, A. F., and Perlmutter, M. (1985, September). *An observational study of preschool children's computing activity.* Paper presented at "Perspectives on the Young Child and the Computer." University of Texas at Austin.

Saint Paul Public Schools. (1985). *Logo: Learning in a computer culture.* St. Paul, MN: Author.

Shade, D. D., Nida, R. E., Lipinski, J. M., and Watson, J. A. (1986). Microcomputers and preschoolers: Working together in a classroom setting. *Computers in the Schools, 3*, 53–61.

Shade, D. D., and Watson, J. A. (in press). Microworlds, mother teaching behavior, and concept formation in the very young child. *Early Child Development and Care.*

Sherman, J., Divine, K. P., and Johnson, B. (1985, May). An analysis of computer software preferences of preschool children. *Educational Technology,* pp. 39–41.

Shrock, S. A., Matthias, M., Anastasoff, J., Vensel, C., and Shaw, S. (1985, January). *Examining the effects of the microcomputer on a real world class: A naturalistic study.* Paper presented at the annual convention of the Association for Educational Communications and Technology, Anaheim, CA.

Silfen, R., and Howes, A. C. (1984). A summer reading program with CAI: An evaluation. *Computers, Reading and Language Arts, 1*(4), 20–22.

Sivin, J. P., Lee, P. C., and Vollmer, A. M. (1985, April). *Introductory computer experiences with commercially-available software: Differences between three-year-olds and five-year-olds.* Paper presented at the annual meeting of the American Educational Research Association, Chicago.

Strand, E., Gilstad, B., McCollum, P., and Genishi, C. (1986, April). *A descriptive study comparing preschool and kindergarten Logo interaction.* Paper presented at the annual meeting of the American Educational Research Association, San Francisco.

Swigger, K., and Campbell, J. (1981). Computers and the nursery school. In D. Harris and L. Nelson-Heern (Eds.), *Proceedings of the National Educational Computing Conference* (pp. 264–268). Iowa City, IA: National Educational Computing Conference.

Swigger, K. M., Campbell, J., and Swigger, B. K. (1983, January/February). Preschool children's preferences of different types of CAI programs. *Educational Computer Magazine,* pp. 38–40.

Swigger, K. M., and Swigger, B. K. (1984). Social patterns and computer use among preschool children. *AEDS Journal, 17*, 35–41.

von Stein, J. H. (1982). An evaluation of the microcomputer as a facilitator of indirect learning for the kindergarten child. *Dissertation Abstracts International, 43*, 72A. (University Microfilms Order No. DA8214463)

Wallace, J. M. (1985). Write first, then read. *Educational Leadership, 42*, 20–24.

Watson, J. A., Chadwick, S. S., and Brinkley, V. M. (1986). Special education technologies for young children: Present and future learning scenarios with related research literature. *Journal of the Division for Early Childhood, 10*, 197–208.

Watson, J. A., Nida, R. E., and Shade, D. D. (1986). Educational issues concerning young children and microcomputers: Lego with Logo? *Early Child Development and Care, 23*, 299–316.

Weir, S. (1987). *Cultivating minds: A Logo casebook.* New York: Harper and Row.

Wright, J. L., and Samaras, A. S. (1986). Play worlds and microworlds. In P. F.Campbell and G. G. Fein (Eds.), *Young children and microcomputers* (pp.73–86). Reston Publishing, 11480 Sunset Hills Rd., Reston, VA 22090.

52. Technological Priorities in the Education of Young Children, by Warren W. Buckleitner and Charles F. Hohmann, pp. 245–47.

Childhood Education, vol. 63, no. 5, June 1987, pp. 337–40. Reprinted by permission of Warren W. Buckleitner and Charles F. Hohmann and the Association for Childhood Education International, 11141 Georgia Avenue, Suite 200, Wheaton, MD. Copyright © 1987 by the Association.

Becker, H. J. (1986, June). Instructional uses of school computers. Baltimore, MD: *The Johns Hopkins University, Center for Social Organization of Schools, 1.*

Berrueta-Clement, J. R., Schweinhart, L. J., Barnett, W. J., Epstein, A. S., and Weikart, D. P. (1984). Changed lives: The effects of the Perry preschool program on youths through age 19. *Monograph No. 8.* Ypsilanti, MI: High/Scope Foundation.

Buckleitner, W. W. (1986, Winter). Hallmarks of quality software. *The High/Scope ReSource*, 12–13.

Clements, D. H. (1985, Spring). Computers in early childhood education. *Educational Horizons*, 124–128.

Cuffaro, H. K. (1984, Summer). Microcomputers in Education: Why is earlier better? *Teacher's College Record, 85*(4), 559–568.

Hohmann, C. F. (1985, May). Using the computer in small group activities. *Key Notes, 1*(2).

Lazar, I., Darlington, R., Murray, H., Royce, J., and Snipper, A. (1982). The lasting effects of early education: A report from the Consortium for Longitudinal Studies. *Monographs of the Society for Research in Child Development, Serial no. 195, 47* (2–3), 64.

Report on Preschool Programs. (1985, June). P. 8.

Schweinhart, L. J., Weikart, D. P., and Larner, M. B. (1986). Consequences of three preschool curriculum models through age 15. *Early Childhood Research Quarterly, 1*, 15–45.

Sheingold, K. (1984, May). The microcomputer as a medium for young children. *Technical Report no. 26.* New York: Bank Street College of Education, Center for Children and Technology.

Tan, L. E. (1985). Computers in pre-school education. *Early Childhood Development and Care, 19*, 319–336.

Section Eight: Parents and Community Involvement

53. In Designing a Preschool Program, We Went Straight to the Source: Parents, by Robert L. Zorn, pp. 250–52.

Reprinted with permission from *The American School Board Journal*, February 1988. Copyright 1988, the National School Boards Association. All rights reserved.

54. Is 'Parenting' Essential to Good Teaching? by James P. Comer, M.D., pp. 253–58.

NEA Today, vol. 6, no. 6, January 1988, pp. 34–40. Copyright © 1988 by the National Education Association of the United States.

"Alienation and the Four Worlds of Childhood." Urie Bronfenbrenner. *Phi Delta Kappan*, Feb. 1986.

Today's children feel increasing societal and personal pressures. By making caring an essential part of their curriculum, schools can help students build a character strength that can only come from a sense of belonging—something often lacking in the hurried, complex, modern American life.

"Education for Community." James Comer. *Common Decency.* Alvin Schorr, ed. Yale University Press, 1986.

True educational reform should help students achieve a sense of community and purpose both now, within their school—and in the future, in adult society. Teachers can play a key role in helping students develop a sense of belonging that is so necessary for overall life success. Parents, teachers and administrators must work together to design educational programs that meet specific needs of children in a caring, democratic environment.

The Feeling Child: Affective Development Reconsidered. Nancy Curry, ed. Haworth Press, 1986.

Through the writings of several educators and psychologists, this volume emphasizes that knowledge of a child's emotional life can help teachers better understand and educate that child. Today too much emphasis is placed on cognitive skills and strategies. By consulting ever-increasing research on how infants and children grow emotionally, educators can reassess their classroom interactions and curriculums and adapt child-oriented approaches to achieve more successful outcomes.

"Home-School Relationships as They Affect the Academic Success of Children." James Comer, *Education and Urban Society*, May 1984.

Because children's interpersonal and psychosocial experiences have great impact on their ability to succeed in school and adult life, parent-teacher cooperation is crucial if children are to develop academically, socially, and emotionally. Teachers who are sensitive to both the developmental needs of their students and to the goals and aspirations of their students' parents can facilitate positive learning by designing their curriculum and classroom interactional environment to address those needs and goals.

"Integration of Mental Health Principles in the School Setting." Barbara Biber. *Prevention of Mental Disorders in Children.* Gerald Caplan, ed. Basic Books, 1961.

Increasing evidence documents the close connection between learning functions (cognitive development) and personality formation (social/emotional development), showing that teachers and school environment play an important role in influencing students' mental health as well as their academic success. Effective, caring teachers greatly aid development of students' positive feelings about themselves; realistic perceptions of themselves and others; independence, curiosity, and creativity; relatedness to the world around them; and strength to cope with whatever comes their way. Without attention to these skills, student academic growth is limited.

The Learning Child. Dorothy Cohen. Pantheon Books, 1972.

This book describes the developmental and educational stages of 5- to 11-year-olds in the context of home and school, and offers practical guidelines for parents and teachers. It stresses the importance of both the role of the teacher over classroom methods or materials, and of understanding the close interconnections between emotional/social and cognitive development.

Lucy Sprague Mitchell: The Making of a Modern Woman. Joyce Antler. Yale University Press, 1987.

The educational philosophy and strategies of Lucy Sprague Mitchell, founder of Bank Street College of Education, are explored as the core of a comprehensive history of "progressive education" in the United States. Mitchell's approach, greatly influenced by the work of John Dewey, emphasizes the importance of children's emotional/social development, interactive learning-by-doing curriculums, and teacher-child cooperation and respect within the classroom environment. Effective teachers show consistent warmth, understanding, gentleness, sense of humor, and insight into the social, emotional, physical, and cognitive needs of the children they seek to teach.

The Montessori Method. Maria Montessori. Schocken Books, 1964.

Like a loving, concerned parent, the school must offer young children a consistent, supportive environment geared to their particular level of development. Children learn by interacting directly with carefully selected learning materials presented to them by teachers striving to move them toward independent, self-directed achievements. Teachers must be sensitive to and understand the learning tasks faced at each stage of development, from the sensori-motor levels of the very young to the intellectual and moral development of older students.

"New Lenses for Viewing Elementary Schools." Allan Shedlin. *Phi Delta Kappan*, Oct. 1986.

The best elementary schools celebrate the uniqueness of individual students, teachers, and families, and strive to create environments where students and adults respect and feel comfortable with one another. There is a balance between caring about each student as an individual and caring about what the students are learning. Subjective (affective) and objective (academic) factors must both be considered in determining the quality of a school.

Schools of Tomorrow. John Dewey and Evelyn Dewey. E. P. Dutton & Co., 1962.

Teachers teach best if they are sensitive to their students' growth patterns and needs. Schools would be more effective if they trusted and respected children more, let them learn naturally from play and other semi-independent activities, and helped them in their attempts to prepare for an adult world of work and social responsibilities.

55. Making Conferences Work for Parents, Teachers, and Children, by Gail Bjorklund and Christine Burger, pp. 259–63.

Young Children, vol. 42, no. 2, January 1987, pp. 26–31. Copyright © 1987 by the National Association for the Education of Young Children. Reprinted with permission.

Berger, E. H. (1981). *Parents as partners in education.* St. Louis, MO: Mosby.

Chinn, P. C., Winn, J., and Walters, R. H. (1978). *Two-way talking with parents of special children: A process of positive communication.* St. Louis, MO: Mosby.

Croft, D. J. (1979). *Parents and teachers: A resources book for home, school, and community relations.* Belmont, CA: Wadsworth.

Hymes, J. L. (1974). *Effective home-school relations.* Carmel, CA: California AEYC.

Ireton, H., and Thwing, E. (1972). *Minnesota Child Development Inventory.* Minneapolis: Behavior Science Systems, P.O. Box 1108, Minneapolis, MN 55440.

Ireton, H., and Thwing, E. (1979). *Minnesota Preschool Inventory.* Minneapolis: Behavior Science Systems, P.O. Box 1108, Minneapolis, MN 55440.

Kamii, C., and DeVries, R. (1973). Piaget for Early Education. In M. Day and R. Parker (Eds.), *The Preschool in Action.* Boston: Allyn & Bacon.

Morrison, G. S. (1978). *Parent involvement in the home, school and community.* Columbus, OH: Merrill.

Nedler, S. E., and McAfee, O. D. (1979). *Working with parents.* Belmont, CA: Wadsworth.

57. Literacy Environments: Bridging the Gap Between Home and School, by Jon Shapiro and Ray Doiron, pp. 266–70.

Childhood Education, vol. 63, no. 4, April 1987, pp. 263–69. Reprinted by permission of Jon Shapiro and Roy Doiron and the Association for Childhood Education International, 11141 Georgia Avenue, Suite 200, Wheaton, MD. Copyright © 1987 by the Association.

Applebee, A. N. (1980). Children's narratives: New directions. *The Reading Teacher, 34,* 137-142.

Applebee, A. N. (1978). *The child's concept of story: Ages two to seventeen.* Chicago: University of Chicago Press.

Bissex, G. L. (1984). The child as teacher. In H. Goelman, A. Oberg and F. Smith (Eds.), *Awakening to literacy.* Portsmouth, NH: Heinemann.

Bissex, G. L. (1980). *Guys at work: A child learns to write and read.* Cambridge, MA: Harvard University Press.

Cazden, C. (1983). Adult assistance to language development: Scaffolds, models and direct instruction. In R. Parker and F. Davis (Eds.), *Developing literacy: Young children's use of language.* Newark, DE: International Reading Association.

Chomsky, C. (1972). Stages in language development and reading exposure. *Harvard Educational Review, 42,* 1-33.

Downing, J. (1970). Children's concepts of language in learning to read. *Educational Research, 12,* 106-112.

Goodman, Y. (1980). The roots of literacy. *Claremont Reading Conference Yearbook, 44,* 1-32.

Hardy, B. (1977). An approach through narrative. In M. Silka (Ed.), *Towards a poetics of fiction.* Bloomington, IN: Indiana University Press.

Harste, J., Woodward, V., and C. Burke. (1984). *Language stories and literacy lessons.* Portsmouth, NH: Heinemann.

Heath, S. B. (1985). Critical factors in literacy development. In K. Egan and A. Luke (Eds.), *Literacy, society and schooling.* New York: Cambridge University Press.

Holdaway, D. (1979). *Foundations of literacy.* Sydney, Australia: Ashton Scholastic.

Juliebo, M. F. (1985). To mediate or not to mediate? That is the question. *Language Arts, 62,* 848-856.

Read, C. (1971). Preschool children's knowledge of English phonology. *Harvard Educational Review, 41,* 1-34.

Snow, C. (1983). Literacy and language relationships during preschool years. *Harvard Educational Review, 53,* 165-189.

Teale, W. H. (1984). Reading to young children: Its significance for literacy development. In H. Goelman, A. Oberg and F. Smith (Eds.), *Awakening to literacy*. Portsmouth, NH: Heinemann.

Wells, G. (1986). *The meaning makers*. Portsmouth, NH: Heinemann.

Wells, G. (1985). Preschool literacy related activities and success in school. In D. Olson, N. Torrance and A. Hildyard (Eds.), *Literacy, language and learning*. Cambridge, MA: Cambridge University Press.

58. Communicating with Parents About Beginning Reading Instruction, by Dorene D. Ross and Elizabeth Bondy, pp. 271–75.

Childhood Education, vol. 63, no. 4, April 1987, pp. 270–75. Reprinted by permission of Dorene D. Ross and Elizabeth Bondy and the Association for Childhood Education International, 11141 Georgia Avenue, Suite 200, Wheaton, MD. Copyright © 1987 by the Association.

Allington, R. (1983). The reading instruction provided readers of differing reading abilities. *Elementary School Journal, 83*, 548–559.

Anderson, R. C., Hiebert, E. H., Scott, J. A., and Wilkinson, I. A. (1985). *Becoming a nation of readers*. Washington, DC: National Institute of Education.

Bondy, E. (1984). *Children's definitions of reading: Products of an interactive process*. Paper presented at the annual conference of the American Educational Research Association, Chicago, IL.

Bussis, A. (1982). Burn it at the casket: Research, reading instruction and children's learning of the first R. *Phi Delta Kappa, 64*, 237–241.

Butler, A., and Turbill, J. (1984). *Toward a reading-writing classroom*. Rozell, NSW: Primary English Teaching Association, Australia.

Cazden, C. (1978). Environments for language learning. *Language Arts*, 681–682.

Davy, B. (1983). Think aloud—Modeling the cognitive processes of reading comprehension. *Journal of Reading, 27*, 44–47.

Durkin, D. (1978–79). What classroom observations reveal about reading comprehension instruction. *Reading Research Quarterly, 14*, 515–544.

Elkind, D. (1986). Formal education and early childhood education: An essential difference. *Phi Delta Kappan, 67*, 631–636.

Goodman, Y. (1984). The development of initial literacy. In

H. Goelman, A. Oberg and F. Smith (Eds.), *Awakening to literacy*. Portsmouth, NH: Heinemann.

Holdaway, D. (1979). *The foundations of literacy*. Sydney, Australia: Ashton Scholastic.

Park, B. (1982). The big book trend—A discussion with Don Holdaway. *Language Arts, 59*, 815–821.

Pellegrini, A., and Galda, L. (1985). Social dramatic play and literacy. *Dimensions, 13*, 12–14.

Roney, R. C. (1984). Background experience is the foundation of success in learning to read. *Reading Teacher, 38*, 196-199.

Rosenshine, B. (1980). Skill hierarchies in reading comprehension. In R. Spiro, B. Bruce, and W. Brewer (Eds.), *Theoretical issues in reading comprehension: Perspectives for cognitive psychology, linguistics, artificial intelligence and education*. Hillsdale, NJ: Lawrence Erlbaum Associates.

Smith, F. (1973). *Psycholinguistics and reading*. New York: Holt, Rinehart & Winston.

Sponseller, D. (1982). Play and early education. In B. Spodek (Ed.), *Handbook of research in early childhood education*. New York: The Free Press.

Strange, M. (1978). Considerations for evaluating reading instruction. *Educational Leadership, 36*, 178–181.

Taylor, J. (1977). Making sense: The basic skill in reading. *Language Arts, 54*, 668–672.

Teale, W. (1982). Toward a theory of how children learn to read and write naturally. *Language Arts, 59*, 555-570.

Section Nine: Child Behavior and Discipline

59. The Banning of Corporal Punishment: In Child Care, School and Other Educative Settings in the United States, by John R. Cryan, pp. 278–83.

Childhood Education, vol. 63, no. 3, February 1987, pp. 146–53. Reprinted by permission of John R. Cryan and the Association for Childhood Education International, 11141 Georgia Avenue, Suite 200, Wheaton, MD. Copyright © 1987 by the Association.

Baker v. Owen, 395 F.Supp. 294 (N.D.N.C. 1975) S.4.3, affirmed 96 S.Ct. 210 (1975).

Black, H. C. (1968). *Black's law dictionary*. St. Paul, MN: West Publishing Co.

Bongiovanni, A. (1977, February). *A review of the effects of punishment: Implications for corporal punishment in the schools*. Paper presented at the Conference on Child Abuse, Children's Hospital, National Medical Center, Washington, DC.

Corcoran, C. (1975, July). *Report on suspensions and corporal punishment*. Vermont State Department of Education.

Glaser v. Marietta, 351 F.Supp. 555 (W.D.Pa. 1972) S.4.3.

Hall v. Tawney, 621 F.2d. 607 (c.a.4, 1981).

Hapkiewicz, W. G. (1975, April). *Research on corporal punishment effectiveness: Contributions and limitations*. Paper presented at the annual meeting of the American Educational Research Association, Washington, DC.

Hiner, N. R. (1979). *Children's rights, corporal punishment, and child abuse (Changing American attitudes, 1870-1920)*. Bulletin of the Menninger Clinic, *43* (3), 223–248.

Hyman, I. A. (1978). A social science review of evidence cited in litigation on corporal punishment in the schools. *Journal of Clinical Child Psychology, 7* (3), 195–199.

Hyman, I. A., and D'Alessandro, J. (1984). Good, old-fashioned discipline: The politics of punitiveness. *Phi Delta Kappan, 66* (1), 39–45.

Hyman, I. A., and Lally, D. M. (1981). Corporal punishment in American education: A historical and contemporary dilemma. In J. R. Cryan (Ed.), *Corporal punishment in the schools: Its use is abuse* (pp. 8–15). Toledo, OH: The University of Toledo.

Hyman, I. A., and Wise, J. A. (Eds.). (1979). *Corporal punishment in American education.* Philadelphia: Temple University Press.

Ingraham v. Wright, 97 S.Ct. 1401 (1977).

Lamberth, J. (1979). The effects of punishment on academic achievement: A review of recent research. In I. A. Hyman and J. A. Wise (Eds.), *Corporal punishment in American education* (pp. 384–393). Philadelphia: Temple University Press.

Manning, J. (1979). Discipline in the good old days. In I. A. Hyman and J. A. Wise (Eds.), *Corporal punishment in American education* (pp. 50–61). Philadelphia: Temple University Press.

Many states still condone corporal punishment in schools: More creative discipline urged. (1982, August). *Psychiatric News,* 17, p. 21.

Maurer, A. (1984). *1001 alternatives to corporal punishment,* Vol. 1. Berkeley, CA: Generation Books.

Maurer, A. (Ed.). (1985-86, Winter). *The last resort,* Vol. 14, 2. Newsletter of the Committee To End Violence Against the Next Generation.

Maurer, A. (1981). The case against physical punishment in schools. In J. R. Cryan (Ed.), *Corporal punishment in the schools: Its use is abuse* (pp. 16–25). Toledo, OH: The University of Toledo.

Maurer, A. (1981). *Paddles away: A psychological study of physical punishment in schools.* Palo Alto, CA: R & E Research.

Maurer, A., and Wallerstein, J. S. (1983). *The influence of school corporal punishment on learning: A statistical study.* A publication by the Committee To End Violence Against the Next Generation, Berkeley, CA. Reprinted with permission.

Maurer, A., and Wallerstein, J. S. (n.d.). *The influence of school corporal punishment on crime.* A publication by the Committee To End Violence Against the Next Generation, Berkeley, CA. Reprinted with permission.

Memoir of William Ellery Channing. (1851). *I,* 23. Boston: William Crosby & H. P. Nichols.

Montgomery, E. (1867). Reminiscences of Wilmington, Delaware. *American Journal of Education,* 17 (September), 189.

More fascinating facts FYI. (1986, January). *Reader's Digest,* p. 172.

National Committee for the Prevention of Child Abuse. (1983). Policy statement on corporal punishment in the schools and custodial settings.

National Education Association. (1972). Report on the task force on corporal punishment (Library of Congress No. 22-85743). Washington, DC.

Rose, T. L. (1984). Current uses of corporal punishment in American public schools. *Journal of Educational Psychology,* 76 (3), 427–441.

Rosenshine, B., and Furst, N. (1971). Research in teacher performance criteria. In B. O. Smith (Ed.), *Research in teacher education* (pp. 37–72). Englewood Cliffs, NJ: Prentice-Hall.

Taylor, L., and Maurer, A. (1985). *Think twice: The medical effects of physical punishment.* Berkeley, CA: Generation Books.

Van Dyke, H. T. (1984). Corporal punishment in our schools. *Clearinghouse,* 57, 296–300.

Watson, J. F. (1870). *Annals of Philadelphia and Pennsylvania* (pp. 290–292). Philadelphia: Larry Stuart Co.

Williams, G. J. (1979). Social sanctions for violence against children: Historical perspectives. In I. A. Hyman and J. A. Wise (Eds.), *Corporal punishment in American education* (pp. 25–40). Philadelphia: Temple University Press.

60. A Cognitive Approach to Behavior Management, by Jerold P. Bauch, pp. 284–86.
Dimensions, vol. 15, no. 4, July 1987, pp. 25–27. © 1987, Southern Association on Children Under Six, Little Rock, Arkansas. Reprinted with permission.

*For more information about this program, contact: Deborah Smith, Outreach Coordinator, CCYC, Box 9, Peabody College of Vanderbilt University, Nashville, TN 37203.

Burns, S., Brooks, P., Haywood H. C., and Cox, J. (1983). *Cognitive small group units.* Nashville, TN: Cognitive Education Outreach Project; Peabody College of Vanderbilt University.

Feuerstein, R., Rand, Y., Hoffman, M. B., and Miller, R. (1980). *Instrumental enrichment.* Baltimore: University Park Press.

Haywood, H. C., Brooks, P., and Burns, S. (1986a). Development and evaluation of the cognitive curriculum for young children. In M. Schwebel and C. Maher (Eds.), *Facilitating cognitive development: Principles, practices and programs.*

**Editor's Note: For another view on this issue, see Kamii, C., and DeVries, R. (1980). *Group games in early education. Implications of Piaget's theory.* Washington, DC: NAEYC.

New York: Haworth Press.

Haywood, H. C., Brooks, P., and Burns, S. (1986b). *Cognitive curriculum for young children: Experimental version.* Nashville, TN: Cognitive Early Education Group.

Haywood, H. C., and Weatherford, D. L. (1986). Cognitive-mediational behavior management. In H. C. Haywood, P. Brooks, and S. Burns (Eds.), *Cognitive curriculum for young children: Experimental version.* Nashville, TN: Cognitive Early Education Group.

Weatherford, D. L. (1986). Cognitive curriculum for young children. *Human intelligence international newsletter,* 7, 6–7.

61. Corporal Punishment in the Schools, by John H. Meier, pp. 287–89.
Childhood Education, vol. 58, no. 4, March/April 1982, pp. 235–37. Reprinted by permission of John H. Meier and the Association for Childhood Education International, 11141 Georgia Avenue, Suite 200, Wheaton, MD. Copyright © 1982 by the Association.

62. Child Abuse and Neglect: Prevention and Reporting, by Barbara J. Meddin and Anita L. Rosen, pp. 290–94.
Young Children, vol. 41, no. 4, May 1986, pp. 26–30. Copyright © 1986 by the National Association for the Education of Young Children. Reprinted with permission.

American Humane Association. (1983). *Highlights of official child neglect and abuse reporting*. Denver, CO: Author.

Education Commission of the States (1976, March). *A comparison of the states' child abuse statutes* (Report No. 84). Denver, CO: Author.

Kempe, H., and Helfer, R. (Eds.). (1972). *Helping the battered child and his family*. Philadelphia: Lippincott.

Jalongo, M. R. (1985, September). When young children move. *Young Children* 40(6), 51–57.

Jirsa, J. (1981). Planning a child abuse referral system. *Social Work in Education*, 3(2), 10.

Kadushin, A. (1978). *Child welfare strategy in the coming years*. Washington, DC: National Association of Social

Workers.

Illinois Public Law. (1979, November). *The abused and neglected child reporting act* (Public Act 81–1077).

McCaffrey, M., and Tewey, S. (1978, October). Preparing educators to participate in the community response to child abuse and neglect. *Exceptional Children*, 45(2), 115.

Underhill, E. (1974). The strange silence of teachers, doctors, and social workers in the face of cruelty to children. *International Child Welfare Review*, (21), 16–21.

U.S. Department of Health and Human Services. (1981). *Study findings: National study of the incidence and severity of child abuse and neglect*. Washington, DC: Superintendent of Documents.

Section Ten: The Future

63. Societal Influences on Children, by Joan Isenberg, pp. 296–301.

Childhood Education, vol. 63, no. 5, June 1987, pp. 341–48. Reprinted by permission of Joan Isenberg and the Association for Childhood Education International, 11141 Georgia Avenue, Suite 200, Wheaton, MD. Copyright © 1987 by the Association.

A healthy personality for each child. (1951). A digest of the factfinding report to the Midcentury White House Conference on Children and Youth. Raleigh, NC: Heath Publications Institute.

Bee, H. (1985). *The developing child*, (4th ed.). Cambridge, MA: Harper & Row.

Berns, R. M. (1985). *Child, family and community*. New York: Holt, Rinehart & Winston.

Bloom, B. (1964). *Stability and change in human characteristics*. New York: Wiley.

Bronfenbrenner, U. (1985a). The parent/child relationship and our changing society. In L. E. Amold, (Ed.), *Parents, children and change*. Lexington, MA: Lexington Books.

Bronfenbrenner, U. (1985b). The three worlds of childhood. *Principal*, 64(5), 7–11.

Bronfenbrenner, U., and Crouter, A. C. (1983). Work and family through time and space. In S. B. Kamerman and C. D. Hayes (Eds.), *Families that work: Children in a changing world*. Washington, DC: National Academy Press.

Bronfenbrenner, U. (1979). *The ecology of human development*. Cambridge, MA: Harvard University Press.

Bruner, J. (1960). *The process of education*. Cambridge, MA: Harvard University Press.

Coleman, M., and Skeen, P. (1985). Play, games and sport. Their use and misuse. *Childhood Education*, 61(3), 192–197.

Comstock, G. A. (1975). *Effects of television on children: What is the evidence?* Santa Monica, CA: The Rand Corp., #P5412.

Damon, W. (1983). *Social and personality development: Infancy through adolescence*. New York: W. W. Norton.

Elkind, D. (1986). Formal education and early childhood education: An essential difference. *Phi Delta Kappan*, 67(9), 631–636.

Elkind, D. (1984). *All grown up and no place to go: Teenagers in crisis*. Reading, MA: Addison-Wesley.

Elkind, D. (1982, March). Misunderstandings about how children learn. *Today's Education*, 24–25.

Elkind, D. (1981). *The hurried child*. Reading, MA: Addison-Wesley.

Erikson, E. (1963). *Childhood and society*, (2nd ed.). New York: W. W. Norton.

Fox, B. J. (1986). *Teach your child to read in 20 minutes a day*. New York: Warner.

Friesen, D. (1984). Too much too soon. *Principal*, 6(4), 14–18.

Galambos, N. L., and Garbarino, J. (1983). Identifying the missing links in the study of latchkey children. *Children Today*, 40, 2–4.

Gerbner, G., and Gross, N. (1978). Demonstration of power. *Journal of Communication*, 29, 177–184.

Glick, P. C. (1979). Children of divorced parents in demographic perspective. *Journal of Social Issues*, 35, 170–182.

Helms, D. B., and Turner, J. S. (1986). *Exploring child behavior*, (3rd ed.). Belmont, CA: Wadsworth.

Harris, A. C. (1986). *Child development*. New York: West

Herzog, E., and Sudia, C. E. (1973). Children in fatherless families. In B. Caldwell and H. N. Riccuti (Eds.), *Review of child development research, 3*. Chicago: University of Chicago Press.

Hetherington, E. M. (1979). Divorce: A child's perspective. *American Psychologist*, 34, 851–858.

Hetherington, E. M., Cox, M., and Cox, R. (1978). The aftermath of divorce. In J. H. Stevens, Jr. and M. Matthews (Eds.), *Mother-child, father-child relations*. Washington, DC: National Association for the Education of Young Children.

Hofferth, S. L. (1979). Day care in the next decade, 1980–1990. *Journal of Marriage and the Family*, 4, 649–658.

Hoffman, L. W. (1974). Effects of maternal employment on the child: A review of the research. *Developmental Psychology*, 10, 204–228.

Hunt, J. McV. (1961). *Intelligence and experience*. New York: Ronald Press.

Ledson, S. (1985). *Teach your child to read in 60 days*. New York: Berkley.

Martens, R. (1978). *Joy and sadness in children's sports*. Champaign, IL: Human Kinetics.

McElroy, M. (1982). Consequences of perceived parental pressure on the self-esteem of youth sport participants. *American Corrective Therapy Journal*, 36(6), 164–167.

Moncure, J. (1985). *My first steps to reading*. Haddam, CT: Children's Reading Institute.

National Center for Health Statistics. (1983). *Report on marriage and divorce today*, 7, 3–4.

National Institute of Mental Health. (1982). *Television and behavior: Ten years of scientific progress and implications for the eighties*. Washington, DC: U.S. Government Printing Office.

Newsweek. (1983, March). Bringing up superbaby, p. 62.

Papalia, D. E., and Olds, S. W. (1986). *Human development* (3rd ed.). New York: McGraw-Hill.

Postman, N. (1985). The disappearance of childhood. *Childhood Education*, 61(4), 286–293.

Postman, N. (1983, March). The disappearing child. *Educational Leadership*, 10–17.

Postman, N. (1982). *The disappearance of childhood*. New York: Delacorte.

Postman, N. (1982). Disappearing childhood. *Childhood Education*, 58(2) 66–68.

Robinson, S. L. (1985). Childhood: Can it be preserved? An interview with Neil Postman. *Childhood Education*, 61(3), 337–342.

Santrock, J. W., and Wasnak, R. A. (1979). Father custody and social development in boys and girls. *Journal of Social Issues*, 35, 112–125.

Seefeldt, C. (1985). Tomorrow's kindergarten: Pleasure or pressure? *Principal*, 64(5), 12–15.

Seligson, M., Genser, A., Gannett, E., and Gray, W. (1983, December). *School-age child care: A policy report*. Wellesley, MA: Wellesley College Center for Research on Women.

Smith, R. E., and Smoll, F. L. (1978). Sport and the child: Conceptual and research perspectives. In F. L. Smoll and R. E. Smith (Eds.), *Psychological perspectives in youth sports*. New York: Wiley.

Spodek, B. (Ed.). (1986). *Today's kindergarten: Exploring the knowledge base, expanding the curriculum*. New York: Teachers College Press.

Stein, A., and Friedrich, L. (1975). Impact of television on children and youth. In E. M. Hetherington (Ed.), *Review of child development research*, 5. Chicago: University of Chicago Press.

Suransky, V. P. (1982). *The erosion of childhood*. Chicago: University of Chicago Press.

Thomas, M. H. (1982). Physiological arousal, exposure to a relatively lengthy aggressive film, and aggressive behavior. *Journal of Research in Personality*, 16, 72–81.

Umansky, W. (1983). On families and the re-valuing of childhood. *Childhood Education*, 59(4), 260–266.

Wallerstein, J. S., and Kelley, J. B. (1980). *Surviving the breakup: How children actually cope with divorce*. New York: Basic Books.

Wallerstein, J. S., and Kelley, J. B. (1975). The effects on parental divorce: Experiences of the child in later latency. *American Journal of Orthopsychiatry*, 46, 256–269.

Wallerstein, J. S., and Kelley, J. B. (1976). The effects of parental divorce: Experiences of the child in later latency. *Journal of the American Academy of Child Psychiatry*, 14, 600–616.

Winn, M. (1983). *Children without childhood*. New York: Pantheon.

64. Developmental and Experiential Programs: The Key to Quality Education and Care of Young Children, by Barbara Day and Kay N. Drake, pp. 302–4.

Educational Leadership, vol. 44, no. 3, November 1986, pp. 25–27. Reprinted with permission of the Association for Supervision and Curriculum Development and Barbara Day and Kay N. Drake. Copyright © 1986 by the Association for Supervision and Curriculum Development. All rights reserved.

Day, B. D., and K. N. Drake. *Early Childhood Education: Curriculum Organization and Classroom Management*. Alexandria, Va.: Association for Supervision and Curriculum Development, 1983.

Elkind, D. "Formal Education and Early Childhood Education: An Essential Difference." *Phi Delta Kappan* 67 (1986): 631–636.

Leeper, S. H., R. I. Witherspoon, and B. D. Day. *Good Schemes for Young Children*. 5th ed. New York: Macmillan, 1984.

Phyfe-Perkins, E. *An Ecological Assessment of Two Preschool Environments*. Cited in E. Phyfe-Perkins, "Effects of Teacher Behavior on Preschool Children: A Review of Research."

(ERIC Reports ED 211–176, 1981.)

Plowden, Bridget, et al. *Children and Their Primary Schools: A Report on the Central Advisory Council for Education*. London: Her Majesty's Stationery Office, 1966.

Tryon, C., and J. W. Lilienthal. *Developmental Tasks: The Concept and Its Importance, Fostering Mental Health in Our Schools*. Washington, D.C.: ASCD, 1950.

Wilson, B. L. "Effect of Task and Authority Structure on Students' Task Engagement." Paper presented at the meeting of the American Educational Research Association, Montreal, Quebec, Canada, April 1983. (ERIC Document Reproduction Service Number ED 230–416.)

65. Upon What Can We Build Our Children's Educational Future? by Walter Hodges, pp. 305–8.

Dimensions, October 1987, pp. 4–7. © 1987, Southern Association on Children Under Six, Little Rock, Arkansas. Reprinted with permission.

Bereiter, C. and Engelmann, S. (1966). *Teaching disadvantaged children in the preschool*. Englewood Cliffs, NJ: Prentice-Hall.

Berrueta-Clement, J. R.; Schweinhart, L. J.; Barnett, W. S.; Epstein, A. S.; and Weikart, D. P. (1984). *Changed lives: The effects of the Perry Preschool Program on youths through age 19*. Ypsilanti, MI: High/Scope Press.

Bronfenbrenner, U. (1974). *A report on longitudinal evaluations of preschool programs. Volume II: Is early intervention effective?* Washington, DC: Department of Health, Education and Welfare, Publication No. (OHD) 74-25.

Coleman, J. S., et al. (1966). *Equality of educational opportunity*. Washington, DC: U.S. Government Printing Office.

Consortium. (1978). *Lasting effects after preschool*. Washington, DC: Superintendent of Documents, U.S. Government Printing Office.

Dunn, L. M. (1960). Special education for the mildly retarded—Is much of it justifiable. *Exceptional Children, 55*, 5–22.

Featherstone, J. The primary school revolution in Britain: I. Schools for children; II. How children learn; III. Teaching children to think. *The New Republic*, August-September, 1967, 1–16.

Gray, S. W.; Ramsey, B. R.; and Klaus, R. A. (1982). *From 3 to 20: The early training project*. Baltimore: University Park Press.

Harrington, M. W. (1962). *The other America*. Baltimore: Penguin Books.

Hodges, W. L.; McCandless, B. R.; and Spicker, H. M. (1971). *Diagnostic teaching for preschool children*. Arlington, VA: Council for Exceptional Children.

Hunt, J. McV. (1961). *Intelligence and Experience*. New York: Ronald Press.

Heber, R. R. (1978). Sociocultural mental retardation—A longitudinal study. In D. Forgays (Ed.*), Primary prevention of psychopathology: Volume 2. Environmental influences*. Hanover, NH: University Press of New England.

Jensen, A. R. How much can we boost IQ and scholastic achievement? *Harvard Educational Review, 39*, 1–123.

Kamii, C. and DeVries, R. (1978). *Physical knowledge in preschool education*. Englewood Cliffs, NJ: Prentice-Hall.

Madden, J.; O'Hara, J.; and Levenstein, P. (1984). Home again: Effects of the Mother-Child Home Program on mother and child. *Child Development, 55*, 636–647.

Pines, M. (1966). *Revolution in learning: The years from birth to six*. New York: Harper & Row.

Skeels, H. M. (1966). Adult status of children with contrasting early life experiences. *Monographs of the Society for Research in Child Development, 31*, 1–65.

Skinner, B. F. (1968). *The technology of teaching*. New York: Appleton-Century-Crofts.

Stebbins, L. B.; St. Pierre, R. G.; Proper, E. C.; Anderson, R. B.; and Cerva, T. R. (1977). *Education as experimentation: A planned variation model. Volume IV-A: An evaluation of Follow Through*. Cambridge, MS: Abt Associates, Inc. (Also see *Volume II-A National Evaluation: Patterns of effects*. U.S. Department of Health, Education and Welfare.)

Weikart, D. P. and Schweinhart, L. (1980). *Young children grow up: The effects of the Perry Preschool program on youths through age 15*. Ypsilanti, MI: High/Scope Press.

White, S.; Day, M.; Freeman, P.; Hartmann, S.; and Messenger, K. *Federal programs for young children: Review and recommendations. Volume III: For Federal program planning*. Washington, DC: Superintendent of Documents.

66. BACK to Basics or FORWARD to Fundamentals? by Alice V. Keliher, pp. 309–10.

Young Children, vol. 41, no. 6, September 1986, pp. 42–44. Copyright © 1986 by the National Assoiation for the Education of Young Children. Reprinted with permission.

Hess, R. D., and Shipman, V. C. (1965). Early blocks to children's learning. *Children, 12*(5).

Keliher, A. V. (1933). Where are the progressives going? *Progressive Education Magazine, 10*(5), 278.

Keliher, A. V. (1954, December). *Educational Fundamentals—1954*. Paper presented at the United Parents' Association, New York.

Keliher, A. V. (1962). Believing and doing. *Childhood Educa-*

tion, 40, 62–65.

Keliher, A. V. (1982). Back to basics or forward to fundamentals? *SCOPE, Bulletin of the Arizona Association for Supervision and Curriculum Development, 8*(1), 3–6.

Taylor, C. (1961). A tentative description of the creative individual. *Human Variability and Learning, Bulletin of the Association for Supervision and Curriculum Development*.

67. The Future of Education, by Wilson Riles, pp. 311–14.

Childhood Education, vol. 58, no. 4, March/April 1982, pp. 202–5. Reprinted by permission of Wilson Riles and the Association for Childhood Education International, 11141 Georgia Avenue, Suite 200, Wheaton, MD. Copyright © 1982 by the Association.

68. Early Schooling and the Nation's Future, by Ernest L. Boyer, pp. 314–17.

Educational Leadership, vol. 44, no. 6, March 1987, pp. 4–6. Reprinted with permission of the Association for Supervision and Curriculum Development and Ernest L. Boyer. Copyright © 1987 by the Association for Supervision and Curriculum Development. All rights reserved.

NEA POLICY ON
EARLY CHILDHOOD EDUCATION

Resolution C–3. Early Childhood Development and Kindergarten

The National Education Association supports the inclusion of prekindergarten childhood education programs within the public school system. These programs should include prekindergarten screening, child care, child development, appropriate developmental curriculum, and special education. The Association further supports kindergarten programs that are developmentally appropriate and that adequately prepare the child for transition into first grade. The Association urges that federal legislation be enacted to assist in funding and organizing the implementation of such programs.

The Association believes that early childhood programs must be staffed by trained and certified/licensed personnel and trained support staff. It supports training programs that will lead to credentials consistent with the educational standards in each state. The Association recommends that minorities, the poor, and the elderly be recruited to work in such programs.

The Association advocates the establishment of fully funded, early childhood special education programs. These programs should be readily accessible, make available those services necessary to assist handicapped children from birth, and be staffed by certified teachers, qualified support staff, and therapists.

The Association urges its affiliates to seek legislation to ensure that early childhood developmental programs offered primarily through the public schools be fully funded and available on an equal basis and culminate in mandatory kindergarten with compulsory attendance. The Association supports regulations requiring students starting kindergarten to have reached five years of age by September 1 of that year. (75, 88)